Technology and Society

Technology and Society
A Bridge to the 21st Century

Edited by

Linda S. Hjorth

Barbara A. Eichler

Ahmed S. Khan

John Morello

Prentice Hall

Upper Saddle River, New Jersey   *Columbus, Ohio*

Library of Congress Cataloging-in-Publication Data
Technology and society: a bridge to the 21st century / edited by
   Linda S. Hjorth . . . [et al.].
      p.   cm.
    ISBN 0-13-618547-9
     1. Technology—Social aspects.   I. Hjorth, Linda S.
  T14.5.T44168   2000
  303.48′3—dc21   98-54924
                                       CIP

Publisher: Charles E. Stewart, Jr.
Associate Editor: Kate Linsner
Production Editor: Alexandrina Benedicto Wolf
Production Coordination: Linda Zuk, WordCrafters
Cover Design Coordinator: Karrie Converse Jones
Cover Photo: The Stock Market
Cover Designer: Tanya Burgess
Production Manager: Deidra Schwartz
Marketing Manager: Ben Leonard

This book was set in Times Roman by The Clarinda Company and was printed and bound by R.R. Donnelley & Sons Company. The cover was printed by Phoenix Color Corp.

© 2000 by Prentice-Hall, Inc.
Pearson Education
Upper Saddle River, New Jersey 07458

Printed in the United States of America

10 9 8 7 6 5 4 3 2 1

ISBN: 0-13-618547-9

Prentice-Hall International (UK) Limited, *London*
Prentice-Hall of Australia Pty. Limited, *Sydney*
Prentice-Hall of Canada, Inc., *Toronto*
Prentice-Hall Hispanoamericana, S. A., *Mexico*
Prentice-Hall of India Private Limited, *New Delhi*
Prentice-Hall of Japan, Inc., *Tokyo*
Prentice-Hall (Singapore) Pte. Ltd., *Singapore*
Editora Prentice-Hall do Brasil, Ltda., *Rio de Janeiro*

If you are thinking a year ahead, sow seed. If you are thinking 10 years ahead, plant a tree. If you are thinking 100 years ahead, make people aware. By sowing seed once, you harvest once. By planting a tree, you will harvest tenfold. By opening the minds of people, you will harvest a hundredfold.

CHINESE PROVERB

To the students who, in their quest for knowledge, consistently reinforce our desire to present varied ideas within the field of technology and society.

LINDA STEVENS HJORTH

To my family, my students, and colleagues whose very capable adoption of technology, along with their arguments for the value of humankind, always inspire me.

BARBARA A. EICHLER

To Tasneem, my parents, my students, and all seekers of truth and wisdom.

AHMED S. KHAN

To our students and our families for their patience, support, and prayers.

JOHN MORELLO

Preface

ISSUES EXPLORED IN THE TEXT

One of the underlying issues explored in *Technology and Society: A Bridge to the 21st Century* is whether we are in charge of technology or whether technology controls us. At what point does technological dependency cause social problems? And to what extent are we, as caring social beings, concerned about technological impact? This text encourages readers to analyze and reflect on technology's impact on the global village economically, politically, and environmentally. The new century will usher in an urgent challenge to resolve the conflicts among our technological, environmental, and social worlds. The ability to understand the impact of technology on our lives and on succeeding generations will be essential to reaching the goals of survival, peaceful coexistence, ethical living, safety, and prosperity.

The chapters in this text are designed to stimulate, inspire, and provoke awareness of technology's impact on society. They are supported by a variety of features intended to supplement and complement learning, critical analysis, and social awareness.

FEATURES

- *Flowcharts:* One of the unique features of the text is the use of flowcharts as logical, interactive maps that emphasize the problems, possible solutions, and points of direction and significance of the chapters and case studies. Many of the flowcharts have been class-tested and we have found that students like them because they appeal to students' kinesthetic and problem-solving learning style. The visual process of flowcharting the information presented in the readings seems to increase insight and critical thinking skills.

- *Internet Exercises:* The Internet exercises are designed to enable students to: (a) become familiar with the knowledge dissemination mode of the ever-expanding Internet; and (b) incorporate the Internet's multimedia resources to enhance learning.

- *Useful Web Sites:* Considering the vast scope and rate of change of technological growth, it is difficult to cover all facets of technology and related issues of its impact on society. Therefore, each part concludes with a list of web sites that can be used by the reader to supplement and enhance the content of the part.

- *Questions:* Each article concludes with questions to integrate knowledge and synthesize understanding of social issues impacted by technology. The questions also create excitement and wonderment about the tenacity of technology and its impact on the quality of life.

- *Statistics:* Boxes containing statistics, percentages, and bar graphs enhance many readings. They provide the reader the opportunity of comprehending the magnitude of the social issue presented from a more numerical format.

ORGANIZATION OF THE TEXT

Part I encourages students to try to clarify and sort out the many ways we look at and define technology. This section begins with an extensive timeline, highlighting technology from the most primitive forms to the most sophisticated. It continues to analyze the question, *"Why study science and technology in society?"* and encourages the reader to understand the progression and impact of technology from the perspective of a *Homo habilis* to those living in the new century. Readers are asked to consider and evaluate the mismatch between man and the newly created world of technology.

Part II investigates the impact of technology on energy development and conservation. This section provides a survey of renewable and nonrenewable energy technologies and discusses the issues and challenges of economic growth within the domains of sustainable environment.

Part III presents a variety of ecological issues and challenges to help the reader understand how technological developments correlate to a healthy environment. The part begins with an overview of the major ecological risks for the 21st century, followed by three articles that provide a global view of the consequences of increased and intense resource use. Tables and graphs promote empirical understanding. Five case studies address more specialized and local issues of the environment. We hope that the reader will understand the urgency and sensitivity of our environmental decisions in the new century.

Part IV offers a series of articles and case studies on the topic of population growth. This section gives the reader an understanding of the global exponential population growth that is facing the world and its associated problems, with some suggested strategies for improving this dilemma. Third world countries' special problems are included in this discussion.

Part V discusses the impact of technology on war and politics. It asks, among other questions, if there is a point at which having impressive military technologies makes war more acceptable to a society. It also asks if societies have fooled themselves into believing that developing these resources will really save it from risking its far more important and irreplaceable human resources.

Part VI confronts the need for ethical behavior in the use of technology. This question is analyzed further through the cases of individuals who had to make ethical decisions about technological use that cost them their jobs. The remaining studies deal with instances in which technology failed. These accidents could have been avoided if someone had spoken up. Many such accidents are the result of human error or the abuse of technology, either in its construction or in its use. By reading this section students will gain a greater understanding of personal and social responsibility attached to technological development and implementation.

Part VII, "Health and Technology," is a far-reaching survey of some of the greatest accomplishments of modern medicine and its greatest ethical concerns. A medical timeline illustrates the rapid growth of medical technology. It is followed by articles that persuade the reader to reconsider the use of some medical technologies; question the overuse of antibiotics; evaluate the use of animals for organ transplants (xenotransplants); and wonder about physician-assisted suicide.

Part VIII explores the state and impact of technology in the developing countries and provides an insight into the intrinsic and extrinsic problems and their potential solutions.

Part IX presents a time and space approach enabling the reader to reflect on the issues of the previous eight parts and to project their development and applications to the future. The purpose of this approach is to refocus and converge the thoughts across the "bridge of now" so that they guide us to the "bridge of the 21st century."

Part IX begins by crossing over the bridge into the 21st century and envisioning a preferred future. Specific case studies of new technological applications that will affect our lives in health, medicine, and the military—as well as future predictions—guide this chapter. "Bridges to Your 21st Century Understanding" highlight special progress on topics mentioned above. Part IX concludes with commentaries from the authors presenting our own interpretation as we walk across the bridge to the 21st century.

The nine parts are organized in a pattern that encourages a developmental understanding of technology and its impact on energy use, population, ecology, war, social responsibility, medicine, third-world countries, and the future. A psychologist, an anthropologist, an engineer, and a historian worked long and hard to make the book interesting. This diversity has added depth, scope, and encompassing views that we hope will play a positive and decisive role in the decisions you make regarding the use of technology in the future.

Our hope in undertaking this effort is that readers will better understand the complex relationship between technology and society, as well as the reasons that technological development sometimes causes society to worry and wonder about its impact—and that they will marvel, at the same time, at its potential for doing good.

ACKNOWLEDGMENTS

We gratefully acknowledge the valuable input of the following reviewers: Ward Deutschman, Briarcliff College; Tony Obradovich, DeVry Institute of Technology; Richard Quinn, New Jersey Institute of Technology; Nathan Strong, Golden Gate University; and Richard Wertz, New England Institute of Technology. In addition, special thanks are extended to Charles Stewart and Kate Linsner for their support in the creation of this project.

Contents

xviii   Contents

PART

I

History of Technology

A monument dedicated to the men and women workers of the Industrial Revolution in Birmingham, England. Photo Courtesy of Ahmed S. Khan.

Have you ever heard the old saying, "Necessity is the mother of invention"? What do you think it means? Often it is interpreted to mean that things are created to take care of a need. Want to preserve an idea? Invent writing. Need to get someplace fast? Invent the auto, train, or airplane. Got a neighbor who keeps trespassing on your property? A fence might be the answer, and in extreme cases, firearms have proven most persuasive.

It seems as if human development and technological development have proceeded hand in hand. Indeed, as we survey all that we have done with the technology that we have developed it would be hard to resist indulging in a moment of self-congratulation. But before we break our arms patting ourselves on the back, as some might say, we should recognize that there is a growing chorus of voices which are asking whether, in fact, technology has become humanity's master and not the other way around. Maybe the old saying that began this introduction ought to read "Invention is the mother of necessity." The inference here is that those things people never dreamed of having a few hundred years ago have become the things that people today couldn't dream of *not* having. Some equally disturbing questions brought about by the use of technology are "Has technology helped everyone, or just the few who can understand or afford it?" and "Have we become so dependent on technology that we have attached our spiritual as well as material happiness to it?

This part of the text is a diverse collection of views covering history, sociology, and anthropology and is expressed by people with equally diverse and even controversial points of view. As you examine the technology time line, imagine the impact that each new technology had on humans and how the technology changed individual and societal lifestyles forever.

The chapter on "The Evolution of Despair," by Robert Wright, challenges the notion that technological development helps everyone. Wright argues that, because of technology, we value our lives not by what we are, but rather by what we possess. He presents a historical perspective of technology that forces the reader to think more critically about the development of technologies.

"The Great Leap Forward," by Jared Diamond, traces human development over the centuries and poses several questions about human evolution. One question remains from Diamond's work: Even though Darwinists have shown, through bones and other evidence, that humans evolved and were not instantaneously and separately created, how and when did humans acquire the unique characteristics of language, art, writing, and mastery over machines?

As you'll see, the selections presented are not short on controversy. Will you agree with everything you read? Not likely. But the material will hold your interest. And if what you read here makes you think about technology and society, in the past, present, and future, the selections will have achieved their purpose.

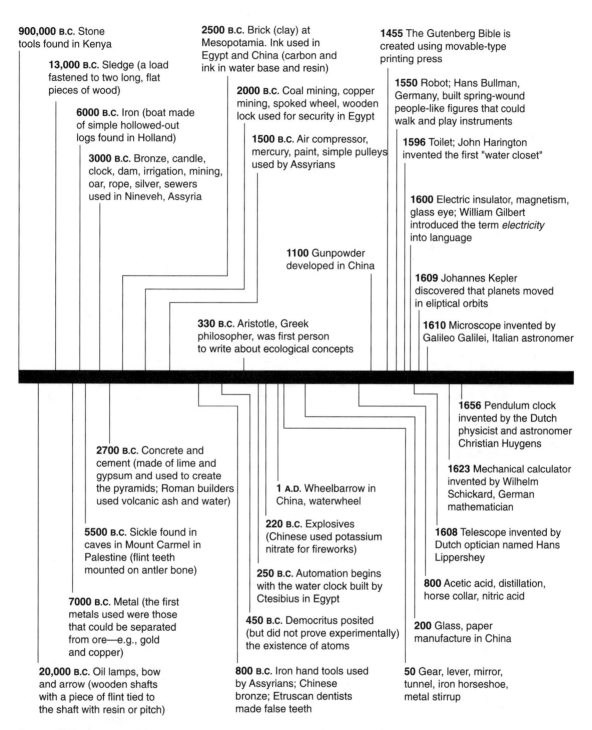

900,000 B.C. Stone tools found in Kenya

13,000 B.C. Sledge (a load fastened to two long, flat pieces of wood)

6000 B.C. Iron (boat made of simple hollowed-out logs found in Holland)

3000 B.C. Bronze, candle, clock, dam, irrigation, mining, oar, rope, silver, sewers used in Nineveh, Assyria

2500 B.C. Brick (clay) at Mesopotamia. Ink used in Egypt and China (carbon and ink in water base and resin)

2000 B.C. Coal mining, copper mining, spoked wheel, wooden lock used for security in Egypt

1500 B.C. Air compressor, mercury, paint, simple pulleys used by Assyrians

1100 Gunpowder developed in China

330 B.C. Aristotle, Greek philosopher, was first person to write about ecological concepts

1455 The Gutenberg Bible is created using movable-type printing press

1550 Robot; Hans Bullman, Germany, built spring-wound people-like figures that could walk and play instruments

1596 Toilet; John Harington invented the first "water closet"

1600 Electric insulator, magnetism, glass eye; William Gilbert introduced the term *electricity* into language

1609 Johannes Kepler discovered that planets moved in eliptical orbits

1610 Microscope invented by Galileo Galilei, Italian astronomer

2700 B.C. Concrete and cement (made of lime and gypsum and used to create the pyramids; Roman builders used volcanic ash and water)

5500 B.C. Sickle found in caves in Mount Carmel in Palestine (flint teeth mounted on antler bone)

7000 B.C. Metal (the first metals used were those that could be separated from ore—e.g., gold and copper)

20,000 B.C. Oil lamps, bow and arrow (wooden shafts with a piece of flint tied to the shaft with resin or pitch)

1 A.D. Wheelbarrow in China, waterwheel

220 B.C. Explosives (Chinese used potassium nitrate for fireworks)

250 B.C. Automation begins with the water clock built by Ctesibius in Egypt

450 B.C. Democritus posited (but did not prove experimentally) the existence of atoms

800 B.C. Iron hand tools used by Assyrians; Chinese bronze; Etruscan dentists made false teeth

1656 Pendulum clock invented by the Dutch physicist and astronomer Christian Huygens

1623 Mechanical calculator invented by Wilhelm Schickard, German mathematician

1608 Telescope invented by Dutch optician named Hans Lippershey

800 Acetic acid, distillation, horse collar, nitric acid

200 Glass, paper manufacture in China

50 Gear, lever, mirror, tunnel, iron horseshoe, metal stirrup

1743 First passenger elevator invented for use by Louis XV of France at Versailles palace

1756 Dentures (Prussian dentist Philip Pfaff described steps to make wax impressions and cast models for missing teeth)

1666 Isaac Newton discovered gravity

1745 Electric capacitor (The first storage device for an electric charge was invented by Edwald von Kliest of Germany); first working electric capacitor (Leyden jar invented by Peter van Musschenbroek at University of Leyden)

1676 Andre Felibien invented the screwdriver

1757 Achromatic lens (John Dolland of England invented lenses made of two kinds of glass for the telescope)

1698 Steam pump invented by Thomas Savery, an English military engineer (pump used to drain water from mines)

1718 Machine gun invented by James Puckle in England; fired 63 rounds in seven minutes

1758 First railroad passenger car made of wood (Great Britain)

1749 Electricity (Benjamin Franklin discovered that electricity has two states: positive and negative)

1760 First bifocals were designed by Benjamin Franklin (U.S.)

1725 Punched card (Basile Bouchon of France used punched paper to control a loom)

1752 Diving suit (Englishman John Smeaton invented an air pump that fit into a diving bell)

1776 David Bushnell (U.S.) built a hand-cranked submarine

1714 Thermometer invented by Gabriel Danile Fahrenheit in Poland

1748 Electroscope, an instrument that detects electric charges, invented by Jean Antoine Nollet of France; steel-nibbed pen invented by Johann Janssen in france

1769 First automobiles had three wheels, was powered by a steam engine, and had a top speed of 3 mph; they were bulky and inefficient

1681 Barograph, a device for recording atmospheric pressure, invented by English physicist Robert Hooke

1661 Pollution control (John Evelyn of England) proposed methods for preventing smoke from polluting the air

1744 "Franklin stove" designed by Benjamin Franklin in United States; widely adopted in Europe decades later

1764 Spinning jenny (Invented by English weaver Hames Hargreaves, the machine could do the work of 30 spinning wheels)

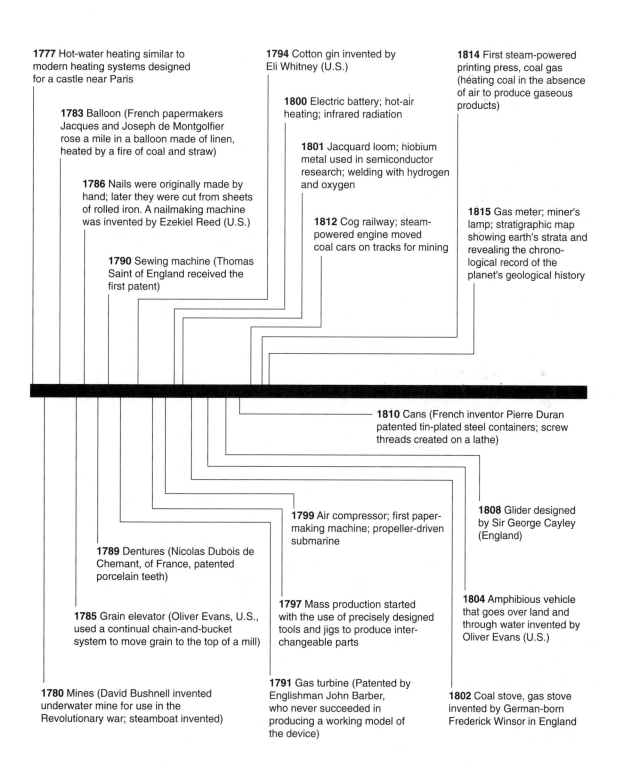

1777 Hot-water heating similar to modern heating systems designed for a castle near Paris

1783 Balloon (French papermakers Jacques and Joseph de Montgolfier rose a mile in a balloon made of linen, heated by a fire of coal and straw)

1786 Nails were originally made by hand; later they were cut from sheets of rolled iron. A nailmaking machine was invented by Ezekiel Reed (U.S.)

1790 Sewing machine (Thomas Saint of England received the first patent)

1794 Cotton gin invented by Eli Whitney (U.S.)

1800 Electric battery; hot-air heating; infrared radiation

1801 Jacquard loom; hiobium metal used in semiconductor research; welding with hydrogen and oxygen

1812 Cog railway; steam-powered engine moved coal cars on tracks for mining

1814 First steam-powered printing press, coal gas (heating coal in the absence of air to produce gaseous products)

1815 Gas meter; miner's lamp; stratigraphic map showing earth's strata and revealing the chronological record of the planet's geological history

1810 Cans (French inventor Pierre Duran patented tin-plated steel containers; screw threads created on a lathe)

1799 Air compressor; first papermaking machine; propeller-driven submarine

1808 Glider designed by Sir George Cayley (England)

1789 Dentures (Nicolas Dubois de Chemant, of France, patented porcelain teeth)

1785 Grain elevator (Oliver Evans, U.S., used a continual chain-and-bucket system to move grain to the top of a mill)

1797 Mass production started with the use of precisely designed tools and jigs to produce interchangeable parts

1804 Amphibious vehicle that goes over land and through water invented by Oliver Evans (U.S.)

1780 Mines (David Bushnell invented underwater mine for use in the Revolutionary war; steamboat invented)

1791 Gas turbine (Patented by Englishman John Barber, who never succeeded in producing a working model of the device)

1802 Coal stove, gas stove invented by German-born Frederick Winsor in England

5

1828 Electric resistor; match (containing potassium and antimony); Ohm's law (formula relating voltage to current and resistance in electric circuits)

1833 Steam brake; plunger-fill fountain pen; reproduction of images in photography; term *scientist* was coined at the British Association for the Advancement of Science

1851 Plastic (Nelson Goodyear, U.S., patented the first synthetic plastic, which he called ebonite)

1830 Lawn mower; achromatic microscope; first commercial sewing machine, washing machine (wooden bin for water; heavy blades stirred the clothes)

1840 Auto speedometer; wire rope (cable); pesticides: first large-scale eradication of pests with chemicals in Europe

1855 Dry cleaning; seismograph; weather station

1857 Air compressor; Bunsen burner; first elevator installed in American department store; fluorescent lightning

1842 Facsimile transmission: First model invented by Scottsman Alexander Bain using a pendulum to create images on a shellac-coated piece of metal

1841 Auto ignition system, circuit breaker, and fuse theory stated by James Prescott Joule (England)

1860 First internal combustion engine in a carriage. Internal combustion engine ran on air and coal gas

1831 Electric motor; electric generator; electric transformer; electromagnetic waves; reaper; safety fuse

1850 Electrically controlled mine explosive; mirror (use of silver deposited onto glass); railroad switchyard; crank-operated washing machine (U.S.)

1856 Blast furnace; micrometer gauge; pasteurization to prevent fermentation in wine

1829 Circuit breaker and fuse; geothermal energy, non-Euclidean geometry; punch card used by Charles Babbage for his mechanical calculator (never finished)

1837 Diving suit; electric motor; electric vehicle; telegraph was patented by Morse, but the first message wasn't sent until 1844

1852 Airship: first successful flight (17 miles); gyroscope (points continuously to true north)

1868 First tilting dental chair invented. First electric dental drill invented. (The drill wasn't put on the market until 1872 and wasn't used until the 1890s due to the lack of electricity)

1862 Rapid-firing machine gun; acoustics of music

1865 Genetics (Gregor Mendel of Austria conducted experiments crossbreeding various strains of garden peas.) Electrolytic refining of copper

1876 Telephone patent was granted to Alexander Graham Bell by the U.S. Supreme Court. Elisha Gray filed for, and failed to receive, the patent two hours after Bell

May 24, 1844. Samuel Morse, inventor of the telegraph, sends a message from the Supreme Court chamber while being watched by Annie Ellsworth, Dolly Madison, Henry Hill, and other dignitaries. Credit: U.S. Capitol Historical Society

1877 Duplicating was invented by Thomas Alva Edison. Carbon microphone created by Emile Berliner and Thomas Alva Edison. Moving-coil microphone invented by Charles Cuttris and Werner Siemens; phonograph was patented by Thomas Alva Edison. Emile Berliner invented a wax phonograph record that produced a fuzzy sound

1864 Nitroglycerine used as a detonator by Alfred Nobel. James Clerk Maxwell created a set of four equations that described the relation between electricity and magnetism

1869 Sir William Herschel (England) devised fingerprint identification system; steam-powered monorail system invented in Syria; periodic table of elements created; stock ticker (printer of stock prices) invented by Thomas Alva Edison; DNA discovered by Johann Friedrick Miescher; automatic air brake invented for railroad cars

1876 Carpet sweeper invented by Melville Bissell (U.S.); J. Willard Gibbs, American physicist, wrote about the general principles of physical chemistry

1861 Color photography (Thomas Sutton and James Clerk Maxwell took pictures, made positive transparencies, and projected them on a screen); tanker named *Elizabeth Watts* was the first ship built in the United States to carry oil from Pennsylvania to London

1867 Barbed wire patented. Dynamite patented. First successful torpedo invented. First commercial typewriter invented

1866 Ernst Heinrich Haeckle was the first to use the term *ecology*

1870 Refrigerator invented and manufactured using ammonia

1878 Solar heating could run a steam engine. Incandescent lightbulb was created by Sir Joseph Swan, but wasn't produced until 1881

1880 Analog computer was designed by the Scottish physicist Lord Kelvin. The machine could not be built, but was the model for a successful computer built by Vannevar Bush in 1930; card-driven electromechanical tabulator invented by Herman Hollerith (U.S.)

1882 Successful development of central electric power plants caused an increase in usage of electrical home appliances; plastic-covered bandage invented by Paul Beiersdor, a German pharmacist; first power station distributed electricity, supplying current for lights in New York City; first motion picture camera invented by Etienne-Jules Marey in France. It took 12 photographs each second

1892 Electric radiator patented; first gas tractor invented

1893 First gasoline car built by Charles and Frank Duryea (U.S.)

1895 X-rays were discovered by German physicist Wilhelm Roentgen. Walter Bradford Cannon was the first to use X-rays for diagnostic reasons; he fed bismuth subnitrate into a small animal and followed it through the digestive system by means of X-rays

1896 Global warming was studied by Swedish physical chemist Svante A. Arrhenius. He wrote about the negative impact that burning fossil fuels could have on the earth's temperature

1888 Magnetic recording started with an article written by Oberlin Smith, who suggested using fabric strips containing iron filings to record sound on magnetic tapes; first ballpoint pen, spray carburetor for cars, pneumatic bicycle tires, electric railroad, electric transformer, radio waves

1888 Electrical streetcars were implemented in Richmond, Virginia. Frank J. Sprague designed a pole that received power from overhead wires

1900 Rigid airship was launched by Count Ferdinand von Zeppelin (Germany). Quantum theory was created by German physicist Max Planck. Eighty different types of optical glasses created

1881 Time and motion studies conducted by Frederick Taylor.

1885 Successful three-wheeled auto built by Karl Benz

1897 First rigid airship (dirigible) built; diesel engine invented; electron discovered; first working drilling rig developed off the California coast

1879 Incandescent lightbulb invented by Thomas Alva Edison

1883 Automobile ignition system was created by Etienne Lenoir (France) and Karl Benz (Germany)

1901 First hearing aid patented, called the "Telephone-Transmitter"; first successful internal combustion tractor built; first tractor company, Hart-Parr Tractor, opened in Charles City, Iowa; first patented vacuum cleaner that had a five-horsepower piston engine for operation.

1907 Electric washing machine invented by Alva J. Fisher (U.S.); first electric vacuum cleaner invented by J.M. Spangler (U.S.); first intra-uterine device (IUD) made from silkworm gut

1903 Four-cylinder model of aircraft engine producing 12 horsepower developed by Orville and Wilbur Wright

1911 First acknowledged bombing from aircraft (Lieutenant Favotti of the Italian army dropped bombs on a Turkish camp in Libya)

1906 First teleprinter invented; sends coded signals recorded on paper tapes encoded into a typewriter

1913 Assembly lines introduced by Henry Ford; zipper with interchangeable identical teeth invented

1920 Hair dryers with electric heating emerged in the United States

1921 Polygraph (lie detector) was invented

1914 Automatic pilot for airplanes invented

1923 First metallic intrauterine device (IUD) invented

1915 Sonar invented for detection of submarines; synthetic rubber invented by the Germans during WWI

1905 First milking machine introduced in America

1912 First commercial fuel injection design created; first parachute jump from an airplane; first gas mask invented to protect WWI firefighters and soldiers from chlorine gas fumes

1904 First patented gyrocompass; automotive hydraulic brakes invented; first subway line opened in New York City

1902 Walter Sutton (U.S.) discovers that chromosomes carry genetic code

1910 Neon light; seaplane invented by Henri Fabre (France); genes: Thomas Hunt Morgan (U.S.) published studies about fruit flies which proved that genes were encoded in chromosomes

1924 First self-winding wristwatch patented in England

1931 Van de Graaf generator was invented to separate electrons from protons

1926 Aerosol spray was invented by Eric Rotheim (Norway)

1926 First rocket fired using liquid fuel

1935 Self-propelled combine harvester. First parking meter; meters were installed in New York in 1951 and London in 1957. Nylon. First radar created that could detect planes 40 miles away. First heart-lung machine; the inventors shut off a cat's heart and lungs and used the machine to keep it alive. They tried the machine on a human patient, but he passed away

1930 Car-washing machines became available. The cars were washed by hand as workers pulled them through on tracks; diesel-powered railroad engines were commonly used; freon gas was discovered for use in refrigerators

Liquid telephone. "Mr. Watson, come here; I want you!" were the first historic words articulated over an electric telephone on March 10, 1876. Courtesy of AT&T Photo Center.

1938 Teflon created and first used on gaskets and valves for atomic bombs. Teflon-coated pans were not sold until 1960.

1944 Missiles were developed during WWII

1942 Cotton picker invented by International Harvester; picked only ripe cotton

1946 Nuclear magnetic resonance (NMR) was discovered by Felix Bloch and Edward Purcell, who shared the Nobel Prize for physics in 1952 for their invention

1940 Color television invented: regular television services didn't start until 1954

1937 U.S. Army adopted the Garand semiautomatic rifle that used eight rounds of clips

1929 Magnetic recording of sound invented

1928 Radio beacon for aircraft was an early form of electronic navigation

1925 Microfilm invented by a bank clerk; used to photograph checks

1932 Automatic transmission was invented by Richard Spikes (U.S.)
1933 First pair of practical contact lenses

Henry Ford introduced assembly lines in 1913. Courtesy of Ford Motor Company.

1947 "Automation" was coined. Instant camera was invented by Edwin Land

1948 Computer memory (electron beam shot from cathode-ray tube to display data on a computer screen); Long-playing record; transistor invented, making most vacuum tubes obsolete; Velcro invented

1949 EDSAC, first computer built with a program. Inventor Harold Lyons harnessed molecular vibrations to create the atomic clock; High-quality phonograph records running at 45 revolutions per minute and $33\frac{1}{3}$ revolutions per minute became available

1951 Birth control pill: 19-Norsteroid was created and found to suppress ovulation. Computer memory: Whirlwind computer created magnetic core memory

1953 Computer printer developed by Remington Rand Company for the Univac. Speed of printer was 600 lines per minute

1955 Hard disk produced by IBM staff; fiber optics created by Narinder S. Kapany (India); first nuclear submarine built in U.S.

1947 Computer-aided process (California Institute of Technology devised ways to use computers to help design aircraft)

1950 Artificial intelligence was introduced as a theory in a paper written by Alan M. Turing (England). Bugging devices were created; solar energy (in Odeillo, France, a 130-ft-high device consisting of 9,500 mirrors focused on a solar oven, creating temperatures of approximately 7,000 degrees Fahrenheit); rigid printed circuits. Nobel prize awarded for semiconductor property studies by Sir Nevill Francis Mott (England) and Philip Warren Anderson (U.S.); detergents first sold in American stores; linear electric motors (produce motion in a straight line); Linus Pauling expresses concern that nuclear fallout is harmful

1954 Measles vaccine; first industrial robot built by George Devol; silicon batteries invented at Bell Labs; genetic code: George Gamow (U.S.) suggested that nucleic acids act as a genetic code during the formation of enzymes

1952 Polio vaccine created by Jonas Edward Salk

1959 First space probe launched by Soviet Union; it was a lunar probe sent to measure radiation and ionization near the moon. First copier using xerography placed on sale

1958 Electric lawnmower invented; artificial intelligence: The Perceptron, an intelligent machine modeled after the human brain, was developed by Frank Rosenblatt (U.S.); Hovercraft (vehicle supported by a cushion of air when in motion) invented

1961 First human in space, Russian cosmonaut Yuri A. Gagarin. First U.S. astronaut, Alan B. Shephard, entered space a few weeks after Gagarin. First electronic watch using a mercury cell invented by Bulova

1968 CAD/CAM system to drive several numerical control machines developed by MIT and the U.S. Air Force; Microchip created by Robert N. Noyce (U.S.)

1965 Artificial sweetener: James M. Schlatter (U.S.) discovered aspartame

1970 Cable introduced to communities

1972 Laser disks developed, but did not become commercially available until 1984

1973 First nuclear magnetic resonance image of human tissue. Skylab launched, with three different crews operating the vehicle for a total of 170 days. They took over 150,000 photos and used more than 45 miles of magnetic tape

1967 Artificial left-heart ventricle implanted in patient

1969 US Apollo 11 made successful landing on the moon. Neil Armstrong (U.S.) and Edwin E. Aldrin (U.S.) walked on the moon for approximately two hours

1962 DDT banned as an insecticide, due to Rachel Carson's book, *The Silent Spring*

1957 Rotary-piston engine containing a triangular-shaped piston rotated within a casing invented by Felix Wankel (Germany). First pacemaker built. Russians launched a satellite

1960 Long-term dialysis made possible because of a Teflon™ and Silastic™ shunt that could be left in a patient's wrist for years and that connected an artificial kidney machine to the patient

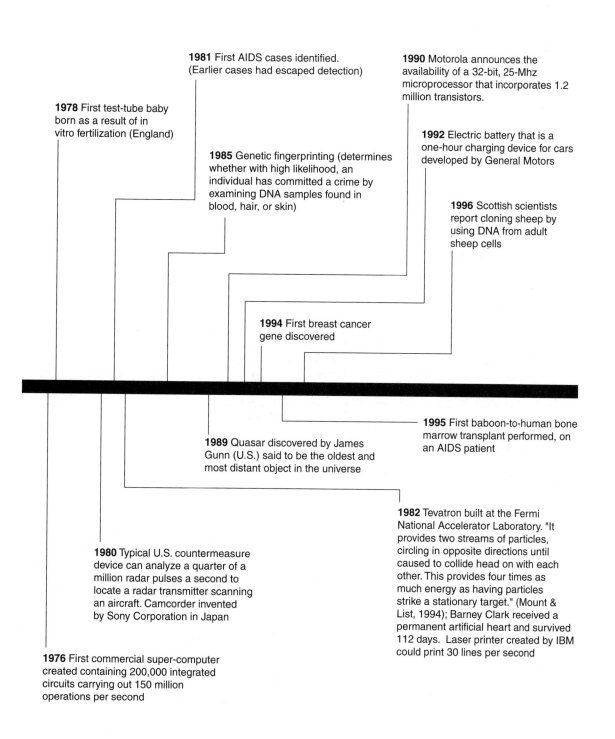

1978 First test-tube baby born as a result of in vitro fertilization (England)

1981 First AIDS cases identified. (Earlier cases had escaped detection)

1990 Motorola announces the availability of a 32-bit, 25-Mhz microprocessor that incorporates 1.2 million transistors.

1985 Genetic fingerprinting (determines whether with high likelihood, an individual has committed a crime by examining DNA samples found in blood, hair, or skin)

1992 Electric battery that is a one-hour charging device for cars developed by General Motors

1996 Scottish scientists report cloning sheep by using DNA from adult sheep cells

1994 First breast cancer gene discovered

1995 First baboon-to-human bone marrow transplant performed, on an AIDS patient

1989 Quasar discovered by James Gunn (U.S.) said to be the oldest and most distant object in the universe

1982 Tevatron built at the Fermi National Accelerator Laboratory. "It provides two streams of particles, circling in opposite directions until caused to collide head on with each other. This provides four times as much energy as having particles strike a stationary target." (Mount & List, 1994); Barney Clark received a permanent artificial heart and survived 112 days. Laser printer created by IBM could print 30 lines per second

1980 Typical U.S. countermeasure device can analyze a quarter of a million radar pulses a second to locate a radar transmitter scanning an aircraft. Camcorder invented by Sony Corporation in Japan

1976 First commercial super-computer created containing 200,000 integrated circuits carrying out 150 million operations per second

1 Why Study Science and Technology in Society?

ROBERT MCGINN

. . . .

INTRODUCTION

On March 23, 1986, the front page of a large San Francisco peninsula newspaper displayed exactly four news stories. One concerned a tentative $350 million settlement of tens of billions of dollars of damage claims filed against the Union Carbide Corporation. The suits were brought by lawyers for thousands of victims of the largest known industrial disaster in history: the December 1984 toxic gas leak at the company's pesticide plant in Bhopal, India, which took over 2,000 lives and inflicted about 200,000 casualties.

A second item related the detonation the previous day, deep beneath the Nevada desert and in the face of domestic and international protest, of a nuclear bomb roughly ten times as powerful as the weapon that destroyed Hiroshima in August 1945.

A third article described the case of a California man who, since suffering traumatic head injuries in an automobile accident in February 1983, had been in a comatose state in a convalescent home. In the wake of the American Medical Association's then recently adopted policy declaring it ethically appropriate for physicians to withhold or withdraw feeding tubes from hopelessly comatose patients, the article related the efforts of the man's brothers to obtain a court order authorizing the removal of his feeding and hydration tubes so that he could "die."

The fourth story reported the imminent approval by the city of Palo Alto, California, of a contract that would make it and a number of adjacent communities part of what would become at that time the nation's largest subscriber-owned cable-TV system.

These news items have one characteristic in common: They all involve *phenomena of science or technology in society*. While the proportion of front-page newspaper stories with significant science- or technology-in-society components rarely approaches the four-out-of-four level, it is often substantial. It might seem, therefore, that the pervasiveness and importance of science and technology in contemporary society are already widely recognized. However, many writers or readers do not recognize that the twin forces of science and technology lie behind numerous examples as disparate as those just related. Nor do they grasp the many and varied reasons that study of science and technology in society is worth while. Let us begin by exploring this question.

THE IMPORTANCE OF SCIENCE AND TECHNOLOGY IN CONTEMPORARY SOCIETY

Military, Economic, and Medical Significance

Science and technology are intimately bound up with three leading concerns of citizens and governments in contemporary societies: military power, economic strength, and medical well-being. Historically speaking, the outcome

Excerpted from *Science, Technology and Society*, by McGinn, Robert, 1991. Reprinted by permission of Prentice-Hall, Inc., Upper Saddle River, NJ.

of World War II depended heavily on the superior scientific and technological capabilities of the United States and its allies. Today those technical resources remain vital to the national security of many governments. One indication of the continuing perceived military importance of science and technology is that in 1988, about three-quarters of the approximately $60 billion U.S. federal government research and development budget went for military-related projects.[1]

Regarding national economic strength, consider the following. First, since the conclusion of the Civil War, when the industrialization of the U.S. economy began in earnest, technology has played a major role in increasing the country's productivity,* a factor critical to long-term economic growth and an increasing standard of living. Indeed, technological change is credited as responsible for almost half of the increase in productivity achieved in the United States since World War II, a contribution far greater than those of capital, education, resource allocation, or economies of scale.[2] Second, of the ten U.S. industrial corporations with the highest sales in 1987, seven were science or technology companies:† General Motors (1), Ford (2), IBM (4), General Electric (6), AT&T (8), DuPont (9), and Chrysler (10).[3] Third, high-technology goods—specifically, commercial aircraft and products in the semiconductor, computer, and office equipment sector—were, along with chemicals and crops, among the few bright spots in the troubled U.S. balance-of-trade picture in the 1970s and 1980s.[4] Such facts underscore the central importance of science and technology in the contemporary U.S. economy.‡ Indeed, science-and-technology capability is likely to be an increasingly important factor in national economic competitiveness for the foreseeable future.

These two forces have also played an important role in greatly increasing the scope and efficacy of medical care in this century, from advances in diagnosis and surgery to vaccines, therapeutic drugs, prosthetic devices, and rehabilitative apparatus. On a personal level, my father's quality of life improved markedly as a result of an artificial hip implant; my wife's cholesterol level declined dramatically as a result of taking an anticholesterol drug; and my son's survival, after being born two months prematurely, was due not only to the efforts of highly competent medical professionals, but also to drugs that accelerated his lungs' development *in utero* and to the high-technology equipment in the intensive-care pediatric nursery in which he spent his first three weeks. As with military strength and economic well-being, the substantial individual and public health benefits afforded by technical advances achieved in recent decades are widely recognized and highly valued in contemporary industrial societies, even though they have carried increasingly steep price tags. The conditions that enable such advances to be realized are complex, fragile, and subject to change. Although they are often taken for granted, they should not be; their evolution and problems deserve close study.

It is not just the military, economic, and medical importance of science and technology in contemporary society that warrants study of such phenomena. The unfolding of such developments has raised a number of difficult social issues that also merit careful consideration. For example, to what extent has the domination of many nations' research and development budgets by military-related projects impeded or promoted the growth of their civilian economies? How should scientific and technological research be organized and funded, and what kinds of political-economic incentives should be enacted to promote sustainable, more equitable national and international economic growth? How can societies ensure that cutting-edge advances in medical science and technology are made available to the needy at home and abroad who are neither covered by public health insurance nor able to afford the going market prices? These are but three of myriad complex policy issues that, taken together, strongly suggest that science and technology in society is a subject of vital practical as well as academic importance.

Human Successes and Failures

The forces of science and technology have been centrally involved in many—indeed, in a seemingly disproportionate number—of the episodes widely viewed as notable human (as opposed to merely individual) successes and failures in recent decades. Notable examples of this trend include the landing on the moon, polio vaccines, civilian jet aircraft transportation, the discovery of the

---

* *Productivity* here means "amount of output generated per unit of input," where *output* typically refers to goods and services, and *input* typically refers to labor (e.g., labor time) or labor and capital combined.

† By *science or technology companies,* I mean private firms whose main products or services require substantial, ongoing, in-house technical research and development efforts.

‡ The pivotal economic role of science and technology in contemporary society has not gone unrecognized in the non-capitalist world. In 1985, the president of the Soviet Union, Mikhail Gorbachev, declared that "The [Communist] party views scientific and technological progress as the main lever for the solution of all economic and social issues" (Erich Bloch, "Basic Research and Economic Health: The Coming Challenge," *Science,* 232, May 2, 1986, 595).

double-helical structure of deoxyribonucleic acid (DNA), the Green Revolution, antibiotics, the personal computer, and the confirmation of the big bang theory of the origin of the universe. The failure side of the ledger includes the Bhopal, Chernobyl, and *Challenger* space-shuttle disasters; the pesticide DDT; the Ford Pinto; building collapses and airplane crashes traceable to defective engineering; and various forms of environmental degradation and human disease caused in part by irresponsible scientific and technological practices. Determining the factors contributing to such successes and failures is a worthwhile intellectual endeavor.

While spectacular at the species level, on the individual human level such successes and failures often mean that certain persons and groups reap substantial benefits from such episodes while others fail to realize them, incur serious harms, or are put at risk of incurring harm. This skewed distribution of benefits, costs, and risks has elicited intense study by both friends and critics of the practices and contexts of science and technology in contemporary society and increased public interest in how these forces are exploited and to what effects.

Threats to Human Survival

As suggested by the news story about the underground bomb detonation, the social significance of science and technology in the contemporary era rests to no small degree on threats to human survival posed by development or use of some of their most potent products: nuclear weapons, products designed for chemical or biological warfare, toxic or lethal by-products of manufacturing or energy-generation processes, and products that threaten the viability of the ecosystem. Understanding the conditions that lead to the creation and irresponsible use of such substances and developing means by which their production and diffusion might be restricted or prevented is a task as difficult as it is urgent.

Ethical Dilemmas

The story about the effort of the comatose patient's brothers to secure court permission to remove his feeding and hydration tubes epitomizes yet another reason that the study of science and technology in contemporary society merits attention. Exploitation of advanced scientific knowledge and technological devices and systems has on occasion given rise to situations in which these advances seem to have turned upon their beneficiaries, creating excruciating ethical and legal dilemmas. Application of these

technical capabilities has sometimes even had tragic outcomes; an example is the prescription to pregnant women of supposedly therapeutic drugs that actually proved to be carcinogenic or to deform fetuses, such as the antimiscarriage drug diethylstilbestrol (DES) and the tranquilizer and sedative thalidomide. The ethical conflicts posed by such science- and technology-based dilemmas require careful analysis. The lessons they teach about problematic aspects of established ethical ideas and assumptions and related social practices in the face of rapid, potent scientific and technological change must be absorbed so that appropriate changes can be made.

Disparities in Human Well-Being

Any list of specific science- or technology-based human successes such as that given above lacks at least one crucial item of a more general nature. It is both a major reason that science and technology are held in high esteem in contemporary society and that, at the same time, some scholars and political figures have leveled intense criticism at the international political-economic context of science and technology. On the one hand, these two forces have made possible the possession of a cornucopia of often sophisticated material goods by hundreds of millions of citizens of the industrialized countries of the West and in Japan.

However, millions of people, in both less and more developed countries, have not partaken of this lavish banquet. . . . .[C]onsider the magnitude of the gap between the historically unprecedented average levels of material affluence enjoyed in societies in which industrialization is well advanced and those characteristic of less developed societies. Understanding the genesis of this gap and developing effective strategies for decreasing it are clearly issues of great intellectual and practical importance.

The existence of such glaring disparities and the widespread belief that scientific and technological resources will be required to diminish them provide another reason that these forces have taken on growing social importance.

Social Conflict

The persistent social conflict witnessed in the last quarter-century is not without precedent in the history of the United States. What is new, however, is something that has greatly magnified the social importance attributed to science and technology in the contemporary era. Much social conflict, not reducible to economic or racial differences, has been occasioned by developments in technology and science. For example, in the last two decades such conflict in the United States has swirled around such issues as the location of recombinant-DNA laboratories in or near residential communities, landing rights for the Concorde Supersonic Transport, the Love Canal incident, the Karen Ann Quinlan and Baby Jane Doe cases, the use of laboratory animals in medical research, the Dalkon Shield intrauterine device, the proliferation of high-rise office buildings in urban centers, research on "surplus" embryos, and the neutron bomb, to name but a few. Such struggles have taxed society's capacity for conflict resolution. . . .

Social and Cultural Roles

Finally, a less obvious but no less important ground of the social importance of science and technology in the contemporary era lies in various influential social and cultural roles that these forces have assumed.

Science. (1) *Combatting Irrationality.* Beginning in the eighteenth century, science became imbued with a skeptical view of and approach to traditional knowledge claims. It came to be assigned the task of weaning the populace from myth, superstition, and resultant irrational belief and behavior. One may observe science serving this function in the influential mid-eighteenth century classic *L'Encyclopédie* of Denis Diderot and Jean d'Alembert. That social function remains operative today. One clear mission of much twentieth century science—and of many contemporary scientists—is to deflate narcissism and combat assorted noxious claims to inherent superiority associated with various "isms," including racism, sexism, ageism, ethnocentrism, and anthropocentrism.

(2) *Preeminent Source of Cognitive Authority.* In the twentieth century, a new social role for science has emerged. Science has become recognized as the leading source of cognitive authority in modern Western life. For centuries in the West, when there was an important dispute over past, present, or future reality in some area of life, leaders of society often turned to a sacred book or religious sage for assistance in making the necessary determination. In the twentieth century, such a tendency persists in certain religious sub-communities and in many individual lives; witness the popularity of biblical literalism and astrology. However, there is now a relatively firm social consensus about the direction in which to turn in such instances: to science.

In contemporary Western society the situation faced by Galileo has been reversed. Rather than scientists being compelled to renounce their empirical findings because they are not in accord with the a priori positions of some church, mainstream religions conduct their business on an intellectual playing field whose parameters are set by the established findings of modern science. To the extent that a religion refuses to recognize and adapt itself to the existential claims and boundary conditions laid down by this preeminent cognitive authority, it forfeits the support of consistent believers in the knowledge claims of modern science. Scientists are the high priests of the twentieth century, and most of the faithful laity defer to the authority conferred by their specialized expertise.

Confirmation of the powerful cognitive authority of science in contemporary Western society is not difficult to find. In 1981, public hearings were held before a U.S. Senate committee considering whether to adopt a bill declaring the fetus a person from the moment of conception.[5] The point of the proposed legislation was that if the fetus was so declared, then abortion would be outlawed, for the fetus would be entitled to the due process protection guaranteed all persons by the Fourteenth Amendment to the Constitution. It is revealing that both supporters and opponents of the measure called scientists to testify for their respective sides, focusing particularly on the pseudoempirical question "When does human life begin?" Neither side wished the conflict to be perceived as one between its own morality and its adversary's science.

So-called creation science illustrates the same gambit. Instead of the issue of the origin of human life being seen as a conflict between religious and scientific authority, some creationists frame the issue as a dispute between "our science" and "their science." Finally, public disclosure in recent years of a number of cases of scientific misconduct has engendered intense discussion within the scientific community. Responses have ranged from attempts to come to grips with the phenomenon to denials that it constitutes a significant problem. Such reactions are explicable partly because such episodes threaten to undermine modern science's cultural role as the ultimate cognitive authority, something that plays no small role in its ability to attract continuing substantial public financial support.

Technology. (1) *Sustaining the Private Corporation.* Technology has long been important in individual and group survival struggles, whether in hunting-and-gathering or agricultural societies. In more recent times it has become vital in sustaining the life of that pivotal modern social institution, the private corporation. Indeed, outside of government, the dominant role played by technology in contemporary society is that of helping corporations survive and increase their profits, something assumed to translate into substantial benefits for society at large. In the late twentieth century, in most influential circles of the Western world, corporation-controlled technological innovation is regarded as the leading contributor to and sine qua non of continued and enhanced societal well-being.

(2) *Source of Personal Identity.* This socioeconomic role, reflecting the interests of producers and owners, is complemented by a sociopsychological one involving consumers. As religion, race, class, sex, and nationality become less able to serve as compelling sources of individual identity in achievement-oriented post-traditional society, the items of technology a person possesses have, along with work, become increasingly important sources of identity and self-esteem. For people without prestigious positions or meaningful work, such items may well become the primary source of these psychological goods. Reminiscent of philosopher Ludwig Feuerbach's materialist dictum "You are what you eat," in contemporary Western society identity and esteem are increasingly rooted in the individual's personal technological inventory. As personal identity becomes more fragile in modern society, producers suggest that one can secure an identity and garner self-esteem by acquiring and displaying the "right"—read "state-of-the-art, high-tech"—artifacts.

(3) *Social Integration and Stratification.* Finally, modern technology has taken on an important sociological role. It is used in various ways to counteract centrifugal tendencies (e.g., the weakened bonds of family and community) characteristic of large-scale, highly mobile twentieth century societies such as the United States. It carries out this integrative role by promoting shared political awareness, common value orientations, and similar consumption patterns, as well as by facilitating intermittent contact between parties at a distance. At the same time, modern technology also serves as a powerful social stratifier. Desire for possession of or control over the sometimes scarce fruits of technological activity fuels feverish struggles for individual, institutional, and national prestige.

"SCIENCE, TECHNOLOGY, AND SOCIETY": A NEW FIELD OF STUDY

In response to the growing importance of science and technology in contemporary society—and to the increasing

recognition of that importance—the last two decades have witnessed the birth and growth of a new academic field: "science, technology, and society," most often referred to simply as "STS." STS does not refer to the kinds of preparatory studies or advanced work in various technical fields pursued by aspiring or practicing scientists and engineers. Rather, it refers to study *about* rather than *in* science and technology. More precisely, STS refers to the study of science and technology *in society*—that is, the study of the ways in which technical and social phenomena interact and influence each other. For example, among the topics studied by STS scholars are the contributions of science and technology to the transformation of social institutions like work and the family, the influence of science and technology on economic growth and international affairs, and ethical and value issues raised by scientific and technological innovations. Other STS scholars, reversing the arrow of influence, study the ways in which science and technology are affected by social factors, such as ideology, political and economic forces, and cultural values.

Besides consideration of the often controversial "external" relationships of science and technology—that is, of their links to social phenomena outside their respective realms—the STS field also encompasses "internal" study of science and technology. *Internal* here does not refer to the inner technical details of scientific and technological work, although that may sometimes be relevant, even essential, to both "externalist" and "internalist" studies. Rather, it refers to studies of phenomena such as the general natures and interrelationships of science and technology, the social structures and reward systems of the professions of science and engineering, and social aspects of everyday scientific and technological activity. The latter category includes the ways in which veteran scientists and engineers initiate and socialize new colleagues, and social factors in the processes by which scientists and engineers adopt or resist proposed changes in theory or practice. . . .

Besides their increasing social importance and the growing recognition of that importance, phenomena of science and technology in society are studied by scholars because they are interesting and complex sociocultural phenomena. Surprising though it may seem, the respective natures and functioning of science and technology in society are not yet well understood, especially in the case of technology. The philosophy, history, and sociology of science are fairly long-standing academic specialities. In contrast, the history and especially the philosophy and sociology of technology are still in early stages of development. There is thus considerable room for original scholarly work on intrinsically interesting, intellectually challenging subject matter.

THE RISE OF CONCERN OVER SCIENCE AND TECHNOLOGY IN SOCIETY: HISTORICAL PERSPECTIVE

One factor in the growth and persistence of concern over science and technology in contemporary society is, then, obvious: These forces are pervasive, potent, and problematic. They do more to shape the character and agenda of modern societies than do most other factors. For an adequate explanation of the *increase* in concern over science and technology in society, however, we must go back at least a half-century.

World War II

Perhaps the most important technical undertaking of the first half of this century was the Manhattan Project, culminating, in August 1945, in the horrors of Hiroshima and Nagasaki. This episode, together with the participation of many German scientists and engineers in the Nazi war effort, raised the issue of the social responsibility of scientists and engineers to a new level of awareness, at least among certain technical practitioners. In the wake of the dropping of the atomic bomb, physicist J. Robert Oppenheimer, director of the Manhattan Project, acknowledged the radically altered relationship of science, technology, and society spawned by the atomic age: "The physicists have known sin."[6]

1945–1960

In the years following World War II, between, say, 1945 and 1960, such concerns remained largely dormant. On the whole, the emerging affluence made possible in part by technology and science during this period, and the increasing role of the federal government in funding scientific and technological work, served effectively to suppress public consideration of these issues. However, development of the H-bomb and its deployment for possible use in war with the Soviet Union or Communist China kept the embers of concern from being completely extinguished.

Precipitating Factors: Twin Crises of War and Environment

In the 1960s this situation changed radically. Public awareness of environmental degradation, galvanized by

Rachel Carson's classic *Silent Spring,* began to increase. As the decade progressed, social protest over the war in Vietnam also grew in scope and intensity. In both cases "science" and "technology" were implicated. From toxic chemical waste disposal, oil-rig and tanker spillages, and strip mining to Agent Orange, napalm, and antipersonnel bombs, many untoward occurrences were debited by significant sectors of society to the accounts of advanced technology and science—and their practitioners.

Initial Responses

Society at Large.   In the late 1960s and early 1970s, a number of developments took place in various industrial societies that reflected the growing public awareness of and concern with issues of science and technology in society. In the United States, Congress passed the National Environmental Policy Act of 1969, which mandated the preparation and approval of environmental impact statements before proceeding with public or private projects "requiring planning permission or state funding or any kind of state license, permission or aid."[7] The following year, complementary legislation was enacted resulting in the establishment of a government agency—the Occupational Safety and Health Administration (OSHA)—charged with protecting workers against dangerous or unhealthy work environments. In 1972, Congress passed the Technology Assessment Act, creating an in-house Office of Technology Assessment (OTA) to supply members of Congress with information useful in considering policy issues with important scientific or technological components. In 1973 the United States experienced an "energy crisis" spawned by the Arab oil boycott. This episode fueled discussion about whether society should pursue wind, tidal, geothermal, solar, and other "soft-path" energy technologies so as to conserve energy as well as environmental and financial resources. Finally, this crisis gave new impetus to the ongoing debate about "appropriate technology" for Third World countries, particularly ones hit hard by enormous increases in the prices of petroleum-based products. In sum, by the early 1970s, STS issues had become the focus of heightened governmental concern.

The Academic World.   In American colleges and universities, protest over the war in Vietnam gave rise in the mid- to late 1960s to what was widely seen as an "antitechnology mood" among students. This was an important factor, but not the only one, in the emergence in the late 1960s and early 1970s of programs devoted to study of the social relations of science and technology. Programs were inaugurated at Cornell, Penn State, and the State University of New York at Stony Brook in 1969, and at the Massachusetts Institute of Technology (MIT), the Universities of Washington and Michigan, and Stanford University shortly thereafter.

Motives among the pioneers of such programs were varied. Some early participants wished to subject recent scientific and technological practice to intense, sometimes tendentious critical analysis. Others wished to use such programs as forums in which to defend the existing practice of science and technology in the universities—including, at times, in their own besieged professions, departments, and research laboratories. Such scholars often spoke of the need for "balanced" consideration of the impact of science and technology on society. However, to them this influence was almost always wholly benign, and they sought to impart to their students a keen appreciation of this fact.

Still other scholars became involved out of a belief that the study of STS subject matter could fill an embarrassing intellectual gap in the curricular offerings of the late twentieth century university. Some went further, holding that interdisciplinary study of science and technology in society held the potential for becoming a new and important mode of integrative undergraduate liberal education for the contemporary era. The campus turmoil spawned by the war in Vietnam had as one of its by-products the dismantling of many established general education requirements. Some early STS supporters saw its interdisciplinary courses as an exciting way of linking up in an organic way students' specialized bodies of knowledge with important intellectual and social concerns beyond the purview of their respective majors. STS courses provided an innovative form of liberal education appropriate for the technological era.

Such courses afforded valuable perspectives and imparted needed skills to different sectors of the undergraduate student body. The study of STS, it was believed, would help tomorrow's decision makers in medicine, law, business, education, engineering, science, and journalism grapple more effectively with the real-life STS issues that they would inevitably face with increasing frequency in their future careers.

The emergence of STS courses and programs in American universities in the late 1960s and early 1970s was a welcome if belated attempt by a number of traditionally structured educational organizations to adapt themselves to an aspect of social reality that had become too obvious and important to continue to ignore.

Survival and Consolidation

The 1970s.   With the winding down and termination of the major triggering episode—the war in Vietnam—in the early 1970s, one might have expected STS concern to go the way of other short-lived educational reform movements. This demise would be doubly expectable given the inflation-driven budget crunches faced by colleges and universities in the period from 1973 to 1976. However, in the mid- to late 1970s, in both the academy and society at large, interest in STS matters increased, fueled by a series of controversial scientific and technological developments. Vexing questions raised by technologies such as nuclear power, computers, genetic engineering, and technologies of human reproduction and life prolongation, issues first raised by startling episodes like Three Mile Island, national defense computer system malfunctions, and the birth of the world's first "test-tube baby," demanded serious consideration. STS programs, congressional hearings, and special features in the print and visual media offered arenas in which such discussions could and often did take place.

1980 to the Present.   In the first half of the 1980s there was little opposition in society or in academia to technology and science per se. On the contrary, science and technology tended to be viewed as redemptive, at least as having essential roles to play in America's struggle against economic decline in the face of vigorous challenges from Japan and other newly industrialized countries (NICs) of Asia. However, even in an atmosphere of scientific and technological boosterism, provocative STS issues like the Reagan administration's Strategic Defense Initiative (SDI, the "Star Wars" program), the first artificial heart implants, and increasing unemployment in the manufacturing sector due in part to automation were and have remained the subjects of lively debate, within and outside the academy.

In the mid-1980s, STS concern received new impetus from philanthropic foundation efforts to promote a basic grasp of scientific, technological, and mathematical thinking and methods among nontechnical college and university students. The motivation for this effort was twofold. "Technical literacy" is seen by some as a precondition for enhanced public understanding of technology and science, something essential for realizing meaningful participatory democracy in the contemporary era. The other motive is economic rather than political: The deteriorating levels of mathematical and scientific learning in American society at large are believed to jeopardize future American economic competitiveness.

The late 1980s witnessed the emergence in academia of a small but growing number of autonomous programs and departments devoted to the study of STS at the doctoral level. In the United States, such endeavors were launched mostly at institutes of technology, such as MIT, Rensselaer Polytechnic Institute, and Virginia Polytechnic Institute. Whether such ventures can thrive only in such specialized educational environments or are forerunners of counterparts at leading research universities remains unclear. The outcome is likely to hinge in part on whether STS, or, as it is called at some institutions, "science and technology studies," achieves recognition as a legitimate field of scholarly activity, as did such equally inter- or multidisciplinary enterprises as religious studies, linguistics, and education.

Conclusion

We have discussed some reasons that science and technology in society is an important topic and indicated the major factors behind the emergence of the STS field. Widespread concern over science and technology in contemporary society was precipitated by twin crises of war and environment. In the last analysis, however, it is the potency, complexity, and rapidity of development of these forces in contemporary society, coupled with the scope, magnitudes, and often controversial character of the social changes associated with them, that have made STS concern and activity a vital and probably permanent feature of the contemporary social and intellectual landscapes.

Endnotes

1. *New York Times,* August 26, 1988, p. A10.
2. Erich Bloch, "Basic Research and Economic Health: The Coming Challenge," *Science,* 232, May 2, 1986, 595.
3. The other three (Exxon [2], Mobil [5], and Texaco [8]) were oil companies whose business is also research and development–intensive. See *The World Almanac and Book of Facts: 1989* (New York: Pharos Books, 1988), p. 140.
4. Michael L. Dertouzos, Richard K. Lester, and Robert M. Solow, *Made In America* (Cambridge, Mass.: MIT Press, 1989), p. 7.
5. *Congressional Quarterly,* February 28, 1981, p. 386, and April 25, 1981, pp. 729–730. See also *New York Times,* April 24, 1981, p. A16, and April 25, 1981, p. A7.
6. J. Robert Oppenheimer, *The Open Mind* (New York: Simon & Schuster, 1955), p. 88.
7. Ernest Braun, *Wayward Technology* (Westport, Conn.: Greenwood Press, 1984), p. 99.

Questions

1. How will studying technology and science correlate to your personal and professional future? Provide two examples and two quotes from McGinn's work to support your answer.
2. What significance does the study of technology and science maintain in the military, economic and medical fields?
3. Provide three situations where technology has been supportive and three in which it has been destructive.
4. How can technology cause social conflict? Provide an example. Use source citations to support presented information.

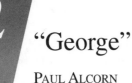

"George"

PAUL ALCORN

● ●

He was a small creature, no more than forty inches in height, and he was, as usual, hungry. His brain was about half the size of modern Homo sapiens, about 650 cubic centimeters, and he lived on a wide, flat plain in Africa, where the tall grass and clutches of low-branched trees made a hunter's paradise for him and his fellow creatures. His kind would one day be known as Homo habilis, but that was nearly two million years in the future. For our purposes, we will call him George.

As I have said, he was hungry. It was a characteristic of his species. Warm blooded and a hunter, George and his companions spent much of their time ranging out across the plain near their most recent campsite in search of food. They were omnivorous, as likely to devour the tough nutty fruit of a nearby berry bush as the raw flesh of some small reptile or insect that failed to escape their notice in time. From day to day, George and his fellows satisfied their internal furnace with the fuel of whatever they could find, always searching for the great kill that would allow them to gorge themselves and replenish the dwindling supply of protein gathered from the last great kill some days or even weeks earlier.

Today they were near the high rock carapace to the east, though they had no concept of direction in those terms. It was merely the "high place over there, where the sun rises." George was scouting ahead of the pack, a chore he seemed to relish. A loner, he would often run ahead,

somehow enjoying the prospect of being the first to sight a potential prey, hoping to be the first to wrestle it to the ground, to pound it to death with his clenched hands, or to tear its throat with his teeth.

The band was in the narrow passage that led into the center of the mound of rocks, close to where a fellow hunter had perished only days before at the hands of another predator, a huge cat creature with claws to tear at the throat and jaws to sink deeply into the flesh and break the victim's neck. George had seen it happen. He remembered it all too well. He was cautious, listening and sniffing the air, remembering what had happened to . . . who was it? His simple consciousness forgot those things easily, but the memory of the danger remained solidly in his mind.

The others were far behind him and out of sight as he turned into the natural bowl formed by the circle of high, flat rocks near the center of the carapace. He could feel the eyes on him, almost smell death in the air. Instinctively, he knew he was not alone. Turning quickly, he scanned the rocks above, seeking any telltale clue of whatever was lurking there. He spun so quickly and jerked his head about so violently in his panic that he nearly missed the low, flat, black furred head, the huge yellowish eyes that stared back at him.

Above George and a little to his left was the same sleek creature that had made a meal of his fellow hunter only days before. George panicked. He turned and leaped to the side of a sheer rock, clinging with his toes and fingertips as the cat made a lunging pass at him. The panther missed the small ape-man by inches. George scrambled toward the summit of the rock, churning his legs wildly in search of

Excerpted from *Social Issues in Technology: A Format for Investigation*, 2d ed., by Paul A. Alcorn, © 1997. Reprinted by permission of Prentice-Hall, Inc., Upper Saddle River, NJ.

some foothold, reaching out blindly with his hands for any purchase further up the rock face. Lacerations appeared on his knees and thighs as he slid against the sharp black obsidian. His fingers numbed as they bit again and again into the narrow, knifelike crevices above. But he was making progress. Below him, the cat yowled and paced, panting heavily and leaping toward the fleeing figure.

Springing with all its might, the huge panther nearly reached George, who pulled forward with a last great effort and reached a wide ledge nearly halfway up the rock face. As he slid himself onto the strip of rock and flattened himself against the wall, a single stone slipped over the edge and fell, striking the huge cat squarely on the nose. With a howl, the panther retreated. George kicked another rock toward the beast, then another, missing both times. In panic, he grabbed several more and hurled them toward the beast, striking him again, this time dead center at the skull. The panther slumped to the ground, stunned by the blow. George grabbed for another loose rock and another, improving his aim with each throw, grasping larger and larger rocks until at last he found himself holding heavy slabs of obsidian over his head with both hands and hurling them down on the lifeless victim. He struck the creature again and again and again.

In the night, belly taut, legs splayed out before him, George lay with the other hunters in the natural bowl of the rocks stuffed with the meat of the dead panther. He was smiling, staring up into the night sky at the bright starlit veil, a swath of white that spread across the sky like a river in the firmament. Absently, he licked his hand and passed the thick saliva over the crusted scratches on his belly and legs. Around him, the sound of night creatures echoed off the surrounding walls as predator and prey continued the struggle for survival.

In his right hand, George clutched at a single round stone, about three inches long across its short axis and weighing nearly half a pound. He felt safe now. He knew that he could fend off any attack. Tomorrow he would try his luck again with his newfound weapon. Tomorrow he would try it against one of the doglike scavengers of the plain or use it to bring down a bird near the river. Perhaps he would never need to be hungry again. Had he not slain the mighty panther singlehandedly? Had he not proven himself the greatest hunter of them all? Who knew what he might be able to do the next time? Who could really know?

Questions

1. Who was George? Describe him in detail.
2. Reflect on George's life; how was his life different from that of humans today? Write a minimum of three paragraphs on the differences.
3. How does the last paragraph of this article correlate to the importance of technology in the life of *homo habilis?*

3

The Evolution of Despair

ROBERT WRIGHT

[I] attribute the social and psychological problems of modern society to the fact that society requires people to live under conditions radically different from those under which the human race evolved . . .

—THE UNABOMBER

There's a little bit of the unabomber in most of us. We may not share his approach to airing a grievance, but the grievance itself feels familiar. In the released excerpts of his still unpublished 35,000-word essay, the serial bomber complains that the modern world, for all its technological marvels, can be an uncomfortable, "unfulfilling" place to live. It makes us behave in ways "remote from the natural pattern of human behavior." Amen, VCRs and microwave ovens have their virtues, but in the everyday course of our highly efficient lives, there are times when something seems deeply amiss. Whether burdened by an overwhelming flurry of daily commitments or stifled by a sense of social isolation (or, oddly, both); whether mired for hours in a sense of life's pointlessness or beset for days by unresolved anxiety; whether deprived by long workweeks from quality time with offspring or drowning in quantity time with them—whatever the source of stress, we at times get the feeling that modern life isn't what we were designed for.

And it isn't. The human mind—our emotions, our wants, our needs—evolved in an environment lacking, for example, cellular phones. And, for that matter, regular phones, telegraphs and even hieroglyphs—and cars, railroads and chariots. This much is fairly obvious and, indeed, is a theme going back at least to Freud's *Civilization and Its Discontents*. But the analysis rarely gets past the obvious: when it does, it sometimes veers toward the dubious. Freud's ideas about the evolutionary history of our

species are now considered—to put it charitably—dated. He hypothesized, for example, that our ancestors lived in a "primal horde" run by an autocratic male until one day a bunch of his sons rose up, murdered him and ate his flesh—a rebellion that not only miraculously inaugurated religion but somehow left a residue of guilt in all subsequent descendants, including us. Any questions?

A small but growing group of scholars—evolutionary psychologists—are trying to do better. With a method less fanciful than Freud's, they're beginning to sketch the contours of the human mind as designed by natural selection. Some of them even anticipate the coming of a field called "mismatch theory," which would study maladies resulting from contrasts between the modern environment and the "ancestral environment," the one we were designed for. There's no shortage of such maladies to study. Rates of depression have been doubling in some industrial countries roughly every 10 years. Suicide is the third most common cause of death among young adults in North America, after car wrecks and homicides. Fifteen percent of Americans have had a clinical anxiety disorder. And, pathological, even murderous alienation is a hallmark of our time. In that sense, the Unabomber is Exhibit A in his own argument.

Evolutionary psychology is a long way from explaining all this with precision, but it is already shedding enough light to challenge some conventional wisdom. It suggests, for example, that the conservative nostalgia for the nuclear family of the 1950s is in some ways misguided—that the household of Ozzie and Harriet is hardly a "natural" and healthful living arrangement, especially for wives. Moreover, the bygone American life-styles that do look fairly natural in light of evolutionary psychology appear to have been eroded largely by capitalism—another challenge to conservative orthodoxy. Perhaps the biggest surprise from evolutionary psychology is its depiction of the "animal" in us. Freud, and various thinkers since, saw "civilization" as an oppressive force that thwarts basic animal urges such as lust and aggression, transmuting them into psychopathology. But evolutionary psychology suggests that a larger threat to mental health may be the way civilization thwarts civility. There is a kinder, gentler side of human nature, and it seems increasingly to be a victim of repression.

The exact series of social contexts that shaped the human mind over the past couple of million years is, of course, lost in the mists of prehistory. In trying to reconstruct the "ancestral environment," evolutionary psychologists analyze the nearest approximations available—the sort of technologically primitive societies that the Unabomber extols. The most prized examples are the various hunter-gatherer societies that anthropologists have studied this century, such as the Ainu of Japan, the !Kung San of Southern Africa and the Ache of South America. Also valuable are societies with primitive agriculture in the few cases where—as with some Yanomamo villages in Venezuela—they lack the contaminating contact with moderners that reduces the anthropological value of some hunter-gatherer societies.

None of these societies is Nirvana. Indeed, the anthropological record provides little support for Jean-Jacques Rousseau's notion of the "noble savage" and rather more for Thomas Hobbes' assertion that life for our distant ancestors was "nasty, brutish, and short." The anthropologist Napoleon Chagnon has written of his first encounter with the Yanomamo: "The excitement of meeting my first Indians was almost unbearable as I duck-waddled through the low passage into the village clearing." Then "I looked up and gasped when I saw a dozen burly, naked, filthy, hideous men staring at us down the shafts of their drawn arrows!" It turned out that Chagnon "had arrived just after a serious fight. Seven women had been abducted the day before by a neighboring group, and the local men and their guests had just that morning recovered five of them in a brutal club fight." The men were vigilantly awaiting retaliation when Chagnon popped in for a chat.

In addition to the unsettling threat of *mano-á-mano* violence, the ancestral environment featured periodic starvation, incurable disease and the prospect of being eaten by a beast. Such inconveniences of primitive life have recently been used to dismiss the Unabomber's agenda. The historian of science Daniel Kevles, writing in the *New Yorker,* observes how coarse the "preindustrial past" looks, once "stripped of the gauzy romanticism of myth." Regarding the Unabomber's apparent aim of reversing technological history and somehow transporting our species back toward a more primitive age, Kevles declares, "Most of us don't want to live in a society like that."

Quite so. Though evolutionary psychologists would love somehow to visit the ancestral environment, few would buy a one-way ticket. Still, to say we wouldn't want to live in our primitive past isn't to say we can't learn from it. It is, after all, the world in which our currently malfunctioning minds were designed to work like a Swiss watch. And to say we'll decline the Unabomber's invitation somehow to turn the tide of technological history isn't to say technology doesn't have its dark side. We don't have to slavishly emulate, say, the Old Order Amish, who use no cars, electricity or alcohol; but we can profitably ask why it is that they suffer depression at less than one-fifth the rate of people in nearby Baltimore.

The barbaric violence Chagnon documented is in some ways misleading. Though strife does pervade primitive societies, much of the striving is subtler than a club fight. Our ancestors, it seems, competed for mates with guile and hard work. They competed for social status with combative wordplay and social politicking. And this competition, however subtle, had Darwinian consequences. Anthropologists have shown, for example, that hunter-gatherer males successful in status competition have better luck in mating and thus getting genes into the next generation.

And getting genes into the next generation was, for better or worse, the criterion by which the human mind was designed. Mental traits conducive to genetic proliferation are the traits that survived. They are what constitute our minds today; they are us, we are designed to steer genes through a technologically primitive social structure. The good news is that doing this job entailed some quite pleasant feelings. Because social cooperation improves the chances of survival, natural selection imbued our minds with an infrastructure for friendship, including affection, gratitude and trust. (In technical terms, this is the machinery for "reciprocal altruism.") And the fact that offspring carry our genes into posterity accounts for the immense joy of parental love.

Still, there is always a flip side. People have enemies—social rivals—as well as friends, feel resentful as well as grateful, feel nervously suspicious as well as trusting.

Their children, being genetic conduits, can make them inordinately proud but also inordinately disappointed, angry or anxious. People feel the thrill of victory but also the agony of defeat, not to mention pregame jitters. According to evolutionary psychology, such unpleasant feelings are with us today because they helped our ancestors get genes into the next generation. Anxiety goaded them into keeping their children out of harm's way or adding to food stocks even amid plenty. Sadness or dejection—after a high-profile social failure, say—led to soul-searching that might discourage repeating the behavior that led to the failure. ("Maybe flirting with the wives of men larger than me isn't a good idea.") The past usefulness of unpleasant feelings is the reason periodic unhappiness is a natural condition, found in every culture, impossible to escape.

What isn't natural is going crazy—for sadness to linger on into debilitating depression, for anxiety to grow chronic and paralyzing. These are largely diseases of modernity. When researchers examined rural villagers in Samoa, they discovered what were by Western standards extraordinarily low levels of cortisol, a biochemical by-product of anxiety. And when a Western anthropologist tried to study depression among the Kaluli of New Guinea, he couldn't find any.

One thing that helps turn the perfectly natural feeling of sadness or dejection into the pathology known as depression is social isolation. Today one-fourth of American households consist of a single person. That's up from 8% in 1940—and, apparently, from roughly zero percent in the ancestral environment. Hunter-gatherer societies, for all their diversity, typically feature intimacy and stability: people live in close contact with roughly the same array of several dozen friends and relatives for decades. They may move to another village, but usually either to join a new family network (as upon marriage) or to return to an old one (as upon separation). The evolutionary psychologists John Tooby and Leda Cosmides see in the mammoth popularity of the TV show *Cheers* during the 1980s a visceral yearning for the world of our ancestors—a place where life brought regular, random encounters with friends, and not just occasional, carefully scheduled lunches with them; where there were spats and rivalries, yes, but where grievances were usually heard in short order and tensions thus resolved.

As anyone who has lived in a small town can attest, social intimacy comes at the price of privacy: everybody knows your business. And that's true in spades when next-door neighbors live not in Norman Rockwell clapboard homes but in thatched huts.

Still, social transparency has its virtues. The anthropologist Phillip Walker has studied the bones of more than 5,000 children from hundreds of preindustrial cultures, dating back to 4,000 B.C. He has yet to find the scattered bone bruises that are the skeletal hallmark of "battered-child syndrome." In some modern societies, Walker estimates, such bruises would be found on more than 1 in 20 children who die between the ages of one and four. Walker accounts for this contrast with several factors, including a grim reminder of Hobbesian barbarism: unwanted children in primitive societies were often killed at birth, rather than resented and brutalized for years. But another factor, he believes, is the public nature of primitive child rearing, notably the watchful eye of a child's aunts, uncles, grandparents or friends. In the ancestral environment, there was little mystery about what went on behind closed doors, because there weren't any.

In that sense, Tooby and Cosmides have noted, nostalgia for the suburban nuclear family of the 1950s—which often accompanies current enthusiasm for "family values"—is ironic. The insular coziness of Ozzie and Harriet's home is less like our natural habitat than, say, the more diffuse social integration of Andy Griffith's Mayberry. Andy's son Opie is motherless, but he has a dutiful great-aunt to watch over him—and, anyway, can barely sit on the front porch without seeing a family friend.

To be sure, keeping nuclear families intact has virtues that are underscored by evolutionary psychology, notably in keeping children away from stepfathers, who, as the evolutionary psychologists Martin Daly and Margo Wilson predicted and then documented, are much more prone to child abuse than biological fathers. But to worship the suburban household of the 1950s is to miss much of the trouble with contemporary life.

Though people talk about "urbanization" as the process that ushered in modern ills, many urban neighborhoods at mid-century were in fact fairly communal; it's hard to walk into a Brooklyn brownstone day after day without bumping into neighbors. It was suburbanization that brought the combination of transience and residential isolation that leaves many people feeling a bit alone in their own neighborhoods. (These days, thanks to electric garage-door openers, you can drive straight into your house, never risking contact with a neighbor.)

The suburbs have been particularly hard on women with young children. In the typical hunter-gatherer village, mothers can reconcile a homelife with a work life fairly gracefully, and in a richly social context. When they gather food, their children stay either with them or with aunts, uncles, grandparents, cousins or lifelong friends. When they're back at the village, child care is a mostly public task—extensively social, even communal. The anthropologist Marjorie Shostak wrote of life in an African hunter-gatherer village, "The isolated mother burdened with bored small children is not a scene that has parallels in !Kung daily life."

Evolutionary psychology thus helps explain why modern feminism got its start after the suburbanization of the 1950s. The landmark 1963 book *The Feminine Mystique* by Betty Friedan grew out of her 1959 conversation with a suburban mother who spoke with "quiet desperation" about the anger and despair that Friedan came to call "the problem with no name" and a doctor dubbed "the housewife's syndrome." It is only natural that modern mothers rearing children at home are more prone to depression than working mothers, and that they should rebel.

But even working mothers suffer depression more often than working men. And that shouldn't shock us either. To judge by hunter-gatherer societies, it is unnatural for a mother to get up each day, hand her child over to someone she barely knows and then head off for 10 hours of work—not as unnatural as staying home alone with a child, maybe, but still a likely source of guilt and anxiety. Finding a middle ground, enabling women to be workers and mothers, is one of the great social challenges of our day.

Much of this trouble, as the Unabomber argues, stems from technology. Suburbs are largely products of the automobile. (In the forthcoming book *The Lost City,* Alan Ehrenhalt notes the irony of Henry Ford, in his 60s, building a replica of his hometown—gravel roads, gas lamps—to recapture the "saner and sweeter idea of life" he had helped destroy.) And in a thousand little ways—from the telephone to the refrigerator to ready-made microwavable meals—technology has eroded the bonds of neighborly interdependence. Among the Aranda Aborigines of Australia, the anthropologist George Peter Murdock noted early this century, it was common for a woman to breast-feed her neighbor's child while the neighbor gathered food. Today in America it's no longer common for a neighbor to borrow a cup of sugar.

Of course, intensive interdependence also has its downside. The good news for our ancestors was that collectively fending off starvation or saber-toothed tigers forged bonds of a depth moderners can barely imagine. The bad news was that the tigers and the starvation sometimes won. Technology is not without its rewards.

Perhaps the ultimate in isolating technologies is television, especially when linked to a VCR and a coaxial cable.

Harvard professor Robert Putnam, in a recent and much noted essay titled "Bowling Alone," takes the demise of bowling leagues as a metaphor for the larger trend of asocial entertainment. "Electronic technology enables individual tastes to be satisfied more fully," he concedes, but at the cost of the social gratification "associated with more primitive forms of entertainment." When you're watching TV 28 hours a week—as the average American does—that's a lot of bonding you're not out doing.

As the evolutionary psychiatrist Randolph Nesse has noted, television can also distort our self-perception. Being a socially competitive species, we naturally compare ourselves with people we see, which meant, in the ancestral environment, measuring ourselves against fellow villagers and usually finding at least one facet of life where we excel. But now we compare our lives with "the fantasy lives we see on television," Nesse writes in the recent book *Why We Get Sick: The New Science of Darwinian Medicine,* written with the eminent evolutionary biologist George Williams. "Our own wives and husbands, fathers and mothers, sons and daughters can seem profoundly inadequate by comparison. So we are dissatisfied with them and even more dissatisfied with ourselves." (And, apparently, with our standard of living. During the 1950s, various American cities saw theft rates jump in the particular years that broadcast television was introduced.)

Relief from TV's isolating and at times depressing effects may come from more communal technologies. The inchoate Internet is already famous for knitting congenial souls together. And as the capacity of phone lines expands, the Net may allow us to, say, play virtual racketball with a sibling or childhood friend in a distant city. But at least in its current form, the Net brings no visual (much less tactile) contact, and so doesn't fully gratify the social machinery in our minds. More generally the Net adds to the information overload, whose psychological effects are still unknown but certainly aren't wholly benign.

This idea that modern society is dangerously asocial would surprise Freud. In *Civilization and Its Discontents,* he lamented the tension between crude animal impulses and the dictates of society. Society, he said, tells us to cooperate with one another, indeed, even to "love thy neighbor as thyself"; yet by our nature, we are tempted to exploit our neighbor, "to humiliate him, to cause him pain, to torture and to kill him. *Homo homini lupus* [Man is a wolf to man]." The Unabomber, too, in his mode as armchair psychologist, celebrates our "WILD nature" and complains that in modern society "we are not supposed to hate anyone, yet almost everyone hates somebody at some time or other." This sort of cramping of our natural selves, he opines, creates "oversocialized" people. He seems to agree with Freud's claim that "primitive man was better off in knowing no restrictions of instinct."

Yet evolutionary psychology suggests that primitive man knew plenty of "restrictions of instinct." True, hatred is part of our innate social repertoire, and in other ways as well we are naturally crude. But the restraint of crude impulses is also part of our nature. Indeed, the "guilt" that Freud never satisfactorily explained is one built-in restrainer. By design, it discourages us from, say, neglecting kin through unbridled egoism, or imperiling friendships in the heat of anger—or, at the very least, it goads us to make amends after such imperiling, once we've cooled down. Certainly modern society may burden us unduly with guilt. After erupting in anger toward an acquaintance, we may not see him or her for weeks, whereas in the ancestral environment we might have reconciled in short order. Still, feeling guilty about spasms of malice is no invention of modern civilization.

This points to the most ironic of evolutionary psychology's implications: many of the impulses created by natural selection's ruthless imperative of genetic self-interest aren't selfish in any straightforward way. Love, pity, generosity, remorse, friendly affection and enduring trust, for example, are part of our genetic heritage. And, oddly, some of these affiliative impulses are frustrated by the structure of modern society at least as much as the more obviously "animal" impulses. The problem with modern life, increasingly, is less that we're "oversocialized" than that we're undersocialized—or, that too little of our "social" contact is social in the natural, intimate sense of the word.

Various intellectual currents reflect this shortage of civility in modern civilization. The "communitarian" movement, lately championed by Democratic and Republican leaders alike, aims to restore a sense of social kinship, and thus of moral responsibility. And various scholars and politicians (including Putnam) are now bemoaning the shrinkage of civil society, that realm of community groups, from the Boy Scouts to the Rotary Club, that once not only kept America shipshape but met deep social needs.

The latest tribute to civil society comes in Francis Fukuyama's book *Trust,* whose title captures a primary missing ingredient in modern life. As of 1993, 37% of Americans felt they could trust most people, down from 58% in 1960. This hurts; according to evolutionary psychology, we are designed to seek trusting relationships and to feel uncomfortable in their absence. Yet the trend is hardly surprising in a modern, technology-intensive econ-

omy, where so much leisure time is spent electronically and so much "social" time is spent nurturing not friendships but professional contacts.

As scholars and public figures try to resurrect community, they might profitably draw on evolutionary psychology. Prominent communitarian Amitai Etzioni, in highlighting the shortcomings of most institutionalized child care, has duly stressed the virtues of parents' "co-oping," working part time at day-care centers. Still, the stark declaration in his book *The Spirit of Community* that "infants are better off at home" gives short shrift to the innately social nature of infants and mothers. That women naturally have a vocational calling as well as a maternal one suggests that workplace-based, cooperative day-care centers may deserve more attention.

Residential planners have begun to account implicitly for human nature. They're designing neighborhoods that foster affiliation—large common recreational spaces, extensive pedestrian thoroughfares and even, in some cases, parking spaces that make it hard to hop from car to living room without traversing some turf in between. In effect: drive-in, hunter-gatherer villages.

Still, many nice features of the ancestral environment can't be revived with bricks and mortar. Building physically intimate towns won't bring back the extended kin networks that enmeshed our ancestors and, among other benefits, made child rearing a much simpler task than it is for many parents today. Besides, most adults, given a cozy community, will still spend much of the day miles away, at work. And even if telecommuting increasingly allows them to work at home, they won't be out bonding with neighbors in the course of their vocations, as our ancestors were.

One reason the sinews of community are so hard to restore is that they are at odds with free markets. Capitalism not only spews out cars, TVs and other antisocial technologies; it also sorts people into little vocational boxes and scatters the boxes far and wide. Economic opportunity is what drew farm boys into cities, and it has been fragmenting families ever since. There is thus a tension within conservative ideology between laissez-faire economics and family values, as various people have noted. (The Unabomber complains that conservatives "whine about the decay of traditional values," yet "enthusiastically support technological progress and economic growth.")

That much modern psychopathology grows out of the dynamics of economic freedom suggests a dearth of miracle cures: Utopian alternatives to capitalism have a history of not working out. Even the more modest reforms that are imaginable—reforms that somewhat blunt moderniza-tion's antisocial effects—will hardly be easy or cheap. Workplace-based day care costs money. Ample and invit-ing public parks cost money. And it costs money to create good public schools—which by diverting enrollment from private schools offer the large communal virtue of making a child's neighborhood peers and schoolyard friends one and the same. Yikes: taxes! Taxes, as Newt Gingrich and others have patiently explained, slow economic growth. True enough. But if economic growth places such a strain on community to begin with—a fact that Gingrich seems to grasp—what's so bad about a marginally subdued rate of growth?

Besides, how large is the psychological toll? Evolu-tionary psychology suggests that we're designed to com-pare our material well-being not so much with some ab-solute standard but with that of our neighbors. So if our neighbors don't get richer—and if the people on *Lifestyles of the Rich and Famous* don't get richer—then we should-n't, in theory, get less happy than we already are. Between 1957 and 1990, per capita income in America more than doubled in real terms. Yet, as the psychologist David My-ers notes in *The Pursuit of Happiness,* the number of Americans who reported being "very happy" remained constant, at one-third. Plainly, more gross domestic prod-uct isn't the answer to our deepest needs. (And that's espe-cially true when growth only widens the gap between rich-est and poorest, as it has done lately.)

There is a lesson here not just for policymakers but also for the rest of us. "It is human nature always to want a lit-tle more," writes the psychologist Timothy Miller in the recent book *How to Want What You Have,* perhaps the first self-help book based explicitly on evolutionary psychol-ogy. "People spend their lives honestly believing that they have almost enough of whatever they want. Just a little more will put them over the top; then they will be con-tented forever." This is a built-in illusion, Miller notes, en-grained in our minds by natural selection.

The illusion was designed to keep us constantly striving, adding tiny increments to the chances that our genes would get into the next generation. Yet in a modern environment—which, unlike the ancestral environment, features contra-ception—our obsession with material gain rarely has that effect. Besides, why should any of us choose to pursue maximum genetic proliferation—or relentless material gain, or anything else—just because that is high on the agenda of the process that designed the human mind? Nat-ural selection, for better or worse, is our creator, but it isn't God: the impulses it implanted into our minds aren't neces-sarily good, and they aren't wholly beyond resisting.

Part of Miller's point is that the instinctive but ulti-mately fruitless pursuit of More—the 60-hour workweeks, the hour a month spent perusing the Sharper Image cata-log—keeps us from indulging what Darwin called "the so-cial instincts." The pursuit of More can keep us from better knowing our neighbors, better loving our kin—in general, from cultivating the warm, affiliative side of human nature whose roots science is just now starting to fathom.

Questions

1. Name three theorists presented in this article, and de-scribe their opinions about technology and society.
2. Has technology made life better? Provide three spe-cific examples. List three examples that illustrate technology's negative effect.
3. What part, if any, might technology play in the in-crease of depression, suicide, and homicide in Amer-ica?
4. "For sadness to linger on into debilitating depression, for anxiety to grow chronic and paralyzing. These are largely diseases of modernity." What does this quote mean to you? List two examples to help you explain it.
5. Why do you think there is no reported depression among the Kalui in New Guinea?

4

The Great Leap Forward

JARED DIAMOND

One can hardly blame nineteenth-century creationists for insisting that humans were separately created by God. After all, between us and other animal species lies the seemingly unbridgeable gulf of language, art, religion, writing, and complex machines. Small wonder, then, that to many people Darwin's theory of our evolution from apes appeared absurd.

Since Darwin's time, of course, fossilized bones of hundreds of creatures intermediate between apes and modern humans have been discovered. It is no longer possible for a reasonable person to deny that what once seemed absurd actually happened—somehow. Yet the discoveries of many missing links have only made the problem more fascinating without fully solving it. When and how did we acquire our uniquely human characteristics?

We know that our lineage arose in Africa, diverging from that of chimpanzees and gorillas sometime between 6 million and 10 million years ago. For most of the time since then we have been little more than glorified baboons. As recently as 35,000 years ago western Europe was still occupied by Neanderthals, primitive beings for whom art and progress scarcely existed. Then there was an abrupt change. Anatomically modern people appeared in Europe, and suddenly so did sculpture, musical instruments, lamps, trade, and innovation. Within a few thousand years the Neanderthals were gone.

Insofar as there was any single moment when we could be said to have become human, it was at the time of this Great Leap Forward 35,000 years ago. Only a few more

Jared Diamond/© 1989. Reprinted with permission of *Discover* Magazine.

dozen millennia—a trivial fraction of our 6-to-10 million-year history—were needed for us to domesticate animals, develop agriculture and metallurgy, and invent writing. It was then but a short further step to those monuments of civilization that distinguish us from all other animals—monuments such as the *Mona Lisa* and the Ninth Symphony, the Eiffel Tower and Sputnik, Dachau's ovens and the bombing of Dresden.

What happened at that magic moment in evolution? What made it possible, and why was it so sudden? What held back the Neanderthals, and what was their fate? Did Neanderthals and modern peoples ever meet, and if so, how did they behave toward each other? We still share 98 percent of our genes with chimps; which genes among the other 2 percent had such enormous consequences?

Understanding the Great Leap Forward isn't easy; neither is writing about it. The immediate evidence comes from technical details of preserved bones and stone tools. Archeologists' reports are full of such terms as "transverse occipital torus," "receding zygomatic arches," and "Chatelperronian backed knives." What we really want to understand—the way of life and the humanity of our various ancestors—isn't directly preserved but only inferred from those technical details. Much of the evidence is missing, and archeologists often disagree over the meaning of the evidence that has survived.

I'll emphasize those inferences rather than the technical details, and I'll speculate about the answers to those questions I just listed above. But you can form your own opinions, and they may differ from mine. This is a puzzle whose solution is still unknown.

To set the stage quickly, recall that life originated on Earth several billion years ago, the dinosaurs became extinct around 65 million years ago, and, as I mentioned, our ancestors diverged from the ancestors of chimps and gorillas between 6 and 10 million years ago. They then remained confined to Africa for millions of years.

Initially, our ancestors would have been classified as merely another species of ape, but a sequence of three changes launched them in the direction of modern humans. The first of these changes occurred by around 4 million years ago: the structure of fossilized limb bones shows that our ancestors, in contrast to gorillas and chimps, were habitually walking upright. The upright posture freed our forelimbs to do other things, among which toolmaking would eventually prove to be the most important.

The second change occurred around 3 million years ago, when our lineage split in two. As background, remember that members of two animal species living in the same area must fill different ecological roles and do not normally interbreed. For example, coyotes and wolves are obviously closely related and, until wolves were exterminated in most of the United States, lived in many of the same areas. However, wolves are larger, they usually hunt big mammals like deer and moose, and they often live in sizable packs, whereas coyotes are smaller, mainly hunt small mammals like rabbits and mice, and normally live in pairs or small groups.

Now, all modern humans unquestionably belong to the same species. Ecological differences among us are entirely a product of childhood education: it is not the case that some of us are born big and habitually hunt deer while others are born small, gather berries, and don't marry the deer hunters. And every human population living today has interbred with every other human population with which it has had extensive contact.

Three million years ago, however, there were hominid species as distinct as wolves and coyotes. On one branch of the family tree was a man-ape with a heavily built skull and very big cheek teeth, who probably ate coarse plant food; he has come to be known as *Australopithecus robustus* (the "robust southern ape"). On the other branch was a man-ape with a more lightly built skull and smaller teeth, who most likely had an omnivorous diet; he is known as *Australopithecus africanus* (the "southern ape of Africa"). Our lineage may have experienced such a radical division at least once more, at the time of the Great Leap Forward. But the description of that event will have to wait.

There is considerable disagreement over just what occurred in the next million years, but the argument I find

most persuasive is that *A. africanus* evolved into the larger-brained form we call *Homo habilis* ("man the handyman").

Complicating the issue is that fossil bones often attributed to *H. habilis* differ so much in skull size and tooth size that they may actually imply another fork in our lineage yielding two distinct *habilis*-like species: *H. habilis* himself and a mysterious "Third Man." Thus, by 2 million years ago there were at least two and possibly three protohuman species.

The third and last of the big changes that began to make our ancestors more human and less apelike was the regular use of stone tools. By around 2.5 million years ago very crude stone tools appear in large numbers in areas of East Africa occupied by the protohumans. Since there were two or three protohuman species, who made the tools? Probably the light-skulled species, since both it and the tools persisted and evolved. (There is, however, the intriguing possibility that at least some of our robust relatives also made tools, as recent anatomical analyses of hand bones from the Swartkrans cave in South Africa suggest. See "The Gripping Story of Paranthropus," by Pat Shipman, in last month's issue.)

With only one human species surviving today but two or three a few million years ago, it's clear that one or two species must have become extinct. Who was our ancestor, which species ended up instead as a discard in the trash heap of evolution, and when did this shakedown occur?

The winner was the light-skulled *H. habilis,* who went on to increase in brain size and body size. By around 1.7 million years ago the differences were sufficient that anthropologists give our lineage the new name *Homo erectus* ("the man who walks upright"—*H. erectus* fossils were discovered before all the earlier ones, so anthropologists didn't realize that *H. erectus* wasn't the first protohuman to walk upright). The robust man-ape disappeared somewhat after 1.2 million years ago, and the Third Man (if he ever existed) must have disappeared by then also.

As for why *H. erectus* survived and *A. robustus* didn't, we can only speculate. A plausible guess is that the robust man-ape could no longer compete: *H. erectus* ate both meat and plant food, and his larger brain may have made him more efficient at getting the food on which *A. robustus* depended. It's also possible that *H. erectus* gave his robust brother a direct push into oblivion by killing him for meat.

The shakedown left *H. erectus* as the sole protohuman player on the African stage, a stage to which our closest living relatives (the chimp and gorilla) are still confined. But around one million years ago *H. erectus* began to expand his horizons. His stone tools and bones show that he reached the Near East, then the Far East (where he is represented by the famous fossils known as Peking man and Java man) and Europe. He continued to evolve in our direction by an increase in brain size and in skull roundness. By around 500,000 years ago some of our ancestors looked sufficiently like us, and sufficiently different from earlier *H. erectus,* to be classified as our own species, *Homo sapiens* (the "wise man"), although they still had thicker skulls and brow ridges than we do today.

Was our meteoric ascent to *sapiens* status half a million years ago the brilliant climax of Earth history, when art and sophisticated technology finally burst upon our previously dull planet? Not at all: the appearance of *H. sapiens* was a non-event. The Great Leap Forward, as proclaimed by cave paintings, houses, and bows and arrows, still lay hundreds of thousands of years in the future. Stone tools continued to be the crude ones that *H. erectus* had been making for nearly a million years. The extra brain size of those early *H. sapiens* had no dramatic effect on their way of life. That whole long tenure of *H. erectus* and early *H. sapiens* outside Africa was a period of infinitesimally slow cultural change.

So what was life like during the 1.5 million years that spanned the emergence of *H. erectus* and *H. sapiens?* The only surviving tools from this period are stone implements that can, charitably, be described as very crude. Early stone tools do vary in size and shape, and archeologists have used those differences to give the tools different names, such as hand-ax, chopper, and cleaver. But these names conceal the fact that none of these early tools had a sufficiently consistent or distinctive shape to suggest any specific function. Wear marks on the tools show that they were variously used to cut meat, bone, hides, wood, and nonwoody parts of plants. But any size or shape tool seems to have been used to cut any of these things, and the categories imposed by archeologists may be little more than arbitrary divisions of a continuum of stone forms.

Negative evidence is also significant. All the early stone tools may have been held directly in the hand; they show no signs of being mounted on other materials for increased leverage, as we mount steel ax blades on wooden handles. There were no bone tools, no ropes to make nets, and no fishhooks.

What food did our early ancestors get with those crude tools, and how did they get it? To address this question, anthropology textbooks usually insert a long chapter entitled something like "Man the Hunter." The point they make is that baboons, chimps, and some other primates prey on small vertebrates only occasionally, but recently surviving

Stone Age people (like Bushmen) did a lot of big-game hunting. There's no doubt that our early ancestors also ate some meat. The question is, how much meat? Did big-game hunting skills improve gradually over the past 1.5 million years, or was it only since the Great Leap Forward—a mere 35,000 years ago—that they made a large contribution to our diet?

Anthropologists routinely reply that we've long been successful big-game hunters, but in fact there is no good evidence of hunting skills until around 100,000 years ago, and it's clear that even then humans were still very ineffective hunters. So it's reasonable to assume that earlier hunters were even more ineffective.

Yet the mystique of Man the Hunter is now so rooted in us that it's hard to abandon our belief in its long-standing importance. Supposedly, big-game hunting was what induced protohuman males to cooperate with one another, develop language and big brains, join into bands, and share food. Even women were supposedly molded by big-game hunting: they suppressed the external signs of monthly ovulation that are so conspicuous in chimps, so as not to drive men into a frenzy of sexual competition and thereby spoil men's cooperation at hunting.

But studies of modern hunter gatherers, with far more effective weapons than those of early *H. sapiens,* show that most of a family's calories come from plant food gathered by women. Men catch rats and other small game never mentioned in their heroic campfire stories. Occasionally they get a large animal, which does indeed contribute significantly to protein intake. But it's only in the Arctic, where little plant food is available, that big-game hunting becomes the dominant food source. And humans didn't reach the Arctic until around 30,000 years ago.

So I would guess that big-game hunting contributed little to our food intake until after we had evolved fully modern anatomy and behavior. I doubt the usual view that hunting was the driving force behind our uniquely human brain and societies. For most of our history we were not mighty hunters but rather sophisticated baboons.

To return to our history: *H. sapiens,* you'll recall, took center stage around half a million years ago in Africa, the Near East, the Far East, and Europe. By 100,000 years ago humans had settled into at least three distinct populations occupying different parts of the Old World. These were the last truly primitive people. Let's consider among them those whose anatomy is best known, those who have become a metaphor for brutishness: the Neanderthals.

Where and when did they live? Their name comes from Germany's Neander Valley, where one of the first skeletons was discovered (in German, *thal*—nowadays spelled *tal*—means "valley"). Their geographic range extended from western Europe, through southern European Russia and the Near East, to Uzbekistan in Central Asia, near the border of Afghanistan. As to the time of their origin, that's a matter of definition, since some old skulls have characteristics anticipating later "full-blown" Neanderthals. The earliest full-blown examples date from around 130,000 years ago, and most specimens postdate 74,000 years ago. While their start is thus arbitrary, their end is abrupt: the last Neanderthals died around 32,000 years ago.

During the time that Neanderthals flourished, Europe and Asia were in the grip of the last ice age. Hence Neanderthals must have been a cold-adapted people—but only within limits. They got no farther north than southern Britain, northern Germany, Kiev, and the Caspian Sea.

Neanderthals' head anatomy was so distinctive that, even if a Neanderthal dressed in a business suit or a designer dress were to walk down the street today, all you *H. sapiens* would be staring in shock. Imagine converting a modern face to soft clay, gripping the middle of the face from the bridge of the nose to the jaws, pulling the whole mid-face forward, and letting it harden again. You'll then have some idea of a Neanderthal's appearance. Their eyebrows rested on prominently bulging bony ridges, and their nose and jaws and teeth protruded far forward. Their eyes lay in deep sockets, sunk behind the protruding nose and brow ridges. Their foreheads were low and sloping, unlike our high vertical modern foreheads, and their lower jaws sloped back without a chin. Yet despite these startlingly primitive features, Neanderthals' brain size was nearly 10 percent greater than ours! (This does not mean they were smarter than us; they obviously weren't. Perhaps their larger brains simply weren't "wired" as well.) A dentist who examined a Neanderthal's teeth would have been in for a further shock. In adult Neanderthals front teeth were worn down on the outer surface, in a way found in no modern people. Evidently this peculiar wear pattern resulted from their using their teeth as tools, but what exactly did they do? As one possibility, they may have routinely used their teeth like a vise, as my baby sons do when they grip a milk bottle in their teeth and run around with their hands free. Alternatively, Neanderthals may have bitten hides to make leather or wood to make tools.

While a Neanderthal in a business suit or a dress would attract your attention, one in shorts or a bikini would be even more startling. Neanderthals were more heavily muscled, especially in their shoulders and neck, than all but the most avid bodybuilders. Their limb bones, which took the force of those big muscles contracting, had to be considerably thicker than ours to withstand the stress. Their arms and legs would have looked stubby to us, because the lower leg and forearm were relatively shorter than ours. Even their hands were much more powerful than ours; a Neanderthal's handshake would have been bone-crushing. While their average height was only around 5 feet 4 inches, their weight was at least 20 pounds more than that of a modern person of that height, and this excess was mostly in the form of lean muscle.

One other possible anatomical difference is intriguing, although its reality as well as its interpretation are quite uncertain—the fossil evidence so far simply doesn't allow a definitive answer. But a Neanderthal woman's birth canal may have been wider than a modern woman's, permitting her baby to grow inside her to a bigger size before birth. If so, a Neanderthal pregnancy might have lasted one year, instead of nine months.

Besides their bones, our other main source of information about Neanderthals is their stone tools. Like earlier human tools, Neanderthal tools may have been simple hand-held stones not mounted on separate parts such as handles. The tools don't fall into distinct types with unique functions. There were no standardized bone tools, no bows and arrows. Some of the stone tools were undoubtedly used to make wooden tools, which rarely survive. One notable exception is a wooden thrusting spear eight feet long, found in the ribs of a long-extinct species of elephant at an archeological site in Germany. Despite that (lucky?) success, Neanderthals were probably not very good at big-game hunting; even anatomically more modern people living in Africa at the same time as the Neanderthals were undistinguished as hunters.

If you say "Neanderthal" to friends and ask for their first association, you'll probably get back the answer "caveman." While most excavated Neanderthal remains do come from caves, that's surely an artifact of preservation, since open-air sites would be eroded much more quickly. Neanderthals must have constructed some type of shelter against the cold climate in which they lived, but those shelters must have been crude. All that remain are postholes and a few piles of stones.

The list of quintessentially modern human things that Neanderthals lacked is a long one. They left no unequivocal art objects. They must have worn some clothing in their cold environment, but that clothing had to be crude, since they lacked needles and other evidence of sewing. They evidently had no boats, as no Neanderthal remains are known from Mediterranean islands nor even from North

Africa, just eight miles across the Strait of Gibraltar from Neanderthal-populated Spain. There was no long-distance overland trade: Neanderthal tools are made of stones available within a few miles of the site.

Today we take cultural differences among people inhabiting different areas for granted. Every modern human population has its characteristic house style, implements, and art. If you were shown chopsticks, a Schlitz beer bottle, and a blowgun and asked to associate one object each with China, Milwaukee, and Borneo, you'd have no trouble giving the right answers. No such cultural variation is apparent for Neanderthals, whose tools look much the same no matter where they come from.

We also take cultural progress with time for granted. It is obvious to us that the wares from a Roman villa, a medieval castle, and a Manhattan apartment circa 1988 should differ. In the 1990s my sons will look with astonishment at the slide rule I used throughout the 1950s. But Neanderthal tools from 100,000 and 40,000 years ago look essentially the same. In short, Neanderthal tools had no variation in time or space to suggest that most human of characteristics, *innovation.*

What we consider old age must also have been rare among Neanderthals. Their skeletons make clear that adults might live to their thirties or early forties but not beyond 45. If we lacked writing and if none of us lived past 45, just think how the ability of our society to accumulate and transmit information would suffer.

But despite all these subhuman qualities, there are three respects in which we can relate to Neanderthals' humanity. They were the first people to leave conclusive evidence of fire's regular, everyday use: nearly all well-preserved Neanderthal caves have small areas of ash and charcoal indicating a simple fireplace. Neanderthals were also the first people who regularly buried their dead, though whether this implies religion is a matter of pure speculation. Finally, they regularly took care of their sick and aged. Most skeletons of older Neanderthals show signs of severe impairment, such as withered arms, healed but incapacitating broken bones, tooth loss, and severe osteoarthritis. Only care by young Neanderthals could have enabled such older folks to stay alive to the point of such incapacitation. After my litany of what Neanderthals lacked, we've finally found something that lets us feel a spark of kindred spirit in these strange creatures of the Ice Age—human, and yet not really human.

Did Neanderthals belong to the same species as we do? That depends on whether we would have mated and reared a child with a Neanderthal man or woman, given the opportunity. Science fiction novels love to imagine the scenario. You remember the blurb on a pulpy back cover: "A team of explorers stumbles on a steep-walled valley in the center of deepest Africa, a valley that time forgot. In this valley they find a tribe of incredibly primitive people, living in ways that our Stone Age ancestors discarded thousands of years ago. Are they the same species as us?" Naturally, there's only one way to find out, but who among the intrepid explorers—male explorers, of course—can bring himself to make the test? At this point one of the bone-chewing cavewomen is described as beautiful and sexy in a primitively erotic way, so that readers will find the brave explorer's dilemma believable: Does he or doesn't he have sex with her?

Believe it or not, something like that experiment actually took place. It happened repeatedly around 35,000 years ago, around the time of the Great Leap Forward. But you'll have to be patient just a little while longer.

Remember, the Neanderthals of Europe and western Asia were just one of at least three human populations occupying different parts of the Old World around 100,000 years ago. A few fossils from eastern Asia suffice to show that people there differed from Neanderthals as well as from us moderns, but too few have been found to describe these Asians in more detail. The best characterized contemporaries of the Neanderthals are those from Africa, some of whom were almost modern in their skull anatomy. Does this mean that, 100,000 years ago in Africa, we have at last arrived at the Great Leap Forward?

Surprisingly, the answer is still no. The stone tools of these modern-looking Africans were very similar to those of the non-modern-looking Neanderthals, so we refer to them as Middle Stone Age Africans. They still lacked standardized bone tools, bows and arrows, art, and cultural variation. Despite their mostly modern bodies, these Africans were still missing something needed to endow them with modern behavior.

Some South African caves occupied around 100,000 years ago provide us with the first point in human evolution for which we have detailed information about what people were eating. Among the bones found in the caves are many of seals and penguins, as well as shellfish such as limpets; Middle Stone Age Africans are the first people for whom there is even a hint that they exploited the seashore. However, the caves contain very few remains of fish or flying birds, undoubtedly because people still lacked fishhooks and nets.

The mammal bones from the caves include those of quite a few medium-size species, predominant among which are those of the eland, an antelope species. Eland bones in the caves represent animals of all ages, as if people had somehow managed to capture a whole herd and kill every individual. The secret to the hunters' success is most likely that eland are rather tame and easy to drive in herds. Probably the hunters occasionally managed to drive a whole herd over a cliff: that would explain why the distribution of eland ages among the cave kills is like that in a living herd. In contrast, more dangerous prey such as Cape buffalo, pigs, elephants, and rhinos yield a very different picture. Buffalo bones in the caves are mostly of very young or very old individuals, while pigs, elephants, and rhinos are virtually unrepresented.

So Middle Stone Age Africans can be considered big-game hunters, but just barely. They either avoided dangerous species entirely or confined themselves to weak old animals or babies. Those choices reflect prudence: their weapons were still spears for thrusting rather than bows and arrows, and—along with drinking a strychnine cocktail—poking an adult rhino or Cape buffalo with a spear ranks as one of the most effective means of suicide that I know. As with earlier peoples and modern Stone Age hunters, I suspect that plants and small game made up most of the diet of these not-so-great hunters. They were definitely more effective than baboons, but not up to the skill of modern Bushmen and Pygmies.

Thus, the scene that the human world presented from around 130,000 years ago to somewhat before 50,000 years ago was this: Northern Europe, Siberia, Australia, and the whole New World were still empty of people. In the rest of Europe and western Asia lived the Neanderthals; in Africa, people increasingly like us in anatomy; and in eastern Asia, people unlike either the Neanderthals or Africans but known from only a few bones. All three populations were still primitive in their tools, behavior, and limited innovativeness. The stage was set for the Great Leap Forward. Which among these three contemporary populations would take that leap?

The evidence for an abrupt change—at last!—is clearest in France and Spain, in the late Ice Age around 35,000 years ago. Where there had previously been Neanderthals, anatomically fully modern people (often known as Cro-Magnons, from the French site where their bones were first identified) now appear. Were one of those gentlemen or ladies to stroll down the Champs Elysées in modern attire, he or she would not stand out from the Parisian crowds in any way. Cro-Magnons' tools are as dramatic as their skeletons; they are far more diverse in form and obvious in function than any in the earlier archeological record. They

suggest that modern anatomy had at last been joined by modern innovative behavior.

Many of the tools continue to be of stone, but they are now made from thin blades struck off a larger stone, thereby yielding roughly ten times more cutting edge from a given quantity of raw stone. Standardized bone and antler tools appear for the first time. So do unequivocal compound tools of several parts tied or glued together, such as spear points set in shafts or ax heads hafted to handles. Tools fall into many distinct categories whose function is often obvious, such as needles, awls, and mortars and pestles. Rope, used in nets or snares, accounts for the frequent bones of foxes, weasels, and rabbits at Cro-Magnon sites. Rope, fishhooks, and net sinkers explain the bones of fish and flying birds at contemporary South African sites.

Sophisticated weapons for killing dangerous animals at a distance now appear also—weapons such as barbed harpoons, darts, spear-throwers, and bows and arrows. South African caves now yield bones of such vicious prey as adult Cape buffalo and pigs, while European caves are full of bones of bison, elk, reindeer, horse, and ibex.

Several types of evidence testify to the effectiveness of late Ice Age people as big-game hunters. Bagging some of these animals must have required communal hunting methods based on detailed knowledge of each species' behavior. And Cro-Magnon sites are much more numerous than those of earlier Neanderthals or Middle Stone Age Africans, implying more success at obtaining food. Moreover, numerous species of big animals that had survived many previous ice ages became extinct toward the end of the last ice age, suggesting that they were exterminated by human hunters' new skills. Likely victims include Europe's woolly rhino and giant deer, southern Africa's giant buffalo and giant Cape horse, and—once improved technology allowed humans to occupy new environments—the mammoths of North America and Australia's giant kangaroos.

Australia was first reached by humans around 50,000 years ago, which implies the existence of watercraft capable of crossing the 60 miles from eastern Indonesia. The occupation of northern Russia and Siberia by at least 20,000 years ago depended on many advances: tailored clothing, as evidenced by eyed needles, cave paintings of parkas, and grave ornaments marking outlines of shirts and trousers; warm furs, indicated by fox and wolf skeletons minus the paws (removed in skinning and found in a separate pile); elaborate houses (marked by postholes, pavements, and walls of mammoth bones) with elaborate fireplaces; and stone lamps to hold animal fat and light the long Arctic nights. The occupation of Siberia in turn led to the occupation of North America and South America around 11,000 years ago.

Whereas Neanderthals obtained their raw materials within a few miles of home, Cro-Magnons and their contemporaries throughout Europe practiced long-distance trade, not only for raw materials for tools but also for "useless" ornaments. Tools of obsidian, jasper, and flint are found hundreds of miles from where those stones were quarried. Baltic amber reached southeast Europe, while Mediterranean shells were carried to inland parts of France, Spain, and the Ukraine.

The evident aesthetic sense reflected in late Ice Age trade relates to the achievements for which we most admire the Cro-Magnons: their art. Best known are the rock paintings from caves like Lascaux, with stunning polychrome depictions of now-extinct animals. But equally impressive are the bas-reliefs, necklaces and pendants, fired-clay sculptures, Venus figurines of women with enormous breasts and buttocks, and musical instruments ranging from flutes to rattles.

Unlike Neanderthals, few of whom lived past the age of 40, some Cro-Magnons survived to 60. Those additional 20 years probably played a big role in Cro-Magnon success. Accustomed as we are to getting our information from the printed page or television, we find it hard to appreciate how important even just one or two old people are in preliterate society. When I visited Rennell Island in the Solomons in 1976, for example, many islanders told me what wild fruits were good to eat, but only one old man could tell me what other wild fruits could be eaten in an emergency to avoid starvation. He remembered that information from a cyclone that had hit Rennell around 1905, destroying gardens and reducing his people to a state of desperation. One such person can spell the difference between death and survival for the whole society.

I've described the Great Leap Forward as if all those advances in tools and art appeared simultaneously 35,000 years ago. In fact, different innovations appeared at different times: spear-throwers appeared before harpoons, beads and pendants appeared before cave paintings. I've also described the Great Leap Forward as if it were the same everywhere, but it wasn't. Among late Ice Age Africans, Ukrainians, and French, only the Africans made beads out of ostrich eggs, only the Ukrainians built houses out of mammoth bones, and only the French painted woolly rhinos on cave walls.

These variations of culture in time and space are totally unlike the unchanging monolithic Neanderthal culture.

They constitute the most important innovation that came with the Great Leap Forward: namely, the capacity for innovation itself. To us innovation is utterly natural. To Neanderthals it was evidently unthinkable.

Despite our instant sympathy with Cro-Magnon art, their tools and hunter-gatherer life make it hard for us to view them as other than primitive. Stone tools evoke cartoons of club-waving cavemen uttering grunts as they drag women off to their cave. But we can form a more accurate impression of Cro-Magnons if we imagine what future archeologists will conclude after excavating a New Guinea village site from as recently as the 1950s. The archeologists will find a few simple types of stone axes. Nearly all other material possessions were made of wood and will have perished. Nothing will remain of the multistory houses, drums and flutes, outrigger canoes, and world-quality painted sculpture. There will be no trace of the village's complex language, songs, social relationships, and knowledge of the natural world.

New Guinea material culture was until recently "primitive" (Stone Age) for historical reasons, but New Guineans are fully modern humans. New Guineans whose fathers lived in the Stone Age now pilot airplanes, operate computers, and govern a modern state. If we could carry ourselves back 35,000 years in a time machine, I expect that we would find Cro-Magnons to be equally modern people, capable of learning to fly a plane. They made stone and bone tools only because that's all they had the opportunity to learn how to make.

It used to be argued that Neanderthals evolved into Cro-Magnons within Europe. That possibility now seems increasingly unlikely. The last Neanderthal skeletons from 35,000 to 32,000 years ago were still full-blown Neanderthals, while the first Cro-Magnons appearing in Europe at the same time were already anatomically fully modern. Since anatomically modern people were already present in Africa and the Near East tens of thousands of years earlier, it seems much more likely that such people invaded Europe rather than evolved there.

What happened when invading Cro-Magnons met the resident Neanderthals? We can be certain only of the result: within a few thousand years no more Neanderthals. The conclusion seems to me inescapable that Cro-Magnon arrival somehow caused Neanderthal extinction. Yet many anthropologists recoil at this suggestion of genocide and invoke environmental changes instead—most notably, the severe Ice Age climate. In fact, Neanderthals thrived during the Ice Age and suddenly disappeared 42,000 years after its start and 20,000 years before its end.

My guess is that events in Europe at the time of the Great Leap Forward were similar to events that have occurred repeatedly in the modern world, whenever a numerous people with more advanced technology invades the lands of a much less numerous people with less advanced technology. For instance, when European colonists invaded North America, most North American Indians proceeded to die of introduced epidemics; most of the survivors were killed outright or driven off their land; some adopted European technology (horses and guns) and resisted for some time; and many of those remaining were pushed onto lands the invaders did not want, or else intermarried with them. The displacement of aboriginal Australians by European colonists, and of southern African San populations (Bushmen) by invading Iron Age Bantu-speakers, followed a similar course.

By analogy, I suspect that Cro-Magnon diseases, murders, and displacements did in the Neanderthals. It may at first seem paradoxical that Cro-Magnons prevailed over the far more muscular Neanderthals, but weaponry rather than strength would have been decisive. Similarly, humans are now threatening to exterminate gorillas in central Africa, rather than vice versa. People with huge muscles require lots of food, and they thereby gain no advantage if less-muscular people can use tools to do the same work.

Some Neanderthals may have learned Cro-Magnon ways and resisted for a while. This is the only sense I can make of a puzzling culture called the Chatelperronian, which coexisted in western Europe along with a typical Cro-Magnon culture (the so-called Aurignacian culture) for a short time after Cro-Magnons arrived. Chatelperronian stone tools are a mixture of typical Neanderthal and Cro-Magnon tools, but the bone tools and art typical of Cro-Magnons are usually lacking. The identity of the people who produced Chatelperronian culture was debated by archeologists until a skeleton unearthed with Chatelperronian artifacts at Saint-Césaire in France proved to be Neanderthal. Perhaps, then, some Neanderthals managed to master some Cro-Magnon tools and hold out longer than their fellows.

What remains unclear is the outcome of the interbreeding experiment posed in science fiction novels. Did some invading Cro-Magnon men mate with some Neanderthal women? No skeletons that could reasonably be considered Neanderthal-Cro-Magnon hybrids are known. If Neanderthal behavior was as relatively rudimentary and Neanderthal anatomy as distinctive as I suspect, few Cro-Magnons may have wanted to mate with Neanderthals. And if Neanderthal women were geared for a 12-month pregnancy, a hybrid fetus might not have survived. My inclination is to take the negative evidence at face value, to accept that hybridization occurred rarely if ever, and to doubt that any living people carry any Neanderthal genes.

So much for the Great Leap Forward in western Europe. The replacement of Neanderthals by modern people occurred somewhat earlier in eastern Europe, and still earlier in the Near East, where possession of the same area apparently shifted back and forth between Neanderthals and modern people from 90,000 to 60,000 years ago. The slowness of the transition in the Near East, compared with its speed in western Europe, suggests that the anatomically modern people living around the Near East before 60,000 years ago had not yet developed the modern behavior that ultimately let them drive out the Neanderthals.

Thus, we have a tentative picture of anatomically modern people arising in Africa over 100,000 years ago, but initially making the same tools as Neanderthals and having no advantage over them. By perhaps 60,000 years ago, some magic twist of behavior had been added to the modern anatomy. That twist (of which more in a moment) produced innovative, fully modern people who proceeded to spread westward into Europe, quickly supplanting the Neanderthals. Presumably, they also spread east into Asia and Indonesia, supplanting the earlier people there of whom we know little. Some anthropologists think that skull remains of those earlier Asians and Indonesians show traits recognizable in modern Asians and aboriginal Australians. If so, the invading moderns may not have exterminated the original Asians without issue, as they did the Neanderthals, but instead interbred with them.

Two million years ago, several protohuman lineages existed side-by-side until a shakedown left only one. It now appears that a similar shakedown occurred within the last 60,000 years and that all of us today are descended from the winner of that shakedown. What was the Magic Twist that helped our ancestor to win?

The question poses an archeological puzzle without an accepted answer. You can speculate about the answer as well as I can. To help you, let me review the pieces of the puzzle: Some groups of humans who lived in Africa and the Near East over 60,000 years ago were quite modern in their anatomy, as far as can be judged from their skeletons. But they were not modern in their behavior. They continued to make Neanderthal-like tools and to lack innovation. The Magic Twist that produced the Great Leap Forward doesn't show up in fossil skeletons.

There's another way to restate that puzzle. Remember that we share 98 percent of our genes with chimpanzees.

The Africans making Neanderthal-like tools just before the Great Leap Forward had covered almost all of the remaining genetic distance from chimps to us, to judge from their skeletons. Perhaps they shared 99.9 percent of their genes with us. Their brains were as large as ours, and Neanderthals' brains were even slightly larger. The Magic Twist may have been a change in only 0.1 percent of our genes. What tiny change in genes could have had such enormous consequences?

Like some others who have pondered this question, I can think of only one plausible answer: the anatomical basis for spoken complex language. Chimpanzees, gorillas, and even monkeys are capable of symbolic communication not dependent on spoken words. Both chimpanzees and gorillas have been taught to communicate by means of sign language, and chimpanzees have learned to communicate via the keys of a large computer-controlled console. Individual apes have thus mastered "vocabularies" of hundreds of symbols. While scientists argue over the extent to which such communication resembles human language, there is little doubt that it constitutes a form of symbolic communication. That is, a particular sign or computer key symbolizes a particular something else.

Primates can use as symbols not just signs and computer keys but also sounds. Wild vervet monkeys, for example, have a natural form of symbolic communication based on grunts, with slightly different grunts to mean *leopard, eagle,* and *snake.* A month-old chimpanzee named Viki, adopted by a psychologist and his wife and reared virtually as their daughter, learned to "say" approximations of four words: *papa, mama, cup,* and *up.* (The chimp breathed rather than spoke the words.) Given this capability, why have apes not gone on to develop more complex natural languages of their own?

The answer seems to involve the structure of the larynx, tongue, and associated muscles that give us fine control over spoken sounds. Like a Swiss watch, our vocal tract depends on the precise functioning of many parts. Chimps are thought to be physically incapable of producing several of the commonest vowels. If we too were limited to just a few vowels and consonants, our own vocabulary would be greatly reduced. Thus, the Magic Twist may have been some modifications of the protohuman vocal tract to give us finer control and permit formation of a much greater variety of sounds. Such fine modifications of muscles need not be detectable in fossil skulls.

It's easy to appreciate how a tiny change in anatomy resulting in capacity for speech would produce a huge change in behavior. With language, it takes only a few seconds to communicate the message, "Turn sharp right at the fourth tree and drive the male antelope toward the reddish boulder, where I'll hide to spear it." Without language, that message could not be communicated at all. Without language, two protohumans could not brainstorm together about how to devise a better tool or about what a cave painting might mean. Without language, even one protohuman would have had difficulty thinking out for himself or herself how to devise a better tool.

I don't suggest that the Great Leap Forward began as soon as the mutations for altered tongue and larynx anatomy arose. Given the right anatomy, it must have taken humans thousands of years to perfect the structure of language as we know it—to hit on the concepts of word order and case endings and tenses, and to develop vocabulary. But if the Magic Twist did consist of changes in our vocal tract that permitted fine control of sounds, then the capacity for innovation that constitutes the Great Leap Forward would follow eventually. It was the spoken word that made us free.

This interpretation seems to me to account for the lack of evidence for Neanderthal-Cro-Magnon hybrids. Speech is of overwhelming importance in the relations between men and women and their children. That's not to deny that mute or deaf people learn to function well in our culture, but they do so by learning to find alternatives for an existing spoken language. If Neanderthal language was much simpler than ours or nonexistent, it's not surprising that Cro-Magnons didn't choose to associate with Neanderthals.

I've argued that we were fully modern in anatomy and behavior and language by 35,000 years ago and that a Cro-Magnon could have been taught to fly an airplane. If so, why did it take so long after the Great Leap Forward for us to invent writing and build the Parthenon? The answer may be similar to the explanation why the Romans, great engineers that they were, didn't build atomic bombs. To reach the point of building an A-bomb required 2,000 years of technological advances beyond Roman levels, such as the invention of gunpowder and calculus, the development of atomic theory, and the isolation of uranium. Similarly, writing and the Parthenon depended on tens of thousands of years of cumulative developments after the Great Leap Forward—developments that included, among many others, the domestication of plants and animals.

Until the Great Leap Forward, human culture developed at a snail's pace for millions of years. That pace was dictated by the slowness of genetic change. After the Great Leap Forward, cultural development no longer depended on genetic change. Despite negligible changes in our anatomy, there has been far more cultural evolution in the past 35,000 years than in the millions of years before. Had a visitor from outer space come to Earth before the Great Leap Forward, humans would not have stood out as unique among the world's species. At most, we might have been mentioned along with beavers, bowerbirds, and army ants as examples of species with curious behavior. Who could have foreseen the Magic Twist that would soon make us the first species, in the history of life on Earth, capable of destroying all life?

Questions

1. What three changes took place in human development to distinguish humans from apes?
2. What physical characteristics are evident in the development of *homo erectus?*
3. Approximately when did the Great Leap Forward occur?
4. What misconceptions does the author mention regarding popular beliefs about Neanderthals?
5. What conclusions might be drawn from the fact that tools used 40,000 years ago by Neanderthals differed little from those used by them 100,000 years ago?
6. What human behaviors have been found in the investigation of Neanderthal societies?
7. What are some basic differences between the Neanderthal and the Cro-Magnon of the Great Leap Forward?
8. Speculate why today's society would find a more comfortable link with Cro-Magnon society than with Neanderthal society.
9. Discuss why a possible encounter between Cro-Magnon and Neanderthal societies might have meant an end to Neanderthal life.

Conclusion

The history of technology is an ongoing process, constantly being updated, as illustrated by the "Technology Time Line." The question that students often ask is, Why do I need to study science, technology, and society? This question is answered by Robert McGinn through an in-depth explanation of the ethical side of technology.

As you read "'George,'" what did you think? Can you imagine what life might have been like at that time? "The Evolution of Despair," written by Robert Wright, presents a historical view of technology interspersed with divergent and ethical "antidotes." What were your thoughts about the Unabomber quote that started the article? Do you agree with Wright's viewpoint, or do you believe that it is too negative?

Despite the diversity of each writer's viewpoint, one thing should be clear: Each article within this part of the text tries to underscore the tangled and complex relationship that has developed over time between human beings and the technology they use. Authors may differ on the extent of the relationship or just which of the two is in control, but they don't deny that there are strong positive and negative relationships between humans and the technologies they employ.

Part 2, "Energy," will take you in a more contemporary direction. You will spend some time looking at the history of technology as it relates to energy and human consumption.

Internet Exercise

Use any of the Internet search engines (e.g., Alta Vista, Yahoo, Infoseek, etc.) to research and compare the following countries and ethnic or cultural groups in terms of technological achievement, according to the criteria in the table that follows:

Countries:

- USA
- Myanmar (formerly Burma)
- Amazon Indians
- England
- Pakistan
- Australian Aborigines
- Japan
- Brazil
- The Hottentots
- Singapore
- Vietnam
- The Amish

Country	Population	Education	Politics	Religion	Communi-cations	Technological Level	State of Environment	Language
USA								
Mynamar (Burma)								
Amazonian Indians								
Pakistan								
Japan								
Australian Aborigines								
Brazil								
Hottentots								
Singapore								
Vietnam								
Amish								
England								

Useful Web Sites

URL	Site Description
http://www.hrc.wmin.ac.uk/campaigns/ef!htmls/ind dom.html	Industrial Domestication
http://www.wrols.com/zenithco/	Islamic Contributions to Science (700 A.D. to 1500 A.D.)
http://www.colby.edu/sci.tech/STS.html	Science, Technology, and Society
http://www.tao.btc.uwe.ac.uk/~paul/ad_astra/ 21/Nano.html	21st Century: Second Industrial Revolution
http://www.iee.org.uk/Archives/links.htm	Sites for the History of Technology
http://www.asap.unimelb.edu.au/hstm/hstm_bin.htm	World Wide Web Virtual Library History of Science, Technology, and Medicine
http://www.it.njit.edu/njIT/catalog/graduate/ 92/59.html	Science, Technology, and Society

Energy

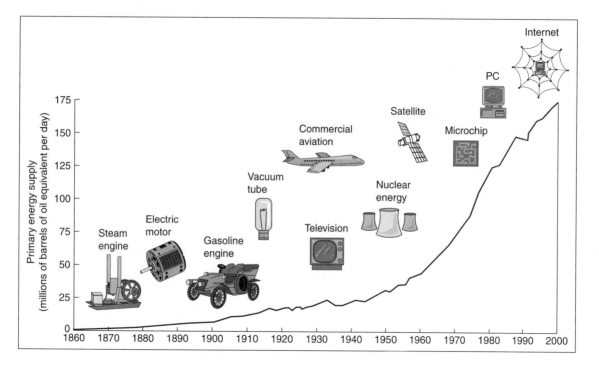

The Energy is the go of things.

JAMES CLARK MAXWELL

Energy is the most basic element of progress for all economies—the pivotal force that sustains life and ensures a standard of living and, ultimately, the standard of life. Energy technologies are society's most basic infrastructure that enables economic growth.

In the pre-Industrial Revolution era, the population of planet earth was small, and energy needs were limited to cooking and heating. Energy could be exploited without serious damage to the atmosphere, hydrosphere, or geosphere. But the dawn of the Industrial Revolution created an energy-hungry genie whose appetite for hydrocarbons has grown to such a degree that it is jeopardizing future prospects for a sustainable environment (Figures P2.1, P2.2).

Since the Industrial Revolution, atmospheric carbon dioxide levels have risen from an estimated 280 parts per million to 362 parts per million, the highest in 150 years (Figure P2.3). The mainstream scientific community, including the Intergovernmental Panel on

Figure P2.1
World fossil fuel use, 1950–96.
Source: *Vital Sign 1997,* Worldwatch Institute.

Source: BP, DOE, UN, PlanEcon

Figure P2.2
Fossil fuel use by type of fuel, 1950–96.
Source: *Vital Sign 1997,* Worldwatch Institute.

Source: BP, DOE, UN, PlanEcon

Figure P2.3

Atmospheric concentration of carbon dioxide, 1764–1996.

Source: *Vital Sign 1997,* Worldwatch Institute.

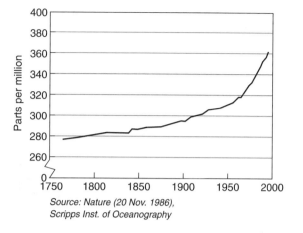

Source: *Nature (20 Nov. 1986),*
Scripps Inst. of Oceanography

Climatic Change, with 2,500 of the world's leading atmospheric scientists, now finds evidence that human activity is indeed altering the earth's climate (Figure P2.4). In 1996, worldwide carbon emissions from the burning of fossil fuels climbed to 6.25 billion tons, reaching a new high for the second year in a row (Figures P2.5, P2.6).

The world's output of goods and service is growing fast. In 1996 it expanded by 3.8 percent, up modestly from 3.5-percent growth in 1995. The gross world product (GWP) climbed from $26.9 trillion to $28.0 trillion (1995 dollars) over the same period, and GWP per person increased from $4,733 to $4,846. If the world economy keeps a similar growth trend into the 21st century, the increased use of fossil fuels would be catastrophic for the environment of the planet. According to some estimates, the entire biosphere (i.e., the earth) provides at least $33 trillion worth of free materials every year, in comparison to the GWP of $28 trillion. The economies of the earth would grind to a halt without the services of ecological life-support systems.

Since the Industrial Revolution, the world has become increasingly dependent on fossil fuels. Modern civilization is actually based on nonrenewable resources, putting a finite

Figure P2.4

Average temperature at the earth's surface, 1866–1996.

Source: *Vital Sign 1997,* Worldwatch Institute.

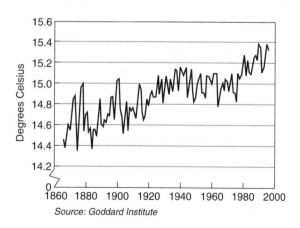

Source: *Goddard Institute*

Figure P2.5
World carbon emissions from
burning of fossil fuel, 1950–96.
Source: *Vital Sign 1997,* Worldwatch
Institute.

Figure P2.6
Carbon emissions from burning
of fossil fuel, by economic re-
gion, 1950–96.
Source: *Vital Sign 1997,* Worldwatch
Institute.

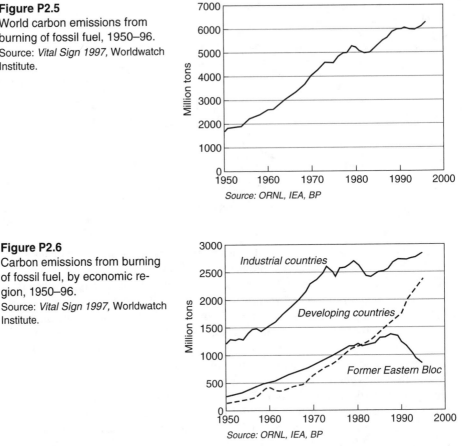

limit on the length of time our civilization can exist. The following facts illustrate the magnitude of the energy problems the world faces today:

- The United States is responsible for almost 25 percent of the world's total energy consumption. Americans use 1 million gallons of oil every two minutes.

- The United States, the largest single source of carbon emissions, is responsible for 23
  percent of the emissions of this climate-changing gas.

- The energy currently wasted by U.S. cars, homes, and appliances equals more than
  twice the known energy reserves in Alaska and the U.S. outer continental shelf.

- Americans could cut energy consumption in half by the year 2030 simply by using energy more efficiently and by using more renewable energy sources.

- A human being living at survival level needs about 2,000 kilocalories of energy per
  day. Americans consume 230,000 kilocalories of energy a day, 115 times the level
  needed for survival.

Energy (noun):

1. The capacity for vigorous activity.
2. The ability of matter or radiation to do work either because of its motion (kinetic energy), or because of its mass (released in nuclear fission, etc.), or because of its electric charge, etc.
3. Fuel and other resources used for the operation of machinery, etc.

> *"Energy is the go of things"*
> James Clark Maxwell
>
> $E = mc^2$
> Albert Einstein

The capacity of doing work.

Work is done when a body is moved by a force. The rate of doing work is known as power. Power is energy spent per time unit. The Units of energy are as follows:

- ergs
- joules
- calories
- watts
- kilowatt hours (kwh)

- BTUs
- horsepower
- foot-pounds
- barrels of oil
- metric tons of coal

Energy is interchangeable with matter and takes many forms (Figure P2.7):

kinetic
potential
electrical
magnetic
heat
chemical
nuclear
sound
light
mass

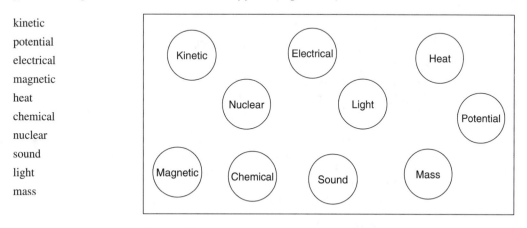

Figure P2.7
Universal set of energy.

The approximate amount of total energy as mass and radiation in the universe is equal to 4.5×10^{58} kwh, which is a small fraction of the amount of energy as gravitation in the universe.
The sun's daily output energy is 8.33×10^{25} kwh.
The earth receives 4.14×10^{15} kwh of energy daily.

- If just 1 percent of America's 140 million car owners were to tune up their cars, nearly a billion pounds of carbon dioxide could be eliminated.
- One-fifth of the world's population now accounts for 70 percent of the globe's energy use.
- China, the world's fastest growing economy, accounts for 14 percent of carbon emissions, mainly because of its heavy dependence on coal.
- One person in Western Europe uses as much energy as 80 people in sub-Sahara Africa.
- A U.S. citizen uses as much energy as 330 citizens of Bangladesh.
- Coal has been mined for 800 years, but over half of it has been extracted in the past 37 years.
- Petroleum has been pumped out of the ground for about 100 years, but half of it has been consumed during the past 25 years.
- If the rest of the world used energy at the same rate as the United States, global energy use would be four times as large as it is, and its impact on environment would be increased manyfold.

Table P2.1
Units of Conversion between Energy and Power

1 watt (w) = 1 joule (j) for 1 second
1 kilowatt (kw) = 1,000 watts
1 megawatt (mw) = 1,000 kilowatts (10^6 watts)
1 gigawatt (gw) = 1,000 megawatts (10^9 watts)
1 terawatt (tw) = 1,000 gigawatts (10^{12} watts)
1 twh = 1 billion kwh
1 kw (capacity) = 8,760 kilowatt-hours (kwh; maximum annual production)
1 kwh = 1.34 horsepower-hours (hph)
1 kwh = 3,415 BTU
1 hph = 2,547 BTU
1 hph = 18 ft^3 CH_4 (methane) using internal combustion
1 metric ton coal equivalent = 8,000 kwh (heat equivalent)
1 ton = 2,000 pounds
1 metric ton = 2205 pounds
1 short ton = .9072 metric tons
1 million metric tons of crude oil of petroleum products = 4 × 10^{13} BTU
1 million metric tons of coal = 2.8 × 10^{13} BTU
1000 million m^3 of natural gas = 3.6 × 10^{13} BTU
1 barrel of crude oil = 5.8 × 10^6 BTU
1 watt-hour = 3.6 × 10^3 joules
1 BTU = 1.055107 × 10^3 joules
1 calorie = 4.184 joules
1 foot-pound = 1.356 joules
1 metric ton coal equivalent (MTCE) = 8,000 kwh (1,000 kwh = .125 MTCE)
1,000 ft hydrogen = 79 kwh
1 langley = .21622 kwh per square foot

The world as a whole could not sustain the rate of energy consumption now enjoyed by the industrial nations. The Third World is trying to industrialize, but the high energy costs are adding to staggering debt loads. A reduction in the use of oil by the industrial nations is essential for world peace and global justice and also for environmental protection and long-term sustainability of the planet.

According to some estimates, most of the increases in energy demand will probably occur in the developing world, where population growth rates are high and industrialization and urbanization are under way. In contrast, demand is expected to remain stable or drop in the industrialized countries, where population growth rates are low. Demand could stabilize or decline in eastern Europe and former Soviet republics, depending on the success of economic reforms. Much hinges on consensus and whether sustainable policies are enacted.

A report by the World Resources Institute concludes that if efficiency is strenuously pursued in all countries, global energy demand in 2020 will be only 10 percent higher than in 1980, even with the expected growth in population. Energy use in the Northern Hemisphere would have to be cut in half, while that in the Southern Hemisphere would grow, and living standards in the Third World in 2020 could then be comparable to those of Western Europe in the mid-seventies. The use of renewable energy sources (hydroelectric, biomass, wind power, solar thermal, and photovoltaic sources) will contribute to sustainability and justice, and in most cases the environmental impact will be lower than that of fossil fuels.

As we discuss the energy issue in relation to our future, our challenge will be to support world economic growth and unprecedented energy needs in a sustainable approach, a formula that demands both economic feasibility and preservation of the environment. This part of the text investigates present energy technologies and concerns and future strategies that will lead the reader to become aware of both future challenges and their potential solutions.

Man strides over the earth, and deserts follow in his footsteps
ANCIENT PROVERB

5 Energy

IAN BARBOUR

Until 1800, all world civilizations were based on wood, wind, water, and animal power. The Industrial Revolution in the nineteenth century was the product of technologies powered by coal. The growth of twentieth-century industrial nations was fueled by coal and cheap oil. In the 1960s it was hoped that nuclear reactors would supply much of the world's future energy needs. But by the 1980s it was clear that each of these sources entails high environmental and social costs. Yet we have done little to develop the renewable sources that might replace them or the conservation and efficiency measures that could reduce energy demand.

One-fifth of the world's population now accounts for 70 percent of the world's energy use, which is more than nine times as much per person as in the remaining four-fifths of the world. One person in Western Europe uses as much energy as eighty people in sub-Saharan Africa.[1] A U.S. citizen uses as much as 330 citizens of Bangladesh.[2] The world as a whole could not sustain the rate of energy consumption now enjoyed by industrial nations, which industrialized when coal and oil were relatively cheap. The Third World is trying to industrialize at a time when high energy prices are hindering development plans and adding to already staggering debt loads.

Values are present in energy decisions, whether recognized or not. There are inescapable trade-offs among diverse values: health, justice, participation, economic de-

velopment, environmental protection, and sustainability. We will look mainly at the social and ethical issues in energy choices, but we cannot ignore technical and economic questions. We must ask both what is technically feasible and what is ethically desirable. Who benefits and who bears the costs and risks of various energy systems? Which technologies accelerate the concentration of economic and political power? Which sources are most promising for developing countries? Which policies take into account the needs of future generations? We will look successively at fossil fuels, nuclear power, renewable sources, and the possibilities for conservation.

I. FOSSIL FUELS

Oil, natural gas, and coal contain energy that arrived from the sun for millions of years, captured in prehistoric plant life and preserved in the geological strata of a few regions of the earth. Fossil fuels supply 88 percent of the world's purchased energy (excluding nonmarket fuels such as firewood). It is estimated that identified global reserves of oil would last for 44 years, natural gas for 60 years, and coal for three centuries at current depletion rates.[3] However, their geographical distributions are very uneven and their political and environmental costs are very high.

1. Oil and Global Justice

Since 1900, oil has been central in the *military and political involvement* of Britain, France, Germany, Turkey, and then the United States in the Middle East. Japan attacked Pearl Harbor in 1941 because its oil supplies had been cut

---

OIL AND INDIGENOUS PEOPLES

"Manuel Echeverria told us that if we didn't permit the company [to proceed with oil development], the government would take our land."
—Humberto Piaguaje, president of the Secoya Indigenous Organization of Ecuador, commenting on the "pressure tactics" used by Occidental Petroleum Company to open the indigenous lands to oil development

"Echeverria threatened that if the indigenous organizations 'continued to make the situation difficult' [by not signing an agreement to allow oil development], they [Occidental] would come with the military."
—Piaguaje, recounting the discussions leading to the signing of an agreement in the presence of Ecuadorian Army major Hernán Altimirano

"Protesters clashed with security forces over plans to privatize the nationalized petrochemical industry and the [Mexican] state oil company's failure to compensate Tabasco for trashing the local environment."
—Andrew Wheat in *Multinational Monitor,* on the occupation of 60 installations of Petróleos de Mexico (Pemex) in 1996

"In the wells where we got drinking water, there is foam so thick on the surface that you have to remove it with your hand."
—A Tabasco university researcher quoted in "Human Rights and Environment in Tabasco," a June 1996 Global Exchange report

"The democratically elected government-in-exile of Burma filed a lawsuit in September against Unocal, charging the multinational oil company with wide-scale human rights violations in connection with construction of a natural gas pipeline in Burma."
—Russell Mokhiber in *Multinational Monitor*

"Of course we know that there has been an environmental cost, and we certainly don't claim that our record is perfect. But the measure of an ethical company is not whether it ever gets things wrong but how it puts things right."
—B. R. H. Anderson, Chairman and Managing Director of Shell Petroleum Development Company of Nigeria, in a letter to *Harper's,* after the "execution" of Nigerian activist Ken Saro-Wiwa for his protest against Shell's exploitation of Nigerian indigenous land

Reprinted with permission from Worldwatch Institute, Washington, D.C.

---

off and its stores of oil were running low.[4] More recently, three oil price shocks—caused by the OPEC oil embargo in 1973, the Iranian crisis in 1979, and Iraq's invasion of Kuwait in 1990—have brought home the world's dependence on Middle Eastern oil. World oil reserves were 50 percent higher in 1990 than in 1973, but most of the new discoveries were in the Middle East which now holds two-thirds of the world's reserves.[5]

Oil production has been declining in the U.S. since 1970, and it is now falling in the former Soviet Union, Britain, and several other non-OPEC nations. The cost of drilling for deeper deposits and in inaccessible locations (such as Alaska and the North Sea) has been growing. Higher prices encouraged some conservation measures, and world oil consumption fell during the early 1980s. But following the price drop in 1986 it rose again and by 1990 was back to the levels of the late seventies. In 1990, the United States imported almost half its oil, and its current policies will lead to increased dependence on imports in the future.[6]

The prospect that Saddam Hussein might control or influence a large part of *Middle Eastern oil production* was clearly a major factor in the 1991 military intervention by the United States (with some support from other allies). Iraq's invasion of Kuwait and efforts to acquire nuclear weapons posed a threat of further aggressive actions. In the future, nations dependent on Middle Eastern oil will continue to be vulnerable to political changes in a region of long-standing conflicts and great inequalities. Saudi Arabia's autocratic royal family will be under great pressure from Islamic fundamentalists and from impoverished Arab countries that lack oil resources. Imported oil is the largest and fastest-growing component of the U.S. trade deficit. In addition, the military costs of oil imports should really be included in their true costs. For example, keeping shipping lanes open in the Gulf in 1985 cost $200 per barrel of oil shipped, eight times its world price.[7]

Dependence on imported oil has had a devastating impact on the *Third World.* We have seen that oil is crucial for agriculture because it is the main feedstock for fertilizer and petrochemicals as well as the fuel for tractors and irrigation pumps. The profligate use of oil in industrial nations together with OPEC policies in the seventies drove up world prices, and by 1981 developing nations were spending an average 61 percent of their export earnings on oil imports.[8] The high price of kerosene, an oil derivative, accelerated the depletion of firewood and other traditional sources used for heating and cooking.

Within industrial countries, *the politics of oil* are extremely complicated because oil plays such a large part in national life. In the past, oil use has been heavily subsidized through depletion allowances, import quotas, and highway construction funds. A powerful lobby was formed by a coalition of diverse interests: oil companies and oil-producing states; auto, insurance, and highway construction companies; and labor unions. The oil lobby has made large contributions to the campaign funds of the members of Congress who are on committees dealing with energy, and it has actively opposed all attempts to raise auto fuel economy standards. Of the 20 largest U.S. companies 7 are oil companies, and many other industries, such as autos, plastics, and petrochemicals, are dependent on oil.[9] Oil companies have also reduced competition by "vertical integration" (control of oil imports, domestic production, refining, pipelines, and service stations). They have used extensive television and magazine advertising to present their interpretation of the energy situation and the policies they favor.

The use of oil also has serious *environmental consequences.* The Exxon Valdez accident off the Alaska coast in 1989 dramatized the damage to wildlife and coastal beauty that a single human error can perpetrate. Other oil spills have been caused by severe storms, and we can expect such spills to continue, though we could reduce some of the consequences by requiring double-hulled tankers and better standby equipment for more rapid containment. The fuel burned in cars and trucks is a major contributor to urban air pollution, which constitutes a serious hazard to human health. According to the American Lung Association, auto air pollution adds $40 billion to annual American medical bills.[10] The nitrogen oxides and ozone-forming hydrocarbons can be controlled by catalytic converters. But the combustion of any oil product adds carbon dioxide to the air, accelerating global warming from the greenhouse effect discussed below.

The *reduction of oil use* by industrial nations is thus essential for world peace and global justice and also for environmental protection and long-term sustainability. Since transportation accounts for two-thirds of U.S. oil use, and more than half the oil used in many other countries, auto fuel economy standards, alternative fuels, and public transportation are promising starting points, as we will see in section IV. Most conservation measures and renewable energy sources have low environmental impacts, and they rely on local or regional materials, diminishing the international competition for fossil fuels that are so unevenly distributed geographically.

2. Coal and the Environment

The known reserves of coal are larger than those of oil, but the human and environmental costs are greater.

1. Human and Environmental Costs of Mining   The long history of *mine accidents and black lung disease* is a classic instance of high risks falling on one group while benefits accrue to other people. The appalling conditions faced by generations of miners have gradually improved in response to labor union demands and legislated safety standards. Following the U.S. mine safety law passed in 1969, fatalities per million working hours fell from 1.2 in 1970 to 0.3 in 1977, and the incidence of lung disease also dropped sharply. Since then enforcement of safety and ventilation standards has improved somewhat, but even stricter standards and better enforcement would not impose an unreasonable economic cost.[11]

It is sometimes claimed that it is justifiable for *workers to be exposed to higher risks* than the public because the risks are voluntarily accepted. However, a coal miner usually has little geographical mobility or job mobility and may have no alternative to working in a mine. Another defense of occupational hazards is that high-risk jobs, such as the construction of tall buildings, often offer a wage premium. But rates of compensation for comparable risks vary widely, and mine workers have usually been poorly paid compared to industrial workers. Some compensation for injury has been provided under workman's compensation laws and under specific legislation providing payments to miners with black lung disease. It would serve the interests of justice and offer greater incentives to safety if the cost of these payments were paid by those who benefit, such as the consumers of coal-fired electricity.

There are also considerable *environmental impacts* from the mining of coal. Deep-mining wastes have depressed land values, polluted streams, and marred areas of great natural beauty around the world. The strip mining of surface coal has left large areas denuded and subject to rapid erosion. In the United States, a 1977 law required replanting and reclamation measures to be sustained for five years (or ten years in arid areas) with costs passed on to coal users. But reclaimed land often can only be used for pasture, and in semiarid regions, with fragile ecosystems and scarce water, it will take decades for healthy plant life to be restored and some areas will probably remain wastelands.[12]

2. Air Pollution and Acid Rain   Burning coal has even greater human and environmental costs than mining it. Coal contains sulfur compounds which form sulfur dioxide in stack emissions, and these in turn combine with moisture to produce sulfates. These sulfates in *urban air* are a major source of respiratory illness and fatality. Tall smokestacks reduce local sulfate levels but at the expense of increased acid rain at distant points.

Since the late sixties the effects of *acid rain* on the forests and lakes of Europe and North America have been increasing. By 1988, 52 percent of the forests in West Germany had been affected. The U.N. Environmental Program estimates that more than a third of Europe's total forest area has been damaged. In some parts of Eastern Europe, only bare trunks and eroded hillsides mark what were once great forests. Crop losses from sulfates and ozone are difficult to determine, but one recent study puts losses at 5 to 10 percent of production in the United States. In half of the lakes in eastern North America, many species of fish and plants have been wiped out by acidification. In Greece, public monuments and statues have deteriorated more in the last 25 years than in the previous 2400 years.[13]

Effective *pollution control technologies* for acid emissions can be installed. Passing the combustion gases through limestone scrubbers removes 85 percent of the sulfur dioxide. Scrubbers and use of low-sulfur coal account for most of the 28 percent drop in sulfur dioxide emissions in the United States between 1970 and 1987. In 1977, Congress required scrubbers on all new plants, but during the eighties the utilities and eastern coal-producing states lobbied effectively against legislation to require the installation of scrubbers on older plants. By 1990, only 30 percent of U.S. coal-fired capacity had scrubbers, compared to 85 percent in West Germany and over 90 percent in Japan. Japan and Germany are also adding catalytic reducers to remove the nitrogen oxides that produce smaller amounts of acid rain. In Japan, pollution control adds 25 percent to the cost of coal-generated power, but an air pollution disaster has been averted. Newer "clean coal technologies," such as fluidized bed combustion and multistage combustion, offer the prospect of cheaper control of both these air pollutants.[14]

The technology to control sulfur and nitrogen emissions is available, and its installation is primarily a matter of *political will*. The cost of the damage from the emissions clearly exceeds the costs of the control technology, but indirect costs do not appear on industrial balance sheets. During the eighties the U.S. administration gave economic growth priority over environmental preservation, and the conflict of regional interests undermined repeated congressional attempts to strengthen clean air laws. However, greater public interest in clean air and a more pragmatic administration finally produced tighter air emission laws, though still below the standards sought by environmentalists; the 1990 Clean Air Amendments required cutting sulfur dioxide emissions in half by the year 2000. A 1988 directive of the European Economic Community seeks to lower sulfur dioxide levels to 57 percent of the 1980 levels by 2003, and a group of nine countries has pledged a 50 percent reduction.[15]

3. Global Warming: The Greenhouse Effect   The burning of all fossil fuels entails the formation of *carbon dioxide* (CO_2). The enormous quantities released into the air by fossil fuels have increased the CO_2 content of the air by 25 percent in the past hundred years. At the present emission rate it will have doubled by 2030. Coal is the worst offender, releasing 24 kilograms of CO_2 per billion joules of heat produced; oil is next (20 kg.), and natural gas produces least (14 kg.). In the United States, coal-burning utilities account for a third of the CO_2 emitted, oil-burning vehicles another third, and fuels burned in homes and industry the final third.[16]

The average annual temperature fluctuates erratically from year to year. Nevertheless, there is a very high correlation between past CO_2 levels and the general *trend of temperature changes*. Core samples from glaciers substantiate this correlation over a period of 160,000 years (including a large temperature change during the last ice age), and it holds for the past 130 years for which there are historical records. In the latter period the change in average temperature has been small, amounting to only 1° F. But the five warmest years in the last century were all in the 1980s. It is known on theoretical grounds that CO_2 increases the reflectivity of the upper atmosphere, trapping more heat in the lower atmosphere.

The prediction of *future global warming* is uncertain because climate effects are very complex and only partially understood. Computer models for atmospheric conditions involve simplifying assumptions about winds, humidity, clouds, oceans, and so forth. One widely quoted study concludes that at present emission rates the CO_2 concentration would double by 2030, and the average surface temperature would rise between 3 and 5.5° C (5 to 10° F), with larger changes in the earth's temperate zones.[17] The melting of polar ice would raise sea levels by somewhere between 8 inches and 5 feet, flooding some coastal areas and contaminating groundwater with salt. Wind and rainfall patterns would be drastically changed, affecting agriculture in many parts of the world. (These effects would of course be worse if emission rates increased or if they continued for a longer time interval.) Climatologists recognize the uncertainties in these calculations, but they are virtually unanimous that the magnitude of the potential consequences is so great that we must not only intensify research on the problem but initiate preventive policies.[18] Such policies would be a form of insurance. The greenhouse effect may turn out to be smaller than current estimates, but it could be greater, and it would be much more difficult to reverse later.

The main way to reduce global warming is to *reduce the use of fossil fuels*. If this is accomplished by conservation measures and greater efficiency, the reduction will at the same time cut down on other environmental impacts from fossil fuels. A report by the National Academy of Sciences says that the United States could cut its carbon emissions by 40 percent with no impact on life-styles.[19] Forests absorb CO_2 from the atmosphere as well as providing wildlife habitats and protection against soil erosion. Slowing the destruction of forests would slow global warming, and in the tropics it would help to preserve endangered species and highly erodible soil. Planting trees would have many environmental benefits, but it will have to be done very extensively to make a dent on the CO_2 accumulation.

Apart from conservation, switching from coal and oil to *natural gas* is the most effective way of reducing carbon dioxide emissions during the next decade. Natural gas is more abundant globally than oil and more widely dispersed, including extensive known deposits in the Third World (and many areas have not yet been explored). Gas fueled combined-cycle plants are highly efficient in generating electricity because the burning gases are used to drive one turbine directly and then the heat is used to generate steam to drive a second turbine. The greater efficiency, together with the smaller amount of CO_2 released per unit of heat, means that only two-fifths as much CO_2 is emitted as at a coal-burning plant of equivalent capacity, and the sulfur dioxide emissions are negligible. Several nations are experimenting with vehicles driven by cylinders of compressed natural gas. Mexico City is planning to use them on its city buses to reduce air pollution. Natural gas development is also much less environmentally destructive than coal mining. Natural gas is the most promising fuel during the transition to sustainable sources.[20]

A *carbon tax* would be an effective way for industrial nations to reduce carbon dioxide emissions, but it would have to be introduced gradually to avoid severe economic dislocations. Such a tax would favor natural gas over coal and oil, and it would strongly favor nuclear, solar, and conservation technologies that release no CO_2 once they are installed. If part of the tax receipts was invested in efficiency improvements, and part was offset by reductions in other taxes, the economy as a whole would be strengthened rather than weakened. By 1991, Finland, Sweden, and the Netherlands had introduced small carbon taxes, and the European Community was making plans for a carbon tax to be instituted in all European nations.[21] Some Third World countries, especially China, have extensive coal deposits and will find it very difficult to avoid expanding their use of coal as they seek more rapid economic growth. But the efforts of industrial nations to develop alternatives to fossil fuels would help all developing nations in making the transition to sustainable sources.

II. NUCLEAR POWER

In 1990, 421 nuclear plants were operating in twenty-six countries (with 96 more under construction), generating 17 percent of the world's electricity. In many industrial nations the percentage of electricity coming from nuclear plants was even higher: 19 in the U.S., 22 in Britain, 28 in

Japan, 34 in the former West Germany, 45 in Sweden, and 75 in France.[22] But in virtually every Western nation, plans to start construction of new plants have been halted by public opposition and by escalating costs (now estimated as twice those for coal-fired plants per kilowatt-hour). All orders for new nuclear plants in the United States since 1973 were subsequently canceled. The industry blames additional safety requirements, regulatory delays, and high interest payments during long construction times (up to eighteen years) for costs of up to $5 billion per plant, ten times the original estimates. A few of the critics of nuclear power are reconsidering it in the light of the greenhouse dangers of coal and the possibility of new "inherently safe" reactor designs. Let us look successively at reactor safety, radioactive waste disposal, and prospects for the future.

1. Reactor Safety and Risk Acceptability

The history of nuclear reactors in the United States supports the *contextualist thesis* . . . that the design of a technology is not inevitable but is the product of choices made in particular social contexts. In the early 1950s, reactor designers had a choice of fuels (natural uranium, enriched uranium, or plutonium), moderators (light water, heavy water, or graphite), coolants (water, liquid metal, or gas), temperature (boiling water, pressurized water, or high temperatures), and reactor size and configuration. The U.S. Navy urgently wanted a nuclear submarine, which required a high energy density and a readily available design—most easily fulfilled by a pressurized light water reactor (LWR) using enriched uranium. The first commercial LWR at Shippingport was designed to serve also as the prototype for an aircraft carrier reactor.

These choices strongly influenced subsequent decisions. By the time the Atomic Energy Commission (AEC) and the private utilities and reactor contractors chose designs for commercialization in the late fifties, LWRs had a substantial head start from the Navy program. Their decisions were based more on cost and current availability than on safety considerations (though liquid sodium coolants were ruled out partly for safety reasons). In Congress, the Joint Committee on Atomic Energy concurred that these decisions were in the national interest.[23]

The next crucial stage was *the very rapid upscaling* in size and numbers that occurred between 1965 and 1970. A hundred reactors were ordered, many of them seven times as large as the largest with which there had been any operating experience. At such sizes, containment structures

could not be counted on to withstand a major accident, and plants were being built near population centers. As successive problems emerged, new safety equipment was added on (such as emergency cooling systems and redundant pumps and instruments), but the basic design was not changed. Until 1965, nuclear technology still had considerable flexibility, but by 1970 large-scale light water reactors had developed a momentum of their own, sustained by heavy financial investment and institutional commitments. The industry was locked in before it could learn from experience.[24] In Britain nuclear reactors were owned by the government and alternative designs were tried, but similar problems were present. Long lead times and huge capital investment in large plants with which there had been no previous experience produced an inflexible system, and mistakes were difficult and costly to correct.[25]

The U.S. Atomic Energy Commission's mandate to *regulate* nuclear power was compromised by its conflicting mandate to *promote* nuclear power. The AEC was secretive, suppressed information and internal dissent, and virtually excluded participation by citizens or independent experts. As often happens, a "cozy triangle" of a government agency, a legislative committee, and a private industry shared a common interest in promoting a particular technology.[26]

During the seventies the nuclear industry faced a variety of *unexpected problems.* Demand for electricity grew much more slowly than had been anticipated. As new safety measures were added, regulations became more complex and delays in construction and licensing extended the construction time to 10, 12, or in one case 18 years. High interest rates further escalated construction costs. Vocal opposition to nuclear plants was often associated with the growing environmental and antiwar movements. Communities woke up to plans for nearby plants, formulated without their involvement, and they protested vehemently and started court challenges. Some of the objections were widely overblown, but others pointed to problems that turned out to be valid. Public confidence in both government bureaucracies and large corporations was eroding. One could no longer simply "trust the experts," for knowledgeable experts now spoke out on both sides. The Nuclear Regulatory Commission was established in 1974 with authority only for regulation, but much of its staff and many of its attitudes and procedures were taken over with little change from the AEC.

Then came two major *reactor accidents.* At Three Mile Island in 1979, a partial meltdown occurred and 90 percent of the fuel rods burst, but very little radiation escaped from the containment vessel. At Chernobyl in 1986 an explosion and fire in a graphite-moderated reactor spread large quantities of radiation across Europe. Thirty-one workers at the plant died within a few weeks. It has been estimated that the radiation will result in the death of 28,000 from delayed cancer over the next fifty years.[27] Both accidents were the result of human errors, which in the Three Mile Island case were compounded by a stuck valve and misread instruments. Previous calculations of reactor risks had failed to allow adequately for unlikely combinations of mechanical failures, system interactions, and operator misjudgments. With complex, tightly coupled systems it is impossible to anticipate all possible linkages among human errors and component failures, and events can occur too rapidly for analysis and corrective action.[28] The credibility of reassurances from the industry and the government was undermined, and public support of nuclear power dwindled in both the United States and Europe.

How should we deal with the risk of reactor accidents? Risk analysis defines risk as the *probability* of an event multiplied by the *magnitude* of its harmful consequences. Current estimates of the probability of a nuclear accident are higher than those in the midseventies, but the calculated risk remains less than many other risks that we accept, such as those in driving an auto. Nuclear proponents say that public anxiety about nuclear accidents is therefore irrational. In reply, social scientists point out that the *acceptability of a risk* involves many factors in addition to probability and consequences. In general, we are more willing to accept risks that are familiar, voluntarily accepted, personally controlled, reversible, and equitably distributed—and necessary to obtain a desired benefit. Nuclear power scores poorly on all these characteristics.[29] Nuclear power is thus less acceptable than conventional risk analysis suggests.

In addition, there may be valid reasons for giving *low-probability catastrophes* more weight than risk-benefit analysis assigns. One accident with 50,000 victims is more socially disruptive and receives more media coverage than 50,000 one-victim accidents. A study by a national laboratory in 1982 calculated that a major nuclear accident near an urban area with unfavorable winds could cause losses as high as $150 billion and 140,000 deaths.[30] The probability of rare events and human errors can seldom be estimated with the same accuracy as high-probability events, and underestimation of the probability of a disaster would have enormous consequences. Again, complex large-scale systems are more vulnerable to disruption than smaller and simpler systems, and they can create human overloads. Fi-

nally, risk analysis of nuclear plants assumes stable social conditions and leaves out the possibility of wars, civil conflicts, or deliberate acts of sabotage, terrorism, or threat.

Any evaluation of technological risks will be influenced by assumptions about *human nature* and *social institutions*. The biblical understanding of human fallibility would lead one to be cautious about situations in which errors can have disastrous consequences. I suggested earlier that the social dimension of sin is expressed in institutional self-interest. It should be no surprise that organizations put their own goals ahead of the public interest or underestimate risks that could be reduced by expenditures on safety. If we live in a world of stark injustice and growing gaps between rich and poor nations, it seems unrealistic to leave out the effects of social unrest and political instability. Nuclear reactors would be vulnerable in situations of conflict, and they would be tempting targets for blackmail by terrorists. Moreover, their large scale and cost represent a concentration of economic and hence political power that makes it difficult for citizens to participate in decisions about them. In short, catastrophe avoidance should be given heavier weight than traditional risk analysis assigns, but it cannot be the only criterion for choosing technologies, since benefits and alternatives must be considered along with risks.

2. Radioactive Wastes and Future Generations

The risks from high-level radioactive wastes extend over very long periods of time. Many of the waste products must be isolated for a thousand years, and plutonium itself is still dangerous after 100,000 years. A huge backlog of military and commercial wastes has already accumulated around the world. Several nations are hoping to create *permanent repositories* in which solidified wastes would be stored in concrete casks in tunnels excavated deep in salt beds or solid rock. The repositories must be isolated from groundwater, since even very slow leaching would contaminate underground aquifers. Most scientists believe that suitable geological formations can be found, but at each of the sites proposed so far, geologists have been concerned about possible changes in groundwater flow induced by fractures, earthquakes, or climate changes.

Both *scientific uncertainties* and *public opposition* have plagued all attempts to establish such repositories. In Germany, the Gorleben salt dome was selected as the first site, but it was discovered that groundwater is eroding the salt and the geological structures are not stable. Gorleben has been the scene of large public protests, and the repository opening has been put off from 1998 to 2008 at the earliest. In France, the opening of a repository has been postponed to 2010, and no site has yet been named. Japan hoped to locate a burial site in a remote and poor prefecture, but despite the offer of a large subsidy, opposition from the governor and the diet was strong. Japan has signed an agreement with China to conduct research on an underground facility in Shanxi province, in return for assistance with the Chinese nuclear program.[31]

Three ethical issues can be identified in planning for nuclear waste disposal.

1. Regional Justice   Radioactive waste disposal is an extreme case of local risks for national benefits. Utilitarians may assert that the total benefits outweigh the total risks, but justice is violated if some people benefit and others sustain the risks. People recognize that the wastes must go somewhere, but they assert, "Not in my backyard." The U.S. National Waste Policy Act of 1982 permitted an individual state to veto a site within its borders, but the veto could be overridden by a majority of both houses of Congress. In 1987 Congress instructed the Department of Energy (DOE) to proceed with detailed underground studies at Yucca Mountain, Nevada, and to abandon plans to study two other western sites concurrently. Both DOE and Congress also capitulated to political pressures to abandon plans to investigate possible sites for a second repository in several eastern states. Nevada has responded by a series of court challenges. The date for opening the first repository has been postponed from 1998 to 2010, to allow for further negotiation and scientific studies.

Fairness in *selection procedures* can help to mitigate the injustice in sacrificing local interests for the national good. But DOE did such a poor job of scientific research that it was criticized by several other government agencies. And Nevadans felt that they had been betrayed politically when the original agreement to build one western and one eastern site was violated. Another way of mitigating injustices is to require the beneficiaries to compensate those who bear the risks. The 1982 act authorizes DOE to provide *compensation to host states,* paid for by a users' fee on the electricity generated from nuclear fuel. In 1987 amendments to the act, the state hosting the first site would receive $10 million per year until the site opens and $20 million per year thereafter. This seems inadequate compensation when there are uncertain health risks, social impacts, and public fears that might stigmatize local communities. Another form of compensation would be the funding of hospitals and health care centers in the area to monitor radiation risks and to provide greater local participation in health decisions.[32] But we must resist the temptation to buy off depressed communities or Native American reservations and to deprive them of an ongoing voice in their own health and safety.

2. Intergenerational Justice   Justice is violated when the current generation benefits from electricity and passes on to future generations some of the resulting risks. According to Rawls, an intergenerational decision is fair if you would accept it when you did not know in which generation you would live. I also mentioned in chapter 3 the biblical view of a covenant between generations and the idea that God's purposes span the generations. Here is a case where the longevity of the risks forces us to think beyond the short time frame of political processes and economic calculations. The present generation has a responsibility to pay for the costs of reducing the risks to posterity. The standards of the Environmental Protection Agency (EPA) specify that radiation released from a nuclear waste depository should not cause more than 1,000 deaths in 10,000 years (which is the time it will take for the level of radiation in typical reactor wastes to fall to that of the uranium ore from which the fuel was extracted).

If we considered the welfare of future generations, would we favor storing radioactive wastes permanently or retrievably? While a *permanent* site costs more initially, it entails no future maintenance costs, and sabotage and terrorism could not occur because the wastes are buried in solid rock. But a *retrievable* site offers two advantages: it would be far easier and cheaper to get at the wastes if problems did show up; and the wastes would be accessible if future generations wanted to reprocess them (to reclaim some of the potential nuclear energy still present) or to use them in a future technology not now imagined.

Alvin Weinberg advocates *retrievable storage* with tight security measures to guard against flooding, drilling, or sabotage. He describes it as a "Faustian bargain" of energy growth at the expense of long-term vigilance. He says it would require a "nuclear priesthood" of highly disciplined technicians to maintain surveillance and guard the buried wastes.[33] But is it realistic to count on the stability of social institutions on a time scale of 10,000 years? No social order in history has lasted more than a few centuries. The occurrence of two world wars and many smaller wars and revolutionary upheavals in this century suggests that in a fast changing world we should use methods that do not depend on human institutions over periods of many generations.

On balance it seems to me that our obligations to future generations would best be fulfilled by *permanent sealed repositories,* but that the first couple of sites should be left open and carefully monitored for leakage or other problems for several decades so that any modifications could be made before they are sealed. From current fees a substantial endowment fund should be set aside, and interest from it would cover future monitoring and modification costs and underwrite insurance against accidents. It is conceivable that a new technology might allow long-lived isotopes in plant wastes to be transmuted into isotopes with shorter half-lives, in order to keep more of the risks within our own generation. But with current technologies this would be extremely expensive, and permanent sealed repositories seem a more promising way of avoiding significant risks to future generations.

3. Public Confidence In many nations, including France, Britain, the United States, and the Soviet Union, the *credibility of government agencies* planning nuclear waste disposal was undermined by their secrecy and their historic failure to protect the public and the environment. In many cases the same agency was responsible for nuclear weapons production, nuclear power generation, and nuclear waste disposal—and for public health and safety regulations. A 1982 report by the Office of Technology Assessment (OTA) of the U.S. Congress noted the erosion of public confidence in the Department of Energy and proposed an independent Waste Management Agency to sponsor scientific research and to encourage greater participation by citizens, state agencies, and independent experts.[34] But DOE has continued to manage the disposal of wastes, and public confidence has not been restored. While some public hearings have been held, DOE has provided only limited opportunities for access to information and for independent scientific review, and it has not been sensitive to the diversity of interests involved or the intensity of public opposition.[35] The controversies over waste disposal, like those over reactor safety, point to the importance of public involvement and the full inclusion of social and environmental costs in the planning of large scale technological projects.

3. The Future of Nuclear Power

If waste disposal problems can be solved, should nuclear power be reconsidered now that coal seems to pose such a threat in the environment? A 1984 OTA study concluded that a revival of the nuclear industry could occur only under two conditions. First, public trust in the government agencies and in the utilities would have to be restored. Second, only simpler, smaller reactors with inherent safety features and standardized designs might achieve acceptable safety and reduce construction and licensing times.[36] By 1990 DOE and the reactor vendors were considering smaller, standardized modular reactors that could be built in factories rather than on site and that would incorporate passively stable features.[37]

Passively stable ("inherently safe") reactors rely on the laws of nature, rather than on human intervention or mechanical systems, to limit the effects of any malfunctions. In smaller reactors, emergency cooling can be obtained by gravity flow from water in elevated tanks or by the natural circulation of water, helium, or air—without the use of complex systems of controls, pumps, and valves. Reactor cores can be designed so that the reaction itself slows down as the temperature rises. The uranium fuel can be formed into pellets, each surrounded by layers of graphite and ceramic that withstand temperatures far higher than do the metal-clad fuel rods currently used. A 135-megawatt graphite-moderated helium-cooled reactor (one-seventh the size of many current reactors) and a 155 megawatt reactor cooled by liquid sodium are among the designs under consideration in the United States. Canada's 300-megawatt heavy water reactor has an excellent operating record, and Sweden is working on a light water reactor in which naturally circulating borated water is used to slow down the reaction and to cool the core.[38]

Morone and Woodhouse hold that if we learn from the mistakes of the past we would develop a second generation of nuclear reactors only *slowly and cautiously.* We would incorporate safety in the initial design rather than by complex add-on systems. We would do research for a decade on diverse types of passive design, and then for a second decade we would develop prototypes of several alternatives for testing at a remote site so that we could learn from experience and make modifications. The whole process would be open to scrutiny by the OTA, independent experts, and environmentalists. After two decades, when both the greenhouse effect and the prospects for solar energy are clearer, a decision about commercialization could be made.[39]

Such a cautious research program on smaller passively stable reactors would *keep options open.* Along with a satisfactory resolution of waste disposal, it might lead to a restoration of public confidence in the nuclear industry. But I could support such a program only if it were funded at a level considerably lower than that for research on conservation and renewable sources. Moreover, given current attitudes in the industry and DOE, the program is not likely to be cautious and open or to restore public confidence. It would probably divert funds from alternatives and encourage the belief that we do not have to take conservation seriously. For at least the next decade, measures to *conserve* electricity will almost certainly cost less than the *production* of an equivalent amount of electricity from a new generating plant of any kind. During that interval we can expect the cost of solar sources to continue to fall if we allocate more funds to research on them. Even if smaller standardized reactors do achieve an acceptable level of safety, they are not likely to be competitive with solar sources if the true costs of the whole nuclear fuel cycle are included.

In the past, nuclear power has been *heavily subsidized* by public funds. The initial research was publicly funded, and free enriched uranium was supplied to private reactors. The Price-Anderson Act of 1957 limits a utility's liability from a reactor accident to $60 million, even though recent government studies put the damage from the maximum credible accident at $150 billion. Federal subsidies to the nuclear industry were still $12 to $15 billion a year in the mid-eighties. Waste disposal research and management will undoubtedly cost many times the disposal fees collected to date, and the safe dismantling of reactors at the end of their useful life (thirty or forty years) could cost up to $30 billion each.[40] The British government, as part of its privatization program, tried to sell off its nuclear plants in 1989, but private investors were not interested when they discovered the estimated costs of decommissioning and waste disposal.[41] Even with simpler modular reactors, the high cost of all these processes would have to be included in any realistic appraisal.

Breeder reactors and the *reprocessing* of spent fuel would reduce the cost of nuclear fuel. Breeder reactors are highly efficient, deriving sixty times as much energy from a ton of uranium as light water reactors do and extending reserves by making low-grade ores economical. Reprocessing plants are operating in Britain, France, and India; they take spent fuel and separate out the plutonium so that it can be recycled as reactor fuel. Japan is planning to ship its used fuel to Europe and bring the reprocessed plutonium back again in convoys, which would be a tempting target for terrorists. The United States rejected both breeders and reprocessing because they involve the transportation of plutonium, of which a small quantity could easily be diverted to make nuclear weapons. A nation that wants to make nuclear weapons now has to set up breeders or reprocessing or uranium enrichment plants—all of which are complex, expensive, large-scale operations. But if plutonium were circulating in nations around the world, it would be easy for terrorist groups to steal a small quantity. It takes only 20 pounds of plutonium to make a bomb, and 100,000 pounds would be available each year if spent fuel at current levels were being reprocessed and recycled. Plutonium can be handled with relative ease, and theft during storage or shipment would be tempting to small nations or revolutionary groups.[42]

It is of course difficult to prevent *the proliferation of nuclear weapons.* There are several routes for acquiring them. Several nations have not signed the Nonproliferation Treaty of 1968, and they do not allow the inspection of their facilities by the International Atomic Energy Agency. Even with stricter and universal international inspection, some diversion of weapons-grade material could occur. But the widespread circulation of plutonium would make acquisition of a bomb much easier. Even if it were intended only for purposes of extortion, events could get out of hand, especially in the midst of tensions between major powers or Middle Eastern rivalries. If nuclear war is the largest catastrophe that threatens both humanity and the planet, anything that even slightly increases the risk of its occurrence must weigh heavily in policy choices. Effective and verifiable arms control would be easier if plutonium were not readily available. I would thus be opposed to breeders and reprocessing even if they posed no safety problems. I also support proposals for international jurisdiction over the crucial portions of the current fuel cycle (uranium enrichment and waste disposal), preferably at regional international centers.[43]

I have not discussed *fusion* because the temperatures necessary for a self-sustaining reaction have proved so difficult to achieve even in the laboratory. In 1991 a European team produced a fusion reaction of 1.7 million watts for two seconds, releasing much less energy than was used to initiate the reaction but more than had been released in any previous experiments. The experimenters cautioned that commercial fusion remains at least fifty years away.[44] Fusion has the advantage that its main fuel, heavy hydrogen, is present in small quantities in ordinary water; if tritium is also needed, it could be produced in the fusion installation. Fusion technology would escape the problems of highly radioactive fuels and wastes that occur with fission, but the temperatures of millions of degrees and the local radioactivity produced would entail their own risks. Moreover, if commercial fusion can be achieved it will probably be only with very large-scale equipment that could not be scaled down.[45]

In short, I would favor a modest program of research on small passively stable reactors and on fusion, in order to keep future options open. But I believe that most of our efforts should be directed toward renewable sources and conservation because they are more promising alternatives for the next few decades.

III. RENEWABLE SOURCES

Renewable energy sources contribute to sustainability and justice, and in most cases the environmental impacts are lower than those of fossil fuels. Many forms of renewable energy involve decentralized systems amenable to local ownership and participation by individuals and communities. Their direct economic costs are only just beginning to be competitive with coal and oil, but these costs could be reduced by appropriate policy initiatives, and the indirect costs are far lower.

1. Solar Energy and Sustainability

An inherent feature of all renewable sources is their sustainability. Their energy will keep on arriving from the sun without depletion for millions of years. Using solar energy is living off income, whereas using fossil fuels is living off capital. One nation's use of solar energy does not affect the amount available to other nations or to future generations. While solar technologies often require considerable initial investment, the fuel itself is free; using it does not drive up the price for other people. Moreover, sunlight is available in all parts of the earth. There are regional variations in the duration and intensity of sunshine, but these are smaller than the huge geographical disparities in the distribution of fossil fuel and uranium reserves. Solar sources are thus compatible with both international and intergenerational justice. They fulfill Rawls's criterion of justice: they are the sort of technology you would try to develop if you did not know in which nation or in which generation you would live.

The main obstacle to renewable energy has been the costs, though in most cases costs have fallen dramatically and would undoubtedly fall faster with more research and with mass production. There are also some environmental problems, though these are seldom as serious as those from fossil fuels. In particular, none of these technologies produces the main greenhouse gas, carbon dioxide, and none of them except biomass produces air pollutants or soil erosion. Renewable systems cannot be turned into military weapons, and they cannot produce sudden catastro-

phes (except for the failure of large dams). The very diversity of solar technologies and their geographical dispersal would diversify the risks. By reducing dependence on foreign oil, they would contribute to world stability and peace and reduce balance-of-payment deficits. In terms of environmental impacts, renewable sources appear in general to be worse than nuclear plants operating normally, but better than coal or oil, for equivalent energy production. But the materials and the fabrication of the equipment for renewable technologies require energy that in many cases would come initially from fossil fuels.

1. *Hydroelectricity.*   Electricity generated from water power has for decades been cheaper than that from any other source. Nearly a fifth of the world's electricity is now water generated. North America has developed 59 percent of its potential hydropower, Europe 36 percent, Asia 9 percent, Latin America 8 percent, and Africa only 5 percent. But large dams entail great environmental costs: inundation of forests, farmland, and homes; accumulation of sediments; and harm to fish migration and aquatic life. In some parts of the world, small dams produce electricity with only modest environmental impacts. China, for example, has 90,000 small water turbines providing electricity in rural areas.[46]

2. *Water and Space Heating.*   In Israel, 65 percent of domestic water heating comes from rooftop solar collectors, which since 1980 have been required on all new residences up to nine stories high. In most countries, space heating with passive solar design and good insulation pays for itself in fuel savings in a decade or two, but most consumers want a more rapid payback on their investment. Building contractors are more interested in keeping the initial home price down than in reducing long-term costs. Retrofitting old houses is expensive, so solar heating does little to help low-income families. But if the cost of oil and gas rises, solar heating will become more attractive when combined with conservation measures.[47]

3. *Biomass.*   Twelve percent of the world's primary energy today comes from organic matter, mainly wood, but a serious fuelwood crisis has occurred in the Third World from the cutting of trees with little replanting. Brazil obtains 62 percent of its automotive fuel from sugar cane converted to ethanol, which was competitive with oil in 1981; but with oil prices lower in the late eighties, government subsidies were continued largely because the program creates 450,000 jobs and helps rural development instead of sending billions of dollars overseas for oil. But

ethanol from crops uses scarce agricultural land. If 40 percent of the entire U.S. corn crop were converted to ethanol it would meet only 10 percent of the nation's auto fuel demand.[48]

A more promising alternative is the planting of fast-growing trees, shrubs, or grasses on marginal land or rangeland, or the integrated cultivation of trees and crops (agroforestry). The burning or fermenting of forest and municipal wastes is another energy source. Crop and animal wastes can be fermented in tanks to create a biogas fuel, with the residue returned to the land as fertilizer. The growth of such biomass absorbs as much carbon dioxide as is released when it is burned, so it produces no net greenhouse effect, and sulfur emissions are low, but careful design and management is needed to limit soil erosion.[49]

4. *Wind Power.* Electricity generated by turbines at windy sites now costs 6 to 8 cents per kilowatt-hour (kwh), which is competitive with current U.S. utility purchases during peak demand periods (when utilities pay a premium in order to avoid having to build new plants) and is approaching the cost of electricity from new coal plants (5 centers per kwh). After some failures in the 1970s, the wind industry expanded in the early 1980s, especially in California, but it has slowed since 1985 when oil prices fell, federal tax credits were eliminated, and federal funds for research on renewable sources were cut by 85 percent. Turbines at windy sites could supply 20 percent of current U.S. electricity demand, and costs would fall with improved designs and mass production. They could be located in mountains or deserts or on farming and ranching lands, with little interference to other activities. India is planning for 10,000 turbines producing 1000 megawatts by 1995, and the Netherlands hopes to reach the same goal by 2000.[50]

5. *Solar Thermal Electricity.* Sunlight can be concentrated by parabolic reflectors to produce steam to drive generators. In California, 350 megawatts of solar thermal electricity are being produced at costs competitive with peak rates, and the costs are expected to fall in the nineties as larger and more efficient units are installed. Already their costs (8 cents per kilowatt-hour) are lower than that of electricity from recent nuclear plants (10 to 12 cents per kwh). Solar steam can also be used for process heat in nearby industries.[51]

6. *Photovoltaic Cells.* Electricity from PVs has the greatest potential for the future. The costs of both crystalline silicon and thin films of amorphous silicon fell dra-

matically in the eighties but are still prohibitive except for remote locations (communications, navigation aids, or isolated villages). In 1991 Texas Instruments announced plans to market flexible solar roof panels that look like metallic sandpaper; because they are made from metallurgical grade silicon, they are expected to cost a fifth of current PVs and would be competitive with coal-generated electricity. PVs create no carbon dioxide or air pollution (except in the fabrication of the equipment). The materials used—iron and silicon—are abundant. The land area needed for solar cells is comparable to that for coal plants of equivalent capacity if land strip-mined during thirty years is included. Panels in deserts, rocky areas, or roadside rights-of-way, or on factory or home rooftops would avoid competing with other land uses. Their modular character is adaptable to small or large arrays. PVs to supply all current U.S. electricity would require a square of land 100 miles on a side—a ninth the area of Arizona, or a fifth of the national area used by the U.S military.[52]

Wind, solar thermal, and PVs share one limitation: they all provide energy *intermittently,* varying with time of day and weather. They are useful for feeding electricity into a grid, thereby reducing the consumption of fossil fuels and avoiding the construction of new plants for daytime peak loads. Solar thermal can be combined with gas turbines in hybrid systems; gas takes over when there is no sunlight. But before wind or PVs could be used as the main source for baseloads, less expensive ways of *storing electricity* must be found. A dozen auto manufacturers, including Ford, GM, and Toyota, are planning to produce electric cars by 1995. Sodium-sulfur or nickel-cadmium batteries are an improvement on lead-acid batteries, but they are bulky and expensive.[53]

Photovoltaic-generated electricity passing through water releases *hydrogen* that can be stored and used for transportation or residential heating. Hydrogen produced from PVs in sunny desert areas could be compressed and distributed inexpensively in a pipeline system like that now used for natural gas. Autos would have to carry the hydrogen in high-compression tanks or in the form of metal hydrides. Hydrogen could also be burned in fuel cells on electric-powered cars, with twice the efficiency of internal combustion motors. If 150,000 square miles (2 percent of the world's desert areas) were used for PVs producing hydrogen, they could supply as much energy as all fossil fuels today. Hydrogen appears very promising in the long run, since it burns so cleanly; it emits no carbon dioxide, sulfur dioxide, or particulates. But extensive research is still needed on its production, storage, and combustion.[54]

Only *a combination of these renewable sources* could reduce the consumption of fossil fuels significantly. By one recent estimate, if total energy consumption remains constant, the U.S. supply in 2020 could be 7 percent nuclear, 4 percent hydro, 6 percent wind, 18 percent biomass, 24 percent solar, and 42 percent fossil fuels (as compared to 86 percent today).[55] But such a shift will take a concerted effort.

Under the influence of market forces alone the transition will be slow because market prices neglect many *environmental and human costs,* even when some of the externalities have been internalized through emission standards and environmental and safety regulations. As I have said, the market takes a short-term view and discounts costs and risks to future generations. When irreplaceable resources such as oil are used up, potential benefits are transferred from the future to the present. Neither the environment nor our grandchildren enter current economic calculations. A study in the former West Germany estimates the external costs of coal (not including global warming) at 2.4 to 5.5 cents per kilowatt-hour, and those of nuclear power at 6 to 13 cents.[56] In the United States, the state regulatory agencies often compare alternatives (including conservation) before they approve the plans of utilities for constructing new plants. The Wisconsin agency adds 15 percent to coal plant figures to reflect external costs, and in New York 25 percent is added.[57]

Moreover, fossil and nuclear fuels have been *heavily subsidized* in the past. For decades, oil was subsidized by depletion allowances, tax credits, highway construction funds, and regulated prices. Some of the subsidies to the nuclear industry were mentioned earlier. By one estimate the total annual U.S. energy subsidy in 1984 was $44 billion, mostly for coal, oil, and nuclear fuels.[58] Because the energy industry has invested heavily in these technologies, most of its research and its political influence supports continued use of these fuels. The cumulative expenditures on solar research since World War II are a minute fraction of that spent on other sources, so it is not surprising that it lags behind. Of the $7 billion that twenty-one industrial nations spent on energy research in 1989, 47 percent went to nuclear fission, 15 percent to fossil fuels, 12 percent to fusion, and only 7 percent to renewables and 5 percent to conservation.[59]

In the late 1970s under Carter, *national policies* to stimulate renewable energy technologies were adopted in the United States, but these were mostly revoked during the 1980s under Reagan. Federal funding for renewable research and development fell from $718 million in 1980 to $115 million in 1989. With the new concern for global warming and the dangers of dependence on imported oil, the time has come to reinstate tax credits for renewables and restore research and development funds at least to their former level. These could be financed by a tax on imported oil, higher taxes at the pump, or the proposed carbon tax. Or they could be paid for by a small fraction of the funds released if the space station and Star Wars research were canceled. Purchases of solar equipment and fuels for government facilities, offices, and vehicles would also help to create economies of scale. The diverse long-term benefits of renewable energy would justify such policies.

2. Decentralization and Participation

[Let us] define freedom *as participation in the decisions that affect one's life.* [We] distinguish three forms of freedom: (1) participation in policy decisions through political processes, (2) participation in economic decisions through the marketplace, and (3) participation in work-related decisions through activities in the workplace. All three forms of participation are very limited when the individual faces a large centralized organization, such as those that produce fossil or nuclear energy. Oil companies are among the world's largest financial institutions, wielding immense economic and political power. Nuclear plants require huge capital investments, so they can be built only by large private utilities or government agencies.

By contrast, some forms of solar technology can be owned and controlled by *individuals and communities,* which would encourage local self-reliance and a plurality of centers of decision—counteracting the trend toward the concentration of economic and political power. Biomass involves many actors: growers, harvesters, processors, and distributors. A biomass system would be coordinated by the market and by government policy, but it would have room for many local initiatives. Economies of scale may rule out very small operations, but intermediate-scale activities can be efficient. Solar heating and insulation and rooftop photovoltaics offer scope for small businesses in the installation and repair of equipment, drawing on local skills and shops that would integrate well with existing building trades. Solar technology is more labor-intensive than coal-fired plants and oil refineries, which produce fewer jobs per dollar than any other major industry. The manufacturing and installation of solar components would be well dispersed geographically.[60]

Community-level systems can be run as cooperatives, small companies, or municipal utilities. The burning of municipal wastes to produce electricity helps to solve the waste disposal and landfill problems faced by many cities. Wind generators and small dams can be locally owned and operated.

With any form of fuel, the *cogeneration* of heat and electricity substantially improves efficiency. Two-thirds of the energy input into most electric plants is simply wasted as heat. Instead, the heat can be used in industrial processes or in community-level systems. District heating, integrated systems, and the recovery of energy from urban sewage and agricultural residues are best carried out locally.

Decentralized systems offer *flexibility* in adapting to local conditions. Solar sources are diverse and can be matched to local resources and to differing end-use and temperature needs. They typically involve shorter construction times than large installations. In addition, they are *less vulnerable* to sabotage, terrorism, or catastrophic accidents. The stakes are smaller when errors or accidents do occur. Careful design and monitoring for environmental damage may be necessary, but not the elaborate safety precautions and security measures that nuclear plants require. Finally, the costs and the benefits of small-scale systems *tend to fall on the same people.* In the case of large power plants, nearby communities receive much of the pollution and environmental degradation, while most of the benefits go elsewhere; it is not surprising that local opposition to the siting of large plants has been rising. Decentralized systems offer a more just distribution of costs and benefits and the prospect of less vehement community opposition.[61]

Critics of decentralization say that small-scale systems are neither efficient nor socially desirable. Solar components such as photovoltaics will have to be mass-produced to be cheap enough to be widely adopted. Like the auto, solar equipment can be individually owned and decentralized in use, but it can be cheaply produced only with the economies of scale possible in large factories. Moreover, with the existing distribution of economic power it is likely that many forms of solar energy will be controlled by large companies. The social regulation of such companies may be difficult, but it is not impossible. Even decentralized systems require central regulation. A million smoky wood stoves would be no improvement on coal-burning plants when it comes to air pollution.

Even if local self-sufficiency were possible it might not be *equitable;* an urban ghetto or a rural village would receive much poorer electric service than an affluent suburb. By stressing local self-reliance, say their critics, decentralists have neglected the importance of social integration and cooperation for the common good. Most people are more interested in the cost and convenience of energy than in local control; they are willing to pay someone else to deliver energy to them. Critics also fear that renewable sources will not be adequate to meet energy demands; severe shortages would lead to slower economic growth, rationing, and government intervention to allocate scarce supplies. Authoritarian responses to scarcity might leave us with more centralization than we have now.[62]

Furthermore, the correlations between *energy systems* and *social structures* are loose and ambiguous. Solar enthusiasts and nuclear enthusiasts sometimes share the assumption that the right technology, the "technical fix," will solve our social problems. But the social and institutional context in which a technology is deployed is often crucial in determining its ultimate social consequences. Nevertheless, we must acknowledge that some technologies have distinctive potential that can be supported by deliberate social policies. The relationships between scale, efficiency, justice, and participation have to be examined separately for each part of an energy system if we are to understand the trade-offs between local participation and other values.

My own conclusion is that a *mix of small and large systems,* adapted to varied tasks and conditions, is preferable to either type alone. For example, the dispersed production of electricity reduces transmission and distribution costs, which constitute half of the consumer's electric bill. But the electric grid offers convenience and reliability in service, and it allows power to be transferred between regions with different peak-load hours or unused capacity. Local sources should therefore be tied into networks wherever possible. Large blocks of electricity for heavy industry and urban areas will probably require central generation. Some photovoltaic installations and some biomass production can be locally controlled, but competition for scarce land may make large solar arrays in remote areas or large plantations of plants or trees for fuel desirable.

But a mix of scales will require a deliberate effort to develop the *untapped potential of small systems.* In the past we have subsidized large-scale technologies. Past investment in such systems has created a momentum for their perpetuation, whereas the constituencies for the small are diffuse and less well organized. The centralization/decentralization debate also involves differences in value priorities and in visions of the future, to which we will return in the final chapter.

IV. CONSERVATION

Conservation is the most cost-effective response to energy shortages. Most ways of reducing energy demand are cheaper than increasing supply by an equivalent amount. It costs less to save than to produce a barrel of oil or a kilowatt-hour of electricity. But conservation also furthers every one of the values discussed in this volume. Conservation in industrial nations reduces global inequities in energy consumption. It cuts the waste of the irreplaceable resources that future generations will need. It is essential for the transition to sustainable sources. Conservation measures seldom harm the environment. A dollar spent on conservation is seven times as effective in cutting carbon dioxide emissions as a dollar spent on nuclear power. Reducing oil imports diminishes a major cause of international conflict. We will look particularly at two values that might seem incompatible with reduced energy use: economic development and personal fulfillment. Finally, we examine the distinctive needs and opportunities of the Third World.

1. Energy and Economic Development

In chapter 2, I said that we should seek economic development: selective economic growth that does not jeopardize equitable distribution, resource sustainability or environmental protection. The conservation of energy and other resources can make a major contribution to economic development.

Until the oil embargo of 1973, the graphs of U.S. energy consumption and gross national product rose on similar curves, and it was assumed that demand would continue to rise in a growing economy. Restricting energy growth, it was said, would automatically restrict economic growth. But from 1973 to 1987, U.S. energy consumption actually fell, while the GNP grew by 35 percent.[63] The nations in the International Energy Agency lowered their energy use per unit of GNP by 24 percent from 1973 to 1989.[64] While higher oil prices did initially result in somewhat slower economic growth, the combined effect of various conservation measures showed that, over a longer period, economic growth can be at least partially uncoupled from energy consumption. But since 1988, with oil prices lower, energy use has started to rise again.

Forms of economic growth that are compatible with *rapid reduction in energy consumption* in industrial nations are essential to global justice and the transition to sustainable solar sources. The United States spends 10 percent of its GNP on energy, while Japan spends only 4 percent, but even Japan has barely begun to fulfill the potential for conservation. Four forms of conservation are most promising:

1. *Transportation.* Transportation fuel comprises two-thirds of U.S. oil use. In response to fuel economy standards introduced by Congress in 1975, the average fuel economy of new cars doubled from 14 miles per gallon (mpg) in 1975 to 28 mph in 1985, but the standards were subsequently relaxed.[65] The auto industry continued to oppose higher standards, and in early 1992 Congress

was still unwilling to require more than the current standard (27.5 mpg average for the new cars produced by any company). Readily available technologies could produce cars with 38 mpg, and the extra cost would be offset by the savings on fuel.[66] The Volvo LPC 2000 gets 81 mpg on highways, and the four-to-five-passenger Toyota AXV prototype achieved 98 mpg on the combined urban/highway test administered by the EPA.[67]

Mass transit and railways are far more efficient than autos and trucks, produce much less carbon dioxide and harmful air emissions, and would reduce the congestion that is paralyzing many cities. Frequent, rapid service with small buses using express lanes will attract urban riders. Electric trolleys and light railway vehicles are much less expensive than underground subway systems, and parking spaces for autos and bicycles can be provided at suburban stops. City centers should be reserved for pedestrians and bicycles. Public transportation also helps low-income families, many of whom do not own cars.[68]

2. *Buildings.* Large savings are possible in commercial and residential heating and cooling. In office buildings, better insulation, thermal reflective glass, more efficient lighting, and the recovery of waste heat from ventilated air can cut energy input in half. For new homes, insulation standards, building codes, and loan requirements could lead to much lower heat losses. Superinsulated homes in Sweden save 89 percent on heating bills and pay for their additional cost in five years. But housing stock turns over slowly; more rapid savings can come from retrofitting existing houses with insulation and weatherstripping, saving up to 50 percent on heating bills. Yet many home owners are reluctant to invest in such improvements unless the payback time is three or four years—a shorter period than they expect in other investments. Renters have little incentive to improve their landlords' houses, and landlords and housing contractors do not pay the energy bills. Some utility companies are taking an active role in home energy audits, subcontracting and guaranteeing the installation of insulation, and arranging loan repayment from the saving in future fuel bills. By helping to control demand, utilities can avoid having to build costly new power plants. But the institutional obstacles to energy conservation in homes can be overcome only by stronger governmental leadership, including housing standards, efficiency ratings, and low-interest loans to low-income families.[69]

3. *Industry.* Many companies have already reduced their energy demand substantially. More efficient equipment

and processes have been introduced in such energy-intensive industries as steel, aluminum, paper, glass, and chemicals. New techniques have been used for waste heat recovery and for the cascading of processes requiring successively lower temperatures. Process steam can be cogenerated with electricity, at twice the efficiency of separately generated electricity. The recycling of materials usually takes far less energy than primary extraction from raw materials. A shift is also occurring within industry from the energy-intensive processing of basic materials to fabrication, finishing, and high-tech products. Electronic systems use few materials and little energy, and they can be used to monitor and control the flow of materials and energy in other industrial processes.[70]

4. *Electricity.* In the past, low electricity rates were offered to large users, partly to promote sales and partly because of economies in distribution and billing. Today, "inverted rate structures" are proposed to discourage heavy use. "Lifeline rates" would start with a low price for a basic block of electricity for minimal needs per person, with rising rates thereafter. This would offer some help to low-income families and would encourage conservation. Lower off-peak rates would produce some shift in demand away from peak-load periods. For appliances, testing and labeling, and perhaps efficiency standards, would be helpful. Some air conditioners and refrigerators on the market are twice as efficient as others. Heat pumps can use the same equipment for heating in winter and cooling in summer. Lighting consumes 20 percent of U.S. electricity, and this could be greatly reduced. A 15-watt fluorescent bulb produces the same amount of light as an ordinary 75-watt bulb. It lasts thirteen times as long, more than repaying its higher initial cost; if the electricity is coal generated, each bulb saves a ton of carbon dioxide and twenty pounds of sulfur dioxide emissions during its life.[71]

Apart from conservation and efficiency measures, selective growth requires other *changes in the economy.* The energy-intensive manufacturing sector has been shrinking while the service sector has been growing (including health care, financial services, information services, and education), and this shift can be carried further. Sudden and severe energy shortages do indeed result in economic and social disruption. The 1973 oil embargo led to job layoffs and economic recession; minority groups were laid off first and low-income families were hardest hit. But gradual shifts toward efficiency and services produce a stronger economy that spends less on energy and is less vulnerable to future oil crises or price fluctuations.

Expenditures on energy conservation also create *more employment* than expenditures on energy production. A European Community study found that conservation expenditures produced more jobs than traditional energy investments.[72] A U.S. study concluded that every dollar invested in conservation produced twice as many jobs as a dollar invested in conventional energy industries.[73] Home insulation and public transportation are labor-intensive, and the jobs are well distributed geographically. Higher energy prices usually result in some substitution of labor for energy. The shift to less energy-intensive products will of course decrease jobs in some industries, but the new industries and services that replace them will more than compensate for such losses.

Issues of justice in conservation do require special attention. The paradox is that the poor cannot afford the higher initial costs for energy-efficient homes or appliances, and they end by paying more in the long run in higher utility bills. They live in poorly insulated homes and they spend a much larger fraction of their income on energy than more affluent people do. The poorest tenth of the population spends 34 percent of its income directly for energy, while the richest tenth spends only 2 percent.[74] It is misguided, however, to try to keep energy prices low to protect the poor, for this reduces incentives for conservation. Instead, both financial and energy services should be targeted especially on low-income families: fuel assistance in emergencies only, home insulation subsidy, a revised utility rate structure, greater support for public transportation, and so forth.

Conservation does involve some risks to *health and environment,* but they are relatively small. Raw materials and energy are needed to fabricate insulating materials. Some insulation gives off formaldehyde, which causes respiratory illness. Sealing a house tightly against air leakage allows a buildup of radon gas (a cause of lung cancer) from cement, bricks, or soil in some regions; this can be avoided with air ventilation and a heat exchanger, but at considerable cost.[75] Smaller cars save energy and pollute less, but the fatality rate in accidents is higher. Conservation does entail environmental and health risks, but in most cases these are less than the risks from equivalent energy production. Overall, conservation gets high marks on each of the criteria we have been using.

2. Life-Styles and Personal Fulfillment

Improvements in efficiency allow people to obtain the same goods and service with a lower expenditure of energy.

These pragmatic conservation measures would require very little sacrifice and would not harm *the quality of life*. Comparisons of 35 industrial nations have shown no correlation between energy use and a varied set of social indicators (including life expectancy, literacy, unemployment, crime, suicide rates, and environmental quality indexes).[76] Another study showed that Sweden had a GNP per capita close to that of the United States and outranked the U.S. on almost every social indicator but used 40 percent less energy per capita. In Sweden, heavy gasoline taxes, smaller cars, and excellent public transportation (aided by geographical compactness) had produced higher transportation efficiency, while commercial and residential use of energy was much less wasteful. Britain came out between Sweden and the United States in energy use and on most of the social indicators.[77]

The conservation measures described above rely on technical changes, economic incentives, and legislated standards, but they would be more effective if accompanied by relatively minor *changes in individual behavior.* Turning thermostats down in winter, turning off unused lights, using public transportation, or recycling glass, paper, and aluminum cans may seem inconsequential, but many small actions add up to significant savings. Educational programs can increase awareness of the importance of conservation and of simple ways to save energy. Psychologists have shown the importance of social reinforcement and group support in behavior change.[78] But the political constituency for conservation is difficult to mobilize because the benefits are diverse, long-run, and widely diffused, whereas well-organized and powerful groups in industry, labor, and government receive immediate benefits from continued dependence on fossil and nuclear fuels.

Changes in life-styles could further reduce energy consumption by altering the goods and services people seek rather than simply providing the same goods and services more efficiently. A consumer society encourages a high demand for material goods, highly processed and packaged foods, and energy-intensive products. During the 1970s, a significant number of young people in North America and Europe were disillusioned with the prevailing materialism and individualism and the stresses of a competitive society. They sought alternative sources of satisfaction in personal growth, human relationships, smaller communities, and greater harmony with nature, and they adopted more frugal life-styles. Some of them joined communes or new religious movements. Others tried to find meaningful work, family life, spiritual growth, and fulfilling activities within traditional institutions.[79] Some of these experi-

ments were short-lived, but others continued in the 1980s, expressing values that are neglected among the dominant goals of industrial societies.

In whatever form they are expressed, *new views of personal fulfillment* can lead to lower levels of resource consumption and energy use. I do not believe that moral exhortation or appeals to austerity or sacrifice will have much influence today. But a revitalization of Western religious traditions could bring new perceptions of the good life and a new recognition of less resource-intensive sources of satisfaction that would alter patterns of consumption in affluent nations. [What is needed is a] shift from the prevailing industrial paradigm to a *postindustrial paradigm* more appropriate to an interdependent world with finite resources. But such paradigm shifts occur slowly except in response to severe crises. In the meantime, the practice of individual frugality must be combined with political efforts for effective legislation, economic incentives, and efficient technologies, which are the most promising social paths to energy conservation today.

3. Energy in the Third World

The Third World is highly dependent on *fossil fuels*. The disastrous impact of higher oil prices was mentioned earlier. Oil has played a vital role in transportation, agricultural irrigation, and fertilizer production. Only a few Third World countries have coal deposits, and the release of greenhouse gases makes increased use of coal problematic. Several developing nations have significant natural gas deposits, and others have not yet been explored; these could be very helpful during the next decades, though they would require the construction of pipeline systems. *Nuclear power* has played a negligible role in the South. It is expensive and perpetuates dependence on equipment and exports from the North. A second generation of smaller, passively stable reactors might be useful in urban and industrial centers in the more advanced developing countries, but most areas lack the electrical grids necessary for distributing large blocks of electricity.

Waterpower and *biomass* account for nearly half the primary energy use of the Third World, but fuelwood, the chief source in rural areas, has been used much faster than it has been replaced . . . . [D]eforestation without replanting has resulted in severe soil erosion and flooding as well as fuelwood shortages. Cheap *solar technology* would be a great boon to the sun-rich Third World. It would reduce dependence on other nations for expertise and fuel. Solar cookers, solar water pumps, methane digesters, small hydroelectric dams, windmills, and photovoltaic cells would be especially helpful. They would encourage national self-reliance and fit in with local cultures.[80]

Conservation might seem insignificant in developing countries, since the amount of energy that could be saved is so much smaller than that wasted in affluent nations. But in fact conservation is crucial for future prospects in all countries. The Brundtland Commission concluded that with strong conservation programs the global energy consumption in 2030 could be only 10 percent higher than in 1980 (rather than growing by a factor of three as in some projections). The report emphasizes the fuelwood crisis, pointing out that an open fire uses eight times the energy of a gas stove of equivalent cooking capacity. It sees promise in biogas, small dams, and solar installations. It advocates incentives for tree planting, community woodlots, and the combination of food and energy production in agroforestry. With careful planning, fast-growing trees could be used efficiently, and replanting would prevent the soil erosion that attended previous fuelwood use.[81]

A report by the World Resources Institute (WRI) concludes that if *efficiency* is strenuously pursued in all countries, global energy demand in 2020 would be only 10 percent higher than in 1980, even with the expected growth in population. Energy use in the North would have to be cut in half, while that in the South would grow, and living standards in the Third World in 2020 could be comparable with those of Western Europe in the midseventies. For $4 billion, a highly efficient wood stove costing $10 could be provided to 400 million rural households in the Third World. Stoves of even higher efficiency would burn biogas from crop and animal residues or produce gas from the partial oxidation of other forms of biomass. The study urges intensive research on better technologies for the conversion of biomass to liquid fuels for transportation. It also advocates the electrification of all villages, using local resources whenever feasible.[82]

The World Resources Institute study looks at energy end use in the framework of a development strategy focused on *basic human needs*. It points out that a quarter of World Bank loans have been for energy but mostly for large projects such as dams or central power plants. "Over 90 percent of energy development aid has gone to building large systems for generating and transmitting electricity . . . . Less than 1 percent of international aid has been used to improve energy efficiency, and most of this 1 percent has gone to the industrial sector."[83] Such aid has paid for foreign consultants and equipment, benefiting the donors, but it has done little to develop indigenous techni-

cal capacities. It has favored cities and heavy industries over rural areas and small-scale technologies. The WRI report advocates self-reliant development, production for local needs, and the expansion of industries producing equipment for agriculture and rural areas rather than for export or the urban elite. It suggests that a shift from materials processing to fabrication and finishing would also reduce energy use and increase employment opportunities.

Some authors hold that developing nations will have to use large-scale electric generation (such as large dams and nuclear and coal-fired plants) if their *electricity demands* continue growing at current rates (7 percent per year, with demand increasing fourfold in twenty years).[84] They hold that developing countries are likely to give industrial growth higher priority than environmental impacts, except where the latter are already serious and obvious (urban respiratory problems, for instance). While some development of such capital-intensive technologies may be necessary, they tend to perpetuate foreign dependency and trade deficits, and the benefits will be short-lived. Third World countries should rather seek to develop their own distinctive renewable sources and seek the transfer of technologies more directly related to basic human needs.

V. CONCLUSIONS

By the criteria of evaluation outlined in earlier chapters, the "hard path" of fossil fuel and nuclear expansion is less desirable than the "soft path" of renewable energy and conservation for both industrial and developing nations. Dependence on *imported oil* has been a source of global injustice, international conflict, and environmental damage. Some of the environmental impacts of *coal* can be reduced by improved combustion and emission control technologies, but others, especially the greenhouse effect, are likely to be very serious. *Natural gas* is preferable environmentally and is crucial for the transitional period, but reserves are unevenly distributed and are not indefinitely sustainable.

Nuclear fuels are sustainable for many centuries (especially with breeder reactors) and environmental risks are low in normal operation. But we have seen that economic costs are high, accidents are potentially catastrophic, and uncertainties about radioactive waste disposal are unresolved (though probably resolvable). The risk of diversion of plutonium to nuclear weapons counts against breeders and reprocessing, and all nuclear plants are vulnerable to human errors, institutional failures, and extortion by terrorists. I expressed support for a program of careful, open research on fusion and on smaller, passively stable reactors—but only as forms of insurance in the unlikely event that promising solar sources (especially photovoltaics) and storage methods (such as hydrogen) remain costly despite intensive research and development efforts.

Renewable sources, by contrast, correlate well with all of the values I have defended. They are compatible with justice because they are available to all countries, more evenly distributed than fossil or nuclear fuels, and more readily subject to national self-determination. They reduce threats to world peace from conflicts over oil and from the proliferation of nuclear weapons. They are compatible with participation because they are diverse, predominantly small-scale and decentralized, and amenable to community ownership and local control. They are uniquely sustainable because they do not significantly deplete resources. Their environmental impact on air and water is lower than that of fossil fuels, and problems of land use and soil erosion can be controlled by careful management.

Whatever sources of energy are used, *conservation* can be justified in every nation in terms of all the values we have been discussing. Efficiency research and conservation efforts have had a small role in the budgets of most national governments and international agencies, and yet these measures are essential to economic development and selective growth. A strenuous conservation program is also required if we are to shift a large fraction of total supply from fossil to renewable fuels without highly disruptive energy shortages.

I have argued that the combination of *renewable sources* and *conservation* would not jeopardize economic development in the long run, though it would involve some increased costs and displacements in the short run. Employment opportunities are greater on the "soft path" than on the "hard." Finally, the understanding of personal fulfillment that I have defended does not require ever higher levels of individual consumption in affluent nations but encourages more frugal life-styles that would give additional support to public policies for conserving energy and other resources.

For several decades we will have to use *a mix of "hard" and "soft" technologies,* even as we try to rely increasingly on the latter. Such diversity would allow flexibility in adapting to new developments and to differing local conditions. Keeping diverse options open would hedge our bets and allow creative responses to technological advances, changing economic costs, and new knowledge of environmental impacts—all of which, along with our value priorities, will influence our future policy judgments.

Notes

1. World Commission on Environment and Development, *Our Common Future* (Oxford: Oxford University Press, 1987), p. 14.
2. *World Development Report* (Washington, DC: World Bank, 1981).
3. U.S. Geological Survey estimates from C. D. Masters et al., "Resource Constraints in Petroleum Production Potential," *Science* 253 (1991): 146–152.
4. Daniel Yergin, *The Prize: The Epic Quest for Oil, Money, and Power* (New York: Simon and Schuster, 1991).
5. Carl Berhens and Robert Bamburger, "Why Can't We Have a Real Energy Policy?" *Congressional Research Service Review* (March-April 1991), p. 2.
6. Energy Information Administration, "Annual Energy Outlook 1991" (Washington, DC: Department of Energy, 1991).
7. Joseph Romm, "Needed: A No-regrets Energy Policy," *Bulletin of the Atomic Scientists* 47, no. 6 (1991): 31; see also Harold Hubbard, "The Real Cost of Energy," *Scientific American* 264, no. 4 (1991): 36–42.
8. Jose Goldemberg et al., *Energy for Development* (Washington, DC: World Resources Institute, 1987), chap. 1.
9. Yergin, *Prize,* p. 13.
10. "Auto Pollution Health Costs Calculated," *Washington Post,* Jan. 21, 1990. See also James Cannon, *The Health Costs of Air Pollution* (New York: American Lung Association, 1985).
11. Carl Bagge, "Coal: Meeting the Energy Challenge," in *Perspectives on Energy,* 2d ed., ed. Lon Ruedisili and Morris Firebaugh (New York: Oxford University Press, 1978).
12. National Academy of Sciences, *Surface Mining: Soil, Coal, and Society* (Washington, DC: National Academy Press, 1981); Walter Rosenbaum, *Environmental Politics and Policy,* 2d ed. (Washington, DC: Congressional Quarterly Press, 1991), pp. 261–66.
13. Hilary French, "Clearing the Air," in *State of the World 1990,* ed. Lester Brown (New York: W. W. Norton, 1990).
14. Sandra Postel, "Protecting Forests from Air Pollution and Acid Rain," *State of the World 1985,* ed. Lester Brown (New York: W. W. Norton, 1985); William Fulkerson et al., "Energy for Fossil Fuels," *Scientific American* 263, no. 3 (1990): 82–89.
15. Rosenbaum, *Environmental Politics,* chap. 6; "A Decade's Acrimony Lifted in the Good of Clean Air," *Congressional Quarterly,* Oct. 27, 1990, 3587–92.
16. Christopher Flavin, "Slowing Global Warming," in *State of the World 1990.*
17. Stephen Schneider, *Global Warming: Are We Entering the Greenhouse Century?* (San Francisco: Sierra Club Books, 1989); Schneider, "The Changing Climate," *Scientific American* 261, no. 9 (1989): 70–79. An estimate of global warming in the range of 2 to 9° F is given in National Academy of Sciences, *Policy Implications of Greenhouse Warming: A Synthesis* (Washington, DC: National Academy Press, 1991).

18. For example, the U.N.'s Intergovernmental Panel on Climate Change estimates that global warming would reduce crop yields in the world's main grain exporting regions by 20 percent; see Martin Parry, *Climate Change and World Agriculture* (London: Earthscan, 1990).

19. National Academy of Sciences, *Policy Implications of Greenhouse Warming.*

20. Christopher Flavin, "Building a Bridge to Sustainable Energy," in *State of the World 1992,* ed. Lester Brown (New York: W. W. Norton, 1992); Walter Vergara et al., *Natural Gas: Its Role and Potential in Economic Development* (Boulder: Westview Press, 1990).

21. Christopher Flavin and Nicholas Lenssen, *Beyond the Petroleum Age: Designing a Solar Economy* (Washington, DC: Worldwatch Institute, 1990); Michael Oppenheimer and Robert Boyle, *Dead Heat: The Race Against the Greenhouse Effect* (New York: Basic Books, 1990).

22. Terrence Price, *Political Electricity: What Future for Nuclear Energy?* (Oxford: Oxford University Press, 1990), p. 4.

23. Steven Del Sesto, *Science, Politics, and Controversy: Civilian Nuclear Power in the United States, 1946–1974* (Boulder: Westview Press, 1979).

24. Joseph Morone and Edward Woodhouse, *The Demise of Nuclear Energy? Lessons for Democratic Control of Technology* (New Haven: Yale University Press, 1989); John L. Campbell, *Collapse of an Industry: Nuclear Power and the Contradictions of U.S. Policy* (Ithaca: Cornell University Press, 1988).

25. David Collingridge, *Technology in the Policy Process: Controlling Nuclear Power* (New York: St. Martin's Press, 1983).

26. Elizabeth Rolph, *Nuclear Power and the Public Safety: A Study in Regulation* (Lexington, MA: Lexington, 1989).

27. Christopher Hohenemser, "The Accident at Chernobyl: Health and Environmental Consequences and Implications for Risk Management," *Annual Review of Energy* 13 (1988): 383–428; see also Viktor Haynes and Marko Bojcun, *The Chernobyl Disaster* (London: Hogarth Press, 1988).

28. Charles Perrow, *Normal Accidents: Living with High-Risk Technologies* (New York: Basic Books, 1984), chap. 2.

29. Baruch Fishoff et al., *Acceptable Risk* (Cambridge: Cambridge University Press, 1981); Paul Slovic and Baruch Fishoff, "Perception and Acceptability of Risk," in *Public Reaction to Nuclear Power: Are There Critical Masses?* (Boulder: Westview Press, 1984).

30. Sandia National Laboratory, "Estimates of the Financial Consequences of Nuclear Power Reactor Accidents" (Washington, DC: Nuclear Regulatory Commission, 1982), cited in Christopher Flavin, "Reassessing Nuclear Power," in *State of the World 1987,* ed. Brown, p. 78.

31. Nicholas Lenssen, "Confronting Nuclear Waste," in *State of the World 1992,* ed. Brown.

32. Gerald Jacob, *Site Unseen: The Politics of Siting a Nuclear Waste Repository* (Pittsburgh: University of Pittsburgh Press, 1990); Charles Walker and Leroy Gould, eds., *Too Hot to Handle: Social and Policy Issues in the Management of Radioactive Wastes* (New Haven: Yale University Press, 1983).

33. Alvin Weinberg, "Social Institutions and Nuclear Energy," *Science* 177 (1972): 27–34.

34. Office of Technology Assessment, *Managing Commercial High-Level Radioactive Waste* (Washington, DC: OTA, 1982).

35. Michael Kraft, "Evaluating Technology through Public Participation: The Nuclear Waste Disposal Controversy," in *Technology and Politics,* ed. Michael Kraft and Norman Vig (Durham: Duke University Press, 1988).

36. Office of Technology Assessment, *Nuclear Power in an Age of Uncertainty* (Washington, DC: OTA 1984).

37. Bernard Cohen, *The Nuclear Energy Option: An Alternative for the 90s* (New York: Plenum Press, 1990), chap. 10.

38. John Taylor, "Improved and Safer Nuclear Power," *Science* 244 (1989): 318–25; Alvin Weinberg, "Engineering in an Age of Anxiety," *Issues in Science and Technology* 6, no. 2 (1989–90): 37–43; Union of Concerned Scientists, *Advanced Reactor Report* (Cambridge, MA: UCS, 1990).

39. Morone and Woodhouse, *Demise of Nuclear Power?*

40. Rosenbaum, *Environmental Politics,* chap. 8.

41. "The Death of the Costliest Delusion," *The Guardian* (London), Nov. 10, 1989.

42. Frederick Williams and David Deese, eds., *Nuclear Nonproliferation: The Spent Fuel Problem* (New York: Pergamon Press, 1980); D. Albright and H. A. Feiveson, "Plutonium Recycling and the Problem of Nuclear Proliferation," *Annual Review of Energy* 13 (1988): 239–66.

43. Robert Williams and Harold Feiveson, "How to Expand Nuclear Power without Proliferation," *Bulletin of the Atomic Scientists* 47, no. 3 (1990): 40–45.

44. *Star Tribune* (Minneapolis), Nov. 11, 1991, p. 1A.

45. J. P. Holdren, "Safety and Environmental Aspects of Fusion Energy," *Annual Review of Energy and The Environment* 16 (1991): 235–400.

46. Cynthia Pollock Shea, "Shifting to Renewable Energy," in *State of the World 1988,* ed. Lester Brown (New York: W. W. Norton, 1988).

47. Rick Bevington and Arthur Rosenfeld, "Energy for Buildings and Homes," *Scientific American* 263, no. 3 (1990): 38–47; Solar Technical Information Program, *Energy for Today: Renewable Energy* (Golden, CO: Solar Energy Research Institute, 1990).

48. Michael Renner, "Rethinking Transportation," in *State of the World 1989,* p. 102. See also H. S. Geller, "Ethanol from Sugar Cane in Brazil," *Annual Review of Energy* 10 (1985): 135–64; Daniel Sperling and Mark De Luchi, "Transportation Energy Futures," *Annual Review of Energy* 14 (1989): 375–424.

49. World Commission on Environment and Development, *Energy 2000: A Global Strategy for Sustainable Development* (London: Zed Books, 1987).

50. Michael Brower, *Cool Energy* (Cambridge, MA: Union of Concerned Scientists, 1990), chap. 4; Paul Gipe, "Wind Power Around the World," *Alternative Sources of Energy* (May 1988), pp. 38–45.

51. Brower, *Cool Energy,* chap 3; Carl Weinberg and Robert Williams, "Energy from the Sun," *Scientific American* 263, no. 3 (1990): 98–107.

52. H. M. Hubbard, "Photovoltaics Today and Tomorrow," *Science* 244 (1989): 297–303; D. E. Carlson, "Photovoltaic Technologies for Commercial Power Generation," *Annual Review of Energy* 15 (1990): 85–98; Ken Zweibel, *Harnessing Solar Power: The Photovoltaics Challenge* (New York: Plenum Press, 1990).

53. Daniel Sperling and Mark DeLuchi, "Transportation Energy Futures," *Annual Review of Energy* 14 (1989): 375–424.

54. Joan Ogden and Robert Williams, *Solar Hydrogen: Moving Beyond Fossil Fuels* (Washington, DC: World Resources Institute, 1989).

55. Brower, *Cool Energy,* p. 23.

56. Olav Hohmeyer, *Social Costs of Energy Consumption* (Berlin: Springer-Verlag, 1988).

57. Susan Williams, Scott Fenn, and Terry Clausen, "Renewing Renewable Energy," *Issues in Science and Technology* 6, no. 2 (1990): 64–70.

58. Richard Heede et al., *The Hidden Costs of Energy* (Washington, DC: Center for Renewable Resources, 1985), cited in Flavin and Lenssen, *Beyond the Petroleum Age,* p. 27.

59. International Energy Agency, *Energy Politics and Programmes of IEA Countries: 1989 Review* (Paris: Organisation for Economic Co-operation and Development, 1990).

60. Amory Lovins, *Soft Energy Paths* (Cambridge, MA: Ballinger/Friends of the Earth, 1977); Flavin and Lenssen, *Beyond the Petroleum Age,* pp. 40–43.

61. K. S. Shrader-Frechette, "Ethics and Energy," in *Earthbound,* ed. Tom Regan (New York: Random House, 1984).

62. On the pros and cons of centralization and decentralization, see Ian Barbour, Harvey Brooks, Sanford Lakoff, and John Opie, *Energy and American Values* (New York: Praeger Publishers, 1982), pp. 72–74 and 130–34.

63. Lee Schipper, Richard Howarth, and Howard Geller, "U.S. Energy Use from 1973 to 1987: Impacts on Improved Efficiency," *Annual Review of Energy* 15 (1990): 457.

64. International Energy Agency, *Energy Policies and Programmes: 1989.*

65. Michael Renner, "Rethinking Transportation," in *State of the World 1989,* p. 103.

66. John Gibbons, Peter Blair, and Holly Gwin, "Strategies for Energy Use," *Scientific American* 261 (Sept. 1989): 136–43.

67. Deborah Gordon, *Steering a New Course: Transportation, Energy, and the Environment* (Cambridge, MA: Union of Concerned Scientists, 1991); Deborah Bleviss and Peter Walzer, "Energy for Motor Vehicles," *Scientific American* 263 (Sept. 1990): 54–61.

68. Marcia Lowe, "Rethinking Urban Transport," in *State of the World 1991.*

69. Christopher Flavin and Alan Durning, "Raising Energy Efficiency," in *State of the World 1988;* Rick Bevington and Arthur Rosenfeld, "Energy for Buildings and Homes," *Scientific American* 263, no. 3 (1990) 38–45.

70. Robert Williams, Eric Larson, and Marc Ross, "Materials, Affluence, and Industrial Energy Use," *Annual Review of Energy* 12 (1987): 99–144.

71. Pietro Nivola, *The Politics of Energy Conservation* (Washington, DC: Brookings Institution, 1986), chap. 4; Arnold Fickett, Clark Gellings, and Amory Lovins, "Efficient Use of Electricity," *Scientific American* 263, no. 3 (1990): 28–37.

72. Olav Hohmeyer et al., *Employment Effects of Energy Conservation Investments in EC Countries* (Luxembourg: European Communities Publications, 1985), cited in Flavin and Lenssen, *Beyond the Petroleum Age,* p. 41.

73. Steven Buchsbaum and James Benson, *Jobs and Energy* (New York: Council on Economic Priorities, 1979); Frederick Buttell, "Labor's Stake in Environmental Quality and Energy Policy," in *Labor and the Environment,* ed. F. Buttell (Westport CT: Greenwood Press, 1984).

74. Robert Paehlke, *Environmentalism and the Future of Politics* (New Haven: Yale University Press, 1989), p. 274. See also Denton Morrison, "Equity Impacts of Some Major Energy Alternatives," in *Energy Policy in the United States: Social and Behavioral Dimensions,* ed. Seymour Warkov (New York: Praeger Publishers, 1978).

75. Henry Hurwitz, "Indoor Air Pollution," *Bulletin of the Atomic Scientists* 37 (Feb. 1981): 61–62, replies on pp. 62–64.

76. Joy Dunkerley, ed., *International Comparisons of Energy Consumption* (Baltimore: Johns Hopkins University Press, 1978).

77. Lee Schipper and Allen Lichtenberger, "Efficient Energy Use and Well-being: The Swedish Example," *Science* 194 (1976): 1001–13.

78. See Warkov, ed., *Energy Policy.*

79. Laura Nader and Stephen Beckerman, "Energy as It Relates to Quality and Style of Life," *Annual Review of Energy* 3 (1978): 11–28; Richard Carlson, Willis Harman and Peter Schwartz, *Energy Futures, Human Values, and Lifestyles* (Boulder: Westview Press, 1982).

80. Christopher Flavin, "Electrifying the Third World," in *State of the World 1987;* Amulya Reddy and Jose Goldemberg, "Energy for the Developing World," *Scientific American* 263, no. 3 (1990): 62–73.

81. World Commission on Environment and Development, *Our Common Future* and *Energy 2000.*

82. Jose Goldemberg et al., *Energy for Development.*

83. Ibid., p. 18.

84. For example, T. J. Wilbanks, "Implementing Environmentally Sound Power Sector Strategies in Developing Countries," *Annual Review of Energy* 15 (1990): 255–76.

Questions

1. Why are fossil fuels used so prevalently?
2. Name five problems associated with the worldwide accelerated use of energy.
3. What is the effect of coal on the environment?
4. What effect does burning fossil fuels have on the environment? What is the main way to reduce global warming?
5. What effect could radioactive wastes have on future generations?
6. What are three ethical issues that can be identified in planning for nuclear waste disposal?
7. How does the energy issue relate to the ecological issues of populations and pollution? What are some of your conclusions?
8. What is the correlation between reducing energy consumption and one's lifestyle?

6

Beyond the Gulf Crisis: An Energy Strategy for the '90s

CHRISTOPHER FLAVIN

• •

President Bush has demonstrated that the U.S. commitment to protect Persian Gulf oil is more than rhetorical. He has not yet done the same regarding our domestic energy policy, which continues to founder in a sea of rhetoric nearly devoid of clear goals or programs. While the United States has spent more than a decade preparing its troops to fight a desert war in the Persian Gulf, it has allowed its oil imports to rise so high that U.S. vulnerability to events in this politically unstable region has been greatly increased.

Deputy Secretary of Energy W. Henson Moore explained the administration's perspective in early 1990 when he wrote, "We anticipate a decade of relative stability" in world oil markets. He attempted to sum up the Bush energy policy but did not even mention the problem of rising U.S. oil imports. The Energy Department was apparently no better prepared than the rest of the administration, which was providing Saddam Hussein with high-tech weapons only weeks before his tanks overran Kuwait.

THE UNITED STATES AND THE PERSIAN GULF

Even without Saddam Hussein, the world oil situation has been deteriorating steadily in recent years. The Middle East's share of the world oil market is rising at more than one million barrels per day each year, the world is again as dependent on the Persian Gulf as it was in 1980. In-

deed, since 1980, the Middle East's share of world oil reserves has risen from 59 percent to 68 percent. Meanwhile, production in the United States and the Soviet Union, the two largest producers, is falling. Contrary to Secretary Moore's conclusions, steep oil price hikes during the '90s are a virtual certainty, even without Saddam Hussein's assistance.

OPEC is not only back in the driver's seat, but is increasingly dominated by the major Persian Gulf producers, such as Saudi Arabia and Iraq. One-fifth of global reserves are now under Iraq's direct control, and over one-half are in the immediate area of the Persian Gulf. Before this crisis, the major Middle Eastern producers still had three million barrels per day worth of spare capacity, most of which is now being used to help weather the embargo of Iraq and Kuwait. But current trends would eliminate all that reserve by the mid-'90s, leaving almost no reserve margins in case of future political upheavals.

The United States bears considerable responsibility for the deterioration in the world oil picture. Throughout the '80s, the Reagan Administration sought to eliminate virtually every government program aimed at reducing oil dependence. It has now been over a decade since the Congress passed significant legislation to reduce U.S. oil consumption. The Bush Administration has eased back on the rhetoric, but is in most respects carrying on with a Reagan-like energy policy. The short-run response to the Persian Gulf crisis is similarly weak. Drivers are exhorted to pump up their tires, and local officials are encouraged to scrap environmental limits in order to save a few thousand barrels of oil.

Reprinted by permission from M. E. Sharpe, Armonk, NY 10504. ("Beyond the Gulf Crisis: An Energy Strategy for the '90s," by Christopher Flavin, *Challenge: The Magazine of Economic Affairs,* Nov/Dec 1990, pp. 4–10.)

President Bush has failed to project a vision of the country's energy future or to make the tough political choices that are needed. As a former oil company executive, he waxes enthusiastic about oil drilling in several of the country's valuable protected areas. But the oil in question is by all accounts minimal; pursuit of that oil is a feeble attempt to resurrect a policy that has failed on its own terms. This policy can be redirected when the Department of Energy delivers its National Energy Strategy to the President in December. Unfortunately, it is not yet even clear whether the administration has embraced the obvious goal of reducing U.S. oil imports. To carry through on that goal, the United States would need to develop a convincing way to improve the energy efficiency of the U.S. economy—particularly of the motor vehicles that now account for nearly two-thirds of U.S. oil consumption. Improved efficiency is far and away the quickest and most cost-effective means of reducing oil dependence. It would also boost the nation's economic competitiveness and strengthen its environmental health.

THE U.S. OIL OUTLOOK

From the mid-'70s until 1986, the U.S. energy situation improved considerably, under the dual influence of high oil prices and an array of policies designed to do everything from weatherizing buildings to commercializing alcohol fuels. As a result, the U.S. economy has grown by 50 percent since 1973, while energy use has increased by less than 7 percent. The U.S. economy is nearly 30 percent more energy-efficient than it was in 1973, which has made it possible to cut the national fuel bill by $150 billion annually. U.S. oil imports fell from a high of nearly nine million barrels per day in 1978 to just five million barrels per day in 1985.

During the past five years, U.S. oil consumption has risen rapidly, and import dependence has again grown to nearly nine million barrels per day. The American Petroleum Institute, the National Petroleum Council, and the U.S. Department of Energy have all released major studies that point with alarm to these trends and argue that U.S. economic health and national security will be threatened by the forces now at work.

The decline in domestic U.S. oil production is a major factor in this deterioration. As the world's pioneering oil producer, the United States has already heavily exploited its oil reserves and has a reserves-to-production ratio of just nine years, far lower than the 100-plus years available to most Persian Gulf producers. The heavy investments

that went into U.S. oil exploration a decade ago delayed the decline in production that began in 1971. However, even when prices were at their zenith, U.S. oil production in the lower forty-eight states was still 20 percent below its peak level. Today it is 35 percent below its peak. Meanwhile, oil from Alaska's North Slope, which temporarily compensated for declines elsewhere, peaked at about two million barrels per day in 1988 and has declined by over 12 percent since then.

Far from being a victim of world oil market fluctuations, the U.S. oil industry benefited from the OPEC-led price increases of the '70s. These high prices temporarily misled U.S. oil producers into thinking they could still compete with low-cost Middle Eastern oil. To the contrary, U.S. oil production will inevitably decline. Interior Department figures show that of the country's thirteen largest oil fields, seven are at least 80 percent depleted.

As finding oil in the United States has become more difficult, the amount of oil discovered per foot of exploratory well has fallen to less than half the rate that prevailed in the early '70s. The average U.S. oil well yields just fourteen barrels of oil, compared to 2,500 barrels in Saudi Arabia. As oil becomes more difficult to find and extract, average U.S. oil extraction costs have reached at least five times those in the Middle East. The U.S. industry can no longer compete at the world price. The 1.6 million barrel per day decline in U.S. oil production since 1985 is among the steepest ever recorded, but it is only the beginning of a downward trend. The Department of Energy's *Annual Energy Outlook* projects that crude oil production in the lower forty-eight states will fall from 6.12 million barrels per day in 1988 to 4.9 million barrels per day in 2000 at crude oil prices of $28 per barrel.

While domestic production was falling, consumption was up 10 percent between 1985 and 1989. By 1989, imports made up 42 percent of consumption. In three of the first seven months of 1990, the United States imported more oil than it produced. The cumulative decline in oil and natural gas liquids production in the continental United States and Alaska could increase U.S. dependence on oil imports to 75 percent by the year 2000.

In short, the United States no longer has an abundant, low-cost energy resource that can substitute for other economic weaknesses. Indeed, in the future the U.S. energy picture is likely to grow closer to that of Europe and Japan, which lack cheap domestic energy sources and yet have been able to develop economies that function well in a high energy cost environment. The United States uses around twice as much oil per unit of GNP and per person as do the European nations.

OIL SUPPLY OPTIONS

Still, the inclination of the oil industry and the Bush Administration is to deal with the country's energy problems by pursuing the increasingly difficult goal of expanding the country's oil output. Given the declining U.S. oil resource base, this is an uphill battle. The agenda of the oil companies centers on opening up pristine areas in Alaska and off the coast of California for drilling. While these projects would undoubtedly boost oil company profits, they would hardly alter the country's dangerous level of oil dependence. The Arctic Refuge is an example. Damage to the ecology of the Refuge is virtually guaranteed. At the same time, the Interior Department's official figures show that the chances are against finding enough oil to be extracted. In the recent past, oil companies have estimated much higher success rates for Alaska and offshore oil projects, invested hundreds of millions of dollars in their development, and come up completely dry.

The Interior Department's 1987 report, *Arctic National Wildlife Refuge, Alaska, Coastal Plain Resource Assessment,* calls attention to the belief that, "the 1902 acre area is currently the unexplored area in the United States with the greatest potential to contain giant and supergiant fields"—a statement that reflects not the oil riches of the Refuge but the meager oil exploration prospects now remaining in the United States. The Interior Department's mid-range estimate of the Arctic Refuge resource is only 3.2 billion barrels. That is about as much oil as the United States consumes every six months, or far less than one percent of worldwide ultimately recoverable oil resources. This is an important figure because it is the overall world supply/demand balance that determines oil prices. Even when global supplies are tight, price will not be appreciably affected by the small amounts of Arctic National Wildlife Refuge oil.

The Department of the Interior also focuses at some length on the presumed economic benefits of 3.2 billion barrels of oil, estimated at $79.4 billion (undiscounted). This figure looks impressive, but the United States currently has an *annual* energy bill of over $400 billion; these revenues spread over a thirty-year period would be less than one percent of the annual national energy bill. Moreover, this oil would still have to be paid for by consumers; the benefits to the economy and job creation would be limited. If 3.2 billion barrels of oil are extracted from the Arctic Refuge over thirty years, as estimated by the Interior Department, then production will average 290,000 barrels

per day. This would restore only a fraction of the oil production the United States is projected to lose by the turn of the century—the earliest that this new oil could be made available. Oil thought to be available in offshore California fields is even smaller in magnitude.

Since 1985, U.S. oil imports have risen by over three million barrels per day, or ten times the projected yield of Arctic Refuge oil. Further increases in U.S. oil imports are, as the Department of Energy points out, almost guaranteed in the years ahead. Trying to stem this tide with Arctic Refuge oil is like trying to stop a major fire with a teacup.

Even in the unlikely event that oil is extracted from the Arctic Refuge, this "success" would have an almost imperceptible impact on the U.S. energy situation. U.S. oil import dependence would at best be lowered by a few percentage points for a limited period of time, delaying by less than a year the major energy adjustments the United States must make. Indeed, there is something pathetic about the world's first major oil producer desperately sucking oil out of a national treasure to maintain wasteful practices that our industrial competitors are abandoning.

Even if continuing to expand fossil fuel consumption could achieve the economic goals claimed, it would undermine our environmental future. Fossil fuels are the main source of air pollution now choking rural areas and cities alike. In addition, rising levels of carbon dioxide and other gases are irrevocably altering the world's climate, and according to scientists could make the world warmer fifty years from now than at any time in human history.

The main cause of this phenomenon is fossil fuel consumption, which adds six billion tons of carbon to the atmosphere each year, more than one ton for each person on the planet. Although there is now evidence that global temperatures have already begun to rise, the implications of such a warming are fully understood. They could well include serious disruptions in agriculture and the flooding of densely populated coastal areas. In response, several governments have begun to develop energy policies aimed at reducing emissions of greenhouse gases. As the Netherlands, Denmark, and Japan all recognize, improved energy efficiency will have to play the largest role in reducing carbon dioxide output over the next two decades, and this can only occur with active government intervention. Fortuitously, these policies will also help to reduce oil consumption.

A FAILED ENERGY POLICY

From the mid-'70s until the mid-'80s, the United States was well on the road to easing its oil dependence. Oil imports had fallen to just one-third of consumption as energy efficiency improved throughout the economy. These gains were in part a result of higher energy prices, but they were also induced by a series of successful energy policies. While synthetic fuels projects collapsed and nuclear research programs led nowhere, other policies led to notable gains. These include energy price deregulation, energy conservation and renewable energy tax credits, minimum efficiency standards for cars and appliances, home weatherization programs, federal and state utility reforms, and federal funding of research and development on energy-efficient and renewable energy technologies.

The improved energy efficiency of the U.S. economy since 1973 has saved the equivalent of 5 billion barrels of oil in 1989, or 14.5 million barrels per day. This is fifty times the potential contribution from the Arctic Refuge, and studies indicate that energy efficiency's contribution could be doubled to the equivalent of more than 20 million barrels of oil per day by 2000. President Reagan entered office determined to eviscerate most of these programs, claiming that energy was a matter for the private sector, not for public policy. Initially, he sought to abolish the Department of Energy and then appointed a dentist to be his first Secretary of Energy. Even the solar collectors atop the White House were torn down. Congress saved the Department and resisted many of his policies, but President Reagan eventually got most of what he wanted. By the late '80s, most of the tax credits for energy conservation and renewable energy sources had expired. And federal budgets for key areas of energy research and development had been cut by 80 percent.

The $194 million being spent on all energy efficiency research and development in 1990 is equivalent to about four days' worth of spending on the U.S. military forces now in the Persian Gulf. Nearly 70 percent of the Department of Energy's budget goes to nuclear weapons production and cleanup. The remaining federal energy budget continues to be dominated by spending on fossil fuels and a host of nuclear technologies that have virtually no chance of making a contribution during the next few decades.

The Reagan Administration and Congress also permitted automobile fuel economy standards to lapse at the level achieved in 1986. For several years, the administration even provided the auto industry with exemptions to the standards already in place. As a consequence, new cars rolling off Detroit's assembly lines in 1989 were actually less efficient than those of the previous year. This is a costly reversal. Automobiles are at the root of U.S. oil dependence. Some 43 percent of the country's oil is now used in automobiles. Another 20 percent is used in other forms of transportation such as air travel and trucking. If average fuel economy were just seven miles per gallon higher, we would be importing two million fewer barrels of oil each day, and be in a much better position to withstand the effects of the embargo in Iraq.

REACHING OIL DEPENDENCE

While President Bush used the words "energy conservation" as U.S. troops were on their way to the Persian Gulf, in a year and a half in office he has not proposed any significant policies to reduce dependence on imported oil. The steady rise in U.S. oil imports during the Reagan Administration has continued during the Bush presidency.

Means are available to reverse this trend. We can make our cars, buildings, and industries far more fuel-efficient than they are today. And we can gradually develop clean renewable fuels to run our vehicles. The record of the recent past demonstrates the enormous potential of energy efficiency. Keeping up with our Japanese and European competitors requires continued efforts to improve efficiency and cut national energy bills.

The first step in this direction would be for the United States to develop a "least cost energy plan" that would fairly weigh all new sources of energy supply and conservation, and consider various energy policies on the basis of their ability to achieve national goals. Recent experiences and numerous analytical studies show that improved energy efficiency is the fastest and least expensive means of reducing dependence on foreign oil. Simply raising new car fuel economy from the current average of 27 miles per gallon to 40 miles per gallon would reduce U.S. oil consumption by 2.8 million barrels per day by the year 2005. This is nearly ten times the rate of extraction that the Department of Interior thinks is possible from the Arctic National Wildlife Refuge.

The automotive technologies to accomplish these goals are at hand. Prototype vehicles that run over 70 miles per gallon have been developed, though they have not yet reached the marketplace. These include improved engines, more efficient transmissions, and greater use of lightweight synthetic materials. The projected additional cost for a 40-mile-per-gallon car is $500, according to Marc Ledbetter of the American Council for an Energy-Efficient Economy. This sum would be more than offset by gasoline savings of over $2,000 during the life of a typical car. Overall, such technologies can save gasoline at a cost of about 43 cents per gallon or one-third the current retail price.

Strong programs are also needed to continue the energy efficient revolution that began to sweep U.S. buildings in the '70s and '80s. These programs can greatly reduce the use of natural gas, freeing up gas to replace oil in other sectors. However, in recent years, the federal government has provided little support for those who are considering reducing their household or office energy consumption. This year the Bush Administration recommended an 85 percent cut in federal grants in this area. Energy efficiency improvements that have occurred so far only scratch at the potential to develop new energy-efficient technologies. Refrigerators, air conditioners, lights, and buildings can all be powered at a fraction of their current energy requirements.

The past decade's efficiency improvements were driven largely by high energy prices which have since fallen. Moreover, the government has yet to address seriously the market imperfections that cause underinvestment in energy efficiency. Without energy policy reforms, the efficiency potential will not be realized, and oil imports will remain high. One strategy that has been effectively employed in New England is to encourage utilities to invest hundreds of millions of dollars in improved energy efficiency by rewarding them with high rates of return on those investments.

BEYOND OIL

Ultimately, freeing the world of oil dependence will mean harnessing the world's abundant reserves of renewable energy resources such as solar, wind, and biomass energy. None of these offers an immediate large-scale alternative to liquid petroleum, but over the coming decades they can begin to form the basis of a non-fossil-fuel transportation system.

While steady progress has occurred in many of the technologies to harness these resources, it has been slowed by low oil prices and declining federal budgets. The U.S. government spends a pittance on all of these technologies combined—$138 million annually or one-fifth the estimated cost of a B-2 bomber. Nonetheless, a host of renewable energy technologies have made it to the commercial market, producing power from wind turbines, solar power plants, and geothermal facilities at competitive prices. California, which is the hotbed of this activity, has 17,000 wind turbines in place and gets over 40 percent of its electricity from renewable energy sources. Renewable energy has greatly reduced California's consumption of oil and natural gas. These results stem not just from California's abundant resources but from a concerted state effort to encourage renewable energy development.

Renewable energy technologies deserve at least as much support as they received a decade ago—$1 billion annually in 1990 dollars. With such a commitment, private investment would itself increase rapidly, and renewable energy sources would begin to make a significant additional contribution to U.S. energy supplies before the '90s were out.

Using renewable energy for transportation will require substantial investments in delivery, storage, and combustion systems. Electric vehicles, for example, can run on electricity coming from any source. General Motors, Fiat, and other companies already have such vehicles under development. Even more promising is the prospect of non-polluting hydrogen cars. Hydrogen can be produced directly from water, using solar or other renewable energy sources. The hydrogen can then be moved around the country by pipeline and stored in large tanks.

It will take time to develop a hydrogen-based transportation system, but Germany already has an integrated national program to develop all aspects of a hydrogen-powered transport system—to be centered around massive solar installations in southern Europe and northern Africa. Involved in the program are research institutes, pipeline companies, engineering firms, and the automobile industry. Mercedes Benz and BMW already have prototype hydrogen-powered cars.

TOWARDS A NATIONAL ENERGY STRATEGY

The concerted German effort highlights a major weakness of U.S. energy policy. It has no clear goals, resources are scattered over miscellaneous technologies, and funding is guided by today's shortsighted industrial interests rather than by a strategic view of the country's energy future. If we continue in this direction, we will not only sacrifice our national security and environment, but the economy as well. The Germans and Japanese, for example, are now outspending us on key solar technologies that are likely to become major competitive industries in the future.

The coming months will be a window of opportunity for U.S. energy policymaking, which is often driven by crisis. Not only is there the chance to consider important new legislation, but President Bush is scheduled to unveil a National Energy Strategy that has been underway for more than a year. With the dangerous implications of our lack of an energy policy now clearly demonstrated, the National Strategy provides an opportunity to implement a plan to reduce oil dependence and improve energy efficiency. Steps to improve automobile fuel economy, to boost energy efficiency research and development budgets, and to reinstate programs encouraging home weatherization are among the policy steps that would help curb our dependence on the Persian Gulf.

Unfortunately, Secretary of Energy James Watkins now appears to be retreating from the notion he voiced a year ago of a strong, comprehensive energy strategy. Rather, the Secretary has spoken recently of lists of options to be delivered to the President in December, at which point they may well be eviscerated by White House political advisors and lobbyists from the energy and auto industries. Meanwhile, just this September, the Bush Administration successfully defeated the most effective short-run policy—legislation before the U.S. Senate that would have raised U.S. new car fuel economy to 40 miles per gallon by the year 2000.

The United States can no longer afford to lurch from one oil crisis to another. The stakes will only grow as the Middle East's share of the world oil market continues to increase in the years ahead. The technology is available to end this explosive cycle. With American lives now on the line and with tens of billions of dollars likely to be spent in the Gulf in the next year alone, it is high time we got serious about "energy security."

Questions

1. Why was the Gulf War fought?
   a. To liberate Kuwait.
   b. To maintain a cheaper supply of oil.
   c. President Bush wanted to punish President Saddam Hussein.
   d. All of the above.
   Explain your answer with facts and opinions.
2. What energy policies were formulated by the Reagan and Bush administrations to reduce U.S. dependence on foreign oil?
3. During the 1980s, did Congress pass any legislation to encourage oil consumption and oil dependence? Explain your answer.
4. Compare U.S. oil strategies during the following eras:
   a. 1960s
   b. 1970s
   c. 1980s
   d. 1990s
5. How can the United States avoid future oil crises and oil wars? List and explain three ways.

7

The Immortal Waste

Ahmed S. Khan

Barbara A. Eichler

Since December 1942—when Enrico Fermi successfully initiated the first nuclear fission reaction (Table 7.1)—millions of tons of nuclear waste have been accumulated as a result of a global race for power generation and weapon production. Today, in thirty nations 426 nuclear power reactors generate one sixth of the world's electricity production. Ninety-seven power reactors are under construction. A typical 1000 MW power reactor generates a large amount of nuclear waste. However, the significant part of the nuclear waste generated world wide is contributed by the nuclear weapons production. The International Atomic Agency (IAEA) has classified nuclear waste into three categories: high, intermediate and low level nuclear waste. (Table 7.2). The classification is based on waste's source, temperature and half-life.

For the last fifty years scientists have proposed various methods and techniques (Tables 7.3–7.4) for the permanent storage of nuclear waste but various governments around the world have not given serious consideration to this problem. As a result of this neglect, 80,000 tons of irradiated fuel and hundreds of thousands of tons of radiated waste are sitting in temporary storage sites.

Unlike chemical waste, whose toxicity can be neutralized or reduced by various techniques in order to minimize the adverse effects on environment and humans, the nuclear waste is radioactive (Table 7.5) and the potency of radioactivity can only be eliminated by natural decay. Depending on the type of element, it can take hundreds and thousands or even millions of years (Tables 7.6–7.8) for material decay to occur.

Accidental or intentional released radiation can rapidly spread through air and water to contaminate the environment. Radioactive waste from Soviet and U.S. weapons facilities has spread thousands of kilometers from the source contaminating the environment and people.

According to a 1991 study commissioned by International Physicians of Nuclear War "the fallout from the atmospheric atomic bomb testing has spread around the globe and will eventually cause an estimated 2.4 million cancer deaths." The accident at Chernobyl released 50 million curies into the environment, whereas the bombing of Hiroshima and Nagasaki released an estimated 1 million curies. The radiation released from Chernobyl will be responsible for an estimated 14,000 to 475,000 cancer deaths.

Nuclear energy provides over 17 percent of the world's electricity and displaces approximately 6 million barrels of oil per day. Today 426 nuclear power plants in 30 countries generate 318,271 MW. By 2000, in 32 countries 511 nuclear plants are estimated to generate 406,226 MW. In the U.S. 110 nuclear plants provide 19% of electricity. By 2000 more than 20% of electricity will be provided by 119 nuclear power plants. At first look the nuclear energy appears to be clean (i.e., it does not contribute to atmospheric emissions, but it generates the immortal nuclear waste, which possesses the greatest threat to the environment and people).

At present there is no permanent depository for high level nuclear wastes in the world. Yet there are about 426 nuclear power plants operating worldwide. Each nuclear

Table 7.1
Nuclear Energy: Chronology of Research and Development

1905	Albert Einstein developed the theory of the relationship between mass and energy. $E = mc^2$ i.e., energy is equal to the mass times the square of the speed of light.
1932	Preliminary work done by Frederic and Joliot-Curie led to the discovery of the neutron by James Chadwick of England.
1934	Enrico Fermi carried out a series of experiments in Rome that showed neutrons could cause the fission of many kinds of elements including uranium atoms.
1938	German scientists Otto Hahn and Fritz Strassman bombarded uranium with neutrons from a radium–beryllium source, and discovered a radioactive barium isotope among residual material. This indicated a new type of reaction–*fission*–took place. Some mass of uranium was converted to energy, thereby verifying Einstein's theory.
Dec. 2, 1941	A group of scientists led by Fermi initiated the first self-sustaining nuclear chain reaction in a laboratory at the University of Chicago.
July 16, 1945	The first atomic bomb was tested at Alamogordo, New Mexico, by the U.S. army under the code name "Manhattan Project."
Aug. 1, 1946	The Atomic Energy Act of 1946 established the AEC to control nuclear energy development and explore the peaceful uses of nuclear energy.
Dec. 20, 1951	The experimental Breeder Reactor I at Arco, Idaho, produced the first electric power from nuclear energy.
Dec. 8, 1953	President Eisenhower delivered his "Atoms for Peace" speech before the United Nations.
Jan. 21, 1954	The U.S. Navy launched the first nuclear-powered submarine, the U.S.S. *Nautilus,* which was capable of cruising 115,000 km (62,500 nautical miles) without refueling.
Aug. 30, 1954	President Eisenhower signed the Atomic Energy Act, which permitted and encouraged the participation of private industry in the development and use of nuclear energy and permitted greater cooperation with U.S. allies.
Jan. 10, 1955	The Atomic Energy Commission (AEC) announced the Power Demonstration Reactor Program. The AEC would cooperate with industry to construct and operate experimental nuclear power reactors.
Aug. 8–20, 1955	The first United Nations International Conference on peaceful uses of atomic energy was held in Geneva, Switzerland.
Sept. 2, 1957	The Price-Anderson Act granted financial protection to the public and to AEC licensees and contractors in the occurrence of a major accident involving a nuclear power plant.
Oct. 1, 1957	The International Atomic Energy Agency (IAEA) is established in Vienna, Austria, by the United Nations to promote the peaceful use of nuclear agency.
Dec. 2, 1957	The world's first large-scale nuclear power plant began operations in Shippingport, Pennsylvania.
July 21, 1959	The world's first nuclear powered merchant ship N.S. Savannah was launched in Camden, New Jersey.
Nov. 25, 1961	The U.S. Navy commissioned the world's largest ship, the U.S.S. *Enterprise*—a nuclear powered aircraft carrier capable of cruising up to 20 knots for distances up to 740,800 km (4,000,000 nautical miles) without refueling.
April 3, 1965	The first nuclear reactor in space (SNAP-10A) was launched.
March 5, 1970	The Treaty for Non-proliferation of Nuclear Weapons was ratified by the United States, the United Kingdom, the Soviet Union and 45 other nations.
1971	A total of 22 commercial nuclear power plants were in full operation in the United States.
August 1974	The federal government released the results of a safety study by Dr. Norman Rasmussen of MIT, which concluded that a meltdown in a power reactor would be extremely unlikely.

(continued)

Table 7.1
Nuclear Energy: Chronology of Research and Development, *(continued)*

Oct. 11, 1974	The Energy Reorganization Act of 1974 divided AEC functions between two newly formed agencies—the Energy Research and Development Administration (ERDA) and Nuclear Regulatory Commission (NRC).
1976	A total of 61 nuclear power plants with an aggregate capacity of 42,699 megawatts were producing 8.3% of electricity generated in the U.S.
March 28, 1979	The worst accident in a commercial reactor occurred at Three Mile Island (TMI) nuclear power station near Harrisburg, Pennsylvania. The cause was the loss of coolant from the reactor core due to mechanical and human errors. Without the cooling water surrounding the fuel, its temperature exceeded 5,000 degrees Farenheit, causing melting and damage to the reactor core. Due to the accident, the radioactive material normally confined to the fuel was released into the reactor's cooling water system.
1979	After the Three Mile Island accident the Nuclear Regulatory Commission (NRC) imposed stricter safety regulation and more rigid inspection procedures in order to improve the safety of nuclear reactors.
	The 12 percent of electricity produced commercially in the United States was generated by 72 licensed nuclear reactors.
1981	The Shippingport power station was shut down after 25 years of service.
1984	A total of 83 nuclear power reactors generated 14 percent of the electricity produced in the United States.
1986	The worst accident in nuclear history—the Chernobyl disaster—took place in the former Soviet Union on April 26.

Table 7.2
Nuclear Waste Classification

Type	Characteristics
High Level	Produced in two ways:
	(a) By reprocessing spent fuel to recover isotopes that can be used again as fuel.
	(b) Reactor fuel rods which contain long lived isotopes (with half-life of 30 years or more) Contains transuranic (heavier than uranium) elements.
	Most are harmful, highly radioactive, and must be handled and transported with shielding. Must be isolated from humans and environment for thousands of years.
	By 1990, 26,400 cubic meters of high level waste was generated.
Intermediate Level	Produced as reactor by-products and other material such as equipment, tools, etc. that have become radioactive.
	Less harmful, but cannot be handled and transported without shielding.
	By 1990, 3,400 cubic meters of Intermediate level waste was generated. IAEA estimates that by 1995 the rate of generation will be 3,800 cubic meters per year.
Low Level	Produced due to contamination of metal, paper, rags, etc. by radioactive material at power reactors, medical equipment, and other non-military sources.
	Contains no transuranic elements.
	Least harmful, can be handled and transported without shielding.
	By 1990, 370,000 cubic meters of low level waste was generated.

Source: "Nuclear Waste: The Challenge is Global," *IEEE Spectrum*, July 1990.

Table 7.3
Technical Options for Dealing with Irradiated Fuel

Method	Process	Problems	Status
Antarctica Ice Burial	Bury waste in ice cap	Prohibited by international law; low recovery potential, and concern over catastrophic failure	Abandoned
Geologic Burial	Bury waste in mined repository hundreds of meters deep	Difficulty predicting geology, groundwater flows, and human intrusions over long time period	Under active study by all nuclear countries as favored strategy
Long-term Storage	Store waste indefinitely in specially constructed buildings	Dependent on human institutions to monitor and control access to waste for long time period	Not actively being studied by gov'ts, though proposed by nongovernmental groups
Reprocessing	Chemically separate uranium and plutonium from fission products in irradiated fuel; decreases radioactivity by 3 percent	Increases volume of waste by 160-fold; poor economics; increases risk of nuclear weapons proliferation	Commercially under way in four countries; total of 16 countries have reprocessed or plan to reprocess irradiated fuel
Seabed Burial	Bury waste in deep ocean sediments	Possibly prohibited by international law; transport concerns; nonretrievable	Under active study by consortium of 10 countries
Space Disposal	Send waste into solar orbit beyond earth's gravity	Potential launch failure could contaminate whole planet; very expensive	Abandoned
Transmutation	Convert waste to shorter-lived isotopes through neutron bombardment	Technically uncertain whether waste stream would be reduced; very expensive	Under active study by United States, Japan, Soviet Union, and France

Source: Worldwatch Institute, *State of the World,* 1992, Norton.

power plant yields about 30 tons of high level waste. Therefore in very simplistic terms not accounting for various types of reactors, the world's high level nuclear waste approaches 15,000 tons annually.

In 1988, the United States proposed its only licensed permanent high level waste dumping site 1200 feet under Yucca Mountain, Nevada, for its 110 operating nuclear plants. Since the proposal of Yucca mountains, however, there remains little progress in this site becoming a reality since the plan is fraught with problems and technical difficulties. In the meantime, the U.S. Department of Energy says it cannot offer a permanent storage site until 2010 at

Table 7.4
Selected Country Programs on High-Level Waste Burial

Country	Earliest Planned Year	Status of Program
Argentina	2040	Granite site at Gastre, Chubut, selected.
Belgium	2020	Underground laboratory in clay at Mol.
Canada	2020	Independent commission conducting four-year study of government plan to bury irradiated fuel in granite at yet-to-be-identified site.
China	none announced	Irradiated fuel to be reprocessed; Gobi desert sites under investigation.
Finland	2020	Field studies being conducted; final site selection due in 2000.
France	2010	Three sites to be selected and studied; final site not to be selected until 2006.
Germany	2008	Gorleben salt dome sole site to be studied.
India	2010	Irradiated fuel to be reprocessed; waste stored for 20 years, then buried in yet-to-be-identified site.
Italy	2040	Irradiated fuel to be reprocessed and waste stored for 50–60 years before burial in clay or granite.
Japan	2020	Limited site studies; cooperative program with China to build underground research facility.
Netherlands	2040	Interim storage of reprocessing waste for 50–100 years before eventual burial, possibly in the seabed or in another country.
Soviet Union	none announced	Eight sites being studied for deep geologic disposal.
Spain	2020	Burial in unidentified clay, granite, or salt formation.
Sweden	2020	Granite site to be selected in 1997; evaluation studies under way at Aspo site near Oskarshamn nuclear complex.
Switzerland	2020	Burial in granite or sedimentary formation at yet-to-be-identified site.
United States	2010	Yucca Mountain, Nevada, site to be studied and, if approved, receive 70,000 tons of waste.
United Kingdom	2030	Fifty-year storage approved in 1982; explore options including seabed burial.

Source: Worldwatch Institute, *State of the World,* 1992, Norton.

Table 7.5
Types of Radiation

Mode of Radiation	Sources	Penetrating Power	Approx. Distance Traveled in Air	Shielding Material
alpha α	Fission and fission products	Very small	5 cm	Paper
Beta β	Fission, fission products, activation products	Small	300 cm at 1 MeV	Water, plastic, wood
Gamma γ	Fission, fission products, activation products	Very large		Lead, plastic, paraffin
Neutron n	Fission	Very large		Water, plastic, paraffin

Table 7.6
Radioactive Decay

Type of Radiation	Nuclide	Half-Life
α	uranium-238	4.47 billion years
β	thorium-234	24.1 days
β	protactinium-234	1.17 minutes
α	uranium-234	245,000 years
α	thorium-230	8,000 years
α	radium-226	1,600 years
α	radon-222	3.823 days
α	polonium-218	3.05 minutes
β	lead-214	26.8 minutes
β	bismuth-214	19.7 minutes
α	polonium-214	0.000164 second
β	lead-210	22.3 years
β	bismuth-210	5.01 days
α	polonium-210	138.4 days
	lead-206	stable

Source: *Radiation Doses, Effects and Risks,* United Nations Environment Programs, Nairobi, Kenya.

the earliest and the wastes continue to pile up. Some of the problems associated with the Yucca mountain plan are as follows.

LOCATION PROBLEMS

- The Department of Energy did not follow Nevada procedures and did not receive proper state authorization for the site.
- Nevada does not want the repository—NIMBY (Not in My Back Yard)—and passed a resolution in 1990 against storing radioactive wastes anywhere in Nevada's borders.
- The dump site was based wholly on political considerations and science's role in this decision was minimal.
- There is a young active volcano within 7 miles of the site and 32 active faults on the site itself. This renders the site unstable and also suggests that through these faults, contaminated water could escape through a network of geologic cracks. (Federal requirements prohibit the construction of a nuclear waste repository where water can travel 5 km from the burial site in less than 100 years.)

Table 7.7
Half-Lives of Radioactive Elements

Element (Symbol-Mass No)	Half-life (years)	Decay Mode
Uranium		
U-232	72	α, β
U-233	1.59×10^5	α, β
U-235	7.03×10^8	α, β
U-236	2.34×10^7	α, β
U-238	4.46×10^9	α, β
U-239	23.5 minutes	α, β
Plutonium		
Pu-239	2.41×10^4	α, β
Tellurium		
Te-130	2×10^{21}	β
Indium		
In-115	5.1×10^{14}	β

- The site is probably among the most highly mineralized areas on the continent. Two of North America's largest gold mines are 15 to 20 miles away, and gold and silver have been found at Yucca Mountain, making the site vulnerable to prospectors.
- Two years of planning have progressed for this site.

Table 7.8
Radioactivity and Thermal Output Per Metric Ton of Irradiated Fuel from a Light-Water Reactor

Age (years)	Radioactivity (curies)	Thermal Output (watts)
At Discharge	177,242,000	1,595,375
1	693,000	12,509
10	405,600	1,268
100	41,960	299
1,000	1,752	55
10,000	470	14
100,000	56	1

SOURCES: Ronnie B. Lipschultz, *Radioactive Waste: Politics, Technology and Risk* (Cambridge, MA: Ballinger Publishing Company, 1980); J.O. Biomeke et al., Oak Ridge National Laboratory, *Projections of Radioactive Wastes to Be Generated by the U.S. Nuclear Power Industry,* National Technical Information Service, Springfield, VA, February 1974.

Table 7.9
Major Nuclear Accidents

United States	Soviet Union
1951, Detroit Accident in a research reactor. Overheating of fissionable material because permissible temperatures had been exceeded. Air contaminated with radioactive gases.	**September 1957** Accident at reactor near Chelyabinsk. A spontaneous nuclear reaction occurred in spent fuel, causing a substantial release of radioactivity. Radiation spread over a wide area. The contaminated zone was enclosed within a barbed wire fence, and ringed by a drainage channel. The population was evacuated and the topsoil removed; livestock was destroyed and buried in pits.
24 June 1959 Meltdown of part of fuel rods due to failure of cooling system at experimental power reactor in Santa Susanna, California.	**7 May 1966** Prompt neutron power surge at a nuclear power station with a boiling-water nuclear reactor in the town of Melekess. Two people were exposed to severe doses of radiation.
3 January 1961 Steam explosion at an experimental reactor near Idaho Falls, Idaho. Three people died.	**7 January 1974** Explosion of reinforced concrete gasholder for the retention of radioactive gases in No. 1 reactor of Leningrad nuclear power station.
5 October 1966 Partial core melt due to failure of cooling system at the Enrico Fermi reactor, near Detroit.	**6 February 1974** Rupture of intermediate loop in No. 1 reactor at the Leningrad nuclear power station due to boiling of water. Three people were killed. Highly radioactive water with pulp from filter powder discharged into the environment.
19 November 1971 Almost 53,000 gallons (200,000 liters) of water contaminated with radioactive substances from an overflowing waste storage tank at Monticello, Minnesota, flowed into the Mississippi River.	**October 1975** Partial destruction of the core at No. 1 reactor of the Leningrad nuclear power station. About one and a half million curies of highly radioactive gases were discharged into the environment.
28 March 1979 Core melt due to loss of cooling at the Three Mile Island nuclear power station. Radioactive gases released into the atmosphere and 172,000 cubic feet of liquid radioactive waste was discharged into the Susquehanna River. Population evacuated from vicinity of disaster.	**31 December 1978** No. 2 unit at the Byeloyarsk nuclear power station was heavily damaged by a fire started when a roof panel in the turbine fell onto a fuel tank. The reactor was out of control. In the effort to supply emergency cooling water to the reactor, eight persons were exposed to severe doses of radiation.
7 August 1979 About one hundred people received a radiation dose six times higher than the normal permissible level due to the discharge of highly enriched uranium from a plant producing nuclear fuel near the town of Irving, Texas.	**September 1982** Destruction of the central fuel assembly of No. 1 reactor at the Chernobyl nuclear power station due to errors by the operational staff. Radioactivity was released into the immediate vicinity of the plant and into the town of Pripyat, and staff doing repair work were exposed to severe doses of radiation.
25 January 1982 A broken tube in a steam generator in the R.E. Ginna nuclear power plant, near Rochester, New York. A breakdown in the cooling system caused a leak of radioactive substances into the atmosphere.	**October 1982** Explosion of generator in No. 1 reactor of the Armyanskaya nuclear power station. The turbine hall burned down.
30 January 1982 Near the town of Ontario, New York, a breakdown in the cooling system caused a leak of radioactive substances into the atmosphere.	**27 June 1985** Accident in No. 1 reactor of the Balakovo nuclear power station. During start-up activities, a relief valve burst. Fourteen people were killed. This accident was due to errors made in haste and nervousness by inexperienced operational staff.
28 February 1985 At the Virgil C. Summer nuclear power station, in Jenkinsville, South Carolina, the reactor became critical too soon, leading to an uncontrolled nuclear power surge.	
19 May 1985 At the Indian Point 2 nuclear power station, near New York City, there was a leakage of several hundred gallons of radioactive water, some of which entered the environment outside the facility.	
1986 Webbers Falls, Oklahoma, explosion of a tank containing radioactive gas at a uranium enrichment plant. One person was killed, eight others injured.	

Table 7.10

List of Nuclear Reactors

	Reactors In Operation	Electricity Generated (megawatts)	Percent of Electricity	Reactors Under Construction
NORTH & CENTRAL AMERICA				
Canada	18	12,185	15.6	4
Cuba	0	0	0	2
Mexico	1	654	—	1
U.S.	110	98,331	19.1	4
SOUTH AMERICA				
Argentina	2	935	11.4	1
Brazil	1	628	.7	1
EUROPE				
Belgium	7	5,500	60.8	0
Bulgaria	5	2,585	32.9	2
Czechoslovakia	8	3,264	27.6	8
East Germany	6	2,102	10.9	5
Finland	4	2,310	35.4	0
France	55	52,588	74.6	9
Hungary	4	1,645	49.8	0
Italy	2	1,120	—	0
Netherlands	2	508	5.4	0
Romania	0	0	0	5
Spain	10	7,544	38.4	0
Sweden	12	9,817	45.1	0
Switzerland	5	2,952	41.6	0
U.K.	39	11,242	21.7	1
West Germany	24	22,716	34.3	1
Yugoslavia	1	632	5.9	0
ASIA				
China	0	0	0	3
India	7	1,374	1.6	7
Iran	0	0	0	2
Japan	39	29,300	27.8	12
Pakistan	1	125	0.2	1
South Korea	9	7,200	50.2	2
Taiwan	6	4,924	35.2	0
USSR	46	34,230	12.3	26
AFRICA				
South Africa	2	1,842	7.4	0
TOTALS	426	318,271	—	97

Source: International Atomic Energy Agency (IAEA), Vienna.

TECHNICAL PROBLEM

- The site will accommodate 63,500 tons of high-level waste. Radioactive waste already exceeds 22,500 tons (which, according to the Department of Energy, should remain isolated from the environment for 10,000 years). It would take 28 years every workday to fill the site. By the end of 28 years there will be tens of thousands more tons of waste to deal with and there will be no room for the new waste. Additionally, trucks and other means of moving the waste would be arriving from all parts of the country at 90 minute or more frequent intervals, posing serious safety and transportation questions.

During the past half-century, a number of major nuclear accidents has taken place at various nuclear reactors in the Soviet Union and the United States (Table 7.9), resulting in the contamination of environment. But it was the accident at Chernobyl that finally destroyed the myth of nuclear energy being a clean energy source. At a little past 1:24 a.m. on April 26, 1986, two mammoth explosions blew apart Unit Four of the Chernobyl nuclear power plant. The plant is located about 70 miles north of Kiev, the capital of Ukraine, a republic of the former Soviet Union. The roof of the plant was blown off and radioactive gasses and materials were released in the atmosphere, reaching up to eleven hundred meters. According to

---

Scenario I

Los Angeles, July 12, 20XX

The powerful earthquake (7.7 on the Richter scale) that shook the city this morning has severely damaged the core of XXXXXX nuclear reactor. A radioactive gas cloud has escaped into the atmosphere. Efforts are being made to contain the radioactivity.

Response:

Discuss how this accident could have been avoided. Are nuclear power stations better or worse than fossil fuel power generating stations?

Scenario II

Dateline: January 30, 20XX

A ship containing 50,000 cubic meters of nuclear waste returned to New York after visiting South America, Africa, and Asia in search of potential dump sites. All Third-World countries have refused to accept the nuclear waste, despite lucrative offers.

Today, the U.S. nuclear waste volume has reached 10 million cubic meters, compared with 500,000 cubic meters in the 1990s. Due to the saturation of temporary storage sites for nuclear waste, and because of a lack of proper planning and development of permanent storage for nuclear waste in the last century, the world's nuclear waste volumes have reached alarming levels. The potential leakage from temporary storage sites poses the greatest threat to the environment.

Action Item/Response:

Going back to 1960, draw a time-line, and label it by proposing appropriate action taken in each decade that could have prevented the nuclear waste dilemma the world faces today.

Time line: _____

1950   1960   1970   1980   1990   2000   2010   2020   2030   20XX

Scenario III

Dateline: February 19, 20XX

Today the U.N. Security Council passed a resolution demanding the African republic of BANGO to accept 500,000 tons of nuclear waste for permanent storage. All African and Third-World countries have protested against this resolution. The government of BANGO has announced that it will not comply with the U.N. resolution. The U.N. is also considering a proposal for establishing common storage sites in Third-World countries for the nuclear waste generated by developed countries.

Response:

Discuss the implications of the U.N. resolution against BANGO. Is the U.N. justified in asking Third-World countries to accept the nuclear waste generated by the developed countries?

Scenario IV

St. Louis, April 1, 20XX

A train carrying high-level nuclear waste from a nuclear power plant in Illinois collided with an east-bound freight train while crossing a bridge over the Mississippi River. The cars containing waste canisters were badly damaged. Due to the colossal impact of the accident, many canisters ripped open and some fell into the river.

Response:

Discuss the impact of this accident on the environment. Should the transfer of high-level waste by train be allowed to continue?

---

recent estimates, more than 50 million curies were released as a result. The cause of the accident was the flawed design of the RBMK reactor (large power boiling reactor). After the accident, Soviet scientists were reluctant to modify the design of the RBMK reactor, but eventually modified it to make it safer. Forty RBMK type reactors are still operating in Eastern Europe and former Soviet states. And in 25 countries, 426 atomic power plants (Table 7.10) continue to operate and generate enormous amounts of nuclear waste.

What appear to be a clean source of energy are a few megawatts of low-cost power for today's consumption. But in the long run, these will cause an immortal radioactive contamination of the environment. With the growing amount of nuclear waste and limited technical options for its storage and disposal, it is just a matter of time until major accidents happen, resulting in contamination of the environment.

If there ever was an element that deserved a name associated with hell, it is plutonium. This is not only because of its use in atomic bombs—which certainly would amply qualify it—but also because of its fiendishly toxic properties, even in small amounts.

—ROBERT E. WILSON

References

Grossman, D., and Shulman, S. (1989). A nuclear dump: The experiment begins. *Discover.* March, pp. 49–56.

Lenssen, N. (1992). Confronting the nuclear waste. *State of the World.* New York, W. W. Norton & Company.

Raloff, J. (1990). Fallout over Nevada's nuclear destiny. *Science News,* Jan. 6, 1990, vol 13, pp. 11–12.

State of the World (1992). New York, W. W. Norton & Company.

Newton, D. (1994). Chernobyl Accident. *When Technology Fails.* Detroit, MI. Gale Research Inc.

Questions

1. Define the following:
   a. Fission
   b. Low-level nuclear waste
   c. Intermediate-level nuclear waste
   d. High-level nuclear waste
   e. Alpha (α) radiation
   f. Beta (β) radiation
   g. Gamma (γ) radiation
   h. Isotope
2. What methods are being employed for the interim storage of commercial spent fuel and high-level nuclear waste?
3. Do you think that Yucca Mountain is a safe place for the permanent storage of nuclear waste? Explain your answer by citing facts.
4. Do you think that nuclear energy is a "clean" source of energy?
5. With more than 426 operational nuclear plants worldwide and 97 plants under construction, is the chance for a nuclear accident growing larger or smaller? What might be the consequences of a major nuclear accident?
6. What alternatives are there to nuclear energy?
7. "Considering the potential risks involved with nuclear technology and the past experiences at Three Mile Island and Chernobyl, the worldwide development of new nuclear plants should be stopped." Do you agree with this statement? Explain your answer.
8. A number of developing countries are constructing nuclear power plants for their growing energy needs. Due to scarce resources, for the majority of the developing countries, nuclear energy appears to be the most viable solution for their growing demand for energy. The developed countries are trying to prevent the transfer of nuclear technology to Third-World countries. Should Third-World nations be denied access to nuclear technology? Support your answer. What alternative sources would you recommend?

Hydroelectric Power

AHMED S. KHAN

BARBARA A. EICHLER

Hydroelectric power is the conversion of the gravitational pull of falling water of rivers and controlled release of water reservoirs through turbine generators. Hydroelectric power (Tables 8.1–8.3) provides a clean and efficient means of producing electric power. It supplied 21 percent of electricity worldwide in 1986, less than coal and oil but more than nuclear power. In 1984, the global yearly production of hydro energy amounted to about 1,700 billion kilowatt hours (kWh); an additional 550 was under construction. The estimated underdeveloped global hydroelectric potential is 5–50 trillion kW-hours per year. Southeast Asia, South America, and Africa contain respectively 16%, 20%, and 27% of the world's theoretical hydroelectric potential.

According to the World Bank, 31 developing countries doubled their hydropower capacity between 1980 and 1985, much of it with small-scale projects. Small-scale hydropower generation provided almost 10 billion watts worldwide by 1983. China is the world leader, with about 90,000 small hydropower stations supplying electricity to rural areas.

In the United States by early 1988, according to the Federal Energy Regulatory Commission (FERC), more than 2,000 hydro projects were operating. But according to the Environmental Protection Agency (EPA), there were 15,000 private hydro dams. So far, America has dammed about 17% of its 3.5 million miles of natural rivers, mostly during the last hundred years.

Throughout history there have been instances of dam failure and discharge of stored water, which have caused considerable loss of life and great damage to property. Advances in soil mechanics and structural engineering have

revolutionized dam construction and hence increased safety aspects. However, it is estimated that about 150,000 dams around the world present a potential hazard to life or property; there have been 200 failures since 1900. Table 8.4 lists major failures resulting in major loss of life.

ADVANTAGES

1. No air, thermal, chemical pollution in electricity generation.
2. Low production costs.
3. High efficiency (about 90%) converting from water to electrical energy.
4. Water reservoir can provide potential flood protection for downstream currents.
5. Groundwater reserves are increased by recharging from the dam's water reservoir.

Table 8.1
History of Hydro Power

B.C.	Use of water wheels.
1000	Development of water driven blast furnace.
1500	Use of water pumping works.
1882	First hydro-electric power station built at Fox River in Appleton, Wisconsin with a capacity of 25 kW.
1885	First large hydro-electric power station built at Niagara Falls, New York.
1936	Hoover Dam built with a capacity of 1345 MW.

Table 8.2
Power Generation Capacity of Major Dams of World

Name of Dam/Location	Capacity (MW)
Guri, Venezuela	10,000
Churchill Falls, Canada	5,225
Bratsk, Siberia, Russia	4,150
Grand Coulee Dam, Washington	4,200
Aswan Dam, Egypt	2,100
Terbala Dam, Pakistan	3,500
Hoover Dam, Nevada	1,345
Mangla, Pakistan	1,000
Three Gorges Dam, China	18,200
expected completion date: 2009	

Table 8.3
Estimated Hydro-Power Potential of World

Region	Potential (1000 MW)	Percent Developed
Africa	437	10%
Asia (excluding CIS republics)	684	5%
Europe (excluding CIS republics)	215	50%
Commonwealth of Independent States (CIS)	269	10%
North America	330	30%
South America	288	8%
Oceania	37	20%

Source: *The Energy Factbook* by Richard C. Dorf. New York: McGraw-Hill.

Table 8.4
Major Dam Failures

Year	Dam	Country
1626	San Ildefonso	Bolivia
1802	Puentes	Spain
1864	Bradfield	England
1889	Johnstown	U.S.
1890	Walnut Grove	U.S.
1895	Bouzey	France
1911	Austin	U.S.
1916	Bila Densa	Czechoslovakia
1917	Tigra	India
1923	Gienco	Italy
1928	St. Francis	U.S.
1935	Alla S. Zerbimo	Italy
1948	Fred Burr	U.S.
1959	Malpasset	France
1961	Kuala Lumpur	Malaya
1961	Babi Yar	Soviet Union
1963	Baldwin Hills	U.S.
1963	Vaiont	Italy
1972	Buffalo Creek	U.S.
1976	Teton	U.S.
1977	Kelly Barnes	U.S.
1979	Machhu II	India

The International Commission on Large Dams (ICOLD) was formed in 1928 by 6 countries with the purpose of developing and exchanging dam design experience, and it has grown to 76 member countries. In 1982 ICOLD established a committee on dam safety to define common safety principles, integrate efforts, and develop guidelines, and in 1987 ICOLD published "Dam Safety Guidelines."
Source: *McGraw-Hill Encyclopedia of Science & Technology,* 7th Edition, p. 20.

6. Dam's water reservoir can store large volume of water for long periods of time; thus, downstream flow can be controlled for water quality and seasonal stream extreme conditions.

DISADVANTAGES

1. High construction cost.
2. Limited feasible sites for dam construction.
3. Electrical power production may be discontinued due to severe drought conditions.
4. Dam construction causes loss of land suitable for agriculture.
5. Construction of dams impacts the ecological cycles of the rivers and surrounding landscape.
6. Silt accumulation and sedimentation changes flow and land drainage patterns.
7. Water stored in the dam's reservoir by impounding the river is low in oxygen; therefore, the water issued from the dam is low in oxygen and affects the species of the water stream.
8. Dam construction prevents up-stream migration of fish.

References

Dorf, R. (1981). *The Energy Factbook*. New York, McGraw-Hill.

Gabel, M. (1975). *Energy, Earth, and Everyone*. San Francisco, Straight Arrow Books.

Knoepfel, H. (1986). *Energy 2000: an Overview of the World's Energy Resources in the Decades to Come*. New York, Gordon and Breach Science Publishers.

McGraw-Hill Encyclopedia of Science and Technology, 7th ed. New York, McGraw-Hill.

World Resources 1988–89, a Report by World Resources Institute. New York, Basic Books.

Questions

1. Define the following:
   a. KWh
   b. Hydroelectric
   c. EPA

2. List some advantages (+) and disadvantages (−) of hydroelectric power:

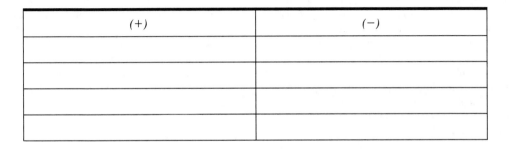

(+)	(−)

9

Solar Energy

Ahmed S. Khan

Barbara A. Eichler

The sun was the major source of energy before the Industrial Age (Table 9.1). In today's electro-optics industrial age, it still remains a vast reservoir of energy which can fulfill today's and tomorrow's growing demands for energy. According to A.B. Lovins, "Solar power in general has several unique implications which do not arise from its obvious advantages. For example, it could help to redress the severe temperate and tropical zones; its diffuseness is a spur to decentralization and increased self-sufficiency of population; and as the least sophisticated major energy technology it could greatly reduce tensions resulting from the uneven distribution of fuels and from limited transfer of technology."

The sun is a continuous source of energy. The mass of the sun is 2.2×10^{27} tons. The sun converts its mass into energy at a rate of 4.2 million tons per second which is 0.02×10^{18} percent of its mass per second. At this rate the sun is expected to radiate energy for billions of years.

Solar radiation is earth's main income energy. Outside the earth's atmosphere the sun provides energy at a rate of 1,353 watts/m normal to sun. Considering the diametral plane of earth (1.27×10^{14} m) the solar input is 1.73×10^{17} watts. But only a small fraction of this reaches earth's surface. The majority of solar energy incident on earth is lost due to reflection by the atmosphere, scattering by clouds, water particles and dust particles (Figure 9.1). The average solar radiation reaching earth's surface is approximately 630 watts per meter. The energy emitted by the sun is spread over a broad band of electromagnetic spectrum. Most of the solar radiation lies in the range of

0.3 micrometer (μm) to 1.3 μm. The solar radiation does not come with constant intensity during the day. The average intensity varies with cloud cover, latitude, season, and time of the day. Solar energy could be used in a number of applications (Figure 9.2). In its intrinsic form the solar radiation can be used for heating. For other applications it needs to be converted into other forms of energy.

ADVANTAGES

1. Continuous source of energy.
2. Clean source of energy.
3. Safe source of energy.

Table 9.1
Use of Solar Energy

B.C.	Solar heat for distillation of liquids and drying agricultural products.
1913	Solar power electrical plants in Egypt.
1960	Use of solar water heaters in Florida.
1967	Use of silicon solar cells in Japan for isolated radio repeaters.
1968	Development of large-scale mirrored solar oven. Produces one megawatt of power per day.
1974	Breakthrough in mass production of photovoltaic cells.
1980s	Afghan refugees in Pakistan use 100,000 solar cookers for preparing food.

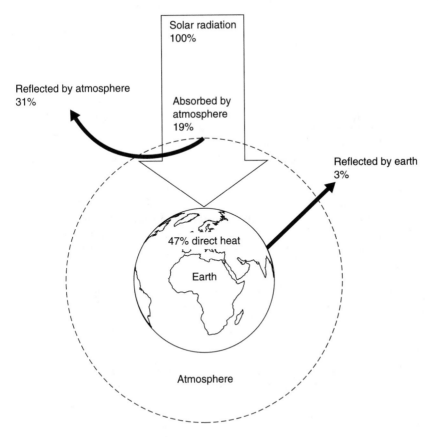

Figure 9.1
Solar radiation incident on earth.

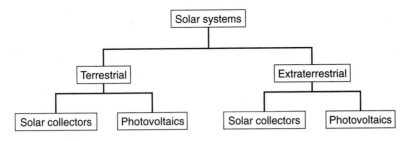

Figure 9.2
Classification of solar energy systems.

TERRESTRIAL SYSTEMS

Terrestrial systems consist of flat-plate or concentrating collectors which transfer solar heat to a carrying medium such as water. The impounded heat can be stored or converted immediately to work. Terrestrial collectors are subject to the intermittent nature of solar cycles and local climates.

EXTRATERRESTRIAL SYSTEMS

The amount of solar power available for power generation in a geosynchronous orbit (35,800 Km from earth) is about 15 times that available on earth. The idea of an orbital solar power station was presented by P.E. Glaser in 1973. According to Glaser, a 5000 MW orbital power station employs concentrators to reflect sunlight on photoelectric solar cells assembled into two large arrays each 4.33 km × 5.2 km in dimension. The generated electrical power is converted into microwave power which can be transmitted towards earth in a focused beam with the help of a 1 km diameter antenna. At earth the microwave radiation is received by a 7.12 km diameter antenna. The received microwave power can be converted into DC or 60 Hz AC for power distribution. The power density of microwaves varies as a function of its frequency—the higher the frequency, the higher is the power density. The high frequency microwaves can cause damage to living tissue.

SCENARIO

Fort Worth, Texas: March 1, 20XX

TERASOLAR-I, the first orbital solar power generating station (Figure 9.3), has completed its twentieth year of service in space. During its twenty year service it has provided an average of 8,000 MW

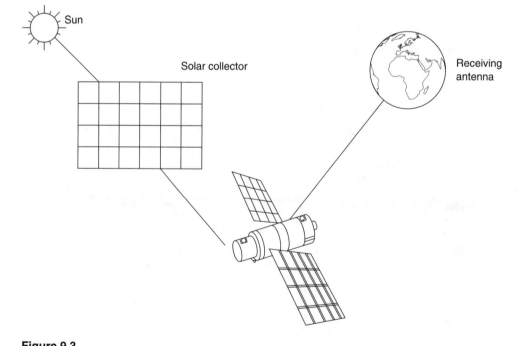

Figure 9.3
TERASOLAR-I, an orbital solar power-generating station.

(45% of power consumption of Texas) of power to a receiving station. The station transmits power at 30 GHz. Originally the power station was designed to use a microwave frequency band of 300 MHz, but to decrease the size of the orbital transmitting antenna and earth's receiving antenna, and in order to cut the cost of the project, the use of a 30 GHz band was approved. A recent medical survey in Dallas reports that the number of cases of cancer has increased by 30%.

Response

Do you think that the radiation from the orbital solar power station is responsible for an increase in the number of cancer cases in the Fort Worth area? How could this have been avoided? Going back into the 20th century, develop an energy strategy that could have avoided this situation.

DISADVANTAGES

1. Average power is not steady and depends on cloud cover, season, latitude, and time of day.
2. Not available at night.
3. Needs to be converted into other forms (e.g., electrical) for useful applications.
4. Extraterrestrial solar energy will increase the heat burden of the biosphere.

References

Dorf, R. (1981). *The Energy Factbook*. New York, McGraw-Hill.

Gabel, M. (1975). *Energy, Earth, and Everyone*. San Francisco, Straight Arrow Books.

Knoepfel, H. (1986). *Energy 2000: An Overview of the World's Energy Resources in the Decades to Come*. New York, Gordon and Breach Science Publishers.

World Resources 1988–89, A Report by World Resources Institute. New York, Basic Books.

Figure 9.4
An array of photovoltaic (PV) solar panels.

Questions

1. Define the following:
   a. Terrestrial systems
   b. Extraterrestrial systems
2. List some advantages (+) and disadvantages (−) of solar energy:

(+)	(−)

10 Wind Power

AHMED S. KHAN

BARBARA A. EICHLER

The atmosphere is a reservoir of solar radiation. The wind is continuously regenerated in the atmosphere as the solar radiation is converted into kinetic energy. The winds are local as well as regional. It is estimated that the average power available from shifting air masses all over the earth is 1.8×10^{15} watts. Wind power available at any location depends on its topographical features. The earth's surface offers resistance to wind, thereby decreasing its power density. In some locations, a wind power density of 500 W/m 10^2 is available, at a nominal height of 25 m from the ground.

The use of wind power dates back thousands of years. It was employed for grinding of grain and pumping of water. Table 10.1 lists the history of wind power.

Wind power can be used to turn vanes, blades, or propellers attached to a shaft. The revolving shaft spins the rotor of a generator, which produces electricity.

ADVANTAGES

1. Continuous source of energy.
2. Clean source of energy, no emissions into atmosphere.
3. Does not add to thermal burden of earth.

DISADVANTAGES

1. For most locations the wind power density is low.
2. The wind velocity must be greater than 7 mph to be usable in most cases.
3. Problem exists in variation in the power density and duration of wind.

Table 10.1
History of Wind Power

1000 B.C.	Wind power of sailing ships
1850	Use of windmills in America
1894	First use of wind power for electric generation by Arctic explorer Nasen
1929	Development of electric wind turbine, 20 meters in diameter, in Bourget, France
1931	Development of 100 kW wind turbine capacity in Yalta, USSR
1941	Development of 1,250 kW capacity wind turbine in Vermont, USA
1950	Development of 10-kW Hutter wind generator consisting of 200-foot blades atop 475-foot tower.
1951	Development of Thomas 6,500-kW generator, consisting of 200-foot blades atop 475-foot tower.
1954	In USSR, the number of wind power plants reached 29,500 with a total capacity of 1 billion kWh.
1957	Development of 200-kW fully automated unit with three 45-foot blades mounted on a 75-foot tower, in Denmark
1960	600 kW Gedser generator designed
1980s	Advances in wind power generators

4. Wind power may have some environmental effects, depending on the location and number of wind power plants (local climate, bird migration patterns, etc.).

References

Dorf, R. (1981). *The Energy Factbook.* New York, McGraw-Hill.

Gabel, M. (1975). *Energy, Earth, and Everyone.* San Francisco, Straight Arrow Books.

Knoepfel, H. (1986). *Energy 2000: An Overview of the World's Energy Resources in the Decades to Come.* New York, Gordon and Breach Science Publishers.

World Resources 1988–89, A Report by World Resources Institute. New York, Basic Books.

Figure 10.1
Wind turbines provide clean, emission-free energy.
Photo by Laima Druskis, © 1988.

Questions

1. How is wind power used to generate electricity?
2. List the advantages (+) and disadvantages (−) of wind power:

(+)	(−)

11 Wind Power: Small, But Growing Fast

CHRISTOPHER FLAVIN

Wind power is now the world's fastest growing energy source. Global wind power generating capacity rose to 4,900 megawatts at the end of 1995, up from 3,700 megawatts a year earlier (see Figure 11.1). Since 1990, total installed wind power capacity has risen by 150 percent, representing an annual growth rate of 20 percent.

By contrast, nuclear power is growing at a rate of less than 1 percent per year, while world coal combustion has not grown at all in the 1990s.

If the world's roughly 25,000 wind turbines were spinning simultaneously, they could light 122 million 40-watt light bulbs or power over a million suburban homes. In the windy north German state of Schleswig-Holstein, wind power already provides 8 percent of the electricity.

Although it now generates less than 1 percent of the *world's* electricity, the rapid growth and steady technological advance of wind power suggest that it could become an important energy source for many nations within the next decade. The computer industry has demonstrated the potentially powerful impact of double digit growth rates. The fact that personal computers provided less than 1 percent of world computing power in 1980 did not prevent them—a decade later—from dominating the industry, and changing the very nature of work.

Wind power is being propelled largely by its environmental advantages. Unlike coal-fired power plants, the leading source of electricity today, wind power produces no health-damaging air pollution or acid rain. Nor does it

produce carbon dioxide—the leading greenhouse gas now destabilizing the world's atmosphere.

In many regions, wind power is now competitive with new fossil fuel-fired power plants. At an average wind speed of 6 meters per second (13 miles per hour) wind power now costs 5–7 cents per kilowatt-hour, similar or slightly lower than the range for new coal plants. As wind turbines are further improved, with lighter and more aerodynamic blades as well as better control systems, and as they are produced in greater quantity, costs could fall even further, making wind power one of the world's most economical electricity sources.

The modern wind power industry established its roots in Denmark and California in the early 1980s. Spurred by government research funds, generous tax incentives, and guaranteed access to the electricity grids, a sizable wind industry was created. However, development slowed dramatically at the end of the decade as government tax incentives were withdrawn and utilities became more resistant to higher-cost electricity.

Even as political support for wind power waned in the late 1980s, the technology continued to mature. Many of the small turbines installed in the early days were expensive and unreliable, but the lessons learned from those first generation turbines were soon translated into new and improved models. The turbines that entered the market in the early 1990s incorporated advanced synthetic materials, sophisticated electronic controls, and the latest in aerodynamic designs.

In an effort to make wind power more economical, most companies have built larger and larger turbines. In

Figure 11.1
World wind energy-generating
capacity, 1980–95.

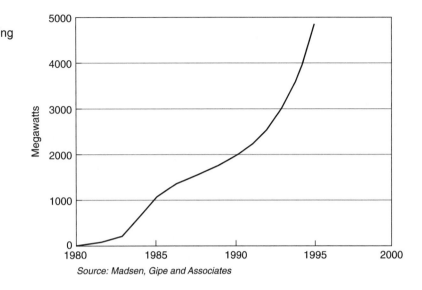

Source: Madsen, Gipe and Associates

Germany, the average turbine installed in 1995 had a capacity of 480 kilowatts, up from 370 kilowatts in 1994 and 180 kilowatts in 1992. Several manufacturers will soon introduce machines that can generate between 1,000 and 1,500 kilowatts—with blade spans as great as 65 meters.

The 1,290 megawatts of wind generating capacity added in 1995 was almost double the capacity added a year earlier, and up sixfold from the 1990 figure (see Figure 11.2). In 1995, the country with the most new capacity was again Germany, which added 505 megawatts, the most any country has ever installed in a single year. India added 375 megawatts, followed by Denmark with 98 new megawatts, Netherlands with 95, and Spain with 58.

The European wind industry is now growing at an explosive pace: altogether, Europe had 2,500 megawatts of wind power capacity at the end of 1995, up nearly threefold from 860 megawatts in 1992 (see Figure 11.3). The United States still led the world with 1,650 megawatts of wind power capacity at the end of 1995, but Germany was closing in fast with 1,130 megawatts. Denmark ranked third with 610 megawatts, and India fourth at 580 megawatts.

Europe is now home to most of the world's leading wind power companies, which are introducing larger and more cost-effective models. Unlike the United States, where most development has consisted of large groups of 20 to 100 turbines, called "wind farms," Denmark and Germany have pursued a decentralized approach to wind power development. Most of their machines are installed

one or two at a time, across the rural landscape. This has made them popular with local communities, which benefit from the additional income, public revenues, and jobs that result.

Europe's leadership also stems from the financial incentives and high purchase prices established for renewable energy in response to concern about the atmospheric pollution caused by fossil-fuel-fired power plants. In Germany, this approach has allowed determined investors and

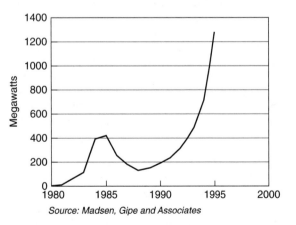

Source: Madsen, Gipe and Associates

Figure 11.2
Annual additions to world wind energy-generating
capacity, 1980–95.

Figure 11.3
Wind-generating capacity, by region, 1980–95.

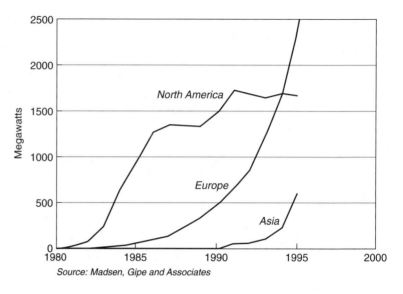

Source: Madsen, Gipe and Associates

environmental advocates to beat back efforts by the electric utilities to reverse the 1991 "electricity in-feed law," which provides a generous price of about 11 cents per kilowatt-hour to electricity generators relying on solar, wind, and biomass energy. In a landmark vote in 1995, the Bundestag decided to uphold the law, though it remains under review by the courts.

Wind energy is also advancing rapidly in the Netherlands, Spain, and the United Kingdom. The U.K. has Europe's largest wind power potential, and hundreds of megawatts of projects are now being planned. European wind industry leaders are also hopeful that sizable wind power markets will soon emerge in Finland, Greece, Ireland, and Sweden, each of which has a large wind resource. Even France, the last bastion of the European nuclear industry, embarked on a sizable wind power development plan in 1995, aimed at adding 250 to 450 megawatts of wind power over the next decade.

Just as wind energy development is taking off in Europe, it has stalled in the United States, where the industry is buffeted by uncertainty about the future structure of the electricity industry. In fact, the country's total wind capacity has hardly increased since 1991. The country that led the world into wind power in the 1980s actually saw a net decline of 8 megawatts in its installed capacity in 1995. Some 50 megawatts were added—mainly in Texas—but 58 megawatts of old turbines were torn down in California. Kenetech, the leading U.S. wind power company, filed for bankruptcy in May 1996 after the combined effects of a

slow market and mechanical problems with its new turbine led to large financial losses.

Prospects for developing nations are far brighter. Although most wind turbines are currently installed in industrial countries, much of the world's wind power potential is in the developing world. The leader so far is India, which is the first developing country with a real commercial market for wind power. India's roughly 3,000 wind turbines have virtually all been installed since the government opened the electricity grid to independent power producers and enacted tax incentives for renewable energy investments in the early 1990s. According to the government, 730 megawatts had been installed by April 1, 1996, which would make India the world's most active wind market in early 1996. However, uncertainty surrounding the Indian elections in May has slowed the pace of development since then.

Some of India's wind turbines are being imported, but others are manufactured in India, either by domestic companies or in joint ventures with foreign companies. Already, the Indian industry has more than 20 indigenous manufacturers and suppliers. In the windy southern state of Tamil Nadu, hundreds of jobs have been created as a result.

Many other developing countries, including Argentina, Brazil, China, Egypt, Mexico, and the Philippines are surveying their wind resources and installing small numbers of turbines on an experimental basis. Although none of these countries has yet encouraged or even permitted the development of a sustained, market-driven wind industry, some may be on the verge. China, for example, has just 36 megawatts installed but has plans to reach 1,000 megawatts by the year 2000.

In most developing countries, wind power development will be driven not by environmental concerns, as it is in industrial countries, but by a desperate need for electricity, which is in short supply throughout the Third World. In areas such as western China and northeast Brazil, wind power is the only indigenous source of electricity ready to be developed on a large scale.

The global wind energy potential is roughly five times current global electricity use—even excluding environmentally sensitive areas. In the United States, where detailed surveys have been conducted, it appears that wind turbines installed on 0.6 percent of the land area of the 48 contiguous states—mainly in the Great Plains—could meet one-fifth of current U.S. power needs—double the current contribution of hydropower. By comparison, the total cropland used to grow corn in the United States is nearly 3 percent of the country's land area. And unlike corn, wind power does not preclude the land from being used simultaneously for other purposes, including agriculture and grazing.

Other countries that have enough wind potential to supply most or all their electricity include Argentina, Canada, Chile, Russia, and the United Kingdom. China's wind energy potential is estimated by the government at 253,000 megawatts, which exceeds the country's current generating capacity from all sources by 40 percent. Much of that potential is located in Inner Mongolia, near some of the country's leading industrial centers.

India's potential is estimated at 80,000 megawatts, which equals the country's total current generating capacity. Europe could obtain between 7 and 26 percent of its power from the wind, depending on how much land is excluded for environmental reasons. Offshore potential in Europe's North and Baltic Seas is even greater.

Wind power cannot fully replace fossil fuels, but it has the potential to meet or exceed the 20 percent of world electricity provided by hydropower. Moreover, though wind power is more abundant in some areas than others, it is in fact one of the world's most widely distributed energy resources. More countries have wind power potential than have large resources of hydropower or coal.

Combined with other renewable energy sources such as solar and geothermal power, and by a new generation of gas-fired micro-power plants located in office and apartment buildings, wind power could help transform the world electricity system. These technologies could quickly replace coal and nuclear power—which together now supply two-thirds of the world's electricity—and allow a sharp reduction in world carbon emissions.

Questions

1. What percentage of the world's total electricity is produced by wind power?
2. Can wind power compete with new fossil-fuel-fired plants?
3. Compare the wind-generating capacities of Asia, Europe, and North America.
4. Why have wind energy projects stalled in the United States?
5. Discuss the factors that are responsible for the development of wind power projects in the Third World.
6. Will wind power someday replace fossil fuel power?

12 The Electric Car Arrives—Again

Seth Dunn

It was two bicycle mechanics from Massachusetts, Charles and Frank Duryea, who rolled out the first commercially manufactured automobiles—13 of their Duryea Motor Wagons—in Detroit in June of 1896. Dubbed "horseless carriages," they ran on a noisy new invention known as the internal-combustion engine—and a pungent fuel called gasoline. Soon, cars were spreading across the countryside—their costs falling rapidly, thanks to Henry Ford's assembly lines—and the world was moving toward a heavy dependence on oil.

One casualty of the internal-combustion engine's triumph was the electric car, which had become quite popular in the 1890s. Proclaimed as quieter, cleaner, and simpler than the engine-driven car, the electric vehicle was widely expected to dominate the automotive market of the twentieth century. Instead, it quietly disappeared as automobile companies chose to pour billions of dollars into developing, and incrementally improving, the internal combustion engine. The electric auto, it seemed, was destined for the scrap heap of technological wrong turns.

It may have taken a century, but suddenly the electric car has returned from the dead. Its comeback has been fueled in large part by the engine-induced smog now filling urban areas like Athens, Bangkok, and Los Angeles—just as the manure piling up in the streets of America's cities a hundred years ago prodded the search for alternatives to the horsedrawn carriage. After years of false starts and heated debate, electric cars are on the road again: already an esti-

mated 7,500 "engineless carriages" are now in use worldwide.

The most telling sign of life for this comeback invention came last December with the appearance of General Motors' long-awaited electric sports car, the EV1, in Saturn showrooms in southern California and Arizona. With its high-profile launch, the world's biggest automaker joined a rapidly growing list of companies around the world marketing, or set to market, electric cars—among them Honda, Mercedes, Peugeot, and Renault. These giants will do battle with a quickly growing army of some 250 entrepreneurial startups, each with visions of becoming the next Henry Ford.

While the electric cars on the market so far are expensive and can only travel limited distances, they are taking carmakers in new directions. With the push of government mandates soon to be overtaken by the pull of market opportunities, the drive to produce the most practical, economical electric car is quickly becoming a competitive auto race. As Michael Gage, President of CALSTART, a California electric vehicle consortium, puts it, "We are entering the tornado."

THE WHIRRING NINETIES

This time it was a maker of flying machines, Paul MacCready, who got the creaky wheels of car innovation turning. MacCready, inventor of the first human-powered aircraft to fly across the English Channel—a bicycle-like device that earned him "engineer of the century" plaudits from his contemporaries—had designed a solar-powered

Reprinted with permission from Worldwatch Institute, Washington, DC., March/April 1997, pp. 19–25.

102

car, the Sunraycer, for GM. In 1987, the Sunraycer won the first Solar Challenge race, crossing Australia on the equivalent of five gallons of gasoline. GM then asked MacCready's firm, AeroVironment, to build a concept electric car for the company.

Three years later, the resulting prototype—called the Impact—was greeted with such unexpected plaudits at a Los Angeles auto show that then-President Jack Smith brashly vowed to begin mass-producing the car immediately. In doing so, he gave this second automotive revolution a much-needed push. The actual jumpstart came later that year, when the California Air Resources Board—at the time facing worsening air pollution in Los Angeles and other cities, and greatly encouraged by GM's vow—passed the toughest auto emissions standards in the world. Most notable was the industry-shaking requirement that 2 percent of cars sold in the state by the seven major carmakers in 1998 be "zero-emission," with the share rising to 10 percent by 2003.

Auto-industry lobbyists immediately turned on their own creation and—joined by the oil industry—began a bitter right to roll back the electric car mandate. At times, it seemed some of these companies had devoted more money to badmouthing zero-emission cars than to designing them. This certainly appeared to be the case for Chrysler, whose chairman—in the midst of scaling back its program—went so far as to declare, "There is absolutely no economic basis for electric vehicles in the world."

Eventually, the lobbying paid off, and California legislators lifted the 1998 mandate. But the big automakers are still required to make the more stringent 10 percent target in 2003, which means that some 800,000 zero-emissions cars should be on California's roads by 2010. This would be a giant leap from the approximately 2,300 electric cars in use in the entire country today.

ROADBLOCKS

Whether these targets will be met depends on whether prospective consumers can be helped around the immediate barriers of cost and range. At today's low-volume production levels, electric cars are more expensive to buy or lease than conventional cars with internal-combustion engines. The problem is not the electric motor, a highly evolved technology used in everything from tiny dentist drills to huge freight locomotives. In fact, today's electric motors are already between four and five times as efficient as internal combustion engines.

The biggest roadblock for electric cars is, and always has been, storing the electricity needed to run them. The

EV1—the product of the California mandate and a $345 million investment by GM—carries 1,175 pounds of lead-acid batteries (the same kind used to start conventional cars), but has a range of just 70 to 90 miles between recharges (the electric equivalent of refueling, recharging takes three hours, using a 220-volt inductive "paddle" at home or in public charging stations—of which California already has more than 400). In part because of the cost of the battery, the EV1s now on the market in California and Arizona lease for as much as $34,000 over 3 years.

But the energy–weight ratio of lead-acid batteries has been cut by 60 percent over the last decade, and further gains are likely down the road. Virtually all of the major carmakers are working hard to lower the cost of more advanced batteries with greater energy density—including nickel–metal-hydride models that could double the EV1's range to between 150 and 200 miles. Other alternatives in the works include nickel–cadmium and lithiumion batteries, and even flywheels—mechanical batteries consisting of a rapidly spinning disk made of synthetic materials.

These new batteries are still too expensive for wide commercial use, but experts at California's Air Resources Board believe that they should be on the market soon. The next advance is expected to come from Honda, whose Formula One race car engineers are now fully devoting their work to electric cars, and whose solar car has displaced GM's as the Solar Challenge champion. Honda plans to launch its EV Plus in California this May. Billed as the first family-oriented electric car, the compact four-seater will be equipped with nickel-metal-hydride batteries which give it a range of 125 miles—but at substantial cost: the batteries alone go for an eyepopping $40,000. Whether people will be willing to pay $500 a month (though this does include insurance and roadside service) to lease a car that is virtually indistinguishable from a standard economy car is uncertain; Honda expects to lease just 300 of the cars over the next three years.

Ironically, the limitations of today's batteries have made these first electric cars far more advanced than they otherwise might have been. Forced to stretch the range of bulky batteries, designers threw away the book on conventional automotive design and construction. In the search for a commercially viable electric car, automakers—for the first time in decades—turned their engineers loose on truly revolutionary concepts.

Author Michael Schnayerson, who was given inside access to GM's program, notes in his book *The Car That Could* how engineers struggled for eight years to fuse unconventionality and practicality, garnering 23 electronics and aerospace patents and a slew of engineering achievements. The EV1's aluminum car frame is the world's lightest; its teardrop-shaped body has aerodynamics equal to a modern fighter plane; and its brakes can regenerate, recharging the battery. With a super-efficient electric motor and low-resistance tires, it accelerates from zero to sixty miles per hour in less than nine seconds—faster than most conventional cars.

With these technological wonders, the EV1 has impressed most of those who have test-driven it. But the far greater challenge ahead for electric cars will be to make their way from the engineering track to the suburban garage. Although many buyers may be lured by the "zero-emission" label, performance, convenience, and cost are the benchmarks by which the cars must ultimately be judged.

ALTERNATE ROUTES

Automakers are taking a variety of approaches to "niche marketing" their first-generation electric cars. GM, for example, appears to be aiming at young, wealthy environmentalists—perhaps Hollywood stars and executives looking for a fast, sporty, pollution-free car that can speed through Beverly Hills. This is, after all, a group already accustomed to spending $30,000 to $40,000 for a Mercedes or Lexus. (Including tax incentives, the monthly lease rate for the EV1 falls to between $480 and $640 per month—less than the figure for luxury cars like the Cadillac DeVille.)

So far, the strategy seems to be working. Thanks to a major ad campaign, demand for the EV1 has been stronger than GM anticipated, with about 50 cars leased out on the very first day. GM's electric car expert, Robert Purcell, believes the EV1 will assume a "second car" role for commuting (the average U.S. commute is less than 35 miles) and for short trips. Purcell notes similarities to the microwave oven, which was unpopular at first but which eventually caught on as a second oven. While production plans have been kept under wraps, Detroit's labor press estimates that at least 80 EVs were made last year.

European automakers appear to be targeting a different set: green-oriented urban dwellers. The City Bee, for example, is a lightweight, fully recyclable two-seater with limited range, developed by the Norwegian consortium PIVCO. Scheduled for assembly in Europe and California later this year, it will cost around $10,000 at a production volume of 10,000, and is intended only for use in the inner city, and for quick rental at rail stations.

A multitude of other small companies, meanwhile, are preparing their own models for production. And the "urban car" niche has now begun to attract bigger players as well, resulting in some intriguing partnerships. German auto giant Mercedes-Benz and Swiss watchmaker Swatch have teamed up to develop a "Smart" car: a two-seater that can be built in under five hours, using plastic parts with interchangeable color schemes like those of the Swatch watches. The Smart car has proven crashworthy even though it is less than 10 feet long. Cast as a modern version of the "runabouts" seen at the turn of the century, and aimed at a younger audience, it can use electric as well as other drive systems. Some 200,000 Smart cars, a sizable percentage of which could be electric, are scheduled to roll out in Europe in March 1998 at a price of between $10,000 and $13,000.

Other European automakers are taking a more conservative approach to marketing electric cars, at much lower cost, by converting conventional cars into electrics. One of the leaders is Peugeot, which has put out a car using nickel-cadmium batteries, with a range of 50 miles. Having successfully tested 500 of its cars in the city of La Rochelle, the Peugeot-Citroen group believes there will be around 100,000 electric cars in Europe by 2000 and plans to grab a quarter of the market; it produced more than 4,000 in 1996.

Renault, meanwhile, sold 215 of its electric conversions in the first six months of last year. It will make 1,000 cars this year, and expects to continue increasing output in 1998. On a smaller scale, Fiat and Volkswagen are selling conversions, which they are reportedly making at a rate of about one a day, in Swiss cities. These conversions have a more limited range than cars designed to be electric from the start, but they allow the automakers to enter the market and gain experience without a huge up-front investment.

Much as L.A.'s smog sped the move to electric cars, air pollution and congestion in Europe have prompted some carmakers to rethink the car's conventional ownership and role in transportation. In France, Peugeot and Citroen are involved with the design of a transit system that will allow Parisian commuters to rent electric cars over short distances under a credit card-like system. Renault plans, as part of a consortium of electric utilities, carmakers, and government agencies, to operate 50 such "multiuser" cars in one of the city's high-tech suburbs. Similar efforts are underway in Switzerland. Swiss carmaker Horlacher will soon offer a lightweight "instant taxi," while Fiat has begun to rent electric cars in Geneva.

Whatever the route to consumers, proponents note that, despite their current high price and limited range, electric cars already have a number of advantages over today's cars. Their relative noiselessness, practicality, and simplicity appeal to many drivers. Electric cars cost less to refuel and service, and have many fewer parts to break down. Their owners are likely to spend less time on maintenance, and if they recharge at home, will rarely have to go to the service station. These time savings have real value in today's busy world. On a lifecycle basis, then, the cost gap between cars that pollute and those that don't is not all that great, even now; with another decade of battery development and mass production, it could be closed entirely.

Air regulators in California and New England argue further that if the avoided costs of urban air pollution, acid rain, and global climate change were included, electric cars would look like a steal. Of course, a fair comparison must include the emissions from the power plants that are used to charge the batteries. Fortunately, emissions from stationary power sources are easier to control than those from vehicles.

More importantly, running cars on electricity opens up a host of new fuel options not based on oil—including renewable resources such as wind power and solar energy. Already, some of the municipal governments promoting electric cars are erecting solar cells on the roofs of their parking garages to recharge them. The California city of Sacramento, for example, through the involvement of automakers, utilities, and local authorities, has installed more than 70 charging stations.

TOOL KITS

As the Sacramento example suggests, governments can play an important role in accelerating the transition to electric cars. Several of them, in fact, offer incentives that can lessen the electric car's initial cost. In the United States, federal and state tax credits and local rebates are available in many areas: customers in Los Angeles, for example, can use a 10 percent federal tax credit and a $5,000 rebate from the South Coast Air Quality Management District.

A 5,000-franc subsidy, meanwhile, is available to those buying electric cars in France. Paris and several other French cities add on tax credits, as do Switzerland, Austria, and Denmark. Switzerland already has about 2,000 electric cars in operation, and aims to use tax incentives to help make 8 percent of its cars electric by 2010. Germany, with more than 2,400 electric cars, gives its customers federal tax exemptions and state-level subsidies. Electric cars are exempt from sales taxes (which are typically high in Europe) in Italy, Norway, Sweden, and the United King-

dom. In Japan, which has the ambitious if distant goal of producing 200,000 electric vehicles by 2000, buyers may see costs cut in half by federal tax credits, incentives, and depreciation allowances—and even further by municipal governments.

Spurred by these and other less-noticed but important policies and programs—installing recharging stations, setting up demonstration projects, funding battery research and development—an electric car industry appears to be taking shape. Consortiums like CALSTART—a network of 200 government agencies, environmental groups, and aerospace, defense, and electric power companies—are helping these groups work horizontally (in contrast to today's "vertical" auto industry) to start programs and attract funding. Electric-vehicle associations in North America, Europe, and Asia report growing memberships, and are holding well-attended conferences and exhibitions each year to share the latest surveys, technologies, and production plans.

Surprisingly, the production hub for cost-competitive electric cars may turn out not to be in today's auto industry powers, the United States and Japan, but in the developing countries. With the world's most polluted urban air, some of these countries are just starting to develop automobile industries and make the associated investment in oil refineries, service stations, and the like—and therefore have less vested interest in the internal-combustion engine. Their industrialists recognize that if they are already making computers and televisions, electric cars should be within reach.

This notion has already taken hold in Asia, where prospective electric-car manufacturers have held extensive discussions with potential manufacturing partners. Thailand, which offers tax exemptions to electric car makers, is producing electric versions of its three-wheeled "tuk-tuk" taxi. Korean car makers Daewoo and Hyundai are working to produce lightweight electric cars for sale by the end of 1997 and 1998, respectively. China, which hopes to have several carmaking plants by 2000, plans to link domestic and foreign makers. One fledgling Chinese car maker has cut a deal with Peugeot-Citroen to produce a small electric model.

As their production picks up, electric cars' prices will fall noticeably. Comparing their price history with that of the traditional automobile, Daniel Sperling of the University of California at Davis estimates full-scale production could reduce the cost of electric cars to well below half the current level. And new technological breakthroughs will not be needed for costs to plummet, according to Tufts

University's Global Development and Environment Institute. The Institute projects price declines analogous to those that have occurred in personal computers, for example, with the costs of an electric car approaching—and with government support, falling below—those of conventional cars. And some analysts believe electric cars will be competing with gasoline-powered cars, *without* subsidies, within a decade. Table 12.1 lists major commercial or near-commercial cars.

BACK TO THE FUTURE?

Once the electric car catches up to today's cars by lowering upfront costs and extending range, its continued success will depend on the ability of manufacturers to lure consumers with inexpensive, battery-powered versions of commuter, family, or sports cars. Gage of CALSTART foresees "an improved driving experience" analogous to the shift from long-playing records and cassettes to the compact disc: the former worked, but the latter is better. Carmakers may also, however, find themselves dusting off hundred-year-old advertising pitches. As *Scientific American* observed in 1896, "The electric automobile . . . has the great advantage of being silent, free from odor, simple in construction, capable of ready control, and having a considerable range of speed."

Perhaps that praise was premature, but precisely a century later, *Scientific American* has returned to the topic—and suggests that the tables have turned. Writes Sperling of UC-Davis in a recent issue: ". . . it seems certain that electric-drive technology will supplant internal-combustion engines—perhaps not quickly, uniformly, nor entirely—but inevitably. The question is when, in what form and how to manage the transition." Those words, ironically, recall a very similar statement anticipating the adoption of the internal combustion engine a century ago. After watching the Duryea brothers race their wagons one afternoon in 1895, a young inventor named Thomas Edison boldly announced, "it is only a question of time when the carriages and trucks in every large city will be run with motors."

While technological dreams do not always come true, the electric car now seems to have more than a fighting chance. The major limitations of today's models are within sight of being overcome: indeed, a host of companies are betting billions of dollars on their ability to make that happen. And they cannot but be pleasantly surprised by the initial response to the EV1: according to Saturn dealers, the waiting list of several hundred hopeful lease holders continues to grow. As any car executive will tell you, the Model T took off when its costs were cut in half and cheap gasoline became an available fuel: now, they seem to be

Table 12.1

Major Commercial or Near-Commercial Electric Cars

Car and Model	Battery	Range (miles)	Location	Date
"GROUND-UP" ELECTRIC CARS				
General Motors EV1	lead–acid	70–90	US	1996
American Honda EV	nickel–metal hydride	125	US	1997
			Japan	1997
Solectria Sunrise	various	120	US	1998
SMALL ELECTRIC CARS				
PIVCO City Bee	nickel–cadmium	60–70	Europe	1997
			US	1997
Mercedes/Swatch "Smart"	various	various	Europe	1998
MODIFIED CONVENTIONAL CARS				
Peugeot 106	nickel–cadmium	50	Europe	1994
Citroen AX	nickel–cadmium	50	Europe	1994
Renault Clio	nickel–cadmium	50	Europe	1996
Fiat Panda Elettra	lead–acid	36	Europe	1996
Volkswagen CitySTROMER	lead–acid	30–54	Europe	1996
Solectria Force	various	60	US	1994

musing, might the electric car do likewise once its prices fall and batteries improve dramatically?

But larger forces, as much as the battery, will determine how far the electric car ultimately goes. On these counts, it seems to have a good deal riding in its favor. Its biggest constituency has always been women, who have far more purchasing power today. And its advantages, curious virtues in 1897, have become serious necessities by now, as the burdens of the gasoline culture grow heavier. Urban air pollution, congestion, dependence on oil imports, and global warming: these mounting societal concerns are recharging the electric car.

Still, if it is to avoid the fate of its predecessors, the EV1 and its companions must now handle the rocky road test of the market by selling, leasing, or renting. Making inroads on today's car population will not happen overnight, yet GM's model is already gracing the pages of the *The New York Times'* Automobile Section, alongside the conventional competition. This, perhaps, is the real story of the electric car's reemergence, lost amid the press conferences and television ads: that, true to the invention's own nature, its entry into the mainstream may resemble less a loud revving than a quiet hum.

References

CALSTART. (1996, October). *Electric Vehicles: An Industry Prospectus.* Burbank, CA, CALSTART, Inc.

Flavin, C., and N, Lenssen. (1994). *Power Surge: Guide to the Coming Energy Revolution.* New York, W.W. Norton & Co.

MacKenzie, J. (1994). *The Keys to the Car.* Washington, DC, World Resources Institute.

Natural Resources Defense Council. (1996). *Green Auto Racing.* Washington, DC, NRDC.

Schiffer, M.B. (1994). *Taking Charge: The Electric Automobile in America.* Washington, DC, Smithsonian Institution Press.

Shnayerson, M. (1996). *The Car That Could: The Inside Story of GM's Revolutionary Electric Vehicle.* New York, Random House.

Sperling, D. (1995). *Future Drive: Electric Cars and Sustainable Transportation.* Washington, DC, Island Press.

Questions

1. Does the electric car reduce pollution? What are some of the pro and con arguments?
2. Discuss the roadblocks that are in the way of mass production of electric cars.
3. How do you think we can safely dispose of a high volume of used batteries that are a waste product of electric car technology? Is any ecologically safe approach being considered? If so, which?
4. Compare the marketing strategies of U.S. and European electric-car manufacturers.
5. Discuss the role of the oil industry in the development and success of the electric car.

ONE STEP FORWARD, A HUNDRED STEPS BACK?

Reduction in carbon emissions by World Bank-funded projects measure in the thousands of tons per year . . . but the emissions generated by bank-funded projects measure in the millions of tons.

Selected Fossil Fuel Power Plants Financed in Part by the World Bank in the 1990s

Location	Plant Description	Estimated Cost ($ billion)	Annual Carbon Emissions (million tons)
Tuoketo, China	3,600 MW, coal fired	4	7.19
Dolana Odra, Poland	1,600 MW, coal fired	0.3	3.196
Paiton, Indonesia	1,230 MW, coal fired	1.8	2.457
Pangasaman, Philippines	1,200 MW, oil fired	1.4	2.397
Hub River, Pakistan	1,469 MW, oil fired	2.4	2.345

Selected Global Environment Facility Energy Projects, Some Cofinanced by the World Bank

Location	Project Description	Estimated Cost ($ millions)	Annual Carbon Emissions (thousand tons)
Leyte, Luzon, Philippines	440 MW, Geothermal	1,300	872
Countrywide, Indonesia	Installation of 200,000 PV systems	118	120
Nine cities, China	Energy-efficiency upgrades of industrial boilers	101	41–68
Guadalajara and Monterrey, Mexico	Dissemination of high-efficiency lighting (1.7 million fluorescent lamps)	23	32
Tejona, Costa Rica	20 MW	31	16

Source: *Banking against Warming,* Christopher Flavin, Worldwatch, November/December 1997, pp. 32–33

CO_2 EMISSIONS

The combined 1995 population of Africa, Asia, Oceania, and Central and South America, which that year had a total of 200 million motor vehicles: 4.40 billion.

The 1995 population of the United States, which also had a total of 200 million motor vehicles: 0.27 billion.

The amount of carbon dioxide that a car getting 27.5 miles per gallon emits over 100,000 miles: 31,752 kilograms.

The amount of carbon dioxide that a human walking that same distance would produce: 59 kilograms.

Source: *Matters of Scale.* Reprinted with permission from Worldwatch Institute, Washington, D.C. November/December 1997, p. 39.

DIRECTIONS: CIRCLE THE RIGHT ANSWER

Ho, ho, ho—this is Santa Claus reporting from high in the stratosphere. I am moving along in my fusion-energized sleigh and looking over the earth with its many problems, but also with its many joys and successes. The love among mankind is still omnipresent, and the progress of man moves forward because of the visionaries, risk-takers and other leaders who blend technology with the future of the world in mind.

I still do see some problems, however. I look down through the stratosphere and see too few ozone molecules (O, O_2, O_3, O_4, O_5), which are gobbled up from the use of (TCBs, DDTs, CO_2, SO_2, CFCs). Because of this increased (infrared, visible, ultraviolet, X rays, gamma rays) radiation exposure from the decreased ozone layer, plants and animals will be more exposed, which may have harmful effects.

I see an increase of electric cars, which are now about (10, 20, 30, 80, 90 percent) efficient and about (10, 14, 30, 8, 12) percent of the population-owned cars. The emissions from cars is principally (NO, SO_2, CO_2), which is a primary cause of (tornados, hurricanes, global warming). About (1/2, 1/3, 1/5, 1/6, 1/4) of the world is rich and industrialized, and the other part of the world would be happy if I gave them a lump of coal to keep them warm. I would wish that the whole world would use (coal, nuclear, solar, oil) energy, as it would be the cleanest source of energy.

There are many other things I need to tell you. But I am running out of time. I just want to wish you the merriest holiday ever and one that is filled with love and concern for your families and your fellow earth creatures. Have a wonderful new year filled with lasting and priceless gifts!

Conclusion

During the past 50 years, the global economy has increased fivefold, world population has doubled, and world energy use has tripled. Will these trends continue in the 21st century? Increased production and use of fossil fuel could have severe local and regional impacts. Locally, air pollution takes a toll on human health. Acid precipitation and other forms of air pollution can degrade downwind habitats, especially in lakes, streams, and forests. On a global level, the increased burning of fossil fuels will result in increased emissions of greenhouse gases, which in turn could lead to global warming and other adverse climate changes.

As we enter a new millennium, population pressures and the deterioration of the environment present a challenge to humankind: how to satisfy the ever-growing appetite of the energy-hungry genie–how to develop and use energy sources that are friendly to the environment. We face a dilemma: Energy technologies often enhance material well-being across the planet, but the continuation of current trends could lead to a degraded planet, yielding an uncertain existence for future generations.

According to some estimates, by the year 2010, world population will total 7 billion, and the gross world product will have doubled. It is predicted that, if energy consumption styles do not change, world energy consumption will increase by 50 to 60 percent. Carbon dioxide emissions will also increase by 50 to 60 percent. Therefore, as we plan for the future, we must use energy sources that enable us to sustain our environment. Appropriate energy policies at the individual, national, and international levels, along with efficient energy technologies and conservation efforts, could play an important role in achieving a balance between economic growth and a sustainable environment.

The next part explores the impact of increased energy consumption on the ecology of our planet.

Internet Exercise

1. Use any of the Internet search engines (e.g., Alta Vista, Yahoo, Infoseek, etc.) to re-search the following:

    a. When did the oil tanker *Exxon Valdez* (Figure P2.8) run aground on Bligh Reef in Prince William Sound in Alaska?

    b. How much oil was spilled into the Sound?

    c. What was the major cause of the accident?

    d. How did the construction of the *Exxon Valdez* contribute to the accident?

    e. What are the short-term and long-term effects of the oil spill in Prince William Sound?

    f. List the 10 largest oil spills to date.

    g. Compare the Prince William Sound oil spill with the Persian Gulf War oil spill in terms of size and short-term and long-term effects.

    h. What actions should be taken by multinational oil companies, governments, and international organizations to prevent future oil spills?

2. Use any of the Internet search engines (e.g., Alta Vista, Yahoo, Infoseek, etc.) to re-search the following questions:

    a. Where is Chernobyl (Figure P2.9) located?

    b. What happened on April 26, 1986, at Chernobyl?

Figure P2.8
The *Exxon Valdez* floats serenely in the midst of an oil spill in the waters of Prince William Sound, Alaska, flanked by another tanker.
Courtesy of U.S. Coast Guard.

Figure P2.9
A blasted wall at the Chernobyl nuclear
plant stands next to a smokestack.
Courtesy of Photo Researchers, Inc.

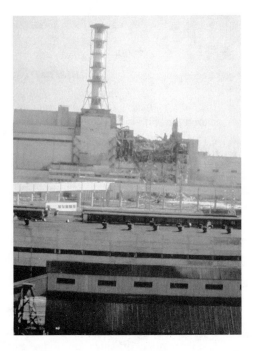

c. What was the cause of the accident at Chernobyl?

d. What are the short-term and long-term effects of the nuclear disaster at Chernobyl?

3. Use any of the Internet search engines (e.g., Alta Vista, Yahoo, Infoseek, etc.) to research the following:

a. Define the following terms:

(i)   Fossil fuel

(ii)   Acid rain

(iii)   Global warming

(iv)   Greenhouse effect

(v)   Radioactive waste

(vi)   GNP

(vii)   Per capita oil consumption

b. Determine the electricity consumption per capita for the following developed and
developing countries:

Developed Country	Electricity Consumption per Capita (kWh)	Developing Country	Electricity Consumption per Capita (kWh)
United States		Bangladesh	
France		China	
Japan		Ethiopia	
Australia		Ghana	
Norway		India	
Sweden		Indonesia	
Switzerland		Kenya	
Italy		Malaysia	
Singapore		Pakistan	
United Kingdom		Venezuela	
Germany		Zimbabawe	

c. What alternative energy sources look promising for the energy demands of the 21st
century?

d. What percentage of the world's total electricity is produced by hydroelectric
power?

e. Compare the features of large dams with those of small dams.

f. Complete the following table:

Country	Hydroelectric Power-Generating Capacity (MW)
United States	
Mexico	
Canada	
Egypt	
China	
Brazil	
Pakistan	
India	
Russia	
Japan	
Argentina	
Venezuela	
Italy	

g. What percentage of the world's total electricity is produced by solar power?

h. Will solar power someday replace fossil fuel as a source of energy? Why? Why not? Explain your answer.

i. Complete the following table:

Country	Solar Power-Generating Capacity (MW)
United States	
Mexico	
Canada	
Nigeria	
China	
Brazil	
Pakistan	
India	
South Africa	
Japan	
Malaysia	
Indonesia	
Australia	

j. Determine the wind power-generating capacity for the following developed and developing countries:

Developed Country	Wind Power-Generating Capacity (MW)	Developing Country	Wind Power-Generating Capacity (MW)
United States		Brazil	
France		China	
Japan		Nigeria	
Australia		Ghana	
Norway		India	
Sweden		Indonesia	
Switzerland		Jordan	
Italy		Malaysia	
Singapore		Pakistan	
United Kingdom		Viet Nam	
Germany		Zimbabwe	

k. Visit NASA's Multimedia Gallery at http://www.nasa.gov. The site contains a large collection of photos of the earth taken from space by various space shuttle missions and depicting the impact of different types of human interaction. Answer the following questions:

(i) List the impact of the construction of dams on ecology and soil erosion in the developing and the developed countries.

(ii) List those bans in the United States where the impact of construction on ecology and soil erosion is most evident.

Trends of the 20th Century

1. Figure P2.10 illustrates some trends of the 20th century. Do you agree or disagree with these trends? Express your degree of agreement or disagreement by marking an X in the appropriate box in the following table, and explain your response:

Trend	Degree of Agreement or Disagreement				
	Strongly Disagree	Disagree	No Opinion	Agree	Strongly Agree
Fossil fuel consumption					
Family values					
Pollution					
Humanity					
Population					
Availability of resources					
State of environment					
Stress					
Moral and ethical values					
Materialism					

2. Chart the following trends into the 21st century and explain your opinion.

Figure P2.10
Trends of the 20th century.

A Bridge to Your 21st Century Understanding

Suppose you were the Chernobyl plant director in 1986. What decisions and actions would you have taken to prevent the disaster? Complete the following flowchart by listing your decisions and actions in chronological order.

Beyond the Bridge: Explore
Future Options . . .

1. The gigantic increase in the use of fossil fuels in the 20th century has wreaked havoc on the earth's atmosphere. What kind of risks does the increased fossil fuel consumption impose on society at personal, national, and international levels? What efforts must be made to minimize these risks? Complete the following table:

	Personal Level	*National Level*	*International Level*
Risks			
Efforts			

Figure P2.11
Impact of increased fossil fuel consumption.

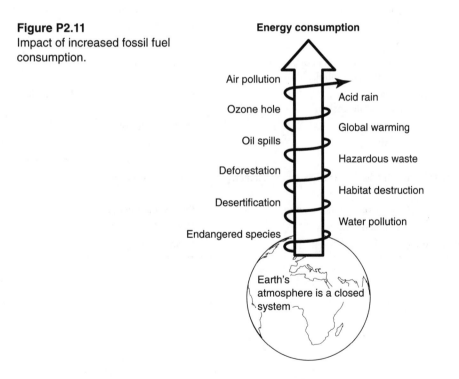

2.   What types of options and policies must be adopted at personal, national, and international levels to change 20th-century's styles of consumption of fossil fuels?

	Personal Level	National Level	International Level
Options/Policies			

3.   What types of renewable and alternative energy technologies will promote economic growth for a sustainable environment in the 21st century?

4.   Can the impact of technology in the 20th century be reversed? Yes or No? Explain your answer.

Useful Web Sites

URL	Site Description
http://www.er.doe.gov	U.S. Department of Energy
http://www.nrel.gov/business/international	Alternative Energy Sources
http://www.solar-energy.vegan.org	What's Solar Energy?
http://www.fsec.ucf.edu	Florida Solar Energy Center
http://www.nei.org	Nuclear Energy Institution
http://www.eagle2.online.discovery.com/dco/doc/10 12/world/science/chernobyl/weblinks.html	Chernobyl Web links
http://www.ponderosa-pine.uoregon.edu/Bi220/Blesofsky/menu.html	Genetic Effects of Chernobyl Incident
http://www.worldwatch.org	Worldwatch Institute
http://www.worldbank.org	World Bank
http://www.undp.org	United Nations Development Program
http://www.lib.umich.edu/libhome/Documents.center/ stats.html	Statistical Resources on the Web
http://www.sandia.gov/Renewable_Energy	Renewable Energy Sources
http://www.hooverdam.com/Gallery	Hoover Dam Photo Gallery
http://www.eren.doe.gov/wind	Wind Power

PART

III

Ecology

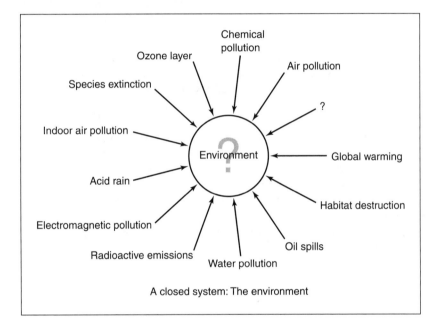

Chemical pollution

Ozone layer

Species extinction

Air pollution

Indoor air pollution

?

Environment

Global warming

Acid rain

Electromagnetic pollution

Habitat destruction

Radioactive emissions

Oil spills

Water pollution

A closed system: The environment

Looking into the environment of
the past, present, and future.
Photo courtesy of Ahmed S.
Khan

The term "environment" simply means the world that is all around us. This definition, then, includes no less than all of our natural world—our ecosystem. The study of ecology examines the mutual relationship between organisms and this natural world, the environment, and therefore analyzes the changes and effects on our whole environment due to organisms and their tools. Of course, one chapter or part of a book can hardly deal with such an all-embracing subject, but it can give an overview of some of the major issues of our ecosystem as man, along with the powerful and unpredictable use of technology, changes its balance, supportive systems, and even beauty. This part's purpose, then, is to enhance awareness, thought, understanding, responsibility, strategies, and involvement for a future environment that is desirable, inhabitable, and sustainable. As this part of the text is presented, historical, social, and economic views will be discussed along with the issues and articles in order to give a more complete understanding of the issues from differing perspectives.

HISTORICAL BACKGROUND AND MAJOR ISSUES

The environmental movement formally began in the United States on Earth Day 1970, when the American public began to awaken to the ecological destruction surrounding it. At that time, pollution controls did not exist for cars; people and cities dumped untreated sewage into the nation's rivers, some of which were so filled with chemical waste that they actually caught fire; and industrial cities were clouded with pungent, acid smoke. Since then, many of these problems have diminished and have been effectively addressed. The Environmental Protection Agency (EPA), established in 1970, monitors air quality around the country, and toxic emissions from smokestacks, factories, and incinerators have been sharply reduced. Mandatory pollution-control standards on automobiles have led to a drop

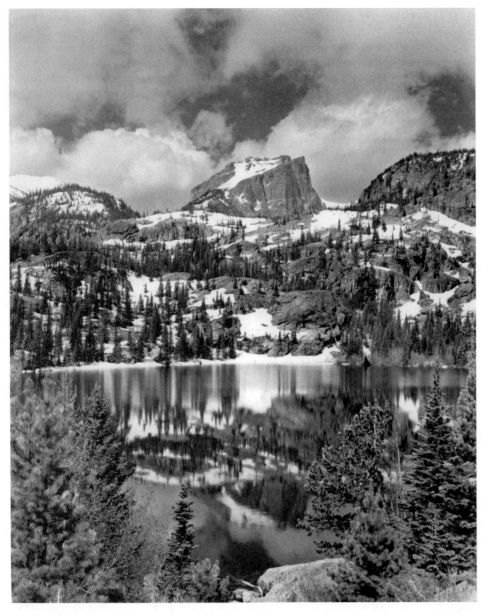

The power and resources of our delicate environment. Photo courtesy of Union Pacific Railroad.

When the environment is finally forced to file for bankruptcy because its resource base has been polluted, degraded, dissipated, and irretrievably compromised, the economy will go down with it.

TIMOTHY WIRTH, U.S. DEPARTMENT OF STATE

in lead emissions, and recycling as a way of reducing solid waste has made a significant impact on the health of the environment.

As, however, our use of materials continues to grow on a worldwide basis, along with an exponentially increasing population growth and level of need, new environmental strategies cannot help but involve an ecological cost of use and cost of the pollution of our supportive natural resources. Based on the findings of a scientific advisory group, the EPA has ranked world environment issues in the following manner.

High risk: Habitat destruction, global warming, ozone-layer depletion, species extinction, loss of biological diversity

Medium risk: Herbicides and pesticides, surface water pollution, airborne toxic substances

Low risk: Oil spills, radioactive materials, groundwater pollution

Human health risk: Indoor air pollution, outdoor air pollution, exposure of drinking water to chemicals

For an overview of and a brief introduction to the high-risk issues, a small discussion of each of the major issues in that category follows.

Habitat Destruction

Habitat destruction includes the destruction of wildlands that harbor the biological diversity of earth. Estimates of the total number of plant and animal species are between 10 million and 80 million, of which only about 1.4 million species have been identified. The biodiversity's mass extinction at unprecedented rates has already begun to cause the loss of 50,000 invertebrate species per year (nearly 140 each day) in the rain forests. By the year 2050, it is believed that 25% of the earth's species will become extinct if rain forest destruction is continued. Other habitats, such as islands, wetlands, and freshwater lakes, are also losing great proportions of their life-forms due to environmental loss and degradation. Rain forests are home to at least half of the planet's species and have been reduced by nearly half of their original area (from 14% of the earth's land to only 6% presently), losing an area about the size of the state of Washington each year due to deforestation. During the past 30 years, about one-third of the world's rain forests have disappeared. Tropical rain forests are lush habitats filled with more diversity of life than any other habitat. A typical patch of rain forest covering four square miles contains 750 species of trees, 750 species of other plants, 125 species of mammals, 400 species of birds, 100 species of reptiles, and 60 species of amphibians. The rich plant life supports food chains that include many of the world's most spectacular animals: brightly colored frogs, eagles, monkeys, tigers, sloths, army ants, and so on. Many rain forest species cannot survive in any other type of environment and are, like all species, biologically unique. The destruction of species that accompanies deforestation becomes a large-scale loss of species to the earth and mankind. For example, of the 3,000 plant species that have anticancer properties, 70% are found in tropical rain forests. Rain forests also have an impact on world climate, affecting the chemistry and ecology of the ocean, consuming huge quantities of CO_2, producing a large percent of the world's oxygen, and slowing global warming. The Amazon River basin, one of the largest rain forests, holds 66% of the Earth's freshwater and produces 20% of the earth's oxygen. (Refer to Tables P3.1 and P3.2 for comparisons of deforestation by country.)

Table P3.1
Deforestation in the Megadiversity Countries, Eighties

Country	Share of World's Land Area	Share of World's Flowering Plant Species[1]	Annual Deforestation Rate[2]	
	(percent)		(square kilometers)	(percent)
Brazil	6.3	22	13,820[3]	0.4
Colombia	0.8	18	6,000	1.3
China	7.0	11	n.a.	n.a.
Mexico	1.4	10	7,000	1.5
Australia	5.7	9	n.a.	n.a.
Indonesia	1.4	8	10,000	0.9
Peru	1.0	8	2,700	0.4
Malaysia	0.2	6	3,100	1.5
Ecuador	0.2	6	3,400	2.4
India	2.2	6	10,000	2.7
Zaire	1.7	4	4,000	0.4
Madagascar	0.4	4	1,500	1.5

[1]Based on total of 250,000 known species; because of overlap between countries, figures cannot be added. [2] Closed forests only. [3]1990 figure.

Sources: Jeffrey A. McNeely et al., *Conserving the World's Biological Diversity* (Gland, Switzerland, and Washington, D.C.: International Union for Conservation of Nature and Natural Resources (IUCN) et al., 1989); World Resources Institute, *World Resources 1990–91* (New York: Oxford University Press, 1990); Ricardo Bonalume, "Amazonia: Deforestation Rate Is Falling," *Nature,* April 4, 1991; Walter V. Reid, "How Many Species Will There Be?" in J. Sayer and T. Whitmore, eds., *Tropical Deforestation and the Extinction of Species* (Gland, Switzerland: IUCN, forthcoming).

From *State of the World 1992:* A Worldwatch Institute Report on Progress Toward a Sustainable Society by Lester Brown, et. al, eds. Copyright © 1992 by the Worldwatch Institute. Reprinted by permission of W.W. Norton & Company, Inc.

Wetlands are also important environmental ecosystems that provide habitats for many species of animals and plants; a third of the endangered or threatened species in the United States live in or are dependent on them. Wetlands are the nurseries for many fish, all amphibians, and many birds and mammals. Wetlands also filter, purify, and hold water, even eliminating pesticides and other toxins by speeding up degradation by microbes. They store water, slow down its flow, and buffer floods and erosion. Coastal wetlands are spawning grounds for between 60% and 90% of U.S. commercial fisheries, and hunting depends entirely upon wetland habitats. Wetlands are among the most productive natural ecosystems on earth in terms of total biological mass per unit of area. Since colonial times, half of the wetlands in the United States have been destroyed, with only about 105 million acres remaining (excluding Alaska). (Refer to Table P3.3 for more detailed information on the loss of state wetland acreage.)

Species Extinction

Biological diversity faces a rate of species extinction greater than any since the mass extinctions of the dinosaurs 65 million years ago. As mentioned previously, a minimum of 50,000 invertebrate species alone are rendered extinct per year, which comes to about 140

Table P3.2
Tropical Forest Area and Rate of Deforestation for 87 Countries, 1981–90 (in thousand hectares)

Region/Subregion	Number of Countries Studied	Total Land Area	Forest Area 1980	Forest Area 1990	Area Deforested Annually 1981–90
LATIN AMERICA	**32**	**1,675,700**	**923,000**	**839,000**	**8,300**
Central America and Mexico	7	245,300	77,000	63,500	1,400
Caribbean subregion	18	69,500	48,800	47,100	200
Tropical South America	7	1,360,800	797,100	729,300	6,800
ASIA	**15**	**896,600**	**310,800**	**274,900**	**3,600**
South Asia	6	445,600	70,600	66,200	400
Continental Southeast Asia	5	192,900	83,200	69,700	1,300
Insular Southeast Asia	4	258,100	157,000	138,900	1,800
AFRICA	**40**	**2,243,400**	**650,300**	**600,100**	**5,000**
West Sahelian Africa	8	528,000	41,900	38,000	400
East Sahelian Africa	6	489,600	92,300	85,300	700
West Africa	8	203,200	55,200	43,400	1,200
Central Africa	7	406,400	230,100	215,400	1,500
Tropical Southern Africa	10	557,900	217,700	206,300	1,100
Insular Africa	1	58,200	13,200	11,700	200
Total	**87**	**4,815,700**	**1,884,100**	**1,714,800**	**16,900**

Note: Figures are preliminary estimates.
Source: World Resources Institute, *World Resources 1992–93* (1992).

Table P3.3
States with Most Wetland Acreage, 1780s–1980s

State	Wetlands in 1780s Acres	Wetlands in 1780s Percent of Area	Wetlands in 1980s Acres	Wetlands in 1980s Percent of Area	Percent Lost
Alaska	170,200,000	45.3%	170,000,000	45.3%	−0.1%
Florida	20,325,013	54.2	11,038,300	29.5	−46
Louisiana	16,194,500	52.1	8,784,200	28.3	−46
Minnesota	15,070,000	28.0	8,700,000	16.2	−42
Texas	15,999,700	9.4	7,612,412	4.4	−52
North Carolina	11,089,500	33.0	5,689,500	16.9	−49
Michigan	11,200,000	30.1	5,583,400	15.0	−50
Wisconsin	9,800,000	27.3	5,331,392	14.8	−46
Georgia	6,843,200	18.2	5,298,200	14.1	−23
Maine	6,460,000	30.4	5,199,200	24.5	−20

Note: Ranked by wetlands acreage in the 1980s.
Source: U.S. Dept. of Interior, Fish and Wildlife Service, *Wetlands in the United States, 1780s to 1980s* (1990).

Table P3.4
Endangered and Threatened Species, 1995

Group	Endangered U.S.	Endangered Foreign	Threatened U.S.	Threatened Foreign	Total Listed
Mammals	55	252	9	19	335
Birds	76	177	16	6	275
Reptiles	14	65	19	14	112
Amphibians	7	8	5	0	20
Fishes	68	11	37	0	116
Snails	15	1	7	0	23
Clams	51	2	6	0	59
Crustaceans	14	0	3	0	17
Insects	20	4	9	0	33
Arachnids	5	0	0	0	5
Total animals	**325**	**520**	**111**	**39**	**995**
Flowering plants	406	1	90	0	497
Conifers	2	0	0	2	4
Ferns and others	26	0	2	0	28
Total plants	**434**	**1**	**92**	**2**	**529**
Total species	**759**	**521**	**203**	**41**	**1,524**[1]

Note: Separate populations of a species, listed both as endangered and threatened, are tallied twice. For example, the grizzly bear is included as threatened in the U.S. and endangered in Mexico. Eight other species are counted twice: leopard, gray wolf, bald eagle, piping plover, roseate tern, chimpanzee, green sea turtle, and olive ridley sea turtle.
Source: U.S. Fish and Wildlife Service, *Box Score of U.S. List of Endangered and Threatened Species,* Apr. 30, 1995.
Permission granted by Andrews & McNeel.

extinctions each day. The world's 10 to 80 million species are threatened by deforestation, loss of wetlands, and urban sprawl, as well as shifting climate and vegetation zones. Another cause for animal and plant loss is the change to monocultures in agriculture, which is the production of only one strain of crop for food that then becomes vulnerable to disease and other threats. Although it may be weakened when it is renewed, the U.S. Endangered Species Act of 1966 is the chief protector of species in the United States, and the Convention on International Trade in Endangered Species of Wild Fauna and Flora (CITES), signed in 1975 by 122 nations, continues to be one of the main forces in the preservation of species internationally. To abate the trend toward species extinction, governments around the world have set aside a total of about 16.4 million square miles of protected lands in about 3,500 parks and preserves. In addition, many countries try to identify species threatened with extinction so that these species may be carefully monitored and protected.

The following are some of the selected endangered species of the world: cheetah, African chimpanzee, Dugong (sea cow), gibbon, gorilla, jaguar, leopard (three species), monkey (many species), orangutan, giant panda, rhinoceros, tiger, whale (eight species), wolf, birds (over 1,000 of 9,672 species), reptiles (many species of alligators, crocodiles,

Table P3.5

Endangered and Threatened Species in the U.S., 1967–95

Year	New Listings	Total Listings	Year	New Listings	Total Listings
1967	78	78	1982	13	803
1968	0	78	1983	29	832
1969	0	78	1984	48	880
1970	323	401	1985	61	941
1971	0	401	1986	46	987
1972	9	410	1987	60	1,047
1973	21	431	1988	46	1,093
1974	3	434	1989	35	1,128
1975	10	444	1990	53	1,181
1976	194	638	1991	86	1,267
1977	20	658	1992	82	1,349
1978	36	694	1993	73	1,422
1979	69	763	1994	128	1,550
1980	23	786	1995	49	1,599
1981	4	790			

Note: As of May 31, 1995. Separate populations of a species, listed both as endangered and threat-
ened, are tallied twice. This table includes emergency listings, but does not subtract de-listed species.
Source: U.S. Fish and Wildlife Service, unpublished data.
Permission granted by Andrews & McNeel.

iguanas, and sea turtles), amphibians (all frogs and toads in the United States), fish (many
species), plants (about 21%, or 4,200 of 20,000 species; as many as 750 plant species in the
United States could become extinct by the first years of the 21st century). (Refer to Tables
P3.4, P3.5, and P3.6 for a more detailed breakdown of data on endangered species.)

Global Warming

Many experts today think that the earth has begun to warm significantly over the past century—by about 1°F—and could further warm 3° to 5°F over the next 50 to 60 years. If this
estimate is true, the effects would be enormous, considering that the earth's temperature
has only risen 9 degrees since the last ice age 12,000 years ago. Such an increase in warming would cause polar ice caps to melt, thus causing a rise in the sea level worldwide, destroying coastal areas, islands, water supplies, forests, and agriculture in many parts of the
world. Global warming is caused from gases in the atmosphere that prevent sunlight from
being reflected away from the earth. Usually, sunlight that reaches the surface of the earth
is partly absorbed and partly reflected. The absorbed light heats the surface and is later released as infrared radiation. Gases (called "greenhouse gases") that are not released collect
the heat and keep it in the atmosphere. The earth's atmosphere is only 0.03% CO_2, but together with other gases, can trap 30% of the reflected heat and maintain the earth's average
temperature at about 59°F.

   Since the 1800s, an unprecedented amount of the four primary greenhouse gases (carbon dioxide, chlorofluorocarbons (CFCs), methane, and nitrous oxide) have been released
into the atmosphere. The worst of these gases are CFCs, which, in addition to contributing

Table P3.6
Observed Declines in Selected Animal Species, Early Nineties

Species Type	Observation
Amphibians[1]	Worldwide decline observed in recent years. Wetland drainage and invading species have extinguished nearly half New Zealand's unique frog fauna. Biologists cite European demand for frogs' legs as a cause of the rapid nationwide decline of India's two most common bullfrogs.
Birds	Three fourths of the world's bird species are declining in population or threatened with extinction.
Fish	One third of North America's freshwater fish stocks are rare, threatened, or endangered; one third of U.S. coastal fish have declined in population since 1975. Introduction of the Nile perch has helped drive half the 400 species of Lake Victoria, Africa's largest lake, to or near extinction.
Invertebrates	On the order of 100 species lost to deforestation each day. Western Germany reports one fourth of its 40,000 known invertebrates to be threatened. Roughly half the freshwater snails of the southeastern United States are extinct or nearly so.
Mammals	Almost half of Australia's surviving mammals are threatened with extinction. France, western Germany, the Netherlands, and Portugal all report more than 40 percent of their mammals as threatened.
Carnivores	Virtually all species of wild cats and most bears are declining seriously in numbers.
Primates[2]	More than two thirds of the world's 150 species are threatened with extinction.
Reptiles	Of the world's 270 turtle species, 42 percent are rare or threatened with extinction.

[1]Class that includes frogs, toads, and salamanders. [2]Order that includes monkeys, lemurs, and humans.
Source: Worldwatch Institute, based on sources documented in endnote 13.
From *State of the World 1992:* A Worldwatch Institute Report on Progress Toward a Sustainable Society by Lester R. Brown, et al, eds. Copyright © 1992 by the Worldwatch Institute. Reprinted by permission of W.W. Norton & Company, Inc.

to the greenhouse effect, are also destroying the stratospheric ozone, which shields the earth's surface from ultraviolet rays. The United States, Russia, Japan, and various countries in Europe have agreed to a 100% phaseout of CFCs by the year 2000. Concentrations of carbon dioxide have increased by 25% within the last century. As the greenhouse gases increase in concentration, they will produce a domino effect that could cause environmental chaos in weather patterns, warming patterns, and sea level. Many scientists speculate that global warming is occurring; however, agreement with regard to global warming is not definite, and the issue remains very contested.

The Ozone Layer

The chemical ozone (O_3) exists as smog at ground level, where we have an abundance of it, causing pollution, and in the stratosphere, where we do not have enough of it, causing a very serious weakening of the ozone shield, which protects us from the sun's ultraviolet rays and other types of radiation. A significant reduction of the ozone layer would lead to an increase in skin cancers and cataracts, the loss of small ocean algae and bacteria, and the breakdown of other natural systems. Chlorofluorocarbons (CFCs), chemicals manufactured since the 1930s for refrigeration, insulation, and packaging, add chlorine to the atmosphere and absorb the ozone in the stratosphere. CFCs are very stable and have lifetimes of 75 to 110 years. They drift into the upper atmosphere, where their chlorine components are released. The freed chlorine atoms find ozone molecules and react, creating chlorine monoxide. In a subsequent reaction, the chlorine monoxide releases its oxygen atom to form molecular oxygen, and the chlorine atom is freed again to repeat the process. With the long lifetime of chlorine, each chlorine atom can destroy about 100,000 molecules of ozone before the chain reaction ends. Ice crystals in the Antarctic and Arctic accelerate the process, producing "ozone holes" near both poles. Studies indicate that stratospheric ozone has declined at least 4% to 8% over the northern hemisphere in the past decade. To combat this process, major nations of the world have agreed to eliminate CFC use and production by 2000. However, NASA indicates that adverse effects on the ozone layer from CFCs will continue until at least 2020.

There are many environmental issues that need to be discussed. The issues, articles, and case studies of this part of the book begin to show our environmental needs, causes, perspectives, problems, and successes. The articles and case studies not only indicate the issues themselves, but also societal and economic responses, since these responses are where effects and actions are rooted. The three chapters, entitled "The Grim Payback of Greed," "Young at Risk," and "Fisheries: Exploiting the Ocean—What Will Be Left?" provide a global analysis of the consequences of increasing intense resource use by man in the environment. The last five chapters, entitled "Buried Displeasure: The Love Canal," "What Will Happen to the Endangered Species Act?", "Air Poisons around the World," "Earth Day: 25 years," and "Rain Forests May Offer New Miracle Drugs" are readings in the field of ecology that deal with more specialized issues in specific locations that have focused outcomes and lessons to man and his future decisions. The articles and case studies were selected for the central issues and reactions that represent, but the variety of issues and case studies available is, of course, as endless as the sea of everyday occurrences and events. The articles and case studies selected were chosen because they wrestle with central issues and responses that enhance awareness and decision making for our future world. These studies also consistently underscore the vital necessity to acknowledge the increasing value and importance of the world around us—our life-sustaining world, the environment.

AN ECONOMIC VIEW OF ECOLOGY

In acknowledging the value of our ecosystem, 13 researchers, in a May 1997 report in the journal *Nature,* tried to establish the economic value of the annual worth of earth's natural goods and services—the annual worth of our ecosystem. This value is estimated at $33 trillion and includes earth's basic services and products, from beaches and forest lumber to

Understanding the many types of value of our ecology. Photo courtesy of Ahmed S. Khan.

oceans' regulation of carbon dioxide. In comparison to the total ecosystem's worth, the world's annual gross national products alone total about $18 trillion.

The actual worth of our ecosystem is probably much larger than $33 trillion, since the calculations were conservative, not all-inclusive, and came from the conversion of a variety of ecosystem values from more than 100 studies. For example, the relationship of shrimp-harvest yields to the local wetlands was calculated to the average value of a hectare (about 2.5 acres) of wetland, which was then applied to the international size of that habitat. Recreational value came from people's reports of willingness to pay for access to lakes, reefs, and other recreational areas. The estimates omit ecosystem services in desert and tundra areas, since these areas have not been studied in terms of ecosystem values. The study also omits services in urban areas like green spaces in New York's Central Park.

The most valuable ecosystems per hectare turned out to be estuaries and wetlands, since they have been studied the most. Other ecosystems will probably increase in value as they also become more studied and understood. This field of ecological economics is a brand new field, only about a decade old. This study is just a starting point, according to the researchers, and they acknowledge many limitations to it. However, even as a starting point, the power of the analysis is the acknowledgment of the per-hectare value of the various habitats, the assignment of value to processes and areas taken for granted, and the way in which the assignment of value will influence local decisions and conservation when it comes to planning.

Questions

1. Is the term "ecosystem" the same as the term "environment"? What are some different connotations of the two terms?

2. How have attitudes toward the environment changed from the 1970s?

3. Why do you think the EPA's world environmental issues are prioritized as they are? Why are some of the issues labeled as high risk, others as medium risk, and yet others as low risk? Explain.

4. Why is the loss of species an issue? Do we have to have so many species?

5. Why is the loss of rain forests an issue? Give three significant reasons.

6. Give three reasons why wetlands are important.

7. What do you think we can do to prevent habitat destruction? Creatively think of three workable ideas.

8. What can the industrial world do to help abate the extinction of species?

9. What causes global warming? What are the four gases mostly responsible for heat absorption of the atmosphere?

10. Explain how CFCs destroy ozone. What can be done to combat CFC use? Give some specific and practical ideas.

11. Why is it a good idea to place economic value on earth's natural habitat and goods and services? Explain.

12. Refer to the title page of this chapter. Why is the environment a "closed system"? Explain.

Questions About the Tables

1. Compare the information contained in Table 3.1 and Table 3.2. What common conclusion can be drawn from this material? What are some of the differences between the various pieces of information presented?

2. Summarize in a short written paragraph the overall conclusions in Table 3.1 and in Table 3.2. Compare the results.

3. Summarize the information contained in Table 3.3. What conclusions do you draw, and what action might you take from these conclusions?

4. Read Tables 3.4, 3.5, and 3.6. Compare Table 3.4 to Table 3.6. Explain the differences in the information and how the information is presented. Does Table 3.5 confirm the findings in Table 3.4, or does it confuse the data? Explain.

5. Summarize in a short written paragraph the findings and conclusions from each of Tables P3.4, P3.5, and P3.6.

ECOLOGICAL STATISTICS

Global facts

- Over 40% of all tropical forests have been destroyed and another acre is lost each second.

- Each year, humankind adds six to eight billion tons of carbon to the atmosphere by burning fossil fuels and destroying forests, pumping up the concentration of greenhouse gases responsible for global warming—an effect that could raise temperatures by three to ten degrees by the year 2050.

- While the U.S. makes up only 5% of the world's population, we produce 72% of all hazardous waste and consume 33% of the world's paper.

- Worldwide, thousands of pounds of plutonium are being produced, used and stored under conditions of inadequate security. Using current technology, only two pounds of plutonium is required to make a nuclear device.

- The annual catch in 13 of the world's 15 major fishing zones has declined and in four of those—three in the Atlantic and one in the Pacific oceans—the catch has shrunk by a startling 30%.

Land facts

- Taxpayers will lose over one billion dollars over the next decade as the Forest Service spends more money on building logging roads and preparing commercial timber sales than it makes on selling the timber.

- In 1992, taxpayers subsidized the clearcutting of our Alaskan rain forest with an estimated $40 million.

- Mining companies are allowed to buy our public lands for less than five dollars an acre—and they pay no royalties on the gold and other minerals they extract. This taxpayer giveaway, combined with the cost of massive environmental damage and cleanup, amounts to a billion dollars every year.

- Grazing has led to soil erosion, watershed destruction and ruin of wildlife habitat on millions of acres of our public lands. Taxpayers subsidized grazing fees with $1.8 billion during the years 1985–1992.

Air facts

- As many as 70,000 people nationwide may die prematurely from heart and lung disease aggravated by particulate air pollution.

- More than 100 million Americans live in urban areas where the air is officially classified by the EPA as unsafe to breathe.

- In many urban areas, children are steadily exposed to high levels of pollutants, increasing the risk of chronic lung disease, cell damage and respiratory illnesses.

- Dioxin and other persistent pollutants that are released into the air accumulate in our waterways, wildlife, food supply and human bloodstreams. These poisons may cause cancer and reproductive disorders in human beings and other animal species.

"Ecology Facts" from *25 Year report 1970–1995*. (1995). New York, New York, Natural Resources Defense Council.

Ecology Vocabulary Exercise

As you proceed through this part of the book and your reading and research of the issues, keep a listing of ecological terms and organizations that you would like to know more about. Use various resources to define and learn more about them, including other texts, articles, encyclopedias, and the Internet (refer to the Internet exercise at the end of Part III).

ECOLOGICAL STATISTICS, *continued*

Water facts

- Millions of pounds of toxic chemicals, like lead, mercury and pesticides, pour into our waterways each year contaminating wildlife, seafood and drinking water.

- One-half of our nation's lakes and one-third of our rivers are too polluted to be completely safe for swimming or fishing.

- Raw sewage, poison runoff and other pollution have caused 8,000 beach closures or advisories over the past five years.

- We are losing once pristine national treasures—like the Everglades, Lake Superior, and the Columbia River System—to toxic pollution, chemical spills, development, and diversion of freshwater flows.

- All but one species of the magnificent ocean-going salmon in the Pacific Northwest face a growing risk of extinction throughout most of their range, due to habitat degradation and overfishing.

Energy facts

- The United States is responsible for almost 25% of the world's total energy consumption. We use one million gallons of oil every two minutes.

- Energy currently wasted by U.S. cars, homes and appliances equals more than twice the known energy reserves in Alaska and the U.S. Outer Continental Shelf.

- We could cut our nation's energy consumption in half by the year 2030 simply by using energy more efficiently and by using more renewable energy sources. In the process, we would promote economic growth by saving consumers $2.3 trillion and by producing one million new jobs.

- When just 1% of America's 140 million car owners tune up their cars, we eliminate nearly a billion pounds of carbon dioxide—the key cause of global warming—from entering the atmosphere.

Health and habitat facts

- In 1991, 2.2 billion pounds of pesticides were used in the U.S.—eight pounds for every man, woman and child.

- A 1991 NRDC study found that pesticide use can be reduced in nine major U.S. crops by 25 to 80%.

- Americans are exposed to 70,000 chemicals, some 90% of which have never been subjected to adequate testing to determine their impact on our health.

- In the early 1990s, 116 million Americans drank water from systems that violated the Safe Drinking Water Act.

- As of 1994, 1.7 million American children, ages one to five, suffered from lead poisoning.

- Of the trash that we Americans throw away every day, 30% by weight is packaging alone. In 1993, we threw away 14 billion pounds of plastic packaging.

The grim residue. Photo ©
Eugene Gordon, 1984.

The Grim Payback of Greed

ALAN DURNING

A man is rich in proportion to the things he can afford to let alone.

HENRY DAVID THOREAU

Early in the age of affluence that followed World War II, an American retailing analyst named Victor Lebow proclaimed that an enormously productive economy "demands that we make consumption our way of life . . . . We need things consumed, burned up, worn out, replaced and discarded at an ever increasing rate."

Americans have responded to Mr. Lebow's call, and much of the world has followed. The average person today is four-and-a-half times richer than were his great-grandparents at the turn of the century. That new global wealth is not evenly spread among the Earth's people, however. One billion live in unprecedented luxury; one billion live in destitution.

Overconsumption by the world's fortunate is an environmental problem unmatched in severity by anything but perhaps population growth. Their surging exploitation of resources threatens to exhaust or inalterably disfigure forests, soils, water, air and climate.

Of course the opposite of overcompensation—poverty—is no solution either to environmental or human problems. Dispossessed peasants slash-and-burn their way into the rain forests of Latin America, and hungry nomads turn their herds out onto fragile African rangeland, reducing it to desert.

If environmental destruction results when people have either too little or too much, we are left to wonder how much is enough. What level of consumption can the Earth

Reprinted with permission from Worldwatch Institute. Durning, A. (May–June 1991). "The Grim Payback of Greed." *International Wildlife.* Vol. 21, No. 3, pp. 36–39.

support? When does having more cease to add appreciably to human satisfaction?

The consuming society: Skyrocketing consumption is the hallmark of our era. The trend is visible in statistics for almost any per capita indicator. Worldwide, since midcentury the intake of copper, energy, meat, steel and wood has approximately doubled; car ownership and cement consumption have quadrupled; plastic use has quintupled; aluminum consumption has grown sevenfold; and air travel has multiplied 32 times.

Moneyed regions account for the largest waves of consumption since 1950. In the United States, the world's premier consuming society, on average people today own twice as many cars, drive two-and-a-half times as far, use 21 times as much plastic and travel 25 times as far by air as did their parents in 1950. Air conditioning has spread from 15 percent of households in 1960 to 64 percent in 1987, and color televisions from 1 to 93 percent. Microwave ovens and video cassette recorders found their way into almost two-thirds of American homes during the eighties alone.

The eighties were a period of marked extravagance in the United States; not since the Roaring Twenties had conspicuous consumption been so lauded. Between 1978 and 1987, sales of Jaguar automobiles increased eightfold, and the average age of first-time fur-coat buyers fell from 50 to 26. The select club of American millionaires more than doubled its membership from 600,000 to 1.5 million over the decade, while the number of American billionaires reached 58 by 1990.

Japan and Western Europe have displayed parallel trends. Per person, the Japanese of today consume more than four times as much aluminum, almost five times as much energy and 25 times as much steel as people in Japan did in 1950. They also own four times as many cars and eat nearly twice as much meat. In 1972 one million Japanese traveled abroad; in 1990, the number was expected to top ten million. As in the United States, the eighties were a particularly consumerist decade in Japan, with sales of BMW automobiles rising tenfold.

Like the Japanese, West Europeans' consumption levels are only one notch below Americans'. Taken together, France, West Germany and the United Kingdom almost doubled their per capita use of steel, more than doubled their intake of cement and aluminum and tripled their paper consumption since mid-century. Just in the first half of the eighties, per capita consumption of frozen prepared meals—with their excessive packaging—rose more than 30 percent in every West European country except Finland; in Switzerland, the jump was 180 percent.

The cost of wealth: Long before all the world's people could achieve the American dream, however, the planet would be laid waste. Those in the wealthiest fifth of humanity are responsible for the lion's share of the damage humans have caused to common global resources. They have built more than 99 percent of the world's nuclear warheads. Their appetite for wood is a driving force behind destruction of the tropical rain forest and the resulting extinction of countless species. Over the past century, their economies have pumped out two-thirds of the greenhouse gases that threaten the Earth's climate, and each year their energy use releases perhaps three-fourths of the sulfur and nitrogen oxides that cause acid rain. Their industries generate most of the world's hazardous chemical wastes, and their air conditioners, aerosol sprays and factories release almost 90 percent of the chlorofluorocarbons that destroy the Earth's protective ozone layer. Clearly, even 1 billion profligate consumers are too much for the Earth.

Beyond the environmental costs of acquisitiveness, some perplexing findings of social scientists throw doubt on the wisdom of high consumption as a personal and national goal: Rich societies have had little success in turning consumption into fulfillment. A landmark study in 1974, for instance, revealed that Nigerians, Filipinos, Panamanians, Yugoslavians, Japanese, Israelis and West Germans all ranked themselves near the middle of a happiness scale. Confounding any attempt to correlate affluence and happiness, poor Cubans and rich Americans were both found to be considerably happier than the norm, and citizens of India and the Dominican Republic, less so. As Oxford psychologist Michael Argyle writes, "There is very little dif-ference in the levels of reported happiness found in rich and very poor countries."

As measured in constant dollars, the world's people have consumed as many goods and services since 1950 as all previous generations put together. Since 1940, Americans alone have used up as large a share of the Earth's mineral resources as did everyone before them combined. If the effectiveness of that consumption in providing personal fulfillment is questionable, perhaps environmental concerns can help us redefine our goals.

In search of sufficiency: Some guidance on what the Earth can sustain emerges from an examination of current consumption patterns around the world. For three of the most ecologically important types of consumption—transportation, diet and use of raw materials—the world's people are distributed unevenly over a vast range. Those at the bottom fall below the "too little" line, while those at the top, in what could be called the cars-meat-and-disposable class, consume too much.

About 1 billion people do most of their traveling, aside from the occasional donkey or bus ride, on foot, many of them never going more than 100 kilometers from their birthplaces. Unable to get to jobs easily, attend school or bring their complaints before government offices, they are severely hindered by the lack of transportation options.

The massive middle class of the world, numbering some 3 billion, travels by bus and bicycle. Kilometer for kilometer, bikes are cheaper than any other vehicles, costing less than $100 new in most of the Third World and requiring no fuel.

The world's automobile class is relatively small: Only 8 percent of humans, about 400 million people, own cars. Their cars are directly responsible for an estimated 13 percent of carbon dioxide emissions from fossil fuels worldwide, along with air pollution, acid rain and a quarter-million traffic fatalities a year.

The global food consumption ladder has three rungs, as well. At the bottom, the world's 630 million poorest people are unable to provide themselves with a healthful diet, according to World Bank estimates.

On the next rung, the 3.4 billion grain-eaters of the world's middle class get enough calories and plenty of plant-based protein, giving them the most-healthful basic diet of the world's people. They typically receive less than 20 percent of their calories from fat, a level low enough to protect them from the consequences of excessive dietary fat.

The top of the ladder is populated by the meat-eaters, those who obtain close to 40 percent of their calories from fat. These 1.25 billion people eat three times as much fat per person as the remaining 4 billion, mostly because they eat so much red meat. The meat class pays the price of its diet in high death rates from the so-called diseases of affluence—heart disease, stroke and certain types of cancer.

The Earth also pays for the high-fat diet. Indirectly, the meat-eating quarter of humanity consumes nearly 40 percent of the world's grain—grain that fattens the livestock they eat. Meat production is behind a substantial share of the environmental strains induced by the present global agricultural system, from soil erosion to overpumping of underground water.

In raw material consumption, the same pattern emerges. About 1 billion rural people subsist on biomass collected from the immediate environment. Most of what they use each day—about a half-kilogram of grain, 1 kilogram of fuelwood, and fodder for their animals—could be self-replenishing renewable resources. Unfortunately, because these people are often pushed by landlessness and population growth into fragile unproductive ecosystems, their minimal needs are not always met.

These materially destitute billion are part of a larger group that lacks many of the benefits provided by modest use of nonrenewable resources—particularly durable things like radios, refrigerators, water pipes, high-quality tools, and carts with lightweight wheels and ball bearings. More than 2 billion people live in countries where per capita consumption of steel, the most basic modern material, falls below 50 kilograms a year. In those same countries, per capita energy use—a fairly good indirect indicator of overall use of materials—is lower than 20 gigajoules per year (compared to 280 gigajoules in the United States).

Roughly 1.5 billion people live in the middle class of materials' use. Providing each of them with durable goods every year uses between 50 and 150 kilograms of steel and 20–50 gigajoules of energy.

At the top of the heap is the throwaway class, which uses raw materials extravagantly. A typical resident of the industrialized fourth of the world uses 15 times as much paper, 10 times as much steel and 12 times as much fuel as a Third World resident. The extreme case is the United States, where the average person consumes most of his own weight in basic materials each day—18 kilograms of petroleum and coal, 13 kilograms of other minerals, 12 kilograms of farm products and 9 kilograms of forest products, or about 115 pounds total.

In the throwaway economy, packaging becomes an end in itself, disposables proliferate and durability suffers. Four percent of consumer expenditures on goods in the United States goes for packaging—$225 a year. Likewise, the Japanese use 30 million disposable single-roll cameras each year, and the British dump 2.5 billion diapers. Americans toss away 180 million razors annually, enough paper and plastic plates and cups to feed the world a picnic six times a year and enough aluminum cans to make 6,000 DC-10 airplanes.

In transportation, diet and use of raw materials, as consumption rises on the economic scale, so does waste—both of resources and of health. Yet despite arguments in favor of modest consumption, few people who can afford high consumption levels opt to live simply. What prompts us, then, to consume so much?

The cultivation of needs: "The avarice of mankind is insatiable," wrote Aristotle 23 centuries ago, describing the way that as each of our desires is satisfied, a new one seems to appear in its place. That observation, on which all of economic theory is based, provides the most obvious answer to the question of why people never seem satisfied with what they have. If our wants are insatiable, there is simply no such thing as enough.

Much confirms this view of human nature. The Roman philosopher Lucretius wrote a century before Christ: "We have lost our taste for acorns. So [too] we have abandoned those couches littered with herbage and heaped with leaves. So the wearing of wild beasts' skins has gone out of fashion . . . . Skins yesterday, purple and gold today—such are the baubles that embitter human life with resentment."

Nearly 2,000 years later, Russian novelist Leo Tolstoy echoed Lucretius: "Seek among men from beggar to millionaire, one who is contented with his lot, and you will not find one such in a thousand . . . . Today we must buy an overcoat and galoshes, tomorrow, a watch and a chain: the next day we must install ourselves in an apartment with a sofa and a bronze lamp; then we must have carpets and velvet gowns: then a house, horses and carriages, paintings and decorations."

What distinguishes modern consuming habits from those of interest to Lucretius and Tolstoy, some would say, is simply that we are much richer than our ancestors and consequently have more ruinous effects on nature. There is no doubt a great deal of truth in that view, but there is also reason to believe that certain forces in the modern world encourage people to act on their consumption desires as rarely before.

The search for social status in massive and anonymous societies, omnipresent advertising messages, a shopping culture that edges out nonconsuming alternatives, government biases favoring consumption and the spread of the commercial market into most aspects of private life—all these things nurture the acquisitive desires that everyone has. Can we, as individuals and as citizens, act to confront these forces?

A culture of permanence: When Moses came down from Mount Sinai, he could count the rules of ethical behavior on the fingers of his two hands. In the complex global economy of the late twentieth century, in which the simple act of turning on a light sends greenhouse gases up into the atmosphere, the rules for ecologically sustainable living run into the hundreds.

The basic value of a sustainable society, though, the ecological equivalent of the Golden Rule, is simple: Each generation should meet its needs without jeopardizing the prospects of future generations to meet their own needs.

What is lacking is the thorough practical knowledge—at each level of society—of what living by that principle means. For individuals, the decision to live a life of sufficiency—to find their own answer to the question "How much is enough?"—is to begin a highly personal process. The goal is to put consumption in its proper place among the many sources of fulfillment and to find ways of living within the means of the Earth. One great inspiration in this quest is the body of human wisdom passed down over the ages.

Materialism was denounced by all the sages, from Buddha to Muhammad. These religious founders, observed historian Arnold Toynbee, "all said with one voice that if we made material wealth our paramount aim, this would lead to disaster." The Christian Bible echoes most of human wisdom when it asks, "What shall it profit a man if he shall gain the whole world and lose his soul?"

For those people experimenting with voluntary simplicity, the goal is not ascetic self-denial. What they are after is personal fulfillment: they just do not think consuming more is likely to provide it.

Still, shifting emphasis from material to nonmaterial satisfaction is hardly easy: It means trying both to curb personal appetites and to resist the tide of external forces encouraging consumption.

Many people find simpler living offers rewards all its own. They say life can become more deliberate as well as spontaneous, and even gain an unadorned elegance. Others describe the way simpler technologies add unexpected qualities to life.

Realistically, however, voluntary simplicity is unlikely to gain ground rapidly against the onslaught of consumerist values. The call for a simpler life has been perennial through the history of North America, from the Puritans of Massachusetts Bay to the back-to-the-landers of the 1970s. None of these movements ever gained more than a slim minority of adherents.

It would be naive to believe that entire populations will suddenly experience a moral awakening, renouncing greed, envy and avarice. What can be hoped for is a gradual weakening of the consumerist ethos of affluent societies. The challenge before humanity is to bring environmental matters under cultural controls, and the goal of creating a sustainable culture—a culture of permanence—is a task that will occupy several generations.

The ultimate fulfillment: In many ways, we might be happier with less. Maybe Henry David Thoreau had it right when he scribbled in his notebook beside Walden Pond. "A man is rich in proportion to the things he can afford to let alone."

For the luckiest among us, a human lifetime on Earth encompasses perhaps a hundred trips around the Sun. The sense of fulfillment received on that journey—regardless of a person's religious faith—has to do with the timeless virtues of discipline, hope, allegiance to principle and character. Consumption itself has little part in the playful camaraderie that inspires the young, the bonds of love and friendship that nourish adults, the golden memories that sustain the elderly. The very things that make life worth living, that give depth and bounty to human existence, are infinitely sustainable.

Questions

1. How much richer are Americans than at the turn of the century?

2. What is another major cause (other than consumption) of severe environmental problems?

3. What two groups are most destructive to the environment? Give two examples from each of the groups.

4. Name three statistics of the industrialized countries' (1/5 world population) destruction of global resources.

5. Give some evidence that refutes the idea of consumerism as an avenue for happiness.

6. Which world class of people do the least damage to the environment? Give three examples.

7. Why do the industrialized nations keep accelerating their consumerism?

8. What can be done to curb this exponential consumerism?

Table 13.1

Generation and Recovery of Selected Materials in U.S. Municipal Solid Waste, 1960–93 (millions of tons)

Item and Material	1960	1965	1970	1975	1980	1985	1990	1993
Gross waste generated[1]								
Paper and paperboard	29.9	38.0	44.2	43.0	54.7	61.5	73.3	77.8
Glass	6.7	8.7	12.7	13.5	15.0	13.2	13.2	13.7
Metals								
Ferrous	9.9	10.1	12.6	12.3	11.6	10.9	12.3	12.9
Aluminum	0.4	0.5	0.8	1.1	1.8	2.3	2.7	3.0
Other nonferrous	0.2	0.5	0.7	0.9	1.1	1.0	1.2	1.2
Plastics	0.4	1.4	3.1	4.5	7.8	11.6	16.2	19.3
Rubber and leather	2.0	2.6	3.2	3.9	4.3	3.8	4.6	6.2
Textiles	1.7	1.9	2.0	2.2	2.6	2.8	5.6	6.1
Wood	3.0	3.5	4.0	4.4	6.7	8.2	12.3	13.7
Other	0.1	0.3	0.8	1.7	2.9	3.4	3.2	3.3
Materials recovered[2]								
Paper and paperboard	5.4	5.7	7.4	8.2	11.9	13.1	20.9	26.5
Glass	0.1	0.1	0.2	0.4	0.8	1.0	2.6	3.0
Metals								
Ferrous	0.1	0.1	0.1	0.2	0.4	0.4	1.9	3.4
Aluminum	0.0	0.0	0.0	0.1	0.3	0.6	1.0	1.1
Other nonferrous	0.0	0.3	0.3	0.4	0.5	0.5	0.8	0.8
Plastics	0.0	0.0	0.0	0.0	0.0	0.1	0.4	0.7
Rubber and leather	0.3	0.3	0.3	0.2	0.1	0.2	0.2	0.4
Textiles	0.0	0.0	0.0	0.0	0.0	0.0	0.2	0.7
Wood	0.0	0.0	0.0	0.0	0.0	0.0	0.4	1.3
Other[3]	0.0	0.3	0.3	0.4	0.5	0.5	0.8	0.7
Percent of gross discards recovered								
Paper and paperboard	18.1%	15.0%	16.7%	19.1%	21.8%	21.3%	28.6%	34.0%
Glass	1.5	1.1	1.6	3.0	5.3	7.6	19.9	22.0
Metals								
Ferrous	1.0	1.0	0.8	1.6	3.4	3.7	15.4	26.1
Aluminum	0.0	0.0	0.0	9.1	16.7	26.1	38.1	35.4
Other nonferrous	0.0	60.0	42.9	44.4	45.5	50.0	67.7	62.9
Plastics	0.0	0.0	0.0	0.0	0.0	0.9	2.2	3.5
Rubber and leather	15.0	11.5	9.4	5.1	2.3	5.3	4.4	5.9
Textiles	0.0	0.0	0.0	0.0	0.0	0.0	4.3	11.7
Wood	0.0	0.0	0.0	0.0	0.0	0.0	3.2	9.6
Other	0.0	100.0	37.5	23.5	17.2	14.7	23.8	22.1

Note: 1. Generation before materials recovery or combustion. Does not include construction or demolition debris or industrial process wastes. 2. Recovery of postconsumer wastes for recycling and composting; does not include converting fabrication scrap. 3. Recovery of electrolytes in batteries; probably not recycled.

Source: Environmental Protection Agency, *Characterization of Municipal Solid Waste in the United States: 1994 Update* (1995). Permission granted by Andrews & McNeel.

9. Explain briefly the major points in the "Payback of Greed." What did you learn from this article?
10. Define the consuming society. Do you think that this will continue to be a problem in the next few decades? Why? Why not?
11. How has wealth affected ecological issues? Does materialism create ecological concerns? How?
12. What is the ultimate fulfillment?
13. How can the payback of greed be stopped?

Table 13.2
Municipal Solid Waste Generated, Recovered, Combusted, and Discarded, 1960–93

Category	1960	1965	1970	1975	1980	1985	1990	1993
Millions of tons								
Generation	87.8	103.4	121.9	128.1	151.5	164.4	195.7	206.9
Materials recovery	5.9	6.8	8.6	9.9	14.5	16.4	33.4	45.0
Recovery for recycling	5.9	6.8	8.6	9.9	14.5	16.4	29.2	N.A.
Recovery for composting	0.0	0.0	0.0	0.0	0.0	0.0	4.2	N.A.
Discards after recovery[1]	81.9	96.6	113.3	118.2	137.0	148.1	162.3	N.A.
Combustion	27.0	27.0	25.5	18.5	13.7	11.7	31.9	32.9
With energy recovery	0.0	0.2	0.4	0.7	2.7	7.6	29.7	N.A.
Without energy recovery	27.0	26.8	25.1	17.8	11.0	4.1	2.2	N.A.
Discards to landfill or other[2]	54.9	69.6	88.2	99.7	123.3	136.4	130.4	129.0
Percent of total generation								
Generation	100.0%	100.0%	100.0%	100.0%	100.0%	100.0%	100.0%	100.0%
Materials recovery	6.7	6.6	7.1	7.7	9.6	9.9	17.0	21.7
Recovery for recycling	6.7	6.6	7.1	7.7	9.6	9.9	14.9	N.A.
Recovery for composting	0.0	0.0	0.0	0.0	0.0	0.0	2.1	N.A.
Discards after recovery[1]	93.3	93.4	92.9	92.3	90.4	90.1	82.9	N.A.
Combustion	30.8	26.1	20.6	14.4	9.1	7.1	16.3	15.9
With energy recovery	0.0	0.2	0.3	0.5	1.8	4.6	15.2	N.A.
Without energy recovery	30.8	25.9	20.3	13.9	7.3	2.5	1.1	N.A.
Discards to landfill or other[2]	62.5	67.3	72.4	77.8	81.4	82.9	66.6	62.4

[1]Does not include residues from recycling or composting processes. 2. Does not include residues from recycling, composting, or combustion processes.
Source: Environmental Protection Agency, *Characterization of Municipal Solid Waste in the United States: 1994 Update* (1995). Permission granted by Andrews & McNeel.

Table 13.3

Worldwide Growth in Selected Human Activities and Products 1970–1990

	1970	*1990*
Human population	3.6 billion	5.3 billion
Registered automobiles	250 million	560 million
Kilometers driven/year (OECD countries only)		
by passenger cars	2584 billion	4489 billion
by trucks	666 billion	1536 billion
Oil consumption/year	17 billion barrels	24 billion barrels
Natural gas consumption/year	31 trillion cubic feet	70 trillion cubic feet
Coal consumption/year	2.3 billion tons	5.2 billion tons
Electric generating capacity	1.1 billion kilowatts	2.6 billion kilowatts
Electricity generation/year		
by nuclear power plants	79 terawatt-hours	1884 terawatt-hours
Soft drink consumption/year (U.S. only)	150 million barrels	364 million barrels
Beer consumption/year (U.S. only)	125 million barrels	187 million barrels
Aluminum used/year for beer and soft drink containers (U.S. only)	72,700 tonnes	1,251,900 tonnes
Municipal waste generated/year (OECD countries only)	302 million tonnes	420 million tonnes

Reprinted from *Beyond the Limits* copyright © 1992 by Meadows, Meadows and Randers. With permission from Chelsea Green Publishing Co, White River Junction, Vermont.

Questions on the Tables

1. Read and analyze Tables 13.1 and 13.2. Compare in both tables the growth of waste generated historically.

2. Compare in both tables the growth and percentages of materials recovered historically.

3. Draw conclusions from the previous two exercises. What further actions would you recommend to continue this process of material recovery and recycling efforts?

4. What are your observations about discards to landfills? What conclusions would you draw and what action would you recommend with the knowledge that a large percentage of current landfills are closing with few new ones opening?

5. Compare Tables 13.1 and 13.2 to the information in "The Grim Payback of Greed." Does the data in the tables correspond to that in the article? Explain.

14 Young at Risk

Children get 12 percent of their lifetime exposure to dioxin in their first year of life. On a daily basis, the infant is getting about 50 times the exposure an adult gets during what may be a critical developmental stage.

EPA TOXICOLOGIST LINDA BIRNBAUM

During the eight years after an industrial dioxin (a group of chlorine-based chemicals from wastes of papermaking incineration of chlorinated plastics and other processes) pollutant explosion in Seveso, Italy, an unusual scarcity of male babies being born was noticed—twice as many girls were born as were boys—differing from the usual ratios of baby boys slightly outnumbering girls. In addition, excess cancers turned up among Seveso's adults. Clinical pathologist Polo Mocarelli theorized that the dioxin interfered with hormonal balances in developing embryos, either making normal male growth impossible or killing males. Such an effect of dioxin affecting sex ratios is well known in wildlife. For example, crossed bills in double-crested cormorants with the presence of dioxin in the Great Lakes region during the 1980s occurred almost always in females; scientists speculated that the males died before they hatched with this deformity (Monks, 1997, p. 18).

Dioxins are a chemical byproduct of many common industrial processes; most (84%) is released as air pollution from waste incineration. Ironically, 53% of dioxin release comes from medical-waste incineration, due to the high level of plastic garbage accumulated by the medicine industry. To add to this negative picture, the EPA says that the dioxins stored in the environment are 15 to 36 times that of known annual emissions, and the amount found on the ground from unidentified sources in the United States is two to five times that from identified sources (Mazza, 1996, p. 2).

Dioxins have already been established in animal studies as one of the most potent carcinogens; they have also been linked to human illnesses that affect almost every major body system, including diabetes, bronchitis, irregular heartbeat, and nervous-system and thyroid disorders. One of the most comprehensive studies of dioxins by the Environmental Protection Agency in 1994 found that dioxins are more prevalent and dangerous in the population than previously reported. According to the EPA study, the average American has accumulated dioxins amounting to nine parts per trillion in his or her body. Studies have shown that dioxins begin to slow the action of the immune system at about seven parts per trillion, which leads to the conclusion that the dioxin insult to the body is already above the level that has been shown to cause harm (Mazza, 1996, p. 1).

A growing body of scientific literature and observation strongly suggests that the young of most animals are far more susceptible to toxins (such as dioxins, PCBs, and other chemicals) than adults. "Children and animal young eat and breathe more for their body weights than adults do, so they get bigger proportional doses of whatever is out there," explains Herbert Needleman of the University of Pittsburgh, who pioneered studies linking lowered intelligence with early childhood exposures to lead. Significantly, in 1993, the National Academy of Sciences concluded that infants and children are not sufficiently protected by pesticide regulations, since the risks have been calculated for adults. These various toxins can not only cause cancer, but also affect the young's immune systems, brains, and reproductive organs. "It's important for us to realize that if we're seeing abnormalities in wildlife, similar mechanisms may exist in humans. We are just another species in the ecosystem; if other species are harmed, we may be too," says University of Florida zoologist Louis Guillette (Monks, 1997, p. 20).

DEFORMED NEWBORNS

In Minamata, Japan, in the 1950s, before people understood the effects of industrial pollution, mercury discharges from a chemical plant poisoned the seafood that habitated the surrounding area and those who ate it. By the 1960s, evidence of the harm of the mercury began to mount from poisonings for which animals died and people became sick. Fishermen noticed that seabirds were dying; feral cats that ate scavenged fish became stiff legged; cerebral palsy and mental retardation significantly increased in children; and adults were frequently ill. At the time of the Minamata poisonings, science held that the womb was a protected environment capable of filtering out harmful substances. However, in Japan, many women who ate the contaminated fish did not become ill themselves, but they gave birth to children with severe mental retardation and physical deformities. That incident changed scientists' thinking to hypothesize that in actuality, the womb was not protective from toxins, but instead the fetus was sharing the mother's toxic load and in a way was actually protecting the mother, since the fetus was absorbing some of the mercury, thus reducing the mother's exposure to it. The fetus received at least the same doses as did its mother—and the fetus was far more susceptible to toxic pollutants.

Not only are the young exposed to toxic chemicals in the womb, but mothers also unload toxins in their milk to the young. The milk from many species, ranging from beluga whales to dairy cows, have measurable concentrations of chemicals, including dioxins, PCBs, and various pesticides. Children, in their first year of life, get 12 percent of their lifetime exposure to dioxin, and on a daily basis, during their critical developmental months, infants get about 50 times the exposure of an adult. Milk is still recommended for its antibodies, protection, and nourishment, and its benefits clearly outweigh its potential risks, but exposure of the young to toxins is increasing and is of growing concern (Monks, 1997, p. 20).

Another study, which took place from 1987 to 1992 by the EPA, indicated strong evidence that lake trout embryos exposed to dioxin could develop a lethal syndrome called "blue sac." The yolk sac of young healthy trout is a rich golden color. During the first month or so, when the fry (baby fish) rely exclusively on the yolk for nutrients, they become vulnerable to blue sac syndrome, where fluid leaks out of the blood vessels and into the yolk sac, turning it milky and slightly blue. Many conditions can cause blue sac, but this study confirmed that certain dioxins, like chemicals found in the Great Lakes at very small concentrations of just 60 parts per trillion (ppt), will cause 50% of lake trout fry to develop the blue sac disorder—making this fish the most vulnerable known. (This finding is in comparison to the same mortality rate of rainbow trout from the same chemicals at 400 ppt.) (Raloff, 1997, pp. 306–7.)

DAMAGED IMMUNITY

Along the coast of Florida, bottlenose dolphins' firstborn calves die between the ages of three and six. In four generations of dolphins in the past 25 years, only one firstborn is known to have survived. Although the cause of the deaths is not certain, high levels of toxins exist in the fat of marine mammals. Research suggests that mother dolphins unload as much as 80% of their accumulation of pollutants into each of their calves, most likely through nursing. The firstborn calf receives the highest dose through the mother's accumulated toxins. The chemicals found in Florida dolphins' blubber are some of the most deadly and long-lived contaminants of the industrial age, including dioxins and PCBs (although banned, PCBs are still found in insulation of electrical systems). The toxins are so persistent and widely distributed, moving into the food chain from the soil and water, that people and other animals continue to be exposed to them worldwide. "What we are seeing now is the impact of damage that was done over the last few decades," says biologist Randall Wells of the Chicago Zoological Society.

The evidence is that these and other toxic chemicals that are still being manufactured can interfere with the immune system. In 1987, about 700 bottlenose dolphins, half of the migrant Atlantic population, died and washed up along the Atlantic coastline of the United States from New Jersey to Florida. Analysis determined that they were killed by infectious disease and that their bodies contained high levels of PCBs, DDT, and other compounds that suppress the immune system, evidence that scientists think explains the dolphins' susceptibility to disease. If these chemicals are damaging immunity in adult dolphins, they may be doing even more harm to juveniles, because mammalian immune systems aren't fully functional until months or years after birth, according to immunologist Garet Lahvis of the University of Maryland School of Medicine (Monks, 1997, p. 22).

Regarding the Inuits, an Eskimo people in the Canadian Arctic, researchers from Quebec are analyzing the relationship of unusually high rates of infectious disease among the Inuit children and exposure to toxic chemicals. Even though no polluting industries operate near the region, contaminants enter the ecosystem from high-altitude winds and migrant wildlife. The contaminants accumulate in greater density with every link up the food chain, as PCBs, pesticides, and other organochlorines progress from plant and fish to seal, whales, polar bears, and humans. Inuit babies in their first year of life have rates of infectious disease that are 20 times greater than those of babies in southern Quebec, and Inuit women have rates of PCBs in their breast milk that are 7 times greater than those of women from the urban, industrialized south of Quebec. With the Inuits, acute ear infections are common, causing hearing loss for nearly one in four among the Inuit children, and the usual childhood immunizations do not work very well. In another study of the Inuits, conducted in 1993, it was found that babies nursed by mothers with the highest contaminant levels in their milk were afflicted with more acute ear infections than were bottle-fed Inuit babies. The babies with the highest exposures to contaminants also produced few of the helper T cells that play an important role in eliminating bacteria and other harmful invaders. Even though there may be other factors causing these problems, the data suggest that contaminants remain a significant factor. In the Netherlands, researchers have concluded that even infants with mild exposures to contaminants may experience weakened immunity; a correlation was discovered between PCB–dioxin exposure and suppressed levels of disease-fighting white blood cells that would cause immune-system changes (although not extreme) that could persist throughout life or provoke autoimmune diseases.

In nonmammalian species, biologist Keith Grasman of Wright State University has measured immune suppression that is mediated by T cells in young Caspian terns and herring gulls from contaminated colonies around the Great Lakes between 1992 and 1994. Grasman states that the same PCB and organochlorine pollutants that are found in these birds have also been measured in seals, dolphins, humans, and other species with similar T-cell immune problems. Many chicks with suppressed immune systems die before they leave the breeding grounds. Some contaminated terns do grow and migrate south, but most never return to breed (Monks, 1997, p. 23–24).

LOWERED INTELLIGENCE

Since the metabolism of young animals is faster than that of adults, and because young animals do not excrete con-

taminants or store them away in fat in the same ways that adults do, babies and young get continuous exposure to toxins at the time that all of their organs, including their brains, are still developing. In an adult, a blood–brain barrier guards the brain from potentially harmful chemicals in the body, but in a child, that barrier does not become fully developed until six months after birth.

The developing brains of the young of various wildlife species are also far more sensitive to toxic contaminants than are the brains of the adults of the species. As an example, in the late 1980s, great blue heron hatchlings from dioxin-contaminated colonies in Canada developed gross asymmetries and other abnormal changes in brain structures. The susceptibility of human young to such toxic effects was evidenced from an accidental PCB poisoning in Taiwan in 1979. In the Taichung province of Taiwan, more than 2,000 people were exposed to PCB-contaminated cooking oil, resulting in "Yu-Cheng," or oil disease. In the first three years after the accident, many newborns died, and others developed blotch patches of dark skin and fingernail and toenail deformities. As the children grew, they were mentally slower than other kids their age and displayed hyperactive and other behavioral problems. These developmental delays and IQ deficits have not gone away as the children have aged. The exposed mothers continued to deliver babies with problems as late as 1985, even though the accident occurred in 1979. As Walter Rogan of the National Institute of Environmental Health Sciences (NIEHS), who studied the case, explains it, a large portion of the PCBs that these women consumed ended up being stored in their fat, a process that happens with many toxic chemicals. During pregnancy, women mobilize a lot of body fat, and the contaminants in the fat are also passed to their children—even years later, as in the case of Yu-Cheng. The same mechanism also applies to low-level toxic exposures from food, air, and water, for which even small amounts of pollutants—accumulated by women throughout their lives—can have lasting consequences for a child exposed to the pollutants in the womb.

A Michigan study found persistent intellectual deficits in children exposed before birth to much lower doses of PCBs than those in the case of Yu-Cheng. In 1981, two Wayne State University psychologists, Sandra and Joseph Jacobson, measured PCB levels in mothers and newborn infants. Since consumption of fatty fish from contaminated water is a major source of PCB exposure, the Jacobsons selected mothers for their study who had eaten Lake Michigan salmon or lake trout during the years before their children were born. The infants with the highest exposures

Dioxin's Effect on Fish Raises Questions of Effects on Higher Animals

Pollutants are considered dioxinlike if they connect to the Ah receptor in cells (a protein that reacts to these pollutants and turns genes on or off). The receptor was identified in fish in 1988 after being recognized in mammals in 1986. Since then, researchers have been examining other lower species to see how far down the evolutionary ladder this receptor exists and the accompanying vulnerability to dioxin with it. Scientists at Woods Hole Oceanographic Institution have been examining various types of animals for this Ah receptor and have so far found sharks to be the most primitive animal with the Ah receptor. (Sea lampreys have something that resembles the receptor, but this substance does not appear to bind to dioxinlike compounds.)

Scientists have also been using lower animals as a useful model of the common effects of dioxins on all animals. So far, it has been found from a joint study between Cornell University and the University of Wisconsin-Madison that dioxinlike chemicals target the cardiovascular system of lower animals as they do in mammals. Using zebra fish, which have transparent embryos, scientists found that the

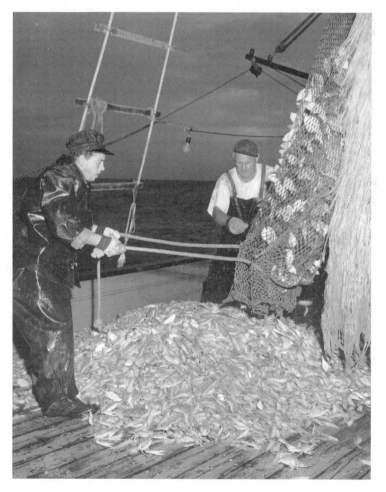

What can be the plan for future fisheries? Photo credit: Florida State News Bureau.

Dioxin's Effect on Fish Raises Questions of Effects on Higher Animals, *continued*

pollutants slow blood flow feeding the head and gills and also slow the heart's rate. Richard Peterson, of the University of Wisconsin-Madison, says that there appears to be a pruning of these blood vessels, which may account for the head malformations that often accompany blue sac syndrome. Dioxinlike compounds also appear to weaken blood vessels once they form, which may explain why blood vessels become leaky in blue sac.

The dioxin chemicals trigger early death in blood vessel cells caused by oxidant damage. This effect may trace to the ability of dioxins to turn on genes that increase the production of detoxifying enzymes which start a process that releases oxidative compounds which do not respond to normal controls. The overproduction of oxidants can damage the vessels. Because there is no reason to suspect that this effect occurs only in fish, scientists are also searching for it in birds, reptiles, and mammals—including humans.

Reprinted with permission from *Science News,* the weekly newsmagazine of science, copyright © 1996, 1997 by Science Service. Excerpted from Raloff, J. (1997, May 17). Those old dioxin blues. *Science News,* Vol. 151, p. 307.

grew more slowly than other babies and at 4 years old had poorer short-term memory. By the time they were 11 years old, the 30 most exposed children had average IQs six points lower than those of the least exposed group. Twenty-three percent of the high-exposure kids were two years behind in reading, while 10% of the least exposed group were two years behind. The Jacobsons also found that fish-free diets did not guarantee lower PCB levels, since there were some very highly exposed children from mothers who did not eat the fish. The exposure might have come from other fatty foods, such as butter, cheese, beef or pork, but there is no way of knowing the source, since exposure to toxins is a societal problem. As Jacobson said, "We are all walking around with PCBs in us." (Monks, 1997, p. 24)

SEXUAL IMPAIRMENT

Sexual development in the growing fetus may be as sensitive to toxic effects as the brain is. When certain chemicals bind to hormone receptors, they can interfere with the work of natural hormones in the development of male or female organs, resulting in any number of reproductive disorders. These chemicals, known as endocrine disrupters, include PCBs, dioxins, and many pesticides. The growing body of evidence suggests reason for concern about the effects of endocrine-disrupting chemicals found in the environment. Among the Yu-Cheng children of Taiwan, the boys with high PCB exposures had smaller than average penises. University of Florida biologists found the same phenomenon in alligators born in a lake poisoned by

pesticides. In the highly polluted St. Lawrence River, biologists found a male beluga whale with a fully developed set of female organs in addition to the whale's male apparatus. This male carried a very high load of endocrine-disrupting contaminants in its blubber.

In South Florida, 13 of the 19 male panthers that still survive have undescended testicles. Because such males produce abnormal sperm and have low sperm counts, biologists are worried about the potential for saving the endangered animals from extinction. It is suspected that environmental endocrine-disrupting chemicals may be contributing to these cats' sexual abnormalities. The panthers are exposed to heavy doses of pesticides and toxic metals such as methyl mercury from their diet of raccoons, which ingest the pollutants in fish. It is possible that most of the problems of the Florida panther could be attributed to pesticides. If this assertion is true, then the introduction of female Texas cougars to improve the panthers' genetic diversity may not accomplish much. If all of the panthers' habitat is contaminated, the animal may not be able to be saved.

According to a 1996 study by U.S. and European scientists, data from several countries show substantial increases since the 1950s in the number of baby boys born with undescended testicles and other sexual abnormalities. One London study found that 5.2% of low-birthweight boys born in the 1980s had undescended testicles, as compared with 1.74% from the 1950s. Testicular cancers nearly doubled among older teenagers in the United States between 1973 and 1992.

Many of the health effects documented in young wildlife from toxic contamination may not apply to human children, but wildlife can give indicators as to where to look for problems and answers. Deformed frogs in Minnesota may yield clues about the reasons for high rates of birth defects among the region's farm children. Links are being established everywhere between environmental toxic contaminants and the health of young wildlife and children. The warnings found in wildlife may help us to do something about environmental toxicities before we permanently contaminate and deform the animal world of which we are a representative part. (Monks, 1997, p. 25)

References

Mazza, P. (1996, February 21). "Love Canal is everywhere: The pervasive threat of dioxin." Available: http://www.tnews.com/test/dioxin.html.

Monks, V. (1997, June–July). Children at risk. *National Wildlife,* Vol. 35, No. 4, pp. 18–27.

Raloff, J. (1997, May 17). Those old dioxin blues. *Science News.* Vol. 151, pp. 306–307.

Questions

1. Why are the young of most animals more susceptible to toxins than adults?
2. Why do you think infants and children are not sufficiently protected by pesticide regulations? How do you think we can use pesticide regulations to better protect infants and children? Explain some specific ideas.
3. What does the case study in Minamata, Japan, teach us about the effects of toxic pollution on fetuses? How are infants doubly exposed to pollutants?
4. What does the study regarding blue sac syndrome in lake trout embryos teach us about dioxins?
5. Give three examples of damaged immunity caused by dioxin and PCB contamination.
6. Give two examples of lowered intelligence caused by toxic pollution. Why are the young particularly susceptible to toxins affecting intelligence? Do you think that the examples in the article can support the claim that such toxins affect intelligence in humans? Explain.
7. Give two examples of sexual impairment caused by toxic pollution. Do you think that the examples in the article can support the claim that such toxins affect sexual impairment in animals and humans? Explain.
8. What is the reason that animals should be so closely watched for their reactions to chemical toxins? Why is the issue of the young such a special case?
9. How can evidence of the effects of chemical toxins, especially on the young, be made more apparent to determine clearer relationships and, hence, approaches to prevention? Outline appropriate studies that could be carried out to this end.
10. How can such chemical toxic pollution be prevented? What worldwide plan would realistically prevent such pollution and casual dumping?

Table 14.1
The 50 Worst Superfund Waste Sites, 1994

State	Site	City/County	Score (Rank)	When Listed
Arkansas	Vertac, Inc.	Jacksonville	65.46 (32)	Oct. 1981
California	McCormick & Baxter Creosoting Co.	Stockton	74.86 (5)	Feb. 1992
California	Stoker Company	Imperial	65.51 (30)	July 1991
California	Riverbank Army Ammunition Plant	Riverbank	63.94 (36)	June 1988
Colorado	Rocky Flats Plant (USDOE)	Golden	64.32 (35)	Oct. 1984
Delaware	Tybouts Corner Landfill[1]	New Castle County	73.67 (6)	Oct. 1981
Delaware	Army Creek Landfill	New Castle County	69.92 (18)	Oct. 1981
Florida	Stauffer Chemical Co.	Tarpon Springs	70.71 (12)	Feb. 1992
Florida	Stauffer Chemical Co.	Tampa	63.62 (39)	Feb. 1992
Hawaii	Pearl Harbor Naval Complex	Pearl Harbor	70.82 (11)	July 1991
Idaho	Triumph Mine Tailings Piles	Triumph	90.33 (1)	May 1993
Indiana	U.S. Smelter & Lead Refinery Inc.	East Chicago	70.71 (12)	Feb. 1992
Iowa	Mason City Coal Gasification Plant	Mason City	69.33 (20)	Jan. 1994

Continued

Table 14.1
The 50 Worst Superfund Waste Sites, 1994, *continued*

State	Site	City/County	Score (Rank)	When Listed
Maine	Portsmouth Naval Shipyard	Kittery	67.71 (24)	June 1993
Massachusetts	Industri-Plex	Woburn	72.42 (9)	Oct. 1981
Massachusetts	Nyanza Chemical Waste Dump	Ashland	69.22 (21)	Oct. 1981
Massachusetts	Baird & McGuire	Holbrook	66.35 (27)	Dec. 1982
Michigan	Berlin & Farro	Swartz Creek	66.74 (26)	July 1982
Michigan	Liquid Disposal, Inc.	Utica	63.28 (42)	July 1982
Minnesota	FMC Corp. (Fridley Plant)	Fridley	65.50 (31)	July 1982
Missouri	Big River Tailings/St. Joe Minerals	Desloge	84.91 (3)	Feb. 1992
Montana	Silver Bow Creek/Butte Area	Silver Bow/Deer Lodge	63.76 (37)	Dec. 1982
Montana	East Helena Site	East Helena	61.65 (49)	Sept. 1983
New Hampshire	Somersworth Sanitary Landfill	Somersworth	65.56 (29)	Dec. 1982
New Hampshire	Keefe Environmental Services	Epping	65.19 (34)	Oct. 1981
New Hampshire	Sylvester[1]	Nashua	63.28 (42)	Oct. 1981
New Jersey	Lipari Landfill	Pitman	75.60 (4)	Oct. 1981
New Jersey	Helen Kramer Landfill	Mantua Township	72.66 (8)	July 1982
New Jersey	Price Landfill[1]	Pleasantville	71.60 (10)	Oct. 1981
New Jersey	CPS/Madison Industries	Old Bridge Township	69.73 (19)	Dec. 1982
New Jersey	GEMS Landfill	Gloucester Township	68.53 (23)	July 1982
New Jersey	Lone Pine Landfill	Freehold Township	66.33 (28)	Oct. 1981
New York	Pollution Abatement Services[1]	Oswego	70.80 (12)	Oct. 1981
North Carolina	General Electric Co.—Shepherd Farm	East Flat Rock	70.71 (12)	Feb. 1992
Ohio	Arcanum Iron & Metal	Darke County	62.26 (47)	Dec. 1982
Pennsylvania	Bruin Lagoon	Bruin Borough	73.11 (7)	Oct. 1981
Pennsylvania	East Tenth Street	Marcus Hook	67.68 (25)	Jan. 1994
Pennsylvania	Tysons Dump	Upper Merion Township	63.10 (44)	Sept. 1983
Pennsylvania	McAdoo Associates[1]	McAdoo Borough	63.03 (45)	Oct. 1981
South Dakota	Whitewood Creek[1]	Whitewood	63.76 (37)	Oct. 1981
Texas	French, Ltd.	Crosby	63.33 (40)	Oct. 1981
Texas	Motco, Inc.[1]	La Marque	62.66 (46)	Oct. 1981
Texas	Sikes Disposal Pits	Crosby	61.62 (50)	Oct. 1981
Utah	Murray Smelter	Murray City	86.60 (2)	Jan. 1994
Utah	Kennecott (South Zone)	Copperton	70.71 (12)	Jan. 1994
Utah	Wasatch Chemical Co. (Lot 6)	Salt Lake City	63.31 (41)	Jan. 1987
Utah	Petrochem Recycling/Ekotek Plant	Salt Lake City	62.18 (48)	July 1991
Washington	Pacific Sound Resources	Seattle	70.71 (12)	May 1993
Washington	Hanford 200-Area (USDOE)	Benton County	69.05 (22)	June 1988
Washington	Hanford 300-Area (USDOE)	Benton County	65.23 (33)	June 1988

1. Site is also its state's top priority.
Source: Environmental Protection Agency, *National Priorities List* (February 1994). Permission granted by Andrews & McNeel.

Table 14.2
Superfund Hazardous Waste Sites, Selected Years, 1981–95

Year	Number of Sites	Year	Number of Sites
1981	115[1]	1989	981
1982	418[1]	1990	1,187
1983	406	1992	1,183
1984	538	1993	1,202
1986	703	1994	1,287
1987	802	1995	1,296

[1]Proposed sites only. Final sites not calculated until release of first National Priorities list in 1983.
Source: Environmental Protection Agency, *National Priorities List. Supplementary Materials* (February 1995).

Table 14.3
States With Most National Priority List Hazardous Waste Sites, 1995

State	Nonfederal	Federal	Total
New Jersey	101	6	107
Pennsylvania	96	6	102
California	73	23	96
New York	78	4	82
Michigan	77	1	78
Florida	54	5	59
Washington	35	20	55
Minnesota	38	3	41
Wisconsin	40	0	40
Ohio	33	5	38
Illinois	33	4	37

Source: Environmental Protection Agency. *National Priorities List. Supplementary Materials* (February 1995).

Table 14.4
Common Hazardous Chemicals Requiring National Response Center Notification (partial list)

Substance	Remarks	Amount to be Reported if Released
Acetic acid	Vinegar is generally 2% acetic acid, but acetic acid is used in many manufacturing processes. Toxic as vapor at 10 parts per million in air.	5.000 lbs. (2,270 kg)
Acetone	Toxic chemical (1,000 parts per million in air) used in large amounts as solvent for resins and fats.	5,000 lbs. (2,270 kg)
Aluminum sulfate	Used sometimes in dyeing or in foam fire extinguishers	1,000 lbs. (454 kg)
Ammonia	Use as fertilizer does not need to be reported; however it is toxic and extremely hazardous; emergency planning required if 500 lbs. possessed.	100 lbs. (45.4 kg)
Benzene	Used in drugs, dyes, explosives, plastics, detergents, and paint remover; can cause cancer; toxic.	10 lbs. (4.54 kg)
Chlorine	Widely used to disinfect water, the gas is toxic at concentration of one part per million in air extremely hazardous; requires emergency planning if 100 lbs. is possessed.	10 lbs. (4.54 kg)
Cumene	Additive for high-octane fuels; toxic to skin at 50 parts per million in air.	5,000 lbs. (2,270 kg)
Cyclohexane	Petroleum derivative.	1,000 lbs. (454 kg)
Ethylbenzene	Toxic at 100 parts per million in air.	1,000 lbs. (454 kg)
Ethylene dichloride	Additive to gasoline that combines with lead to make "Ethyl" gasoline; also used in making plastics.	100 lbs. (45.4 kg)

Table 14.4
Common Hazardous Chemicals Requiring National Response Center Notification (partial list), *continued*

Substance	Remarks	Amount to be Reported if Released
Ethylene oxide	Widely used in making plastics; toxic at 50 parts per million in air; extremely hazardous; requires emergency planning if 1,000 lbs. possessed.	1–10 lbs. (0.454 kg–4.54 kg)
Formaldehyde	Used in wood substitutes and plastics; toxic and may cause cancer; extremely hazardous; requires emergency planning if 500 lbs. possessed.	100 lbs. (45.4 kg)
Hydrochloric acid	Used in petroleum, manufacturing, and metals industries; toxic; as the gas hydrogen chloride, it is extremely hazardous and requires emergency planning if 500 lbs. possessed.	5,000 lbs. (2,270 kg)
Methanol	Commonly called wood alcohol; used as antifreeze, solvent, and starting material for other compounds; toxic.	5,000 lbs. (2,270 kg)
Nitric acid	Used in preparing fertilizers and explosives; toxic and extremely hazardous; requires emergency planning if 1,000 lbs. possessed.	1,000 lbs. (454 kg)
Phenol	Used in making plastics; vapor is toxic to skin at 5 parts per million in air; extremely hazardous; requires emergency planning if 500 pounds possessed and further planning if 10,000 pounds possessed.	1,000 lbs. (454 kg)
Phosphoric acid	Used as flavoring agent, in pharmaceuticals, and in manufacturing fertilizers; toxic.	5,000 lbs. (2,270 kg)
Sodium hydroxide	Commonly known as lye or as caustic soda; toxic.	1,000 lbs. (454 kg)
Styrene	Used in manufacture of styrene plastics and artificial rubber; toxic.	1,000 lbs. (454 kg)
Sulfuric acid	Most common chemical used in U.S; toxic and extremely hazardous; emergency planning required if 1,000 lbs. possessed.	1,000 lbs. (454 kg)
Toluene	Used in making explosives, drugs, and dyes; toxic.	1,000 lbs. (454 kg)
Vinyl chloride	Used to make plastics and aerosols; causes cancer; toxic.	1 lb. (0.454 kg)
Xylene	Used to make other compounds; toxic.	1,000 lbs. (454 kg)

Source: Environmental Protection Agency, *Title 3 List of Lists* (Jan. 1990). Permission granted by Andrews & McNeel.

Questions About the Tables

1. Examine Tables 14.1–14.3. Draw numeric and locale conclusions. What do you conclude from this data on hazardous waste sites?
2. Read the list of chemicals in Table 14.4. How often do you use any of these chemicals? How do you dispose of them? Were you aware of their classification as hazardous before examining Table 14.4?
3. Are you aware of the health hazards of the chemicals listed in Table 14.4? Please list the health hazards of which you are aware for any of the chemicals mentioned. Share this knowledge in discussion.
4. Discuss approaches to chemical dumping and chemical disposal.
5. Research superfund hazardous waste site dumps. What progress is being made? How much money is being spent?
6. How should we dispose of hazardous wastes? Discuss some plausible methods.

Fisheries: Exploiting the Ocean— What Will Be Left?

15

Developing countries hire private companies to conduct surveillance and enforcement of new fisheries laws. These companies are zealous: One has proposed to watch over fisheries from a blimp, which could descend to launch a patrol boat.

MICHAEL PARFIT

Technology has applied its increasing power to the fish of the ocean . . . and there is now trouble at sea. "There are too many fishermen and not enough fish" (Parfit, p. 9). Fifty years of rapidly improving fishing technology has created an immensely powerful industrial fleet—37,000 freezer trawlers that catch and process a ton or more of fish an hour, manned by about a million people worldwide. This fleet contrasts with small-boat fishermen, who probably number about 12 million, but who catch only about half the world's fish.

The problem is that fish stocks are being damaged by pollution, by destruction of wetlands that serve as nurseries and provide food, by the waste of unprofitable fish (called "bycatch"), and, most of all, by overfishing. These practices have caused the collapse of some fish stocks and the fishing of many important groups of fish beyond sustainable capacity. At this point, the annual catch from the sea has peaked at about 78 million metric tons and seems somewhat stable, but the cost of this fishing intensity will be felt with future shortages of certain types of fish and in future sustainable yields. Although technology has helped quadruple the world's catch of seafood since 1950, a nearly empty basket is typical for what a lone fisherman has to show for hours of work—a complaint heard around the world. Morocco and most small coastal or island countries are extremely worried about overharvesting and want to reduce fish quotas taken in their waters by foreign fleets. One Moroccan official asserts, "People using traditional techniques will not survive. The waters are being emptied by industrial fishing." One marine scientist says, "We've come to our reckoning, the next ten years are going to be

very painful, full of upheaval for everyone connected to the sea" (Parfit, 1995, pp. 2–11).

According to the U.N. Food and Agriculture Organization (FAO), almost two thirds of the world's 200 commercially important distinct fish populations are either exploited or fished to the edge. The FAO states that there is an urgent need for the development of effective measures to reduce and control fishing capacity and effort. The visual images of overfishing are very apparent when

- trawlers line up abreast to sweep the life from the sea with nets so large that each could drag up a dozen jumbo jets;
- vessels called "long-liners" trail out thousands of baited hooks on lines stretching 80 miles across the ocean; and
- Japan's squid fleet is so enormous that its lights to draw squid to its nets in the north Pacific can be seen by orbiting astronauts.

Within two decades, giant vessels have combined the latest technology, including satellite navigation, spotter planes, fish-scanning sonar, and lightweight nets, to capture the "limitless" bounty of the seas into finite resources. Big trawling vessels can pull up at least 20,000 pounds of fish in 20 minutes (Hanley, 1997, pp. 1–2).

The problem isn't easily resolvable, and it could grow into a catastrophe. Fishing is a 70-billion-dollar-a-year industry with strong roots in national pride, profits, and age-old traditions of freedom. As governments struggle to solve the problems at sea, they inevitably create laws that challenge traditional freedoms. Throughout the world seas, fishing vessels are attacked in competitive territorial battles and ownership of waters. Such examples as the following are common:

- In Patagonia, an Argentinian gunboat chases and fires on a vessel from Taiwan; the crew is rescued, but the trawler sinks.

- In the North Atlantic, the Stern trawler REX is arrested west of Scotland for trespassing in British waters. REX is officially multinational to evade fishing laws and is owned by Icelanders, registered in Cyprus, and crewed by fishermen from the Faroe Islands.

- In the South Atlantic, a patrol boat from the Falkland Islands chases a Taiwanese squid boat 4,364 nautical miles from home waters, all the way past South Africa. The boat gets away.

There has been an increasing aggressiveness of the law on the free oceans, which began after World War II, such that by the 1970s, most nations pushed their territorial control from 12 to 200 nautical miles offshore in order to grab valuable fishing grounds, thereby pushing the boats of other nations (the "distant-water fleets") far out to sea. Now, 200 nautical miles is not enough. Many fish roam from national to international waters, where they are taken by intense fishing methods outside of any nation's control. Therefore, nations whose roaming salmon, cod, or pollock are caught before they get home fight with those nations that intercept them. Furthermore, more and more countries are taking the fight to sea. In Canada, the Great Banks of Newfoundland were in danger of fishing collapse, necessitating that Canada shut down its own fishery there, putting about 40,000 people out of work. However, distant-water trawlers from Spain, Portugal, and other nations continued to fish just outside the 200-mile limit, making Canada very angry and distrustful. Typical strong offensive responses from Canada or other nations in this situation included strategies of using spy planes to record any suspicious ship's activities, shooting at poachers, implementing blockades, employing patrol boats, and making arrests.

Such fishing-rights arguments have made the oceans a sort of oceanic Wild West, with one state acting as the self-appointed lawmaker, as well as sheriff and judge. In actuality, except for the past few decades, most of the sea was indeed like the Old West: free, wild, unregulated, and a place of opportunity for any brave enough to venture forth.

But declining populations of fish and feuding fishermen, along with the power of technology, are proving that even the limits of the grandest piece of the planet—our seas—have been reached (Parfit, 1995, pp. 10–20).

HIGH-TECH FISHING VESSELS AND METHODS

The number of fishing vessels has doubled since 1970 to more than a million. Not only has the number doubled, but also the types of fishing vessels used have radically changed to types of superefficient floating ship factories where all fish from the ship's enormous fishing path is processed onboard and where all products are used—nothing is wasted. A typical new factory ship is 376 feet long and both operates as a mothership for fleets of smaller vessels and catches its own fish, processing and packaging fish at sea as it catches them. The typical "technological kit" of such ships includes a variety of gigantic nets (some large enough to swallow the Statue of Liberty), highly powerful lights that act as bait, literally miles of fishing lines that dangle lures or baited hooks, sonar arrays and computers to locate and track the fish, and sensors on the net. The fish are not so much strained from the sea by the nets, but are instead herded by the net's cables and winchlike leading edges. A typical factory ship is capable of processing more than 600 metric tons of pollock a day into surimi, the protein paste used in imitation seafood products. All processing occurs onboard, including the tasks of processing into various products, quick freezing, and packaging. To keep morale high among the 125 crew members of such ships, living decks on the ships are separated from work decks and typically can include well-decorated cafeterias, gymnasiums, bathrooms with Japanese soaking tubs, and television in most of the crew's cabins (Parfit, 1995, pp. 16–17).

THE DIMINISHING CATCH

Nearly 40% of the world's oceans have been locked up by territorial claims and exclusive fishing zones. The 200-nautical-mile coastal boundaries have not stopped the overexploitation of species. Rich nations buy into poor countries' waters. High-tech fleets grab fish migrating outside protected coastal zones. And the fish just keep getting scarcer and smaller. After peaking in 1989, and despite a temporary rise in the Pacific ocean catch, the tonnage of sea-food harvested worldwide has reached a foreboding plateau. Meanwhile, demand continues to grow, with an annual per-capita consumption of 66.6 kilograms (147

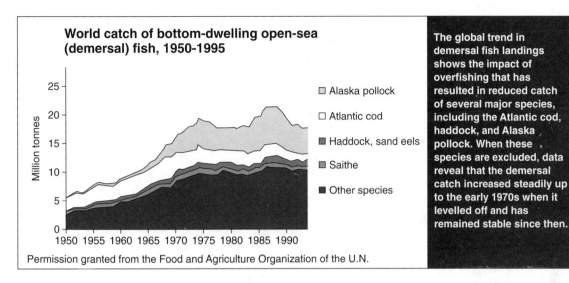

Figure 15.1
World catch of bottom-dwelling open-sea (demersal) fish, 1950–1995.
Source: Food and Agriculture Organizations of the United Nations.

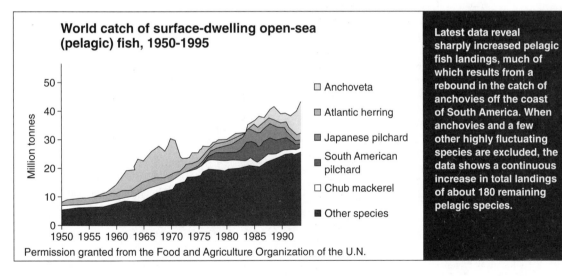

Figure 15.2
World catch of surface-dwelling open-sea (pelagic) fish, 1950–1995.
Source: Food and Agriculture Organizations of the United Nations.

World total fish production in marine waters, 1950-1993
After increasing steadily for more than 30 years, the world catch of ocean fish dropped sharply in 1990 and now appears to have peaked at a level between 85 and 90 million tons per year. FAO estimates that catches of 70 percent of marine species have reached or exceeded sustainable levels.

Source: Food & Agriculture Organization of the U.N.

Figure 15.3
Total fish production, 1950–1993.
Source: Food and Agriculture Organizations of the United Nations.

pounds). Japan has the world's biggest appetite; China is gaining rapidly in bulk catches. (See the accompanying graphs.) Some of the species being caught include the following:

Salmon: Hydropower, pollution, and logging have diminished salmon-spawning streams worldwide. The North Pacific waters remain the healthiest waters for salmon.

Shrimp: About one quarter of all shrimp consumed are raised in man-made ponds. Viruses recently devastated farmed stocks in China, Ecuador, and Texas.

Herring, sardines, anchovies: These small open-ocean fish are used mainly for industrial purposes, such as the production of fish meal and fertilizer (although they remain a delicacy in many countries). Herring has been heavily fished in both the Atlantic and Pacific. Anchovies are caught mainly off the Pacific coast of South America, where populations fluctuate dramatically, depending on the El Niño phenomenon.

Cod, pollock, haddock: These fish are the mainstays of human consumption and have been heavily exploited. The cod fishery in the northwest Atlantic

recently collapsed, and in Newfoundland, it completely disappeared. Pollock is still plentiful, and much of it is processed into fish sticks and fast food. Cod, haddock, and flounder stocks have collapsed in New England.

Jacks, sauries, capelins: Used both for eating and industrial purposes, these fish are prey for larger, more favored fish such as cod or tuna.

Redfish, seabreams, roughies. When more easily accessible fish stocks run out, fishermen turn to alternative species. Redfish, a restaurant basic, have been fished commercially since the 1930s. Orange roughy fishing began only in the 1970s. The danger is that little is known about the biology of these alternative food fishes. Some scientists think that orange roughies may live longer than humans. If this is true, then orange roughies will need ample time to replenish from intense fishing.

Tuna, billfish: These fish are the glamour fish of the industry, where they command luxury prices. A two-bite portion of sushi made from prime meat from the bluefin tuna can cost $75 in Japan. Large fish are hunted with harpoons and spotter planes (Parfit, 1995, pp. 12–13).

THE SEAS . . . NOW AND THEN . . .

When my father began diving in the Mediterranean Sea in the early forties, the water was clean. Great beds of sea-grass and algae thrived there, along with dense schools of fish and rich invertebrate fauna. Gorgonians were abundant, and so were huge groupers and spiny lobsters. It was the rich sea-floor community the world was seeing in the early Cousteau films.

Since those days, the Mediterranean coast has become densely populated. Industries, hotels, and homes line the coast. Sewage and other wastes stream into the sea. Sadly, the same waters where the first Aqua-lung divers discovered the sea's beauty and diversity are today biologically impoverished. And this scene—where urban development meets the water—is spreading rapidly around the world today.

JEAN-MICHEL COUSTEAU (1990)

The very survival of the human species depends upon the maintenance of an ocean clean and alive, spreading all around the world. The ocean is our planet's life belt.—Marine Explorer Jacques-Yves Cousteau (1980)

Our seas have changed, and the unlimited bounty of the sea is endangered. This doesn't mean that the sea is ruined, however. It is more like a forest than a mine in that it will keep producing as long as we do not plunder it without restraint, and that is just what we do not know how to do yet. The Dust Bowl did not kill American agriculture; it just changed it into a big industry—highly regulated and tidy. Fishing may go the same route. Fish farming has produced the only productive growth in recent years and will continue to grow, as will the regulation of the sea itself. We will still have fish, but not the fish or traditions or industries that we have known.

SOME FACTS

- The world fishing fleet has doubled in size over the past two decades and now includes 37,000 "industrial" vessels of more than 100 tons. U.S. and other government subsidies encouraged this growth.

- The ocean catch has exploded from 18 million tons in 1950 to 90 millions tons in recent years. Fish stocks began to decline in the 1990s, and production could no longer increase at the same rates. If the same fishing practices continue, the average marine catch could decline by 10 million tons a year.

- Impact on seafood prices has been moderate due to aquaculture of new fish, shrimp, and scallop farms in China, Thailand, and elsewhere.

- Fishing jobs directly or indirectly employ about 200 million people in the world. There are an estimated 3 million fishing vessels made up of mostly small vessels in developing countries. The 3 million vessels include the supertrawlers of 37,000 ships of more than 100 tons. These ships caught 90.7 million tons of marine and inland fish in 1995. Aquaculture produced 21.3 million tons in 1995 (Hanley, 1997, pp. 1–2).

THE MAGNUSON FISHERY CONSERVATION AND MANAGEMENT ACT

The enactment of the Magnuson Fishery Conservation and Management Act (MFCMA) in 1976 extended fishery jurisdiction to 200 nautical miles offshore and established the current federal fishery management structure. This act, however, did little to preserve fisheries—its intended objective. By banishing foreign competition from U.S. coastal waters and offering generous subsidies to U.S. fishers, it has encouraged thousands of new U.S. boats and, in most cases, imposed no restrictions on the amount of fish an individual fisher could take. As a result of this "open access" policy, U.S. fisheries have become packed with competing boats in an intense, dangerous race for any fish left in the water. In 1992, eight lives were lost in a frenzied race for halibut in which the entire season was compressed into a 48-hour time period. MFCMA also intensifies problems by letting fishery managers use economic and social factors to modify scientists' estimates of levels for sustainable catches. Then, because of monetary and social pressure, the managers reset the allowable catch to be high.

The Environmental Defense Fund would like Congress to reauthorize a Magnuson Act that defines and prohibits overfishing and requires the allowable catch to be ecologically sustainable rather than based on short-term economic demands. One suggested scheme would assign each fisher a tradable share of the total allowable catch. Such shares, called Individual Transferable Quotas (ITQs), could be used or sold, giving fishers an equitable base and vested interest in the fishery's future. Through market forces, ITQs would reduce fishing by ending the race for fish, since as fish populations again increase, ITQs would increase in value, giving fishers a strong incentive to help fish populations recover (EDF is advocating reforms to reduce overfishing, 1994, pp. 1–2).

The MFCMA was reauthorized and signed by President Clinton on October 11, 1996. The reauthorization focuses more on the issues of habitat degradation, overfishing, bycatch (discards and other fish), and funding, and for many people, it did not strengthen sustainable yield approaches enough. Provisions for ITQs remain controversial. The strength, effects, and direction of the MFCMA reauthorization will be a central ecological issue that affects us all and that we should watch carefully (Buck, 1996).

References

Buck, E. H. (1996, December 4) 95036: Magnuson Fishery Conservation and Management Act reauthorized. *Congressional Research Service Issue Brief,* pp. 1–14. Available: http://www.cnie.org/nle/mar-3.html.

EDF is advocating reforms to reduce overfishing. (1994, January). *EDF Letter.* Vol. XXV, No. 1, pp. 1–2. Available: http://www.edf.org/pubs/EDF-Letter/1994/Jan/c_overfish.html.

Hanley, C. J. (1997, July 21). Fishermen endanger "limitless' seas". *Chicago Tribune* pp. 1–2.

New bill seeks to reverse crashes of fish populations. (1994, July). *EDF Letter.* Vol. XXV, No. 4, pp. 1,3.

Parfit, M. (1995, November). Diminishing returns, exploiting the ocean's bounty. *National Geographic.* Vol. 188, No. 5, pp. 2–37.

Questions

1. What has caused the depletion of worldwide fish stocks?

2. In what way has the increase of technology contributed to the depletion of the world's fish stocks?

3. Explain why nations are using warlike tactics to protect their national fishing waters?

4. Why are the oceans of the past compared to the Wild West? What has changed?

5. What is the role of floating fish factories in the depletion of fish stocks? What do you think can be a sustainable approach for the future with the existence and use of these fish factory trawlers?

6. Devise a plan for future world fisheries that accounts for sustainable yields, the use of high technology, and national fishing rights. Contrast that plan with current practices.

7. Explain the cause and effect of the 200-mile offshore coastal waters fishing jurisdiction.

8. What is the future of the small independent fisherman? Explain.

9. What was the result of the Magnuson Fishery Conservation and Management Act in 1976 on world fisheries? Explain both the positive and negative results.

10. How could the Magnuson Act be rewritten to deal with some of the problems of world fisheries? Research the new reauthorization of the 1996 Magnuson Act. What are its strengths and weaknesses?

11. Explain the concept of Individual Transferable Quotas (ITQs).

12. Consult Tables 15.1 and 15.2 for fishing data patterns for discussion.

13. Research open sea and fishery areas. In what ocean is the largest catch found?

14. Refer to Figure 15.1, 15.2, and 15.3. Which fish is the most caught dermesal fish in the world catch? Which fish is the most caught pelagic fish in the world catch?

15. Refer to Figure 15.3. Why do you think that total fish production has peaked? Which species do you think are fished the most? Which species of fish do you feel we still have abundant supplies of?

Table 15.1

Dying Seas

Sea Threat	Baltic	Bering	Black	Caspian	Mediter-ranean	South China	Yellow
Over-fishing	H	H	H	H	H	H	H
Eutrophication	M	N	M	L	L	M	M
Dams	L	N	H	H	M-H	M	M
Organo-Chlorines	H	M	M	L	M	M	M
Heavy Metals	M	L	H	M	M-H	H	H
Oil Drilling	L	L	H	H	M	H	H
Population (millions)	80	1.4	165	45	360	517	250
Area (Thousands of sq. km)	370	420	2,292	371	2,500	3,685	404

Key: H = High, M = Medium, L = Low, N = Negligible
Source: Dying Seas, Worldwatch, January/February 1995. Reprinted with permission from Worldwatch Institute.

Table 15.2

World Commercial Catch of Fish, Crustaceans, and Mollusks,[1] by Country, 1988–93
(in thousands of metric tons; liver weight)

Country	1988	1989	1990	1991	1992	1993
China	10,358	11,220	12,095	13,135	15,007	17,568
Peru	6,641	6,854	6,875	6,949	6,871	8,451
Japan	11,966	11,173	10,354	9,301	8,502	8,128
Chile	5,209	6,454	5,195	6,003	6,502	6,038
United States[2,3]	5,956	5,775	5,868	5,486	5,588	5,939
Russia	—	—	—	7,047	5,611	4,461
India	3,125	3,640	3,794	4,044	4,232	4,324
Indonesia	2,795	2,948	3,044	3,252	3,442	3,638
Thailand	2,642	2,700	2,786	2,968	3,240	3,348
South Korea	2,731	2,841	2,843	2,521	2,696	2,649

(1) Does not include marine mammals and aquatic plants. (2) Includes weight of clam, oyster, scallop, and other mollusk shells. (3) Statistics on quantities caught by recreational anglers in the U.S. are excluded.
Source: U.S. Dept. of Commerce, Natl. Oceanic and Atmospheric Admin., Natl. Marine Fisheries Service

Questions About the Tables

1. According to Table 15.1, where are the biggest threats to the seas? How does this result compare with the threats mentioned in the previous case study?

2. What does Table 15.1 tell you about the health of the seas? Select one of the threats and outline a plan to help abate some of the damage.

3. Examine Table 15.2. What countries have increased or decreased their yields during the five-year period of 1988–1993? Explain these behaviors.

A Bridge to Your 21st Century Uunderstanding

Complete and discuss the following flowchart.

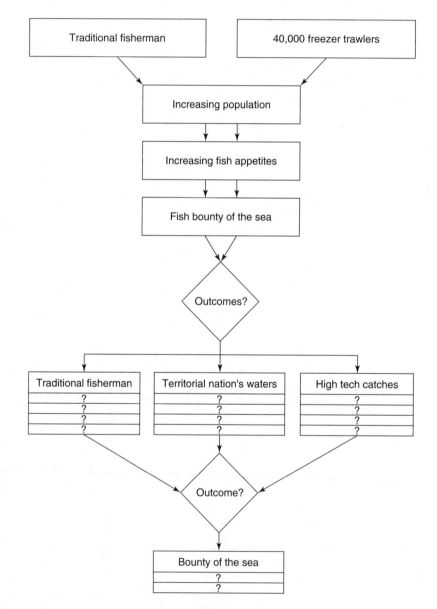

Fisheries: Exploiting the Oceans—What Will Be Left?

Buried Displeasure: The Love Canal

16

Love Canal was the dream community of William T. Love. He imagined a village nestled in the rolling hills and orchards near the Niagara River in upstate New York. The success of the venture, begun back in 1894, depended on the construction of a canal that would connect the two branches of the Niagara River. The canal would tap the power of the rapids just before Niagara Falls and produce hydroelectric power, which would attract business and industry to the area.

But Love's dream was not to be. Economic difficulties caused many of his backers to pull out of the scheme. The only trace of Love's plan was a three thousand foot long, sixty foot wide canal. In 1927, the area was annexed to the city of Niagara Falls. Around 1946, the city was approached by the Hooker Chemical Company, which was looking for a place to dump chemical wastes. Love Canal seemed like the perfect spot, sparsely populated, and the thick clay-like soil provided perfect protection against any possible leakage. Hooker began dumping chemical wastes into the canal that year, and for every year until 1952. At least 150 chemicals were placed in Love Canal, including Dioxin, the most toxic man-made chemical known. There was little public awareness at the time about the dangers of these chemicals, and their connection with nervous system disorders, kidney problems, respiratory distress, deafness and birth defects.

The potential for a technological disaster at Love Canal mounted during the 1950's. The post-war Baby Boom had created a pressing need for housing and schools. Officials in Niagara Falls began looking at Love Canal as a place to expand. In 1953, the Niagara Falls Board of Education announced it intended to acquire Love Canal for the purpose of building an elementary school in the area. Hooker, aware the land could be taken from them via eminent domain, sold the land to the city for $1, but made city officials sign a deed acknowledging that the area had been used as a chemical dump site, and absolving Hooker of any deaths or loss or damage to property once construction began. The 99th Street School was built on the central part of the canal, and the city sold the southern part to developers. As the bulldozers began tearing away the top soil, the rain and snow gradually began to seep into the drums and containers holding the chemical wastes, and in time a chemical mixture, leachate, began to flow out of Love Canal. The leachate which began to appear in the late 1950's produced skin burns on a few children who were playing in the area. But that was nothing compared to the complaints that began surfacing in the 1970's as the danger of Love Canal became apparent. Heavy rains during that decade forced the buried chemicals to the surface, and with them came increased reports of miscarriages, birth defects, liver abnormalities and cancer. In 1978 over 200 families were forced from their homes after toxic fumes were detected in their basements. Two years later, the Federal Government and the state of New York, reacting to an Environmental Protection Agency report, moved an additional 800 families out of the Love Canal area.

Love Canal remained a near ghost town throughout the 1980's as the E.P.A., Hooker Chemical, the School Board and City of Niagara Falls as well as numerous insurance companies thrashed out the legal and possibly criminal costs of this disaster. In 1988, Love Canal residents

159

received a $20 million settlement, in addition to the $30-$40,000 each family received for their homes. Individual claims were in the $2-$4,000 range. By 1990, 1,000 cases were still pending.

ONE PERSON MAKES A DIFFERENCE

Lois Gibbs was a housewife living in Love Canal in 1978. She discovered an epidemic of miscarriages, birth defects, nervous-system problems, and respiratory disorders across the neighborhood and also that the neighborhood had been built next to a huge toxic waste dump. She became a neighborhood organizer and ultimately became responsible, as much as anyone, for bringing this toxic disaster into the public forum and causing responsible parties to pay for victim relocation. She continued to become one of the most prominent grassroots environmental activists in the United States, founded the Citizens Clearinghouse on Harzardous Wastes, and has written extensively on toxic hazards, the prevention of new ones, and approaches for communities with existing toxic dumps. Ms. Gibbs has also written on the effects of dioxin as a potent carcinogen, as well as a cause of illnesses affecting almost every major system of the body, such as diabetes, chronic bronchitis, irregular heartbeat, nervous disorders, thyroid and immune system disorders, and a variety of reproductive system disorders, including birth defects, miscarriages, and lowered fertility. Gibbs recommends a strong dose of democracy as a cure for toxic environmental problems. She concludes, "The job is too big for some national organization or remote coalition to achieve on our behalf . . . Our country's power is vested in the people, and the people must act" (Mazza, 1996).

SOME INFORMATION TO CONSIDER

- Manufacturing wastes are being created at an accelerating pace of 6% per year, which means that the total waste production is doubling every 12 years.
- In the 12 years since the problems with Love Canal were found, American industry has pumped out a total

amount of toxic waste equal to all of the toxic waste created prior to Love Canal (from the years 1880–1978).

- The Niagara River has the greatest concentration of toxic dumps anywhere on the North-American continent, with 65 huge chemical dumps along the banks of the river. Love Canal, at 20,000 tons of toxins, is not the largest of these dumps, since the Hyde Park dump contains 80,000 tons of toxins, the "S" site contains 70,000 tons, and the 102 Street Site contains 80,000 tons; all of these sites are within a few hundred yards of the river (Montague, 1990).

When Lois Gibbs founded the Citizens Clearinghouse for Hazardous Waste (CCHW) in 1981, its main focus was to help community groups suffering from the effects of toxic dump sites like Love Canal, but it has expanded its programs to address a broad range of environmental issues, including toxic waste, solid waste, air pollution, incinerators, medical waste, radioactive waste, pesticides, sewage, and industrial pollution. The CCHW is a now a 16-year-old nonprofit environmental organization and remains the only national organization started and led by grassroots organizers. As of 1996, CCHW has worked with over 80 community-based groups nationwide, and Lois Gibbs remains Executive Director of CCHW (Gibbs, 1996).

References

Excerpted from Ferell, O.C. and John Fraedrich. *Business Ethics.* New York: Houghton Mifflin, 1991. Additional information provided by researchers Denise Schultz, Paula Ingerson and Joanne Hammond.

"Lois Gibb's biography page." (1996). Available: http://www.medaccess.com/newsletter/n10415/gibbiog.htm.

Mazza, P. (1996, February). "Love Canal is everywhere: The pervasive threat of dioxin." pp. 1–3. Available: http://www.tnews.com/text/dioxin.html.

Montague, P. (1990, June). The Niagara River—part I: How industry survived Love Canal. *Rachel's Hazardous Waste News #186.* Environmental Research Foundation, Annapolis. pp. 1–3. Available: http://xp0.rtknet.org/E3540T132.

What Will Happen to the Endangered Species Act?

17

The motivation and purpose of the Endangered Species Act is to provide some regulations for the mutual coexistence of humans and all other species within the demands of each population. Increased grazing, logging, mining, and many other environmentally dependent businesses in the United States threaten the existence of many animal and plant species. Efforts to protect these "human dependents of the world" are the result of the landmark Endangered Species Act (ESA) legislation, which gives endangered wildlife an advantage over human business and profits. The conservation efforts of the ESA present a serious (and at times highly emotional) conflict in many affected areas to economic operations and result in unemployment and loss of private property rights. Opponents believe that the ESA ignores the economic considerations and interests of the specific location, while supporters believe that the ESA ensures and preserves the species and a variable gene pool. The debate then becomes the following: Can the Endangered Species Act accommodate increasing human demands and decreasing biodiversity?

In 1973, President Richard Nixon signed the Endangered Species Act into law; the ESA's main purpose is to maintain a list of endangered or threatened species. Based on the assumptions that each life-form may prove invaluable in ways we cannot yet measure and that each is entitled to exist, the act gave the federal government sweeping powers to prevent extinction. No commitment of this magnitude to other life-forms had ever been made before. This act provides guidance to two agencies: the Fish and Wildlife Service and the National Marine Fisheries Service, whose main responsibilities are to stop further endangerment of species. The services then strive to protect wildlife and remove them from the list when they have gained recovery. The decision is to be based solely on scientific data rather than on economic and political aspects. In 1973, the U.S. list contained 109 names; in 1995, the total included more than 900 (1,400 including foreign species), with 3,700 officially recognized candidates waiting to be listed (Chadwick, 1995, pp. 7–9).

Conjecture regarding possible removal of the ESA brings much reaction from both critics and supporters, businessmen and environmentalists. Of course, businessmen who depend on the land for revenue would not mind seeing the removal of the ESA altogether, and other opponents of the act feel that the ESA is poorly written and simply stands in the way of economically beneficial activities.

Endangered Species: A species that could become extinct in the future.
Threatened Species: A Species that could become endangered soon.
Recovery Point: The time at which the measures provided by the Endangered Species Act are no longer necessary.

161

On the other side, supporters stand on the foundation that one cannot put a price on the value of a species. There are, however, many additional problems aside from economic issues with the way that the ESA is written and managed.

The ESA categories of threatened, endangered, and secure are not well defined and allow for different views of interpretation. Since the ESA gives the government the ability to prioritize the future of a species above any human disturbance that may cause a decline of that species, the vague interpretations allow groups to twist ESA categories to their own needs or to define data differently. The resulting ambiguity yields conflicting reports of population statuses, inaccurate information, and ineffective—and even destructive—action taken on a species population. The ESA lacks population guidelines for each species so that it can be accurately categorized and protected. Without that clear frame of reference, the protection of a species becomes very difficult and arbitrary while human impacts are steadily increasing.

Another problem is that the ESA is used as a last-chance approach. After a species qualifies for the ESA due to decreased numbers, the situation is already extremely dire. In these cases, the act is dealing with the last population of a species, and action has to be taken immediately to curb extinction. Such desperation forces the government to make drastic strategies to save the species, and so a more balanced approach involving the needs of local human populations and economics are not considered. Such last-minute recovery plans magnify tensions and are not nearly as effective when the act has to salvage a species that is nearly lost. If the act could practice planned "preventive medicine" instead of "reactive medicine," resources would be more strategically used, productivity would be increased, and both humans and animal species would experience decreased tension.

An additional problem is that the ESA does not adequately take into account the amount of habitat required for a species' numbers to increase. The ESA does not make provisions for species that need larger tracts of land or for the construction of habitat bridges, which link smaller tracts of land together to allow cross-movement. Instead, the ESA protects islands of habitat surrounded by urban influence, allowing very little chance of survival for nomadic species such as the fox, wolf, grizzly bear, lynx, cougar, and many others. The larger nomadic predators need very large tracts of land to search for food. The ESA does make good attempts at preserving national parks as large areas of habitat, but national parks are not usually biodiverse ecosystems that meet the food needs of these species and are appealing more for their aesthetic beauty. Then, typically, when the large predators roam from their small habitats in search of food, they are shot when entering an agricultural or populated area. Conflict then arises because the ESA prohibits shooting an endangered species, but humans feel betrayed by the government for simply defending their land, lives, and resources (The Endangered Species Act, 1997, p. 1).

Other problems exist in processing and interpreting the list of species on the ESA. Some of the removals from the list exaggerate the rate of success of the ESA. In 1993, the Burneau Host Spring Snail was removed from the list after a federal judge ruled that it was listed erroneously; this species was one of 8 others removed out of a total of 21 species because of listing errors. Another example is that of the Rydberg milvetch (a member of the pea family), which existed only in Southwestern Utah in 1905 and is believed to be extinct. However, in 1980, taxonomists decided that a dozen populations of a close relative (the plataua) should be counted as Rydberg milvetches, and the species was removed from the list even though the plant was not the same one.

The species that were delisted because their status had improved also need correct interpretation. The Arctic peregrin falcon was struck from the list in October 1995, but its improvement probably had more to do with the reduction of pesticides than changes in hunting laws and the protection of habitat. Also, the smallness of recovery numbers may be a basic reflection of the dangers faced by the species at the time of the listing rather than the ineffectiveness of recovery tactics. The belief is that, allowing for data errors, extinctions, and other extraneous factors, success stories under the ESA can be misinterpreted and the effectiveness of the act can not be realistically appraised (Is Endangered Species Act in Danger, 1995).

According to most sources, the ESA does fundamentally work, but the act would prove more effective if changes were made. The ESA has many success stories: the palau dove, palau flycatcher, palau owl, Atlantic brown pelican, and the gray whales. The increase in the numbers of red wolves within the continental United States is due mostly to anti-shooting laws as set forth by the ESA. The ESA, in conjunction with the banning of DDT, has increased many populations of birds, including the bald eagle. The ESA has also funded the recovery of some severely endangered species, such as the California condor.

According to research numbers, the ESA does help to slow rates of extinction; however, it also has been suggested that many species go extinct while waiting for ESA recognition (Endangered Species Act, 1997, p. 2).

When first written in 1973, the ESA appeared to be the answer for increased environmental concern and pressure for diminishing species. There remain some fundamental problems, however, that are now prompting views that species-recovery planning and implementation processes are not working very well, and these problems also agitate involved parties pitting business interests against environmentalists and federal agencies.

Some of the ESA classic case studies include the Northern Spotted Owl, the Snail Darter, The Red-Cockaded Woodpecker and the Gnatcatcher.

Northern Spotted Owl
Habitat: Northwest Old Growth Forests
Status: Threatened

The government declared 8 million acres off-limits to chainsaws, saving the environment as well as the owl, but taking away thousands of jobs and millions of dollars in timber sales in a depressed area. Controversy surrounded the importance of economics versus endangered species. The conclusion was that new regulations for national forest use were created, emphasizing conservation, not consumption. Management of both federal and state forest timberlands has shifted from lumber production to environmental protection. The city of Sweet Home has new industries moving into the region, with the emergence of strong growth opportunities (Mitchell, 1997).

Snail Darter
Habitat: Little Tennessee River
Status: Endangered

Work in the middle of the construction of the Tellico Dam in the Little Tennessee River was halted due to concern over the future of the snail darter (a tiny fish). Criticisms of the ESA began, due to the costs of salvaging a species versus completing the half-finished multimillion-dollar dam. Supporters of the ESA argued that the snail darter existed only in the Little Tennessee River, but other populations have since been found. The conclusion was that the fish were transplanted and the dam was completed.

Red-Cockaded Woodpecker
Habitat: Southeast Old Pine Forests
Status: Endangered

The woodpecker inhabits the old growth pine forest ecosystem and passes its nest from one generation to the next. The loss of 88 million acres of pine forest due to development threatens the woodpecker as well as many other potentially endangered species. The conclusion of this case is as yet unresolved.

Gnatcatcher
Habitat: Sage Shrub Ecosystem of California
Status: Endangered

The gnatcatcher blocked the future construction of a development in southern California. Supporters said that the planned site of the development was the only remaining location for the species, while opponents said that preservation attempts were prohibiting the construction of a development with high property values. To break the impasse, Secretary of the Interior Bruce Babbit changed the classification of the species to "threatened" rather than "endangered" to allow continuing "controlled development" to the area. In return, the developing companies had to set aside a certain percentage of sage shrub habitat to ensure the recovery and future of the gnatcatcher. A 1992 report by the Fish and Wildlife Service gives the following data:

Species	Number of in 1990	Number of in 1992
Improving	57	69
Stable	181	201
Declining	219	232
Extinct	11	14
Unknown	113	195

This report indicates an increase of 11 to 14 extinct species and 219 to 232 species declining, showing approximately the same number of species improving as declining. This data does not represent the ESA well, since with most species in decline due to the pressure of human encroachment and the loss of habitat, the ESA as written in 1973 could be interpreted as an inadequate protection of species (Endangered Species Act, 1997, p. 2).

RECENT DEVELOPMENTS

Secretary of the Interior Bruce Babbit has proposed revisions to the Endangered Species Act that include a spirit of compromise to replace the old era of confrontation. The core of his proposal of 1997 is to appease both sides, such that environmentalists have more land set aside for preservation and property owners can use portions of their land without enduring excessive bureaucratic and legal entanglements. His proposal incorporates 10 policy changes, representing the most sweeping changes in the law's 24-year history, and reacts to many criticisms of the ESA. The criticisms recently have been so vocal that some legislators have wanted to repeal the entire act, and various classic controversies such as those of the spotted owl and snail darter fueled that approach. However, since then there have been administrative reforms that have been field tested, have been proven to work, and will be less subject to shifting political whims.

Some of the policies that Babbit wants to incorporate into the law include the following:

- allowing property owners with five acres or less to be exempted from some restrictions;

- encouraging local and state governments and Indian tribes to play a larger role in the protection of wildlife with private land management;

- focusing more on helping threatened species boost their numbers so that they do not end up on the endangered species list;

- enacting a "no surprises" policy where property owners can agree to set aside lands that shelter endangered

wildlife or donate money to a conservation project. In exchange, the U.S. Fish and Wildlife Service will give the property owners authorization to destroy the habitat on other portions of their land that they plan to develop. In order to obtain the authorization, owners have to devise thorough, comprehensive plans. Once the deal is struck, the wildlife plan would be unchangeable. If another endangered species not covered by the plan shows up later, the United States would pay the cost of protecting it.

Since 1994, when Babbit first introduced the no-surprises policy, 200 habitat recovery plans have been established and another 200 are forthcoming. More than 18 million acres of developable lands have been set aside for wildlife under the plans. However, some scientists say that the policy is bad science, since it is impossible to make a plan that will consider long-term dynamic needs for species that will occur over the next 50 to 100 years. Also, critics say that allowing land owners to write their own environmental plans represents a conflict of interest that can lead to abuse. Babbit's approaches, at the very least, conserve the law while defusing ownership and economic tension (Haynes, 1997).

References

Is Endangered Species Act in danger? (1995, March 3). *Science,* p. 267.
The Endangered Species Act (1997). Available: http://gladstone.uoregon.edu/-cait/mainbody.htm.
Chadwick, D. H. (1995, March). Dead or alive: The Endangered Species Act. *National Geographic,* pp. 2–41.
Haynes, V.D. (1997, July 27). U.S. wants to amend endangered species law. *Chicago Tribune,* Section 1, p. 4.
Mitchell, J. G. (1997, March). In the line of fire: Our national forests. *Scientific American,* Vol. 191, No. 3, pp. 57–58.

Further Reading

Graham, F., Jr. (1994, July/August). Winged victory. *Audubon,* pp. 36–49.
Horton, T. (1995, March/April). The Endangered Species Act: Too tough, too weak, or too late? *Audubon,* p. 68.
Kohm, K. (1991). *Balance on the Brink of Extinction.* Washington, D.C.: Island Press.
Korn, P. (1992, March 30). The case for preservation. *The Nation,* p. 414.
Mann, C. C., and Plummer, M. L. (1995, January/February). California vs. Gnatcatcher. *Audubon,* pp. 40–48.
National Research Council. (1993). *Science and the Endangered Species Act.* National Research Publishing Company.
Rauber, P. (1996, January/February). "An End to Evolution." *Sierra,* p. 28.

Spending by States on Endangered Species

37% Birds

33% Mammals

13% Fishes

8% Plants

5% Invertebrates

4% Reptiles/Amphibians

Source: 1996 Endangered Species Survey, International Association of Fish and Wildlife Agencies

Questions

1. Do you think that the Endangered Species Act is needed? Do you think that this legislation was too strong or too weak in 1973? If you were to change the law now, how would you change it?
2. Where do you stand in your political view on the environment? Could you be regarded as a critic or supporter of the ESA? Explain in detail your reasons. Should the ESA be eliminated? If so, what should take its place? If not, why not?
3. Name some significant successes of the ESA. Support your list of successes with the role and contribution of the ESA for these successes.
4. Name some of the problems of the ESA, and give some suggestions to correct those problems.
5. Research some of the classic ESA cases (e.g., bald eagle, gnatcatcher, northern spotted owl, California condor, milvetch), and present arguments for and against ESA involvement with and protection of these species.
6. Do you feel that the ESA works? Give arguments for and against your conclusions.
7. Do you feel that Babbit's proposal strengthens or weakens the ESA's power and effectiveness? Explain your answer. Do you like Babbit's revisions? Explain.
8. If you were to change Babbit's proposal, how would you change it?
9. What is meant by a "no surprises" policy? Do you feel that this is a necessary component to Babbit's proposal? Why or why not?
10. Research the species that the ESA lists. Does your research support or refute the utilization of the ESA?
11. What is your overall reaction to the issue of ESA? Give your views regarding the environmental, ethical, economical, and political aspects of this issue.

A Bridge to Your 21st Century Understanding

Complete and discuss the following flowchart.

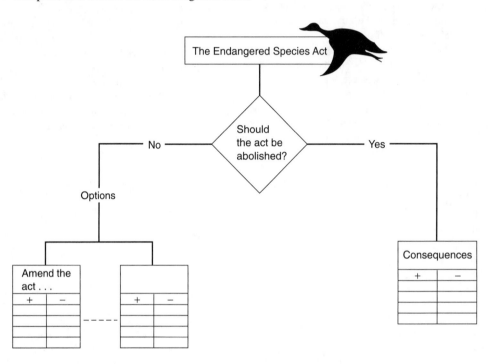

Air Poisons around the World

18

There are studies showing that on days when there are more particulates in the air, more people die. You can't get more basic that that . . . . This country has a law called the Clean Air Net, which says that Americans should be able to breathe without harm.

JOHN H. ADAMS, EXECUTIVE DIRECTOR, NATURAL RESOURCES DEFENSE COUNCIL

Air pollution in its many forms—sulfur dioxide, ozone, fine particles, carbon monoxide and nitrogen oxide—is causing a deathly fog around the world. "From Hong Kong to Mexico City, the toll taken in terms of human death and disease caused or aggravated by air pollution almost certainly is measured in the millions," says Dr. Alfred Munzer, past president of the American Lung Association and respiratory specialist.

In Japan, various respiratory illnesses suffered by thousands of citizens living in heavily polluted areas of Japan were deemed indisputably to be caused by sulfur dioxide. The next year the Japanese government set up a tracking program and medical reimbursements for certified victims of air pollution ranging from bronchitis to asthma. Even though the program monitored only sulfur dioxide and was limited to just a few industrial areas, it still certified more than 90,000 air pollution victims before it was stopped in 1988 because of pressure from polluters. Since no other nation has routinely collected this kind of data on air pollution and human health, this number serves as an indicator of a world-wide unprecedented problem.

Sulfur dioxide along with fine particles which results in newly formed acidic compounds claim an unbelievable number of victims in all parts of the world. In 1992 when weather conditions trapped sulfur dioxide over the Mae Moh region of Thailand, 4000 residents required medical treatment, cattle died with blistered hides and crops withered. In Poland, medical tracking of army inductees has revealed four times more asthma and three times more bronchitis in areas that were polluted by sulfur dioxide. In

Krakow, men were tracked who lived in the city's most polluted areas for 13 years; the study found losses of lung function similar to smoking.

Ozone, the dominant chemical in smog, is an invisible toxic gas that is the result of reactions of unburnt gasoline with other pollutants. Ozone scars tissue, burns eyes, promotes coughing, wheezing and rapid, painful breathing. Within minutes of entering the lungs, ozone burns through the cell walls. The immune system tries to defend the lungs, but they are stunned by the ozone. Cellular fluid then seeps into the lungs and breathing becomes rapid and painful. In the nose and airways, ozone destroys ciliated cells which the body replaces with thick-walled abnormal squamous cells. With time the lungs stiffen and the ability to breathe drops. Children raised in ozone-polluted areas have unusually small lungs and adults lose up to 75 percent of their lung capacity. The massive cell death that ozone causes triggers pre-cancerous physiological responses.

Mexico City's air which has some of the world's worst ozone pollution rises in the unhealthful ozone levels about 98% of the time. Healthy men newly exposed to Mexico City's air developed pre-cancerous cell alterations in nasal and airway passages. Mexico City residents generally are in the second of three stages of cancer where the third is the production of cancer.

In Los Angeles, one in four fatal accident victims aged from 14 to 25 had severe lung lesions of the sort caused by ozone which is a destructive, irreversible disease in young people. Los Angeles residents exposed to ozone had double the risk of cancer compared to residents of cleaner cities.

Particulates are a catch-all term for everything from road dust to soot to mixtures of pollutants—solids as well as liquids, microscopic and larger grains that vary in the environment. Scientists believe that fine particles which are small enough to lodge deep into the lung are the most dangerous. Fine particles result from the burning of coal, oil and gasoline as well as from the atmospheric change of oxide of sulfur and nitrogen into sulfates and nitrates.

Bangkok police work in gritty air pollution thick with air particulates from motorcycles and thick clouds of burnt diesel fuels from buses and trucks. The effects on these officers include abnormal lung function tests and spots on lungs as well as general congestion. Roughly one out of every nine Bangkok residents has a respiratory ailment caused by air pollution.

The evidence that particulates kill is "absolutely complete" according to University of British Columbia's Dr. David Bates, a foremost air pollution and health expert. Studies from around the world and within the U.S. confirm that as the particulate pollution rises, so do sickness and death.

Carbon monoxide is invisible and oxides of nitrogen almost so—therefore, it is impossible to tell when the air contains dangerous levels of both. These gases are produced when gasoline and other fuels are burned incompletely. Roughly 90 percent of urban CO occurs from motor vehicle tailpipes especially in cities like London. Carbon monoxide, when breathed, starves the body of oxygen which then causes dizziness and unconsciousness.

Oxides of nitrogen form the reddish-brown layer that can be seen from an airplane one mile up. Nitrous oxides cause oxygen and nitrogen in the air to combine which then further cause air and ozone pollution. Like ozone, oxide of nitrogen destroys organic matter such as human tissues and makes organisms more susceptible to bacterial infections and to lung cancer.

Some of the worst air pollution is in the "Black Triangle," where the Czech Republic meets Poland and the former East Germany. More sulfur per square meter falls there than on any other place in Europe. In Poland, high lead levels in soil from the air are unprecedented elsewhere in the Western world. According to experts, the "Black Triangle" is among the most polluted locations in the world. Respiratory disease in children up to 14 years is epidemic. In this triangle, black smoke clings to everything. The World Health Organization has concluded that approximately 15 percent of infant mortality and 50 per-

cent of postneonatal respiratory mortality in the Czech Republic may be connected to air pollution. According to studies, children living in cities with air pollution are as much as 11 months behind in bone growth than those breathing cleaner air. In Poland, lead-laden air pollution is so severe that it causes lead poisoning and intelligence loss where some experts have estimated that 10 to 15 percent of the nation's citizens have been affected.

Governments who are forced to choose between protecting the public and shielding industry from regulation too often choose to sacrifice their men, women and children. The people in Mexico, Japan, Thailand, England, U.S., Poland, the Czech Republic and the rest of the world require a basic quality of life of breathing clean air. Governments must prioritize their efforts to the health of their citizens and utilizing technology for their peoples as well as their economics—otherwise their economic decisions become short-lived like their suffering people. Technology has the capability to provide for both economic and human needs with a priority on the value of all life and the treasured air on which all depends.

U.S. HISTORICAL AND SOCIETAL PROGRESS REGARDING AIR POLLUTION

In the United States in 1973, after a lawsuit initiated by the Natural Resources Defense Council, the Environmental Protection Agency (EPA) created a five-year program to gradually reduce the lead content in gasoline. At that time, tetrethyl lead (TEL) was routinely added to lower grade gasoline to effect more efficient burning and prevent gasoline "knock" caused by uneven combustion. For decades, the nation had allowed the combustion of leaded gas to emit millions of tons of lead into the air, where it was breathed in or deposited in soil and dust. Lead, however, is toxic, even in the smallest amounts. Children with elevated blood–lead levels can suffer lowered IQs, slower neural transmission, hearing loss, and disruption of the formation of hemoglobin red blood cells, and acute lead poisoning causes more massive physiological damage. By the mid 1970s, physiological links were established between lead content in gasoline and health problems in children.

By 1985, after many political battles and opposition by special-interest groups, the EPA proposed stricter regulations with the goal of eliminating gasoline lead entirely by the mid-1990s. Two factors drove this development. One was new health data showing that blood–lead levels previously accepted as safe had adverse effects, and the other was data by Joel Schwartz (formerly of the EPA, now a professor at the Harvard School of Public Health) that illustrated that it would cost industry about $575 million to meet the newest lead standards by 1986—but that sum would be small in comparison to the $1.8 billion saved in 1986 alone from reduced needs for medical care, lower pollution emissions from catalytic converters, greater fuel efficiency, and less vehicle maintenance. As of 1994, the Center for Disease Control (CDC) estimated that still 1 million children under six years of age in the United States had blood–lead levels exceeding recommended thresholds, but the number was significantly reduced from previous data.

Aside from lead, the two worst air pollution components are ozone and fine airborne particles called "particulates." There were several major air pollution disasters during the early part of this century—in Meuse Valley, Belgium, in 1930; in Donora, Pennsylvania, in 1948; and in London in 1950—that demonstrated that high concentrations of air pollution could kill large numbers of people. By the late 1980s, there was accumulating evidence that the particulate matter (tiny suspended particles of soot, soil, mineral, or metal) in this pollution was closely associated with death and illness (Skelton, 1997, pp. 27–29).

FINE-PARTICULATE REGULATIONS NEEDED

The people who are hurt worst are those with the most vulnerable lungs—children, the elderly, and asthmatics. For people with heart or lung disease, fine particulates can cause an earlier death by a year or more. Over the past 10 years, there have been hundreds of studies indicating that the damage caused by these two pollutants is much more serious than previously known and that on days when more particulates are in the air, more people die. Fine particulates are currently the leading air pollution health threat in the country. Researchers believe that about 60,000 Americans may die annually as a result of particulate pollution—a larger number than for any other form of pollution. Currently, however, less than one third of all funds to reduce air pollution are directed toward removing fine particulates (Adams, 1997, p. 2).

Airborne particles have different sources and are of different sizes. Currently, the smallest particulates regulated by the federal government have a diameter of 10 microns or less (referred to as PM-10). The largest of these particulates are dust and dirt, but the smallest of these particulates (PM-2.5) cause the greatest health threat. These very fine particles evade the body's clearance mechanism and penetrate deeply into the lung's most sensitive areas. Additionally, these particulates are mostly byproducts of combustion (from coal-fired power plants, industrial boilers, highway vehicles, and other pieces of machinery) that in themselves form chemicals that are health hazards. In 1971, the EPA set a general limit of particulate standard concentrations at PM-10 or above. But by the end of the decade, it was becoming clear that it was the smallest particulates that were the worst health risks. In 1987, the EPA set a tougher standard limit for particles at PM-10, the first-ever standard limit on fine, inhalable particles. Evidence continued to mount that the lives of thousands of Americans were being shortened by a year or two, on average, from exposure to particulates at levels below the PM-10 standard (Skelton, 1997, p. 29).

Then, additional studies became available that tracked the health of more than 8,000 people from six cities for 14 to 16 years. These studies concluded that fine particles increased the risk of premature death for residents of the most polluted city by 26%. Another study tracked 500,000 people in 151 cities with the results that people living in the most polluted areas with fine particles had a 17% greater risk of mortality. In 1996, a study of 239 cities found that about 64,000 people may die prematurely from heart or lung disease annually due to particulate pollution. In 1996, the EPA finally proposed a tougher particulate standard that included the first-ever standard for the finest, most dangerous particulates, PM-2.5. It is estimated that these new standards and the new law would annually prevent 9,000 hospital admissions, 250,000 cases of aggravated asthma, and 20,000 premature deaths every year. But there is no knowing whether the PM-2.5 standard will survive the final version of the EPA law. There is much industrial pressure for this new standard not to survive. This issue is better put in the following manner: As a standard for the entire and future industrial world, the United States and the world require such protection for rights to and needs for clean air (Skelton, 1997, p. 30).

In 1987, U.S. law required certain industries to disclose their emissions of 320 toxic chemicals. Since the disclosure began, selected industries have reduced those chemical emissions by 31%; however, companies still admitted to 1992 emissions of 3.8 billion pounds of toxic chemicals. Public disclosure has been quite effective in getting industry to clean up its approach, but there is still a long way to go (It's the ecosystem, stupid, 1994). A study in 1997 indicated that industries' quantitative breakdown of emissions was not very accurate in terms of analysis of location, composition, and emission rates and that more accurate methods have to be developed to rely more on actual measurements rather than calculations on paper. In 1997, some of the largest industrial polluters, including oil refineries, coal-power plants, steel companies, and car and truck exhaust pipes, are attempting to ease these standards (Raloff, 1997).

References

Excerpted from
Adams, J. H. (1997, Spring). Past time for clean air. *The Amicus Journal*, p. 2. It's the ecosystem, stupid. (1994, February/March). 26th environmental quality index. *National Wildlife*, p. 40.
Moore, Curtis A. (1995, September/October)
Raloff, J. (1997, June 28). Industries tally air pollution poorly. *Science News*, Vol. 151, p. 396.
Skelton, R. (1997, Summer.) Clearing the air. *The Amicus Journal*, pp. 27–30.

Questions

1. What compounds mentioned in this article cause air pollution? How are each of these compounds created?

2. What can be done to stop the creation of these air pollution compounds?

3. Is such air pollution a significant health risk in your estimation, or is it the necessary price and inconvenience that is a part of the price of technology? What priority would you place on curbing these air pollution compounds?

4. What are some approaches that the industrialized nations can take to curb such air pollution? How can these efforts be made effective?

5. How can the industrialized nations aid the Third-World nations in this effort to clean up the air?

6. What were some of the deciding factors that drove the passage of stricter regulations of lead in gasoline? Explain how economics and society–health arguments won this standard. Do you think that this method is a winning strategy for the passage of proposals rather than the facts of the environmental effects alone? What are the implications of this situation?

7. Why are fine particulates so dangerous?

8. Do you feel that there should be a PM-2.5 standard? How can such a standard be enacted? (You may wish to refer to Question #6 for some ideas.)

9. Has industrial disclosure of toxic emissions helped to reduce industrial chemical emissions? Why do you think this has happened? What are the problems with self-disclosure as far as pollution control? What approaches would you further recommend for reducing levels of emissions?

10. Refer to Tables 18.1, 18.2 and 18.3. Observe the historical improvement of air toxins and air pollutants. Comment on these trends in each of the tables.

11. Refer to Table 18.4: The Common Air Pollutants. Discuss how each pollutant could realistically be minimized in industry, transportation, and domestic uses. How does your plan compare with what is being done today? How can we improve governmental and societal efforts to reduce pollutants?

Table 18.1

Toxics Release Inventory, 1993–94

Reported industrial releases of toxic chemicals into the environment by major manufacturing facilities (excluding power plants and mining facilities) decreased 8.6% from the 1993 figure and 44.1% from the figure for 1988, the baseline year.

Pollutant Releases	1993 mil lb	1994 mil lb	Top Industries, Total Releases	1993 mil lb	1994 mil lb
Air releases	1,672	1,556	Chemicals	1,316	851
Underground injection	576	349	Primary metals	329	313
Land releases	289	289	Paper	216	246
Water releases	271	66	Transportation equipment	136	122
Total	**2,808**	**2,260**	Plastics	127	119
Pollutant transfers			**Carcinogens, air/water/ land releases**		
To recycling	3,252	2,456	Dichloromethane	64	63
To energy recovery	487	464	Styrene	33	40
To treatment	328	319	Chloroform	14	11
To disposal/other	325	298	Formaldehyde	12	12
To publicly owned treatment works	314	255	Tetrachloroethylene	12	10
Total	**4,706**	**3,792**	Benzene	11	10

Source: Environmental Protection Agency

Table 18.2

Emissions of Principal Pollutants 1985–1994

(in thousand short tons)

Source	1985	1986	1987	1988	1989	1990	1991	1992	1993	1994
Carbon monoxide[1]	114,690	109,199	108,012	115,849	103,144	100,650	97,376	94,043	94,133	98,017
Lead	20.1	7.3	6.9	6.5	6.0	5.7	5.3	4.9	4.9	5.0
Nitrogen oxides[2]	22,860	22,348	22,403	23,618	23,222	23,038	22,672	22,847	23,276	23,615
Volatile organic compounds[2]	25,799	24,991	24,777	25,720	23,934	23,600	22,876	22,422	25,575	23,174
Particulate matter	3,220	3,092	2,964	3,067	3,036	2,704	2,674	2,725	2,666	2,688
Sulfur oxides	23,230	22,442	22,204	22,647	22,785	22,433	22,068	21,836	21,517	21,118
Total	**189,819**	**184,079**	**180,366**	**190,907**	**176,127**	**172,430**	**167,671**	**163,877**	**167,171**	**168,617**

(1) The observed increase in carbon monoxide emissions between 1993 and 1994 is attributed to 2 sources: transportation emissions (up 2%) and wildfire emissions (up 160%). (2) Ozone, a major air pollutant and the primary constituent of smog, is not emitted directly to the air but is formed by sunlight acting on emissions of nitrogen oxides and volatile organic compounds.
Source: U.S. Environmental Protection Agency, Office of Air Quality Planning and Standards

Table 18.3

U.S. Lead Emission Estimates, 1985–94

(in short tons)

Source	1985	1986	1987	1988	1989	1990	1991	1992	1993	1994
Fuel combustion	515	516	510	511	505	500	495	491	491	493
Industrial processes	3,402	2,972	3,004	3,090	3,161	3,278	3,081	2,771	2,866	2,868
Transportation	16,207	3,808	3,343	2,911	2,368	1,888	1,704	1,637	1,580	1,596
Natural sources	0	0	0	0	0	0	0	0	0	0
Miscellaneous	0	0	0	0	0	0	0	0	0	0
Total[1]	20,124	7,296	6,857	6,513	6,034	5,666	5,279	4,899	4,938	4,956

(1) Totals may not add because of rounding.
Source: U.S. Environmental Protection Agency, Office of Air Quality Planning and Standards

Table 18.4
The Common Air Pollutants (Criteria Air Pollutants)

Name	Source	Health Effects	Environmental Effects	Property Damage
Ozone (ground-level ozone is the principal component of smog)	Chemical reaction of pollutants; VOCs and NOx	Breathing problems, reduced lung function, asthma, irritated eyes, stuffy nose, reduced resistance to colds and other infections, may speed up aging of lung tissue	Ozone can damage plants and trees; smog can cause reduced visibility	Damages rubber, fabrics, etc.
VOCs[4] (volatile organic compounds); smog-formers	VOCs are released from burning fuel (oil, gas, etc.), solvents, paints, and other products used at work or at home. Cars are an important source of VOCs. VOCs include chemicals such as benzene, toluene, methylene chloride.	In addition to ozone (smog) effects, many VOCs can cause serious health problems such as cancer and other effects	In addition to ozone (smog) effects, some VOCs such as formaldehyde and ethylene may harm plants	
Nitrogen Dioxide (one of the NOx); smog-forming chemical	Burning of gasoline, natural gas, coal, oil etc. Cars are an important source of NO^2.	Lung damage, illnesses of breathing passages and lungs (respiratory system)	Nitrogen dioxide is an ingredient of acid rain (acid aerosols), which can damage trees and lakes. Acid aerosols can reduce visibility.	Acid aerosols can eat away stone used on buildings, statues, monuments, etc.
Carbon Monoxide (CO)	Burning of gasoline, wood, natural gas, coal, oil, etc.	Reduces ability of blood to bring oxygen to body cells and tissues. CO may be particularly hazardous to people who have heart or circulatory (blood vessel) problems and people who have damaged lungs or breathing passages		

continued

Table 18.4, *Continued*
The Common Air Pollutants (Criteria Air Pollutants)

Name	Source	Health Effects	Environmental Effects	Property Damage
Particulate Matter (PM-10); (dust, smoke, soot)	Burning of wood, diesel and other fuels; industrial plants; agriculture (plowing, burning off fields); unpaved roads	Nose and throat irritation, lung damage, bronchitis, early death	Particulates are the main source of haze that reduces visibility	Ashes, soots, smokes and dusts can dirty and discolor structures and other property, including clothes and furniture
Sulfur Dioxide	Burning of coal and oil, especially high-sulfur coal from the Eastern United States; industrial processes (paper, metals)	Breathing problems, may cause permanent damage to lungs	SO_2 is an ingredient in acid rain (acid aerosols), which can damage trees and lakes. Acid aerosols can also reduce visibility.	Acid aerosols can eat away stone used in buildings, statues, monuments, etc.
Lead	Leaded gasoline (being phased out), paint (houses, cars), smelters (metal refineries); manufacture of lead storage batteries	Brain and other nervous system damage; children are at special risk. Some lead-containing chemicals cause cancer in animals. Lead causes digestive and other health problems.	Lead can harm wildlife.	

[4]All VOCs contain carbon (C), the basic chemical element found in living beings. Carbon-containing chemicals are called organic. Volatile chemicals escape into the air easily. Many VOCs, such as the chemicals listed in the table, are also hazardous air pollutants, which can cause very serious illnesses. EPA does not list VOCs as criteria air pollutants, but they are included in this list of pollutants because efforts to control smog target VOCs for reduction.
Source: U.S. Environmental Protection Agency

A Bridge to Your 21st Century Understanding

Complete and discuss the following flowchart.

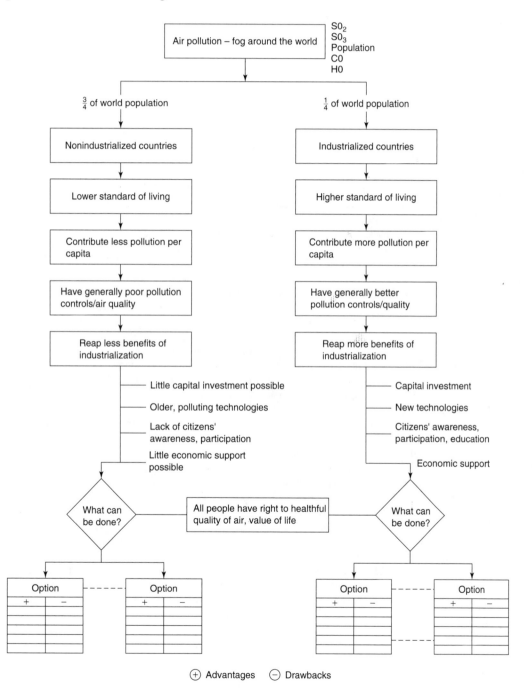

Air pollution – fog around the world

S0₂
S0₃
Population
C0
H0

$\frac{3}{4}$ of world population

$\frac{1}{4}$ of world population

Nonindustrialized countries

Industrialized countries

Lower standard of living

Higher standard of living

Contribute less pollution per capita

Contribute more pollution per capita

Have generally poor pollution controls/air quality

Have generally better pollution controls/quality

Reap less benefits of industrialization

Reap more benefits of industrialization

— Little capital investment possible

— Capital investment

— Older, polluting technologies

— New technologies

Lack of citizens' awareness, participation

Citizens' awareness, participation, education

Little economic support possible

Economic support

What can be done?

All people have right to healthful quality of air, value of life

What can be done?

Option
+	−

Option
+	−

Option
+	−

Option
+	−

⊕ Advantages   ⊖ Drawbacks

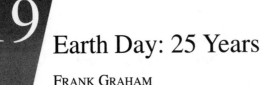

19

Earth Day: 25 Years

FRANK GRAHAM

Rejoicing at grass roots, Mary Lyn Ray epitomizes a generation of activists who answered the call of Earth Day, April 22, 1970, when millions rallied to the cause of the environment. Ray, for one, is rousing her neighbors to keep their corner of New Hampshire green.

It was to have been a teach-in. The National Environmental Teach-In, the organizers called it, hoping to capture the spirit if not the politics of those earlier "sit-ins" of the fractious 1960s. Instead, what emerged on April 22, 1970, was Earth Day, the greatest nationwide street demonstration the United States had witnessed since the tumultuous close of World War II.

Twenty million Americans turned out that day to hear politicians and philosophers pledge allegiance to the planet by deploring its polluted condition. Congress stood in recess, its lawmakers out on the ecological stump. Senator Edward Kennedy, ex-Harvard, stumped at Yale; Senator Barry Goldwater at Adelphi University in Garden City, New York. Margaret Mead, the anthropologist, predicted that the energy required to roll back environmental degradation might well match that of the Industrial Revolution. John V. Lindsay, the mayor of New York City, proclaimed it a day to remember: "This is the first time," he said, "I've walked down Fifth Avenue without getting booed . . . ."

A few speakers feared that the enthusiasm of that day might soon fade away. They needn't have worried. There have been Earth Days each April 22 ever since. A silver anniversary for this sometimes uncertain notion that we the

Graham, F. (April, 1995). "Earth Day: 25 Years." *National Geographic.* Vol. 187, No. 4, pp 123–138.

people are a part of the earth, not apart from it, and that (to borrow from the mountain philosopher John Muir) "when we try to pick out anything by itself, we find it hitched to everything else in the universe."

The original event, 1970, had been the brainchild of Senator Gaylord Nelson of Wisconsin, a longtime battler for clean water and a man regarded by many conservationists as one of the few voices of conscience on Capitol Hill. At the time, Nelson was troubled that the environment remained, as he called it, a "non-issue in the politics of our country" even after all the ecological alarms and disasters of the 1960s. The parching of the Everglades. Blackened beaches from the oil-rig blowouts off Santa Barbara. The perils of pesticides. The smog in Los Angeles. The sewage afloat in Chesapeake Bay.

But these *were* issues to more folks than Gaylord Nelson suspected. And as inquiries from the town began to swamp the senator's staff, Nelson was obliged to hire Denis Hayes, a 25-year-old Harvard Law School student, to take over the operation. With Hayes aboard, the planned festivities evolved into Earth Day, and Environment with an uppercase E was off and running, though not without its fair share of detractors.

From the left came insinuations that Earth Day was a scam to deflect the nation's attention from the war in Vietnam. On the right it was said that the event was a communist plot—the April 22 date that Nelson had selected to avoid a conflict with college exams and spring vacations happened to coincide with the 100th anniversary of Lenin's birth.

The events of that day were as varied as the expectations of the participants. There were trail hikes and talkathons, prayer vigils and publicity stunts. In Washington, D.C., demonstrators poured oil on a sidewalk in front of the Department of the Interior to protest its policies on offshore drilling. At Boston's Logan International Airport, 200 people posed as pallbearers for the United States' planned but never-to-be-built supersonic jetliner.

The gimmicks grabbed the headlines, but for most of the people who turned out for the ubiquitous street fairs and pep rallies, Earth Day One was about as confrontational as a bouquet of tulips. But it wasn't a lark either, or a "springtime skipalong," as one of the national newsweeklies suggested. By year's end, even some skeptics began to concede that the fallout from Earth Day would be writ on the face of America for years to come. At first the most noticeable changes appeared in the law books. Three months before Earth Day, President Richard Nixon had signed the National Environmental Policy Act, requiring review and analysis of public projects. An amended—and tougher—Clean Air Act cleared Congress that year, to be followed by a Clean Water Act, a Marine Mammal Protection Act, an Endangered Species Act, a Safe Drinking Water Act, and a Toxic Substances Control Act, among scores of new federal and state statutes.

And inevitably, as the environmental community scored one victory after another on the regulatory and legislative fronts, a few Americans would come to resent what Earth Day had wrought, perceiving the regulations as infringements on their property rights and decrying the laws as pernicious attacks on liberty and the pursuit of happiness.

But the most surprising legacy of that landmark occasion 25 years ago is neither the backlash nor the passage of statutes, but rather the emerging prominence of grassroots advocates acting as unaffiliated individuals or in small groups to educate a community, save a special place, or squash a project harmful to the commonwealth.

The message on April 22, 1970, was that the planet's plight demands an urgent response from each of us. For a quarter century that message has endured to influence the way thousands of Americans now live their lives. Here are brief profiles of seven of them.

MARY LYN RAY

The heart of Mary Lyn Ray's world is a cluster of green-and-gold valleys ringed by the blue-tinted mountains of central New Hampshire. It is a good piece of country for a woman like Ray, a writer of children's books and a land saver with a strong sense of place.

Unlike most over-40 activists in the environmental movement, Ray sat out Earth Day the first time around. "It just sort of passed me by," she recalls. "I remember thinking, 'How encouraging that so many people care.'"

By 1987, however, Ray had something of her own to care about. More than 150 acres of open fields and woodlands adjoining her home in South Danbury was at risk of being developed into small house lots. And if that happened, it would mark the beginning of the end for the values and traditions vested in the land. She decided to acquire the property herself to protect it.

With help from the nonprofit Society for the Protection of New Hampshire Forests, Ray contrived to purchase the land by using underlying gravel deposits as collateral for a bank loan. When the deposits proved too shallow to meet payments on the loan, Ray sold off her collection of art and antiques and learned to live on the edge of bankruptcy. And, convinced that the land should be preserved beyond her lifetime, she arranged for a conservation easement that precluded development.

That was only for starters. Having limited the use of her own land, Ray felt she could ask her neighbors to think about placing easements on *their* property. By late last year her persistence had helped bring permanent protection to more than 5,000 acres of forest and farmland on Ragged Mountain and the surrounding hills.

"When Mary Lyn sets her sights on something," says Paul Bofinger, president of the Forest Society, "you can see the fire in her eyes. She's bet the farm more than once to make good things happen. We're awful lucky to have her on our side."

JUDITH HANCOCK

Right now Judith Hancock is afloat in Okefenokee National Wildlife Refuge. But you might find her, too, at the wheel of a pickup truck on a backcountry road in Osceola National Forest, near Lake City, Florida, checking out potential threats to wildlife and its habitat. "I hope this one's got a bottom," she says as she accelerates the truck across a mudhole filled by recent rains. An earthy plume oozes over the windshield.

Then, pounding the steering wheel with an open palm, Hancock inquires of a rattled passenger, "Still with me?"

The intensity of Hancock's approach to mudholes mirrors her passion for her unremunerated work. In the Osceola she contended with the U.S. Forest Service over timber plans she considered unfriendly to the endangered red-cockaded woodpecker and the wood stork.

The Earth Day idea was a decade old when Hancock first came to the environmental wars, and the first battle she fought was right here in the national forest, where a consortium of companies had applied for permits to mine phosphate. Hancock was familiar enough with wetland ecology to know that the mining and processing of phosphate rock along the headwaters of rivers can have a devastating effect on them, introducing sediment, excess nutrients, and toxic chemicals to the water. So she joined a citizens campaign to block the miners. The citizens prevailed. Based partly on information supplied by the group, Congress enacted a bill in 1984 prohibiting phosphate mining in the national forest.

Now Judy Hancock leaves the cab of her truck to plunge down a trail through wet woods along the Suwannee River. She pauses to admire large golden silk spiders and a canebrake rattlesnake, and before the day's done, she's picked up enough chiggers to keep a hound scratching for a week.

FATHER PETER KREITLER

Every day is Earth Day for Father Peter Kreitler, a 52-year-old Episcopal priest in Los Angeles, California. Tall and outgoing, with a tidy white beard and the confident, resonant voice of a preacher, Kreitler serves as a kind of diocesan minister to the environment, touring the grittier parts of the city in a relentless war against visual pollution. He knows there are far greater problems to solve in the vast sprawl of Los Angeles, but at the same time he believes that solutions have to start somewhere, even if they're small.

"When people lose respect for themselves and their surroundings," he says, "everything else breaks down. Gangs mark out their territories with graffiti, and litter piles up in the streets. We want to turn those things around." Kreitler founded Earth Service, Inc., which fights blight by helping neighborhood groups organize to paint over wall graffiti and haul trash out of vacant lots. Much of the group's effort is aimed at involving young people in recycling and the planting of trees.

El Padre, as he is identified by the letters on his license plate, was ordained in 1970, just five days after the first Earth Day. He did not participate in the event himself, but he remembers reading about it and being impressed by the number of people who expressed their concern. Later that year he began addressing environmental issues regularly from the pulpit, to the extent that some parishioners would soon be joking about "Father Peter's Save the Whales sermons."

So far Kreitler has been frustrated by the reactions to his environmental ministry from some of his colleagues of the cloth. A couple of years ago he called on several pastors to persuade them to correct such sources of wasted energy as incandescent bulbs. "I didn't get much of a response," Kreitler laments. "When the churches say, 'Let there be light,' they really mean it."

ISAAC EASTVOLD

Isaac Eastvold made his pact with the petroglyphs before Earth Day was conceived. His vow was to keep them from harm's way. The petroglyphs are those drawings carved in stone centuries ago by the ancestors of the Pueblo Indians. Though the art is scattered widely throughout the cliffs and canyons of the American Southwest, one of the greatest remaining petroglyph concentrations lies along the West Mesa escarpment on the outskirts of Albuquerque, New Mexico—right in the path of intense development.

Eastvold, bearded and often stirred to lyricism, has devoted at least half his 54 years to the study and protection of Indian rock art. Profoundly moved by the spiritual images, he first roamed the California desert, photographing petroglyphs for the Bureau of Land Management. Then, in 1985, he and his wife, Sharon, moved to Albuquerque and turned their attention to the rock-art treasures that lay just across the Rio Grande.

"When we got here," Eastvold recalls, "the petroglyphs were under terrific pressure. Vandals were using them for target practice. Big boulders with petroglyphs on them were being carted into the city for residential landscaping. In some areas development was being permitted right up to the rocks."

Eastvold proposed that the petroglyphs be protected in a national monument. Then, assuming the presidency of a new group called Friends of the Albuquerque Petroglyphs, he spearheaded an effort to enlist the support of New Mexico's congressional delegation and forge a consensus among competing city and state interests.

In 1990 his dream came true: Congress established 7,200-acre Petroglyph National Monument under the joint management of the city, the state, and the National Park Service. But the fragile consensus evaporated when the city of Albuquerque proposed building two huge roads through the fledgling monument. Eastvold and Pueblo leaders, who consider the park a major religious site, supported alternative routes recommended by the Park Service, but the city has recently granted subdivision permits blocking those routes.

"One developer threatened to run me out of town and ruin my reputation," Eastvold said. "When I pointed out that this is a place of worship for Native Americans, he laughed in my face and scorned their beliefs as a 'Stone Age religion.' He couldn't understand that the land around the petroglyphs is as vital to their meaning as the great cathedrals are to the paintings they hold."

On occasion Eastvold walks in the monument with Phillip Lauriano, a spiritual leader of the nearby Sandia Pueblo. Lauriano recalls first visiting the petroglyphs with his grandfather nearly 70 years ago. He explains to Eastvold that prayers here "go beyond the great divide to a reservoir of strength and power." The men walk together through a sea of wildflowers—evening primroses, mallows, sunflowers. Hover flies, gemlike and volatile, float in front of the blossoms. Wind rustles the bunchgrass.

"Wind in the grass," says Eastvold, "is the voice of the desert."

MARGARET MILLER

Margaret Miller is telling her husband, Paul, that it's time to go over to Dillon's Super Store and check on the bins. "Mrs. Recycling," they call her in Wichita, Kansas. "I got into recycling," Margaret explains, "because I thought it would be most enlightening for the person who wouldn't ordinarily become involved in environmental issues. It's visible. It gets people thinking."

Miller first came to the attention of Kansans when she took on one of the state's electric utilities by opposing its big Wolf Creek nuclear power plant (she lost) and then organized a consumers coalition seeking representation before the state board that sets utility rates (she won).

In 1989 Miller and two friends asked the Wichita City Council to help them set up a recycling program. "They laughed at us," Miller recalls. "They said people here would never go for it. So we established our own collection in a few parking lots. At the end of 18 months it was taking a fleet of trucks to handle all the waste." Now both the city and the state have pitched in, and local governments throughout Kansas coordinate the collection, reduction, and recycling of waste.

A key to Miller's success is her willingness to cooperate with the business community. "Margaret Miller pioneered recycling in Kansas," says Eric Evenson, manager of a new Weyerhauser Company plant in Wichita. The plant sorts and bales recyclable office papers and other "secondary" fibers for reprocessing. Evenson also credits

Miller with educating the public on how to separate wastes—"and that's a job we could never have done by ourselves."

But the job never ends. Over in the parking lot at Dillon's Super Store, Miller spots a newcomer to the system. "Look at that woman," she says in a low voice. "She's going to put those colored bottles in with the clear ones."

Miller approaches. The miscreant is about to get educated.

PERCY AND ELLA HERON

Percy and Ella Heron's community garden sits at the corner of Inwood Street and Lakewood Avenue in the South Jamaica section of Queens, not far from the great airports of New York City. The garden is enclosed by a high chain-link fence. The gate is padlocked when the garden is not in use. The neighborhood of single-family houses on narrow lots has seen better days, though hardly anyone but the Herons has lived here long enough to remember them.

Percy and Ella Heron moved in here, two houses from the corner, in 1949. Together they and their neighbors tend the community garden, nurturing not only plants in the earth but also ideas in the minds of a younger generation. "We teach the neighborhood children about the soil," says Ella. "We teach about water and where it comes from and why it has to be clean."

Once there had been a house at the corner. Then the house burned, and the city condemned it and tore what remained to the ground. Vacant, the lot attracted garbage and litter until the Herons stepped in, appealed to the city's Department of General Services, and, with its blessing, slowly turned the place into a community garden, one of some 700 now flourishing in New York under the auspices of the department's Operation Green Thumb.

In season, the garden sparkles with roses, azaleas, hydrangeas, daisies, asters, tulips, and daffodils. There are planter boxes with peanuts and okra and tomatoes. Children come to the garden after school to help the Herons with their chores. This is how the ideas get planted.

Now it is time for Earth Day again. It will be, as always, a very special day at the community garden. Last October Ella and Percy Heron and some of their young friends got down on their hands and knees and planted tulip bulbs around the edge of a bed of roses. And what Ella told the kids was, "Don't you forget to come back here on April 22. These tulips might be fixing to bloom for that day."

To People Who Make a Difference

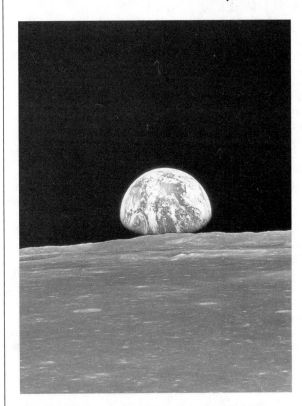

Planet Earth from space. Photo courtesy of NASA Headquarters.

The registry of people who make environmental differences live in every town, county, and province of the world. What is happening notably since the 1970s is that people are becoming aware and concerned; they understand that they can make a difference and change the spread of ecological malaise. They are thinking change and enacting a system. The people mentioned previously are only a few of the people that have altered ways of doing things. Magazines, newspapers, and publications of local organizations all herald individual ecological achievement, but there is still much achievement that goes unacknowledged. The central idea here is that ecological change stems from individual conscience that has held to a commitment to improve some system or aspect that affects our earth. Ecological leadership and change begin with such individuals that care and extend energy and commitment behind their caring. From their actions, there are positive changes, new systems, and new research. This is where the hope for our future lies—with a strong, positive, ecologically minded, innovative dynamic. This box is dedicated to the many individuals who have made a difference and who will make *such* a difference.

Exercise

Research from publications, your local newspapers, and local organizations people who have enacted environment-friendly systems or approaches for ecological improvement. If possible, interview these individuals and give a presentation on their struggles and accomplishments.

Questions

1. What effect did each of these people have on the environment?
2. Why do you feel that all seven of these people are important in helping our planet? Which one do you think is most important?

A Bridge to Your 21st Century Understanding

Choose two people from this article that are the most interesting to you. Create a flowchart on each one.

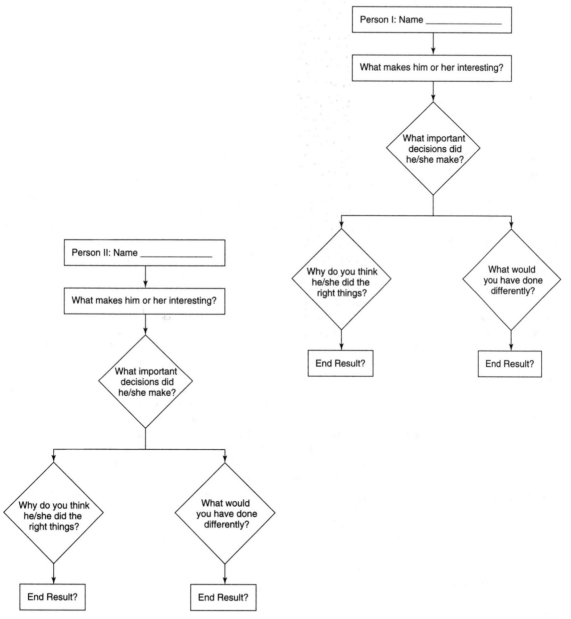

Person I: Name _____

↓

What makes him or her interesting?

↓

What important decisions did he/she make?

Why do you think he/she did the right things?

↓

End Result?

What would you have done differently?

↓

End Result?

Person II: Name _____

↓

What makes him or her interesting?

↓

What important decisions did he/she make?

Why do you think he/she did the right things?

↓

End Result?

What would you have done differently?

↓

End Result?

20 Rain Forests May Offer New Miracle Drugs

In the remote rain forests of Suriname, families have traditionally used local plants to treat common illnesses such as fever and stomachache, and more exotic ailments like leishmaniasis, an Amazon parasite which produces skin lesions. Folklore knowledge not only includes which plants are specific to certain diseases, but also proscribes the methods of preparation and application of the health restoring tinctures.

Synthetic production of drugs has been the primary focus of western pharmaceutical companies since the 1940s. Producing drugs in the laboratory allows these companies to safeguard their investment in research and development through intellectual property legislation enacted via patents and licenses.

In recent times, international drug companies such as Bristol-Myers are refocusing their interest on the natural laboratory that lies beneath the canopy of the rain forest, which is able to offer an albeit undocumented but nevertheless tried and perfected methodology towards drug refinement and employment. Recent discoveries include tree extracts from Indonesia which show promise in fighting HIV infection; a Brazilian shrub which is used to treat diabetes; and fungi and bacteria from the Philippines which show promise in treating a variety of ailments.

The process of searching for new natural medicines is called bioprospecting. Recent technological advances in screening samples of plants, animals and other natural substances for curative ingredients, has made it cost-effective to collect and analyze the large number of specimens needed to hone in viable medicines. In addition, the natural proclivity of diseases such as malaria to build up resistance to drugs has accelerated the need for alternative forms of treatment.

Bioprospecting accounts for 10% of the research budget in most large U.S. drug companies, which can amount to a significant investment for firms such as Merck & Co., which have annual R & D budgets of up to $1 billion. In addition, government agencies such as the National Institutes for Health, the National Science Foundation, and the U.S. Agency for International Development are also turning to bioprospecting. These three agencies will spend $2.3 million searching the rain forests of Costa Rica, Peru, Suriname, and Cameroon, and the deserts of Mexico, Chile, and Argentina.

Bioprospecting successes include the landmark Taxol, a treatment for advanced ovarian cancer found in the bark and needles of the Pacific Yew, and Vinblastine, a drug used for treating cancers including Hodgkin's disease and leukemia found in the rosy periwinkle, a Madagascan plant. Two other natural substances, Michellamine B from a Cameroon vine, and Prostratin, from a Samoan Rubber tree, are showing promise in the fight against AIDS.

Plants are not the only source of potential life saving drugs. On the French Guinea border, the Wayana people eat the heads of soldier ants to obtain a chemical which they believe will ward off malaria.

The search for curative compounds does not only take place in the natural environment. Medicinal plant researchers scour local markets seeking folk cures which

Goering, L. (1995, 12 September). Rain forests may offer new miracle drugs. *Chicago Tribune*, Sect. 1 16.

may lead to the next wonder drug. In addition, these researchers rush to record potential remedies which may be lost to the passing of generations. Traditional cures are often complex combinations of herbs and animal extracts taken together to produce the required effect. Plants which reduce the side effects of curative substances are often taken with their medicinal counterparts. Researchers fear the knowledge of which combinations are effective may be lost as cultures are assimilated into the mainstream, and as the natural environment is destroyed. For example, at least 90% of the plants in the vanishing Brazilian Amazon have never been chemically analyzed.

Another problem is the time it takes to bring a discovered drug to market, often 10 to 15 years. Lab-developed drugs are often cheaper to refine and document for approval; a recent report indicated that Aspirin, derived from Willow tree bark, may have never been approved under the modern approval process due to uncertainties about the specific mechanism which makes it effective.

Researchers are also struggling with the dilemma of how to return part of the profits to the people and countries who provided the cure. In Suriname, bioprospectors have set up a Forest People's Fund, which received an initial $50,000 royalty from Bristol-Myers Squibb, and will receive between 1% and 5% of any royalties from marketed drugs. This program is designed to encourage local conservation of threatened ecosystems with financial incentives.

Thus while bioprospecting is showing increasing promise as a source of medicines and disease fighting drugs, researchers are fighting environmental and cultural destruction in the race to discover the next wonder drug. And while the search for traditional cures accelerates, no such speed-up in the process of bringing these cures to market seems imminent.

RAIN FOREST DIVERSITY AND DESTRUCTION

As stated in the introduction, the rain forests of the world need protection, since they significantly affect world climate, consuming large quantities of CO_2, contributing a large percentage of the world's oxygen, and slowing global warming. Also, the rain forest guards over most of the planet's biodiversity (an umbrella term for the variety of ecosystems, species, and genes present). Scientists theorize that tens of millions of species exist; however, they have described only a small proportion, only between 1.4 and 1.5 million of them. Half of these species that have

been identified live in tropical forests, but scientists estimate that 90% of all existing species live in the rain forest and would be identified if only the scientists had time to study them. The destruction of rain forests is rampant at about the pace of 100 acres a minute (approximately the size of the state of Washington each year). Rain forests now cover about only 5% of the earth's land surface, yet they contain at least half of its plant and animal species. During the past 30 years, about one third of the world's rain forests have disappeared, and this rate is increasing (Jukofsky, 1993, p. 20).

An example of this biological richness and abundance is in a study which found that a single hectare (about 2.5 acres) of rain forest in Peru contained 300 tree species— almost half the number of tree species native to all of North America. In another study, scientists found more than 1,300 butterfly species and 600 bird species within one five-square-kilometer patch of Peruvian rain forest. (The whole United States harbors 400 butterfly species and about 700 bird species.) In the same Peruvian jungle, Harvard entomologist Edward O. Wilson determined 43 ant species in a single tree, about the same number as exists in all of the British Isles (Rice, 1997, p. 48).

ECONOMIC VALUE

One reason that such plant and animal life diversity is vital is that it is essential for creating food, medicines, and raw materials. Wild plants have the genetic resources to breed pest- and disease-resistant crops. An estimated 120 clinically useful prescription drugs originate from 95 species of plants, of which 39 grow in tropical forests. Botanists estimate that from 35,000 to 70,000 plant species that are mostly from tropical forests provide traditional remedies in countries throughout the world. Without the rain forest, these plant species and the vast array of existing and potential medicines derived from them would become forever lost (Rice, 1997, p. 48).

Dr. Robert Balick of the New York Botanical Garden and Dr. Robert Mendelsohn of Yale University have studied the potential economic value that might result from medicines derived from the flora of the rain forest. Effective new drugs are valued at an average of $94 million each to drug companies. They concluded that at least 328 drugs await discovery with a projected value of some $147 billion (Medical Herpetology, 1997).

About half of the Earth's 250,000 flowering plants exist in tropical forests, but less than 1% of them have been thoroughly tested for medicinal uses. Nearly half of all drugs

Table 20.1

The Rain Forest Pharmacy: Partial List

Drug	Derived from	Medical Uses
Atropine	Belladonna	Eases asthma attacks
Cocaine	Coca	Local anesthetics
D-Tubocurarine	Chondodendron tomentosum	Skeletal muscle relaxant
Diosgenin	Mexican Yam	Oral contraceptive
Papain	Papaya	Eases chronic diarrhea
Picrotoxin	Levant berry seeds	Eases schizophrenic seizures
Pilocarpine	Pilocarpus	Glaucoma
Quinine	Cinchona	Malaria
Reserpine	Snakeroot	Tranquilizers and treatment of hypertension
Vinblastine	Rosy periwinkle	Helps Hodgkin's disease
Vincristine	Rosy periwinkle	Helps acute leukemia

Source: Jukofsky, 1993 p. 26

prescribed in the United States have originated from plant life, with 47 medications currently on the market that are derived from the tropical forest, including codeine, quinine, and curare (Drugs and Money Abound in Rain Forests, 1995).

It is hoped that the economic value of studies of the rain forest will emphasize the importance of research and accelerate the conservation of invaluable world resources. However, efforts to slow destruction of the world's rain forests, home to these innumerable species, have met with limited success. Entire plant and animal populations and species are disappearing fast. Factors that cause this loss, aside from deforestation, including acid rain, other types of pollution, and increased UV-B exposure, are being investigated. It is greatly hoped that the discovery of pharmaceutical and other products derived from the rain forest can result in increased support and attention for biodiversity conservation and funds for continuing research (Medical Herpetology, 1997).

References

"Drugs and Money Abound in Rain Forests." *ION Science,* July 1995. Available: http://w.w.winjersey.com/media/IonSci/glance/news795/raindrug.html.

Goering, L. (1995, September 12). Rain forests may offer new miracle drugs. *Chicago Tribune,* section 1, 16.

Jukofsky, D., and Wille, C. (April/May 1993). "They're Our Rain Forests Too." *National Wildlife,* Vol. 31, No. 3, pp. 18–37.

Medical Herpetology. 1997. Available: http://www.worlcorp.com/biodiversity/newsletter/two/herp.htm.

Rice, R. E., Gullison, R. E., and Reid, J. W. (1997, April). "Can Sustainable Management Save Tropical Forests?" *Scientific American.* Vol. 276, No. 4, pp. 44–49.

Questions

1. Should local inhabitants be rewarded for drugs discovered in their region? Can ownership of a renewable living resource (such as a plant) be treated in the same way as a non-renewable resource (such as mineral rights)?

2. The article mentions that it can take 10 to 15 years to gain approval and bring a drug to market. Is there a justification for performing drug trials on patients before full testing has been completed, and the drug proven safe and effective? If a patient has a terminal illness, what guidelines would you suggest in administering experimental medicines?

3. Researchers are concerned that potential cures will be lost to the destruction of the environment and the assimilation of folklore into popular culture. While there is much focus on saving the environment, the preservation of cultural diversity attracts little attention. What responsibility do the western nations have in safeguarding native cultures in the countries which they influence? Conversely, what right do they have in denying modern "civilization" to less technological societies?

4. The goal of the medical community, including drug companies, is to keep people alive for the longest

possible time, regardless of their usefulness to society as a whole. It is also true that the earth has limited resources, and natural law dictates that exponential population growth is not sustainable. This dictates that at some point (or points) mankind will be beset by natural and uncontrollable events such as epidemics which will cull the world's population back to sustainable levels. Extend this logic to produce an argument supporting euthanasia, or other solutions to world over-population. What are the ramifications of such arguments?

5. Project how long the rain forests have to exist given the current rate of destruction. What are some approaches you can think of to stop this rate of destruction?

6. What specifically are the ramifications of our increasing loss of rain forests? From this answer, derive solutions for abating this loss.

7. How effective do you think estimations of the economic value of potential drugs will be to save rain forest diversity? How would you use this strategy of placing an economic value on resources of rain forests to support rain forest conservation?

8. Research a more extensive list of rain forest medicines.

9. The article states that one reason that plant and animal life diversity is vital is for creating food, medicines, and raw materials. What are some other reasons?

A Bridge to Your 21st Century Understanding

Complete and discuss the following flowchart.

⊕ Advantages

⊖ Drawbacks

A Bridge to Your 21st Century Understanding

Complete and discuss the following flowchart.

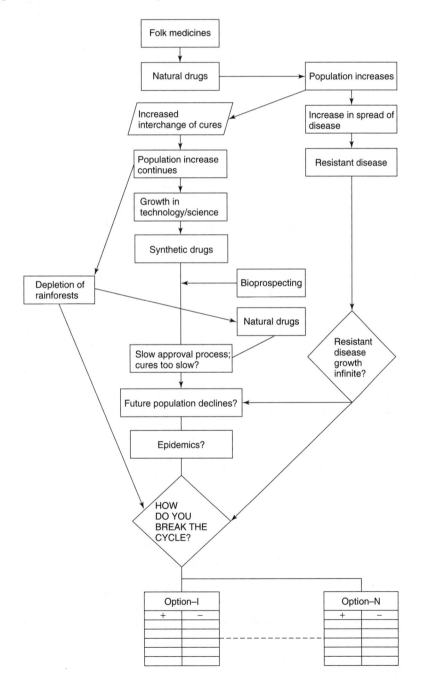

Conclusion

As stated in the beginning of this part of the book, the purpose of this part is to enhance awareness, responsibility, strategies, and involvement for a sustainable, desirable environment. This part has overviewed many major issues that cry out for more results and better solutions. Many of those solutions have begun to be implemented and have already made an important difference—but the issues of this part (and others) remain central and critical to our future and our future quality of life. Your thoughtful awareness and involvement can and will make an important contribution. Therefore, this text is designed so that you may become aware of the issues and the decisions you can make or that can be made to design the future. Your involvement and awareness become the fulcrum for the solution. The flowcharts illustrate this philosophy.

The issues presented are not meant to present a negative picture of ecology, but instead are intended to bring out three different layers of central issues that need to be addressed. The three layers of the overview, the global case study, and the specific case study could be likened to the earth itself with (1) the overview being similar to the atmosphere of ecological understanding; (2) the global case study being comparable to the surface of the earth, with all the interactions of activity that take place on the surface of the globe; and (3) the specific case study being similar to the local activity that then affects global issues and understanding. The three layers of the issues presented then included the following aspects:

1. The overview structural layer in the introduction discussed the history and overview of the high-risk environmental issues of habitat destruction, species extinction, global warming, and depletion of the ozone layer, with an approach with regard to economic value.

2. The text then proceeded to the major global issues of consumerism and waste, long-term effects of pollutants on our animal and human young, and superfunds—what to do with our toxic wastes—and the exploitation of and lack of planning for our world fishing industries.

3. The specific case studies brought to your attention the situations regarding Love Canal, the Endangered Species Act, air pollution, Earth Day, people who have made a difference in environmental causes, and rain forest pharmaceuticals.

It is hoped that from these issues and experiences, you have a better pulse of some of the major ecological issues and are oriented to participate in their solutions.

Our "Ecological" Social–Economic View

Associating fiscal value with the earth's natural goods and services will begin to raise perceptions of ecological value to its real importance and value. The estimation of our ecosystem at $33 trillion seems conservative, but this estimate is a start in bringing to peoples' minds the replaceable and working value of the ecosystem. Pollution controls can be viewed from dollars saved in annual health costs. Raw material costs should include costs of earth materials lost and recovery techniques to the environment. Costs of fish should be raised with monetary penalties when quotas are exceeded. Rain forest conservation approaches can be partially funded through the market of its products and pharmaceuticals. And lastly, threatened and endangered species can receive the funding that is necessary if the extinction of species becomes a heavy debt and monetary liability.

Not all ecological problems can be solved with a credit and debit ledger, but placing true monetary value on an interactive world ecosystem on which we all depend may help unindustrialized countries as well as industrialized countries treasure and account for their resources and level the playing field. Many Third-World countries retain valuable resources without receiving compensation for their use or conservation (e.g., the animals of Africa and Asia, the rainforests of Central America, etc.). It makes good sense to count treasure as treasure.

Bridge to the Future

Many of these issues discussed in this part of the book have been the recipients of some successful efforts at enacting solutions. The Rio de Janeiro Earth Summit of 1992, attended by more than 100 heads of state, addressed many issues with serious intent to makes progress on issues of environment and poverty, but the solutions that came out of this summit are not necessarily working. In the part on the future, Part 9, we will discuss some successes, failures, and future initiatives for ecological progress in the 21st Century.

Internet Exercise

1. Use any of the Internet search engines (e.g., Alta Vista, Yahoo, Infoseek, etc.) to research the following topics:

    a. Updates on rain forest destruction and some programs to conserve rain forests.

    b. Disappearance and malformation of frogs on the earth.

    c. The latest research on global warming—is it or is it not happening?

    d. The latest views on the disappearance of the ozone layer and the laws that try to protect the ozone layer and their effects.

    e. Some of the facts on improvements in conservation due to recycling.

    f. Water pollution and the water we drink.

    g. More information on Superfund.

    h. The latest information on the Magnuson Fishery Conservation and Management Act.

    i. Commercial and recreational fishing catches in your local area for the last decade.

    j. Some of the projects that the Citizens Clearinghouse for Hazardous Waste have undertaken.

    k. New revisions and implications of the Endangered Species Act.

    l. Air pollution in your area.

    m. Water pollution in your area.

    n. The latest laws on air pollution particulates.

    o. A list of people whom you admire who have made a difference ecologically.

    p. New medicines and products derived from flora or fauna in the rain forest.

    q. Garbage production in the last ten years (locally, statewide, or nationally).

    r. Ecological laws passed in the last two years (local, state, or federal).

2. Use any of the Internet search engines (e.g., Alta Vista, Yahoo, Infoseek, etc.) to research the following topics:

    a. Ecosystem, ecosphere, and sythesphere.

    b. Environmental Protection Agency.

    c. Biological diversity.

    d. Chlorofluorocarbons and ozone.

    e. Dioxins.

    f. PCBs.

    g. Pesticides.

h. Hazardous wastes.

i. U.N. Food and Agriculture Organization.

j. Individual Transferable Quotas.

k. Endangered Species Act and threatened species.

l. U.S. Fish and Wildlife Service.

m. Air particulates.

n. Ethnobotany.

o. The words you have listed (see the vocabulary exercise in the introduction) from your research and reading of ecological issues.

Useful Web Sites

URL	Site Description
http:www.medaccess.com/newsletter/ n10415/cchw_ov.htm.	Citizens Clearinghouse for Hazardous Waste
http://www.edf.org	Environmental Defense Fund
gopher://ftp.std.com:70/11periodicals/rachel	Environmental Research Foundation
http://www.audubon.org	National Audubon Society
http://www.nationalgeographic.com	National Geographic Society
http://www.nrdc.org	National Resources Defense Council
http://www.nwf.org/nwf	National Wildlife Federation
http://www.tnc.org	The Nature Conservancy
http://www.sciam.com	Scientific American
http://www.sierraclub.org/RightFrame.html	Sierra Club
http://www.worldwildlife.org	World Wildlife Fund
http://www.yahoo.com/Society_and_Culture ions/Public_Interest_Groups/Environment	Listing of Environmental Organizations
http://www.nasa.gov	NASA
http://www.fao.org	Food and Agriculture Organization of the United Nations

PART

IV

Population

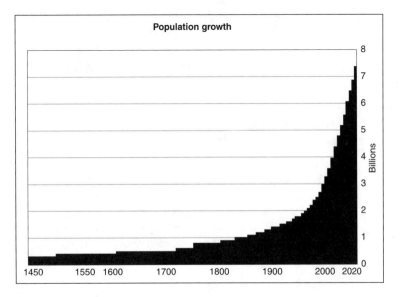

Population growth

Understanding world population is-
sues: A street in Calcutta, India.
Photo courtesy of United
Nations/J.P. LaFonte.

"Humanity is approaching a crisis point with respect to the interlocking issues of population, environment, and development."

STATEMENT FROM 60 SCIENCE ACADEMIES LED BY THE U.S. NATIONAL ACADEMY OF SCIENCES AND BRITAIN'S ROYAL SOCIETY, OCTOBER 1993.

"The decisions that the international community takes over the next several years, whether leading to action or inaction, will have profound implications for the quality of life for all people, including generations not yet born, and perhaps for the planet itself."

STATEMENT MADE AT THE INTERNATIONAL CONFERENCE ON POPULATION AND DEVELOPMENT, CAIRO, 1994.

As you read and reflect upon these pages, you will find many issues—individual, local, national, global, religious, societal, economic, and ecological—that all closely interrelate. Graphs in this part of the book show that we reached our first billion people in world history around 1839; our second billion 90 years later, around 1930; and our third billion 30 years later, in 1960. Currently, we are adding a billion people to the world's population approximately every 15 years or less, which could easily escalate our population count to the U.N. high projection of 11.9 billion by the year 2050. For sustenance, the United Nations recommends an ambitious plan to stabilize population at low to medium projections of 7.9 to 9.8 billion people by 2050. In order for this stabilization to happen, it is necessary to address the following issues that are confronting us:

growth projections
ecological implications

food production

limitation of the earth's natural resources for food production

the issues raised by the 1994 Cairo Conference

population control issues

numbers carrying capacity where country becomes stabilized

specific case studies (such as those of Pakistan, India, Ethiopia, and Mexico)

the interdependent nature of population, poverty, and the local environment

This part on population and the issues that it addresses have many implications, the purpose of which is to help you to be informed and to make informed decisions on the individual, local, national, economic, ecological, and other fronts. There is much to say and more to do, but it all starts with being informed and playing a part in determining a future plan; this is a vital assignment, since we add to the world population approximately

3	people	each second
117	people	each minute
10,600	people	each hour
254,000	people	each day
1,800,000	people	each week
7,700,000	people	each month
93,000,000	people	each year.

All of these numbers translate to a situation in which nine babies are born and three people die every two seconds, resulting in a net increase of three people each second. By the year 2000, annual population growth will increase to 94 million people, and by 2020 it will rise to 98 million. In 2020, 98% of the increase will be from births in developing countries (U.S. Bureau of the Census).

For real-time population numbers, the following Internet addresses access the current second-by-second population clocks and projection numbers to give you a further idea of our exponential patterns of population growth (also refer to the "Useful Web Sites" section at the end of this part):

National population	http://www.census.gov/cgi-bin/popclock
World population	http://sunsite.unc.edu/lunarbin/worldpop
	http://www.census.gov/cgi-bin/ipc/popclockw

Like the other parts of this book, this part presents factual, historical, social, and economic weavings along with the issues and articles to provide a cross-analysis of the issues from differing perspectives. The tables and figures that follow the introductory text give a necessary empirical base to realize the issues numerically before the descriptive discussions of the cases and articles are presented. This format builds an understanding of the issues from both data-based and cross-descriptive views.

MALTHUS VS. DEMOGRAPHIC TRANSITION THEORY

The rapid growth of Europe's population because of more abundant food supplies and better living conditions caused Thomas Malthus (1766–1834), an English economist, to predict uncontrolled population growth and, hence, future doom. In 1798, he wrote the book *An Essay on the Principle of Population,* in which he predicted what became known as the Malthus theorem. His principal argument was that while population grows geometrically (from 2 people to 4 to 8 to 16, etc.), food supply increases arithmetically (from 1 unit to 2 to 3 to 4, etc.), concluding that if births proceed unchecked, the population will outgrow its food supply (Henslin, 1996, pp. 352–353). However, a different and somewhat opposite argument called a three-stage demographic transition theory also exists in which the first stage, Stage I, has high birth rates and high death rates while population remains stable; the second stage, Stage II, experiences high birth rates and low death rates while population surges; and the third stage, Stage III, has low birth rates and low death rates while population stabilizes and the economic quality of life improves. The theory is that all nations proceed through these stages in economic and societal growth before reaching stabilization (Brown, 1987). Consider the following historical world population patterns below.

Historical World Population Trends		
Approximate Year	*Estimated Population*	
1 million B.C.	125	thousand
8000 B.C.	5.3	million
4000 B.C.	86.5	million
1 A.D.	200	million
1000 A.D.	275	million
1650 A.D.	545	million
1750 A.D.	728	million
1839 A.D.	1	billion
1850 A.D.	1.17	billion
1900 A.D.	1.55	billion
1930 A.D.	2.0	billion
1950 A.D.	2.5	billion
1960 A.D.	3.0	billion
1970 A.D.	3.6	billion
1976 A.D.	4.0	billion
1982 A.D.	4.5	billion
1995 A.D.	5.72	billion
PROJECTED		
1998 A.D.	6.0	billion
2025 A.D.	8.5	billion
2050 A.D.	10	billion

Sources: Pytlik, 1985, p. 148; Wright, 1995, p. 356

Questions

1. What are the slowest periods of population gain? What are the most rapid?

2. Using these population figures and those leading to current and future growth, what do you feel are projections for world food supply, economic growth, political stability, and quality of life?

3. Apply your conclusions to the Malthus theorem and the demographic transition theory. Do your conclusions change when you consider these viewpoints? What validity do you think these arguments hold?

4. What will happen after 2050 in terms of population growth? What does the demographic theory project will happen? What does the Malthus theory project will happen with these exponential projections? What theory do you have regarding the future of population growth?

5. What do you project the population numbers to be in the year 3000 A.D.? Give a planned and supported explanation of your projection.

Population Vocabulary Exercise

As you proceed through this part and your reading and research of various issues associated with population topics, keep a listing of terms and organizations dealing with population that you would like to know more about. Use various resources to define and learn more about them, including other texts, articles, encyclopedias, and the Internet (refer to the Internet exercise at the end of this part).

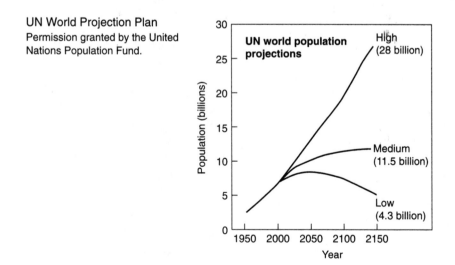

UN World Projection Plan
Permission granted by the United
Nations Population Fund.

WORLD POPULATION CONTINUES TO SOAR

Concern for the exponentially increasing world population is becoming more widespread. One of the most important questions in the world today is whether human beings are wise enough to see what is coming. Today's global population cannot be sustained at the current lifestyle level of the United States, Europe, or Japan. Over the past couple of centuries, the following statements were issued about population growth:

- Around 200 years ago (1798), Englishman Thomas Malthus stated, "Population, when unchecked, increases in a geometrical ratio. Subsistence only increases in an arithmetical ratio."

- About a century later, Charles Darwin said, "Man tends to increase at a greater rate than his means of subsistence; consequently he is occasionally subjected to a severe struggle for existence."

- Nearly 100 years after that (1968), Paul Ehrlich spoke of population calamity in *The Population Bomb*.

OTHER COMMENTS ON THE ISSUE OF CONTINUED INCREASING GROWTH AND THE RESULTING DECREASING WORLD STABILITY

- Joel E. Cohen, in "How Many People Can Earth Hold?", states, "According to every plausible calculation that's ever been done, Earth could not feed even the 695 billion people that the U.N. projected for 2150 if present fertility rates were to continue" (Cohen, p. 100). He quotes Princeton demographer Ansely Coale's conclusions: "Every demographer knows that we cannot continue a positive rate of increase indefinitely. The inexorable arithmetic of compound interest leads us to absurd conditions within a calculable period of time. Logically we must, and in fact we will, have a rate of growth very close to zero in the long run (Cohen, p. 100).

- Lester R. Brown and Hal Kane, in their book *Full House,* explain the following: "The demands of the 90 million people added each year for grain and seafood are being satisfied by reducing consumption among those already here. This is a new situation, one that puts population policy in a new light . . . [This population expansion rate] can devastate local life-support systems" (Brown and Kane, pp. 49–50).

Debate on this issue by nations and their people heatedly continues as the world's population continues to leap geometrically from 2.5 billion in 1950 to 5.6 billion in the 1990s. It is projected that there will be 6 billion people by 2000 and perhaps 9 billion by 2025 or 2030. Overpopulation is one of the chief obstacles to universal well-being. A 1994 Cornell University study concluded that the world can only support 2 billion people at the current standard of living now experienced by the industrialized nations of the world. In 1992, 1,600 prominent world scientists, including half of the living science Nobel laureates, presented a declaration to the world's leaders stating that the continuation of destructive human activities "may so alter the living world that it will be unable to sustain life in the manner that we know" (Brown and Kane, p. 30).

The current global growth pattern adds about the equivalent of Mexico's population (92,202,200 people) to the world every year. The U.S. population climbed to 261.7 million in 1994. The annual year-end estimate shows a gain of 2.5 million people in 1994, for a total of 261,653,497 people. The growth includes a natural increase of 1.7 million people—4 million births minus 2.5 million deaths—plus 733,000 additional people due to immigration and the return of 84,000 Americans from abroad.

REFERENCES

(1) Brown, L.R., and Kane, H. (1994). *Full house: Reassessing the Earth's Population Carrying Capacity.* New York: W.W. Norton & Company.
(2) Cohen, J.E. (1992, November). How many people can earth hold? *Discover.* Vol. 13, pp. 114-120.

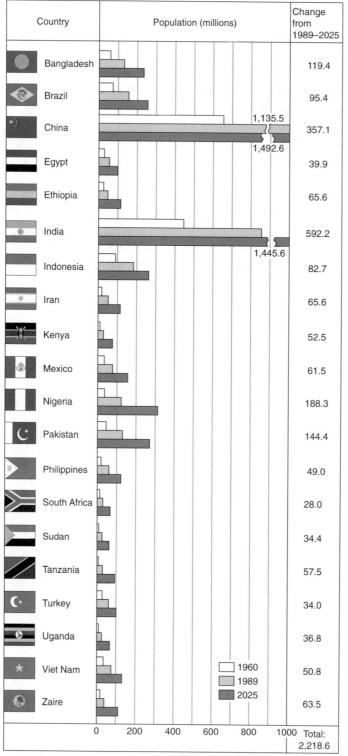

Figure P4.1
High-growth countries. Seventy percent of the projected increase in world population by the year 2025 will occur in these 20 less developed countries. The data are from the United Nations Department of International Economic and Social Affairs.
Reprinted with permission from Ian Worpole.

Questions

1. Using an almanac or the Internet, find the current population figures for the world and for the United States. Chart the new percentage-growth figures. What are your conclusions regarding the various statements quoted in this box?

2. Do you agree with the statements quoted in this box? Why or why not? Build your position on the figures of population growth.

3. Consult world population growth charts. Where are the highest percentages of population growth occurring? What are some of your conclusions about food resources in these areas?

Table P4.1
Annual Rates of Birth, Death and Growth of the Human Population Since 1950

5-Year Period Beginning in Year	Annual Growth Rate (Percent)	Annual Birth Rate (Percent)	Annual Death Rate (Percent)
1950	1.79	3.7	2.0
1955	1.86	3.6	1.7
1960	1.99	3.5	1.5
1965	2.06	3.4	1.3
1970	1.96	3.2	1.2
1975	1.73	2.8	1.1
1980	1.74	2.8	1.0
1985	1.74	2.7	0.98

Source: United Nations Population Fund.

Table P4.2
Percentage Distribution of the World's Population, by Major Area,
1950–2050

Area	1950	1990	2050
Developed countries	29.9%	20.5%	12.4%
Europe	15.6	9.4	4.9
North America	6.6	5.2	3.3
Oceania	0.5	0.5	0.4
USSR[1]	7.2	5.4	3.8
Developing countries	70.1	79.5	87.6
Africa	8.8	12.1	22.6
Latin America	6.6	8.5	9.2
China	22.1	21.5	15.2
India	14.2	16.1	17.0
Other Asia	18.4	21.2	23.7

1. Republics of former Soviet Union.
Source: United Nations Department of International Economic and Social Affairs,
Long-range World Population Projections, 1950–2150 (1992).

Table P4.3
Estimated and Projected Population of Major World Areas, 1950–2050 (in millions)

Area	1950	1990	2000	2025	2050
World	**2,518**	**5,292**	**6,261**	**8,504**	**10,019**
Developed	752	1,089	1,143	1,237	1,233
Europe	393	498	510	515	486
Northern America	166	276	295	332	326
Oceania	13	26	30	38	41
USSR[1]	180	289	308	352	380
Developing	1,766	4,203	5,118	7,267	8,786
Africa	222	642	867	1,597	2,265
Latin America	166	448	538	757	922
China	555	1,139	1,299	1,513	1,521
India	358	853	1,042	1,442	1,699
Other Asia	465	1,121	1,372	1,958	2,379

1. Republics of former Soviet Union.
Source: United Nations Department of International Economic and Social Affairs, *Long-Range World Population Projections, 1950–2150* (1992).

Table P4.4

The World's Largest Urban Areas, Ranked by 1990 Estimated Population (in millions)

The following chart is arranged according to urban areas that had populations of more than three million in 1990. An urban area is a central city, or several cities, and the surrounding urbanized areas, also called a metropolitan area.

Urban area	Country	1950	1970	1990	2000[1]
1. Mexico City	Mexico	3.1	9.4	20.2	25.6
2. Tokyo	Japan	6.7	14.9	18.1	19.0
3. São Paulo	Brazil	2.4	8.1	17.4	22.1
4. New York	United States	12.3	16.2	16.2	16.8
5. Shanghai	China	5.3	11.2	13.4	17.0
6. Los Angeles	United States	4.0	8.4	11.9	13.9
7. Calcutta	India	4.4	6.9	11.8	15.7
8. Buenos Aires	Argentina	5.0	8.4	11.5	12.9
9. Bombay	India	2.9	5.8	11.2	15.4
10. Seoul	South Korea	1.0	5.3	11.0	12.7
11. Beijing	China	3.9	8.1	10.8	14.0
12. Rio de Janeiro	Brazil	2.9	7.0	10.7	12.5
13. Tianjin	China	2.4	5.2	9.4	12.7
14. Jakarta	Indonesia	2.0	3.9	9.3	13.7
15. Cairo	Egypt	2.4	5.3	9.0	11.8
16. Moscow	Russia	4.8	7.1	8.8	9.0
17. Delhi	India	1.4	3.5	8.8	13.2
18. Metro Manila	Philippines	1.5	3.5	8.5	11.8
19. Osaka	Japan	3.8	7.6	8.5	8.6
20. Paris	France	5.4	8.3	8.5	8.6
21. Karachi	Pakistan	1.0	3.1	7.7	11.7
22. Lagos	Nigeria	0.3	2.0	7.7	12.9
23. London	United Kingdom	8.7	8.6	7.4	13.9
24. Bangkok	Thailand	1.4	3.1	7.2	10.3
25. Chicago	United States	4.9	6.7	7.0	7.3
26. Teheran	Iran	1.0	3.3	6.8	8.5
27. Istanbul	Turkey	1.1	2.8	6.7	9.5
28. Dhaka	Bangladesh	0.4	1.5	6.6	12.2
29. Lima	Peru	1.0	2.9	6.2	8.2
30. Madras	India	1.4	3.0	5.7	7.8
31. Hong Kong	Hong Kong	1.7	3.4	5.4	6.1
32. Milan	Italy	3.6	5.5	5.3	5.4
33. Madrid	Spain	1.6	3.4	5.2	5.9
34. St. Petersburg	Russia	2.6	4.0	5.1	5.4
35. Bangalore	India	0.8	1.6	5.0	8.2

Table P4.4

Urban area	Country	1950	1970	1990	2000[1]
36. Bogotá	Colombia	0.6	2.4	4.9	6.4
37. Shenyang	China	2.1	3.5	4.8	6.3
38. Philadelphia	United States	2.9	4.0	4.3	4.5
39. Caracas	Venezuela	0.7	2.0	4.1	5.2
40. Baghdad	Iraq	0.6	2.0	4.0	5.1
41. Lahore	Pakistan	0.8	2.0	4.1	6.0
42. Wuhan	China	1.2	2.7	3.9	5.3
43. Alexandria	Egypt	1.0	2.0	3.7	5.1
44. Detroit	United States	2.8	4.0	3.7	3.7
45. Guangzhou	China	1.3	3.0	3.7	4.8
46. San Francisco	United States	2.0	3.0	3.7	4.1
47. Ahmedabad	India	0.9	1.7	3.6	5.3
48. Belo Horizonte	Brazil	0.4	1.6	3.6	4.7
49. Naples	Italy	2.8	3.6	3.6	3.6
50. Hyderabad	India	1.1	1.7	3.5	5.0
51. Kinshasa	Zaire	0.2	1.4	3.5	5.5
52. Toronto	Canada	1.0	2.8	3.5	3.9
53. Athens	Greece	1.8	2.5	3.4	3.8
54. Barcelona	Spain	1.6	2.7	3.4	3.7
55. Dallas	United States	0.9	2.0	3.4	4.4
56. Katowice	Poland	1.7	2.8	3.4	3.7
57. Sydney	Australia	1.7	2.7	3.4	3.7
58. Yangon	Myanmar	0.7	1.4	3.3	4.7
59. Casablanca	Morocco	0.7	1.5	3.2	4.6
60. Guadalajara	Mexico	0.4	1.5	3.2	4.1
61. Ho Chi Minh City	Vietnam	0.9	2.0	3.2	4.1
62. Chongqing	China	1.7	2.3	3.1	4.2
63. Porto Alegre	Brazil	0.4	1.5	3.1	3.9
64. Rome	Italy	1.6	2.9	3.1	3.1
65. Algiers	Algeria	0.4	1.3	3.0	4.5
66. Chengou	China	0.7	1.8	3.0	4.1
67. Harbin	China	1.0	2.1	3.0	3.9
68. Houston	United States	0.7	1.7	3.0	3.6
69. Monterrey	Mexico	0.4	1.2	3.0	3.9
70. Montreal	Canada	1.3	2.4	3.0	3.1
71. Taipei	China	0.6	1.8	3.0	4.2

1. Projected figures.
Source: United Nations Department of International Economic and Social Affairs, *World Urbanization Projections 1990* (1991).

Table P4.5
World Births, Deaths, and Population Growth, 1994

Characteristic	World	Developed	Developing
Population	5,642,151,000	1,240,354,000	4,401,797,000
Births	139,324,000	16,944,000	122,380,000
Deaths	52,514,000	11,715,000	40,799,000
Natural increase	86,810,000	5,229,000	81,582,000
Births per 1,000 population	25	14	28
Deaths per 1,000 population	9	9	9
Growth rate (percent)	1.5%	0.4%	1.9%

Source: U.S. Bureau of the Census. *World Population Profile 1994* (1994).

Table P4.6
Nations With Highest and Lowest Fertility Rates, 1995 Estimates

HIGHEST FERTILITY RATES				LOWEST FERTILITY RATES			
Country	Fertility Rate per Woman	Country	Fertility Rate per Woman	Country	Fertility Rate per Woman	Country	Fertility Rate per Woman
Yemen	7.4	Ethiopia	6.8	Hong Kong	1.2	Slovenia	1.5
Niger	7.3	Guinea	6.8	Spain	1.2	Austria	1.6
Ivory Coast	7.1	Somalia	6.8	Italy	1.3	Belgium	1.6
Uganda	7.1	Afghanistan	6.6	Germany	1.3	Estonia	1.6
Angola	6.9	Liberia	6.6	Greece	1.5	Latvia	1.6
Benin	6.9	Burundi	6.5	Bulgaria	1.5	Netherlands	1.6
Mai	6.9	Zaire	6.5	Japan	1.5	Portugal	1.6
Malawi	6.9	Laos	6.4	Romania	1.5	Switzerland	1.6
Oman	6.9			Russia	1.5	Ukraine	1.6

Source: United Nations Fund for Population Activities (UNFPA). *The State of World Population 1995* (1995).

Table P4.7
Population Indicators by Region and Nation

Region/Country	Population Estimate ('000s)		Birth Rate Per 1,000 1990 −95	Death Rate Per 1,000 1990 −95	Life Expec- tancy 1990 −95	Percent Urban 1995	Fertility Rate Per Woman 1995
	1995	2025					
World total	**5,716,400**	**8,294,300**	**26**	**9**	**65**	**45%**	**3.0**
More developed regions	1,166,600	1,238,400	14	10	75	75	1.7
Less developed regions	4,549,800	7,055,900	29	9	62	38	3.4
Least developed countries	575,400	1,162,300				22	5.6
AFRICA	**728,100**	**1,495,800**	**43**	**14**	**53**	**34**	**5.6**
Eastern Africa	**227,100**	**494,600**	**48**	**16**	**49**	**22**	**6.2**
Burundi	6,400	13,500	46	17	48	8	6.5
Eritrea	3,500	7,000				17	5.6
Ethiopia	55,100	126,900	49	18	47	13	6.8
Kenya	28,300	63,400	44	10	59	28	6.0
Madagascar	14,800	34,400	45	13	55	27	5.9
Malawi	11,100	22,300	54	21	44	14	6.9
Mauritius	1,100	1,500	18	7	70	41	2.3
Mozambique	16,000	35,100	45	18	47	34	6.3
Rwanda	8,000	15,800	52	18	46	6	6.3
Somalia	9,300	21,300	50	19	47	26	6.8
Tanzania	29,700	62,900	48	15	51	24	5.7
Uganda	21,300	48,100	51	21	42	13	7.1
Zambia	9,500	19,100	46	18	44	43	5.7
Zimbabwe	11,300	19,600	41	11	56	32	4.8
Middle Africa	**82,300**	**189,100**	**46**	**15**	**51**	**33**	**6.2**
Angola	11,100	26,600	51	19	46	32	6.9
Cameroon	13,200	29,200	41	12	56	45	5.5
Central African Republic	3,300	6,400	44	18	47	39	5.5
Chad	6,400	12,900	44	18	48	21	5.7
Congo	2,600	5,700	45	15	52	59	6.0
Gabon	1,300	2,700	43	16	54	50	5.5
Zaire	43,900	104,600	47	15	52	29	6.5
Northern Africa	**160,600**	**268,600**	**34**	**9**	**61**	**46**	**4.0**
Algeria	27,900	45,500	34	7	66	56	3.6
Egypt	62,900	97,300	31	9	62	45	3.7
Libya	5,400	12,900	42	8	63	86	6.2
Morocco	27,000	40,700	32	8	63	48	3.4
Sudan	28,100	58,400	42	14	52	25	5.6
Tunisia	8,900	13,300	27	6	68	57	3.0
Southern Africa	**47,400**	**82,800**	**32**	**9**	**63**	**48**	**4.1**
Botswana	1,500	3,000	38	9	61	28	4.7
Lesotho	2,100	4,200	34	10	61	23	5.0
Namibia	1,500	3,000	43	11	59	37	5.0
South Africa	41,500	71,000	31	9	63	51	4.0

Table P4.7
Population Indicators by Region and Nation, *continued*

Region/Country	Population Estimate ('000s) 1995	Population Estimate ('000s) 2025	Birth Rate Per 1,000 1990 −95	Death Rate Per 1,000 1990 −95	Life Expec- tancy 1990 −95	Percent Urban 1995	Fertility Rate Per Woman 1995
Western Africa	**210,700**	**460,600**	**46**	**15**	**51**	**37%**	**6.3**
Benin	5,400	12,300	49	18	46	31	6.9
Burkina Faso	10,300	21,700	47	18	48	27	6.3
Ghana	17,500	38,000	42	12	56	36	5.8
Guinea	6,700	15,100	51	20	45	30	6.8
Guinea-Bissau	1,100	2,000	43	21	44	22	5.6
Ivory Coast	14,300	36,800	50	15	52	44	7.1
Liberia	3,000	7,200	47	14	55	45	6.6
Mali	10,800	24,600	51	19	46	27	6.9
Mauritania	2,300	4,400	46	18	48	54	5.2
Niger	9,200	22,400	51	19	47	17	7.3
Nigeria	111,700	238,400	45	14	53	39	6.2
Senegal	8,300	16,900	43	16	49	42	5.8
Sierra Leone	4,500	8,700	48	22	43	36	6.3
Togo	4,100	9,400	45	13	55	31	6.3
LATIN AMERICA	**482,000**	**709,800**	**26**	**7**	**68**	**74**	**3.0**
Caribbean	**35,800**	**49,600**	**24**	**8**	**69**	**62**	**2.7**
Cuba	11,100	12,700	17	7	76	76	1.8
Dominican Republic	7,800	11,200	28	6	68	65	2.9
Haiti	7,200	13,100	35	12	57	32	4.7
Jamaica	2,400	3,300	22	6	74	54	2.2
Puerto Rico	3,700	4,600	18	7	75	73	2.1
Trinidad and Tobago	1,300	1,800	23	6	71	72	2.3
Central America	**126,400**	**197,500**	**30**	**6**	**69**	**68**	**3.3**
Belize	200	400	—	—	—	47	3.9
Costa Rica	3,400	5,600	26	4	76	50	3.1
El Salvador	5,800	9,700	33	7	66	45	3.8
Guatemala	10,600	21,700	39	8	65	42	5.1
Honduras	5,700	10,700	37	7	66	44	4.6
Mexico	93,700	136,600	28	5	70	75	3.0
Nicaragua	4,400	9,100	40	7	67	63	4.8
Panama	2,600	3,800	25	5	73	53	2.8
South America	**319,800**	**462,700**	**24**	**7**	**67**	**78**	**2.9**
Argentina	34,600	46,100	20	9	71	88	2.7
Bolivia	7,400	13,100	34	9	61	61	4.6
Brazil	161,800	230,300	23	7	66	78	2.8
Chile	14,300	19,800	23	6	72	84	2.5
Colombia	35,100	49,400	24	6	69	73	2.6
Ecuador	11,500	17,800	30	7	67	58	3.3

Table P4.7
Population Indicators by Region and Nation, *continued*

Region/Country	Population Estimate ('000s)		Birth Rate Per 1,000 1990 -95	Death Rate Per 1,000 1990 -95	Life Expec- tancy 1990 -95	Percent Urban 1995	Fertility Rate Per Woman 1995
	1995	*2025*					
Paraguay	5,000	9,000	33	6	67	53%	4.1
Peru	23,800	36,700	8	65	71	72	3.3
Uruguay	3,200	3,700	17	10	72	90	2.3
Venezuela	21,800	34,800	26	5	70	93	3.1
NORTHERN AMERICA	**292,800**	**369,600**	**16**	**9**	**76**	**76**	**2.0**
Canada	29,500	38,300	14	8	77	77	1.9
United States	263,300	331,200	16	9	76	76	2.1
ASIA	**3,458,000**	**4,960,000**	**26**	**8**	**65**	**35**	**3.0**
Eastern Asia	**1,424,200**	**1,745,800**	**20**	**7**	**72**	**37**	**1.9**
China	1,221,500	1,526,100	21	7	71	30	2.0
Hong Kong	5,900	5,900	13	6	78	95	1.2
Japan	125,100	121,600	11	7	79	78	1.5
Korea, North	23,900	33,400	24	5	71	61	2.3
Korea, South	45,000	54,400	16	6	71	81	1.8
Mongolia	2,400	3,800	34	8	64	61	3.4
South-eastern Asia	**484,300**	**713,400**	**28**	**8**	**63**	**34**	**3.2**
Cambodia	10,300	19,700	39	14	51	21	5.1
Indonesia	197,600	275,600	27	8	63	35	2.8
Laos	4,900	9,700	45	15	51	22	6.4
Malaysia	20,100	31,600	29	5	71	54	3.4
Myanmar	46,500	75,600	33	11	58	26	4.0
Philippines	67,600	104,500	30	7	65	54	3.8
Singapore	2,800	3,400	16	6	74	100	1.7
Thailand	58,800	73,600	21	6	69	20	2.1
Vietnam	74,500	118,200	29	9	64	21	3.7
South Central Asia	**1,381,200**	**2,196,300**	**32**	**10**	**59**	**29**	**3.9**
Afghanistan	20,100	45,300	53	22	43	20	6.6
Bangladesh	120,400	196,100	38	14	53	18	4.1
Bhutan	1,600	3,100	40	17	48	6	5.7
India	935,700	1,392,100	29	10	60	27	3.6
Iran	67,300	123,500	40	7	67	59	4.8
Nepal	21,900	40,700	37	13	54	14	5.2
Pakistan	140,500	284,800	41	10	59	35	5.9
Sri Lanka	18,400	25,000	21	6	72	22	2.4
Western Asia	**168,400**	**304,600**	**34**	**7**	**66**	**66**	**4.3**
Iraq	20,400	42,700	39	7	66	75	5.5
Israel	5,600	7,800	21	7	77	91	2.8
Jordan	5,400	12,000	40	5	68	72	5.4
Kuwait	1,500	2,800	28	2	75	97	3.0

Table P4.7
Population Indicators by Region and Nation, *continued*

Region/Country	Population Estimate ('000s)		Birth Rate Per 1,000 1990 −95	Death Rate Per 1,000 1990 −95	Life Expec- tancy 1990 −95	Percent Urban 1995	Fertility Rate Per Woman 1995
	1995	*2025*					
Lebanon	3,000	4,400	27	7	69	87%	2.9
Oman	2,200	6,100	40	5	70	13	6.9
Saudi Arabia	17,900	42,700	36	5	69	80	6.2
Syria	14,700	33,500	42	6	67	52	5.6
Turkey	61,900	90,900	28	7	67	69	3.2
United Arab Emirates	1,900	3,000	21	4	71	84	4.1
Yemen	14,500	33,700	48	14	53	34	7.4
EUROPE	**727,000**	**718,200**	**13**	**11**	**75**	**74**	**1.6**
Eastern Europe	**308,700**	**299,400**	**14**	**11**	**71**	**70**	**1.6**
Bulgaria	8,800	7,800	13	12	72	71	1.5
Czech Republic	10,300	10,600	—	—	—	65	1.8
Hungary	10,100	9,400	12	14	70	65	1.7
Poland	38,400	41,500	14	10	72	65	1.9
Romania	22,800	21,700	16	11	70	55	1.5
Slovakia	5,400	6,000	—	—	—	59	1.9
Northern Europe	**93,500**	**98,600**	**14**	**11**	**76**	**84**	**1.9**
Denmark	5,200	5,100	12	12	76	85	1.7
Estonia	1,500	1,400	14	12	71	73	1.6
Finland	5,100	5,400	13	10	76	63	1.9
Ireland	3,600	3,900	14	9	75	58	2.1
Latvia	2,600	2,300	14	12	71	73	1.6
Lithuania	3,700	3,800	15	10	73	72	1.8
Norway	4,300	4,700	15	11	77	73	2.0
Sweden	8,800	9,800	14	11	78	83	2.1
United Kingdom	58,300	61,500	14	11	76	90	1.8
Southern Europe	**143,900**	**139,300**	**11**	**10**	**76**	**65**	**1.4**
Albania	3,400	4,700	23	5	73	37	2.8
Bosnia and Herzegovina	3,500	4,500	—	—	—	49	1.6
Croatia	4,500	4,200	—	—	—	64	1.7
Greece	10,500	9,900	10	10	78	65	1.4
Italy	57,200	52,300	10	10	77	67	1.3
Macedonia	2,200	2,600	—	—	—	60	2.0
Portugal	9,800	9,700	12	10	75	36	1.6
Slovenia	1,900	1,800	—	—	—	64	1.5
Spain	39,600	37,600	11	9	78	76	1.2
Yugoslavia	10,800	11,500	—	—	—	57	2.0
Western Europe	**180,800**	**180,900**	**12**	**11**	**76**	**81**	**1.5**
Austria	8,000	8,300	12	11	76	56	1.6
Belgium	10,100	10,400	12	11	76	97	1.6

Table P4.7
Population Indicators by Region and Nation, *continued*

Region/Country	Population Estimate ('000s)		Birth Rate Per 1,000 1990 –95	Death Rate Per 1,000 1990 –95	Life Expec- tancy 1990 –95	Percent Urban 1995	Fertility Rate Per Woman 1995
	1995	*2025*					
France	58,000	61,200	13	10	77	73%	1.7
Germany	81,600	76,400	11	11	76	87	1.3
Netherlands	15,500	16,300	14	9	77	89	1.6
Switzerland	7,200	7,800	13	10	78	61	1.6
OCEANIA	**28,500**	**41,000**	**19**	**8**	**73**	**70**	**2.5**
Australia–New Zealand	**21,700**	**29,000**	**15**	**8**	**77**	**85**	**1.9**
Australia	18,100	24,700	15	8	77	85	1.9
Melanesia	5,800	10,100	32	9	59	21	4.5
New Zealand	3,600	4,400	17	8	76	86	2.1
Papua New Guinea	4,300	7,500	33	11	56	16	4.8
Countries of the former USSR with economies in transition							
Armenia	3,600	4,700	23	6	71	69	2.5
Azerbaijan	7,600	10,100	27	7	70	56	2.4
Belarus	10,100	9,900	16	10	72	71	1.7
Georgia	5,500	6,100	18	9	72	59	2.1
Kazakhstan	17,100	21,700	24	8	69	60	2.4
Kyrgyzstan	4,700	7,100	31	7	68	39	3.5
Moldova	4,400	5,100	21	10	68	52	2.1
Russian Federation	147,000	138,500	16	11	70	76	1.5
Tajikistan	6,100	11,800	40	7	70	32	4.7
Turkmenistan	4,100	6,700	36	8	65	45	3.8
Ukraine	51,400	48,700	14	12	71	70	1.6
Uzbekistan	22,800	37,700	—	—	—	41	3.7

Note: Totals may not add because of rounding numbers. Data for small countries or areas, generally those with population of 200,000 or less in 1990, are not given in this table.
Source: United Nations Populations Fund (UNFPA), *The State of World Population 1995* (1995) and *The State of World Population 1994* (1994).

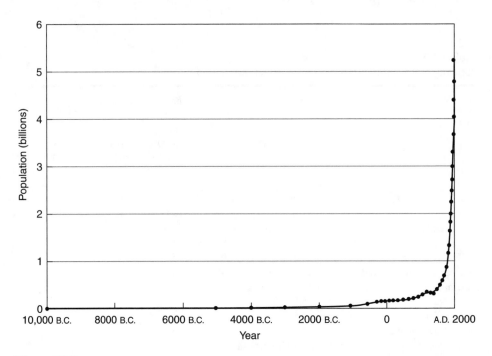

Figure P4.2
Estimated human population from the last ice age to the present.
From *How Many People Can the Earth Support?* by Joel E. Cohen. Copyright © 1995 by Joel E. Cohen. Reprinted by permission of W.W. Norton & Company, Inc.

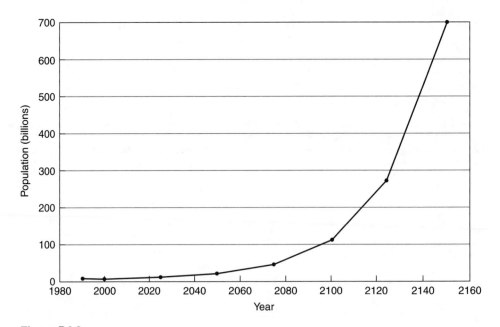

Figure P4.3
United Nations' projection of world population, assuming fertility remains constant at its 1990 levels in different regions.
Source: original figure drawn according to data of United Nations (1992a). Permission granted by the United Nations Population Fund.

Figure P4.4
Where in the World Do They Live?

According to the U.S. Bureau of the Census, 75 of each 100 persons in the world today live in only 22 countries. The other 25 live in any of the remaining 184 countries. Note that 37 people out of every 100 live in China and India.

Of every 100 people in the world in 1991:

21 live in China (mainland)
16 live in India
 5 live in the former Soviet Union
 5 live in the United States
 4 live in Indonesia
 3 live in Brazil
 2 live in Bangladesh
 2 live in Japan
 2 live in Mexico
 2 live in Nigeria
 2 live in Pakistan
 1 lives in Egypt
 1 lives in Ethiopia
 1 lives in France
 1 lives in Germany
 1 lives in Iran
 1 lives in Italy
 1 lives in the Philippines
 1 lives in Thailand
 1 lives in Turkey
 1 lives in the United Kingdom
 1 lives in Vietnam

Source: U.S. Bureau of the Census. *World Population Profile 1991* (1991). United Nations Population Fund.

Questions about the Tables

1. Using the first quote in the introduction, from the U.S. National Academy of Sciences, further explain what is meant by a *crisis point.* Explain this term in factual, empirical terms from the information contained in the introduction.

2. In the history of world population trends, where are the population acceleration points?

3. Table P4.1 seems to indicate that the annual growth rate, birth rates, and death rates are all slowing. Explain why population continues to rise sharply, as indicated in Figure P4.2.

4. Figure P4.3 indicates a U.N. World Projection Plan. Using this figure and other sources, explain what you think is a realistic projection and how it can be attained.

5. Figure P4.1 contains a projection of population growth for various countries. Compare this data with the information in Tables P4.2, P4.3, P4.6, and P4.7 and Figure P4.4. Write a summary of your findings.

6. The box titled "World Population Continues to Soar" states that the world can support only 2 billion people at a universal standard of living now enjoyed by industrialized nations. Interpret this statement from world projections and selected countries' population growth patterns.

7. Discuss the patterns of growth in Tables P4.2 and P4.3.

8. Examine Table P4.4. Relate this information to your findings from Question 7. What countries and areas have the most populated cities? What patterns do you find?

9. Relate Tables P4.5 and P4.6. How are births, deaths, and population growth related to fertility rates? Generalize your findings.

10. Table P4.7 gives important country-by-country profiles. Select 10 countries in various regions and compare their demographic data. What patterns do you find?

11. Consulting Table P4.7, locate the 10 countries with the highest life expectancy and the 10 countries with the lowest life expectancy. What significant patterns do you find?

12. Summarize your findings from Questions 5–12 into well-written paragraphs that strongly support your conclusions.

Putting the Bite on Planet Earth

Don Hinrichsen

Each year, about 90 million new people join the human race. This is roughly equivalent to adding three Canadas or another Mexico to the world annually, a rate of growth that will swell human numbers from today's 5.6 billion to about 8.5 billion by 2025.

These figures represent the fastest growth in human numbers ever recorded and raise many vital economic and environmental questions. Is our species reproducing so quickly that we are outpacing the Earth's ability to house and feed us? Is our demand for natural resources destroying the habitats that give us life? If 40 million acres of tropical forest—an area equivalent to twice the size of Austria—are being destroyed or grossly degraded every year, as satellite maps show, how will that affect us? If 27,000 species become extinct yearly because of human development, as some scientists believe, what will that mean for us? If nearly 2 billion people already lack adequate drinking water, a number likely to increase to 3.6 billion by the year 2000, how can all of us hope to survive?

The answers are hardly easy and go beyond simple demographics, since population works in conjunction with other factors to determine our total impact on resources. Modern technologies and improved efficiency in the use of resources can help to stretch the availability of limited resources. Consumption levels also exert considerable impact on our resource base. Population pressures work in

conjunction with these other factors to determine, to a large extent, our *total* impact on resources.

For example, although everyone contributes to resource waste, the world's bottom-billion poorest and top-billion richest do most of the environmental damage. Poverty compels the world's 1.2 billion bottom-most poor to misuse their environment and ravage resources, while lack of access to better technologies, credit, education, healthcare and family-planning condemns them to subsistence patterns that offer little chance for concern about their environment. This contrasts with the richest 1.3 billion, who exploit and consume disproportionate amounts of resources and generate disproportionate quantities of waste.

One example is energy consumption. Whereas the average Bangladeshi consumes commercial energy equivalent to three barrels of oil yearly, each American consumes an average of 55 barrels. Population growth in Bangladesh, one of the poorest nations, increased energy use there in 1990 by the equivalent of 8.7 million barrels, while U.S. population growth in the same year increased energy use by 110 million barrels. Of course, the U.S. population of 250 million is more than twice the size of the Bangladeshi population of 113 million, but even if the consumption figures are adjusted for the difference in size, the slower growing U.S. population still increases its energy consumption six or seven times faster yearly than does the more rapidly growing Bangladeshi population.

In the future, the effects of population growth on natural resources will vary locally because growth occurs unevenly across the globe. Over the course of the 1990s, the

Reprinted with permission from National Wildlife Federation, Hinrichsen, D. (1994, Sept/Oct.) Putting the Bite on Planet Earth. *International Wildlife*.

Third World's population is likely to balloon by more than 900 million, while the population of the developed world will add a mere 56 million. Asia, with 3.4 billion people today, will have 3.7 billion by the turn of the century; Africa's population will increase from 700 million to 867 million; and Latin America's from 470 million to 538 million. By the year 2000, the Third World's total population is expected to be nearly 5 billion; only 1.3 billion people will reside in industrialized countries.

The United Nations estimates that world population will near 11.2 billion by 2100. However, this figure is based on the assumption that growth rates will drop. If present rates continue, world population will stand at 10 billion by 2030 and 40 billion by 2110.

The United Nations Population Fund estimates that to achieve the 11.2 billion projection, the number of couples using family planning services—such as modern contraceptives—in the developing world will have to rise to 567 million by the year 2000 and to 1.2 billion by 2025. In sub-Saharan Africa this means a 10-fold increase by 2025 in the number of people who use family planning. If these measures do not succeed , human population growth could blast the 11.2 billion figure clear out of the ball park.

Perhaps the most ominous aspect of today's unprecedented growth is its persistence despite falling annual population growth rates everywhere except in parts of Africa, the Middle East and South Asia. Annual global population growth stands at 1.6 percent, down from 2 percent in the early 1970s. Similarly, the total fertility rate (the average number of children a woman is likely to have) has dropped from a global average of six only three decades ago to slightly more than three today.

Population continues to grow because of tremendous demographic momentum. China's annual growth rate, for example, is only 1.2 percent. However, the country's huge population base—1.2 billion people—translates this relatively small rate of growth into a net increase in China's population of around 15 million yearly. Clearly, any attempt to slow population growth is a decades-long process affected by advances in medicine, extended life spans and reduced infant, child, and maternal mortality.

The following pages survey the effects of human population growth on a wide range of natural resources.

PLANTS AND ANIMALS:
THE SHRINKING ARK

Biologists have catalogued 1.7 million species and cannot even estimate how many species remain to be docu-

mented. The total could be 5 million, 30 million or even more. Yet, we are driving thousands of species yearly to extinction through thoughtless destruction of habitat.

A survey conducted recently in Australia, Asia and the Americas by the International Union for Conservation of Nature and Natural Resources—The World Conservation Union (IUCN) found that loss of living space affected 76 percent of all mammal species. Expansion of settlements threatened 56 percent of mammal species, while expansion of ranching affected 33 percent. Logging and plantations affected 26 percent.

IUCN has declared human population growth the number one cause of extinctions. The 10 nations with the worst habitat destruction house an average of 189 people per square kilometer (250 acres), while the 10 that retain the most original habitat stand at only 29 people per square kilometer.

Future population growth poses a serious threat to wildlife habitat. Every new person needs space for housing, food, travel, work and other needs. Human needs vary widely from place to place, but a UN survey found that the average person requires about 0.056 hectares (a hectare is a standard unit of land measurement equal to about 2.47 acres) of nonfarm land for daily living. To this must be added land for food production. This varies with land quality and available technologies, but each newborn person probably will need at least 0.2 hectare of cropland unless food production per acre increases in the years ahead. This will require the conversion of more and more wildland into cropland. In East Asia, for example, the amount of irrigated, high-yield cropland per person is already near the 0.2 hectare limit.

UN consultant and author Paul Harrison estimates, very conservatively, that each new person will need at least a quarter of a hectare. Thus, every billion people that we add to the planet in the years ahead will require 250 million hectares more of agricultural land. Most of this land will have to come from what is currently wildlife habitat. The UN's projected population of 11.2 billion by 2100 would require creation of roughly 20 million square kilometers (8 million sq. mi.) of new cropland—equivalent to more than 80 percent of all forest and woodland in developing countries today.

Conversion of natural habitat for human use can even reduce the value of remaining wild areas for wildlife. When development chops wild lands into fragments, native species often decline simply because the small remnants do not meet their biological needs. For example, studies of U.S. forest birds indicate that species that prefer to nest in forest interiors are more subject to predation and lay fewer eggs when habitat fragmentation forces them to nest along forest edges. A study in southern California indicated that most canyons lose about half of native bird species dependent on chaparral habitat within 20 to 40 years after the canyons become isolated by development, even though the chaparral brush remains. Biologist William Newmark's 1987 study of 14 Canadian and U.S. national parks showed that 13 of the parks had lost some of their mammal species, at least in part because the animals could not adapt to confinement within parks surrounded by developed land.

Habitat loss in North America and in Latin American tropics has caused declines in many bird species that migrate between those regions. The Breeding Bird Survey, a volunteer group that tabulates nesting birds each June, found that 70 percent of neotropical migrant species monitored in the eastern United States declined from 1978 to 1987. So did 69 percent of monitored neotropical migrants that nest in prairie regions. Declining species include such familiar songbirds as veeries, wood thrushes, blackpoll warblers and rosebreasted grosbeaks. As human population growth continues to push development into wild areas, fragmentation will increase and its effects on wildlife survival will intensity.

LAND LOSS: A FOOD CRISIS

Land degradation, a global problem, is becoming acute in much of the developing world. Population pressures and inappropriate farming practices contribute to soil impoverishment and erosion, rampant deforestation, overgrazing of common lands and misuse of agrochemicals.

Worldwide, an estimated 1.2 billion hectares, an area about the size of China and India combined, have lost much of their agricultural productivity since 1945. Every year, farmers abandon about 70,000 square kilometers (27,000 sq. mi.) of farmland because soils are too degraded for crops.

Drylands, including grasslands that provide rich pastures for livestock, have been hardest hit. Although not as extensive as once thought, desertification—the ecological destruction that turns productive land into deserts—still threatens the Middle East and parts of Africa and Asia.

Because of land degradation, large portions of the Sahel, including Burkina Faso, Chad, Mali, Mauritania, Niger and Senegal, can no longer feed their people. Although annual fluctuations in rainfall may interrupt the trend of cropland loss, the Sahel could suffer agricultural

collapse within a decade. Sahelian croplands, as presently farmed, can support a maximum of 36 million people. In 1990 the rural population stood at an estimated 32 million and will exceed 40 million by the end of the decade even if annual population growth slows from the current 3 percent to 2 percent.

Since 1961, food production has matched world population growth in all developing regions except sub-Saharan Africa. In the early 1980s, the UN Food and Agriculture Organization (FAO) predicted that more than half of all developing nations examined in its study of carrying capacity (62 out of 115) may be unable to feed their projected populations by 2000 using current farming technology. Most of the 62 countries probably will be able to feed less than half of their projected populations without expensive food imports.

As a direct result of population growth, especially in developing nations, the average amount of cropland per person is projected to decline from 0.28 hectares in 1990 to 0.17 by 2025.

Three factors will determine whether food production can equal population growth:

1. *New Croplands.* Currently, the amount of new land put into production each year may equal the amount taken out of production for various reasons, such as erosion, salt deposits and waterlogging. Thus, the net annual gain in arable land, despite widespread habitat destruction to create it, may be zero.
2. *New Water Sources.* Agricultural demand for water is expected to double between 1970 and 2000. Already more than 70 percent of water withdrawals from rivers, underground reservoirs and other sources go to crop irrigation.
3. *Agrochemical Use.* Pesticides and fertilizers are boosting crop yields. However, in many areas agrochemicals are too expensive to use, while in other areas they are overused to prop up falling yields. Agrochemicals can pose health hazards, creating another expense for developing nations.

FOREST: THE VANISHING WORLD

The quest for more crop and grazing land has sealed the fate of much of the world's tropical forests. Between 1971 and 1986, arable land expanded by 59 million hectares, while forests shrank by at least 125 million hectares. However, consultant Harrison estimates that during the same period, land used for settlements, roads, industries, office buildings and other development expanded by more than 30 million hectares as a result of growth in urban centers, reducing the amount of arable land in surrounding areas. Consequently, the amount of natural habitat wiped out to produce the 59-million-hectare net in arable land may have exceeded 100 million hectares.

When both agricultural and nonagricultural needs are taken into account, human population growth may be responsible for as much as 80 percent of the loss of forest cover worldwide. Asia produces the highest rate of loss, 1.2 percent a year. Latin America loses 0.9 percent yearly and Africa 0.8 percent.

If current trends continue, most tropical forests will soon be destroyed or damaged beyond recovery. Of the 76 countries that presently encompass tropical forests, only four—Brazil, Guyana, Papua New Guinea and Zaire—are likely to retain major undamaged tracts by 2010, less than a generation away.

Population pressure contributes to deforestation not only because of increased demand for cropland and living space but also because of increased demand for fuelwood, on which half of the world's people depend for heating and cooking. The majority of sub-Saharan Africa's population is dependent on fuelwood: 82 percent of all Nigerians, 70 percent of Kenyans, 80 percent of all Malagasies, 74 percent of Ghanaians, 93 percent of Ethiopians, 90 percent of Somalians and 81 percent of Sudanese.

By 1990, 100 million Third World residents lacked sufficient fuelwood to meet minimum daily energy requirements, and close to 1.3 billion were consuming wood faster than forest growth could replenish it. On average, consumption outpaces supply by 30 percent in sub-Saharan Africa as a whole, by 70 percent in the Sudan and India, by 150 percent in Ethiopia and by 200 percent in Niger. If present trends continue, FAO predicts, another 1 billion people will be faced with critical fuelwood shortages by the end of the decade. Already, growing rings of desolation—land denuded for fuelwood or building materials—surround many African cities, such as Ouagadougou in Burkina Faso, Niamey in Niger and Dakar in Senegal. By 2000, the World Bank estimates, half to three-quarters of all West Africa's fuelwood consumption will be burned in towns and cities.

According to the World Bank, remedying the fuelwood shortage will require planting 55 million hectares—an area nearly twice the size of Italy—with fast-growing trees at a rate of 2.7 million hectares a year, five times the present annual rate of 555,000 hectares.

TROUBLED OCEANS: DISAPPEARING RESOURCES

Population and development pressures have been mounting in coastal areas worldwide for the past 30 years, triggering widespread resource degradation. Coastal fisheries are overexploited in much of Asia, Africa and parts of Latin America. In some cases—as in the Philippines, Indonesia, Malaysia, China, Japan, India, the west coast of South America, the Mediterranean and the Caribbean—economically important fisheries have collapsed or are in severe decline. "Nearly all Asian waters within 15 kilometers of land are considered overfished," says Ed Gomez, director of the Marine Science Institute at the University of the Philippines in Manila.

Overfishing is not the sole cause of these declines. Mangroves and coral reefs—critical nurseries for many marine species and among the most productive of all ecosystems—are being plundered in the name of development.

In 1990, a UN advisory panel, the Group of Experts on the Scientific Aspects of Marine Pollution (GESAMP), reported that coastal pollution worldwide has grown worse over the decade of the 1980s. Experts pointed to an overload of nutrients—mainly nitrogen and phosphorus from untreated or partially treated sewage, agricultural runoff and erosion—as the most serious coastal pollution problem. Human activities may be responsible for as much as 35 million metric tons of nitrogen and up to 3.75 million metric tons of phosphorus flowing into coastal waters every year. Even such huge amounts could be dissolved in the open ocean, but most of the pollution stays in shallow coastal waters where it causes massive algal blooms and depletes oxygen levels, harming marine life near the shores.

Although the world still possesses an estimated 240,000 square kilometers (93,000 sq. mi.) of mangrove swamps—coastal forests that serve as breeding grounds and nurseries for many commercially important fish and shellfish species—this represents only about half the original amount. Clear-cutting for timber, fuelwood and wood chips; conversion to fish and shellfish ponds; and expansion of urban areas and croplands have claimed millions of hectares globally. For example, of the Philippine's original mangrove area—estimated at 500,000 to 1 million hectares—only 100,000 hectares remain; 80 to 90 percent are gone.

Some 600,000 square kilometers (230,000 sq. mi.) of coral reefs survive in the world's tropical seas. Unfortunately, these species-rich ecosystems are suffering widespread decline. Clive Wilkinson, a coral reef specialist working at the Australian Institute of Marine Science, estimates that fully 10 percent of the world's reefs have already been degraded "beyond recognition." Thirty percent are in critical condition and will be lost completely in 10 to 20 years, while another 30 percent are threatened and will be lost in 20 to 40 years. Only 30 percent, located away from human development or otherwise too remote to be exploited, are in stable condition.

Throughout much of the world, coastal zones are overdeveloped, overcrowded, and overexploited. Already nearly two-thirds of the world's population—some 3.6 billion people—live along coasts or within 150 kilometers (100 mi.) of one. Within three decades, 75 percent, or 6.4 billion, will reside in coastal areas—nearly a billion more people than the current global population.

In the United States, 54 percent of all Americans live in 772 coastal counties adjacent to marine coasts or the Great Lakes. Between 1960 and 1990, coastal population density increased from 275 to nearly 400 people per square kilometer. By 2025, nearly 75 percent of all Americans will live in coastal counties, with population density doubling in areas such as southern California and Florida.

Similarly, nearly 780 million of China's 1.2 billion people—almost 67 percent—live in 14 southeast and coastal provinces and two coastal municipalities, Shanghai and Tianjin. Along much of China's coastline, population densities average more than 600 per square kilometer. In Shanghai they exceed 2,000 per square kilometer. During the past few years, as many as 100 million Chinese have moved from poorer provinces in central and western regions to coastal areas in search of better economic opportunities. More ominously, population growth is expected to accelerate in the nation's 14 newly created economic free zones and five special economic zones, all of them coastal.

WATER: DISTRIBUTION WOES

Nearly 75 percent of the world's freshwater is locked in glaciers and icecaps, with virtually all the rest underground. Only about 0.01 percent of the world's total water is easily available for human use. Even this tiny amount would be sufficient to meet all the world's needs if it were distributed evenly. However, the world is divided into water "haves" and "have nots." In the Middle East, north Asia, northwestern Mexico, most of Africa, much of the western United States, parts of Chile and Argentina and nearly all of Australia, people need more water than can be sustainably supplied.

As the world's human population increases, the amount of water per person decreases. The United Nations Educational, Scientific and Cultural Organization (UNESCO) estimates that the amount of freshwater available per person has shrunk from more than 33,000 cubic meters (1.2 million cu. ft.) per year in 1850 to only 8,500 cubic meters (300,000 cu. ft.) today. Of course, this is a crude, general figure. But because of population growth alone, water demand in more than half the world's countries by 2000 is likely to be twice what it was as recently as 1971.

Already some 2 billion people in 80 countries must live with water constraints for all or part of the year. By the end of the 1990s Egypt will have only two-thirds as much water for each of its inhabitants as it has today, and Kenya only half as much. By then, six of East Africa's seven nations and all five nations on the south rim of the Mediterranean will face severe shortages. In 1990, 20 nations suffered water scarcity, with less than 1,000 cubic meters (35,000 cu. ft.) of water per person, according to a study by Population Action International. Another eight experienced occasional water stress. The 28 nations represent 333 million people. By 2025, some 48 nations will suffer shortages, involving some 3 billion residents, according to the study.

China—although not listed as water short because of the heavy amount of rain that falls in its souther region—has, nevertheless, exceeded its sustainable water resources. According to Qu Geping, China's Environment Minister, the country can supply water sustainably to only 650 million people, not the current population of 1.2 billion. In other words, China is supporting twice as many people as its water resources can reasonably sustain without drawing down groundwater supplies and overusing surface waters.

FOSSIL FUELS: ENERGY BREAKDOWN

Human society runs on energy, principally fossil fuels such as oil, gas and coal. These three account for 90 percent of global commercial energy production. Nuclear power, hydro-electricity and other sustainable resources provide the rest.

The industrialized nations, with less than a quarter of the world's people, burn about 70 percent of all fossil fuels. The United States alone consumes about a quarter of the world's commercial energy, and the former Soviet Union about a fifth. In terms of per capita consumption patterns, Canada burns more fuel than any other nation—in 1987 the equivalent of 9 metric tons of oil per person—followed by Norway at 8.9 metric tons of oil per person and the United States at 7.3. By contrast, developing nations on average use the equivalent of only about half a metric ton of oil per person yearly.

Known oil reserves should meet current levels of consumption for another 41 years, up from an estimated 31 years in 1970 thanks to better energy efficiency and conservation measures, along with new oil fields brought into production. Natural-gas reserves should meet current demand for 60 more years, up from 38 years in 1970. Coal reserves should be good for another 200 years.

But our addiction to fossil fuel has resulted in chronic, sometimes catastrophic, pollution of the atmosphere, in some cases far beyond what natural systems or man-made structures can tolerate. A noxious atmospheric cocktail of chemical pollutants is primarily responsible for the death and decline of thousands of hectares of European forests. Acid rain—caused by a combination of nitrogen and sulfur dioxides released from fossil-fuel combustion—has eaten away at priceless monuments and buildings throughout Europe and North America, causing billions of dollars in damages.

Urban air contains a hazardous mix of pollutants—everything from sulfur dioxide and reactive hydrocarbons to heavy metals and organic compounds. Smog alerts are now commonplace in many cities with heavy traffic. In Mexico City, for example, smog levels exceeded World Health Organization standards on all but 11 days in 1991. Breathing the city's air is said to be as damaging as smoking two packs of cigarettes a day, and half the city's children are born with enough lead in their blood to hinder their development.

The only way to stretch fossil fuel reserves and reduce pollution levels is to conserve energy and use it much more efficiently than we do now. Some progress has been made, but the benefits of energy conservation have been realized in only a few industrialized countries.

Recent history has shown what can happen. In the decade following the first oil shock, per capita energy consumption fell by 5 percent in the member states of the Organization for Economic Cooperation and Development (OECD)—consisting of the industrialized countries of Western Europe and North America, plus Japan, Australia and New Zealand—while their per capita gross domestic product grew by a third.

Buildings in the OECD countries use a quarter less energy now than they did before 1973, while the energy efficiency of industry has improved by a third. Worldwide, cars now get 25 percent more kilometers per gallon than they did in 1973. In all, increased efficiency since 1973 has saved the industrialized nations $250 billion in energy costs.

Even more savings could be realized through concerted efforts to conserve energy and improve efficiency. Three relatively simple, cost effective measures could be introduced immediately: 1) making compact fluorescent lamps generally available in homes and offices; 2) tightening up building codes to require better insulation against cold and heat; and 3) requiring lean-burn engines, which get up to 80 kilometers per gallon (50 mpg), in all new compact cars. These three "technical fixes" could save billions of dollars in energy costs.

POLICY: BUILDING A FUTURE

The main population issues—urbanization, rapid growth and uneven distribution—when linked with issues of environmental decline, pose multiple sets of problems for policymakers. The very nature of these interrelated problems makes them virtually impossible to deal with in balkanized bureaucracies accustomed to managing only one aspect of any problem. Population and resource issues require integrated, strategic management, an approach few countries are in a position to implement.

Sustainable-management strategies, designed to ensure that resources are not destroyed by overexploitation, are complicated to initiate because they require the cooperation of ministries or departments often at odds over personnel, budgets and political clout. Most governments lack institutional mechanisms that ensure a close working relationship among competing ministries. Consequently, most sustainable-development initiatives never get beyond words on paper. "We talk about integrated resource management, but we don't do it," admits one Indian official in Delhi. "Our ministries are like fiefdoms, they seldom cooperate on anything."

Fragmented authority yields fragmented policies. Big development ministries—such as industry and commerce, transportation, agriculture, fisheries and forestry—rarely cooperate in solving population and resource problems. Piecemeal solutions dominate, and common resources continue to deteriorate.

The world's population and resource problems offer plenty of scope for timely and incisive policy interventions that promise big returns for a relatively small investment. As little as $17 billion a year could provide contraceptives to every woman who wants them, permitting families throughout the globe to reduce births voluntarily. This approach might produce the same or better results that would government-set population targets, according to one study. Moreover, population specialists recognize that educating girls and women provides a higher rate of return than most other investments. "In fact, it may well be the single most influential investment that can be made in the developing world," says Larry Summers, a former World Bank economist.

But time is at a premium. The decision period for responding to the crises posed by rapidly growing populations, increased consumption levels and shrinking resources will be confined, for the most part, to the next two decades. If human society does not succeed in checking population growth, the future will bring widespread social and economic dislocations as resource bases collapse. Unemployment and poverty will increase, and migrations from poorer to richer nations will bring Third World stresses to the developed world.

Questions

1. How many people are added to the human race each year? Calculate the percentage of growth annually.
2. List some of the stresses on the earth's environment as a result of unprecedented population growth.
3. What are the difficulties of lowering world population rates even if a country's annual growth rate declines?
4. How much land does a person need to survive? How does this impact wildlife, plants and land use?
5. Discuss the problem of land degradation. How much is the average amount of cropland per person projected to decline from 1990 to 2025? Discuss implications. What are possible solutions?
6. How soon will most tropical forests disappear? What are the implications?
7. What are some of the pressures on oceans? What are the ramifications?
8. How much have freshwater supplies shrunk from 1850? What are the issues here?
9. What is the effect of world reliance on fossil fuels? What are some solutions suggested in the article as well as your own?
10. Name some practical solutions to building a future policy that can sustain world population. Aside from suggestions in the article, also name your own possible solutions and approaches.

22

Can the Growing Human Population Feed Itself?

JOHN BONGAARTS

Demographers now project that the world's population will double during the next half century, from 5.3 billion people in 1990 to more than 10 billion by 2050. How will the environment and humanity respond to this unprecedented growth? Expert opinion divides into two camps. Environmentalists and ecologists, whose views have widely been disseminated by the electronic and print media, regard the situation as a catastrophe in the making. They argue that in order to feed the growing population farmers must intensify agricultural practices that already cause grave ecological damage. Our natural resources and the environment, now burdened by past population growth, will simply collapse under the weight of this future demand.

The optimists, on the other hand, comprising many economists as well as some agricultural scientists, assert that the earth can readily produce more than enough food for the expected population in 2050. They contend that technological innovation and the continued investment of human capital will deliver high standards of living to much of the globe, even if the population grows much larger than the projected 10 billion. Which point of view will hold sway? What shape might the future of our species and the environment actually take?

Many environmentalists fear that world food supply has reached a precarious state: "Human numbers are on a collision course with massive famines. . . . If humanity fails to

act, nature will end the population explosion for us—in very unpleasant ways—well before 10 billion is reached," write Paul R. Ehrlich and Anne H. Ehrlich of Stanford University in their 1990 book *The Population Explosion*. In the long run, the Ehrlichs and like-minded experts consider substantial growth in food production to be absolutely impossible. "We are feeding ourselves at the expense of our children. By definition farmers can overplow and overpump only in the short run. For many farmers the short run is drawing to a close," states Lester R. Brown, president of the Worldwatch Institute, in a 1988 paper.

Over the past three decades, these authors point out, enormous efforts and resources have been pooled to amplify agricultural output. Indeed, the total quantity of harvested crops increased dramatically during this time. In the developing world, food production rose by an average of 117 percent in the quarter of a century between 1965 and 1990. Asia performed far better than other regions, which saw increases below average.

Because population has expanded rapidly as well, per capita food production has generally shown only modest change; in Africa it actually declined. As a consequence, the number of undernourished people is still rising in most parts of the developing world, although that number did fall from 844 million to 786 million during the 1980s. But this decline reflects improved nutritional conditions in Asia alone. During the same period, the number of people having energy-deficient diets in Latin America, the Near East and Africa climbed.

Many social factors can bring about conditions of hunger, but the pessimists emphasize that population pressure on fragile ecosystems plays a significant role. One specific concern is that we seem to be running short on land suitable for cultivation. If so, current efforts to bolster per capita food production by clearing more fertile land will find fewer options. Between 1850 and 1950 the amount of arable land grew quickly to accommodate both larger populations and greater demand for better diets. This expansion then slowed and by the late 1980s ceased altogether. In the developed world, as well as in some developing countries (especially China), the amount of land under cultivation started to decline during the 1980s. This drop is largely because spreading urban centers have engulfed fertile land or, once the land is depleted, farmers have abandoned it. Farmers have also fled from irrigated land that has become unproductive because of salt accumulation.

Moreover, environmentalists insist that soil erosion is destroying much of the land that is left. The extent of the damage is the subject of controversy. A recent global assessment, sponsored by the United Nations Environment Program and reported by the World Resources Institute and others, offers some perspective. The study concludes that 17 percent of the land supporting plant life worldwide has lost value over the past 45 years. The estimate includes erosion caused by water and wind, as well as chemical and physical deterioration, and ranks the degree of soil degradation from light to severe. This degradation is least prevalent in North America (5.3 percent) and most wide spread in Central America (25 percent), Europe (23 percent), Africa (22 percent) and Asia (20 percent). In most of these regions, the average farmer could not gather the resources necessary to restore moderate and severely affected soil regions to full productivity. Therefore, prospects for reversing the effects of soil erosion are not good, and it is likely that this problem will worsen.

Despite the loss and degradation of fertile land, the "green revolution" has promoted per capita food production by increasing the yield per hectare. The new, high-yielding strains of grains such as wheat and rice have proliferated since their introduction in the 1960s, especially in Asia. To reap full advantage from these new crop varieties, however, farmers must apply abundant quantities of fertilizer and water.

Environmentalists question whether further conversion to such crops can be achieved at reasonable cost, especially in the developing world, where the gain in production is most needed. At the moment, farmers in Asia, Latin America and Africa use fertilizer sparingly, if at all, because it is too expensive or unavailable. Fertilizer use in

the developed world has recently waned. The reasons for the decline are complex and may be temporary, but clearly farmers in North America and Europe have decided that increasing their already heavy application of fertilizer will not further enhance crop yields.

Unfortunately, irrigation systems, which would enable many developing countries to join in the green revolution, are often too expensive to build. In most areas, irrigation is essential for generating higher yields. It also can make arid land cultivable and protect farmers from the vulnerability inherent in natural variations in the weather. Land brought into cultivation this way could be used for growing multiple crop varieties, thereby helping food production to increase.

Such advantages have been realized since the beginning of agriculture: the earliest irrigation systems are thousands of years old. Yet only a fraction of productive land in the developing world is now irrigated, and its expansion has been slower than population growth. Consequently, the amount of irrigated land per capita has been dwindling during recent decades. The trend, pessimists argue, will be hard to stop. Irrigation systems have been built in the most affordable sites, and the hope for extending them is curtailed by rising costs. Moreover, the accretion of silt in dams and reservoirs and of salt in already irrigated soil is increasingly costly to avoid or reverse.

Environmentalists Ehrlich and Ehrlich note that modern agriculture is by nature at risk wherever it is practiced. The genetic uniformity of single, high-yielding crop strains planted over large areas makes them highly productive but also renders them particularly vulnerable to insects and disease. Current preventive tactics, such as spraying pesticides and rotating crops, are only partial solutions. Rapidly evolving pathogens pose a continuous challenge. Plant breeders must maintain a broad genetic arsenal of crops by collecting and storing natural varieties and by breeding new ones in the laboratory.

The optimists do not deny that many problems exist within the food supply system. But many of these authorities, including D. Gale Johnson, the late Herman Kahn, Walter R. Brown, L. Martel, the late Roger Revelle, Vaclav Smil and Julian L. Simon, believe the world's food supply can dramatically be expanded. Ironically, they draw their enthusiasm from extrapolation of the very trends that so alarm those experts who expect doom. In fact, statistics show that the average daily caloric intake per capita climbed by 21 percent (from 2,063 calories to 2,495 calories) between 1965 and 1990 in the developing countries. These higher calories have generally delivered greater amounts of protein. On average, the per capita consumption of protein rose from 52 grams per day to 61 grams per day between 1965 and 1990.

According to the optimists, not only has the world food situation improved significantly in recent decades, but further growth can be brought about in various ways. A detailed assessment of climate and soil conditions in 93 developing countries (excluding China) shows that nearly three times as much land as is currently farmed, or an additional 2.1 billion hectares, could be cultivated. Regional soil estimates indicate that sub-Saharan Africa and Latin America can exploit many more stretches of unused land than can Asia, the Near East and North Africa.

Even in regions where the amount of potentially arable land is limited, crops could be grown more times every year than is currently the case. This scenario is particularly true in the tropics and subtropics where conditions are such—relatively even temperature throughout the year and a consistent distribution of daylight hours—that more than one crop would thrive. Nearly twice as many crops are harvested every year in Asia than in Africa at present, but further increases are possible in all regions.

In addition to multicropping, higher yields per crop are attainable, especially in Africa and the Near East. Many more crops are currently harvested per hectare in the First World than elsewhere: cereal yields in North America and Europe averaged 4.2 tons per hectare, compared with 2.9 in the Far East (4.2 in China), 2.1 in Latin America, 1.7 in the Near East and only 1.0 in Africa.

Such yield improvements, the enthusiasts note, can be achieved by expanding the still limited use of high-yield crop varieties, fertilizer and irrigation. In *World Agriculture: Toward 2000,* Nikos Alexandratos of the Food and Agriculture Organization (FAO) of the United Nations reports that only 34 percent of all seeds planted during the mid-1980s were high-yielding varieties. Statistics from the FAO show that at present only about one in five hectares of arable land is irrigated, and very little fertilizer is used. Pesticides are sparsely applied. Food output could drastically be increased simply by more widespread implementation of such technologies.

Aside from producing more food, many economists and agriculturists point out, consumption levels in the developing world could be boosted by wasting fewer crops, as well as by cutting storage and distribution losses. How much of an increase would these measures yield? Robert W. Kates, director of the Alan Shawn Feinstein World Hunger Program at Brown University, writes in *The Hunger Report: 1988* that humans consume only 60 per-

cent of all harvested crops, and some 25 to 30 percent is lost before reaching individual homes. The FAO, on the other hand, estimates lower distribution losses: 6 percent for cereals, 11 percent for roots and 5 percent for pulses. All the same, there is no doubt that improved storage and distribution systems would leave more food available for human nutrition, independent of future food production capabilities.

For optimists, the long-range trend in food prices constitutes the most convincing evidence for the correctness of their view. In 1992–93 the World Resources Institute reported that food prices dropped further than the price of most nonfuel commodities, all of which have declined in the past decade. Cereal prices in the international market fell by approximately one third between 1980 and 1989. Huge government subsidies for agriculture in North America and western Europe, and the resulting surpluses of agricultural products, have depressed prices. Obviously, the optimists assert, the supply already exceeds the demand of a global population that has doubled since 1950.

Taken together, this evidence leads many experts to see no significant obstacles to raising levels of nutrition for world populations exceeding 10 billion people. The potential for an enormous expansion of food production exists, but its realization depends of course on sensible governmental policies, increased domestic and international trade and large investments in infrastructure and agricultural extension. Such improvements can be achieved, the optimists believe, without incurring irreparable damage to global ecosystems.

Proponents of either of these conflicting perspectives have difficulty accepting the existence of other plausible points of view. Moreover, the polarity between the two sides of expert opinion shows that neither group can be completely correct. Finding some common ground between these seemingly irreconcilable positions is not as difficult as it at first appears if empirical issues are emphasized and important differences in value systems and political beliefs are ignored.

Both sides agree that the demand for food will swell rapidly over the next several decades. In 1990 a person living in the developing world ate on average 2,500 calories each day, taken from 4,000 gross calories of food crops made available within a household. The remaining 1,500 calories from this gross total not used to meet nutritional requirements were either lost, inedible or used as animal feed and plant seed. Most of this food was harvested from 0.7 billion hectares of land in the developing world. The remaining 5 percent of the total food supply came from imports. To sustain this 4,000-gross-calorie diet for more than twice as many residents, or 8.7 billion people, living in the developing world by 2050, agriculture must offer 112 percent more crops. To raise the average Third World diet to 6,000 gross calories per day, slightly above the 1990 world average, food production would need to increase by 218 percent. And to bring the average Third World diet to a level comparable with that currently found in the developed world, or 10,000 gross calories per day, food production would have to surge by 430 percent.

A more generous food supply will be achieved in the future through boosting crop yields, as it has been accomplished in the past. If the harvested area in the developing world remains at 0.7 billion hectares, then each hectare must more than double its yield to maintain an already inadequate diet for the future population of the developing world. Providing a diet equivalent to a First World diet in 1990 would require that each hectare increase its yield more than six times. Such an event in the developing world must be considered virtually impossible, barring a major breakthrough in the biotechnology of food production.

Instead farmers will no doubt plant more acres and grow more crops per year on the same land to help augment crop harvests. Extrapolation of past trends suggests that the total harvested area will increase by about 50 percent by the year 2050. Each hectare will then have to provide nearly 50 percent more tons of grain or its equivalent to keep up with current dietary levels. Improved diets could result only from much larger yields.

The technological optimists are correct in stating that overall world food production can substantially be increased over the next few decades. Current crop yields are well below their theoretical maxima, and only about 11 percent of the world's farmable land is now under cultivation. Moreover, the experience gained recently in a number of developing countries, such as China, holds important lessons on how to tap this potential elsewhere. Agricultural productivity responds to well-designed policies that assist farmers by supplying needed fertilizer and other inputs, building sound infrastructure and providing market access. Further investments in agricultural research will spawn new technologies that will fortify agriculture in the future. The vital question then is not how to grow more food but rather how to implement agricultural methods that may make possible a boost in food production.

A more troublesome problem is how to achieve this technological enhancement at acceptable environmental costs. It is here that the arguments of those experts who forecast a catastrophe carry considerable weight. There can be no doubt that the land now used for growing food crops is generally of better quality than unused, potentially cultivable land. Similarly, existing irrigation systems have been built on the most favorable sites. Consequently, each new measure applied to increase yields is becoming more expensive to implement, especially in the developed world and parts of the developing world such as China, where productivity is already high. In short, such constraints are raising the marginal cost of each additional ton of grain or its equivalent. This tax is even higher if one takes into account negative externalities—primarily environmental costs not reflected in the price of agricultural products.

The environmental price of what in the Ehrlichs' view amounts to "turning the earth into a giant human feedlot" could be severe. A large inflation of agriculture to provide growing populations with improved diets is likely to lead to widespread deforestation, loss of species, soil erosion and pollution from pesticides, and runoff of fertilizer as farming intensifies and new land is brought into production. Reducing or minimizing this environmental impact is possible but costly.

Given so many uncertainties, the course of future food prices is difficult to chart. At the very least, the rising marginal cost of food production will engender steeper prices on the international market than would be the case if there were no environmental constraints. Whether these higher costs can offset the historical decline in food prices remains to be seen. An upward trend in the price of food sometime in the near future is a distinct possibility. Such a hike will be mitigated by the continued development and application of new technology and by the likely recovery of agricultural production and exports in the former Soviet Union, eastern Europe and Latin America. Also, any future price increases could be lessened by taking advantage of the underutilized agricultural resources in North America, notes Per Pinstrup-Andersen of Cornell University in his 1992 paper "Global Perspectives for Food Production and Consumption." Rising prices will have little effect on high-income countries or on households possessing reasonable purchasing power, but the poor will suffer.

In reality, the future of global food production is neither as grim as the pessimists believe nor as rosy as the optimists claim. The most plausible outcome is that dietary intake will creep higher in most regions. Significant annual fluctuations in food availability and prices are, of course, likely; a variety of factors, including the weather, trade interruptions and the vulnerability of monocropping to pests, can alter food supply anywhere. The expansion of agriculture will be achieved by boosting crop yields and by using existing farmland more intensively, as well as by bringing arable land into cultivation where such action proves economical. Such events will transpire more slowly than in the past, however, because of environmental constraints. In addition, the demand for food in the developed world is approaching saturation levels. In the U.S., mounting concerns about health have caused the per capita consumption of calories from animal products to drop.

Still, progress will be far from uniform. Numerous countries will struggle to overcome unsatisfactory nutrition levels. These countries fall into three main categories. Some low-income countries have little or no reserves of fertile land or water. The absence of agricultural resources is in itself not an insurmountable problem, as is demonstrated by regions, such as Hong Kong and Kuwait, that can purchase their food on the international market. But many poor countries, such as Bangladesh, cannot afford to buy food from abroad and thereby compensate for insufficient natural resources. These countries will probably rely more on food aid in the future.

Low nutrition levels are also found in many countries, such as Zaire, that do possess large reserves of potentially cultivable land and water. Government neglect of agriculture and policy failures have typically caused poor diets in such countries. A recent World Bank report describes the damaging effects of direct and indirect taxation of agricultures, controls placed on prices and market access, and overvalued currencies, which discourage exports and encourage imports. Where agricultural production has suffered from misguided government intervention (as is particularly the case in Africa), the solution—policy reform—is clear.

Food aid will be needed as well in areas rife with political instability and civil strife. The most devastating famines of the past decade, known to television viewers around the world, have occurred in regions fighting prolonged civil wars, such as Ethiopia, Somalia and the Sudan. In many of these cases, drought was instrumental in stirring social and political disruption. The addition of violent conflict prevented the recuperation of agriculture and the distribution of food, thus turning bad but remediable situations into disasters. International military intervention, as in Somalia, provides only a short-term remedy. In the absence of sweeping political compromise, hunger and malnutrition will remain endemic in these war-torn regions.

Feeding a growing world population a diet that improves over time in quality and quantity is technologically feasible. But the economic and environmental costs incurred through bolstering food production may well prove too great for many poor countries. The course of events will depend crucially on their governments' ability to design and enforce effective policies that address the challenges posed by mounting human numbers, rising poverty and environmental degradation. Whatever the outcome, the task ahead will be made more difficult if population growth rates cannot be reduced.

Questions

1. As the population of the world will probably exceed 10 billion by 2050, name the two schools of thought and their positions in dealing with the environment and the future of humanity. What is your view before you read this article?
2. How much has food production increased in the Third World between 1965 and 1990? How much has population expanded during this time period? What is the result?
3. What is the argument in the article concerning the amount of arable land in the developed world and undeveloped world?
4. What is the problem with increased food per hectare from the "green revolution" and irrigation systems?
5. Explain the issue of genetic uniformity.
6. According to the optimists, how much additional land could be cultivated?
7. How can yield improvements be achieved according to the optimists?
8. Explain the argument of the optimists concerning waste, storage and distribution losses of food.
9. How can the potential for food expansion be realized?
10. How much would food production have to rise in order to bring the Third World diet to the level found in the developed world?
11. What do you feel is the role of new technology in boosting this production?
12. Explain the author's view in accomplishing increase in food production. Explain your view.

The 1994 International Conference on Population and Development in Cairo

23

Unless women can manage and control their own fertility, they cannot manage and control their own lives.

KAVAL GULHATI, INDIAN FAMILY PLANNER.

In September 1994, 179 delegations of the United Nations, assembled in Cairo, Egypt, at the International Conference on Population and Development, reached a bold and sweeping plan to stabilize world population. (The conference attendees included not only 179 national delegations, but also 2,500 government delegates, 7 heads of state, 5 vice presidents, 20 deputy prime ministers, 1,200 nongovernmental organizations, and 4,000 journalists. The momentum of the population issue, as it climbed to the top of the global agenda with the sheer magnitude and the percentage of the global community that the conference involved, was, in itself, an important accomplishment.) In the preparatory meetings leading up to the conference, delegates rejected the concept of the high trajectory of population growth reaching 11.9 billion people by 2050. Instead, they recommended an ambitious plan to stabilize world population between the low and medium projections of 7.9 to 9.8 billion—by 2050. Their strategy reflected a sense of urgency—that unless population growth can be slowed quickly, it will push human demands beyond the carrying capacity of many countries, causing environmental degradation, economic decline, and social disintegration (Roush, 1994).

The plan calls for active services to provide family planning to the estimated 120 million women in the world who want to limit the number of their children but lack access to the family planning services. It also addresses the

"Nature's Limits" by Lester R. Brown, from *State of the World 1995:* A Worldwatch Institute Report on Progress Toward a Sustainable Society by Lester R. Brown, et al, eds. Copyright © 1995 by Worldwatch Institute. Reprinted by permission of W.W. Norton & Company, Inc.

underlying causes of high fertility, such as female illiteracy, and strives for universal primary school education for girls, recognizing that as female educational levels rise, fertility levels fall—a relationship that holds across all cultures. The goals of the conference were to achieve gender equality and to permit women to have the right to control and manage their own lives. A major achievement of the Cairo conference was to change the world view of the population issue. From the previous view, which was concerned with demography and contraception, the agenda moved to a focus on the situation of women.

The Cairo conference highlighted the fact that real change in demographic patterns will occur only through fundamental changes in women's lives, such as increases in women's access to education, cash, and credit. Two thirds of the world's illiterate people are women. Women are responsible for over 80% of food production in Africa, but they have very little access to agricultural extension, credit, land titles, or management. Studies show that with better education and an increase of stature in family and community for women, birth rates decline. Ninety-five percent of the growth in population will occur in the developing world, increasing from the current 5–6 billion people to 8.6–12 billion by the year 2100.

There also needs to be an increase in the amount of information regarding reproduction available to adolescents around the world. As there are currently over 1 billion teenagers on the planet and increasingly large numbers of them are unmarried and living in cities, there are radical changes in values of "the young and the restless" as values are beamed around the planet on television, raising questions that do not relate in their culture and the lives of their ancestors (Catley-Carlson, 1994).

The document produced by the conference sets a plan for developing and supportive countries to invest at least 20% of their public expenditures in the social sector. Special focus is placed on a range of population, health, and education programs that would improve the health and status of women. It also requests donor spending on population assistance (currently at about $1 billion) to increase from 1.4% of official development assistance to 4%. One of the prominent themes of the Cairo conference was to try to ensure that the responsibility and funding of this change would be shared by the whole world. These measures, the document states, "would result in world population growth at levels close to the United Nations low [projection] of a global population of 7.8 billion by the year 2050 (Roush, 1994).

The goals set in Cairo will be extremely difficult to achieve, but if the world succeeds in stabilizing human population at 8 or 9 billion, it will satisfy one of the conditions of an environmentally sustainable society. The plan recognizes the earth's natural limits and the urgency to respect those limits. There already is evidence of these limits in the world's declining fish catches, falling water tables, declining bird populations on every continent, rising global temperatures, and the fact that world grain stocks are at their lowest level in 20 years.

In trying to answer the question of how many people the earth can support, we raise the reverse question: What exactly will limit the growth in human numbers? It appears that it is the supply of food that will determine the earth's population carrying capacity. Three natural limits for food production are already slowing food yields: the sustainable yield of oceanic fisheries, the amount of fresh water produced by the hydrological cycle, and the amount of fertilizer that the existing crop varieties can effectively use.

Understanding and respecting the earth's limits is dependent on the urgent recognition of limiting the draw on those resources and translating that recognition into a worldwide population plan for limitation and stabilization. According to the plan developed in Cairo, this can happen best if women have an informed voice in the planning of their families. As the delegates gathered in Cairo debated the plan of action for nine days, the world's population grew by some 2.1 million people (Brown, 1995).

References

Brown, L. (1995). Nature's limits. *State of the World,* 1995 (pp. 3–4). New York: W.W. Norton & Co, 1995.

Catley-Carlson, M.: Interview. (1994, October). Cairo Conference Finds Women's Status Central to Slowing Population Growth, Increasing Food Production. *2020 News & Reviews.* Available: htttp://www.cgiar.org./ifpri/2020/newslet/nv_1094/nv-1094f.htm.

Roush, W. (1994, August 26). Population: The view from Cairo. *Science,* p. 1164. Available: http://www.mit.edu:8001/people/weroush/population.html.

Questions

1. The Cairo conference plan is ambitious on many counts. Identify five areas in which this plan is especially ambitious.

2. What do you think is the response to the conference's resolutions from nations whose religious and cultural convictions do not support the equal status, education, and self-control of women? What can be done about their response?

3. Some sources have said that this conference was one of the most revolutionary of any U.N. conferences. Why do you think this might be so?

4. Relate the World Birth Control Fact Sheet to the U.N. resolutions from the Cairo conference. Given those facts on birth control, what are some of the biggest obstacles to accomplishing the resolutions? Do you think that the resolutions deal with the core of the problem? Why or why not?

A Bridge to Your 21st Century Understanding

Complete and discuss the following flowchart.

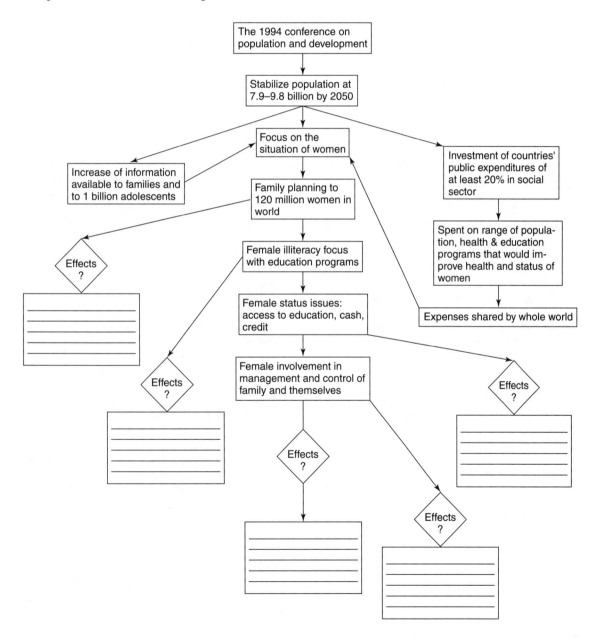

The 1994 conference on population and development

Stabilize population at 7.9–9.8 billion by 2050

Focus on the situation of women

Increase of information available to families and to 1 billion adolescents

Investment of countries' public expenditures of at least 20% in social sector

Family planning to 120 million women in world

Spent on range of population, health & education programs that would improve health and status of women

Female illiteracy focus with education programs

Effects ?

Female status issues: access to education, cash, credit

Expenses shared by whole world

Effects ?

Female involvement in management and control of family and themselves

Effects ?

Effects ?

Effects ?

Effects ?

24

World Birth Control Discussion Issues

SOME WORLD ARGUMENTS AGAINST POPULATION AND BIRTH CONTROL

1. *Progrowth position:* Rapid population growth in a particular country or region is a positive force on grounds of
   (a) economic development (a larger population provides necessary economies of scale and a good labor supply);
   (b) protection of presently underpopulated areas from covetous neighbors;
   (c) differences in fertility among ethnic, racial, religious, or political population segments; and
   (d) military and political power and the strength of a younger age structure.
2. *Revolutionary position:* Population programs are merely a way to hide or placate fundamental social and political contradictions that would lead to a just revolution and therefore could be viewed as inherently counterrevolutionary.
3. *Anticolonial and genocidal position:* The motives of highly developed countries of pushing less developed countries (LDCs) to adopt aggressive population programs are open to suspicion. These more developed countries went through a period of rapid population growth as part of their own development processes,

and their current efforts to restrain population growth in the less developed countries are an attempt to keep control and power by retarding the development of these countries. Population limitation could be seen as attempt of the rich countries to "buy development cheaply" or a racist or genocidal attempt to reduce the size of poor and largely nonwhite populations.

4. *Overconsumption by rich countries position:* Population problems are actually resource-scarcity and environmental-deterioration problems that derive from activities of the rich, highly developed countries and not from high fertility in the LDCs. Even if fertility is too high in the LDCs, this is a consequence of their poverty, which, in turn, results from overconsumption of the world's scarce resources by rich countries.
5. *Agricultural and technological improvement position:* Growing population numbers can be accommodated as they have in the past by improvements in agricultural and industrial technologies. Past Malthusian predictions were incorrect, and the same is true of these new Malthusian predictions and solutions. Overpopulation is really underemployment. A humane and well-structured economy can provide employment and subsistence for all people, no matter what the size of the population.
6. *Distribution problem position:* It is not the population numbers themselves that are causing population problems, but their distribution in space. Many areas of the world or countries are underpopulated; others have too many people condensed into too small an area. Instead of efforts to moderate the rate of growth,

Reprinted by permission of *Foreign Affairs,* July 1974. Copyright 1974 by the Council on Foreign Relations, Inc. Teitelbaum, M. (1974, July). Population and Development: Is a Consensus Possible? *Foreign Affairs,* Vol. 52 No 4.

governments should undertake efforts to reduce more population flows to urban areas and to distribute population on available land.

7. *High mortality and social security position:* High fertility is a response to high death and disease rates; if these levels were reduced, fertility would decline naturally. Living children are the primary way that poor people can achieve security in old age. Therefore, improvements in mortality rates and social security programs would lead to a reduction in fertility.

8. *Status of women position:* High fertility levels are perpetuated by the status and roles of women primarily as procreative agents. As long as women's economic and social status depends largely upon the number of children they bear, there is little possibility that societal fertility levels will decline.

9. *Religious doctrine positions:* The ideology of "Be fruitful and multiply; God will provide" does not recognize population as a serious problem. The other argument holds that while current rates of population growth are a serious problem, the primary instruments to deal with them—modern contraception, surgical sterilization, and abortion—are morally unacceptable; abortion is "murder," and surgical sterilization is "unnatural."

10. *Medical risk position:* Fertility reduction is not worth the medical risks of using the medical means of population programs. Oral contraceptives and intrauterine devices have measurable, if small, short-term risks and possible long-term effects. Sterilization and abortion are operative procedures, both of which have an element of risk, especially when performed outside a hospital.

11. *Progress and development position:* As the social and economic aspects of a society further develop, fertility rates decline. Most of the decline in fertility in LDCs derives from social and economical development than from the success of population control programs. International assistance for development is too heavily concentrated on population programs and is short-changing the focus on general overall development.

12. *Social justice position:* Fertility will not decline and population programs will not be successful until the basic reasons for high fertility—poverty, ignorance, and fatalism—are eliminated through social policies that result in a redistribution of power and wealth among the rich and poor, both within and among nations.

SOME WORLD ARGUMENTS SUPPORTING POPULATION AND BIRTH CONTROL

1. *Population activist position:* Unrestrained population growth is the principal cause of poverty, malnutrition, environmental disruption, and other social problems. The situation is desperate and necessitates action to restrain population growth, even if coercion is required: "Mutual coercion, mutually agreed upon." Population programs are fine as far as they go, but they are wholly insufficient in scope and strength to meet the urgency and reality of the situation.

2. *Services need position:* According to data and surveys, there is a great unmet demand for fertility control in all countries; therefore, the main problem is to provide modern fertility control to already motivated people. Some proponents also hold that the failure of some population service programs is due to inadequate fertility control technologies and that there is an urgent need for technological improvements in this area.

3. *Human rights position:* According to U.N. propositions, it is a fundamental human right for each person to be able to determine the size of his or her own family. Furthermore, some argue that each woman has the fundamental right to the control of her own bodily processes, a rationale that supports contraception and possibly abortion. Health is also a basic human right that population programs support directly and indirectly and includes the direct medical benefits of increased child spacing for maternal and child health and the indirect effects of reducing numbers of dangerous illegal abortions.

4. *Population control and development position:* Social and economic development programs help, but alone are not sufficient to bring about low mortality and fertility levels. Special population programs are also required. Too rapid population growth intensifies other social and economic problems. Some countries might benefit from larger populations, but would benefit more by moderate rates of growth over longer periods of time than by rapid rates of growth over shorter periods of time. Economic, social, and population programs are all interlinked.

Use of contraceptive methods,
by region
Courtesy of UN Population Fund.

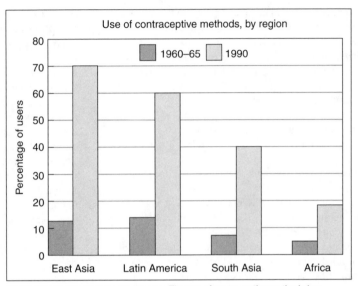

Use of contraceptive methods, by region

For all developing countries on average. The use of contraceptive methods has
grown from less than 10% in the 1960s to more than 50% today.

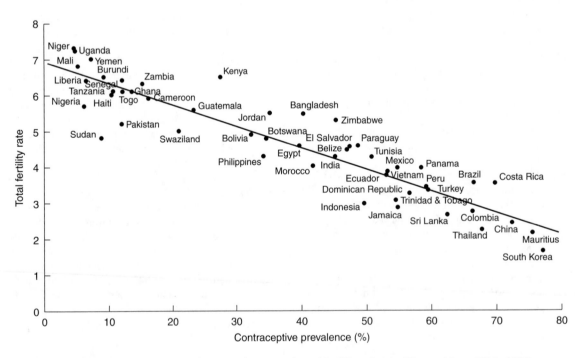

The relationship between contraceptive prevalence and total fertility rates in 50 countries, 1984–1992.
(From Population Reports 1992.)

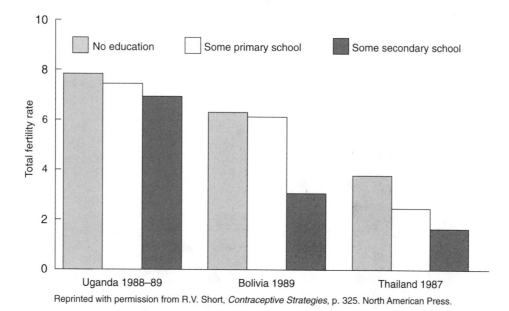

Reprinted with permission from R.V. Short, *Contraceptive Strategies*, p. 325. North American Press.

Total fertility rates in three countries by women's level of education. Before fertility rates start to fall, fertility is high in all groups (Uganda). As educated women are first to reduce their fertility, differences widen amongst groups (Bolivia). Eventually, fertility is low in all groups (Thailand). (From Population Reports 1992.)

Figure 24.5
Percentage Use of Contraceptive Methods Worldwide (1987)

Currently, 390 million couples are using modern contraceptives, about 51% of the total

female sterilization	29
intrauterine devices	20
oral contraceptives	14
condoms	9
male sterilization	8
coitus interruptus	8
rhythm	7
injectables	2
other methods	2
barrier methods	1

Note.   Methods with lowest failure rates predominate in developing countries. Methods with highest failure rates predominate in developed countries.

BIRCH CONTROL

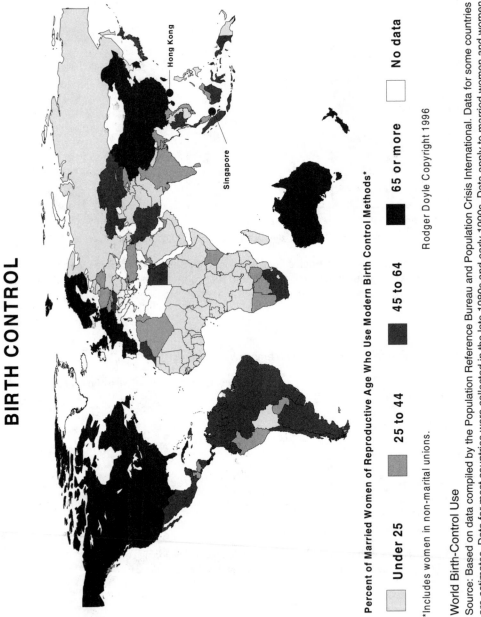

Percent of Married Women of Reproductive Age Who Use Modern Birth Control Methods*

Under 25 | 25 to 44 | 45 to 64 | 65 or more | No data

*Includes women in non-marital unions.

Rodger Doyle Copyright 1996

World Birth-Control Use

Source: Based on data compiled by the Population Reference Bureau and Population Crisis International. Data for some countries are estimates. Data for most countries were collected in the late 1980s and early 1990s. Data apply to married women and women in nonmarital unions. Excerpted with permission from Doyle, R (1996, September). World birth-control use. *Scientific American.* Vol. 275, No. 3, p. 34.

WORLD BIRTH CONTROL FACT SHEET

I. In the past 30 years, there has been a marked decline in world fertility rates, particularly in developing countries.

1. Between 1960–1965, women in developing countries averaged six births over a lifetime while in 1990–1995, they averaged 3.4 births over a lifetime.
2. In east Asia for the past 30 years, births fell 65% and are now below replacement rate of 2.1 children.
3. In other parts of Asia, births declined by about a third, Latin America halved, and Africa only by 10%.

II. In the developed countries, the number of births per woman declined by about 40% and are now below replacement level in all these countries, including the United States.

III. Modern contraceptive methods have played a key role in lowering fertility.

1. Among women of reproductive age who are married (or in nonmarital unions), half now depend on the following methods: female sterilization (most popular), male sterilization, hormonal implants (such as Norplant), injectibles (such as Depo-Provera), intrauterine devices (IUD's), birth control pills, condoms, and diaphragms.
2. The first four methods are almost 100% effective, followed by IUD's, the pill, and the male condom in effectiveness. Diaphragms are among the least effective.
3. Condoms (both the male and female type) are the only methods that provide protection against sexually transmitted diseases, such as AIDS.
4. The percentage of women using modern contraception is as follows:
54% in Asia (39% if China is excluded), 53% in Latin America, 30–40% in the Muslim Middle East and North Africa, 48% in the countries of the southern tip of Africa, <10% in middle Africa, 65–75% in the United States and western Europe, in the former Soviet Union <20% because of short supply.

IV. Growth in birth-control use and decline in fertility in developing countries is closely linked to educational opportunities for women (e.g., sub-Saharan Africa, with the highest fertility rates, has the lowest female educational levels).

1. Increased literacy makes it easier for women to receive reliable information on contraception.
2. The demands of education, particularly at the post-secondary level, cause women to delay marriage and childbearing.

V. Some developing countries, such as China and Cuba, are already below the replacement level of 2.1 children, mostly because of modern birth-control methods.

1. Countries such as Brazil, Indonesia, Vietnam, South Africa, Turkey, Egypt, and India should reach this level within the approximate next ten years.
2. Pakistan and Nigeria, where few women use modern contraception, are at the other extreme and are not likely to reach the replacement rate for several decades.

VI. More historical and traditional methods of birth control include the rhythm method, coitus interruptus, and prolonged breast-feeding (which suppresses ovulation). Worldwide, 7% of all married women (or women in nonmarital unions) of reproductive age depend on these methods, which are far less reliable. The rhythm method is prevalent in Peru, and coitus interruptus is the birth control method of choice in Turkey.

A Day in the Life of the World 1993

100,000,000	Acts of intercourse will take place
910,000	Conceptions will occur
150,000	Abortions will be performed
500	Mothers will die as a result of abortion
384,000	Babies will be born
1,370	Mothers will die of pregnancy-related causes
25,000	Infants in the first year of life will die
14,000	Children aged 1-4 will die
356,000	Adults will get a sexually transmitted disease
250,000	Is the net increase in population of the world

Reprinted with permission from North American Press; Short, R.V. *Contraceptive Strategies,* p. 327.

Questions

1. What positions against population and birth control do you think have the most merit? Why?
2. What positions for population and birth control do you think have the most merit? Why?
3. What positions do you think are the most difficult to address concerning the population issue and the 1994 U.N. resolutions made in Cairo?
4. What do these positions for and against population and birth control tell you about other cultures and societies? What do they tell you about their priorities?
5. What plans might you have to address or change the positions you identified in Questions 1 and 2?
6. Do you think that the U.N. resolutions adequately address the concerns of the positions against birth control?

POPULATION CONTROL

During recent years, many scientists and economists have expressed a concern about the population growth and scarcity of resources. The world population has increased from 3.72 billion (1970) to 5.32 billion (1990) and is projected to be 10 billion by the year 2010. Many experts believe that earth's population is about to surpass the planet's "carrying capacity." Contrary to this, World Bank figures show that food prices have declined dramatically to an historic low—reflecting improvements and a worldwide surplus of grain. The population growth rates in the developed countries are low whereas for the developing countries they are high.

To address the question of population control, the United Nations (UN) held a conference in Cairo. The conference adopted a resolution for the population control. The resolution document, called "Proposed Program of Action for the Cairo Conference," calls for adoption of various birth control methods, including abortion for population control. The majority of the Third-World countries with Catholic and Muslim populations believe that the UN has gone too far in making these recommendations. The UN recommendations are in direct contradiction to the religious beliefs of Catholics and Muslims all over the world. The Pope has formed a Catholic–Islamic alliance to oppose UN recommendations for population control.

- Do you think that the UN is justified in recommending population control strategies that contradict people's religious beliefs?
- In many Third-World countries the majority of people are farmers. Due to a lack of technology and resources, they believe in having large families in order to manage their farms. What population control strategy would you recommend to help Third-World farmers?
- Many Third-World nations believe that population is an asset and that the developed countries are trying to control their future potential through the United Nations. Do you agree with this view? Why? Why not?

JAPAN'S BAN ON THE PILL NOT LIKELY TO CHANGE*

On July 9, 1996, Japanese Health and Welfare Minister Naota Kan announced at the Foreign Correspondent's Club that oral contraceptives, which had been officially banned for more than 30 years, could be approved by the next year. (Health Ministry Officials point out that Kan's prediction was his own personal opinion rather than official policy.) Even if the pill is approved, doctors say that it will not become popular quickly, as opinion polls regularly show widespread misconceptions from women about the pill and its side effects.

Presently, only women with menstrual disorders can legally use the pill in high and middling doses; however, the number of women redirecting the use of the pill from the treatment of such disorders to birth control could be as high as 500,000. Many believe that Japan's abortion rate, one of the highest in the world at 400,000 per year, would be much reduced if pill use were legal.

Kan's announcement was an important encouragement for pill supporters after many disappointments. In 1965, pill approval was denied because of fears that it would corrupt sexual morals. In 1986, the government set up a medical study group to examine the feasibility of the use of a low-dose contraceptive pill that concluded in favor of its introduction, but legislation was never forthcoming. Drug companies petitioned the government in 1990, but fears that condom use (the main form of birth control in Japan) would decline, leading to an increase in the spread of HIV, brought about the pill's rejection in 1992. Another possible approval was lost again in late 1995 with publicity surrounding studies on venous thromboembolic disease and the use of combined oral contraceptives.

Critics argue that the ban is still in place because of a male-dominated bureaucracy that denies women contraceptive freedom. Other important factors that stop the pill from becoming legal are the profits of condom manufacturers, profits of those who perform abortions, and anxiety about Japan's rapidly declining population. Without strong feminist and antiabortion movements to keep the issue alive, complacency has also added to the pill not becoming legalized.

* This law has now been passed—but the issue of women's right to choose is still relevant in Japan and throughout the world.
Excerpted with permission from Gutierrez, E., and Netley, G. (1996, September 28). Japan's ban on the pill seems unlikely to change. *The Lancet*. Vol. 346, p. 886.

25 Fertility Rates: The Decline Is Stalling

LINDA STARKE

· ·

During the 1970s, one of the encouraging developments in population trends was the reduction in the total fertility rate in several key countries, including the world's two largest nations—China and India. (The fertility rate measures the average number of children born to women in their childbearing years.) In China, the rate dropped precipitously, from 6.4 children per woman in 1968 to 2.2 in 1980. In India, the decline was more modest, but still significant: from 5.8 children per woman between 1966 and 1971 to 4.8 children between 1976 and 1981.

These trends helped slow the rate of world population growth from 2.1 percent between 1965 and 1970 to 1.7 percent between 1975 and 1980. At that point, however, the decline in the number of children that women were having in these two population giants stalled.

In China, despite the most aggressive and least democratic population control program in the world, the fertility rate remained around 2.5 throughout much of the 1980s as couples continued to want to marry young and to have two or more children. In India, the overzealous promotion of family planning by the ruling Congress Party through 1977 apparently backfired after the party's defeat, and progress toward lower birth rates ran out of steam.

One important lesson from these experiences is that governments must do more than just supply contraceptives; they need to lower the demand for children by making fundamental changes that improve women's lives and

From the Worldwatch Institute's annual report of key global indicators, *Vital Signs 1993*

increase their access to and control over money, credit, and other resources.

Many countries still register fertility rates above replacement level (see Table 25.1), which is generally 2.1 children per woman or basically two children per couple. The total fertility rate for the world as a whole in 1991 was 3.3, ranging from 1.8 in more developed nations to 4.4 in less developed ones (excluding China). In a number of countries, such as Brazil, Egypt, Indonesia, Mexico, and Thailand, fertility rates have been dropping as they did in the 1970s in China and India. At the same time, many developing countries have not yet entered the demographic transition.

The demographic transition occurs when both birth rates and death rates in a country drop from historically high levels to low ones that translate into a stable population—one that merely replaces itself with each new generation. Traditionally, although not always, death rates have declined first, following the spread of sanitation and improved health care overall. Rapid population growth often follows this first phase of the demographic transition, as the gap between fertility and mortality rates widens for a time. Eventually, however, fertility rates fall too.

At the moment, they remain high in a number of countries. The reasons include unequal rights and opportunities for women, as well as inadequate access to birth control. Whatever the reason, the effect is the same: 67 countries, home to 17 percent of the world population, are at best in the early stages of a transition to low fertility rates. Most of them are in Africa and South

Table 25.1

Population Size, Fertility Rate, and Doubling Time, 20 Largest Countries, 1993

Country	Population (Millions)	Rate (Average Number of Children Per Woman)	Doubling Time (Years)
Italy	58	1.3	3466
Germany	81	1.4	*
Japan	125	1.5	217
United Kingdom	58	1.8	267
France	58	1.8	169
Russia	149	1.7	990
United States	258	2.0	92
China	1,178	1.9	60
Thailand	57	2.4	49
Indonesia	188	3.0	42
Brazil	152	2.6	46
Turkey	61	3.6	32
Mexico	90	3.4	30
India	97	3.9	34
Viet Nam	72	4.0	31
Philippines	5	4.1	28
Egypt	8	4.6	30
Pakistan	122	6.7	23
Iran	3	6.6	20
Nigeria	5	6.6	23

Source: Population Reference Bureau, 1993 World Population Data Sheet (Washington, D.C.: 1993).
*At its current mortality rate, Germany's population is shrinking, and at this fertility rate will never double.

Asia, and their populations are likely to double in 20 to 25 years.

This is leading to a two-tiered demographic world that is every bit as worrying as the world of economics haves and have-nots. Countries such as Nigeria and Pakistan are finding it harder to keep up with the demand for food, health care, jobs, housing, and education than countries that are in the middle of the demographic transition.

As Shiro Horiuchi of Rockefeller University notes, "the demographic gap seems to overlap with a growing gap in economic development." This gap has been growing for more than 20 years. In 1970, 34 percent of the world lived in countries with fertility rates below 5.5. Just five years later, thanks to the dramatic declines in India and especially China, the figure was 80 percent. It has not gained much since then, however, reaching 83 percent by 1985. More than three fourths of the significant declines in fertility rates started in the 1965 to 1970 period, and not many have begun since then.

Even when a country does reach replacement-level fertility, its population can continue growing for decades. There is a built-in momentum created by all the people who have yet to enter their childbearing years. Indeed, the decline in the world's population growth rate stalled in the 1980s in part because even in China, India, and other countries where fertility rates had been dropping, a large number of people who had been born in the 1960s reached childbearing age. So even if couples had two or three children instead of five or six, as their parents did, the population would grow substantially.

For the world as a whole, even if replacement-level fertility had been achieved in 1990, the population would continue to grow until it reached 8.4 billion in 2150 because of all the young people already alive.

This built-in momentum obviously limits how quickly any country can stop population growth. Nevertheless, reaching replacement-level fertility is an all-important first step. The 67 countries that have not yet begun the demographic transition—nations in which invariably the government believes fertility levels are too high—could move in the right direction by providing the contraceptive and health care services that would help couples have only the number of children they desire.

Questions

1. What is the fertility rate?
2. What was the fertility rate as a whole in the world in 1991?
3. How many countries are in the early stages of a transition to low fertility rates? What are the characteristics of this early transition phase? What is the longer term effect of being in the early stages of a demographic transition?
4. Why is this demographic gap overlapping with an economic gap?
5. Why did the decline of the fertility rate stall in the 1980s?
6. Why, if replacement-level fertility had been reached in 1990, would the population continue to grow to 8.4 billion?

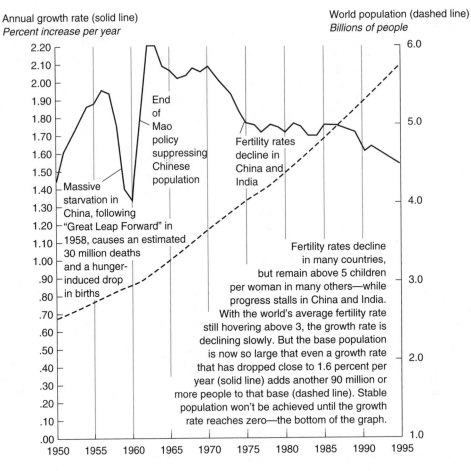

Annual growth rate (solid line)
Percent increase per year

World population (dashed line)
Billions of people

Figure 25.1
World population: Even as the rate of growth declines, the number of humans continues to climb.

Table 25.2
Projected Population Size at Stabilization, Selected Countries

Country	Population in 1986	Annual Rate of Population Growth	Size of Population at Stabilization	Change from 1986
	(million)	(percent)	(million)	(percent)
Slow Growth Countries				
China	1,050	1.0	1,571	+ 50
Soviet Union	280	0.9	377	+ 35
United States	241	0.7	289	+ 20
Japan	121	0.7	128	+ 6
United Kingdom	56	0.2	59	+ 5
West Germany	61	−0.2	52	− 15
Rapid Growth Countries				
Kenya	20	4.2	111	+435
Nigeria	105	3.0	532	+406
Ethiopia	42	2.1	204	+386
Iran	47	2.9	166	+253
Pakistan	102	2.8	330	+223
Bangladesh	104	2.7	310	+198
Egypt	46	2.6	126	+174
Mexico	82	2.6	199	+143
Turkey	48	2.5	109	+127
Indonesia	168	2.1	368	+119
India	785	2.3	1,700	+116
Brazil	143	2.3	298	+108

Source: World Bank, *World Development Report 1985* (New York: Oxford University Press, 1985).

Table 25.3
Countries That Reached Population Stability by 1995

Country	Population Mid-1995	Birth Rate	Death Rate	Annual Rate of Natural Increase Or Decrease[1]
	(million)	(births per thousand population)	(deaths per thousand population)	(percent)
Austria	8	12	10	+0.1
Belarus	10	11	13	−0.2
Belgium	10	12	11	+0.1
Bulgaria	8	10	13	−0.3
Croatia	4	10	11	−0.1
Czech Republic	10	12	11	0
Denmark	5	13	12	+0.1

continued

Table 25.3
Countries That Reached Population Stability by 1995, *continued*

Country	Population Mid-1995	Birth Rate	Death Rate	Annual Rate of Natural Increase Or Decrease[1]
	(million)	(births per thousand population)	(deaths per thousand population)	(percent)
Estonia	2	9	14	−0.5
Finland	5	13	10	+0.3
France	58	12	9	+0.3
Georgia	5	12	10	+0.2
Germany	82	10	11	−0.1
Greece	10	10	9	0
Hungary	10	12	14	−0.3
Italy	58	9	10	0
Japan	125	10	7	+0.3
Latvia	2	10	15	−0.5
Lithuania	4	13	12	0
Norway	4	14	11	+0.3
Poland	39	12	10	+0.2
Portugal	10	12	11	+0.1
Romania	23	11	12	−0.1
Russia	148	9	16	−0.6
Slovenia	2	10	10	+0.1
Spain	39	10	9	+0.1
Sweden	9	13	12	+0.1
Switzerland	7	12	9	+0.3
Ukraine	52	11	14	−0.4
United Kingdom	59	13	11	+0.2
Yugoslavia[2]	11	13	10	+0.3

[1]Does not always reflect exactly the difference between birth rates and death rates shown because of rounding.
[2]Reflects the new Yugoslavia, consisting of Serbia plus Montenegro.
Source: Population Reference Bureau, *1995 World Population Data Sheet* (Washington, D.C.: 1995).

Questions About the Tables

1. What do you think is meant by "stabilization of population rate"?
2. Explain the information in Table 25.2. Why do the rapid-growth countries experience a much larger change of percentage of growth rate than the slow-growth countries?
3. Compare Table 25.3 with Table 25.2. What are the significant differences between stable-growth countries and the rapid-growth countries?
4. Compare your results from Question 3 with the information from Table P4.7 and Table P4.8 at the beginning of this part. Note specifics like fertility rate per woman of Table P4.7 and Table P4.8 which further support Tables 25.2 and 25.3. Select a country and give three specifics from Tables P4.7 and P4.8 which support Tables 25.2 and 25.3.

Population Carrying Capacities: Four Case Studies: Pakistan, India, Ethiopia, and Mexico

26

THE CONCEPT OF POPULATION CARRYING CAPACITY

Population carrying capacity is an approach that many ecologists use to mark and provide a sustainable limit philosophy that measures needed ecological policy. Economists tend to view carrying capacity with more flexibility due to technological and policy interventions so that the approach has a less fixed value.

Population carrying capacity can be defined as "the number of people that the planet can support without irreversibly reducing its capacity or ability to support people in the future." While this is a global-level definition, it applies at a national level too, albeit with many qualifications, for example, international trade, investment and debt. Furthermore, it is a function of factors that reflect technological change, food and energy supplies, ecosystem services (such as provision of freshwater and recycling of nutrients), human capital, people's lifestyles, social institutions, political structures and cultural constraints among many other factors, all of which interact with each other.

Two points are particularly important: that carrying capacity is ultimately determined by the component that yields the lowest carrying capacity; and that human communities must learn to live off the "interest" of environmental resources rather than off their "principal". Thus, the concept of carrying capacity is closely tied in with the

Excerpted from *Population Resources and the Environment: The Critical Challenges.* United Nations Population Fund.

concept of sustainable development. There is now evidence that human numbers with their consumption of resources, plus the technologies deployed to supply that consumption, are often exceeding the land's carrying capacity already. In many parts of the world, the three principal and essential stocks of renewable resources—forests, grasslands and fisheries—are being utilized faster than their rate of natural replenishment.

Consider a specific example—the Earth's carrying capacity with respect to food production. According to the World Hunger Project, the planetary ecosystem could, with present agro-technologies and with equal distribution of food supplies, satisfactorily support 5.5 billion people if they all lived on a vegetarian diet (the 1991 global population is already 5.4 billion). If people derived 15 percent of their calories from animal products, as tends to be the case in South America, the total would decline to 3.7 billion. If they derived 25 percent of their calories from animal protein, as is the case with most people in North America, the Earth could support only 2.8 billion people.

True, these calculations reflect no more than today's food production technologies. Certain observers protest that such an analysis underestimates the scope for technological expertise to keep on expanding the Earth's carrying capacity. We can surely hope that many advances in agro-technologies will come on stream. But consider the population–food record over the past four decades. From 1950 to 1984, and thanks largely to remarkable advances in Green Revolution agriculture, there was a 2.6-fold increase in world grain output. This achievement, representing an average increase of almost 3 percent a year, raised per capita production by more than a third. But from 1985 to 1989, there was next to no increase at all, even though the period saw the world's farmers investing billions of dollars to increase output (fertilizer use alone expanded by 14 percent). These big investments were supported by rising grain prices and by the restoration to production of idled United States cropland. Crop yields had "plateaued"; it appeared that plant breeders and agronomists had exhausted the scope for technological innovation. So the 1989 harvest was hardly any higher than that of 1984. During that same period, there were an extra 440 million people to feed. While world population increased by almost 8.5 percent, grain output per person declined by nearly 7 percent.

To put the case more succinctly, every 15 seconds sees the arrival of another 44 people, and during the same 15 seconds the planet's stock of arable land declines by one hectare. Plainly, this is not to say the first is a singularly causative factor of the second. Many other factors, notably technology, contribute to the linkage. Equally, it is not to deny that there is a strong relationship between the two factors: more people are trying to sustain themselves from less cropland.

Regrettably, there is all too little concise analysis of the concept of carrying capacity. So the evaluation of its nature, and especially of the threat of environmental overloading, must remain largely a matter of judgment. But remember that in a situation of pervasive uncertainty, we have no alternative but to aim for the best assessment we can muster. We cannot defer the question until such time as we have conducted enough research. After all, if we do not derive such conclusions as we can and make explicit planning decisions on their basis, there will be implicit planning decisions taken by large numbers of people who, through their daily lifestyles, are determining the outcome. In other words, decisions on the population–environment nexus will be taken either by design or by default. We must make do with such information and understanding as we have at hand, however imperfect that may be.

To comprehend the concept of carrying capacity in real-world terms, consider the following case studies. Through the experience of four countries, drawn from all three main developing regions, we can discern the strong links between population pressure and the capacity of the natural resource base to support increasing human numbers.

Questions

1. Define "population carrying capacity."
2. What two points underlie carrying capacity?
3. What is the cause of the difference between earth's carrying capacity estimates of food production of 5.5 billion people, 3.7 billion people, and 2.8 billion people, as mentioned in the article? What number do you think will reflect a sustainable world standard of living and why? Explain.
4. What happens every 15 seconds in the way of adding and subtracting to earth's carrying capacity?
5. What do you think of the validity of the concept of carrying capacity? Do you think that this concept can help us design our future, or will we proceed to our future by default?

PAKISTAN

Pakistan, like its neighbour India, suffers much environmental degradation in the form of deforestation, soil erosion, desertification and depletion of water supplies. This resource decline is leading to agricultural problems; indeed, to a growing incapacity of natural environments to support present human numbers. Yet the country's natural resource base is central to the national economy, with agriculture the largest single development sector. In 1985, agriculture accounted for 32 percent of Pakistan's GDP, employed 55 percent of the population and earned 79 percent of all export revenues.

Pakistan's land area of 887,722 square kilometers is mostly semi-arid or arid. At the time of independence in 1947, the populace totalled 31 million people, and the country was self-sufficient in most staple foods. By 1990, the populace totalled 123 million people, and was growing at an annual rate of 2.9 percent, doubling the population in 24 years. Allowing for a further decline in the death rate and some decline in the birth rate, the population is projected to reach 162 million people by 2000 and 248 million by 2020; more than twice as many people in a mere three decades. But it is questionable whether there will be much fertility decline in the foreseeable future. The average family size today is 7 children (technically expressed as 6.7), the highest in southern Asia except for Afghanistan. This is considered to be due, in part, to the poor social status of women, and the general neglect of women's development needs in this predominantly Muslim country. Only 3 percent of women are educated, and the female to male school enrollment ratio is among the 10 lowest in the world.

Between 1947 and 1985, Pakistan's birth rate fell from 45 to only 43 per 1,000 people. But in 1990, it is estimated to have risen to 44 per 1,000. By contrast, the crude death rate has fallen from over 25 to 13 per 1,000 people, still higher than the rate for India (11 per 1,000) and the average for the region (12 per 1,000). Obviously, there is some scope for a further decline in the death rate. The level of contraceptive use among reproductive-age women is only 8 percent, one seventh that recorded for the region. So the population size in 2100 and 2020 could be rather higher than projected. With only a marginal decline in the birth rate and a continuing decline in the death rate, Pakistan could find itself trying to support twice as many people in less than a generation, and more than 400 million by the time it has enjoyed another 45 years of nationhood.

The 3.7 times increase in human numbers since 1947 has been accommodated mainly by three major advances in agriculture during the 1960s. These were: the Indus Basin Treaty that provided a greater volume of riverwater for irrigation; a sharp increase in the number of tubewells supplying access to more underground water; and the introduction of high-yielding varieties of grain. Today, there appears to be little opportunity to gain much more advantage from the first two, while the third provided scant support during the 1980s when grain yields plateaued.

Meantime, the country's natural resource base has experienced growing stress for at least 30 years. Consider three key sectors: forestry, water and agricultural land. A maximum of 3 percent of national territory is still forested, whereas the government believes it should be at least 15 percent. The Director-General of the Pakistan Forestry Institute, referring to deforested watersheds, concludes the country "already faces a grave situation insofar as water for irrigation and power generation is concerned." Yet deforestation seems set to grow worse if only because of growing demand for fuelwood, which in the mid-1980s accounted for 50 percent of the country's energy requirements and almost 90 percent of total wood consumption. There was an acute shortage of fuelwood as far back as 1978, when the annual growth of wood was supplying only 62 percent of the annual harvest. Yet demand for fuelwood is projected to double during the last two decades of this century. So there appears to be little relief for watershed forests in the foreseeable future.

Second, water is in short supply, especially for agriculture. An irrigation network covers almost a fifth of the country, the largest such system in the world. Some 156,000 square kilometres of croplands are irrigated, a full 70 percent of the cropland expanse; a proportion way ahead of Japan's 63 percent, China's 48 percent and India's 33 percent. These irrigated croplands produce 80 percent of the country's food. Irrigated wheatlands, comprising 38 percent of all irrigated croplands, and four times as large an area as rain fed wheatlands, average over 2,000 kilograms of harvest per hectare a year, rain fed wheatlands only around 850 kilograms.

But water is the scarcest input to agriculture, and supplies are likely to run out well before other resources such as land, energy, high yielding grains, fertilizers and pesticides. On four occasions during the 1980s, Pakistan has experienced critical water shortages, leading to inadequate irrigation-water flows for the main crop-growing season. According to the Director of the Pakistan Water and Power Development Authority, "Water supplies presently available for irrigation are already short of optimum crop water requirements. . . Even if all surface supplies and groundwater reservoirs are exploited, water would still fall far short of future requirements."

Indeed, there is little prospect of increasing the water supply at all. The Indus River and its tributaries could provide perhaps another 25 to 30 percent in volume, but this would lead to saltwater intrusions into the river's lower reaches. Nor is there much scope for recycling irrigation water. Recycled flows are usually only half as useful as original withdrawals, because of grossly declining quality as irrigation channels pick up fertilizers, salts, pesticides and toxic elements from croplands.

Fortunately, there could be much greater efficiency in water use. If water use were better regulated and controlled, the expanse of double-cropped lands could theoretically be tripled. But because of incorrect pricing policies for water, among other factors, wheat yields per hectare/metre (the amount of water needed to cover one hectare to a depth of one metre) have increased from 2.17 tons per hectare a year in 1971–76 to only 2.34 tons in the period 1981–86, despite the use of improved seeds and expanded use of fertilizers. In addition, there is widespread leakage of irrigation water: the first 20 percent is lost from conveyance systems, and 40 percent of the remainder from on-farm water courses, with a further 25 percent attrition from runoff due to inefficient application to crops (fields are often far from level). Because of policy constraints—perverse water pricing has persisted for two decades—there seems little hope that efficiency of water use will be improved within the foreseeable future.

Associated with problems of water supply is the phenomenon of salinization. At least 24 percent of Pakistan's croplands are salinized on the surface, and another 29 percent feature below-surface salinization. Together with waterlogging and alkalization, this means that more than 70 percent of the country's croplands are affected by water-related degradation.

As a result of these constraints on the agricultural resource base, in conjunction with the pressures of population growth, there is pervasive land hunger. To sustain a subsistence income through agriculture (consistent with nutritional needs of 2,400 calories per adult per day), an average-size family of 7 persons needed 2.5 hectares of farmland in 1980. But even a decade ago, when the population was 30 percent smaller than today's, two thirds of farm households did not have enough land to support themselves through this means alone. Whereas the amount of cultivated land per rural inhabitant was a third of a hectare in 1983 (already less than the 0.37 of a hectare considered a minimum with agro-technologies available), it is projected to fall to 0.14 of a hectare in the year 2010. Not surprisingly, there is great and growing pressure from agricultural encroachment on the remaining forests. This, in turn, means that deforestation further aggravates water supply problems for downstream agriculture, reducing the carrying capacity of existing farmlands.

This latter phenomenon of positive feedback between factors of environment and development is paralleled by a reinforcing process between environment and population. Deforestation-derived water deficits affect not only agriculture but public health. Water of sufficient quantity and quality is available to only 23 percent of the rural population. As a result, there is a pervasive problem of water related diseases, especially among young children: infant mortality remains a good deal higher than in adjoining states of India.

All this is not to deny Pakistan's remarkable achievement in agriculture. During much of its 43 years of nationhood, Pakistan has been self-sufficient in most major food staples. But by reason of population growth alone, the 1988 level of wheat demand—16 million tons—is projected to reach 25 million tons by 2000 and 40 million tons by 2010; import requirements are projected to grow to 2 million tons and 5 million tons by each date, respectively. These wheat imports, plus imports of edible oil, are projected to cost 37 billion rupees by 2010 (at 1980 prices), exceeding the value of all projected exports in that year by 25 percent.

On a more positive side, there is much room to step up agricultural productivity. Farmers achieve only 25 to 30 percent of demonstrated potential crop yields. Wheat output per hectare is only 85 percent that of India, corn output 47 percent that of Turkey, and rice output 46 percent that of Egypt. And while the expanse of croplands can scarcely be increased by any more because of soil and climate factors, some 100,000 square kilometers of wastelands, or rather wasted lands, could, through careful management, be brought into production for raising livestock. So theoretically, Pakistan eventually could feed at least three times as many people, or almost 350 million. How, then, does this leave the concept of population carrying capacity?

In Pakistan's case, it appears to reflect three key factors. First, for the country to achieve much advance at all beyond its present meagre levels of human welfare (GNP per head $350, with little improvement during the 1980s), it is going to have to tackle the challenge of doing most things right most of the time. In other words, it is going to have to do much better with several leading sectors of development forestry, agriculture, water, public health and population, to name the more relevant—whether through policy reform, improved planning and programming, institutional adaptation, or more advanced and appropriate technology. This "leap ahead" in socio-economic infrastructure has apparently proved beyond the capacities of the government in a situation of growing constraints and stresses on several fronts. Indeed, the challenge would tax the capacities of a nation with vastly more planning experience and with much more extensive infrastructure.

Secondly, and insofar as carrying capacity must be considered a long-term affair, it is questionable whether Pakistan's development record during its four decades of nationhood has been of a sort to prove sustainable into the foreseeable future. There is much evidence that increases in agricultural output have been accomplished at a cost to sustainable productivity, as evidenced by the rundown of the agricultural resource base via land degradation (Salinization, soil erosion) and depletion of resource stocks (forests, surface and groundwater reserves). Technology, in the form of high-yielding grains, fertilizers and pesticides, has enabled food production to keep pace with, or even exceed, population growth for most of the last four decades—a remarkable accomplishment by any standard. But there are signs that the "techno-fix" response to growing human numbers, with their growing aspirations, can no longer maintain its momentum.

The third key factor is that whatever opportunity remains for the nation's carrying capacity to keep on expanding through enhanced agricultural output (sorely limited as this is now turning out to be), it would be taxed in the extreme to keep abreast of population growth at a level of 3 percent a year. Even the most advanced nation would find it difficult to deploy the planning abilities to keep up with a growth rate of that magnitude.

These three factors are crucial to the concept of population carrying capacity for Pakistan. It is difficult to ascertain their individual importance in a conclusive manner, because they have yet to be analyzed (whether in isolation or in combination) to a degree that allows each to be appraised apart from other variables. Nor would a factor-by-factor assessment present the full picture since each interacts with the others in multiple dynamic ways. It may eventually be possible through refined analysis to determine the precise significance of each; to separate out and quantify the carrying-capacity impacts of each, plus their synergistic reinforcing of the other two. Unfortunately, no such analysis has been undertaken.

An operational evaluation of Pakistan's carrying capacity becomes, in essence, a matter of judgment. This judgment should be based upon an informed and considered appraisal of all component factors at issue, together with an assessment of how far the country's problems can be relieved through improved technology, policy changes, institutional innovation and the like in the future. Of course, the future is unknown. But one can usefully speculate in light of the recent past: Pakistan's record during the 1980s surely serves to give warning rather than to inspire hope. Nonetheless, the assessment must remain a matter of judgment—no more and no less.

So while the concept of carrying capacity can still be viewed as something that is putatively expandable in Pakistan's case, there is much evidence to suppose it is practically close to its apparent limits for the foreseeable future—if, indeed, it has not been surpassed already. In these circumstances, it would make sense for Pakistan to respond through two prime strategies: an unprecedented effort to reform agricultural policies together with whatever other measures are necessary to increase food output and to reduce the rate of population growth.

What are the possibilities for population planning? Taking a rather extreme view, were fertility rates to remain constant between 1990 and 2025, total population would grow from approximately 124 million in 1990 to 486 million by 2025. Conversely, were fertility rates to decline to correspond to the United Nations "medium variant" growth projection, total population would rise much less—from approximately 123 million in 1990 to 267 million by 2025. The corresponding reduction in fertility rates to achieve this decline in total population would require bringing the present birth rate down from 47 births per1,000 population in 1985–90, to 20 births per 1,000 by 2020–25.

Fortunately, Pakistan's present demographic trends are not only a matter of deep national concern, but are mobilizing effective action. Since the 1974 United Nations World Population Conference, the government has consistently viewed its rates of population growth as being "too high" and has sought to support family planning and other population programmes to reduce growth. In addition, the government has consistently viewed its spatial distribution patterns as inappropriate and has sought to decelerate rates of rural–urban migration and to promote a more balanced relationship between population and natural resources.

Balancing resources and human requirements has become a high priority in government planning during the last two five-year national development plans. To achieve its objectives, the government has adopted a population welfare programme which utilizes a multi sectoral approach with the specific aim of changing desired family size. This approach encourages active participation of governmental and non-governmental organizations, in conjunction with local communities, and aims at strengthening communication strategies. The government's commitment is reflected in a recent statement by the Minister of Planning and Development that "investment in family planning is a crucial investment for a nation. That is why our population welfare program must rank—and it does— as the top priority in development planning."

A major aim of Pakistan's population welfare program has been to bring about an increase in the small proportion of married women who knew of any contraceptive method in 1984. Only 20 percent of currently married women today know of a source of family planning information or supplies, and only 12 percent have ever used contraception. These figures contrast sharply with Bangladesh where almost 100 percent of married women knew of some contraceptive method in 1985, and 32 percent had used some form of contraception.

Clearly, what is required is the financial and human resources to strengthen and consolidate the existing family

welfare programme of Pakistan in order to support and expand reproductive health and clinical services; to pursue
an integrated clinical training programme for family planning and health personnel; to foster community-based maternal and child health/family planning (MCH/FP) services through family welfare centres; and to expand family
planning service delivery through the involvement of traditional medical practitioners (hakeems). It also requires
the development of research and evaluation capabilities as
regards interrelationships between population, environment and sustainable development; the building up of national capacities in policy analysis; the integration of population factors into national development plans; assistance
to promote training of nationals to assure self-reliance in
population planning in the future; and strategies to promote extensive population education in the formal and
non-formal schooling sector, among workers in urban industry, and among male and female workers in farm settings and rural cooperatives.

Questions

1. What is the main problem for Pakistan's future economic and ecological stability?
2. What are some suggestions that you might have to
   build Pakistan's natural resource base and economic
   stability?
3. How much of a component is fuelwood in terms of a
   source for Pakistan's overall energy consumption?
   What are some viable alternatives to it?
4. What three factors affect Pakistan's carrying capacity?
5. What conclusions or strategies are drawn?
6. Suppose that you have been given the task for recommending ways to increase Pakistan's agricultural production. What ideas would you propose that would
   make Pakistan self-sufficient in food production?

INDIA

India features the second largest population on Earth, 853
million people in 1990. With a population growth rate of
2.1 percent in 1990, and little fertility decline in recent
years, the total is projected to reach slightly more than a
billion in the year 2000 and 1.4 billion by 2020, assuming
the United Nations "medium variant" projection. If, however, fertility rates were to remain constant, India could
end up with a staggering 2.1 billion people by the year
2100. Yet there are many signs the country has already exceeded its carrying capacity, if only through its flagging efforts to feed vast numbers of people.

As in the case of Pakistan, a good part of India's economy depends on its natural resource base. India's territory
comprises 3.29 million square kilometers, of which 1.43
million square kilometers (43 percent) are cultivated, and
of these some 470,000 square kilometers (33 percent) are
irrigated. It is the irrigated lands that have underpinned India's success in turning itself from a food-deficit nation
into a nation with a slight food surplus. But outside the irrigated areas there has been virtually no Green Revolution.
The remaining farmlands are rainfed, featuring ultra-low
levels of productivity. It is in these lands that most of India's impoverished people live.

Irrigation-water supplies are critically dependent on
forested catchments, notably in the Himalayan foothills.
Yet, according to the National Remote Sensing Agency of
India, forest cover declined from nearly 17 percent of national territory in 1970 to just over 14 percent in 1981. The
government believes forest cover should be 25 percent of
the land area. According to the late Prime Minister Rajiv
Gandhi, deforestation has brought the nation "face to face
with a major ecological and socio-economic crisis." Yet,
despite the important links between forest cover and irrigated agriculture, investment in forestry and soil conservation programmes under the sixth five-year plan has been
only 17.9 percent of investment in large scale irrigation
projects. The late Prime Minister Gandhi called for 48,000
square kilometres to be reforested each year, but only one
third of this goal has been achieved to date.

Much of the deforestation is due to excessive fuelwood
gathering as well as agricultural encroachment. In 1982,
fuelwood demand was estimated at 133 million tons,
whereas remaining forestlands could sustain an annual
harvest of only 39 million tons. The gap of 94 million tons
was ostensibly met either by over-cutting (thus compro-
mising future forest production) or by burning cow dung

A Bridge to Your 21st Century Understanding

Complete and discuss the following flowchart.

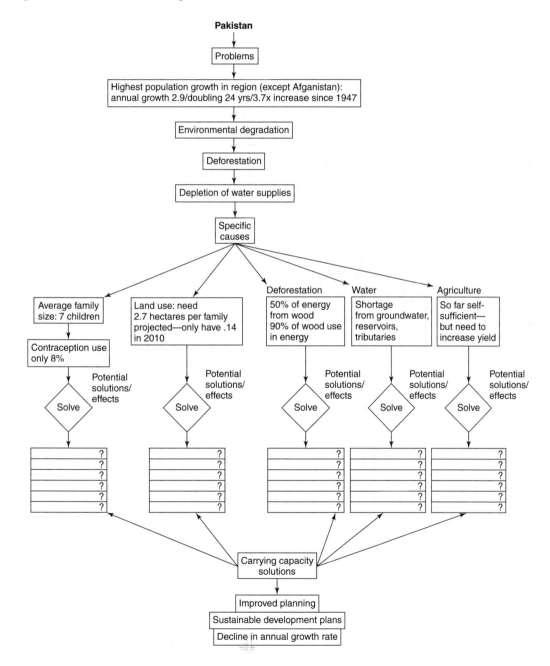

Pakistan

Problems

Highest population growth in region (except Afghanistan):
annual growth 2.9/doubling 24 yrs/3.7x increase since 1947

Environmental degradation

Deforestation

Depletion of water supplies

Specific
causes

Average family size: 7 children	Land use: need 2.7 hectares per family projected—only have .14 in 2010	Deforestation 50% of energy from wood 90% of wood use in energy	Water Shortage from groundwater, reservoirs, tributaries	Agriculture So far self-sufficient— but need to increase yield
Contraception use only 8%				

Potential solutions/effects

Solve

?	?	?	?	?
?	?	?	?	?
?	?	?	?	?
?	?	?	?	?
?	?	?	?	?
?	?	?	?	?

Carrying capacity
solutions

Improved planning

Sustainable development plans

Decline in annual growth rate

and crop residues (which compromises future soil fertility). By the end of this century, the gap will be much larger if India's population continues to grow and its forests continue to contract. Indeed, even if all planned plantations are established, there will be a predicted shortfall of 182 million tons of wood, or double the shortfall in 1982.

Deforestation has already disrupted India's watershed systems, causing increased downstream flooding during the monsoon and water shortages during the dry season. In the Ganges River system, dry season water-flows declined by almost a fifth during the 1970s. Much of India's success in attaining food self-sufficiency by the early 1980s has been due to a doubling of its irrigated area since 1960. Yet because of the degradation of watersheds and the disruption of major water-flows, coupled with a surging demand for municipal and industrial water—partly reflecting the sheer rise in human numbers—India faces the prospect of acute water shortages over much of its territory by the middle of this decade.

Moreover, in 1984, the amount of flood-prone lands nationwide totalled 590,000 square kilometers, compared to only 230,000 square kilometers in 1970. In the Ganges Plains alone, flooding annually affects an area averaging 80,000 square kilometers, including 35,000 square kilometers of valuable croplands. The value of crops lost averages more than $250 million a year, while damage to buildings and public utilities averages around $750 million a year.

On top of this is the problem of land degradation. Some 1.75 million square kilometers are losing agricultural productivity through soil erosion, salinization and waterlogging, with a marked decline in soil fertility and crop yields across an area of a million square kilometres. Soil erosion alone causes Indian farmlands to lose 6 million tons a year of nitrogen, phosphorus and potash. Replacing these critical nutrients through chemical fertilizers requires an annual outlay of around $6 billion. In addition, 130,100 square kilometers of irrigated lands suffer from salinization and waterlogging. Much of this land may eventually have to be taken out of production. Land degradation of all sorts is estimated to cause a loss of 30 to 50 million tons of produce every year.

In addition, there is the growing problem of siltation. Twenty eight of the biggest irrigation projects have a total catchment area of 690,000 square kilometers, of which 220,000 square kilometers are critically eroded and fewer than 20,000 square kilometers have been rehabilitated. In 1980, 12 irrigation reservoirs were filling with sediment at between two and five times the initial rates, and a good number of others at between six and 20 times the initial

rates. If only 20 percent of the live-storage capacity of major and medium sized reservoirs is silted up by the end of this century, it will mean a loss of irrigation potential equivalent to about 40,000 square kilometers, a full tenth of the present irrigated area. Whereas irrigated lands were meeting the needs of 56 percent of India's population in 1975, it is planned they will have to meet the needs of 87 percent of the projected population in the year 2000.

All this is not to discount India's remarkable feat in increasing its wheat production from 10 million tonnes in 1964 to more than 45 million tonnes in 1985, and in raising total food grain production to a record 150 million tonnes in 1984. For almost a quarter of a century the nation has maintained a sufficient rate of growth in food output to keep just ahead of population growth (though with hardly any increase in per capita food output, and a slight decline in average consumption of calories, protein and fat). By the end of the century, however, the nation will need at least 230 million tons of food grain each year to feed its growing population, a 53 percent increase over the 1984 output. These needs notwithstanding, there has been a steady decline in the growth rate of agricultural production since 1960 and, since 1984, there has been virtually no increase at all in food-grain output.

The 1960 to 1984 upsurge in total food production was accomplished primarily in irrigated areas such as those of the Punjab and Haryana States with their level terrain. Additional lands for irrigated agriculture are limited. Not only are watershed supplies of irrigation water becoming irregular, but groundwater stocks have been over-exploited to such an extent that in many areas water tables have dropped by at least one metre. So severe are these water problems that India's future irrigation potential is severely constrained. By 1996, India's food-grain production could well plateau, with per capita output holding at around 204 kilograms, only marginally more than the 195 kilograms of 1985. Thereafter, the growth rate for food-grain production could decrease to only 1.9 percent a year during the period 1996 to 2005, only fractionally higher than the projected growth rate for population. There remains much scope to intensify agricultural production. India has about 20 percent more land under paddy rice than China, yet produces 40 percent less. This anomaly is due primarily to the fact that the agricultural resource base is being progressively depleted through land degradation on several fronts.

Thus, profound questions arise about India's capacity to keep feeding its populace which is projected to expand by 190 million, or an additional 22 percent, by the end of the century. Moreover, the challenge is not only to feed extra people, but also to upgrade nutritional levels among the third of the populace that remains malnourished. If these food-deficient people were to be adequately fed through more efficient and equitable grain distribution, India's grain surplus would be instantly eliminated.

Overall, then, it appears that in certain respects India's renowned Green Revolution has been a short-term success accompanied by long-term costs. India's farmers have posted some impressive results since 1964. But in major measure these advances have been achieved through over-working croplands and over-pumping water stocks. So a key question arises: have Indians been feeding themselves today by borrowing against future food productivity?

Recent trends suggest the outlook is not promising. The annual growth rate in agricultural production in India slipped from an average of 2.8 percent during 1965–75 to 2.2 percent during 1981–85, scarcely above the annual rate for population growth. True, there is some scope for India to purchase food from outside sources. But this depends largely on the strength of its economy, burdened as it is with a foreign debt that totalled $37.3 billion in 1987. While this sum appears slight compared with those of certain Latin America nations, debt servicing nevertheless absorbed nearly 19 percent of India's export earnings.

Furthermore, population growth not only means extra mouths to feed. It exacerbates the problem of landlessness. The total number of landless households was 15 million in 1961, rising to 26 million by 1981, and is projected to reach 44 million by the year 2000. As noted, agriculture accounts for 79 percent of employment nationwide. The total workforce is projected to expand from 224 million in 1980 to 376 million in the year 2000, and the level of unemployment and under-employment is not expected to change from its present level of 33 percent. For off-farm employment to absorb all those who are unemployed and underemployed, non-agricultural sectors would have to grow at more than 12 percent a year, or well over twice the rate during the decade 1975–84. So there is the prospect of a fast-growing pool of rural people without land or adequately remunerative work.

To reiterate a basic point, these food–population issues place a premium on India's continuing access to water in sufficient amounts at appropriate times of the year. While there is often too much water during the monsoon season, there is often too little during the subsequent dry season. According to a number of reports and analyses summa-rized in *The State of India's Environment, 1984–1985,* several parts of India could face severe seasonal water deficits by the turn of the century when irrigation demand is projected to be half as high again as it is today and industry's demand to be at least twice as high. This raises the prospect of strife and conflict over water supplies.

Resource-sharing conflicts over the waters of the Ganges River are also a reality. Rising in Nepal, where watershed degradation is pervasive and pronounced, the river runs for 2,700 kilometers before reaching the Bay of Bengal in the Bangladesh delta. Within its valleylands live more than 500 million Indian and Bangladeshi farmers. Bangladesh, occupying the lower reaches of the Ganges River, makes ever greater demands on the river's flows— and the present deteriorating situation arises from a river basin that is projected to feature almost 200 million more people by the end of the century.

Overall hangs the prospect of climatic change, with potentially critical impacts. Scientists predict that a planetary warming is surely on its way, caused by a buildup of carbon dioxide and other greenhouse gases in the atmosphere. As a result of global warming, monsoon systems may be disrupted which could prove critical insofar as India receives 70 percent of its precipitation from the monsoon. Global warming could also bring on a greater incidence of typhoons and coastal storms along India's coastline, possibly 40 to 50 percent more destructive than today's due to the increased temperature of the ocean surface.

The other side of the carrying capacity equation is population growth. As noted previously, if population growth were to follow the path of the United Nations "constant fertility variant", it will grow from approximately 856 million in 1990 to more than 2 billion by 2025 (implying a constant crude birth rate of about 32 per 12,000 population). Achieving the United Nations "medium variant" projection would result in considerably lower population growth, amounting to about 1.4 billion in 2025; and with the "low variant," an even lower population of 1.3 billion. Achieving the "low variant" would require a drop in crude birth rates from 32 per 1,000 in 1990 to about 13 per 1,000 by 2025.

The government of India has recognized population growth rates as "too high" since the 1974 United Nations Conference on Population and it favours expanded support to increase contraceptive use. Increasingly, policy statements indicate the government considers its population problem to be extremely serious, particularly in relation to alleviating poverty. The basic aim of the government's population policy is to reduce fertility by influencing social variables known to promote fertility reduction, such as health, education and literacy, as well as by implementing a nationwide family planning program. The government also perceives the population's spatial distribution to be inappropriate and it has adopted policies to reduce imbalances in population distribution in relation to natural resources, as well as congestion in urban areas.

Under the fifth five-year national development plan (1980–84), family planning continued to be accorded high priority, with emphasis on program integration and coordination of activities involving all ministries and departments. During the sixth plan, the government sought to extend the delivery of services through the strengthening of health and family planning infrastructure, particularly rural infrastructure, with the aim of making family planning services available on a wider scale and at all levels.

Though statistics from contraceptive prevalence surveys are dated, they reveal that whereas 95 percent of married women knew of some contraceptive method in the early 1980s, only 34 percent were using any method at all. Again, in a country as populous and poor as India, the success of its population policies and family planning programs will be highly contingent on financial and human resources needed to extend its present services. Priorities include upgrading the service delivery capacity of the health care and family welfare network through intensive area development projects; strengthening the data collection and analysis system on interrelationships between population, environment and sustainable development; and strengthening the managerial capability at all levels of India's population program through training, research, and the development and improvement of management information and evaluation systems.

A great deal needs to be done to support India's population education program, both in and out of schools; and to produce additional audio-visual and printed materials for motivation campaigns. Most importantly, additional support for health and family welfare programs aimed specifically at women should be developed, through innovative projects which emphasize the positive role women play as managers of reproduction as well as of natural resources required in everyday household use, notably fuelwood, water, and food security.

Questions

1. What is the evidence that India has exceeded its carrying capacity?
2. What is the cause of much of the deforestation in India?
3. How did food production in India increase from 1960 to 1984? Why are projections of food production not expected to increase? Has the Green Revolution been a success? Why or why not?
4. Compose some creative ideas to increase land irrigation projects without causing further land degradation and water shortages.
5. Explain the problem of landlessness.
6. What is India's problem of water supply?
7. Imagine for a moment that you have been given the job of proposing ways to reduce India's population. What ideas would you propose that would reduce the population without disturbing the nation's culture?

A Bridge to Your 21st Century Understanding

Complete and discuss the following flowchart.

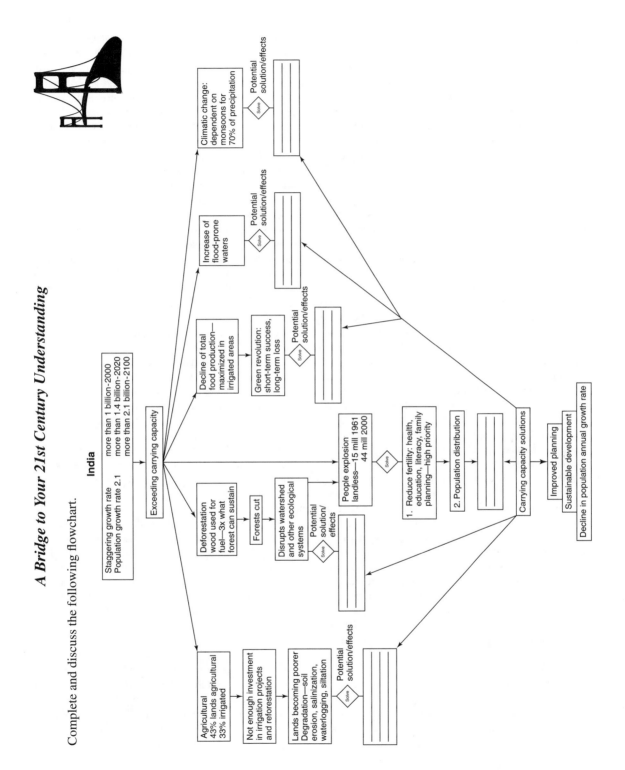

ETHIOPIA

Ethiopia and Kenya are symptomatic of many problems suffered by sub-Saharan Africa as a whole, even though Ethiopia is one of the most impoverished nations, while Kenya is frequently regarded as something of a development success story in the region. Both display many of the adverse repercussions of rapid population growth. But before examining these two countries in detail, and in order to supply a conceptual context for the entire region, let us take stock of some pervasive factors afflicting sub-Saharan Africa as a whole.

Of the region's nearly 450 million people in 1985, some 250 million were chronically malnourished; 150 million were subject to acute food deficits; and 30 million were actually starving. In much if not most of the region, per capita food production has been declining for a full two decades. At least 62 percent of the entire populace endures absolute poverty. As much as 80 percent of croplands and 90 percent of stock-raising lands are affected to some degree by land degradation processes. Yet the population of sub-Saharan Africa, with an annual average growth rate of 3 percent in 1985–90, is projected to reach 722 million by the year 2000 and almost 1.4 billion by 2025, according to the United Nations "medium variant" projection. This ultra-rapid rate of growth operates in conjunction with adverse climatic conditions, characterized by erratic rainfall patterns, frequent droughts and increasing desertification, that have affected the region for most of the past two decades.

Sub-Saharan Africa has continued to feature a fertility rate higher than anywhere else in the world; and since 1960, the region has been growing poorer and hungrier in absolute as well as relative terms. Today's average per capita income of roughly $250 is only 95 percent of real income in 1960; of the 36 poorest countries in the world, 29 are in Africa. Worse, average per capita agricultural production has declined by an average of 2 percent annually since 1970. And the World Bank estimates that production is unlikely to grow at more than 2.5 percent a year for at least the next two decades, even while population growth remains at 3 percent or more a year. As a result, food output per head, which has declined by 20 percent since 1970, is scheduled to decline by a further 30 percent during the next 25 years. The region serves as a prime example of an "adverse outlook" scenario.

In recent years there has been some respite, thanks to better rains. But because of unpromising baseline conditions generally, and particularly in respect to harsh climate,

together with widespread environmental degradation and poor agricultural policies, the return of only moderately adverse weather conditions could quickly trigger a renewed onset of broad-scale famine. If these adverse conditions persist—aggravated, perhaps, by the climatic vicissitudes entrained by the greenhouse effect—the number of chronically malnourished, which totaled 30 million in 1985, could well increase to 130 million by the end of this century. This means that the proportion of starving people would expand from less than 7 percent of the region's population in 1985 to 18 percent by the year 2000.

It is within the context of sub-Saharan Africa as a whole that we should examine the case of Ethiopia. It epitomizes those nations with high population growth rates that must work exceptionally hard to satisfy their basic needs—food, water, shelter, health care, employment and education. When a nation is economically impoverished, it may well find the task all but beyond its means. So human needs overtake the pace of development, until eventually they threaten the very structure and stability of the nation. In Ethiopia, the essentials of everyday life, in terms of food supplies alone, are increasingly maintained by outside agencies rather than by the government. The country's output of cereal grain in 1980, 5.1 million tons, has been theoretically projected to expand to 7.3 million tons in 1991—though in fact, food production declined by an average of 1 percent a year during the 1980s. Despite this projected increase in cereal—grain output in 1991 to 7.3 million tons, Ethiopia's need for cereal imports jumped from 214,000 tons in 1980 to more than 3 million tons by 1991.

As a consequence of the severe imbalance between population and food supplies, plus associated political upheavals, there are now at least 5 million people facing starvation, and a total of almost 15 million people—nearly a third of the population—chronically undernourished. Furthermore, there are now at least 3 million displaced people within Ethiopia and another half million in refugee camps in the Sudan (where they are explicitly recognized as environmental refugees rather than political refugees).

How did Ethiopia get to this state? By the early 1970s, as much as 470,000 square kilometers of Ethiopia's traditional farming areas in the highlands—home to 88 percent of the population—were severely eroded. These formerly fertile upland areas were losing an estimated billion tons of topsoil a year (a more recent and refined estimate puts the loss at 1.5 to 3.5 billion tons a year). This massive soil erosion was due partly to rudimentary agricultural practices, partly to inequitable land-tenure systems, and partly to pressures generated by a population that increased from 20 million in 1950 to 31 million by 1970. The results included a marked fall-off in agricultural production accompanied by food shortages in cities, with ensuing disorders that precipitated the overthrow of Emperor Haile Selassie in 1974.

The Dergue regime did not move fast enough to restore agricultural production. Primarily for this reason, throngs of impoverished peasants started to stream into the country's lowlands, including the Ogaden zone that borders Somalia—a zone of long-standing conflict between the two nations. In Somalia, too, steadily increasing human numbers, together with inefficient agricultural practices, had led to much over-taxing of traditional farmlands. Largely for these reasons (plus some ethnic complications), there was a migration into the Ogaden from the Somali side as well. The result was a clash between the two sides, with an outbreak of hostilities in 1977.

Primarily as a result of a regional arms race and internal conflicts, Ethiopia in 1981 spent $447 million on defence, and Somalia $105 million. Added to the outlays of previous years, the total sum expended in the Horn of Africa because of the Ogaden conflict can be estimated at well over $1 billion during a five-year period. If only a small part of that sum had been allocated ahead of time to reforestation, soil safeguards and associated aspects of restoring the agricultural resource base in the two countries—estimated by the United Nations Anti-Desertification Plan to cost no more than $50 million a year for 10 years—the disastrous outcome could well have been avoided.

According to the United Nations "constant fertility variant" projection, if crude birth rates were to remain at 1990 levels over the next 45 years, total population would increase from 49 million in 1990 to 161 million by 2025. Were crude birth rates brought more into line with the UN "medium variation" projection—requiring a birth-rate decline from 49 per 1,000 in 1985–90 to about 30 per 1,000 in 2020–25 the total population would grow far less, to about 127 million by 2025.

Between 1974 and 1980, the government of Ethiopia perceived its rates of population growth and fertility as "satisfactory", requiring no intervention. Furthermore, it provided little support for family planning services. More recently, the government has changed its position, now viewing population growth and fertility levels as being "not satisfactory" because they are "too high" in relation to family well-being and in particular to maternal and child health. While family planning services were initiated by the Ministry of Health in 1981, only 23 percent of the country's 2,500 health stations, centres and hospitals pro-

vided integrated maternal, child health and family planning services. In 1981, the contraceptive prevalence rate was estimated to be only 2 percent; more recent estimates suggest rates of 2 to 8 percent in urban areas and from 1 to 2 percent in rural areas.

Government priorities include the formulation of a more focused population policy which rationalizes current population growth patterns relative to the country's economic and environmental carrying capacity. Furthermore, in view of the extensive poverty in the country, and limited resources available to the government for population activities, various forms of assistance are urgently needed to strengthen Ethiopia's existing population program. These include strengthening the national maternal and child health care program as part of the government's family welfare goals; greatly expanded population education on relationships between population, environment and sustainable development in primary and secondary schools, as well as in non-formal education; strengthening national capacities for population analysis, studies and training in Ethiopia's major universities and research-oriented nongovernmental organizations; and programs to support and encourage the potential of women in their role as natural resource managers.

The Dergue government, like the Selassie regime before it, has been unable to resolve the problem of growing human numbers seeking to survive off an impoverished natural resource base. Even though Ethiopia has had one of the lowest population growth rates in sub Saharan Africa—around 2 percent a year for most of the time between 1950 and 1980, rising to 2.9 percent in 1990—Ethiopia's population had increased from 20 million in 1950 to about 49 million by 1990.

Questions

1. What is the profile of sub-Saharan Africa as a whole in terms of food production, poverty, and population? What figures does the article provide to support your view?

2. What is the reason that the number of chronically malnourished Ethiopian people of 30 million in 1985 could increase to 130 million by 2000?

3. How did Ethiopia get to the state of being unable to serve its population's basic needs?

4. How did defense spending affect the current population and environmental situation in Ethiopia?

5. What plan might you have to increase population planning participation among Ethiopian people?

A Bridge to Your 21st Century Understanding

Complete and discuss the following flowchart.

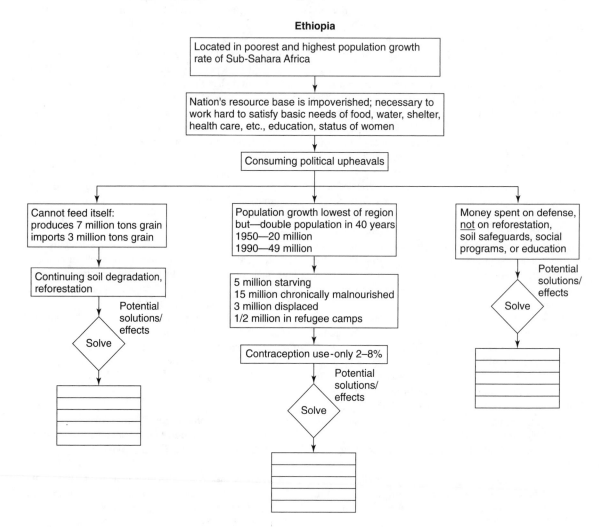

Ethiopia

Located in poorest and highest population growth rate of Sub-Sahara Africa

Nation's resource base is impoverished; necessary to work hard to satisfy basic needs of food, water, shelter, health care, etc., education, status of women

Consuming political upheavals

Cannot feed itself:
produces 7 million tons grain
imports 3 million tons grain

Continuing soil degradation, reforestation

Potential solutions/ effects

Solve

Population growth lowest of region but—double population in 40 years
1950—20 million
1990—49 million

5 million starving
15 million chronically malnourished
3 million displaced
1/2 million in refugee camps

Contraception use-only 2–8%

Potential solutions/ effects

Solve

Money spent on defense, not on reforestation, soil safeguards, social programs, or education

Potential solutions/ effects

Solve

MEXICO

Mexico is more of a middle-income country than the others considered thus far, with a current per capita income of $1,800. But it still illustrates the problems of population growth with respect to environment, albeit problems of a rather different sort from those already reviewed.

Mexico was the first developing country to engage in Green Revolution agriculture, expanding its grain production four-fold between the mid-1950s and the mid-1980s. But its population growth has also been among the most rapid anywhere, increasing from 28 million in 1950 to 89 million by 1990 (a 218 percent increase), making it the second largest populace in Latin America. As a result of the upsurge in human numbers and nutritional needs, plus an increase in environmental degradation, the benefits of the Green Revolution breakthroughs have all but dwindled away in terms of per capita consumption. Mexico has once again become a net food importer.

Because much of the country is dry, it possesses limited agricultural land. In more than 70 percent of these lands, soil erosion is significant: 60 percent medium and growing worse, 12 percent severe. Outright desertification claims 2,250 square kilometres of farmlands each year. At least one tenth of irrigated areas have become highly salinized, and 10,000 square kilometers need urgent (and expansive) rehabilitation if they are to be restored to productivity.

Moreover, the country's remaining forests total only 120,000 square kilometers, and are giving way to large-scale ranchers and small-scale peasants alike. The loss of the forests' "sponge effect" disrupts river flows: in two thirds of arable lands, water supplies constitute the main factor that is limiting agricultural productivity. Because of dwindling water supplies, together with soil erosion, at least 1,000 square kilometers of farmlands are abandoned each year. From the late 1950s to the early 1970s, the area under staple crops—corn, wheat, rice and beans—expanded by almost half, extending into marginal lands with highly erodible soils. At least 45 percent of all farmers occupy those 20 percent of croplands located on steep slopes. By the mid-1970s, these newly opened-up areas were starting to feature declining crop yields—precisely at the time when there was a peak in population growth. Domestic calorie production as a percentage of total supply reached 105 percent in 1970 but, by 1982, it had slipped to 94 percent.

The distribution of agricultural lands is becoming ever more skewed as large farmers buy out small farmers and engage in capital-intensive cash cropping for export. But growing numbers of smallholder peasants impose still greater strains on over-worked croplands, reducing their carrying capacity; and migrating throngs of marginalized farmers are pushed into those lands most susceptible to degradation.

As a result of this agricultural squeeze, there has been a recent upsurge in migration from Mexico's rural areas. Many migrants head for Mexico's cities which, after growing at 5 percent or more a year since 1960, are less and less capable of absorbing new arrivals. For every two rural Mexicans who migrate to the city, one now crosses the border into the United States.

What are some likely future population pressures in Mexico? Despite a remarkable economic performance for much of the period 1960 to 1980, average real wages in 1988 were below the level of 1970; and the economy has generally stagnated or even contracted since 1980 while the population has grown by more than a quarter. Nor does the economic outlook presage much improvement. A realistic prognosis is that within a decade Mexicans could well be poorer than they are today. Just to keep pace with a swelling work force, Mexico will have to create jobs at half the rate the United States achieves, while doing it within an economy only one thirtieth the size, and at an investment cost that could conceivably reach $500 billion by the year 2000. This is an unrealistic expectation. In 1986, a year with poor economic performance because of declining oil prices and growing debt burden, the jobs total actually decreased. Not surprisingly, then, it is an optimistic estimate that foresees "only" 20 million Mexicans without proper employment by the turn of the century. At least half of these will be living in rural areas, where there could be an additional 2 million, perhaps even 4 million, landless peasants. According to Professor J.G. Castañeda of the National University of Mexico, "The consequences of not creating nearly 15 million jobs in the next 15 years are unthinkable. The youths who do not find them will have only three options: the United States, the streets or revolution."

The biggest issues confronting Mexico appear to be population growth and urbanization. The population could more than double between 1990 and 2025 if fertility rates were to remain unchanged. Realizing the United Nations "medium variant" projection—implying a drop in the crude birth rate from 28 per 1,000 in 1990 to about 18 per 1,000 in 2025—would still result in a population of 150 million by 2025, up from 89 million in 1990. Bolder reductions, to achieve the UN "low variant" projection, would imply a further drop in the birth rate to 15 per 1,000 in 2025, resulting in a total population of 132 million.

Since 1974, the government of Mexico has considered its rates of population growth to be "too high", and has promoted policies to lower growth rates, chiefly through fertility reduction by providing support to contraceptive information, education, and supplies. The government has consistently expressed dissatisfaction with imbalances in the growth and distribution of population (including migration patterns), in relation to the distribution of natural resources. In view of these policies, the government has taken steps to integrate specific demographic goals into its overall development planning. In 1974, Mexico adopted a General Population Law with the aim of regulating factors affecting population structure, volume, dynamics and distribution, and it established the National Population Council (CONAPO), which is responsible for formulating plans on population and promoting their integration into economic and social programs. In 1977, the country approved a national family planning policy with the aim of reducing the population growth rate; and in 1979, a regional population policy was adopted, addressed to the specific problems of interregional migration and the geographical distribution of the population.

By 1987, approximately 91 percent of married women knew of at least one contraceptive method, while 53 percent were actually using one method or another. On the one hand, this indicates considerable progress since the contraceptive prevalence rate was only about 30 percent in 1976, grew to 48 percent by 1982 and has now passed 50 percent. On the other hand, approximately 45 percent of married women have yet to be reached by family planning programs—an important goal in view of population and environmental problems.

Recognizing the urgency of the problems at hand, the government is now embarking on several aggressive strategies and programs to enhance the effectiveness of its population policies. For example, it seeks to reduce the population growth rate to 1.8 percent by 1994 and to 1 percent by the year 2000. In order to achieve a better distribution of population, more in line with the development potential of different regions, the government aims to lessen the relative size of the great metropolitan zones and to encourage the growth of small and intermediate cities. The government also seeks to promote the integration of demographic objectives and criteria more explicitly into the country's economic and social planning; and it aims to raise the socio-economic status and role of women as contributors to the economy and as environmental managers.

Questions

1. What is Mexico's current per-capita income?
2. Why hasn't Mexico's Green Revolution grain production growth produced food excess?
3. How would you describe the following events taking place in Mexico: desertification and the sponge effect?
4. What is the effect of large farmers buying out small farmers and using capital-intensive farming approaches rather than the labor-intensive techniques used by small farmers?
5. What will be the consequence of Mexico's being unable to create nearly 15 million jobs in the next 15 years?
6. What are the biggest issues confronting Mexico?
7. How does Mexico plan to make its family planning programs more effective?
8. How can Mexico deal with the high growth of urban areas and the negative impact of such growth? What are short-term and longer term solutions to this problem?

A Bridge to Your 21st Century Understanding

Complete and discuss the following flowchart.

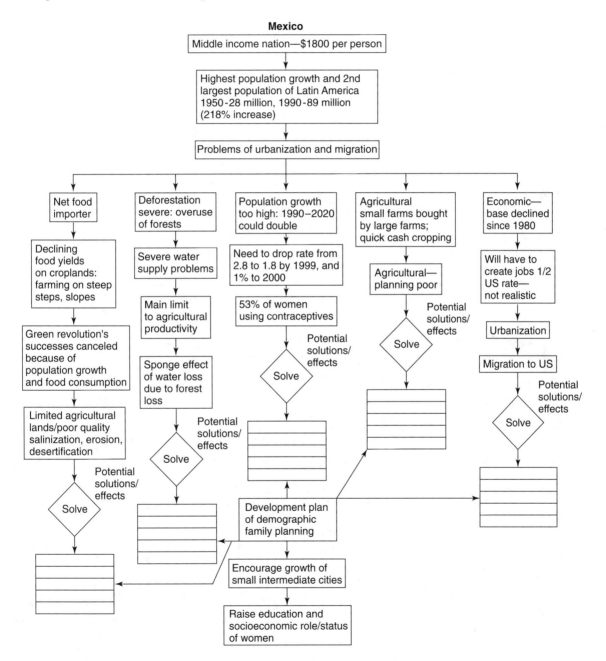

Mexico

Middle income nation—$1800 per person

↓

Highest population growth and 2nd
largest population of Latin America
1950-28 million, 1990-89 million
(218% increase)

↓

Problems of urbanization and migration

Net food importer
- Declining food yields on croplands: farming on steep steps, slopes
- Green revolution's successes canceled because of population growth and food consumption
- Limited agricultural lands/poor quality salinization, erosion, desertification
- Potential solutions/effects — Solve

Deforestation severe: overuse of forests
- Severe water supply problems
- Main limit to agricultural productivity
- Sponge effect of water loss due to forest loss
- Potential solutions/effects — Solve

Population growth too high: 1990–2020 could double
- Need to drop rate from 2.8 to 1.8 by 1999, and 1% to 2000
- 53% of women using contraceptives
- Potential solutions/effects — Solve

Agricultural small farms bought by large farms; quick cash cropping
- Agricultural—planning poor
- Potential solutions/effects — Solve

Economic—base declined since 1980
- Will have to create jobs 1/2 US rate—not realistic
- Urbanization
- Migration to US
- Potential solutions/effects — Solve

Development plan of demographic family planning

Encourage growth of small intermediate cities

Raise education and socioeconomic role/status of women

27

The Humanitarian and Technical Dilemmas of Population Control in China

Su Xiaokang
Translated by Yuan Xue

An important experiment for mankind this century is the control of population growth by state-administered means. The necessity for some controls is beyond dispute from the point of view of global interests as a whole. But the outcome of their implementation and the resulting ethical dilemma in any one particular country is an issue which ultimately concerns values reaching beyond mere economic benefits. It becomes an issue we mankind cannot ignore.

Population controls have created two basic dilemmas. First, the ethics of life is being challenged. This differs from those ethical dilemmas, such as genetic manipulation, facing Western developed countries; instead, it is the conflict between unnatural interference in human reproduction, on the one hand, and traditional values and basic human rights, on the other. Second, the malady that results from applying artificial economic planning to population control shows that the role of the state in population control is suspicious.

An important implication of these two dilemmas is that the assumption of international organizations, such as the United Nations and the World Bank, for instance, and of governments of the Western countries may be turned into a mere illusion. Namely, this is the assumption that by trusting or supporting the population policy of the Chinese government, due to the unavailability of alternatives, the explosion of the Chinese population—the hidden danger of the world—can be solved.

Let us address the first point. China does not have population theories like those in the West, but only a more traditional concept of child bearing that has become a custom for a thousand years or so. This custom regards carrying on the ancestral line as being the first priority of life, thus it is said, "of the three kinds of unfilial acts, having no descendants is the worst." Although it has been seriously challenged since China entered the modern period when traditional families began to disintegrate, this concept still remains today a basic value widely held among the people. The natural economy in the Chinese countryside sustains this basic value; that is, underdevelopment has been maintained mainly by the increase of labor. Therefore, both the rural economy and the concepts of the patriarchal family system stress to a great extent traditional customs such as having an extended family, valuing only the male child and raising children for old-age security. A thorough change of ethical practices before being able to change the rural economy will undoubtedly cause strong social instability.

The unprecedented ethical dilemma in human child-bearing behavior that exists in China stems from the following:

- people make the choice to bear children based on fear;
- for the first time in history, child-bearing has become an illegal action that makes many pregnant women flee

Published by permission of the *Journal of International Affairs* and The Trustees of Columbia University in the City of New York. Xiaokang, Su (Winter, 1996). The humanitarian and technical dilemmas of population control in China. *Journal of International Affairs,* vol. 49, no. 2, pp. 343–347. © The Trustees of Columbia University in the City of New York.

from home in large numbers and hide in wild places to escape forced abortions;

- artificial distortions in demographics, that is, the practice of drowning infant females rages on, causing the numbers of female children proportionately less vis-à-vis those of males.

Officially sanctioned data, i.e., the 1987 population sample survey, shows that the death rate of female infants was 47.15 percent of the total infants of the same age, lower than the 48.33 percent female rate of the total population, and the sex ratio of male and female infants was 112.1 to 100. But according to private estimates by population experts with good knowledge of the situation in the countryside, the female infants that are killed plus the *chaosheng yinge* (infants born beyond the official quota) is expected to reach millions every year in China.

All the above is widely known, but there is more seldom known to the outside world:

- the medical ethics crisis faced by doctors, including those who are being forced to induce abortion for pregnant women and even to kill with drugs some infants more than seven months old that have survived the induced abortion;
- as a consequence of the massive number of induced abortions, dead infants are commonly used in autopsies, organ transplants and in medicine and nutriment research;
- those born without designated official sanction, privately called black children, lose basic living rights, including their grain ration.

Their families often are compelled to leave their home villages and wander destitute, emerging in the outskirts of many Chinese cities in *heicun* and *heitun* (both meaning black villages) where those escaping forced birth control live in close quarters.

The second dilemma is the effect of population control after making people pay such costs. In China, the role of the state in population control has changed drastically. After the Communist takeover in 1949, the regime initially carried out an open and conniving population policy; Mao Zedong believed that "more people make the job easier." As a result, for twenty years, China experienced a continuous population growth rate of over two percent. Its population doubled from 500 million to 1 billion in 38 years,

forming a population-reproduction typology of high birth rate and high natural growth rate unmatched in the world. This process continued until the 1970s, when it was abruptly ended by the sudden appearance of severe measures: the *yitaihua* (one family, one child) policy carried out by the Chinese government through coercion, and the so-called national policy that stated that the growth rate of the population could not go beyond 1.2 percent per year. The question became whether an irrational natural process can be reversed successfully by another kind of extremely radical artificial measure.

China's central leadership has been confronted with a basic difficulty in the practical application of initiating population control within a planned economy. It is a policy applying flawed math to manage a whole population. This results from the following:

- inaccuracy in the vital statistics used as the basis of planning;
- the impossibility of replacing the natural speed of population growth with human-imagined figures;
- the spuriousness of deriving the national population growth rate by adding up that of each province as rigidly laid down by the central government.

The Chinese government continues to carry out one Five-Year Plan after the next. The Seventh Five-Year Plan of Population Control formulated in 1985 required that the population be kept at 1.113 billion. But the vital statistics of 1990 show that the Plan was surpassed by 30 million. Analyzing the reasons for the failure, Peng Peiyun, Director of Chinese Family Planning Committee, said that at the time of formulating the Seventh Five-Year Plan, about 13 million people went without being counted. She also said that the Eighth Five-Year Plan of Population Control and the ten-year population program formulated in 1991 require that the population in China be kept under 1.3 billion by the end of this century. But, again, according to the announcement of the survey issued by the Chinese government in August 1995, the population has already reached 1.2 billion.

There are two questionable factors in Peng's statement. First, it is likely that the publicized figure of 1.2 billion is still an underestimation. Secondly, the Eighth Five-Year Plan is a continuation of the thinking of the Seventh Five-Year Plan with extremely uncertain consequences. There is one element, however, that is known for sure. During this period, women in their prime of child-bearing age have reached 120 million or more. No matter how severe the control, it can not suppress the figure of those born unplanned; furthermore, a harsh and rigid control means an even greater disaster for the rights and interests of women in mainland China, as well as even greater repercussions. This is another reason for the failure of the Seventh Five-Year Population Plan about which Peng Peiyun spoke.

Meanwhile, such severe controls do not take into consideration standards of education and basic knowledge of birth control. Facing an audience of 260 million illiterate or semi-illiterate (22.27 percent of the total population, mostly women in the countryside), the usefulness of the propaganda and preaching of the Chinese government is next to nothing. This factor is both the reason for the masses to resist the birth control policy (the fundamental driving force of the resistance comes from not only the strong and invisible traditional custom and also a more primitive child-bearing impulse), and, at the same time, the major factor for the rudeness in the policy implementation. Such a rudeness is expressed by the cadres at the grass-roots level carrying out the policy and the so-called "birth control work teams" dispatched into villages to impose on those policy-violators forced abortions and economic punishment and, on all women of child-bearing age, preventative oviduct legation. Deviations in policy implementation and excessive retaliations are common occurrences.

In short, to control child-bearing behavior through state planning, as if it were economic behavior, will not only fail like the past economic plans in China, but also expose serious inhumanity. Its limited control effect is gained at the great expense of deprivation of basic human rights, damage to traditional values and sacrifice of innumerable lives. In recent years in China, the newborn population has been approximately 21 million per year with a net increase of 14 million; this growth momentum is expected to continue towards the end of this century, then reaching 17 million (equivalent to a medium-sized country) per year. According to the estimation made by the Chinese government itself, surpassing a population of 1.3 billion by the end of this century will mean China's total population in the middle of the next century will reach between 1.5 and 1.6 billion, or possibly even 1.8 billion if it gets out of control. At that time, the Chinese population issue will truly become a thorny problem for the entire world.

Questions

1. What are the two dilemmas of population control in China?
2. What is the customary philosophy in China on having children? What supports this philosophy?
3. What are some of the ethical implications of state-imposed birth quotas?
4. What are the reasons that China reached the fastest natural growth rate in the world?
5. What are some of the reasoning flaws that China used in its initiation of population control?
6. What are some of the reasons that the population control plan in China is not succeeding as expected?
7. Faced with the exploding population of China, do you think that a government-imposed population quota law is the most effective solution? Why or why not? What approach would you suggest?

Earth's Carrying Capacity: Not Quite So Easy When Applied to Humans

28

We face a real crunch. At issue is whether we can do what is totally unprecedented—feed, house, nurture, educate, and employ as many more people in the space of four decades as are alive today.

GEOGRAPHER ROBERT W. KATES OF ELLSWORTH, MAINE.

With the current worldwide population increasing by 90 million people annually and the last billion people added just in the last 12 years, people over forty years old have actually lived through a doubling of the human population—the first time this has ever happened. This unprecedented growth evokes the concern of how many people the earth can sustain. In four decades, we again will have a doubling of the world's population—the most difficult challenge for mankind yet.

EARTH'S CARRYING CAPACITY DOES NOT ACCURATELY APPLY TO HUMANS

Scientists, in analyzing the demands placed on the earth by human population, usually refer to the "earth's carrying capacity"—the maximum population its ecosystems can sustain indefinitely. This concept works well when defining how many animals a habitat can support, but it breaks down when applied to people, since humans' variety of habits and environmental patterns have a wide variation of resource consumption and waste generation. The typical New Yorker, for example, uses 10 to 1,000 times more resources daily than the average Chilean or Ghanaian. A second reason that the carrying capacity formula doesn't work well is that humans have a great ability to alter their physical environment or culture for survival. Many scientists are beginning to argue that they can't predict how many people the earth can sustain until there exists a better way to account for the various social, cultural, and demographic habits and effects of people.

Wolfgang Lutz, a scientist in Laxenburg, Austria, has a different approach. The formula he uses does not just account for the *number* of people; it estimates environmental impact *(I)* as the product of population *(P)* times affluence *(A)* times the technological efficiency *(T)* of a culture *(I = PAT)*. The formula $I = PAT$ was first developed by scientists Paul Ehrlich and John Holdren to examine the environmental impacts of population in general. Some scientists use this formula to calculate the economic and environmental costs associated with each new birth. There was a problem with the use of this formula in calculations of the impact of CO_2 emissions, however: The formula better correlated with the number of *households* rather than individuals. Within the last couple of decades, there has been a trend toward the existence of more households with fewer members caused by the patterns of divorces, young adults setting up their own households, the postponement of marriage, an increase in life expectancy, and a growing sense of privacy. The trend of more, but smaller, households is most prevalent in the nations that already use the most resources, and this trend could cause substantial impacts. When calculated using households, rather than individuals, in the $I = PAT$ formula, CO_2 emissions were 50% higher than those suggested by the use of individuals in the formula.

FOOD PRODUCTION AS AN EXAMPLE

Population growth impacts food production. Since 1955, nearly one third of the world's cropland (an area larger than China and India combined) has been abandoned be-cause its overuse has led to soil loss, depletion, or degrada-tion. The search for cropland substitute accounts for about 60 to 80% of the world's deforestation; however, the areas being deforested are poorly suited for agriculture and are becoming more difficult to find.

Additionally, about 87% of the world's freshwater is being consumed by agriculture—far more than is con-sumed by any other human activity. Farmers are using sur-face water and are mining underground aquifers. Accord-ing to Population Action International, "farmers are literally draining the continents, just as they are allowing billions of tons of topsoil to erode."

Although at present there is enough of a supply of land and water to feed the earth's existing population, the per-capita availability of cereal grains, the source of 80% of the world's food, has been declining for 15 years. Most na-tions today rely on imports of surplus grains from the re-sources of only a few nations, which account for 80% of all cereal exports, the United States providing the largest share. If the population of the United States doubles in 60 years as projected, then U.S. food and cereal resources will need to be used to feed 520 million Americans. Mean-while, if China's population continues to grow to another 500 million people and if China continues to experience loss of cropland to erosion and unabated industrialization, its demands for imports by 2050 might be more than the world's entire 1993 grain exports. Lester Brown of the Worldwatch Institute says, "Who could supply grain on this scale? No one."

Considering these food demands still does not answer the question of how many people earth can sustain. Joel Cohen, head of the Laboratory of Populations at Rocke-feller University, states that there is no single answer. It will depend, he says, "on the number of people that are willing to wear clothes from cotton (a renewable resource) versus polyester (a nonrenewable petroleum-based prod-uct), how many will eat beef versus bean sprouts, how many will want parks versus parking lots, how many will want Jaguars with a capital J and how many will want jaguars with a small j. These choices will change in time, and so will how many people the Earth can support." If the U.S. population doubles by 2050, the share of its diet from animal products will drop by about half, to perhaps 15%, and food would cost up to 50% of each person's paycheck, which is about what Europeans spend on food now—but this percentage is far more than what U.S. residents typi-cally pay.

OTHER APPROACHES FOR A SUSTAINABLE PLAN

Another idea that addresses the problem of limited re-sources for a growing population is the free-market eco-nomic approach. If world markets were free, the price of goods would rise as the amount of materials grew limited. Rising prices would alert entrepreneurs to the approaching scarcity and provide an entrepreneurial award for new products and creativity. Thomas Lambert of the Center of the Study of American Business feels that resource scarcity will lead to technological developments that leave everyone better off than before. "The entire history of hu-manity indicates that with enough economic freedom, overpopulation relative to natural resources or energy will not occur.

The problem with this free-market argument, according to Thomas Homer-Dixon of the Peace and Conflict Studies Program at the University of Toronto, is that not all things are equal. In areas where young children receive inade-quate nutrition, stimulation, or education, many will not mature adequately to meet the challenge of innovation. Other people face social barriers to innovation such as business corruption, banking difficulties and lack of mone-tary support, politics and poverty, and power group consid-erations. Mr. Homer-Dixon says that as resource scarcity and population stresses rise, "the smarter we have to be so-cially and technically just to maintain our well-being—the more dire the problem, the more quickly we're going to have to respond." Mr. Homer-Dixon is an optimist in that he feels research institution in developing countries will increase the supply of ingenuity. Most of the creativity that is useful in solving scarcity and food production problems is going to be generated locally by people familiar with lo-cal geography, social relations, and resources. To stop the flow of local talent to industrialized nations where greater research opportunities exist, there needs to exist funding of local research by providing scientists in the developing world with monetary and technical resources and with computers, modems, and fax machines—a communication network to peers around the globe.

Global Research on the Environment and Agricultural Nexus (GREAN) is such a proposed organization. GREAN would set up a partnership among U.S. universities and 16 international centers that belong to the Consultative Group on International Agricultural Research. Since the demand for food in developing countries is expected to double by 2025 and triple by 2050, GREAN wants to involve the outstanding scientists of the world (including those in developing countries) in projects aimed at developing sustainable, environmentally friendly food production by and for the world's poorest people (Raloff, 1996, pp. 396–7).

Another approach is to link population to the environment more closely. The 1992 Earth Summit Conference in Rio targeted many environmental issues but largely overlooked population. The 1994 Conference on Population in Cairo led to a comprehensive program of action but overlooked the environment. Establishing such a link helps to balance the intensity and sensitivity of developing countries with the highest population growth rates with the developed countries in terms of their consumptive use of earth's resources—and therefore better designs a whole global cooperative action plan. This type of link could measure use of global materials and resources as a means to reduce CO_2 emissions and other patterns directly related to quality of life and patterns of population. Policies on population aim to decrease fertility rates in a noncoercive fashion and focus on improving the well-being of women. This can be done by helping women avoid unwanted pregnancies, improving girls' education, aiming to achieve greater gender equality, and reducing child mortality, among other methods. Tying environmental actions to population can develop an all-beneficial picture of the improvement of environmental habits and the abatement of consequences that stem from population growth in an equally noncoercive, comprehensive fashion. This process then becomes an all-encompassing and realistic method not only of reducing population, but also of improving the quality of life around the world, with all countries as equal participants in the solution (Gaffin, 1996, p. 7).

As we approach these challenges, Mr. Cohen believes that "neither panic nor complacency is in order. Earth's capability to support people is determined both by natural constraints and by human choices. In the coming half century, we and our children are less likely to face absolute limits than difficult trade-offs" such as population size, environmental quality, and lifestyle. Many people have already been questioning the consumerism of the industrialized countries since the 1950s. Choices will begin to occur when people begin to question what they are buying with their hard-earned money and the real long-term value of

these items. For example, environmentalist mediator Paul Wilson, a lawyer in Portland, Oregon, has spent seven years simplifying his life in terms of his diet and aspirations after realizing that the products he was buying were not worth the hours of work needed to pay for them. His sense is that a transition will occur in which people and their organizations will perceive the imbalance of values in their own way until simple values predominate. Earth's carrying capacity for humans will have to be determined by their own well-chosen choices and strategies (Raloff, 1996, p. 397).

References

Gaffin, S. R., O'Neill, B. C., and Bongaarts, J. (1996, November). Population growth could affect global warming. *Environmental Defense Letter.* Vol. 27, No. 6, p. 7.

Raloff, J. (1996, June 22). The human numbers crunch: The next half-century promises unprecedented challenges. *Science News,* Vol. 149, No. 25, pp. 396–397.

Questions

1. Why doesn't the concept of carrying capacity apply so easily when it comes to people?
2. What is $I = PAT$?
3. What was the problem in using this formula? How was it better correlated?
4. How can this formula be used to project intensity of resource use and carrying capacity? How can it be used to better predict the availability of future resources?
5. How are we going to resolve the inequalities of resource use, according to the article?
6. What are some suggestions for helping unindustrialized countries control accelerating populations and future quality of life issues?
7. What is the free-market approach? What is the problem with using this type of approach?
8. What kind of a population reduction plan can involve industrialized nations as well as unindustrialized or developing countries? Develop an outline of such a plan and present it to your class.

Conclusion

The world is in the thrust of an unprecedented expansion of population. It took hundreds of thousands of years for humans to arrive at a population level of 10 million, which occurred only 10,000 years ago. This number expanded to 100 million people about 2,000 years ago and to 2.5 billion people by 1950. Within the span of a single lifetime, it has more than doubled to 5.5 billion in 1993. The implications of this growth are enormous: some very positive, some extremely threatening, and certainly *all* needing planning, awareness, a world community that works together, and wise choices. It has been stated in this part of the book that we have only a few decades to determine the future path of population growth and all the effects that this path brings with it. The text of this part—from discussions of the effects of this population growth to discussions of the earth's natural limits, from a presentation of the proceedings of the 1994 Cairo conference and the information contained in case studies of Pakistan, India, Ethiopia, Mexico, and China to a presentation of details of some possible plans for alleviating problems of population—alludes to some of the problems and solutions. The problems and solutions are very complex, but it is hoped that this part has begun to sort the issues and makes the reader aware of and involved in the important task of finding and implementing the best course.

Already, progress is being made in many countries of the world, with the reduction of birth rates, an increase in education, and the provision of more medical aid. However, much still has to be accomplished in dealing with the key determinants of rapid population growth of poverty, high childhood mortality, low status and education of women, low adult literacy, and various other negative cultural influences on progress. The common goal is to improve the quality of life for all people and future generations, protecting human social, economic, and personal well-being. This goal involves the participation of all the people on earth in using science and technology wisely, finding substitutes for wasteful practices, educating others about the protection of earth's resources, and actively protecting the natural environment. What happens in Africa or Asia or Puerto Rico affects us all . . . three more of us every second.

Our Population: A Social–Economic View

Environmental degradation is generally the effect of attempts to secure improved standards of food, clothing, shelter, and comfort for growing numbers of people. The impact of the threat to the ecosystem is linked both to human population size and resource use per person. The issues, then, of resource use, waste production, and environmental degradation are accelerated by factors of population growth and further exacerbated by consumptive habits, certain technological developments, social habits, and poor resource management.

As our population continues to increase, the chance of the occurrence of irreversible changes of magnitude also increases. Already, there are indicators of severe environmental stress caused by the growing loss of biodiversity; increase of greenhouse gases; deforestation; ozone depletion; acid rain; loss of topsoil; and world shortages of water, food and fuelwood. The developed countries, with 85% of the gross world product but only 23% of the population, account for the largest use of these resources (Population Summit, 1993).

As the developing countries seek to adopt standards of living and resource patterns from the developed world, the people of the world are further intensifying the already unsustainable demands on the biosphere. For the future, it is important that economic value be placed on the use of earth's resources in a manner similar to that proposed by Green Net National Production or the net national product. Some equitable measures have to be placed on the value of the resources that can sustain the quality of life and the breath of life in each one of us. Productive activities and models to create a sustainable use of our natural resources must happen globally and coordinately, developed world and developing world alike. The placement of monetary values on natural resources would point us in a positive direction toward conservation and somewhat equalize national population imbalances and provide for intelligent resource use.

Bridge to the Future

As we attend to the challenges of increasing food supplies, limiting population growth, and educating societies to 21st-century imperatives, some special progress has been made. Some of these new approaches are alluded to in the part of the book on the future, Part 9. These methods will receive more attention and refinement as we begin to tackle the population problem on the bridge to the 21st Century.

Internet Exercise

1. Use any of the Internet search engines (e.g., Alta Vista, Yahoo, Infoseek, etc.) to research the following topics:

   a. The various population time frames ("popclocks") given in this chapter. Find other resources describing issues of population. Compare the various pieces of data and determine the reasons for any discrepancies.

   b. Malthus and his predictions.

   c. The three-stage demographic theory.

   d. Lester R. Brown and his work with world food projections.

   e. Other world demographic charts not given in this chapter.

   f. Future predictions of world population growth.

   g. The United Nations Population Fund's work.

   h. The International Union for Conservation of Nature and Natural Resources (IUCN) and its work and predictions.

Some ideas taken from the following source: Graham-Smith, F. (1993). Population summit. *Population–The Complex Reality*. Cambridge, England: Cambridge University Press.

i. The Group of Experts on the Scientific Aspects of Marine Pollution (GEASMP) and its work.

j. Figures available from the United Nations Educational, Scientific and Cultural Organization (UNESCO) on population growth, food supply, and education.

k. The Population Council in New York City and its work.

l. Anne H. Ehrlich and Paul R. Ehrlich's predictions and their work.

m. The Club of Rome's Project on the Predicament of Mankind.

n. More information on the 1994 International Conference on Population and Development in Cairo, Egypt.

o. Any country in the world not discussed in this chapter. Research its population growth and find what information you can on its cultural attitudes about population growth and its socioeconomic positions.

p. More information about the pros and cons of birth control.

q. The latest developments on birth control. Also, find information on the latest developments on birth control in relation to various religions and countries.

r. The carrying capacity of earth.

s. Global Research on the Environment and Agricultural Nexus (GREAN).

t. $I = PAT$.

u. The status and education of women and birth control.

v. Abortion rates throughout the world in various countries and the countries' cultural views on abortion.

w. Poverty and population rates around the world.

x. Green Net National Production (NNP).

2. Use any of the Internet search engines (e.g., Alta Vista, Yahoo, Infoseek, etc.) to research the following topics.

a. Birth rate.

b. Death rate.

c. Stabilization of population.

d. Demography.

e. Developed countries.

f. Developing countries.

g. Growth rate.

h. Infant mortality rate.

i. Projections.

j. Vital events.

k. Vital rates.

l. Fertility rate.

m. Exponential growth.

n. Sink (the process of a system).

o. Birth control devices and approaches.

p. Carrying capacity.

q. Environmental degradation.

r. Sustainability.

Useful Web Sites

URL	Site Description
http://www.sunsite.unc.edu/lunarbin/worldpo	World population estimates
http://www.census.gov/cgi-bin/ipc/popclockw	World populations estimates—U.S. Census Bureau
http://www.census.gov.cgi-bin/popclock	U.S. Census Bureau population estimates
http://www.psc.lsa.umch.edu	Domestic/international population research
http://www.cpc.unc/edu	Population Research Institute
http://www.carnell.com/population	Weekly population issues newsletter
http://popindex.princeton.edu	Published population database
http://www.uscusa.org/global/popfaq.html	FAQs about population growth
http://www.jrn.columbia.edu/~wm7/population.html	World population 1700–1994
http://www.carnell.com/population/openews.html	Common myths on population
http://keck.whittier.edu/dallas/Population_lab.html	International population laboratory exercises
http://www.worldvillage.org/index2.html	World Village Project

Boundless humanity. Photo courtesy of United Nations.

War, Politics, and Technology

PART

V

"Peace brings riches; riches bring pride, pride brings anger; anger brings war; wars bring poverty; poverty brings humanity; humanity brings peace; peace, as I have said brings riches; and so the world's affairs go around."

LUIGI DA PORTO, 16TH CENTURY AD

Evolution of killing power

Lethality (vertical axis): 1, 10, 10^2, 10^3, 10^4, 10^5, 10^6, 10^7, 10^8, 10^9, 10^{10}, 10^{11}

Categories (horizontal axis): Sword, Longbow, Flintlock, WWI rifle, Assault rifle, Cannon, WWI tank, WWI fighter-bomber, WWII tank, WWII fighter-bomber, Battle tank, Conv. fighter-bomber, SR NM*, Nuc.-armed fighter bomber, Strat NM**

*Short-range nuclear missile, 20-kiloton warhead   **Strategic nuclear missile

It was probably a clenched fist that provided an end to the first recorded argument. In time, the fist was replaced by a stick. Soon, the stick was modified to accommodate a rock, which was then further modified to sport a sharpened blade. In time, the sticks would give way to the sword, the bow, the flintlock, more sophisticated firearms, artillery, bombs, airplanes, missiles, and so on. As weapons evolved, so did the scale and scope of the conflicts in which they were used. Disputes ranged from the basic disagreement over boundary lines to clashes covering regions, nations, and continents, until even the entire world was occasionally consumed in conflict. The change in scope also precipitated changes in costs. Wars would not be ad hoc affairs, financed simply by robbing petty cash. Budgets would have to reflect the possibility of war. Similarly, leaders realized that weapons were not cheap, but to be victorious, they would have to have them in ever-increasing numbers. This presented a whole new set of problems regarding the raising of funds for these expenditures. Along the line, these leaders realized that weapons, no matter how elaborate and lethal, were useless in the hands of an untrained mob pressed into temporary emergency service. Enter the professional army, followed shortly, or perhaps simultaneously, by the advent of the arms merchants, supplying leaders and their generals with the weapons they needed to wage war. It seemed that as the rise of the nation-state was taking place, the world was also being joined by another institution, the military industrial complex. And with it came the union between those who wielded the power, those who wielded the sword, and those who wielded the forge that made the sword. No longer just an exercise of courage, bravery, and national pride, wars, because of their cost (which could deprive civilian populations of needed services) and the sacrifices involved in their execution, also became exercises in innovation and administration.

This part of the book is about the relationship between war, politics, and technology. You will see as you read along that it makes several points. First, as societies became more dependent upon technology for their weapons, the waging of war became as methodical and calculating as it was passionate. Nations may have rushed into war haphazardly in the past, but the new technology gave them pause to consider the economic, political, and social consequences of such an undertaking. Second, and speaking to the issue of cost, technowars would be expensive. Sacrifices would have to be made. Civilians would have to sacrifice until the conflict was resolved. Sometimes, the ability of a population to do without while resources were allocated for the purchase of military technology became a bigger question mark than the outcome of the war. This Part also offers a general overview of how today's military (primarily that of the United States) gets the technology it needs. It also looks at some examples of military technologies and their development over the years and then concludes with a look at those innovations looming on the horizon of the next century.

29

More War in a Minute: The Sponsorship of Conflict

JOHN MORELLO

• •

Some people think that military technology, like its civilian counterparts, is a result of an autonomous self-directed force. That assumption is far from the actual case. In his book *Technology and Society: The Shaping of People and Things,* Ron Westrum argues that all technologies are propelled by those who take responsibility for their management and benefit from their growth. They are shaped by the institutions that manage them. Technologies need support from groups and organizations that invest resources in developing and managing them. Westrum called groups of this nature *sponsors*. Sponsors are institutions that help to develop technology and decide how and when society will use it. From initial conception to final use, most technologies are shaped by these sponsors and reflect their influence. Sponsors come from various places: government, private industry, the legal system, consumers, even educational institutions. You may never have thought of this, but the school you attend is a sponsor of technology, and the product of that sponsorship is none other than yourself. You will graduate not just with a degree, but with a degree from your university. This is not to say that each of these types of sponsors plays a role in the development of military technologies, but enough of them are present in the creative process to make them all worth investigating.

Westrum has identified three classes of sponsors: *Dominant Clients*, *Dominant Regulators*, and *Monopolistic Makers*. Dominant Clients are those customers that, given their size and their special needs, exert a major influence in the shaping of technology. This kind of relationship is

evident between manufacturers of military products and their customers, the various branches of the military. The demands of the Dominant Clients are met only at great cost. And, surprisingly, according to James Fallows, the author of *National Defense,* the military technologies commissioned by these Dominant Clients are sometimes inferior to the products made available to the civilian market. An example of this phenomenon was the experience of the Lockheed Aircraft Corporation. Traditionally, argues Fallows, Lockheed had made its money selling aircraft to the military. But in the 1970s, the company tried to work both sides of the street by selling the L-1011 to commercial carriers and the C-5A to the Pentagon. According to Gregg Easterbrook, writing in 1984 in *The Atlantic Monthly,** the L-1011 became a star, while the C-5A was a disaster, dogged by technical problems. Additionally, the planes were delivered behind schedule, were nearly a billion dollars over budget, and were the subject of a Congressional investigation, prompted by a civilian Air Force analyst who blew the whistle on the boondoggle. Nonetheless, wrote Fallows, the C-5A was eventually purchased by the Air Force at a price much higher than that originally agreed upon. This case is a good example of the power of a Dominant Client, which gets what it wants regardless of the economic, and possibly social, consequences. For example, said Fallows, if commercial products are not delivered on time or are over budget, the producer pays the penalty. But if military products are not delivered on time or are over budget, the customer is held accountable. That's because of the clout of the Dominant Client.

Excerpted with permission of the author.

Westrum also identified a class of sponsor called *Dominant Regulators*. Dominant Regulators are a different kind of sponsor, but they still play a role in the relationship between technology and the military. One can count among the ranks of Dominant Regulators government institutions such as the Food and Drug Administration (FDA), which ensures that the foods you eat and the medicines you take are safe. The idea for such a regulatory agency surfaced early in the 20th century. In those days, many people bought their medicine through mail-order catalogs that promised miraculous cures, sometimes only to discover that the medicine did nothing except make them sicker. Discontent with this situation prompted the beginnings of the creation of regulations to discern real products from fake ones. But the real turning point came when a reporter named Upton Sinclair went undercover to expose bad working conditions at the Chicago Stockyards. Instead, his book, *The Jungle,* ended up as a horror story about the unsanitary conditions in which meat was prepared for the American consumer. Legend has it that after President Theodore Roosevelt read the account, he couldn't eat meat for several days. In the wake of that and other revelations, Congress passed the Pure Food and Drug Act of 1906, requiring producers of meat and medicine to observe strict laws regarding the purity of production of their products. Ultimately, the FDA was established to oversee food and drug production, requiring new products be submitted for testing prior to marketing. It has the power to ban products from American markets or to remove products from the marketplace until they have been proven safe for consumption. The FDA is one of the nation's most influential Dominant Regulators.

Other Dominant Regulators are not part of the government, but can also wield tremendous influence on which products do and do not reach the market place. Some nongovernmental regulators are called *Standard Setting Organizations* and include institutions such as the Underwriter's Laboratory. The next time you go shopping for a coffee pot, a microwave oven, or some other appliance, check to see if the product has a UL sticker. That sticker means that the manufacturer sent the product to the Underwriter's Laboratory for independent testing. If the tests proved satisfactory, the UL label goes on the product, attesting to its quality. Other Dominant Regulators include groups led by consumer advocate Ralph Nader or groups made up of women, senior citizens, or some other segment of the community brought together to demand changes in a certain product. Parents of small children, for example, might apply pressure to the makers of children's sleepwear to make the sleepwear more flame retardant. Often, the military is regulated by Congress via the numerous congressional committees that oversee military operations.

The efforts of Dominant Regulators are determined by the amount of access consumers have to technology. While the military is not often found in the position of denying itself the technology it feels it needs, it sometimes has been called upon to exercise some restraint. You'll read more about this issue in the chapter about the F-22. Unfortunately, restraint isn't always exercised, and sometimes, the consequences can be deadly. During the Vietnam War, for instance, some servicemen reported that their M-16 rifles would jam in combat. The original form of the M-16, the Armalite AR-15, had been developed to fulfill the need for

The M-16 Rifle. The M-16 was touted by large, influential technology sponsors and was adopted by the army for use during the Vietnam War. It was chosen over a weapon reported to have been more ideal for jungle warfare.
Courtesy of U.S. Army

a high-velocity, small-caliber weapon that would be ideal for jungle warfare. However, the Army lobbied for the M-16, claiming that the AR-15 was inaccurate and did not have the desired range. The lobby effort was successful: The M-16 became the weapon issued to most combat personnel in Vietnam (McNaugher, 1984).

The third and final sponsor class that helps produce our technology for the military is what Westrum has called *Monopolistic Makers.* Simply stated, because a corporation holds such a high percentage of the market share of a given product, anytime it introduces a new technology, it can be reasonably sure that the new product will be used by customers already using its products. For example, IBM and AT&T have had a major influence on the computer and telecommunications fields. Therefore, when the military shops for new technologies, the shopping is done with the understanding that whatever selection the military makes will be used by a large number of its personnel. The occasional difference occurs in the area of interservice rivalries, where one branch of the service campaigns for and gets a technology unique to its own peculiar needs. This factor has produced a certain amount of overlap in the military community, but with more aggressive oversight, it is gradually becoming a thing of the past.

Over the years, the sponsorship of technology by the military has followed the same rate of growth as that of its civilian counterparts. Its *Dominant Clients* tell manufacturers what it wants the technology to do, what it should look like, and what it should cost. *Dominant Regulators* ostensibly should control the conditions under which the technology should be used, and *Monopolistic Makers*

should guarantee a wide range of use of a given technology and some degree of uniformity. There are, however, some notable exceptions between the military and its civilian counterparts. Only until recently have cost, efficiency, and standardization been adopted as criteria in the military procurement process. In addition, one standard that has been unique to the military process has been the search for technologies with an ever-increasing potential for destruction. You see, in the military, the need to be one step ahead of the competition has less to do with market share and more to do with superiority and survival.

References

Easterbrook, G. (1984, August). The Airplane That Doesn't Cost Enough. *Atlantic Monthly.*

Fallows, J. (1981). *National Defense.* New York, Random House.

McNaugher, T. L. (1984). *The M-16 Controversies: Military Organization and Weapons Acquisition.* New York, Praeger Press.

Westrum, R. (1991). *Technologies and Society: The Shaping of People and Things.* Belmont, CA, Wadsworth Publishing.

Questions

1. Define sponsorship.
2. Define "Dominant Client."
3. What is the role of a Dominant Regulator?
4. What Dominant Regulator helps to control the military?
5. What is the role of a Monopolistic Maker?

30

Tanks: The Evolution of Mechanized Warfare

The earliest recorded designs of a motorized tank can be found in the United States dating from the end of the 19th century. E. J. Pennington sketched a four-wheeled contraption that looked more like a boat than a car, with bathtub sides and two guns in the front and rear. But sketches were all that Pennington could produce. A lack of money and vision by America's military establishment had stalled the project. So it was up to a British engineer, F. R. Simms, to breathe life into the design. The result was the War Car, a turn-of-the-century invention boasting a 16-horsepower Daimler engine resting on four steel-tired wheels (Reid, 1976). Britain and other European powers experimented with tanks (actually, armored cars, since track technology hadn't been developed at that time). Yet, despite some intriguing developments, mobile warfare continued to be executed using horsepower that required saddles and oats. World War I, however, changed all that. The "war to end all wars" was also one in which military leaders and their industrial colleagues first glimpsed the potential of mechanized warfare. Some unusual military–industrial alliances were struck as ventures that were experimenting with automobile development became interested in tank development. For example, the British Army joined forces with Rolls Royce, while the Germans signed on with Daimler Benz.

In the first few months of the war, wheeled armored cars enjoyed some success, but their limitations in the new service conditions of Europe soon became obvious to all.

Trench warfare, the machine gun, poison gas, and the mud of no-man's land made them useless. Although many of these conflicts would be solved in time, it was the lack of mobility that made wheeled armored cars obsolete. Tracked vehicles seemed to be the answer (Reid, 1976). The Mark I, designed by the British in 1915, weighed 28 tons and had a top speed of four miles per hour. With armor half an inch thick, it carried a crew of eight: Four operated the tank, and the rest fired two six-pound cannons and four machine guns. Inside the Mark I, ventilation was poor, the heat was overwhelming, and there was no suspension system. The men inside the Mark I bounced around like tennis balls (Fleming, 1995).* Nonetheless, the tank caused a fair amount of consternation when it first appeared on the battlefield in 1916 (Reid, 1976). The age of modern mechanized warfare had arrived.

After the war, there was little additional tank development. Most nations, tired of war and the financial obligations it implied, halted further research and development. Both Britain and France put off new development, despite protests from military thinkers. Things were no better in the United States, where the upper echelons of the military establishment also discounted the tank's value in war. The experience of J. Walter Christie is a good case in point. Christie had studied the tanks of World War I and created a more modern fighting machine. His most important innovation was a suspension system, which allowed tanks to be more mobile in all types of terrain. It also made the ride safer for the members of the crew, who frequently emerged from their tanks with bones dislocated or even broken. Other new features included a more powerful engine and a

A World War I Tank. Tanks like this British M-1 tank first appeared in the early stages of World War I. They were slow, dangerous for their occupants, and fell victim more often to mechanical difficulties than to enemy fire. However, they changed the way in which wars would be fought in the future.
Courtesy of U.S. Signal Corps

bigger main gun mounted on a rotating turret, which vastly expanded the tank's field of fire. But the military wasn't interested, and subordinate officers were warned that further discussion about the tank would prove unhealthy to their careers. When Dwight Eisenhower, then an Army major, wrote an article urging the Army to take a greater interest in mechanized warfare, he was severely rebuked for impugning official military doctrine. Even George S. Patton, who had recognized the value of the tank early on, switched back to the horse cavalry. Christie, desperate and in need of cash, sold his tank design to the Soviet Union, which used it to develop the T-34, one of the best tanks built during World War II (Fleming, 1995). The T-34 would become the first in a new series of Main Battle Tanks (MBTs). MBTs would combine mobility, lethality, and survivability and were destined to be the wave of the future in terms of tank development. The T-34's construction, simplicity of operation, and the firepower of its 76-mm gun proved to be up to the challenge of German armor when Germany invaded the Soviet Union in 1941.

Germany military thinkers had previously realized that the tank could make their armies more effective if they combined both armor and infantry. Tanks, supported by infantry, could go further and wreak more havoc on the enemy. And, in addition to tying troops to tanks, the Germans took the technology a step further. They created entire divisions of tanks, with motorized infantry and artillery in supporting roles. It would take several years of fighting and dying before the Allied powers developed tank technology to challenge the German's Tiger and Mark series of tanks, each sporting heavier armor and greater firepower than the American and British Shermans, Churchills, and Cromwells (Frankland, 1989). The experience of those American and British tankers facing and surviving superior German technology in World War II contributed heav-

ily to the campaign in those two countries to achieve tank superiority in the postwar world. Yes, air power could stop tanks. But what if bad weather grounded the air force? In the final analysis, tanks could only be stopped by better tanks (Fleming, 1995). The Cold War, which pitted the Soviet Union against the United States on a variety of levels, included the race to build a better tank.

However, like before, U.S. tank development in the postwar years neither reflected the advances in the available technology nor kept pace with other nations. The wars that America found itself enmeshed in, in places like Korea and Vietnam, featured terrain that was unconducive to extensive mechanized warfare. Additionally, air power had become the key piece in the U.S. defense puzzle. Therefore, armored technology took a backseat to air-power technology. The result was a series of U.S. tanks, the "M" series, which were big, slow, underequipped in terms of firepower, and fueled with gasoline, making them instant fireballs if hit in the right spot. The M-60 was the last of the series and was described by General James H. Polk, writing in a 1972 issue of *Army Magazine,* as "an inferior tank, part of a tired, old second-rate series."

Other countries were not so hesitant to invest in tank technology. The Russians took their T-34, which had performed so well in World War II, and spun it off into the T-54, 55, 62, and 72. The "T" series, despite its cramped quarters, which occasionally exposed crew to dangerous moving parts, were formidable vehicles with well-sloped armor, low silhouettes, and a weapons system that produced deadly accurate results. And, if imitation is the sincerest form of flattery, consider this: The Israeli Army, which in its wars with Arab neighbors would score brilliant victories using armor, thought so much of the T-62 that, for example, it incorporated captured T-62s into its own armored divisions.

Just as tank technology was developing, so too were efforts to stop tanks. A whole new generation of antitank weapons has been appearing over the years, featuring sophisticated armor-piercing warheads. The new development caused some tank advocates to wonder if their vehicles were destined to be museum pieces and not battlefield pieces. Defenders of the tank now had to look at the problem of defense from a whole new angle—literally. Researchers in Britain discovered that angling the layers of armor on a tank could deflect antitank rounds. This discovery breathed new life into tank development and new enthusiasm among American engineers about their chances for a state-of-the-art vehicle. That enthusiasm was ultimately manifested in the M1A1 Abrams tank. Named after General Creighton Abrams, former Chief of Staff and a veteran of tank operations during World War II, the M1 was an indication that the Army wanted a tank that combined mobility, firepower, and the highest level of survivability for its crew. Although the first M1s were delivered in the 1980s, it was not until the Gulf War in 1991 that designers would learn whether or not they had accomplished their mission. They were not disappointed. As the tanks rolled into battle in 1991, the M1A1s were equipped to deal with the variety of challenges with which Saddam Hussein and his Iraqi Army might present them. The tanks were fitted with an internal cooling system that protected the crew against nuclear, biological, or chemical warfare. They cruised along smoothly at 41 mph, supported by torsion-bar suspension, rotary shock absorbers, and extra long tracks. They were also under 10 feet tall, which made them difficult for enemy gunners to target. The four-person crew used a thermal imaging system to find and track their targets. The 120-mm main gun had a range of 2,500 meters and could be fired on the run with accuracy. The air-cooled gas turbine ran on a number of fuels, including diesel, and was quieter and produced less smoke. And, despite concerns that such a sensitive engine might be prone to breakdowns, especially as a result of sand and dust, those breakdowns could be avoided by regularly changing the filters. The M1A1 will undergo further modifications in the years to come. Its successor, the M1A2, will feature, among other things, a weapons system that will allow it to deal with a number of targets simultaneously.

The tank has finally come of age in an age of high tech. Starting from the days of the Mark I, through the years of the Shermans, the "M" series for the United States, and the "T" series for the Soviet Union, mechanized warfare has taken on a new look both inside and outside. The vehicles are faster, more agile, more durable, and far deadlier. The crews are better trained. And, despite those who might criticize the high-tech features of the M1A1 as well as the tank's high price tag (about $4 million each), there is little question as to whether any weapon other than a fully equipped tank with a well-trained crew can stop a similar vehicle. The nearly 90 years of technological trial and error have finally produced tanks that can truly be said to be up to the task.

References

Fleming, T. (1995, vol.10, no. 3, Winter). Tanks. *Invention & Technology.*

Frankland, N. (1989). *The Encyclopedia of Twentieth Century Warfare.* New York, Crown Publishers.

Reid, W. (1976). *The Lore Of Arms: A Concise History of Weaponry.* New York, Facts On File.

http://www.usmc.mll.

http://www.jmu.edu/rotc/gallery.ml/html.

Questions

1. What year did the first treaded tank appear on the battlefield?
2. What problems did early tanks have that made them as dangerous for those inside as for those outside?
3. What breakthrough did British researchers make after World War II that could help protect tanks?
4. Who was J. Walter Christie, and what contributions did he make to tank development?
5. What features does the M1A1 tank have that make it safer for crew members and more dangerous for enemy forces?

31

The F-22: The Plane Even Congress Couldn't Shoot Down

The F-22 took off in 1992, to great sighs of relief from officials of Lockheed Martin and the Air Force, two sponsors who teamed up in the 1980's to produce a new fighter plane. From 1990, when the YF-22 prototype took to the skies, to April 1991, when the Air Force approved the final design, the mission of the project had been the same: to create a new generation of fighters that would project and defend U.S. interests into the 21st century. Powered by two Pratt and Whitney F-119-PW 100 engines, it will reach speeds in the Mach-2 category, allowing it to cruise for most of its missions at speeds that today's fighters can attain only during a brief stint. It also will be the first agile, supersonic fighter to be stealthy, even more so than its cousin, the F-117 Stealth fighter–bomber. In addition, the F-22 will sport a lethal weapons system, including Advanced Medium Range Air-to-Air Missiles (AM-RAAM), monitored by the latest computer technology and topped off by a helmet-mounted display that supplies pilots with target data wherever they look (Sweetman, 1995).* It even comes with the potential of accommodating two crew members. Very impressive, very complicated, and very expensive. The F-22 could end up costing the Pentagon—and ultimately, the American taxpayers—$100 million per copy, making it one of the costliest weapons systems in the Defense Department's history (Callahan, 1992).**

*Reprinted with permission from *Popular Science* magazine, copyright © 1996, Times Mirror Magazines, Inc.

**Reprinted with permission from *Technology Review,* published by the Association of Alumni and Alumnae of MIT, copyright © 1998.

Furthermore, fiscal problems aren't the only issues keeping Pentagon officials awake at night. Because the F-22 is loaded with those state-of-the-art goodies, will anyone be able to fly it to its full potential? Take the advanced stealth characteristics, for example. It gives the pilot plenty of flexibility, but at the same time, a lot to think about. He or she must weigh the opportunities to attack against the need to remain hidden. Also, different radar systems can lock on to the F-22, depending on its distance from the systems. Add to that the fact that the plane is more visible to radar from the side or the tail than from the front. Therefore, the pilot must worry if he or she is at greater risk when trying to avoid the danger rather than when confronting it face to face. The decision of whether to fight or flee, as well as other decisions, have to be made instantaneously amidst the crushing physical G-load strains of air combat, where planes can be shot down by other planes or by SAM (surface-to-air-missile) sites from miles away. Flying the F-22 requires so much concentration that engineers have worried that pilots may not have the "right stuff" mentally to operate the plane at peak efficiency. So, batteries of elaborate computer and video technology have been built into the F-22 to help the pilot keep track of everything and avoid lapses.

Another issue troubling Defense Department think-tankers is who this plane will be used against. One answer is Russia. The Pentagon has argued that the United States must maintain technological superiority against the possible revival of Soviet power. The chances of such a revival seem unlikely, counter critics. With its economy in shambles and its political structure still shaky, Russia appears to be no threat to the United States now or in the immediate future. Consequently, the Congressional Budget Office, which oversees government expenditures, concluded as early as 1991, the same year as the USSR's collapse, that conditions inside Russia made the need for weapons like the F-22 unnecessary (Callahan, 1992). The CBO recommended that the project be scrapped and that existing fighter aircraft be upgraded to meet America's security needs.

Not so fast, said the Pentagon. Despite its disintegration in 1991, the "evil empire," as Ronald Reagan called it, lives on in the form of its exportable military technology. Two systems that could tip the balance in any confrontation involving the United States and some other adversary are the Sukhoi Su-35, an advanced and deadly fighter, and the Vympel R-77 air-to-air missile. The R-77 is now acknowledged to have a longer range and greater agility than the Air Force's AMRAAM (Sweetman, 1995). And now the R-73E is being tested, which is said to have even more enhanced steering performance. The instant that the R-73E fired, the missile starts to veer sharply towards its target,

The F-22, the latest development in air-power technology. It may be the most unstoppable military plane the world has seen. Even the U.S. Congress couldn't shoot it down.
Courtesy Lockheed Corporation

leaving little or no time for evasive measures. The missile's infrared seeker lets a pilot lock onto any target in front of his or her aircraft. Here, too, the pilot may rely on a head-mounted sighting device, so that all he or she has to do is look at the enemy and press a button to fire (Sweetman, 1995). F-22 supporters say that because of these up-and-coming weapons systems, the F-22 plane is needed more than ever.

If skeptics haven't been swayed by that argument, the price tag of the F-22 will help even less. When all 648 planes are built, sometime around the year 2012, the total cost of the project could exceed $98 billion (Callahan, 1992). And while critics are willing to give the USSR credit for producing its share of sophisticated Cold War hardware, they're also quick to point out that making weapons is one thing, but maintaining them is another. Because of this, they say, Moscow shouldn't be considered a real military threat and the F-22 should be scrapped.

But changing geopolitical circumstances haven't deterred the F-22's supporters. The second threat they see, in the absence of a Russian one, is that of "Third-World Challengers," such as China, North Korea, and even Iraq. However, neither of the first two qualify as legitimate threats to the United States. Sino-American relations can be rocky from time to time, but armed conflict would be unlikely. This is not to say that there hasn't been a degree of sabre rattling the last few years, especially over the mutually sensitive issue of Taiwan, but the differences of opinion have been more over economics than politics or geography. North Korea might seem a better prospect for trouble, but if the country collapses or merges with South Korea (outcomes that have both been predicted), F-22 supporters would no longer have an arena to show what the plane can do. Could the Iraqis recover from the devastation of the Gulf War to cross swords again with the United States? Operation Desert Storm proved that air power would be the primary instrument for winning future wars, thereby justifying further expenditures for airplane technology like the F-22. Indeed, France and Britain are developing new fighter aircraft more advanced than the F-15, America's primary fighter. Presumably, these new fighters could be sold to the Iraqis. Supporters of the F-22 argue that it has the advanced technology to meet these challenges and claim that it was technology that carried the day back in 1991.

On the other hand, Iraq's dismal performance in the Gulf War might also be cause for caution and restraint. It is far from clear that Third-World states, heavily armed with modern weapons, present the extreme danger that Pentagon officials suggest in attempting to justify annual defense expenditures at Cold War levels. In 1991, Iraq had one of the finest integrated air defenses in the developing world, including 16,000 surface-to-air missiles and 7,000 antiaircraft guns. It also had an advanced air force that included more than 900 combat planes, including some of the best French and Soviet fighters available. But, when the war came, the equipment proved nearly worthless. Iraq's air defenses were destroyed; when aircraft did come up to intercept American and other Coalition Force attackers, they proved to be no match (Callahan, 1992).

Furthermore, while the Gulf War showed that highly sophisticated air-power elements can speed victory and save lives, this success shouldn't be an invitation for a Pentagon spending spree. It is not completely clear that the new, big-ticket items were any more responsible for the success of Operation Desert Storm than were some of the older, cheaper, and equally capable weapons already available. For example, much of the success against Iraqi tanks was due in part to the use of the F-111 bomber, a relic of the late 1960s, and the cheapest aircraft in the Air Force, the A-10 Thunderbolt, which has been in operation since 1976. The A-10 was a particularly effective tool in destroying tanks because of its relatively low speed as well as its large fuel capacity, which allows it to remain over the target area much longer than faster jets which consume more fuel. Additionally, it can be retrofitted with certain technologies that increase its striking power. The Gulf War proved that given the weakness of Third-World states, low-tech weapons are still adequate in handling many missions on the modern battlefield. Equally important might be the fact that in the absence of high technologies, knowing how to get the most out of existing technologies can also mean the difference between victory and defeat.

Despite the success of the more modest military technologies in the Gulf War, the F22's makers seem intent on forging ahead with the expensive and questionable aircraft. It would seem as if the project, bereft of any practical justification, is being driven by domestic political concerns, namely those of the company that's building it, the branches of the military that want it, and those political interest groups that stand to profit from its construction. That says little for any genuine concern for global security and says even less for the many other critical needs that the money could address.

References

Callahan, D. (1992, August/September). The F-22: An Exercise in Overkill. *Technology Review,* vol. 95, no. 6, pp. 42–49.

http://www.airforce.com/welcome/welcome.html.

Sweetman, B. (1995, August). Beyond Visual Range: Flying the F-22. *Popular Science.* vol. 247, no. 2, pp. 44–49.

Questions

1. What weapons systems does the F-22 have that makes it different from the F-117?

2. How much is the F-22 expected to cost?

3. What potential enemies does the Pentagon think this plane will be used against?

4. Comment on the following statement: "Potential enemies are far behind us on weapons development. Why do we have to develop new technology when the current technology will work?"

5. What planes could be used in place of the F-22 that might be as effective, yet cheaper?

32 Revealed: Stealth Demonstrator

STUART F. BROWN

• •

Out of a storage hangar somewhere in the black world of military research comes a shovel-nosed secret airplane that can only be described as . . . ugly! Tacit Blue is the experimental aircraft's code name, although insiders struck by its resemblance to a killer whale dubbed it "Shamu."

Tacit Blue was first revealed at a Pentagon briefing on April 30. In late May, the plane went on display at the U.S. Air Force Museum in Dayton, Ohio, for all to see.

The 56-foot-long aircraft has an oversized, curved fuselage and a straight, tapered wing spanning 48 feet. Built by Northrop Corp. (now Northrop Grumman) in Hawthorne, California, under a highly classified $165-million program begun in 1978, Tacit Blue flew in a series of 135 test flights from 1982 to 1985. Although only one complete aircraft was built and flown, Tacit Blue yielded important knowledge about stealthy shapes and materials that influenced the design of the B-2 bomber, F-22 fighter, and several spy drones.

As a "technology demonstrator," the craft helped Northrop engineers validate the complex equations needed to predict the reflection of radar from surfaces with three-dimensional compound contours. In an earlier generation of the technology, Lockheed Skunk Works engineers used a pair of aircraft known as Have Blue to test the radar reflectivity of two-dimensional, faceted surfaces, like those later used in the F-117A stealth attack plane.

At the April 1996 Pentagon briefing, Lt. General George Muellner of the Air Force said Tacit Blue was used

to explore the idea of a single-seat surveillance plane that would fly at altitudes of about 30,000 feet over hostile territory—gathering electronic intelligence and radar images of targets on the ground. Muellner said no operational aircraft based on Tacit Blue were built, because Pentagon officials instead decided to produce the Joint Surveillance Target Attack Radar System (STARS) surveillance and battle-management aircraft, which has a larger, more powerful radar and can look obliquely into hostile territory without flying over it.

Tacit Blue's synthetic-aperture radar, made by Hughes, was designed to test "low probability of intercept" tricks for imaging terrain and objects on the ground without attracting attention. Disguising the radar signal as background noise and coding it so that only its own receiver could interpret the return signal enabled Tacit Blue's operators to gather images undetected.

A pair of Garrett turbofan engines buried in the aft fuselage provided power for the aircraft. These engines are the same type used in business jets. A top-mounted air-inlet duct, and an exhaust nozzle shielded from below by a flat extension of the "Vee" tail, minimized Tacit Blue's visibility to radar and infrared sensors.

Why is the Air Force trotting out a test plane that retired 11 years ago? "The taxpayers invested money in it, and we're trying to declassify things. We're under a presidential order to do that," General Muellner replied. Will more revelations like Tacit Blue be forthcoming from the Air Force? "You know, we continue to explore new technologies all the time," said the general.

Questions

1. What was the job of the plane code-named "Tacit Blue" as a technology demonstrator?
2. How does the technology tested by Tacit Blue differ from the technology used by the F-117A?
3. How does Tacit Blue's V-shaped tail respond to radar?
4. When was the Tacit Blue project begun?
5. What was the ultimate purpose of Tacit Blue?
6. How much did the Tacit Blue program cost? Why was it never made operational?
7. Comment on the following statement: "Since the program never produced a single plane, the Tacit Blue Project was a waste of money."

33

The Wars of Tomorrow

Men like to celebrate the valor of war. But every nation tends to conveniently forget or minimize its own barbarism. Wars tend to bring out the worst in us.

CARL SAGAN

The images on the screen were in black and white and very grainy, much like the first pictures seen in the early days of television. But the resolution was still good enough to make out objects: mostly planes, buildings, and bridges. Suddenly, just as our eyes were adjusting to the picture before us, a projectile zoomed in from out of nowhere and annihilated it. Were we all part of a mass amusement arcade experience? Not exactly. What we were watching were the onboard video cameras of American and Coalition Force planes as they attacked Iraqi positions during the 1991 Gulf War. And the attack was almost secondary to what they attacked with: planes with stealth technology that could evade Iraq's radar detection and antiaircraft systems; cruise missiles that flew fast and low and surgically (most of the time) hit their targets; imaging systems (JSTARS, short for Joint Surveillance Target Attack Radar System) that identified Iraqi tanks at night, in bad weather, or even if they were buried; and global positioning systems (GPS) that helped commanders keep track of air, land, and sea operations. The technological overkill was so impressive that after weeks of bombing raids, ground forces were victorious in only a short period of time. And, as Iraq's military machine was being dismantled, America's military establishment was rebuilding its image in the eyes of many who thought its best days were behind it after the Vietnam experience. Given a well-defined mission with the right tools, America's military achieved victory at low cost: less than 500 Allied lives were reported lost, as opposed to over 200,000 of the Iraqis. America's new military technology made the difference . . . this time. But will our weapons technology give us the edge next time? No one is completely sure.

David Shukman is a BBC television correspondent who specializes in military affairs. His latest book, *Tomorrow's War: The Threat of High Technology Weapons* (1996) lays out a new and potentially frightening scenario for wars in the high-tech age. Shukman argues that the next war will not be measured by megatons, kilotons, or even throw weight. Instead, there will be a new approach to warfare. Information, he says, rather than brute force, will win the day. The potency of modern electronics will be the key, because of their ability to handle and process information. He argues that computers will be the weapon that will make our other, more lethal weapons faster, more accurate, and more intelligent. With the ability to see the enemy's moves in the minutest detail, to analyze information instantly, and to transmit it to a weapon that makes use of it, warfare will be transformed. Information will be the determining factor.

If that's the case, as Shukman sees it to be, then warfare is in for more than just a data boost. War will be decidedly less human, at least on the battlefield. Robots will serve as automated sentries on guard through the night; artillery pieces will fire by themselves. Shukman also predicts that robotlike ants will be used to eat their way through communications cables. Soldiers who must be on the battlefield will have a decided edge. Global positioning systems even more powerful than the ones used in Operation Desert Storm will help tell the soldiers where they are and what's going on around them. JSTARS and AWACS (Airborne Warning and Control Systems) will seem antiquated as the next war unveils communications technologies based on cheap minisatellites to spy from space. Lethal combat may be a thing of the past for the few soldiers on the battlefield as they utilize weapons designed not to kill, but to immobilize instead: sticky foam, sprayed to prevent movement; microwave projectiles to melt sensitive equipment; flash-blinding bombs that cause blindness; acoustic beams that can cause discomfort and unconsciousness for personnel who come in contact with them; and combustion inhibitors that can stop trucks, jeeps, tanks, and planes. These weapons are designed not to kill, but rather to confuse and bewilder the enemy, throwing off communications between the forward and rear areas and stalling any advances.

But all these weapons, Shukman argues, will depend on government decisions to provide the money for their development and the military's good sense regarding their use. Neither path is clearly marked; the military is just as capable of doing the wrong thing with a piece of technology as any civilian operation, and governments tend to fall victim to the mistake of making decisions that might be politically correct in the short term but wrong over the long haul. The extra element of danger in all this is that other societies might not be encumbered by such difficult or deliberative decision processes. More important, the technological lead that many developed nations once enjoyed seems to be fast shrinking. Shukman argues that there is a serious risk that other nations, especially the newly developing societies, might surpass the West by developing or acquiring these new weapons systems first. The technology is certainly available; the only restriction seems to be cost. While Western nations grapple with the political, social, and economic consequences of weapons development (and those consequences are considerable in this age of shrinking financial resources), a process that could take years, Shukman argues that nations with less democratic systems and oversight processes could possess new weapons in half the time. And those weapons might not have to be the result of their own labors. The international arms market could be the one-stop shopping source for nations eager to acquire military technology and nations desperate to raise cash. The end result, he predicts, would be a military nightmare for the world.

In order for the United States to be ready for the next war, various things would have to happen. First, there would have to be tighter international control of technological diffusion—i.e., the spread of technology from one nation to the next. Some sort of ironclad system must be found to keep dangerous technologies from falling into the wrong hands. Some restrictions exist, but they tend to be porous at critical times. Second, and most important, the United States must reevaluate weapons development. Although not out of the realm of the possible, future military efforts the size of Operation Desert Storm may have had their day. The next war will probably be a good deal smaller and occur in terrain that may not be conducive to large numbers of troops, tanks, or heavy bombers. Technologies to fit the era of the smaller wars will be necessary, and they won't be politically attractive. They won't be high profile, nor will they shower any particular military service, producer, or politician with any glory or credit for their acquisition. It will take a mixture of scientific ingenuity and political courage to make these newer, smaller weapons for the next war. But rest assured that if we don't make them, someone else will.

References

Dunnigan, J. (1996). *Digital Soldiers: The Evolution of High-Tech Weaponry and Tomorrow's Brave New Battlefield.* New York, St. Martin's Press.

Shukman, D. (1996). *Tomorrow's War: The Threat of High-Technology Weapons.* New York, Harcourt, Brace, & Company.

Questions

1. Discuss the capabilities of the following weapons: JSTARS and AWACS.
2. The article suggests that information may be more important than firepower or manpower in the next war. What examples can you find which suggest that information technology may replace men and equipment on the battlefield?
3. What, in your opinion, are the ethical issues to be considered in deciding to use nonlethal instead of lethal weapons on the battlefield? Is there such a thing as a nonlethal weapon?
4. How might the following weapons be used in future wars: sticky foam, combustion inhibitors, acoustic beams.
5. What two recommendations does the article make regarding U.S. preparations for future wars?

34

Warfare in the Information Age

Tony Capaccio with Mary Greczyn

Years ago, the world watched as allied troops pummeled Iraq with a dizzying display of high-tech might. Now, as U.S. soldiers began another year in Bosnia, they are again armed with cutting-edge weaponry, making them "the meanest dogs in town," as former Defense Secretary William Perry put it.

But for NATO and U.S. troops, Bosnia is about enforcing a tenuous peace, not about war. While the weapons are impressive, equally important, if unsung, are the systems that enhance "situational awareness." It's what Alvin Toffler and other futurists would call Third Wave Information Warfare. We call it knowing what's going on.

"Awareness" includes images of vehicle and troop movements that are gleaned from airborne and ground sensors and relayed digitally via satellite to command centers as far away as northern Italy. To the individual G.I., "awareness" translates into a more immediate concern—knowing the location of millions of deadly land mines.

Military planners are looking at the Joint Endeavor deployment as a template for future post-Cold War peace "enforcements." If Bosnia is any guide, future military operations will be fought primarily with information, rather than with guns and bombs.

In the following pages, we take a close look at some of the new technologies that are helping the United States wage information warfare in Bosnia. They run the gamut from intelligence-gathering aircraft to new mine-detection equipment aimed at neutralizing the war-torn land's worst killer.

BOSNIA ON THE WEB

Thousands of Americans have dialed the Pentagon's BosniaLink home page since it went online. One of the most popular features is the greeting forum, where you can leave a message of 50 words or less for the troops. The address is *http://www.dtic.dla.mil/bosnia/*. Pentagon public affairs gurus have packaged more than 20,000 messages into CD-ROMs and distributed them throughout Bosnia.

HEAT SEEKER

At least two video Infra-Cams have been deployed for mine clearance. Made by Inframetrics of North Billerica, Massachusetts, the handheld infrared cameras can detect heat "anomalies" from as far away as 100 meters.

Working alongside a soldier sweeping a standard metal detector, the camera operator reads the thermal signature of buried objects. Mines reflecting heat show up as "hot spots" on the camera's view finder, and the molecular structure of disturbed soil reflects heat differently than undisturbed earth. The camera can also find booby traps and unexploded ordnance.

3-D RADAR PICTURES

The Bosnian Joint Endeavor is demonstrating the utility of unmanned aerial vehicles, or drones, in a peacekeeping role. Since mid-March, three predator drones have been flying observation missions at altitudes between 9,000 and 25,000 feet. Equipped with lenses that detect heat sources and take 3-D radar pictures, the drones are capturing images with a resolution approaching one foot. The radar lens can see through clouds.

Predator imagery is beamed, via the multichannel Global Broadcast Satellite network, to headquarters equipped with special receivers. The locations include Tuzla; Sarajevo; Vicenza and Naples, Italy; Stuttgart, Germany; and NATO's central intelligence center in Molesworth, U.K.

MINE CLEARING

Many of the mine-clearing operations in Bosnia have been performed the old-fashioned way—on all fours. That's where a 7-ounce, 28-inch superhard titanium probe comes in handy. It handles the strain of lifting thick ice from mine fields better than fiberglass models.

Special forces teams are using about a hundred of the titanium probes—made by Mission Knives of San Juan Capistrano, California—to pinpoint the exact locations of mines and help extract them, after the mines are flagged by devices such as metal detectors and infrared cameras.

BODY ARMOR

Estimates of the number of land mines in Bosnia range from 1.7 million to 6 million. To protect mine clearance specialists, the Army has dispatched 180 sets of a new body armor system called BASIC (for Body Armor Set, Individual Countermine). It's a 20-pound ensemble consisting of spectacles or a face shield, trousers, and "overboots."

The spectacles and face shield have clear polycarbonate lenses that provide ballistic protection against small and slow-moving fragments. The nylon trousers are filled with Kevlar cloth—the stuff of bulletproof vests. Ankles and feet are protected by an improved version of snug overboots.

The overboot soles, made from thick rubber, have cleats that vent hot gases from exploding mines. An attenuator—a honeycombed metal plate molded into the sole—deflects the blast away from the foot. A Kevlar insole offers added protection.

This month, the Army plans to send 1,147 nylon vests to Bosnia to protect soldiers from snipers. Armor plates made from ceramic tiles slip into pockets on the front and back of each vest.

BLACK-BOX APACHES

The $12 million AH-64 Apache was designed to destroy Warsaw Pact armor with laser-guided Hellfire missiles.

But since December, six Apaches have been enforcing the peace with electronics instead of missiles.

The Apaches are fitted with black boxes, designed by PhotoTelesis of San Antonio, Texas, containing sensors that gather black-and-white analog images as the chopper hovers between two and five miles from an incident. The black boxes digitize the images and transmit four or five per minute over the helicopter's standard FM or UHF radio frequencies to ground stations.

A CODED CRY FOR HELP

Last year, Americans marveled at the survival smarts of downed Air Force Capt. Scott O'Grady but scoffed at the low-tech radios he carried. American rescue aircraft spent six days orbiting dangerous Serb air space hoping to make voice contact with O'Grady.

The downed airman carried a PRC-112 walkie-talkie and a handheld GPS unit, so he could tell rescuers his location. But he risked revealing his position to eavesdropping enemies. That risk has been eliminated with a new radio called Hook 112 from Motorola's Government and Space Technology Group in Scottsdale, Arizona.

It's loaded with a series of pre-coded distress messages that are transmitted in microsecond data bursts impossible to trace. The pilot can initiate a transmission, or messages can be sent automatically in response to electronic "interrogations" from transponders on orbiting American aircraft.

Within 30 minutes, the data burst is bounced off a spy satellite or specially equipped aircraft, transmitted to a ground station, and forwarded to a search-and-rescue center.

SHORTSTOP CATCHES INCOMING SHELLS

Before NATO and U.S. troops arrived, Bosnia's worst carnage was caused by artillery and mortar rounds. Mindful of this, the Army is using electronic Shortstops to confound incoming enemy shells.

Made by Whittaker of Simi Valley, California, the suitcase-size black boxes protect hospitals, airfields, and command posts by tricking incoming shells into premature detonation. A multidirectional antenna detects the signal given off by the proximity fuse of an incoming mortar or artillery round, then manipulates the signal and bounces it back to the round within microseconds. Believing it is at a lower altitude, the fuse detonates hundreds of meters above the target.

FOUR-LEGGED MINE DETECTORS

At least six K-9 Land Mine Detection Systems are in Bosnia. These dogs can find metal and plastic mines buried as deep as three inches. Handlers trail by about 10 meters as the dogs sniff one-meter lanes through dangerous terrain.

The K-9s are also trained to detect clear paths through a mine field to rescue a trapped soldier.

TAKING THE NIGHTMARE OUT OF LOGISTICS

The most unglamorous aspect of any military operation is logistics. But just as the "situational awareness" of battle commanders has been heightened by information technology, so has the logistician's tracking power. A prototype system known as the Logistics Anchor Desk pulls together computerized information from military bases all over the world. The network lets planners match current consumption data with projected trends to determine the amount of supplies needed.

Desk sets have been operating for months in Kaposvar, Hungary; and 1st Armored Division headquarters in Tuzla. Military planners in Europe used the Desk last December to calculate how many of the 10,000 soldiers deploying through Hungary would be there at any one time. The maximum number was 6,000. This prediction saved the Army about $1 million in unnecessary food, bedding, and fuel expenditures.

POCKET ENCYCLOPEDIA

The cliche about good things coming in small packages applies to 500 packages of computer disks distributed to military units deployed in Bosnia. Each three-disk set, running on Windows-based software, provides profiles of 36 different types of anti-tank and anti-personnel mines known to exist in Bosnia.

Called BosniaFile, the software includes a description of each weapon, a picture, the country of origin, metal content, fuse mechanism, shape, diameter, and weight. For example, with the computers that have been issued to each company of soldiers, a G.I. could learn that the cylindrical, plastic PMA-3 antipersonnel device has minimal metallic content that "does render [it] rather difficult to detect."

PICTURES ON DEMAND

One of the most innovative intelligence technologies supporting NATO comes from the national Reconnaissance Office, the secret agency that manages the nation's spy satellites. Called the Flyaway Contingency Package, it's a portable archive of normally top-secret spy-satellite images of Bosnia, with resolutions of one foot or better.

Using the stored images as reference points, military planners have been producing hundreds of custom-made maps with latitude and longitude grids overlaid on the spy imagery. The maps are comparable to the "triptiks" that the AAA prepares for vacationers planning car trips.

The imagery archive can be updated using a classified modem that taps into the spy community's Internet site, called Intell Link.

LASER TARGETING

During three years of NATO support for U.N. peacekeepers, the alliance provided troops for guiding air strikes. "Forward air controllers" literally talked pilots onto their targets. Now the U.S. Air Force has fielded a more advanced version of target location that cuts the chatter and increases accuracy. It's called Sure Strike.

Ground observers aiming a Laser Target Locator—made by Litton Data Systems of Agoura Hills, California—fire off a beam. The laser readings are then fed into a GPS receiver, and the target's coordinates are radioed to a circling F-16. The information generates a "target designation" box on the pilot's cockpit display. The whole process takes about 10 seconds.

Three sets of Sure Strike ground equipment are deployed with U.S. troops. Every F-16 fighter flying Bosnia missions is equipped to receive the information.

ROLLING ROBOT

Bosnia is the proving ground for Panther, a mine-detonating tank. It's a Vietnam-era M60A3 fitted with controls from Omnitech Robotics of Englewood, Colorado. Rollers that extend well beyond the vehicle chassis detonate mines out of reach of the tank's track and suspension. A soldier steers the teleoperated Panther using two cameras mounted on the tank. In May, the Omnitech system replaced a line-of-site kit that required the operator to trail in another vehicle about 500 meters away. U.S. troops are using seven Panthers in Bosnia.

DRESSED FOR WARMTH

Taking its cue from mountain climbers, the Army for years has fielded waterproof Goretex outerwear. Bosnia marks the first time the Army's Extended Cold Weather Clothing

System has been issued as a system of layered wear for an overseas military operation.

The five-layer clothing system, which has been tested successfully down to −60°F, weighs 30 percent less than cotton and wool clothing. The system consists of polypropylene underwear, a fiberpile shirt, nylon overalls, and a liner jacket. These garments are topped with a Goretex parka, hood, and face mask. Intermediate Cold Wet Gloves and Cold Wet Boots, made from Goretex with a Thermalite lining, round out the snowman ensemble.

HOMES AWAY FROM HOME

Joint Endeavor marks the coldest duty for U.S. troops since the Korean War. The Army was ready, deploying by early January the first of six 16-acre modular "tent cities" equipped with heated billets, warm showers, and flush toilets.

The tents provided a respite from the mud and cold U.S. troops encountered during the winter and spring. The modular shelters, erected from aluminum frames and polymer-impregnated fabric, are certified to withstand extreme temperatures ranging from −15°F to 120°F. The tents are equipped with heating and cooling ducts, and electrical outlets.

Each tent city houses 560 soldiers and allows 10-minute showers daily. A laundry system washes and dries up to 15 pounds of clean clothing per soldier every three days. Two modular kitchens per city cook three meals daily. "Morale, welfare, and recreation" facilities furnish diversions ranging from playing cards to TV-VCR units.

VIRTUAL TERRAIN

U.S. flyers who planned bombing runs over Serb territory last fall, and diplomats who later crafted the Dayton peace accord, used an embryonic form of virtual reality to rehearse missions and hash out the political boundaries NATO and U.S. troops enforce today. Called PowerScene, from Cambridge Research Associates in McLean, Virginia, the technology was also deployed with the 1st Armored Division to Tuzla last December.

On a computer terminal, PowerScene depicts the rolling Bosnian terrain in composite videos of commercial, tactical, and spy imagery. The Dayton zones of separation are laid over the terrain imagery. Looking at the land from a perspective 200 feet above the ground, Army terrain analysts preview traffic routes, potential hilltop observation-post locations, and artillery sites.

The PowerScene database contains 3-D digitized terrain elevation data similar to a cruise missile's memory

bank. The Army data depicts terrain elevations every 30 meters, or 100 feet. More than 80 percent of the Bosnian terrain has been digitized.

BATTLEFIELD VIDEOCONFERENCES

Video teleconferences have come of age during the Bosnia mission. During the Sava River bridging operation last December, U.S. engineers at the water's edge used high-resolution video teleconferencing gear from PictureTel of Danvers, Massachusetts, to talk with commanders marshaling troops in Europe. The teleconferences enabled commanders to distribute live video clips showing the extent of the flooding, the condition of roads and rail lines, and the status of equipment shipments. This spring, the 1st Armored Division's 1st and 2nd brigades also received video teleconferencing gear, giving NATO commanders the ability to hold conferences with field units.

The intelligence community has its own, more secure teleconferencing setup, called the Joint Worldwide Intelligence Communications System. Using this system, officials convened a videoconference in Washington, Germany, and Bosnia to decide whether to allow foreign intelligence officers to fly aboard an electronic warfare plane. The issue was resolved after a short discussion, instead of a week of phone calls and faxes.

HUMVEE VIEWS

The Humvee has served as a weapons carrier, ambulance, and jack-of-all-trades jeep. Now the ubiquitous vehicle has another use.

In Bosnia, the Army has converted several Humvees into Long Range Advance Scout Surveillance Systems. These vehicles have forward-looking infrared radar, high-resolution black-and-white cameras, laser range finders, digital compasses, and GPS receivers. The sensors are mounted on a pan-tilt unit that can be raised four meters.

Like the Apache helicopters converted into hovering peacekeepers, the Humvees can transmit four or five digitized pictures per minute over standard Army radios.

JSTARS IN ACTION

Between mid-December and late March, the Air Force's Joint Surveillance Target Attack Radar System (JSTARS) surveillance aircraft logged about 100 flights over Zagreb, Croatia, looking into Bosnia.

JSTARS is a refurbished Boeing 707 that uses a 24-foot-long, canoe-shaped phased-array radar to sweep a

12,400-square-mile area as it flies in a racetrack orbit. When a ground target is detected, the radar signal is processed and displayed on one of 10 JSTARS workstations aboard the aircraft.

Potential moving targets are color-coded into dots: magenta for wheeled vehicles, powder blue for parked, yellow for potential tracked vehicles. The radar images are fired off instantly to ground stations in Sarajevo, Tuzla, Hungary, and NATO's air operations center near Venice.

One of JSTARS' Bosnia missions was to monitor movements around mass grave sites in the northwest areas of Serbheld Bosnia. The radar was programmed to "revisit" a small path around Prijedor every 30 seconds and record movement. Pilots later learned the "sector search" was commissioned by the International War Crimes Tribunal.

SILENT SENTINEL

Special operations forces are using the Remotely Monitored Battlefield Sensor System to covertly monitor traffic. Made by Lockheed Martin, the 35-pound device contains magnetic, passive infrared, and seismic sensors that detect passing vehicles and people. The sensors transmit radio signals to a station up to 15 kilometers away. The signals identify passersby as humans or vehicles, and relay their direction of movement.

Joint Endeavor marks only the second time since the Gulf War that the system has been used in a real-world operation. The Army is also deploying a lighter version that weighs about seven pounds.

SAY IT IN SERBO-CROATIAN

Hoping to solve the vexing problem of translating Serbo-Croatian documents into English, the Army has fielded five briefcase-size Forward Area Language Converters. Each $15,000 system pairs a portable computer with a scanner for text-to-text translations.

For conversations, the Defense Advanced Research Projects Agency created a $1.5 million laptop system that focuses on key phrases but is limited to one-way translation of English into Serbo-Croatian. Soldiers use it at checkpoints and when talking to locals about mine sites.

PREVENTING FRIENDLY FIRE

More U.S. troops were killed during the Gulf War by so-called "friendly fire" than by Iraqi bullets. To prevent a grim repeat, more than 1,200 sets of Thermal Combat ID Panels have been sent to Bosnia. The panels, which are covered with thermal tape, are attached to vehicles with Velcro fasteners. The panels show up as cold spots, giving the vehicles distinctive signatures that are obvious to U.S. troops viewing them through thermal sights.

Questions

1. What does the term "situational awareness" mean with regard to warfare? What types of technologies does it involve?
2. Describe the role of JSTARS in warfare. How might JSTARS be part of a "situational awareness" strategy?
3. Describe how Combat Thermal ID panels might prevent cases of "friendly fire."
4. How are video infrared cameras used to detect land mines?
5. What technologies are available to detect mines with minimal metallic content?
6. How has the Humvee been refitted to serve in Bosnia?

Case Study: Friendly Fire: The Gulf War

35

At 3:00 p.m. on February 26, 1991, elements of the British First Armored Division were crossing the Iraqi desert during the early stages of Operation Desert Storm. In bad weather and poor visibility two British Warrior armored personnel vehicles of that division were attacked by two American A-10 tankbuster aircraft. Nine British soldiers were killed. Friendly fire, the incident of allied forces firing on each other, had claimed more victims. How had it happened?

Even before the start of Desert Storm, Coalition force commanders had been acutely aware of the possibilities of friendly fire incidents. With thousands of allied armor encountering Iraqi forces across hundreds of miles of desert and with close air support a vital part of allied superiority, identification was bound to be a problem. In order to reduce the chances of a mistake by allied aircraft, a system of orange and green recognition panels were introduced, as were huge inverted "V" markers, at least six feet high, painted on the sides of the tanks and on their turrets. The system was tested for aerial visibility and found to be effective.

In the opening stages of the ground war, the British First Armored Division was supposed to outflank Iraqi forces by first heading north, and then turning east to close in on Kuwait. The mission was proceeding smoothly, and by 2:00 p.m. on February 26 eighty Iraqi vehicles had been destroyed. At the time of the attack by the American planes, C Company, including 8th Platoon was in the

process of blowing up some captured Iraqi field artillery. Moments after the charges had been placed and the men had returned to the safety of their armored personnel carriers, two of the vehicles were attacked by two A-10 tankbusters, firing Maverick missiles. The attack took place despite the fact that British vehicles were carrying the brightly colored fluorescent panels as well as the large freshly painted V identification signs. The pilots of the A-10's also had at their disposal high powered binoculars for better identification of their targets. How then could the pilots later claim they thought they were attacking Iraqi T-54 tanks?

Before going any further, it's important to remember the problem facing American aircraft was that the situation on the ground was changing by the hour. With no fixed battle front, the speed of the allied advance had spread Coalition forces across an enormous area of desert. The two A-10's had first contacted one of the AWACS (Airborne Warning And Control) planes to give them a target. After a fruitless search they contacted a forward air controller handling air-ground support in the area of the British First Armored Division. At roughly the same time the pilots began talking to an F-16 pilot who told them of targets off to the east. The A-10's, following the F-16 pilot's instructions, set off looking for a crossroads as he had described. The problem was that the desert was crisscrossed with crossroads, and the A-10's couldn't be sure which one was the right one. Ultimately, the pilots found a crossroads which appeared to have targets of opportunity, made their runs and headed south until they came upon a target consisting of about fifty vehicles. They claimed the British air controller had assured them there were no friendly vehicles within their area of operations. They further claimed that by using their binoculars and making two passes over the target they confirmed the fact the vehicles were in fact Iraqi. They were adamant that there were no Coalition markings on the vehicles they attacked. And, without contacting the air controller for confirmation of the grid reference of the proposed target, they attacked. Nine British soldiers were killed, and to this day many questions remain unanswered.

Questions

1. What steps did Allied commanders take to prevent friendly fire attack on armored vehicles and ground personnel?
2. The pilots claim that ground controllers assured them that no Allied personnel were in their vicinity. Therefore, should the ground controllers share the blame for this accident?
3. How would you prevent this and other incidents like it from happening again?

A Bridge to Your 21st Century Understanding

Complete and discuss the following flowchart.

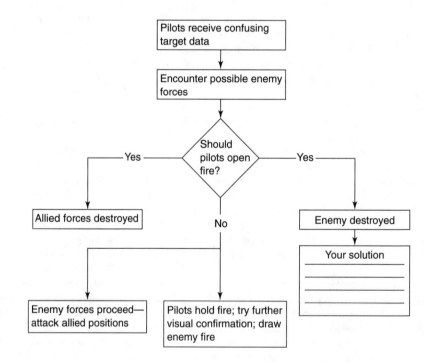

Case Study: The Thresher Tragedy

36

On April 10, 1963, the USS Thresher, an advanced American nuclear-powered submarine, attempted to dive to its maximum operating depth of 10,000 feet. The Thresher never surfaced. Her entire crew of 129 men died in an accident whose cause remains largely undetermined. However, many experts believe carelessness and rushed construction may have contributed to an accident which prevented the Thresher from pulling out of her dive.

Launched on July 9, 1960, the USS Thresher was the first of an advanced class of attack nuclear-powered submarines. Submerged, she could achieve speeds of 30 knots or better, and could go deeper than any previous sub. The Thresher and those like her were to be true submarines, designed to spend long periods of time under water.

During sea trials, however, the Thresher was subjected to a number of problems. On April 30, 1961 the captain ordered a dive. As it descended, instruments suddenly began indicating that the sub was near the pressure limit that the hull could withstand, although all other indicators confirmed that the Thresher was not even approaching its maximum depth. The sub sailed back to drydock, where the instruments were checked and found to have been faulty.

Sea trials resumed in February, 1962, as the Thresher underwent shock tests to determine its ability to withstand underwater explosions. Although it suffered some damage during the four month trial, the submarine passed all the shock tests and went into drydock for nine months of complete overhauls.

On April 9, 1963 the Thresher went out to sea for a series of shallow test dives. After these trials the submarine crossed the Georges Bank area of the Atlantic and into truly deep waters. On the morning of April 10, the Thresher began a depth dive. By 8:53 A.M. the sub had approached its test depth of nearly 10,000 feet. At 9:13 A.M. communication between the Thresher and the Skylark, a submarine rescue ship became garbled. Between 9:14 and 9:17 disaster struck. During those minutes the communications personnel on the Skylark heard the words "test depth," just prior to a muted dull thud. Within a few hours it became apparent the Thresher must have exceeded its design depth and imploded.

A Court of Inquiry was convened to make an official determination as to the cause of the accident. The Court reported that most likely the accident was caused by a cracked fitting in a cooling pipe. Such a break would have filled a small compartment with water, shorting out a power circuit and possibly causing the nuclear reactor to shut down making it impossible to stop the dive. However, during the Court's inquiry, a number of unsettling facts about the history of the rushed construction of the Thresher came to light. Its periscope control had been installed backwards. A spike was found in its air circulation system. At least 20 percent of its hydraulic valves were found to have their 'open' and 'close' indicators reversed. Fourteen percent of 145 pipe joints tested were found to be below standard, and over 2,800 pipe joints were never tested. Still, the Thresher was launched.

The tragedy led the Navy to reevaluate its shipyard quality control procedures, install mechanical values to back up electric ones on its submarines, and perfect a

Schlager, Neil, ed., *When Technology Fails,* Detroit: Gale Research, 1994. Reproduced by permission.

291

ballast expulsion system faster and more powerful than that found on the Thresher.

Questions

1. What early indications signaled that the Thresher was not a seaworthy craft? Identify at least two flaws found in the construction of the Thresher.

2. Discuss the accident from the perspective of liability. Who is responsible? The company who built the submarine? The Navy? The captain of the Thresher?

3. How did the Thresher tragedy change the Navy's construction policies?

A Bridge to Your 21st Century Understanding

Complete and discuss the following flowchart.

Conclusion: A Kinder, Gentler War?

If I knew what they were going to do with this, I would have become a shoemaker!
ALBERT EINSTEIN, AFTER DISCOVERING THAT THE ATOMIC BOMB WAS DROPPED ON HIROSHIMA

This chapter has examined the impact of technology on the making of war. Several things should be evident. First, it should be clear that changes in technology have changed the way in which nations have approached warfare. The cost and complexity of new weapons mean that nations now dash less and deliberate more before entering conflict. In fact, cost alone should be reason enough for pause. As the price of weapons technology climbs, nations operating on a guns-or-butter economy have to decide if having a particular weapon is worth imposing a degree of economic hardship on citizens. Equally important is the question of whether that nation's population would tolerate those hardships for any period of time. Military technology is often acquired because it's believed that it will give one side a distinct advantage over another. But it's often not long before both sides have the technology, and the momentary initiative fades into the carnage produced by stalemate. If you have ever read any early 20th-century history, you might remember just how traumatic an impact technology had on World War I. Poison gas, the airplane, the tank, and the machine gun helped reduce the conflict to a bloody deadlock, which was resolved only when the United States committed enough of its own resources to turn the tide in the Allies' favor. Along the way, though, nations, political systems, and economies groaned and sagged under the costs of war. Some collapsed, some survived, but none ended up the same. In fact, the experience of war and the technology it featured prompted many nations to reassess their role in world affairs. Some nations—the United States, for example—scaled back on military technology, certain that one way to stay out of future conflicts was to refrain from developing systems that made it a likely opponent. There are other, more modern examples of the dubious advantages of military technology. In 1945, the United States was in sole possession of the atomic bomb, which would, it was thought, justify American beliefs that the postwar years would truly be "The American Century." A few years later, however, the Soviet Union exploded its first atomic device. Since then, billions of dollars have been spent amassing enough high-tech weapons to ensure victory in a war that never came. But one war that was lost was the war to improve the quality of life of people. Dollars spent on bombs often meant less for schools, children, the elderly, the environment, or any one of a dozen important domestic issues.

The complexity of these weapons technologies has imposed an additional burden on society. Complicated weapons cannot be left in the hands of temporary, civilian fighting forces, assembled only in times of national crisis. Large, permanent armies would have to be created, dependent upon taxpayer support and tied to commercial interests that have sprung up to produce and sell even newer technologies to them. In time, this alliance of businessmen and generals fused to become what today is known as the military–industrial complex, a well-organized system that has been able to survive and prosper by wielding enormous influence in economic and political circles, as well as by exploiting citizen anxiety that failure to buy this military technology will leave the nation unprepared for some crisis, as yet unknown and unseen. More often than not, this system has been successful in getting what it wants. But its successes have often happened in days when money was plentiful and most needs, social as well as military, could be met. Success could also be attributed to the fact that those times featured a tangible adversary: the Soviet Union. But times have since changed. There is an Evil Empire no longer. And so, just as spending limits have been imposed upon social needs, the time has also come to rein in spending on military technologies. A degree of social restraint and social responsibility should be exercised in the area of military technology. Perhaps, we have reached a point at which having the latest and most expensive technology is no guarantee of success. Rather, the responsible use of existing technology—and the careful, deliberate selection of new technologies—may be the key.

The next part of the book is about exercising social responsibility in the area of technology use. Some of the chapters are about people speaking out about the use or misuse of a technology. Others describe cases for which a specific technology has failed and people either died or were seriously hurt as a result. It is important to remember that technology is rarely applied for the intended purpose of causing people pain. The pain occurs when the technology is either the wrong type for the situation or when it is in the hands of people who do not know how to use it.

Internet Exercise

1. Use any of the Internet search engines (e.g., Alta Vista, Yahoo, Infoseek, etc.) to research the following topics:

   a. A diagram and specifications of the F-22.

   b. A diagram and specifications of the A-10.

   c. The amount of money the United States spent last year on defense.

   d. The amount of money spent on defense last year by any two of the following nations:

      i. Russia

      ii. China

      iii. Saudi Arabia

2. Use any of the Internet search engines (e.g., Alta Vista, Yahoo, Infoseek, etc.) to research the following topics:

   a. A diagram and specifications of the M1A1 Tank.

   b. A diagram—with specifications, if available—of any World War II tank. How does the World War II tank compare with the M1A1 in terms of the following factors?

      i. speed

      ii. crew size

      iii. weapons

      iv. weight

3.   Complete the following table:

Gulf War	
What kinds of advanced weapons were used in the Gulf War?	
How many bombs (kilotons) were dropped during the war?	
How many allied soldiers were killed during the war?	
How many Iraqi soldiers were killed during the war?	
How many Iraqi civilians died during the war?	
How many Iraqi children died due to economic sanctions?	
Why was the Gulf War fought?	
Discuss the impact of technology on the outcome of the war.	

Useful Web Sites

URL	Description
http://www.military-info.com/index.htm	Military information
www.sipri.se	Worldwide military spending
www.lib.umich.edu/libhome/Documents.center/stats.html	Military statistics
www.amsus.org	Military medicine page
www.ucg.com	Defense/military database
www.jstor.org	Journal of military history
www.militaria.com	Web military bookshelf
www.dtic.mil/nms.html	National military strategy
www.psi-research.com	Military and historical links
www.cfcsc.dnd.ca	War, peace, and security www links

PART

VI

Social Responsibility

The explosion of the Challenger. What part did social responsibility play in this disaster?
Courtesy AP/Wide World Photos

Every technology is both a burden and a blessing; not either-or, but this-and-that.

NEIL POSTMAN, AUTHOR, Technopoly: *The Surrender of Culture to Society*

As technologies are embraced as "blessings," this part resonates concerns that techno-users need to partake with immense responsibility so that newly developed technologies will not mature into societal burdens. Technology is more than a mechanism or tool; it is also a catalyst for societal changes. Once technology is introduced, life, thinking, behavior, and social norms change. When cars, microwaves, computers, birth-control pills, penicillin, and other technologies were invented, life as we knew it drastically changed. Our point of reference changed, and our behaviors were altered. With the advent of technology, we arrive places faster, communicate globally, cook quickly, and even look to medical technologies to get us to sleep swiftly. Technologies have been invented, for the most part, to make life "better," but do they also carry a societal or psychological cost?

For hundreds of years, the Kaiapo Indians of the lower Amazon basin were considered to be "skilled farmers and hunters and the fiercest warriors of central Brazil" (Henslin; Simons, 1995, p. 463). They eventually sold gold and mahogany and became a wealthy village. With the newfound wealth, Chief Kanhonk bought a small satellite, which the Indians called the "big ghost," so that they could watch television. Prior to the satellite purchase, the Kaiapos would meet at night to tell stories and share ancestral customs. After the purchase of the satellite, however, children were found straying from their ancestral story-telling traditions to watch Western cartoons instead (Henslin 1995, 464). When studying various cultures, we often find that each has its own story to tell about the impact of technology on the lives, culture, and values of its people.

As technology permeates through all cultures and timespans, sociological and behavioral adaptations develop. For example, in the 1930s, many American children surrounded the radio in their living room to let their imaginations go while listening to Orphan Annie, Terry and the Pirates, or Jack Armstrong and the All American Boy. The words emitted from the radio allowed children to create the characters and backgrounds within the world of their imaginations. No visual cues limited what their minds created. This all changed for their children when television dominated the living rooms of the 1950s. Children no longer relied on their imaginations, as the television presented every visual and auditory detail. Additionally, parents worried that their kids would end up with damaged eyes or receive large amounts of radiation from sitting too close to the television.

This part of the book, on social responsibility, discusses the link between technology and its implications for society. Many of the cases and articles presented within this part provide discussion on more serious issues than those faced by the Kaiapos or American children in the 1930s and 1950s. But the issues remain the same: With each technology introduced at any time in any culture, adaptations seem to follow. Many of the cases presented in this part encourage users of technology to evaluate the technologies with respect and with their own analyses of personal and social responsibility.

Most technologies work to provide progress to those who use them. However, there are times when technologies are misused and harm or death befalls their users. Therefore, it is befitting to start this part of the book with a chapter about ethics and to enhance this concept by correlating ethics to human responsibility and action in the next article, on whistle-blowing. Whistle-blowing is a moral process of telling authorities that harm might occur if changes are not made. When one decides to blow the whistle, he or she is making a personal decision to prevent improper behaviors, often related to the use of technology, from being used in a way that could have a negative impact on others. In this part of the book, cases on the whistle-blowing of Roger Boisjoly and the "nuclear warriors" are presented, followed by the technoethical cases of the Molasses Spill and the Bhopal disaster. This part ends with an exploration of the effects of cybercrime.

As we bridge our way into a new century and prepare to hand our world over to a younger generation, it will be important to consistently evaluate the technologies that we use and their impact on society and the world in which we live. This part of the book supports that endeavor.

References

Henslin, J. (1996) *Sociology: A down-to-earth approach.* Needham Heights, MA. Allyn and Bacon.
Simons, Marlise. (1995) "The Amazon's savvy Indians." *Down to earth sociology: Introductory readings.* 8th ed. New York, Free Press.

It would be a nice world if efficient processes were moral. I don't think that's been the history of the 19th and 20th Centuries. There is such a thing as morality, and morality is higher than economics.

UNIVERSITY OF CHICAGO PROFESSOR ROBERT FOGEL,
ASSESSING THE RESEARCH FINDINGS THAT WON
HIM THE NOBEL PRIZE IN ECONOMIC SCIENCE

37 Ethics

ROBERT McGINN

INTRODUCTION

For at least the last two decades, many of the most divisive ethical issues debated in Western societies have been precipitated by developments in science and technology, including advances in reproductive, genetic, weapons, and life-prolonging technologies. The adoption and alteration of public policy for regulating science- or technology-intensive practices, such as the provision of access to exotic medical treatment, the disposal of toxic waste, and the invasion of individual privacy, have also raised perplexing ethical issues. This chapter is devoted to the analysis of such conflicts.

There is no universally shared criterion for deciding when a conflict of values falls within the province of ethics rather than, say, law. However, the issues and conflicts discussed in this chapter involve values widely regarded as integral to the enterprise of ethics in contemporary Western societies; such values include freedom, justice, and human rights such as privacy. Disputes over whether an agent's freedom should be limited prospectively or its prior exercise punished, whether justice has been denied or done to some party, or whether someone's human rights have been protected or violated, are widely regarded in Western societies as specifically *ethical* disagreements, thus marking them as human value issues or conflicts of special importance in these societies.

As a prelude to analysis of science- or technology-based ethical issues, we will describe a quartet of basic

Science, Technology and Society by McGinn, Robert © 1991. Reprinted by permission of Prentice-Hall, Inc., Upper Saddle River, N.J.

considerations centrally involved in judgments about and the playing out of such conflicts. We will then characterize and analyze a number of important *kinds* of ethical issues and conflicts associated with contemporary science and technology. Where appropriate, we will indicate noteworthy sociocultural factors that, in concert with the technical developments in question, help generate the issue or conflict. All this will pave the way for a key conclusion reached in this chapter: that developments in contemporary science and technology are calling into question the adequacy of traditional ethical thinking. A more comprehensive and sensitive kind of ethical analysis is now required, one more adequate to the complexity and consequences of contemporary scientific and technological processes and products.

CLARIFICATION OF ETHICAL ISSUES AND CONFLICTS

Ethical issues and conflicts, whether or not they are associated with developments in science and technology, can often be usefully clarified if four kinds of considerations pertinent to ethical decision- and judgment-making about controversial actions, practices, and policies are kept in mind.[1]

The Facts of the Matter

One consideration is that of determining, as scrupulously as possible, the facts of the situation underlying or surrounding the conflict in question. Doing so may require ferreting out and scrutinizing purportedly factual assumptions and allegedly empirical claims made by disputants about the conflict situation in question. It may also require ascertaining whether any persuasive accounts of the facts of the matter have been developed by neutral parties. In such efforts, important concerns include unmasking pseudo-facts and factoids posing as bona fide facts, ensuring that the credibility attributed to an account of the facts reflects the reputation and interests of its source, and setting the strength of the evidence required to warrant acceptance of an account of the facts at a level proportional to the gravity of the issue or conflict in question.

Affected Patients and Their Interests

A second kind of clarificatory consideration in thinking about an ethical issue or conflict is that of identifying all pertinent "patients"—that is, all affected parties with a legitimate stake in the outcome of the dispute. Further, all protectable interests of each stakeholder should be delineated and their relative weights carefully and impartially assigned.

Key Concepts, Criteria, and Principles

A third kind of consideration is that of identifying the key concepts, criteria, and principles in terms of which the ethical issue or conflict in question is formulated or debated. For example, the abortion issue hinges critically on the protagonists' respective concepts of what it is to be a "human being" and a "person" as well as what is meant by a "viable" fetus. The ethical (and legal) debate over the withdrawal of technological life-support systems turns sharply on what is meant by "killing" someone as well as on which criteria implicitly or explicitly govern protagonists' use of the key terms "voluntary consent" (to withdrawal or withholding of treatment) and "death."

Ethical Theories and Arguments

A fourth kind of basic consideration to be kept clearly in mind is that ethical disputes often involve two quite distinct kinds of decision-making theories and arguments. *Consequentialist* ethical theories and arguments make determination of the rightness or wrongness of actions and policies hinge exclusively on their estimated *consequences*. The most familiar consequentialist ethical theory is utilitarianism—the view that an action or policy is right if and only if it is likely to produce at least as great a surplus of good over bad, or evil, consequences as any avail-

able alternative. There are different versions of utilitarianism, depending on, among other things, what a given thinker understands by "good" and "bad," or "evil," consequences. For example, so-called hedonic utilitarians, of whom nineteenth century British reformer Jeremy Bentham is perhaps the best known, took pleasure to be the only good, and pain the only bad, or evil. "Ideal utilitarians," such as the early twentieth century British philosopher G. E. Moore, construed "good" and "bad" quite differently, including things like friendship and beauty among goods and their absence or opposites, such as alienation and ugliness, among bads, or evils.[2]

The second kind of ethical theory and argument that often enters into ethical disputes is called deontological. *Deontological* ethical theories and judgments hold that certain actions or practices are inherently or intrinsically right or wrong—that is, right or wrong in themselves, independent of any consideration of their consequences. Different deontological theorists and thinkers point to different things about actions and policies, in light of which they are judged to be right or wrong. Some point to supposedly intrinsic moral properties of actions and policies falling into one or another category. For example, actions such as telling a lie or breaking a promise may be regarded as intrinsically wrong. Others emphasize that a certain course of action is obligatory or impermissible because it is approved or disapproved, or unconditionally mandated or prohibited by some authority, perhaps a deity. As we will see in this chapter, several of the most important kinds of ethical issues and conflicts engendered by developments in science and technology arise from or are exacerbated by the fact that partisans of one position on an issue are consequentialists while their opponents are deontological thinkers (for convenience, deontologists).*

KINDS OF SCIENCE-OR-TECHNOLOGY-BASED ETHICAL ISSUES AND CONFLICTS

We now turn to examination of science- and technology-based ethical issues and conflicts. Given the purpose of this book, our objective here will not be to provide detailed discussions of—much less solutions to—even a select number of the long list of such problems. Rather, we will

---

* In reality, the ethical thinking of denizens of contemporary industrial societies is rarely so black and white. It often incorporates consequentialist, deontological, and perhaps other considerations in uneasy or unstable combinations.

identify and critically analyze the limited number of qualitatively distinct kinds of such disputes. (Eight are considered here.) The aforementioned quartet of basic concerns—facts; patients and interests; concepts, criteria, principles; and ethical theories and arguments—will be used to shed light on the sociotechnical roots and intractability of many of these problems.

Violations of Established World Orders

Some ethical conflicts arise from the fact that scientific or technological breakthroughs make possible actions or practices that, in spite of what some see as their benefits, others believe violate some established order of things whose preservation matters greatly to them. The order of things in question may be regarded as "natural" or as "sacred."

For example, much opposition to recent achievements in biomedicine and genetic engineering flows from beliefs that employing such techniques is *unnatural*. Thus some oppose the technique of *in vitro* fertilization as involving the unnatural separation of human reproduction from sexual intercourse. In a similar vein, the production of farm animals with genes from at least two different animal species ("transgenic animals") is viewed by some critics as a transgression of natural animal-species boundaries, while the use of genetically mass-produced bovine growth hormones to substantially increase the volume of milk produced by cows is opposed by some as "chang[ing] the natural behavior of animals" or as "interrupt[ing] the naturalness of [farmers'] environment."[3]

Opposition to technological violations of natural orders is, however, sometimes based on concern about the long-term consequences of intervention for human or other animal well-being or for ecosystem integrity. For example, some oppose the production of transgenic animals because they believe that the resultant animals will suffer physically as a result of being maladapted. Similarly, some critics of the use of bovine growth hormone to raise milk production levels are primarily concerned with the safety of such milk for young children. The plausibility of such consequentialist ethical thinking hinges on the details of the particular case under consideration, including the estimated magnitudes, likelihoods, and reversibility of the projected consequences of intervention.

Deontological ethical arguments against such intervention as intrinsically wrong take two forms. First, the intervention-free order of nature is regarded as natural and intrinsically "good," while technology is not viewed as part of the natural order but rather as artificial. Therefore, it is concluded, attempts to use technology to intervene in the

natural order are improper. A second argument notes that something has existed or has been done in the so-called natural way from time immemorial and concludes that therefore it should be done or continue to be done in that same way—without technological intervention. Is either the "unnaturalness" or the "longevity" argument persuasive?

It is unclear why the development and transformative use of technology on nature should be seen as "unnatural." The claim that because God created the natural order it should not be "tampered with" by humans is suspect for two reasons. Those holding this idea presumably also believe that the human being was created by the deity, in which case the human is no less "natural" a creation than the "natural order" and indeed is properly regarded as part of that order. Moreover, they also presumably believe that God endowed humans with creative powers, including the ability to devise technics, thereby enabling them to intervene in the natural order. If so, why is it unnatural for natural creatures to use their God-given powers to intervene in the natural order? It seems implausible that the deity would endow its natural creatures with an unnatural power or with a power whose use was unnatural. If it is not the very use of technology to transform nature that is unnatural but only certain uses of it, then these opponents of technological violations of natural orders must clarify what it is that makes some technological interventions "violations" of those orders and others simply harmonious interventions in them.

As for the argument that the existing way of doing something is the proper way because of its longevity, it too fails to convince. That a practice is long-standing may make it familiar or seem natural. But long-standingness cannot by itself justify the view that the practice is proper. That would be drawing an *evaluative* conclusion from a purely *factual* premise. Conversely, a particular technological intervention in a long-established natural order might initially be resisted because it is unfamiliar or deemed unnatural. However, the fact that something runs counter to a long-standing practice does not suffice to show that it is improper. If that were so, then the abolition of slavery would have been improper. In fact, opposition to a practice initially regarded as unnatural because of its novelty or strangeness often diminishes over time as the new way becomes increasingly familiar. Some innovative technical practices eventually come to seem natural and quite proper, as has been the case with the use of antibiotics.

Is there, then, nothing to the concerns about technological violations of established orders as unnatural? Even if the deontological arguments examined here fail to hold water, the concerns they express still warrant serious consideration, for deontological thinking and argument are sometimes disguised or compressed versions of what are at bottom consequentialist thinking and argument. Reference to an innovative practice as unnatural and therefore as intrinsically wrong may be a powerful if deeply misleading way of expressing concern over its possible elusive long-term consequences.

Other scientific and technological developments have made possible practices that are seen by some groups as violations of world orders viewed not so much as natural but as *sacred*. Thus, in the Hasidic community centered in Brooklyn, New York, birth control is forbidden, supposedly on the basis of the Torah.[4] For the Wahabi, a fundamentalist Arabian Muslim sect, television, with its image-reproducing capacity, violates the sacred order related in the Koran. Opposition to certain technologies or technological ways of doing things as violations of sacred orders is less likely to ebb in the minds of such opponents, for the sacred way is apt to be regarded as God's way and, as such, as immutable and thus as something that ought not adapt itself to human technological change.

Violations of Supposedly Exceptionless Moral Principles

Other ethical issues arise from the fact that the use, failure to use, or withdrawal of particular scientific procedures or items of technology is seen by some as violating one or another important moral principle that its adherents believe to be exceptionless. For example, some people are categorically opposed to nuclear weapons on the grounds that their use will inevitably violate the supposedly exceptionless principle that any course of action sure to result in the destruction of innocent civilian lives in time of war is ethically impermissible.

Similarly, the supposedly exceptionless principle that "life must never, under any circumstances, be taken"—put differently, that "life must always be preserved"—is clearly an important ground of the categorical judgment that withdrawal of life-sustaining technologies, whether mechanical respirators or feeding and hydration tubes, is ethically wrong. A third example is the opposition by some to the "harvesting" of fetal tissue for use in treating Parkinson's or Alzheimer's disease, even in a relative. This opposition is often rooted in the supposedly exceptionless principle that "a human being must never be treated merely as a means to some other end, however worthwhile in itself."

Sociologically, opposition to certain scientific and technological developments on the grounds that they involve or may involve violations of some special order of things or some supposedly exceptionless moral principle, reflects a fundamental fact about modern Western industrial societies. While much has been written about their secularization, there remain in such societies significant numbers of people whose ethical thinking is deontological in character, whether or not religiously grounded.

The world views of such individuals contain categories of actions that are strictly forbidden or commanded. For them, the last word on a particular science- or technology-based ethical issue or conflict sometimes hinges solely on whether the action or practice in question falls into one or another prescribed or proscribed category. While deontological thinkers may resort strategically to consequentialist arguments in attempting to change the views of consequentialist opponents, the latter's arguments against their adversaries' deontologically grounded positions usually fall on deaf ears, however well documented the empirical claims brought forward as evidence. Deontological fundamentalists and consequentialist seculars are, in their ethical judgment and decision making, mutual cultural strangers.

An interesting consequence of deontological appeals to supposedly exceptionless moral principles in the context of potent contemporary technologies is the appearance of moral paradoxes. For example, Gregory Kavka has shown that the situation of nuclear deterrence undermines the venerable, supposedly exceptionless "wrongful intention principle"—namely, the principle that "to form the intention to do what one knows to be wrong is itself wrong."[5] Launching a nuclear strike might well be ethically wrong (because of the foreseeable loss of innocent civilian lives). But what about forming the intention to do so if attacked? According to the wrongful intention principle, forming the intention to carry out that wrong action would itself be *wrong*. However, since forming that intention might well be necessary to deter an attack and thus to avoid launching an impermissible retaliatory strike, it might well be ethically *right*. One and the same action—that of forming the intention to retaliate—is therefore both right and wrong, a moral paradox. Thus can technological developments compel reassessment of supposedly exceptionless ethical principles.

Distributions of Science- or Technology-Related Benefits

Some contemporary ethical issues and conflicts arise from the fact that the benefits of developments in science and technology are allocated in ways that do not seem equitable to one or another social group. This is particularly so with respect to medical benefits, whether they be diagnostic tests, surgical procedures, or therapeutic drugs, devices, or services.

Concerns over whether an allocation of such benefits is "distributively just" often emerge when demand for the benefit exceeds its supply and decisions must be made about who will receive the benefit and who will not—sometimes tantamount to deciding "who shall live and who shall die." For example, in the early 1960s, the supply of dialysis units available to the Artificial Kidney Center in Seattle, Washington, was insufficient to meet the needs of those with failed kidneys.[6] Criteria were selected to use in deciding who would be granted access to this beneficial scarce technical resource. Today, the demand for various kinds of human organs often exceeds available supplies. The criterion of "need" is thus by itself insufficient to make allocation decisions. Criteria such as "likelihood of realizing a physiologically successful outcome" seem promising, but are quite problematic, for, as Ronald Munson has argued,

> [T]he characteristics required to make someone a "successful" dialysis patient are to some extent "middle-class virtues." A patient must not only be motivated to save his life, but he must also understand the need for the dialysis, be capable of adhering to a strict diet, show up for scheduled dialysis sessions, and so on. As a consequence, where decisions about whether to admit a patient to dialysis are based on the estimates of the likelihood of a patient's doing what is required, members of the white middle class have a definite edge over others. Selection criteria that are apparently objective may actually involve hidden class or racial bias.[7]

Other criteria, such as "probable post-treatment quality of life" and "past or likely future contribution of the treatment candidate to the community" are no less problematic. Hence, some believe that for such allocations to be distributively just, once need and physiological compatability have been established, a lottery should determine access to the scarce benefit.

On other occasions, it is not the shortage but the high cost of a medical treatment and the inability of all needy patients who want the treatment to afford it that engenders ethical conflict. Science and technology are often central factors in these high costs, for such costs may reflect the high purchase price of a machine or drug paid by a care unit, something which may in turn reflect the device's or substance's high research and development costs. Such situations help pose the contentious ethical issue of whether access to some needed expensive drug or procedure should be permitted to hinge on whether a prospective patient can afford to pay the going market price.

Deontological ethical thinkers who have come to think of medical care as a basic human right may find it morally unthinkable that a person be denied access to such treatment simply because of not being able to afford it (or because, for example, of being "too old"). In contrast, consequentialists, some of whom find the concept of an "absolute right" potentially dangerous, may believe that a particular technically exotic treatment is so expensive that granting everyone in life-or-death need unlimited access to it will effectively preclude many more individuals from getting less expensive, more beneficial, non-life-or-death treatments. Diverging accounts of "the facts of the matter" and different criteria for what makes a treatment "exotic" often bulk large in such judgments.

Consequentialists are apt to believe that individuals do *not* have a moral right to draw without limit on public or insurance-company funds to have their or their family members' lives extended regardless of the quality of the sustained life and the prognosis for its improvement. They may even hold that the financial and social consequences of doing so create a moral obligation to *terminate* such treatment, or at least to cease drawing on public funds to pay for continued treatment. In such ways have advances in science and technology as well as people's varying concepts (e.g., of a life worth living) and divergent ethical theories become intertwined in complex ethical disputes over distributive justice, rights, and obligations.

Infliction of Harm or Exposure to Significant Risk of Harm Without Prior Consent

A fourth category of ethical issues and conflicts engendered by developments in science and technology arises from activities that, while undertaken to benefit one group, inflict harm or impose significant risk of harm on another without the latter's prior consent. Examples of this sort of phenomenon abound and include some research on animals; production of cross-border and multi-generational pollution; the maintenance of carcinogen-containing workplaces; and the operation of "hair-trigger" military defense systems. As with earlier categories, the ethical issues and conflicts here have both technical and social roots.

Most parties to such disputes would agree that, other things being equal, it is always unethical to subject a morally pertinent party to undeserved harm or serious risk of same without the party's freely given prior consent. Let us examine how the consent issue plays out in the four above-mentioned kinds of cases.

In laboratory experimentation on sentient animals, the issue of consent bulks large in the persistent ethical conflict. Consequentialist proponents hold, on cost-benefit grounds, that activities that promise future benefits (including avoidance of suffering) for humans but that (supposedly unavoidably) inflict suffering on existing animals are ethically permissible, perhaps even obligatory. Those carrying out such activities may proceed because since animals cannot consent to anything, they are different in a morally relevant respect from human beings.[8] Hence the consent condition, precluding similar treatment of humans, is, in the case of animals, legitimately waived. Some opponents of such research, often deontologists, also subscribe to the prior-consent principle, but they see animals such as rabbits and monkeys as no less morally relevant patients than are humans. They draw a diametrically different conclusion: Since the consent of laboratory animals cannot be obtained, research activity that produces suffering for animals is ethically wrong or impermissible, even if the suffering is "unavoidable"—computer models that make animal tests unnecessary may not be available—and the benefits of the research could plausibly be shown to exceed its costs. It is not difficult to see why resolution of this disagreement is unlikely to be forthcoming.

Explanation of the rise of ethical conflict over cases of cross-border and multigenerational pollution (e.g., acid rain, dumping toxic chemical or metal waste into multinational bodies of water, and the possibly insecure disposal of nuclear waste), must heed technical factors as well as the problematic issue of consent. But for the capacity of contemporary scientific and technological activities to produce potent geographically and temporally remote effects, these ethical disagreements would simply not arise. Moreover, this "action-at-a-distance" capacity contributes to the tendency either to neglect or to assign modest weights to the legitimate interests of affected patients at considerable geographical or temporal remove. This in turn facilitates proceeding with the activities in the absence of consent of such endangered parties, or, in the case of not-yet-born members of future generations, impartial reflection on whether they would consent if they were informed and in a position to give or withhold it. The facts that the human capacity for empathy tends to diminish rapidly the more remote the injured or endangered party and that the world is organized into a weak international system of sovereign states both contribute to the genesis of such ethical conflicts.

In ethical disputes over workplaces made dangerous because of scientific or technological activities or products, the issue of consent rears its head in a different form. Historically, employers or their representatives argued that maintenance of a dangerous workplace was not unethical because a worker who accepted a job in one thereby voluntarily consented to exposure to all its attendant risks. To the extent that workplace hazards in the early industrial era were primarily threats to worker safety and that a worker

had other less dangerous employment alternatives, such a viewpoint might seem at least minimally plausible. However, as twentieth century industrial workplaces became pervaded with thousands of industrial chemicals of uncertain bearing on worker health, the notion that workers could meaningfully consent to the imposition of any and all risks that their workplaces posed to their health began to ring hollow. Workers had to make decisions to take or keep jobs in ignorance of what, if any, risks they would be or were being exposed to. Put differently, management could proceed with its risk-imposing activities without their workers' informed consent.

This situation came to be viewed by some as a violation of the prior-consent principle, and hence as unethical. Others saw it as ethically permissible because the benefits (to both company and workers) of proceeding in this way supposedly outweighed the (typically undervalued) costs of doing so. The main attempt to mitigate this situation has taken the form of right-to-know legislation: Workers have a right to a safe workplace but not to a risk-free (in particular, carcinogen-free) one. They are, however, entitled to that which is deemed necessary for their giving informed consent to imposition of workplace risks; specifically, they are entitled to "be informed about" all carcinogenic and other toxic substances used in their workplaces. Whether the extensive technical information provided and the way in which it is communicated to workers suffice to ensure their "informed consent" remains an open factual and criteriological question at the core of a persistent ethical issue.

Ethical conflict over the operation of "hair-trigger" military defense systems is also driven by both technical and social factors. Such systems are called "hair-trigger" because they can be set to "fire" on being subjected to slight pressures. Their risk arises from the enormity of destruction that can be unleashed by slight pressure on the sensitive firing mechanism; such pressure can be brought by mistaken "sightings" or misinterpretations of data. The 1988 downing of an Iranian commercial aircraft by the high-tech-equipped U.S.S. *Vincennes* because of misinterpretation of radar and electronic data is a tragic case in point, albeit on a relatively small scale. There have been numerous occasions on which American retaliatory nuclear forces have been activated and on the verge of being unleashed because of what turned out to be mistaken technological indications that a Soviet attack had been launched.

While technological "progress" is partly behind such ethical conflicts, consent is also a factor. In the case of hair-trigger military defense systems (e.g., ones operating on a "launch-on-warning" basis), the public has not been afforded an opportunity to explicitly give or withhold its consent, informed or otherwise, to the imposition of such grave risks. For opponents of such systems, this alone makes them ethically objectionable. For proponents, the astonishing speed of current or emerging offensive military technologies makes the risk of *not* employing hair-trigger defense systems exceed the risk of relying upon them. Moreover, such systems are morally justified, proponents argue, since the people have indirectly consented to such risks by voting democratically for the government that imposes them. The fact that civilian aircraft are permitted to fly over populous areas without their residents having first voted on whether to accept the associated risks does not suffice to show that the people do not consent to the risks imposed on them by this practice. Hence, it would be argued, the consent condition has not been violated and ethical impropriety has not been demonstrated. The same would be true in the case of hair-trigger defense systems. However, the greater the magnitude of the danger involved—enormous in the case of the nuclear war—the lower the risk of its accidental occurrence must be if the explicit securing of consent is to be reasonably set aside as having been implicitly given. The upshot is that the lack of shared criteria for deciding whether citizen consent has been effectively obtained in such cases is central to this acute ethical dispute.

Two morals of this kind of ethical conflict deserve attention. First, the problematics of consent are, to a significant degree, science- and technology-driven. Second, the potency of much contemporary scientific and technological activity is pressuring sensitive ethical analysts to enlarge the domain of morally pertinent patients whose interests are to be taken into account in assessing the ethical propriety of current or proposed actions or policies. This situation is reflected in ongoing struggles over whether to include various kinds of previously excluded stakeholders, such as those far afield who are nevertheless deleteriously affected by potent "spill-over" effects and future citizens whose legitimate interests may be jeopardized by activities designed first and foremost to benefit the presently living. Here, too, the contours of the evaluative enterprise of ethics are being subjected to severe stress by developments in contemporary science and technology.

Science- or Technology-Precipitated Value Conflicts

A fifth kind of science- or technology-based issue or conflict arises when a scientific or technological advance allows something new to be done that precipitates a value conflict, not necessarily between the values of opposed parties, but *between two or more cherished values of one and the same party*. For example, life-extending technologies have engendered situations in which family members are compelled to choose between two values, to both of which they owe allegiance: human life preservation and death with dignity. The crucial point about this increasingly frequent kind of value conflict is that the parties plagued by such conflicts would not be so but for scientific or technological advances.

Most recently, genetic tests allowing those with access to their results to know something of a sensitive nature about the health-related state or genetic predispositions of the person tested have proliferated. This has given rise to value conflicts between testers' or policymakers' concern for the protection of human *privacy* regarding disclosure of test results and their concern for *fairness* to one or another interested party other than the testee.

For example, in 1986 an adoption agency was trying to place a 2-month-old girl whose mother had Huntington's disease, a progressive, irreversible neurological disorder. The prospective adoptive parents indicated that they did not want the girl if she was going to develop the disease. The agency asked a geneticist to determine whether the child had the gene that would sooner or later manifest itself in the disease. The geneticist, while presumably sympathetic to the would-be adoptive parents' seemingly reasonable request, declined to do the testing. He reasoned that since many victims of the disease have claimed that they would have preferred to have lived their lives without knowing they had the "time-bomb" gene for the disease, it would be unethical to test someone so young, that is, at a point before she could decide whether to exercise her right to privacy in the form of *entitlement not to know* that she had the fatal gene.[9]

Tests for various genetic disorders, such as Down's syndrome, sickle cell anemia, and Tay Sachs disease, have been available for some time. In the foreseeable future, however, it is expected that tests will become available for identifying genetic traits that predispose people to more common health problems, such as diabetes, heart disease, and major forms of mental illness: Thus, according to Dr. Kenneth Paigen, "We are going to be able to say that somebody has a much greater or much less than average chance of having a heart attack before age 50 or after age 50."[10]

The potential implications of such advances for matters such as employment eligibility, life insurance qualification, and mate selection are formidable. Will employers with openings for positions with public safety responsibilities (e.g., commercial airline pilots) be permitted to require that applicants take genetic tests that will disclose whether they are predisposed to heart disease or to a genetically based mental disorder such as manic depression? Will insurance companies be permitted to require applicants for life or health insurance to take genetic tests predictive of life expectancy or diabetes? Will prospective spouses come to expect each other to be tested to determine their respective genetic predispositions and whether they are carriers of certain traits of genetic diseases and to disclose the test results?

In the case of companies recruiting for jobs with public safety responsibilities, prohibition of such tests to protect applicant privacy could impose significant safety costs on society. In the insurance case, preventing mandatory disclosure of test results in the name of individual privacy would spread the cost of defending this cherished value over society at large in the form of increased insurance premiums for those *without* life- or health-threatening genetic traits or predispositions. In the case of mate selection, declining to pursue and disclose the results of reliable genetic tests could set up partners for severe strains on their relationship should presently identifiable genetic disorders manifest themselves in the partners or their offspring at a later date.

It remains to be seen how society will resolve the public policy questions raised in such cases by the ethical value conflict between privacy and fairness. However, it is already clear that advances in genetic science are going to pose powerful challenges to society's commitment to the right of individual privacy. The knowledge about the individual afforded by such tests is likely to be of such pertinence to legitimate interests of other parties that the protection afforded individual privacy may be weakened out of concern for fairness to those parties, perhaps to the point of recognizing that under certain conditions they have a right to that knowledge. Put differently, technology is here bringing micro, or personal, justice and macro, or societal, justice into conflict.

Science- or Technology-Engendered "Positive" Rights

Besides conflicts over the values of freedom and justice, issues of "rights," especially "human rights," bulk large in contemporary Western ethics. In recent decades, advances in science and technology have engendered a new ethical issue: that of how best to respond to newly recognized so-called *positive rights.*

In the modern era, some claims have come to be widely recognized as "human rights"—that is, as irrevocable entitlements that people supposedly have simply because they are human beings. Human rights are thus contrasted with civil or institutional rights—rights that people have because they are delineated in specific revocable legal or institutional documents. Among the most widely recognized human rights are "life" and "liberty."

These rights, and some derived from them—privacy, for example, is widely thought to be a kind of special case of liberty—have traditionally been viewed as what philosophers call "negative" or "noninterference" rights—that is, as entitlements *not to be done to* in certain ways. Thus, the right to life is construed as entitlement not to be deprived of one's life or physical integrity. The right to liberty is construed as entitlement not to have one's freedom of action physically constrained or interfered with, unless its exercise has unjustifiably harmed another's protectable interests (e.g., those in life, limb, property, reputation) or poses an unreasonable risk of doing so.

As scientific and technological progress has gathered momentum in recent decades, several rights traditionally viewed as negative have given birth to a number of correlative "positive" rights—in other words, entitlements *to be done to* in certain ways. Consider three examples. Many believe that the right to life, traditionally construed as a negative human right, must, *in the context of new life-preserving scientific and technological resources,* be regarded as having taken on a positive component: entitlement to be provided with whatever medical treatment may be necessary to sustain one's life (independently of ability to pay for it). According to this way of thinking, affirmation of the right to life in the contemporary scientific and technological era requires affirmation of a positive right of access to whatever means are necessary to sustain life. Thus, for example, denial of costly life-sustaining drugs to a patient in need of them on any grounds save scarcity, including concern over the aggregate high cost to society of providing them, is seen by many as a violation of the patient's right to life. Hence, depending on whether the ethical analyst is a deontological or consequentialist thinker, failure to provide these drugs would be deemed categorically or prima facie ethically impermissible.

The right to privacy has traditionally been viewed as a noninterference right, entailing, among other things, entitlement not to have one's home broken into by government authorities without a search warrant issuable by a court only upon proof of "probable cause." However, the computer revolution has put individual privacy interests at risk.

To compensate for this, legislation in the United States and other countries entitles citizens to be provided with certain categories of information being kept on them in computerized files. For example, the U.S. Fair Credit Reporting Act of 1970 entitles each citizen to review and correct credit reports that have been done on them and to be notified of credit investigations undertaken for purposes of insurance, mortgage loans, and employment. Given the exceptional mobility of this information and the potential for severely damaging individual privacy that this creates, protection of the right of individual privacy in the computer era is held to require acknowledgement of countervailing positive rights: entitlement to know what exactly about oneself is contained in computerized government files and to have one's record rectified if it is shown to be erroneous.

A third, somewhat more speculative example involves a special case of the general right to liberty—namely, the traditional negative right of reproductive freedom: entitlement not to be interfered with in one's procreative undertakings, be they attempts to have or to avoid having offspring, including via "artificial" contraceptive means. It remains to be seen whether, in the context of the recent and continuing revolution in reproductive science and technology, the negative right of individual reproductive freedom will engender a positive counterpart: entitlement of those with infertility problems to be provided with (at least some) technical reproductive services enabling them to attempt to have offspring, where access does not hinge on a client's ability to pay or even perhaps on marital status.

As such scientifically and technologically generated positive rights expand, ethical tension will mount. Some deontologists, believing that human rights are "absolute," may conclude that their corresponding positive rights are likewise, hence inviolable. Others, including most consequentialists, while treating rights as claims that always deserve society's sympathetic consideration, may conclude that they cannot always be honored without regard to the social consequences of doing so. The most important consequence of this ethical tension may be that the day is drawing closer when society will have to come decisively to grips with the consequences of philosophical commitment to a concept of rights as "absolute" and "immutable."

Public Harms of Aggregation

Suppose that each of a large number of people carry out essentially the same action. Suppose further that, considered individually, each of these actions has at worst a negligible negative effect on a social or natural environment. Finally, suppose that the aggregated effect of the large number of people doing the same thing is that substantial harm is done to the environment in question. Let us call such outcomes *public harms of aggregation.* Many, if not most, such harms are possible only because, to an unprecedented degree, modern production, communication, and transportation methods have made many scientific and technological processes and products available on a mass basis. A curious moral aspect of such situations is that as the individual acts were assumed to be of negligible negative impact, they are typically regarded as being ethically unobjectionable. Hence, the aggregate effect of a mass of ethically permissible actions may nevertheless turn out to be quite ethically problematic. In ethics, sometimes numbers *do* count.[11]

Consider, for example, the pollutants emitted by each of the approximately 400 million automobiles in the world. The aggregate negative environmental effect of individually innocuous, hence seemingly ethically unproblematic, effects is known by now to be substantial. To the extent that this aggregate effect can be shown to harm people's health, particularly groups at special risk of being affected (e.g., the elderly, young children, and those with respiratory problems), the aggregate effect would begin to be judged as ethically unacceptable and unjust, and the individual pollution-emitting activities might begin to appear as something other than ethically neutral.

An analogy may help clarify this novel ethical situation. Suppose that a populous nation experiences a devastating depression in which many of its people suffer. Suppose that after the fact it is plausibly shown that an important contributing cause of the depression's occurrence was the fact that each family in the country had accumulated a substantial but individually manageable level of consumer debt. If the country was fortunate enough to recover its economic health, would not the new accumulation of a substantial but still manageable amount of consumer debt by an individual family be likely to be regarded as an ethically irresponsible thing to do? If so, the same could be said of an individual car owner's emission of pollution or an individual consumer's failure to recycle.

A somewhat futuristic example of the same pattern from the biomedical realm is that of predetermination of the sex of one's offspring. Given the fact that reproductive freedom is widely viewed as a human right, it is safe to assume that attempts of individual couples—at least married ones—to avail themselves of the latest scientific or technological means to determine the sex of their offspring will be regarded as ethically permissible. However, suppose that in a populous society with a culture biased in favor of male off-spring a significant number of couples opt for predetermination and that a significant sexual imbalance of male over female offspring results. Suppose further that at least some of the ethically problematic consequences envisioned as resulting from this state of affairs come to pass (e.g., increased crime committed by men or heightened male aggressiveness in competition for scarcer female mates).

The upshot of this situation is that twentieth century science and technology may be pushing society toward reevaluation of "permissive" ethical judgments traditionally made about individual actions that are at worst "negligibly harmful." Consequentially speaking, the threshhold of harm necessary to activate negative ethical judgments may be in the process of being reduced by the aggregative potential of modern science and technology in populous societies.

Practitioner Problems

The kinds of science- and technology-based ethical problems considered thus far have something in common: While spawned by developments within the spheres of science and technology, the resultant issues and conflicts unfold, not primarily within those spheres, but in society at large. In contrast, problems in the final category considered here, while related to concerns of society at large, arise primarily *inside* the communities of practitioners of science and technology. They are ethical problems associated with the concrete processes and practices of scientific and technological activity, both those in which these activities unfold and those in which their results are communicated. Such problems are sometimes viewed as falling within the province of "professional ethics," meaning that they are ethical problems that arise in the course of professional practice.

Problems of Execution. Edward Wenk has identified three kinds of ethical issues faced by practicing engineers in their work.[12]

(1) *Distributive Justice.* The first is essentially an issue of distributive justice, involving as it does an allocation of costs, benefits, and risks. This kind of problem arises when an engineer must decide whether to embark upon or proceed with a feasible project that he or she recognizes is likely to expose people to a non-trivial degree of risk to their safety, health, or property without their consent. Beyond answering the question "Can it be done?" about the contemplated project, the would-be ethical engineer must confront the quite different question "Ought it be done?"

For example, from an ethical point of view, should an engineering company accept a lucrative contract to erect a potentially hazardous structure, such as a hydroelectric dam, in a geologically unstable area near a rural village in the absence of the informed consent of its inhabitants?

Other things being equal, if the degree of risk—understood as a function of the estimated magnitude of the harm that could occur and the estimated likelihood of its occurrence—is substantial, then it would be ethically wrong to proceed. If it is negligible, then it would be ethically permissible, perhaps even obligatory, to do so. One problem with this kind of situation is that determination of what constitutes an "acceptable risk" is not a strictly technical question but a social and psychological one. Among other things, the answer to it depends on *what* members of the population at risk believe to be at stake, on *how highly* they value it at the time in question, and on *how seriously* they would regard its loss.

Meridith Thring has extended this analysis in the case of engineers who are independent operatives doing work in research and development. For years, Thring, a university professor of mechanical engineering, had been doing research on industrial robots. However, he eventually came to believe that "the primary aim [of such work] is to displace human labour." For this reason he abandoned work on industrial robots and decided to work only on

> applications where the aim is to help someone to do the job he does now without actually exposing his body to danger or discomfort; or where we need to amplify or diminish his skill and strength. A good example is "telechirics," . . . artifacts that allow people to work artificial hands and arms and operate machines in hazardous or unpleasant environments as if they were there, while they are in fact in comfortable and safe conditions.[13]

Thring implies that it is also ethically incumbent on engineers to consider whether the work they contemplate—here, a research and development project—poses an unacceptable risk to any important nonsafety interest of patients likely to be affected by it—for example, that of not being rendered redundant. At bottom, this too is an issue in distributive justice. For Thring, the ethical engineer must first carefully estimate the costs, benefits, and risks likely to be associated with a possible technological endeavor and then ask "Are those benefits, costs, and risks likely to be allocated to the affected parties in a way that is distributively just?" The engineer may then proceed with the work only if he or she can answer that question in the affirmative.

Similar ethical constraints apply to the initiation or continuance of scientific experiments that pose significant undisclosed risks to the safety, health, or property interests of people participating in or likely to be affected by them. Three of the most ethically repugnant scientific experiments carried out in or on behalf of the United States during this century are of this character and warrant brief description.

Beginning in 1932, U.S. Public Health Service researchers administered placebos to 431 black men in Tuskegee, Alabama. Each experimental subject, induced to come in for blood tests supposedly as part of an area-wide campaign to fight syphilis, was tested for and found to have syphilis. However, *the subjects were neither told that they had the disease nor treated for it.* The purpose of the experiment was to obtain scientific knowledge about the long-term effects of syphilis on mental and physical health. Nontreatment continued for 40 years, long after it became known that penicillin was a cure for syphilis and was widely available. Following press exposure in 1972, the experiment was terminated.[14] A Public Health Service investigation disclosed that of 92 syphilitic patients examined at autopsy, 28 men (30.4 percent) died from untreated syphilis—specifically, from syphilitic damage to the cardiovascular or central nervous systems. Hence, the total number of men who died as a result of nontreatment may have exceeded 100.[15]

In the 1950s, the U.S. Central Intelligence Agency solicited and funded a series of "mind-control experiments." Among the techniques used on experimental subjects were sensory deprivation, electroshock treatment, prolonged "psychological driving," and the administering of LSD and other potent drugs. By one estimate, at least 100 patients went through one series of brain-washing procedures.[16] Many participants in the experiments suffered long-term physical and mental health problems. In 1953, one subject was given a glass of liquor laced with LSD. He developed a psychotic reaction and committed suicide a week later.[17]

As part of its Biological Warfare program, the U.S. Army secretly sprayed bacteria and chemicals over populated areas of the United States (and Panama) during a 20-year period beginning in 1949. At least 239 such tests were carried out. The objective was to determine the country's vulnerability to germ warfare by simulating what would happen if an adversary dropped certain toxic substances on the United States. One frequently used microorganism was *Serratia marcescens.* Its safety was questioned prior to 1950, and strong evidence that it could cause infection or death existed in the late 1950s. Nevertheless, it continued to be used in tests over populous areas for the next decade. Four days after a 1950 spraying over the San Francisco Bay Area, a patient was treated at the Stanford University Medical Center for infection caused by *Serratia,* the first case ever recorded at the hospital. Within the next five months, ten more patients were treated at Stanford for the same infection. One of them died.[18]

Their ethically reprehensible character aside, such cases serve the useful purpose of showing that "freedom of scientific inquiry" is not an absolute, unconditional, or inviolable right. While clearly an important human value, "freedom of scientific inquiry" may, under certain conditions, have to take a backseat to other important values, such as protection of the dignity and welfare of each and every individual human being. We will return to the question of possible limits on scientific inquiry in Chapter 15.

(2) *Whistle Blowing.* Wenk's second kind of ethical issue in engineering is that of "whistle blowing." Engineers—or scientists—may become aware of deliberate actions or negligence on the part of their colleagues or employers that seem to them to pose a threat to some component of the public interest (e.g., public safety, the effective expenditure of public monies, and so on). If the worried practitioner's "in-house" attempts to have such concerns addressed are rebuffed, then he or she must decide whether to "go public" ("blow the whistle") and disclose the facts underlying the concerns.

Problematic phenomena of the sort that impel some practitioners to consider such a course of action are often driven by the huge profits and professional reputations at stake in modern research and development activity. These phenomena can be associated with any of a number of phases of engineering or science projects. Consider, for example, misleading promotional efforts to secure public funding; cheap, unreliable designs; testing shortcuts; misrepresented results of tests or experiments; shoddy manufacturing procedures; intermittently defective products; botched installation; careless or inadequate operational procedures; or negligent waste disposal. A significant number of such cases have come to light in recent years, of which three follow.

At Morton Thiokol, Inc. (MTI), several engineers working on the *Challenger* space shuttle booster project tried to convince management that the fateful January 1986 launch should not be authorized since the already suspect O-ring seal on the booster rocket had not been tested at the unusually cold temperatures prevailing on the day of the tragedy. MTI senior engineer Roger Boisjoly testified before the presidential committee investigating the disaster about what led up to the decision by the company and the National Aeronautics and Space Administration (NASA) to authorize the launch, a process at whose turning point MTI's general manager told his vice president of engineering to "take off his engineering hat and put on his management hat."[19] For his candid testimony, Boisjoly was allegedly subjected to various forms of mistreatment within the company and was placed on extended sick leave.[20]

In 1972, three engineers employed by the San Francisco Bay Area Rapid Transit (BART) system, after receiving no response to their in-house memos of concern, went public about subsequently confirmed safety-related deficiencies that they had detected in the design of BART's Automated Train Control System. They were summarily dismissed for their trouble.[21]

A senior engineer at the Bechtel Corporation, part of a task force assigned to plan the removal of the head of the failed nuclear reactor vessel at Three Mile Island after the famous 1979 accident, became concerned about short-cuts allegedly being taken by his company in testing the reliability of the crane to be used to remove the vessel's 170-ton lid. When he protested the alleged shortcuts, he was relieved of many of his responsibilities. He then went public, was suspended, and later fired.[22]

Sociologically speaking, several things are noteworthy about such cases. Technical employees who find themselves in situations in which they are asked or required to do things that violate their sense of right and wrong are not an endangered species. Results of a survey of 800 randomly selected members of the National Society of Professional Engineers published in 1972 disclosed that over 10 percent felt so constrained. A "large fraction" were sufficiently fearful of employer retaliation that they acknowledged they would rather "swallow the whistle" than become whistle blowers.[23] A major 1983 study of technical employees found that 12 percent of respondents "reported that, in the past two years, they have been in situations in which they voiced objection to, or refused to participate in, some work or practice because it went against their legal/ethical obligations as engineers or their personal senses of right and wrong."[24]

For a number of reasons, engineers have traditionally been loath to criticize their employers publicly. Most obviously, those who feel compelled to "go public" enjoy precious little legal or professional-association protection against employer retaliation, often in the form of firing.

However, as Wenk argues, some reasons that discourage whistle blowing are sociocultural in nature:

> For engineers, a problem arises because most work in large organizations and many find excitement of participation in mammoth undertakings. They learn to value formal social structures, an attitude akin to "law and order." They adopt the internal culture and values of their employer and are likely to be allied with and adopt the perspectives of the people who wield power rather than with the general population over whom power is held. As a consequence, there is less tradition and inclination to challenge authority even when it is known to be wrong in its decisions which imperil the public.[25]

Not without reason, engineers—and, increasingly, scientists in large industrial organizations—tend to see themselves as employees with primary obligations to their employers, not the public. Moreover, the notion that employees retain certain citizen rights—for example, freedom of expression—when they enter the workplace is a relatively new notion in American industrial history. In a classic 1892 opinion, Oliver Wendell Holmes, then Massachusetts Supreme Court justice, wrote:

> There are few employments for hire in which the servant does not agree to suspend his constitutional rights of free speech as well as idleness by the implied terms of the contract. The servant cannot complain, as he takes the employment on the terms which are offered him.[26]

Only in the late twentieth century has this traditional attitude begun to be reversed, partly because the costs of such enforced silence are now viewed as unacceptable to society.

Ethically speaking, the obligation of technical professionals to blow the whistle when it is appropriate to do so arises from several factors. First, much contemporary research and development is supported by public money, as is the graduate education of many scientists and engineers (through government fellowships and loans). Second, the scale of the possible harm to the public interest at stake in many contemporary technical activities is large. The third factor is the following ethical principle of harm prevention: "[W]hen one is in a position to contribute to preventing unwarranted harm to others, then, other things being equal, one is morally obliged to attempt to do so."[27] An engineer or scientist sometimes possesses personal, specialized, "insider" knowledge about a troubling facet of a technical activity or project. Coupled with the credibility attached to testimony provided by authoritative technical professionals (as opposed to claims made by nonspecialist activists), that knowledge puts the scientist or engineer in a special position to make a possibly decisive contribution to preventing unwarranted harm to others or at least to preventing its repetition. This gives rise to a moral obligation to blow the whistle—once all other reasonable steps to rectify the situation "in house" have been taken and failed.

Some have urged that the obligation to responsibly blow the whistle be emphasized during the formal education of scientists and engineers—by the use of actual case studies, for example.[28] Others have stressed the importance of effecting structural and policy changes in the organizations in which technical professionals work and in their professional associations so that whistle blowers are not required to choose between remaining silent and becoming self-sacrificing "moral heroes."[29] A third approach is that of legislation. A measure of protection for whistle-blowers has been built into some federal environmental and nuclear laws, and roughly half the states prohibit the firing of employees who have blown the whistle on their employers for practices violating existing public policies. However, some advocates for whistle-blowers see the need for comprehensive federal legislation allowing whistle-blowers who suffer reprisals to initiate legal action against their employers up to two years after such occurrences.[30]

(3) *Consideration of Long-Term Effects.* Wenk's third and final category of ethical issues confronting engineers in daily practice involves "managing the future." He argues that engineers have a tendency to focus on designing, producing, or installing "hardware" without adequately "anticipat[ing] . . . longer term effects." This is an abdication of the engineer's "professional responsibility." In terms of the "quartet of basic concerns" that we have utilized in this chapter, given the scale and scope of the effects of many contemporary engineering products and projects, engineers who fail to scrutinize their projects with comprehensive critical vision, both with respect to its likely consequences (including possible longer-term ones) and its likely patients or "stakeholders" (including, where appropriate, members of future generations) are guilty of unprofessional and ethically irresponsible conduct. Uncritical allegiance to the deontological dictum "if it can be done, it should be done" no longer confers immunity from charges of ethical impropriety on technical practitioners.

Problems of Communication. Other ethical issues faced by technical practitioners have to do not with possible effects of scientific and technological projects on the safety, health, or property of those who may be affected by them, but with problematic aspects of *practitioners' communication* of and about their work.[31] Issues in this category, most notably ones involving *fraud* and *misrepresentation,* pertain to publication or presentation of claimed findings and to work-related interactions with nontechnical funding or policy-making officials. Cases of fraud have come to light in recent years in which experiments reported on in published papers were in fact never carried out, crucial data were fabricated, and conclusions were drawn from data allegedly known not to support them.[32]

(1) *Fraud.* Falsification of scientific data may not be as infrequent as normally supposed. June Price Tangney surveyed researchers in the physical, biological, behavioral, and social sciences at a large American university. Of 1,100 questionaires distributed, 245 were completed and returned. Half of the respondents were senior researchers with the rank of full professor. Not surprisingly, the survey revealed that 88 percent of the respondents believe that scientific fraud is uncommon. However, 32 percent reported that they had a colleague in their field whom they had at some time suspected of falsifying data.[33] This figure, while suggestive, must be interpreted cautiously. It is not proof that one third of all scientists engage in such misconduct, for not only may suspicions be mistaken, but multiple respondents could have had the same individual in mind.

Whatever the extent of fraud in science, scientists see a number of factors contributing to the phenomenon. Tangney's respondents identified the following as major motivations for fraud: desire for fame and recognition (56 percent), job security and promotion (31 percent), firm belief in or wish to promote a theory (31 percent), and "laziness" (15 percent).[34] Underlying many such factors, she contends, is *the highly competitive nature of contemporary science:* the pressure to publish, the shortage of desirable jobs, and the fierce competition for funds. Beyond contributing to fraud, Tangney argues that such pressures can negate "what might otherwise be a fairly adequate self-policing mechanism in the scientific community." Indeed, the results of her survey call into question the common wisdom about the self-correcting nature of science, via processes like refereeing and publication, for of the aforementioned 32 percent who had suspected a colleague of falsifying data, over half (54 percent) reported that they had taken no action to confirm or disconfirm their suspicions.[35] The competitive nature of contemporary science may have biased the reward system in the profession *against* undertakings aimed at uncovering fraud.

In a highly competitive academic environment, many researchers may feel that, if they raise questions about serious misconduct, their own reputations will be tarnished and their own chances for resources and advancement will be diminished. A scientist may be rewarded for uncovering "legitimate" flaws or shortcomings in a rival's work. However, there generally is little to be gained and much to be lost by attempting to expose a fraud.[36]

(2) *Misrepresentation.* Misrepresentation takes a number of forms in the communication of research findings, including both failure to credit or fully credit deserving contributors and crediting or overcrediting undeserving contributors. It might seem that such acknowledged species of misconduct, however regrettable, do not deserve to be called unethical, except perhaps by deontologists, for whom they fall into forbidden categories of actions regardless of the gravity of their consequences for science or society. However, consequentialists may also selectively regard such practices as unethical, since they can in fact result in serious public harm. In May 1987, a scientist was accused by an investigative panel of scientists appointed by the National Institutes of Health of "knowingly, willfully, and repeatedly engag[ing] in misleading and deceptive practices in reporting results of research."[37] The pertinence of these practices to consequentialist ethical judgment making becomes clear from the panel's finding that the scientist's publications had influenced drug treatment practices for severely retarded patients in facilities around the United States.

Presentations of research findings to groups of peers also offer opportunities for ethically problematic behavior. Such presentations are sometimes used to establish claims of priority in the conduct of certain kinds of research. However, given the intensely competitive nature of the contemporary scientific research enterprise, if the research work is still in progress, it is understandable that scientists may opt to disclose just enough of their findings to serve their priority interests but not enough to reveal their overall strategies or the next steps in their "battle plans." However, quests for priority and resultant recognition may go beyond being unprofessional and become unethical if deliberately misleading or outright false information is disseminated in hopes of sending rivals "off on wild goose chases," diverting them from paths believed potentially fruitful. While making such an ethical judgment may appear open only to a deontological thinker, doing so can also be defended on consequentialist grounds, by, for ex-

ample, appealing to the harm that such deception can inflict on knowledge-sharing institutions like the peer seminar which have usefully served scientific progress and thus, indirectly, human welfare.

The interaction of scientists and engineers with public funding agencies or policy-making officials can also be ethically problematic. Institutional or organizational pressures to obtain funding for research and development ventures or units with significant prestige or employment stakes can induce applicants to resort to various forms of misconduct in hopes of increasing the chances of favorable action by a funding agency. Among these are use of false data, misrepresentation of what has been accomplished to date on a project in progress, and gross exaggeration of what can be expected in the grant period or of the scientific or social significance of the proposed work.

Dealings with makers of public policy often lend themselves to such hyperbole, for policymakers are typically individuals with nontechnical backgrounds who are unable to assess critically the plausibility of the claims made about current or proposed research or development projects. If a prestigious researcher deliberately misrepresents the potential or state of development of a pet project to an influential policymaker in order to enhance the project's funding prospects, then insofar as approval is secured through this deception and at the cost of funding for other worthwhile projects, consequentialist thinkers may join deontologists in judging the practitioner guilty of unethical conduct. This they may do not least on grounds of the long-term consequences for the welfare of society of undermining the integrity of the research funding process.

THE CHALLENGE OF CONTEMPORARY SCIENCE AND TECHNOLOGY TO TRADITIONAL ETHICAL THEORIES

The foregoing discussion of categories of ethical issues and conflicts engendered by developments in science and technology strongly suggests that these forces are putting growing pressure on traditional absolutistic ethical thinking. There are several reasons that the validity and utility of such thinking are being called into question in an era of rapid scientific and technological development.

As we saw, many such theories condemn or praise particular kinds of actions if they but fall into one or another category of supposedly intrinsically good or bad deeds. However, as noted, an action or practice condemned as "unnatural" can come to seem less so over time, especially if the original ethical judgment was predicated on the act's or practice's being unusual or unfamiliar when it first came to attention. Similarly, traditional absolutistic ethical outlooks are sometimes based on static world views born of their subscribers' limited experience. As a culture or subculture dominated by such a world view overcomes its geographical or intellectual isolation and interacts more with the rest of the world, supposedly immutable categories or rules pertaining to "sacred" things or ways tend to loosen up. Adherents of such world views may come to recognize that respectable members of different cultures or subcultures think and act differently than they do about the same matters. Further, new products, processes, and practices can, as noted, have long-term hidden effects. Their eventual eruption and empirical confirmation sometimes call for revision of ethical judgments made before recognition that such subterranean effects were at work. However, such reevaluation is not congenial to absolutistic thinking, which purports to base its unwavering ethical judgments and decisions on something other than consequences. Considerations such as these make it increasingly difficult to sustain absolutistic ethical theories and outlooks in contemporary scientific and technological society.

Besides challenges to its intellectual tenability, contemporary science and technology are calling into question the utility of traditional absolutistic ethical theories—that is, their ability to serve as intelligent guides to action in a world of rapid and profound technical and social change. Such categorical theories and outlooks are helpless when confronted with ethical issues and conflicts of the sorts discussed in the third section of this chapter. For example, such theories shed no light on cases involving the distribution of benefits, costs, and risks associated with scientific and technological developments; intrapersonal conflicts between two venerable ethical values; public harms of aggregation; or the situations of technical professionals torn between loyalty to employers, concern for their families' well-being, and devotion to promoting the public interest. Finally, traditional deontological approaches to ethical thinking offer no incentives to agents to consider whether, in the face of possible unforeseen effects of a technical innovation, expansion of the domain of pertinent patients or the list of their protectable interests might be in order.

This is not to imply that consequentialist theories and thinking are immune from difficulties when confronted by contemporary scientific and technological developments. For example, uncertainty about possible elusive or projected long-term consequences of scientific and technological innovations and developments makes ethical judgments based on such assessments provisional and open to

doubt. However, that is a price that must be paid if ethical judgments and decisions are to be made on an empirical rather than an a priori basis and are to be focused on the bearing of scientific and technological developments on human harm and well-being.

One conclusion of this chapter, then, is that developments in contemporary science and technology call for revisions in traditional ethical thinking and decision-making. One kind of ethical theory deserving serious consideration we will call *qualified neo-consequentialism*. Under this theory, ethical judgments about actions, practices, and policies hinge first and foremost on assessments of their likely consequences. In particular, these assessments must have the following *neo-consequentialist* qualities. They should be

1. *Focused on harm and well-being*—directed to identifying and weighing the importance of consequences likely to influence the harm or well-being of affected patients;*
2. *Refined*—designed to detect or at least be on the lookout for subtle effects that, although perhaps hidden or manifested only indirectly, may nonetheless significantly influence stakeholder harm or well-being;
3. *Comprehensive*—designed to attend to *all* harm- and well-being-related effects—social and cultural as well as economic and physical in nature—of the candidate action, policy, or practice on *all* pertinent patients, remote as well as present, "invisible" as well as influential;
4. *Discriminating*—designed to enable scientific and technological options to be examined critically on a case-by-case basis, in a manner neither facilely optimistic nor resolutely pessimistic, and such that any single proposal can emerge as consequentially praiseworthy and be adopted or as consequentially ill-advised and be rejected in its present form if not outright; and
5. *Prudent*—embodying an attitude toward safety that, as long as a credible jury is still out or if it has returned hopelessly deadlocked, is as conservative as the magnitude of the possible disaster is large.

---

*The reader will note that no account has been presented here of exactly what is meant by human "harm" and "well-being." That substantial task must be left for another occasion. Suffice it to say here that for this writer, "harm" is not reducible to considerations of physiological deprivation, physical injury, and property damage or loss; nor is "well-being" reducible to considerations of material abundance, financial success, and high social status.

Further, the assessments sanctioned by our proposed ethical theory must also meet certain conditions. If an action, policy, or practice is to earn our theory's seal of approval, its projected outcome must not only be likely to yield at least as large a surplus of beneficial over harmful consequences as that of any available alternative, but it must also meet certain additional *qualifications,* two of which will now be briefly discussed.

It is scarcely news that contemporary scientific and technological activities unfold in societies in which those who stand to benefit greatly from their fruits are rarely the same as those likely to bear their often weighty costs and risks. We therefore stipulate that to be ethically permissible or obligatory, the allocation of the scrupulously projected benefits, costs, and risks of a technical undertaking among the various affected stakeholders must also be *distributively just.*

Various criteria have been put forth for evaluating the justice of such distributions.[38] One that deserves serious consideration is John Rawls's famous "difference principle."[39] Imagine, says Rawls, a group of people in "the original position"—that is, convened to formulate from scratch the rules that will govern the first human society, one shortly to come into being. Suppose that these deliberations take place behind "a veil of ignorance"—that individual group members have no knowledge whatsoever of whom or what they will turn out to be (e.g., male or female, black or white, Asian or North American, physically handicapped or not) or of their eventual economic well-being or social status. Then, Rawls contends, the group would eventually reach agreement that it was in each member's best interest that the following rule of justice be adopted: an unequal distribution of any social or economic "good" will be permitted in the society-to-be only if there is good reason to believe that it will *make everyone, including the less fortunate, better off.* Indeed, Rawls eventually offered a stronger version of his principle according to which an unequal distribution of such a good is just only if there is good reason to believe that it will make everyone better off *and* that it will *yield the greatest benefit to those currently worst off.*[40] If either version of this rule is found compelling, it would have to be applied to each predominantly beneficial but unequal distribution of projected science- or technology-based benefits, costs, and risks before the conclusion could be reached that it was ethically permissible or obligatory to proceed with the action, project, or practice in question.

Our neo-consequentialist ethical theory has a second qualification. A science- or technology-related course of action may sometimes be denied ethical approval even if all of the foregoing conditions are met. Even then, it may be proper to withhold ethical approval if the projected harmful consequences (1) *exceed some substantial quantitative threshhold*—either in a single case or when aggregated over multiple cases of a similar sort—and (2) are not *greatly* outweighed by their positive counterparts. In such situations, the decision-making party may decide that it would be prudent to decline the admittedly greater projected benefits offered by the option under consideration.

Ethical decision making that takes no account of the absolute magnitude of an option's projected negative consequences even if they are outweighed by their positive counterparts, or of how the outweighed negative consequences of an individual course of action may aggregate over multiple instances, is deeply flawed. Indeed, allowing "yielding a positive balance of benefit over harm" by itself to compel ethical approval of individual courses of action may even be unjustified on consequentialist grounds, for following that criterion consistently in multiple instances may over time lead to unacceptable public harms of aggregation. For example, assessing the impact on traffic of individual proposed downtown high-rise office buildings solely in terms of the modest number of additional cars each structure may attract into the city may allow the aggregate effect on traffic of approval of a large number of such projects to go unreflected in individual decision-making processes.

Conclusion

Hopefully, the reader will find the qualified neo-consequentialist approach to thinking about ethical issues and conflicts just sketched more adequate to the realities of contemporary scientific and technological practice. In any event, in this chapter we have characterized a number of different kinds of science- and technology-based ethical issues and conflicts, indicated some noteworthy technical and social roots of such problems, and argued that important traditional ethical concepts and modes of thinking are being subjected to increasing pressure by scientific and technological changes in contemporary society. While this stress is being strenuously resisted in some quarters, it is likely in the longer run to lead to major transformations of ethical ideas and thinking.

Endnotes

1. I owe my initial awareness of this framework to a 1972 lecture at Stanford University by ethicist Dr. Karen Lebacqz.
2. See, e.g., William Frankena, *Ethics,* Foundations of Philosophy series, 2nd ed. (Englewood Cliffs, N.J.: Prentice-Hall,

1973), chaps. 2 and 3. See also Mary Warnock, *Ethics Since 1900* (London: Oxford University Press, 1960), chap. 2, pp. 48–52.

3. *Wall Street Journal,* May 4, 1989, p. B4.

4. Stephen Isaacs, "Hasidim of Brooklyn: Fundamentalist Jews Amid a Slumscape," *Washington Post,* "Outlook" section, February 17, 1974, Section B, p. 1.

5. Gregory Kavka, *Moral Paradoxes of Nuclear Deterrence* (Cambridge: Cambridge University Press, 1987), pp. 19–21.

6. Ronald Munson, *Intervention and Reflection* (Belmont, Calif.: Wadsworth, 1979), p. 398.

7. *Ibid.,* pp. 399–400.

8. For example, Carl Cohen argues that animals are not members of any "community of moral agents." Incapable of, among other things, giving or withholding consent, animals, unlike humans cannot have rights thereby precluding involuntary experimentation on them. See Cohen's "The Case for the Use of Animals in Biomedical Research," *New England Journal of Medicine,* 315, no. 14, 1986, 867.

9. Gina Kolata, "Genetic Screening Raises Questions for Employers and Insurers," *Science,* 232, no. 4748, April 18, 1986, 317.

10. *New York Times,* August 19, 1986, p. 21.

11. John M. Taurek, "Should the Numbers Count?" *Philosophy and Public Affairs,* 6, 1977, 293–316.

12. Edward Wenk, Jr., "Roots of Ethics: New Principles for Engineering Practice," American Society of Mechanical Engineers Winter Annual Meeting, Boston, Massachusetts, December 1987, 87-WA/TS-1, pp. 1–7.

13. Meredith Thring, "The Engineer's Dilemma," *The New Scientist,* 92 no. 1280, November 19, 1981, 501.

14. *New York Times,* July 26, 1972, p. 1.

15. *New York Times,* September 12, 1972, p. 23. For a detailed account of this episode, see James H. Jones, *Bad Blood: The Tuskegee Syphilis Experiment* (New York: Free Press, 1981).

16. Harvey Weinstein, *A Father, a Son, and the CIA* (Toronto: James Lorimer and Co. Ltd., 1988).

17. Leonard A. Cole, *Politics and the Restraint of Science* (Totowa, N.J.: Rowman and Allanheld, 1983), p. 111.

18. *Ibid.,* pp. 112–114.

19. Roger Boisjoly, "Ethical Decisions: Morton Thiokol and the Space Shuttle *Challenger* Disaster," American Society of Mechanical Engineers Winter Annual Meeting, Boston, Massachusetts, December 1987, 87-WA/TS-4, p. 7.

20. *Ibid.,* p. 11.

21. Stephen H. Ungar, *Controlling Technology: Ethics and the Responsible Engineer* (New York: Holt, Rinehart and Winston, 1982), pp. 12–17.

22. Rosemary Chalk, "Making the World Safe for Whistle-Blowers," *Technology Review,* January 1988, p. 52.

23. Rosemary Chalk and Frank von Hippel, "Due Process for Dissenting 'Whistle-Blowers.'" *Technology Review,* June/July 1979, p. 53.

24. Chalk, "Making the World Safe," pp. 56–57.

25. Wenk, "Roots of Ethics," p. 3.

26. Chalk and von Hippel, "Due Process," p. 53.

27. Compare this principle with Kenneth Alpern's "principle of due care" and "corollary of proportionate care" in his "Moral Responsibility For Engineers," *Business and Professional Ethics Journal,* 2, Winter 1983, 40–41.

28. Boisjoly, "Ethical Decisions," p. 12.

29. Richard DeGeorge, "Ethical Responsibilities of Engineers in Large Organizations: The Pinto Case," *Business and Professional Ethics Journal,* 1, no. 1, 1981, 12.

30. Chalk, "Making the World Safe," pp. 55–56.

31. For a useful bibliography on this aspect of the problem, see Marcel Chotkowski LaFollette, "Ethical Misconduct in Research Communication: An Annotated Bibliography," published under NSF Grant No. RII-8409904 ("The Ethical Problems Raised by Fraud in Science and Engineering Publishing"), August 1988.

32. See, e.g., William Broad and Nicholas Wade, *Betrayers of the Truth* (New York: Simon & Schuster, 1982), pp. 13–15; and Nicholas Wade, "The Unhealthy Infallibility of Science," *New York Times,* June 13, 1988, p. A18.

33. June Price Tangney, "Fraud Will Out—Or Will It?" *New Scientist,* 115, no. 1572, August 6, 1987, 62.

34. *Ibid.*

35. *Ibid.*

36. *Ibid.,* p. 63.

37. *New York Times,* April 16, 1988, p. 6.

38. For cogent discussion of various criteria of distributive justice, see Joel Feinberg, *Social Philosophy,* Foundations of Philosophy Series (Englewood Cliffs, N.J.: Prentice Hall, (1973), chap. 7.

39. John Rawls, *A Theory of Justice* (Cambridge, Mass.: Harvard University Press, 1971), chaps. 1–3, especially pp. 75–78.

40. For discussion of alternate versions of Rawls's difference principle, see Robert Paul Wolff, *Understanding Rawls* (Princeton, N.J.: Princeton University Press, 1977), pp. 40–41.

Questions

1. How would you define ethics?

2. List three ways that ethics correlates to social responsibility.

3. There are four kinds of considerations that are pertinent to ethical decisions and judgment making. List and describe them.

4. What does the phrase "violations of supposedly exceptionless moral principles" mean?

5. Name a new technology and then provide an example of value-based conflicts that it has created.

Whistle-Blowing

The economic and technological triumphs of the past few years have not solved as many problems as we thought they would, and, in fact, have brought us new problems we did not foresee.

HENRY FORD II

Whistle-blowing occurs when people believe that something is wrong with a system, process, or product and feel personally responsible or morally obligated to let officials know abut the wrongdoing. In an article entitled "Blowing the Whistle: The Organizational and Legal Implications for Companies and Employees," published in *Psychology Today* (1996), it was pointed out that traditionally, whistle-blowers have long histories of successful employment and a firm belief in their organizations. When they perceive that something within their organization as potentially harmful, they become morally convicted to correcting, changing, or reporting the misdeed. Personal responsibility and concern about others is at the heart of their conviction. Whistle-blowers believe that by reporting the misconduct or hazard, their concerns will not be ignored and the problem will be solved. Whistle-blowers tend to have high ethical standards, strong religious beliefs, and a faith that superiors share the same desire as themselves to correct wrongs.

Whistle-blowing often occurs when an individual believes that decision making by a company or the government may be breaking the law, financially profitable but morally wrong, potentially dangerous, or a case of exploitation of management authority (VAOIG, 1998, p. 1). Some factors upon which people blow the whistle include the following: "misleading promotional efforts to secure public funding; cheap, unreliable designs; testing shortcuts; misrepresented test results or experiments; shoddy manufacturing procedures; intermittently defective products; botched installations; careless or inadequate operational procedures; negligent waste disposal" (McGinn, 1991, p. 158). The reality is that whistle-blowers have strong ethical and moral beliefs that carry them through the rough times they are often subjected to after they report the wrongdoing. It is only through family and peer support systems or strong religious beliefs that they can come to terms with the isolation, demotion, intimidation, and threat of loss of work that they may experience after blowing the whistle (Rechtschaffen, 1996, p. 38).

In fact, "[W]histle-blowers are part and parcel of the corporate culture on which they blow the whistle. They are often rather senior because it is those issuing orders who usually have the most control over and the most knowledge about what is occurring within the corporation." (Koehn, 1998, p. 3). Even though whistle-blowing can be personally costly, it remains an important part of social and personal decisions in the face of precarious conflicts. Individuals have to go through soul-searching and heart-wrenching decisions when making the decision to blow the whistle and when dealing with the ramifications of this decision. The two examples of whistle-blowing described in the upcoming text are 1) the classic case of Roger Boisjoly, the chief engineer for the Challenger space shuttle, and 2) the case of the "nuclear warriors."

References

Koehn, D. (1998). Whistleblowing and trust: Some lessons from the ADM scandal. Business Ethics Magazine Articles. Available: http://condor.depaul.edu/eumes/adm.nun.

McGinn, R. (1991). *Science, Technology and Society.* Upper Saddle River, NJ, Prentice Hall.

Presidential Commission on the Space Shuttle *Challenger Accident,* February 25, 1986.

Rechtschaffen, G., and Yardley, J. (1996, March). Whistleblowing and the law: Are you legally protected if you blow the whistle? *Management Accounting.* pp. 38–41.

VAOIG Hotline. *Whistleblowing information.* Available: http://www/va/gov/VAOIG/hotline/wmsue.nun

Case I: Roger Boisjoly, Chief Engineer at Morton Thiokol

"Whistleblowing arises from an unsuccessful attempt to achieve change through the chain of command. When issues are critical and management's response is unsatisfactory, employees have little recourse but to circumvent the chain of command. All too often they are punished in a modern version of blaming the messenger."

ROGER BOISJOLY, CHIEF ENGINEER AT MORTON THIOKOL

One of the saddest days in the history of America's space program was January 28, 1986, the day that the Challenger space shuttle exploded. Six astronauts and a school teacher, Christa McAuliffe, died when the shuttle exploded 73 seconds after liftoff. The nation, transfixed and confused, watched the disaster on their television sets, wondering how something that seemed so good could have pivoted so quickly into terror . . . How could it have happened?

On January 24, 1985, Roger Boisjoly, chief engineer at Morton Thiokol, watched the launch of Flight 51-C and noted that the temperature that day was much cooler than it had been during other recorded launches. When he inspected the solid rocket boosters, he found that "both the primary and secondary-ring seals on a field joint had been blackened" from what he thought might be severe hot gas blowby related to low temperatures (Boisjoly and Curtis, 1987, p. 9). Boisjoly presented his findings to NASA's Marshall Space Flight Center and received tough questioning from the Flight Readiness Review committee. He decided that he needed further evidence before he could positively link low temperatures with hot gas blowby. He further studied the effects of temperature on the seals of Flight 51-B and found that, in fact, there was a direct correlation between low temperatures and the chance for a catastrophe to result (Boisjoly and Curtis, 1987, pp. 9–10).

During the following months, Boisjoly felt frustration that management did not seem to be listening to him about the problem he had discovered. On January 27 (the day before the Challenger disaster), the predicted temperature for the launch was 18 degrees Fahrenheit. This low temperature prompted Morton Thiokol, the Marshall Space Flight Center, and the Kennedy Space Center to discuss their concerns about the safety of the launch, since no shuttle had ever been launched at a temperature lower than 53 degrees Fahrenheit. Boisjoly again stated his concern that the O-rings on the shuttle's solid rocket boosters would stiffen in the cold and lose their ability to act as a seal, potentially causing a fatal disaster (Schlager, 1994, p. 611).

After the meeting, Boisjoly returned to his office and created the following journal entry:

I sincerely hope that this launch does not result in a catastrophe. I personally do not agree with some of the statements made . . . stating that SRM-25 is okay to fly tomorrow. (Boisjoly and Curtis, 1987, p. 13)

On January 28, 1986, as Boisjoly and his engineering team had predicted, the Challenger exploded, and all of those on board died. As the nation mourned, the Rogers Commission was formed to investigate the reason for the explosion. Research after the fact showed that there was "a failure in the joint between the two lower segments of the right Solid Rocket Motor . . . (i.e.) the destruction of the seals that are intended to prevent hot gases from leaking through the joint during the propellant burn. . ." (The Commission, 1986, Vol .4). It was a tragic technological disaster that could have been prevented. The seal had leaked because the booster was used at a temperature below its range of safe operation, something that Roger

Boisjoly had tried to warn management about (Westrum, 1991).

The experience of Roger Boisjoly is representative of what whistle-blowers often face when they make a moral decision to tell the truth. Their truths are based on their own perceptions, values, and morals; the question is why others do not choose to listen or act upon their recommendations.

References

Boisjoly R., and Curtis, E. (1987, October). *Roger Boisjoly and the Challenger disaster: A case study in engineering management, corporate loyalty and ethics.* Lowell, MA, University of Lowell. (Reprinted from the Proceedings of the ASEM Eighth Annual Meeting, October 1987.)

Schlager, N. (1994). *When Technology Fails: Significant Technological Disasters, Accidents and Failures of the Twentieth Century.* Washington, DC, Gale Research.

Westrum, R. (1991). *Technologies and Society: The Shaping of People and Things.* Belmont, CA, Wadsworth Publishing Company. p. 132.

Questions

1. What was the main cause of the Challenger explosion? What do you think might be different about the respective answers of NASA, Morton Thiokol, and Roger Boisjoly to this question? Use the Internet or sources from the library to provide additional information to support your answer.

2. Pretend for a moment that you are Roger Boisjoly. Your recommendation that the launch be postponed has been overridden. What should you do? Provide a detailed explanation as to why you would or would not pick each of the following options.

    a. Resign your position in protest.

    b. Blow the whistle by calling a local radio or television station.

    c. Tell the astronauts and their families of your concerns.

    d. Do nothing.

3. What is your opinion of Roger Boisjoly's role as a whistle-blower? How would you have handled this situation differently?

A Bridge to Your 21st Century Understanding

Complete and discuss the following flowchart.

A Bridge to Your 21st Century Understanding

Complete and discuss the following flowchart.

A Bridge to Your 21st Century Understanding

Complete and discuss the following flowchart.

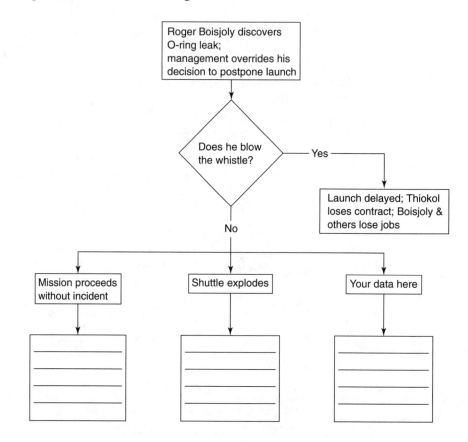

Case II: Nuclear Warriors

ERIC POOLEY

George Betancourt looked up from his desk as George Galatis burst into the office, a bundle of papers under his arm. On that morning in March 1992, the two men—both senior engineers at Northeast Utilities, which operates five nuclear plants in New England—were colleagues but not yet friends. Apart from their jobs and first names, they seemed to have little in common. Betancourt, 45, was extravagantly rebellious—beard, biker boots, ponytail sneaking out the back of his baseball cap—while Galatis, 42, was square-jawed and devout: Mr. Smith Goes Nuclear. But Galatis respected Betancourt's expertise and knew he could count on him for straight answers.

On this day, Galatis wanted to know about a routine refueling operation at the Millstone Unit 1 nuclear plant in Waterford, Connecticut. Every 18 months the reactor is shut down so the fuel rods that make up its core can be replaced; the old rods, radioactive and 250°F hot, are moved into a 40-ft.-deep body of water called the spent-fuel pool, where they are placed in racks alongside thousands of other, older rods. Because the federal government has never created a storage site for high-level radioactive waste, fuel pools in nuclear plants across the country have become de facto nuclear dumps—with many filled nearly to capacity. The pools weren't designed for this purpose, and risk is involved: the rods must be submerged at all times. A cooling system must dissipate the intense heat they give off. If the system failed, the pool could boil, turning the plant into a lethal sauna filled with clouds of radioactive steam. And if earthquake, human error or me-

© 1996 Time Inc., Reprinted by permission.

chanical failure drained the pool, the result could be catastrophic: a meltdown of multiple cores taking place outside the reactor containment, releasing massive amounts of radiation and rendering hundreds of square miles uninhabitable.

To minimize the risk, federal guidelines require that some older plants like Millstone, without state-of-the-art cooling systems, move only one-third of the rods into the pool under normal conditions. But Galatis realized that Millstone was routinely performing "full-core off-loads," dumping all the hot fuel into the pool. His question for Betancourt was, "How long has this been going on?"

Betancourt thought for a minute. "We've been moving full cores since before I got here," he said, "since the early '70s."

"But it's an emergency procedure."

"I know," Betancourt said. "And we do it all the time." What's more, Millstone 1 was ignoring the mandated 250-hr. cool-down period before a full off-load, sometimes moving the fuel just 65 hrs. after shutdown, a violation that had melted the boots of a worker on the job. By sidestepping the safety requirements, Millstone saved about two weeks of downtime for each refueling—during which Northeast Utilities has to pay $500,000 a day for replacement power.

Galatis then flipped through a safety report in which Northeast was required to demonstrate to the Nuclear Regulatory Commission that the plant's network of cooling systems would function even if the most important one failed. Instead, the company had analyzed the loss of a far less critical system. The report was worthless, the NRC

323

1. The plant is shut down, and the reactor vessel is flooded with water. After cool-down, technicians open gates between the vessel and the refueling canal, which leads to the spent-fuel pool, the 40-ft. deep, 30-ft. by 25-ft. body of water where spent fuel is stored.

Refueling bridge

Refueling canal

Fuel assembly

Spent-fuel pool

Storage rack

Reactor vessel

2. Working from the refueling bridge, technicians use a crane to reach into the vessel and grasp a fuel assembly—a bundle of 62 rods—and pull it through the water into the pool. It is placed in a rack with other spent-fuel rods.

3. The process is repeated for each of the 580 fuel assemblies. When the plant is ready to resume operation, two-thirds of the rods are returned to the core along with 190 fresh assemblies. The rest are stored in the pool for future disposal.

TIME diagram by Joe Lertol

hadn't noticed, and the consequences could be dire. If Millstone lost its primary cooling system while the full core was in the pool, Galatis told Betancourt, the backup systems might not handle the heat. "The pool could boil," he said. "We'd better report this to the NRC *now*."

Betancourt saw that Galatis was right. "But you do that," he said, "and you're dogmeat."

Galatis knew what he meant. Once a leading nuclear utility, Northeast had earned a reputation as a rogue—cutting corners and, according to critics, harassing and firing employees who raised safety concerns. But if Galatis wanted to take on the issue, Betancourt told him, "I'll back you."

So began a three-year battle in which Galatis tried to fix what he considered an obvious safety problem at Millstone 1. For 18 months his supervisors denied the problem ex-

isted and refused to report it to the NRC, the federal agency charged with ensuring the safety of America's 110 commercial reactors. Northeast brought in outside consultants to prove Galatis wrong, but they ended up agreeing with him. Finally, he took the case to the NRC himself, only to discover that officials there had known about the procedure for a decade without moving to stop it. The NRC says the practice is common, and safe—if a plant's cooling system is designed to handle the heat load. But Millstone's wasn't. And when Galatis learned that plants in Delaware, Nebraska and New Jersey had similar fuel-pool troubles, he realized the NRC was sitting on a nationwide problem.

Ten years after the disastrous uncontained meltdown at Chernobyl, 17 years after the partial meltdown at Three Mile Island, most Americans probably give only passing thought to the issue of nuclear safety. But the story of

George Galatis and Millstone suggests that the NRC itself may be giving only passing thought to the issue—that it may be more concerned with propping up an embattled, economically straitened industry than with ensuring public safety. When a nuclear plant violates safety standards and the federal watchdog turns a blind eye, the question arises, How safe are America's nuclear plants?

Though the NRC's mission statement promises full accountability—"nuclear regulation is the public's business," it says—the agency's top officials at first refused to be interviewed by TIME. After repeated requests, Chairwoman Shirley Ann Jackson, a physics professor who was appointed by President Clinton last summer, finally agreed to talk. But the veteran official in charge of the agency's day-to-day operations, executive director James M. Taylor, would provide only written answers to TIME's faxed questions.

"The responsibility for safety rests with the industry," Jackson told TIME. "Like any other regulatory body, NRC is essentially an auditing agency." Jackson argued that her agency is tough—"When we catch problems, it never makes the papers"—but added that with 3,000 employees and just four inspectors for every three plants, "we have to focus on the issues with the greatest safety significance. We can miss things."

In fact, Millstone is merely the latest in a long string of cases in which the NRC bungled its mandate and overlooked serious safety problems until whistle blowers came forward (see illustration). The NRC's relationship with the industry has been suspect since 1974, when the agency rose from the ashes of the old Atomic Energy Commission, whose mandate was to promote nuclear power. The industry vetoes commission nominees it deems too hostile (two of five NRC seats are vacant), and agency officials enjoy a revolving door to good jobs at nuclear companies such as Northeast. "The fox is guarding the henhouse," says Delaware Senator Joseph Biden, who is pushing legislation to create an independent nuclear safety board outside the NRC. The Democrat, who is also calling for a federal investigation of NRC effectiveness, believes the agency "has failed the public."

It all comes back to money. "When a safety issue is too expensive for the industry, the NRC pencils it away," says Stephen Comley, executive director of a whistle-blower support group called We the People, which has brought many agency failures to light. "If the NRC enforced all its rules, some of the plants we've studied couldn't compete economically."

In a rare point of agreement with activists, the nuclear industry also says regulations threaten to drive some plants out of business, but it argues that many NRC rules boost costs without enhancing safety. "The regulatory system hasn't kept pace with advances in technology," says Steve Unglesbee, a spokesman for the Nuclear Energy Institute, the industry's p.r. unit. "Industry-wide, our safety record is improving. But NRC creates so many layers of regulation that every plant is virtually assured of being in noncompliance with something."

The NRC suggested as much in a 1985 agency directive on "enforcement discretion," which allowed the agency to set aside hundreds of its own safety regulations. Since 1990, Millstone has received 15 such waivers—more than any other nuclear station. In November, Jackson scaled back the policy, but she says this never endangered public safety. Others disagree.

"Discretionary enforcement was out of hand," says NRC acting Inspector General Leo Norton, who investigates agency wrongdoing but has no power to punish. "We shouldn't have regulations on the books and then ignore or wink at them."

Yet the tensions between cost and safety can only increase as deregulation of the nation's utilities ushers in a new era of rate-slashing competition. In some states, consumers will soon choose their electric company the way they now choose a long-distance telephone carrier. Companies with nuclear plants are at a disadvantage because nuclear-generated electricity can cost twice as much as fossil-generated power. No new plants have been ordered in 18 years, and a dozen have been mothballed in the past decade.

For now, however, nuclear power provides 20% of the electricity consumed in the U.S.; New England depends on nuclear plants for more than half its supply. Long-term, says Northeast senior vice president Donald Miller, Millstone and her sisters will survive only "if we start running them like a business [and] stop throwing money at issues." New England's largest power company, with $6.5 billion in assets and $3.7 billion in revenues last year, Northeast is slashing its nuclear work force of 3,000 employees by one-third over the next five years. Company CEO Bernard Fox says the move will not undermine safety.

George Galatis went to work at Northeast Utilities in June 1982 with a degree from Rensselaer Polytechnic Institute and experience with a top manufacturer of nuclear components. At Northeast, he started in the division that oversees the utility's 15 fossil-fuel plants, then moved to the nuclear group, specializing in performance and reliability. Eric DeBarba, Northeast's vice president of technical services, describes him as a solid engineer. "Nobody here ever questioned his honesty or motives," DeBarba says.

Galatis tells it differently. In March 1992 he began working on Millstone 1, one of three nuclear plants perched on a neck of land that juts into Long Island Sound from the shore of southeastern Connecticut. He was checking specifications for a replacement part for a heat exchanger in the spent-fuel cooling system. To order the proper part, he needed to know the heat load. So he pulled a safety report that should contain the relevant data.

But they weren't there.

"The report didn't contain the safety analysis for what we were doing," says Galatis. "No heat-load calculations." It was then he realized the plant had been routinely operating "beyond design basis," putting 23 million BTUs into a pool analyzed for 8 million, which is, he says, "a bit like running your car at 5,000 r.p.m."

Galatis raised the issue with members of Northeast's division of nuclear licensing. "They tried to convince me they had it analyzed," he says. He asked them to produce the documents, and they could not. Galatis sensed trouble when, in later talks, "they began denying that the first discussions had taken place." In June 1992 he spelled out the problem in a memo, calling the fuel pool a license violation and an "unreviewed safety question"—NRC lingo for a major regulatory headache—and adding other concerns he had found, such as the fact that some of the pool's cooling pipes weren't designed to withstand an earthquake, as they were required to do. Northeast sat on the memo for three months, until Galatis filed an internal notice-of-violation form, and Betancourt, a leader in the spent-fuel field for years, wrote a memo backing him up.

"When I started in the industry, 20 years ago," Betancourt says, "spent fuel was considered the ass end of the fuel cycle. No one wanted to touch it. Everyone wanted to be on the sexy side, inside the reactor vessel, where the action and danger were. No one noticed fuel pools until we started running out of room in them."

In 1982 Congress mandated that the Department of Energy begin to accept nuclear waste from commercial reactors in 1998. Consumers started paying into a federal fund meant to finance a storage site. Though the Energy Department has collected $8.3 billion, no facility has been completed; in a case of NIMBY writ large, no state wants such a site in its backyard. As the nation's stockpile of spent fuel reached 30,000 tons, activists seized the issue as a way to hobble the industry, and the Energy Department announced that a permanent facility planned for Yucca Mountain, Nevada, wouldn't be ready until 2010; Energy

Secretary Hazel O'Leary now puts its chances of opening at no better than fifty-fifty. Bills to create temporary sites are stalled in both houses of Congress.

"Slowly, we woke up to this problem," says Betancourt. The NRC relaxed standards and granted license amendments that allowed plants to "rerack" their rods in ever more tightly packed pools. Sandwiched between the rods is a neutron-absorbing material called Boraflex that helps keep them from "going critical." After fuel pools across the country were filled in this way, the industry discovered that radiation causes Boraflex to shrink and crack. The NRC is studying the problem, but at times its officials haven't bothered to analyze a pool's cooling capacity before granting a reracking amendment. "It didn't receive the attention that more obvious safety concerns got," says Inspector General Norton.

Then, in late 1992, David Lochbaum and Don Prevatte, consultants working at Pennsylvania Power & Light's Susquehanna plant, began to analyze deficiencies in spent-fuel cooling systems. They realized that a problem had been sneaking up on the industry: half a dozen serious accidents at different plants had caused some water to drain from the pools. In the worst of them, at Northeast's Haddam Neck plant in 1984, a seal failure caused 200,000 gal. to drain in just 20 min. from a water channel next to the fuel pool. If the gate between the channel and the pool had been open, the pool could have drained, exposing the rods and causing a meltdown. Says Lochbaum: "It was a near miss."

The NRC insists that the chance of such an accident is infinitesimal. But the agency's risk-assessment methods have been called overly optimistic by activists, engineers and at least one NRC commissioner. The agency's analysis for a fuel-pool drainage accident assumes that at most one-third of a core is in the pool, even though plants across the country routinely move full cores into pools crowded with older cores. If the NRC based its calculations on that scenario, says Lochbaum, "it would exceed the radiation-dose limits set by Congress and scare people to death. But the NRC won't do it." The NRC's Taylor told TIME that the agency analyzes dose rates at the time a plant opens—when its pool is empty. The law, he said, "does not contain a provision for rereview."

Lochbaum and Prevatte reported Susquehanna to the NRC and suggested improvements to its cooling system. The NRC, Lochbaum says, didn't read the full report. He and Prevatte called Congress members, pushed for a public hearing and presented their concerns to NRC staff. Conceding that Lochbaum and Prevatte "had some valid points," the agency launched a task force and in 1993 issued an informational notice to the 35 U.S. reactors that share Susquehanna's design, alerting them to the problem but requiring no action. One of the plants was Millstone 1.

In 1992, Galatis didn't know about Lochbaum's struggle to get fuel-pool problems taken seriously. He did know he would face resistance from Northeast, where the bonus system is set up to reward employees who don't raise safety issues that incur costs and those who compromise productivity see their bonuses reduced. (Northeast says it has a second set of bonuses to reward those who raise safety issues. Galatis never got one.)

"Management tells you to come forward with problems," says Millstone engineer Al Cizek, "but actions speak louder than words." A Northeast official has been quoted in an NRC report saying the company didn't have to resolve a safety problem because he could "blow it by" the regulators. An NRC study says the number of safety and harassment allegations filed by workers at Northeast is three times the industry average. A disturbing internal Millstone report, presented to CEO FOX in 1991 and obtained by TIME, warns of a "cultural problem" typified by chronic failure to follow procedures, hardware problems that were not resolved or were forgotten, and a management tolerant of "willful [regulatory] noncompliance without justification." The report, written by director of engineering Mario Bonaca, changed nothing. "We've been working at this," says Fox, "but making fundamental change in a complex, technical environment is really hard."

A 1996 Northeast internal document reports that 38% of employees "do not trust their management enough to willingly raise concerns [because of] a 'shoot the messenger' attitude" at the company. In recent years, two dozen Millstone employees have claimed they were fired or demoted for raising safety concerns; in two cases, the NRC fined Northeast. In one, Paul Blanch, who had only recently been named engineer of the year by a leading industry journal, was subjected to company-wide harassment after he discovered that some of Millstone Unit 3's safety instrumentation didn't work properly.

Galatis had watched that case unfold. "George knew what he was getting into," says Blanch. "He knew Northeast would come after him. He knew the NRC wouldn't protect him. And he did it anyway."

In January 1993, Galatis pushed for a meeting with Richard Kacich, Northeast's director of nuclear licensing. Galatis outlined the pool's problems and asked for a consultant, Holtec International, to be brought in. Holtec agreed with Galatis that the pool was an unanalyzed safety

question; later the consultant warned that a loss of primary cooling could result in the pool's heating up to 216°F—a nice slow boil.

Galatis sent a memo to DeBarba, then vice president of nuclear engineering, in May 1993. Galatis was threatening to go to the NRC, so DeBarba created a task force to address "George's issues," as they were becoming known. The aim seems to have been to appease Galatis and keep him from going public. DeBarba says the calculations that Holtec and Galatis used were overly conservative and that experience told him there was no problem. The pool hadn't boiled, so it wouldn't boil. If a problem ever developed, there would be plenty of time to correct it before it reached the crisis stage. "We live and work here. Why would we want an unsafe plant? We had internal debate on this topic," DeBarba told TIME. "Legitimate professional differences of opinion." In 1977, he says, the NRC stated, "We could make the choice [of a full-core off-load] if it's 'necessary or desirable for operational considerations.' But that does not mean that what George raised was not an issue. We have rules on this, and we want to get it right."

By October 1993, Galatis was writing to the chief of Northeast's nuclear group, John Opeka, and to Fox, who was then company president. Galatis mentioned the criminal penalties for "intentional misconduct" in dealings with the NRC. Opeka objected to Galatis' abrasive tone but hired another consulting firm, which also agreed with Galatis. Northeast moved on to yet another consultant, a retired NRC official named Jim Partlow.

In December, during a four-hour interview that Galatis calls his "rape case"—because the prosecutor, he says, put the victim on trial—Partlow grilled Galatis about his "agenda" and "motives." After Galatis showed him the technical reports, Partlow changed his mind about Galatis and began questioning Kacich about the apparent violations. In two March 1994 memos to Kacich, Partlow backed Galatis, scolded the utility for taking so long to respond to him and suggested that they should reward Galatis "for his willingness to work within the NU system . . . Let him know that his concern for safety . . . is appreciated."

DeBarba and Kacich created another task force but did not modify the cooling system. Kacich began having conversations with Jim Andersen, the NRC's project manager for Millstone 1, about Galatis' concerns and how to get through the spring 1994 off-load. Andersen, who works at NRC headquarters in Washington, has told the inspector general that he knew all along Millstone was off-loading its full core but didn't know until June 1993 that it was a problem. Even then he did not inform his superiors. In a bow to Galatis, Millstone modified its off-load procedure, moving all the rods but doing so in stages. Before the off-load, Northeast formally reported to Andersen what he'd known for months: that Millstone might have been operating outside its design basis, a condition that must be reported within 30 days.

During the spring outage, a valve was accidentally left open, spilling 12,000 gal. of reactor-coolant water—a blunder that further shook Galatis' faith. He began to see problems almost everywhere he looked and proposed the creation of a global-issues task force to find out whether Millstone was safe enough to go back online. His bosses agreed. But when the head of the task force left for a golf vacation a few weeks before the plant was scheduled to start up, Galatis says, he knew it wasn't a serious effort. So he made a call to Ernest Hadley, the lawyer who had defended whistle blower Blanch against Northeast two years before.

An employment and wrongful-termination lawyer, Hadley has made a career of representing whistle blowers, many of them from Millstone. For 10 years he has also worked with Stephen Comley and We the People. Comley, a Massachusetts nursing-home operator, is a classic New England character, solid and brusque. He founded We the People in 1986 when he realized the evacuation plans for Seabrook Station, a plant 12 miles from his nursing home, included doses of iodine for those too old and frail to evacuate.

"Some of us were expendable," says Comley. "That got me going." For years he was known for publicity stunts—hiring planes to trail banners above the U.S. Capitol—and emotional outbursts at the press conferences of politicians. The NRC barred him from its public meetings until a judge ordered the ban lifted. But Comley's game evolved: instead of demanding that plants be shut down, he began insisting they be run safely. He teamed up with the sharpwitted Hadley to aid and abet whistle blowers and sank his life savings into We the People before taking a dime in donations. Comley, says the NRC's Norton, "has been useful in bringing important issues to our attention. Steve can be a very intense guy. I don't think it's good for his health. But people who seem—not fanatical, but overly intense—help democracy work."

In April, 1994, two years after he discovered the problems with Millstone's cooling system, Galatis reported the matter to the NRC. He spoke to a "senior allegations coordinator," waited months, then refiled his charges in a letter describing 16 problems, including the cooling system, the pipes that couldn't withstand seismic shock, the corporate culture. "At Northeast, people are the biggest safety problem," Galatis says. "Not the guys in the engine room. The guys who drive the boat."

Galatis told DeBarba and Kacich that he was going to the NRC. He continued to experience what he calls "subtle forms of harassment, retaliation and intimidation." His performance evaluation was down-graded, his personnel file forwarded to Northeast's lawyers. DeBarba "offered" to move him out of the nuclear group. He would walk into a meeting, and the room would go suddenly silent. De-Barba says he is unaware of any such harassment.

With missionary zeal, Galatis continued to forward allegations to the NRC. Yet four months passed before Galatis finally heard from Donald Driskill, an agent with the NRC's Office of Investigations (the second watchdog unit inside the NRC, this one tracks wrongdoing by utilities). Galatis felt that Driskill was too relaxed about the case. Driskill talked to Northeast about Galatis' charges—a breach of confidentiality that the NRC calls "inadvertent." When Hadley complained to him about Northeast's alleged harassment of Galatis, Driskill suggested he talk to Northeast's lawyer: "He's a really nice guy."

While playing detective—sniffing through file drawers and computer directories—Galitis found items that he felt suggested collusion between the utility and its regulator. Safety reports made it clear that both on-site inspectors and officials from the NRC's Office of Nuclear Reactor Regulation had known about the full-core off-loads since at least 1987 but had never done anything about them. Now, to clear the way for the fall 1995 off-load, NRC officials were apparently offering Northeast what Galatis calls "quiet coaching." One sign of this was a draft version of an NRC inspection report about the spent-fuel pool that had been E-mailed from the NRC to Kacich's licensing department. "What was that doing in Northeast's files?" asks Inspector General Norton.

On June 10, 1995, Jim Andersen visited the site to discuss Galatis' concerns with Kacich's staff. Andersen wouldn't meet with Galatis but huddled with Kacich's team, trying to decide how to bring Millstone's habits into compliance with NRC regulations, either by requesting a license amendment—a cumbersome process that requires NRC review and public comment—or by filing an internal form updating the plant's safety reports. This was the easier path, but it could be used only if the issue didn't constitute an unreviewed safety question. Andersen told De-Barba and Kacich that the license amendment "is the cleaner way to go," but they weren't sure there was enough time to get an amendment approved before the next off-load, scheduled for October 1995.

NEAR MISSES

The Nuclear Regulatory Commission's Office of the Inspector General—a watchdog that can investigate but not punish—has looked into an array of cases in which safety problems were ignored by NRC staff. Some highlights:

- After a 1975 fire knocked out equipment at the Browns Ferry plant in Alabama, the NRC approved a material called Thermo-Lag as a "fire barrier" to protect electrical systems. Between 1982 and 1991, however, the NRC ignored seven complaints about Thermo-Lag; when an engineer testified that fire caused it to melt and give off lethal gases, the NRC closed the case without action. After more complaints and an inspector general's investigation, the NRC "reassessed." Now, it says, "corrective action is ongoing."

- In 1980 workers at Watts Bar 1, a plant then under construction by the Tennessee Valley Authority, flooded the NRC with some 6,000 allegations of shoddy workmanship and safety lapses—enough to halt construction for five years. The NRC breached confidentiality and identified whistle blowers such as electrical supervisor Ann Harris to the TVA; several were fired. After 23 years and $7 billion, Watts Bar 1 was completed last fall. Though workers say the TVA has abandoned thorough safety inspections in favor of a "random sampling" program, the NRC in February granted an operating license to Watts Bar, the last U.S. nuclear plant scheduled for start-up.

- In the early 1980s, when Northeast Utilities' Seabrook Station in New Hampshire was under construction, Joseph Wampler warned the NRC that many welds were faulty. His complaints went unanswered, and he was eventually fired. Blacklisted, he says, Wampler moved to California and revived his career. But in 1991 the NRC sent a letter summarizing Wampler's allegations—and providing his full name and new address—to several dozen nuclear companies. His career was destroyed a second time; he now works as a carpenter. The NRC fined Northeast $100,000 for problems with the welds.

- In 1990 Northeast engineer Paul Blanch discovered that the instruments that measure the coolant level inside the reactor at Millstone 3 were failing. Blanch was forced out, and the problem went uncorrected. In 1993 the NRC's William Russell told the inspector general that the agency had exercised "enforcement discretion," a policy that allows it to waive regulations. Later Russell said the remark had been taken out of context.

- Last December a worker at the Maine Yankee plant in Bath charged that management had deliberately falsified computer calculations to avoid disclosing that the plant's cooling systems were inadequate. The NRC didn't discover this, the Union of Concerned Scientists told reporters, because it didn't notice that Maine Yankee had failed to submit the calculations for review—though they were due in January 1990.

- In 1988 a technician at the Nine Mile Point plant near Oswego, New York, called the NRC with allegations of drug use and safety violations at the plant. The NRC executive director at the time, Victor Stello Jr., took a personal interest in the matter, but his chief aim seemed to be building a case against Roger Fortuna, the deputy director of the NRC's Office of Investigation, for leaking secrets to the watchdog group We the People. The NRC demanded that We the People head Steve Comley turn over tapes he had allegedly made of conversations with Fortuna. When Comley refused, he was ruled in contempt and fined $350,000 (he still has not paid). The charges against Fortuna were found to be without merit, and when the case came to light—during hearings to confirm Stello as Assistant Secretary of Energy—Stello withdrew his name. "The tension between enforcement and appeasement," a ranking NRC official says, "tugs at this agency every day."

On July 10, Betancourt met with Ken Jenison, an inspector from the NRC's Region 1 office, and gave testimony in support of Galatis' safety allegations. Less than a week later, Betancourt was called to the office of a good-natured human-resources officer named Janice Roncaioli. She complained that he wasn't a "team player," Betan-court says, and ran through the company's termination policies. Rancaioli called Betancourt's account of the meeting "slanted" but would not comment further, citing employee-confidentiality rules.

In a July 14 meeting, Jenison, one official who wasn't going to stand for any regulatory sleight-of-hand, told

DeBarba and Kacich that if Northeast tried to resolve its licensing problems through internal paperwork alone, he would oppose it. Northeast had to get a license amendment approved before it could off-load another full core, and time was running out. DeBarba and Kacich called on Galatis and Betancourt to help them write the amendment request. The plan included, for the first time, the cooling-system improvements Galatis had been demanding for three years. It was a kind of victory, but he felt disgusted. "The organizational ethics were appalling," he says. "There's no reason I should have had to hire a lawyer and spend years taking care of something this simple."

So Galatis helped Kacich with the amendment request, which was filed July 28. Then he and Hadley drew up another document: a petition that asked the NRC to deny Northeast's amendment request and suspend Millstone's license for 60 days. The petition, filed on behalf of Galatis and We the People, charged that Northeast had "knowingly, willingly, and flagrantly" violated Millstone 1's license for 20 years, that it had made "material false statements" to the NRC and that it would, if not punished, continue to operate unsafely.

On Aug. 1, Betancourt was called into DeBarba's office; Roncaioli was present, and DeBarba told Betancourt he was being reassigned. "We want to help you, George," Betancourt recalls DeBarba saying, "but you've got to start thinking 'company.'" It was all very vague and, Betancourt thought, very intimidating. On Aug. 3—the day Betancourt was scheduled to meet with the Office of Investigations—Roncaioli called him to her office again. According to Betancourt, she said she wanted to "reaffirm the meaning" of the DeBarba meeting. Betancourt's wife and children began to be worried that he would be fired. "Why don't you just do what they want you to?" his eldest girl asked. Betancourt didn't know quite how to answer. "Your own daughter telling you to roll over," he says.

After Galatis filed his petition, on Aug. 21, he found himself in many of New England's newspapers. As citizen's groups called meetings, Northeast and the NRC assured everyone that the full-core off-load was a common practice that enhanced safety for maintenance workers inside the empty reactor vessel. "We've been aware of how they off-loaded the full core," NRC spokeswoman Diane Screnci told one paper. "We could have stopped them earlier."

At a citizens' group meeting, Galatis met a mechanic named Pete Reynolds, who had left Millstone in a labor dispute two years before. Reynolds shared some hair-raising stories about his days off-loading fuel. He told Galatis—and has since repeated the account to TIME—that he saw work crews racing to see who could move fuel rods the fastest. The competition, he said, tripped radiation alarms and overheated the fuel pool. Reynolds' job was to remove the big bolts that hold the reactor head in place. Sometimes, he said, he was told to remove them so soon after shutdown that the heat melted his protective plastic booties.

Galatis knew that if such things had happened, they would be reflected in operator's logs filed in Northeast's document room. So, on Oct. 6, he appeared in the room and asked for the appropriate rolls of microfiche. The logs backed up what Reynolds had said: Millstone had moved fuel as soon as 65 hrs. after shutdown—a quarter of the required time. The logs noted the sounding of alarms. Galatis wondered where the resident inspector had been.

The deadline came for Millstone's off-load, but the amendment still had not been granted. Connecticut's Senator Chris Dodd, Representative Sam Gejdenson and a host of local officials were asking about the plant's safety, and Millstone scheduled a public meeting for late October. Senior vice president Don Miller sent a memo to his employees warning them that "experienced antinuclear activists" had "the intention of shutting the station down and eliminating 2,500 jobs." The memo stirred up some of Galatis' colleagues. "You're taking food out of my girl's mouth," one of them told him.

DeBarba assembled a task force to assess what had to be done to get the pool ready for the overdue off-load, but he kept Galatis and Betancourt off the team. The task force came up with six serious problems, most already raised by Galatis. Scrambling to fix the pool in a few weeks, DeBarba hired extra people. The plant shut down anticipating permission to move fuel.

Galatis and Hadley had been waiting two months for a reply to their petition to deny Northeast's amendment. Finally, on Oct. 26, a letter from William Russell, director of the NRC's Office of Nuclear Reactor Regulation, informed them that their petition was "outside of the scope" of the applicable regulatory subchapter. Two weeks later, the NRC granted Northeast's amendment. Millstone started moving fuel the next morning.

Because of Galatis, the plant is still shut down. "What's especially galling," says Hadley, "is that the NRC ignored my client and denied his motion, then validated his concerns after the fact." In late December, Inspector General Norton released his preliminary report. He found that Northeast had conducted improper full-core off-loads for 20 years. Both the NRC's on-site inspectors and headquarters staff, the report said, "were aware" of the practice but somehow "did not realize" that this was a violation. In other words, the NRC's double-barreled oversight system shot blanks from both barrels. Norton blamed bad training and found no evidence of a conspiracy between Northeast and the NRC to violate the license. He is still investigating possible collusion by the NRC after Galatis came forward. What troubled him most, Norton told TIME, is that agency officials all the way up to Russell knew about the off-loads and saw nothing wrong with them. "The agency completely failed," says Norton. "We did shoddy work. And we're concerned that similar lapses might be occurring at other plants around the country."

In a second investigation, the Office of Investigations is looking into Northeast's license violations and the alleged harassment of Galatis and Betancourt. The intense public scrutiny their case has received will, Galatis says, "make it harder for them to sweep this one under the rug."

On Dec. 12, Russell sent a letter informing Northeast that because "certain of your activities may have been conducted in violation of license requirements," the NRC was considering penalties. In an extraordinary move, Russell demanded a complete review of every system at Millstone 1, with the results "submitted Funder oath," to prove that every part of the plant is safe—the global examination Galatis asked for two years ago. The results, Russell wrote, "will be used to decide whether or not the license of Millstone Unit 1 should be suspended, modified or revoked."

Now the pressure is on NRC Chairwoman Jackson to prove her commitment to nuclear safety—and her ability to reform an inert bureaucracy. "I will not make a sweeping indictment of NRC staff," Jackson, a straight-talking physicist who in July 1995 became both the first female and the first African American to run the NRC, told TIME. "Does that mean everybody does things perfectly? Obviously not. We haven't always been on top of things. The ball got dropped. Here's what I'm saying now: The ball will not get dropped again."

In response to the problems Galatis exposed, Jackson launched a series of policies designed to improve training, accountability and vigilance among inspectors and NRC staff. She ordered the agency's second whistle-blower study in two years and a nationwide review of all 110 nuclear plants, to find out how many have been moving fuel in violation of NRC standards. The results will be in by April, along with a menu of fuel-pool safety recommendations. (By using a technique called dry-cask storage, utilities could empty their pools and warehouse rods in airtight concrete containers, reducing risk. In the past, the NRC has ruled that the process isn't cost effective.)

Jackson still refuses to meet with Galatis or even take his phone call. "Mr. Galatis is part of an adjudicatory process," she explains. But in a letter turning down Stephen Comley's request that she meet with him and Galatis, Jackson wrote, "The avenues you have been using to raise issues are the most effective and efficient ways. I see no additional benefit to the meeting."

Asked by TIME if she considered three years and two wrecked careers "the most efficient" way to raise the fuel-pool issue, Jackson offered a thin smile. "I'm changing the process," she said. "When all is said and done, then Mr. Galatis and I can sit and talk."

For Galatis, the endgame should have been sweet. On Dec. 20, a Millstone technical manager fired off a frank piece of E-mail warning his colleagues that "the acceptance criteria are changing. Being outside the proper regulatory framework, even if technically justifiable, will be met with resistance by the NRC. Expect no regulatory relief." De-Barba put 100 engineers on a global evaluation of the plant, and they turned up more than 5,000 "items" to be addressed before the plant could go back online. The company announced a reorganization of its nuclear division in which DeBarba and Miller were both promoted. Miller, who told TIME that "complacency" was to blame for the utility's troubles, was put in charge of safety at Northeast's five nuclear plants. On Jan. 29, the NRC, citing chronic safety concerns, employee harassment "and historic emphasis on cost savings vs. performance," enshrined all three Millstone plants in the agency's hall of shame: the high-scrutiny "watch list" of troublesome reactors. Northeast announced that Millstone would stay down at least through June, at a cost of $75 million. And Standard & Poor's downgraded Northeast's debt rating from stable to negative.

"A hell of an impact," says Betancourt, but "I'm going to lose my job."

"If I had it to do over again," says Galatis, "I wouldn't." He believes his nuclear career is over. (Though still employed by Northeast, he knows that whistle blowers are routinely shut out by the industry.) He's thinking about entering divinity school.

In January, Northeast laid off 100 employees. To qualify for their severance money, the workers had to sign elaborate release forms pledging not to sue the utility for harassment. Four engineers say they were fired in retaliation for their testimony to the NRC four years ago on behalf of whistle blower Blanch. The company denies any connection between the layoffs and Blanch's case. That makes Blanch chuckle. "The two Georges had better watch their backs," he says. "Up at Northeast, they've got long memories."

In the end, Galatis believes, the NRC's recent flurry of activity is little more than window dressing. "If they wanted to enforce the law," he says, "they could have acted when it counted—before granting the license amendment. Whatever wrist slap they serve up now is beside the point."

"I believe in nuclear power," he says, "but after seeing the NRC in action, I'm convinced a serious accident is not just likely but inevitable. This is a dangerous road. They're asleep at the wheel. And I'm road-kill."

Questions

1. What is the solution to the problem of storing nuclear reactive waste?

2. Why was Millstone sidestepping the safety requirements? What would have happened if Millstone lost its primary cooling system while the full core was in the pool?

3. What would you have done if you had been in Galatis's and Betancourt's position? Defend your reasoning for your actions.

4. What part does the NRC play in monitoring the lethality of this situation?

A Bridge to Your 21st Century Understanding

Complete and discuss the following flowchart.

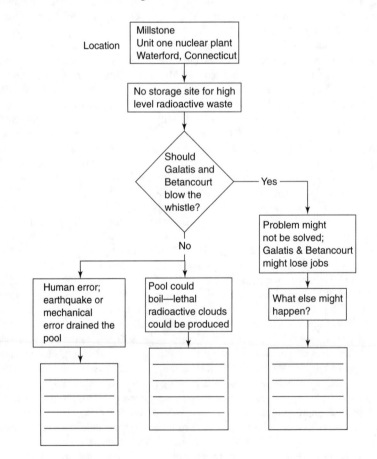

The Great Molasses Flood

41

"Old timers in Boston say that to this very day you can smell a faint whiff of molasses in the old buildings on Commercial Street. But is that only an old timer's tall tale?"

MARJORIE STOVER, AUTHOR

It might be unusual to smell molasses on Commercial Street in Boston today, but on January 15, 1919, there was no doubt that the smell of molasses was in the air. On that mild winter day, "without warning, a massive tidal wave of sweet, sticky death gushed from a fractured steel tank, leaving twenty-one dead, over one hundred and fifty injured and many buildings crushed under nearly 12,000 tons of thick, brown, sugary molasses." (Schlager, 1994).

The problem started when a giant steel-sided storage tank that was 50 feet high and 90 feet in diameter was built by the Purity Distilling Company to contain rum, but instead was being used to store tons of molasses (Cavadias, 1998, p. 1; Stover, 1985, p. 34). The original order for the tank was issued without an engineer's approval, and the only requirement used in making the order was that the tank be able to hold liquids that were 50% heavier than water (Schlager, 1994, p. 246). There were further problems with the tank as well:

> The steel thicknesses for the rings were 5 to 10 percent less than illustrated on the original permit plans. . . . The only way that the tank was tested was by running six inches of water into it. (Schlager, 1996, p. 247)

These problems with the tank caused it to fail. Apparently, employees had noticed that the tank had been leaking molasses, but chose not to report it. However, on January 15, 1919, at 12:40 PM, everyone in the area of 529 Commercial Street in the North End of Boston found out the hard way that the molasses tank had problems. First, they heard sounds similar to the firing of machine guns as the rivets holding together the metal sheets of the tank's body popped out of their holes (Mercan, 1998, p. 2). Then,

they heard a roaring sound as the tank exploded and separated warm molasses poured into the streets. (The molasses was warm because the company had placed steam heating pipes inside of the tank.) Some say that the river of molasses flowed at 35 miles per hour and was at times 15 feet high and 160 feet wide (Cavadias, 1998, p. 1; Mercan, 1998, p. 2; Schlager, 1996, p. 247).

Twenty-one people were killed due to the molasses flow, either by drowning or by being hit by debris. Over 150 people were injured. It was difficult for the rescue workers and their trucks and equipment to get through to help the injured because the gooey liquid stood three feet deep in some places (Stover, 1985, p. 36). A 2.5-ton section of the tank had been thrown onto a playground 182 feet away (Schlager, 1996, p. 247). Another part of the tank broke and tore off a part of the Atlantic Avenue Elevated Railway, causing the railway to collapse. It seems that the pieces of tank were thrown far distances because the fermenting molasses caused pent-up gases to form within the tank, causing the tank to burst apart when the pressure got too high (Mercan, 1998, p. 2). Some survivors had to have their "molasses-stiffened clothing cut off of them, and trapped horses had to be shot" (Cavadias, 1998, p. 1).

The flood of goo engulfed the area and destroyed most everything in its path. Buildings fell off their foundations, basements were filled with molasses, molasses "statues" of people were found, and the tank was left laying in pieces on the ground, as a painful reminder. It was six or seven days before all of the bodies could be found and months before Commercial Street could return to normal (Cavadia, 1998, p. 1; Mercan, 1998, p. 2; Stover, 1985, p. 35; Schlager, 1996, p. 248).

When the tank was examined, two fractures were found in the steel plates; it was these fractures that allowed the tank to be torn apart. Also, it did not help that the tank had been made of materials that were thinner than those called for on the original permit drawings. The tank was a technological failure because it was improperly designed and constructed and because the calculations for the tank's construction were never checked by an experienced engineer. The tank disaster had occurred because of structural weakness and human error. (Schlager, 1996, p. 249).

References

January 15, 1919: A tidal wave of molasses inundates Boston. (1998, August). Available: http://cavadia.com/tidalwave.html.

The great Boston molasses flood. (1998, August). Available: http://www.mercan.com/~kimchee/molass1.nun.

Schlager, N. (1996). *Accidents and Failures of the Twentieth Century.* London, Gale Research, Inc.

Stover, M. *Patrick and the Great Molasses Explosion.* (1985). Minneapolis, Dillon Press, Inc.

Questions

1. If you had been working at the Purity Distilling Company in 1919, what would you have done to prevent this accident from happening?

2. What is the relationship between this case and social responsibility? Why do you think that the employees ignored the leaking tank seams? Why wouldn't anyone question the tank's use when the tank was installed?

A Bridge to Your 21st Century Understanding

Complete and discuss the following flowchart.

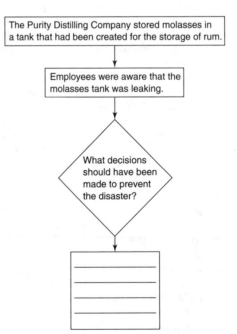

The Toxic Cloud Over Bhopal

42

In the early hours of December 3, 1984 a toxic cloud of methyl isocyanate (MIC) gas from Union Carbide's plant in Bhopal, India, escaped and enveloped the hundreds of shanties and huts surrounding the plant. The deadly cloud drifted in the cool night air through streets in surrounding neighborhoods killing and badly injuring thousands of people. By dawn inhabitants of Bhopal had become victims of the worst industrial accident.

A report drawn up eight months later, by two international trade union confederations, suggested that it was a combination of management mistakes, badly designed equipment and poor maintenance that caused the accident. The gas was formed when a plant employee added water to a methyl isocyanate storage tank. The water caused a reaction that built up heat and pressure in the tank, and quickly converted the chemical into lethal gas that escaped into the atmosphere. The sensors and alarms that could have detected and indicated the increase in pressure and heat in the MIC tank were inoperative. The plant's flare tower that could have been used to burn off the escaping gas was inoperative too. The warning sirens were used with one hour delay. There was no evacuation plan prepared beforehand for such an emergency. The civil authorities and the population of Bhopal were also not informed about the degree of toxicity and the movement of the MIC gas cloud.

Approximately twenty-seven tons of MIC vapor, and fourteen tons of reaction products, were released in the atmosphere over a period of ninety minutes and affected an area of fifteen square miles.

The MIC gas leak was not the first accident at the plant; in the preceding four years there had been six accidents, some of which involved MIC, including one fatality in 1981 which led to an official investigation. The findings of that investigation were not acted upon until after the accident in 1984.

The Union Carbide developed its plant in 1969 at Bhopal, initially as a mixing and packaging plant for pesticides imported from the United States. Later, in 1980 it was expanded to manufacture the pesticides Sevin and Temik. One chemical used in large quantities in the production process was methyl isocyanate (MIC), a highly reactive, volatile and toxic compound. The process that reacted MIC with another compound was considered the leading technology for producing pesticides Sevin and Temik. The development of the plant was part of an Indian government effort to achieve industrial self-sufficiency. The plant was located on the outskirts of Bhopal on land leased to Union Carbide India Limited (UCIL) by the Indian state government of Madhya Pradesh, at an annual rent of about Rupees 500 ($40).

In 1984 Union Carbide reported sales of $9.5 billion, reflecting its position as one of the largest industrial companies in the United States and the world. The international operations were responsible for approximately 30 percent of total sales that year. India was one of three dozen countries where Union Carbide had business interests. In 1984 Union Carbide India Limited (UCIL) celebrated its 50th anniversary. It operated 14 plants with a workforce of 9,000 people. UCIL had sales of about $200 million annually. In 1984 the entire work force at Bhopal plant was Indian. In keeping with the government's interest in promoting self-sufficiency and

The Bhopal Catastrophe

Chemicals Leaked	Approximately twenty-seven tons of Methyl Isocyanate (MIC) vapor and fourteen tons of reaction products
Threshold limit value (TLV) of MIC established by United States Occupational Safety and Health Act (OSHA).	0.02 parts per million over eight hour period.
Exposure area	Fifteen square miles
Deaths	2,352–10,000
People Disabled	17,000–20,000
People Exposed	200,000
People Evacuated	70,000

local control, the last American employed at the plant had left two years before, making the plant an all Indian operation.

The legal dimensions of the Bhopal disaster began when Indian prosecutors brought charges of criminal negligence against the Indian and American management of Union Carbide in the Indian courts. In 1985 the government of India, on behalf of the victims of Bhopal, filed a civil suit against Union Carbide in the Federal District Court in New York City. The U.S. court decided that India was the proper site for any Bhopal action and sent the litigation there for disposition. The Indian government filed suit in India for $3.3 billion. After several years of negotiations, Union Carbide agreed to a settlement of $470 million with the government of Ragiv Ghandi. The dropping of all criminal charges against Union Carbide executives was part of the settlement.

After the elections in India, the government of new prime minister V.P. Singh repudiated the Indian Supreme Court and rejected the $470 million settlement as "totally inadequate". His government announced its intention to return to the original $3.3 billion claim and to pursue criminal charges against Union Carbide executives. Following a lengthy review by the Indian Supreme Court, the original settlement was upheld and the criminal proceedings were reopened. Union Carbide has paid, as ordered, $190 million in interim compensation which the government of India has to distribute among survivors pending the final outcome of the settlement. Presently the Indian government is providing survivors 200 Rupees a month (approximately U.S. $10). These payments are to last as long as the case remains unsettled in the Indian courts. It is expected that the litigation and debate over the criminal

prosecution for negligence and financial compensation will not end soon.

No matter what kind of settlement is reached in courts, the survivors face a nightmare future of uncertainty. Thousands are now suffering from a host of ailments including acute respiratory distress, vomiting blood, conjunctivitis, damaged eyesight, pain in the abdomen and injuries to liver, brain, heart, kidneys and immune system. In addition to these problems, women are also suffering from gynecological complications such as menstrual and reproductive disorders. An epidemiological study of the yearly rate of spontaneous abortions and infant deaths in the years after the accident found the rate in Bhopal to be three to four times the regional rate.

Today, at personal, local, national and international levels, the Bhopal disaster remains a reality. Like Union Carbide's plant in Bhopal, a number of chemical plants belonging to multi-national corporations are operating in the Third World countries. The lack of environmental and occupational safety regulations in the developing countries, coupled with multi-national companies' desire to increase earnings per share at any cost, sets the stage for reoccurrence of the Bhopal catastrophe.

References

Goldsmith, E., and Hildyard, N. (1998). *The Earth Report—The Guide to Global Ecological Issues,* Los Angeles, Price Stern Sloan, Inc.

Gottschalk A.J. (1993). *Crisis Response,* Detroit, Visible Ink Press.

Kurzman, D. (1987). *A Killing Wind,* New York, McGraw-Hill Company.

Schlager, N. (1994). *When Technology Fails,* Detroit, Gale Research.

Questions

1. What lessons should the chemical industry have learned from the Bhopal disaster?
2. What could be done at personal, local, national, and international levels to promote safety in the chemical plants?
3. In the Third World, more than half a million people are poisoned every year by pesticides, but these same pesticides also save millions from starvation. Should the use of pesticides be banned worldwide?
4. What steps and measures could Union Carbide have taken to avert the disaster at Bhopal?
5. How do you feel about the $470 million settlement? Is it an appropriate amount for 200,000 survivors for the rest of their lives?

A Bridge to Your 21st Century Understanding

Complete and discuss the following flowchart.

43 Crime in Cyberspace

GENE STEPHENS

Billions of dollars in losses have already been discovered. Billions more have gone undetected. Trillions will be stolen, most without detection, by the emerging master criminal of the twenty-first century—the cyberspace offender.

Worst of all, *anyone* who is computer literate can become a cybercrook. He or she is everyman, everywoman, or even everychild. The crime itself will often be *virtual* in nature—sometimes recorded, more often not—occurring only in cyberspace, with the only record being fleeting electronic impulses.

But before discussing the infohighway crimes we can expect to see in the years ahead, let's look at the good news: The most-dreaded types of offenses—crimes such as murder, rape, assault, robbery, burglary, and vehicle theft—will be brought under control in the years ahead by a combination of technology and proactive community policing. Creation of the cashless society, for example, will eliminate most of the rewards for robbers and muggers, while computer-controlled smart houses and cars will thwart burglars and auto thieves. Implanted bodily function monitors and chemical drips (such as "sober-up" drugs and synthesized hormones) will keep most of the sexually and physically violent offenders under control.

More importantly, proactive policies—seeking out crime-breeding situations and taking steps to eliminate

them before the crime occurs—may alleviate much of the burgeoning violence among young people. Tender, loving care demonstrated by informed parenting, universal health and day care, mentoring, and communal attention to children's welfare can prevent another generation of starved-for-attention juveniles from becoming criminals.

But cyberspace offenders—ranging in age from preteen to senior citizen—will have ample opportunities to violate citizens' rights for fun and profit, and stopping them will require much more effort. Currently, we have only primitive knowledge about these lawbreakers: Typically, they are seen only as nuisances or even admired as innovators or computer whizzes. But increasingly, the benign "hacker" is being replaced by the menacing "cracker"—an individual or member of a group intent on using cyberspace for illegal profit or terrorism.

Access to cyberspace has begun to expand geometrically, and technology is making the information superhighway even more friendly and affordable for millions of users. But foolproof protective systems can probably never be developed, although some high-tech entrepreneurs are certainly trying. Even if a totally secure system could ever be developed, it would likely disrupt the free flow of information—an unacceptable intrusion to most users. In fact, it is the ease of access that is driving this rapidly expanding field of crime.

What are the major cybercrimes being committed, how, and by whom? More importantly, where is cybercrime headed in the twenty-first century? Let's look at six cyberspace crime categories: communications, government, business, stalking, terrorism, and virtual.

Originally appeared in September–October 1995 issue of The Futurist. Used with permission from the World Future Society, 7910 Woodmont Avenue, Suite 450, Bethesda, Maryland 20814, 301/656-8274. <http://www.wfs.org>.

COMMUNICATIONS CRIMES

Already, cellular theft and phone fraud have become major crimes. Low-tech thieves in airports and bus terminals use binoculars to steal calling-card access numbers as unsuspecting callers punch in their phone codes. Other thieves park vans beside busy interstate highways and use equipment obtained from shopping mall electronics stores to steal cellular phone access codes from the air. Within moments of these thefts, international calls are being made with the stolen numbers in what is becoming a multibillion-dollar-a-year criminal industry.

Phone company employees, meanwhile, are also stealing and selling calling card numbers, resulting in more hundreds of millions of dollars in unauthorized calls. In 1994, an MCI engineer was charged with selling 60,000 calling card numbers for $3 to $5 each, resulting in more than $50 million in illegal long-distance charges. In another case, when a phone company tried to institute a call-forwarding program, crackers quickly defrauded the system of more money than the company stood to make in legal profits.

In the future, the opportunities for hacking and cracking will escalate, with telephones, computers, faxes, and televisions interconnected to provide instantaneous audiovisual communication and transmission of materials among individuals. The wide appeal of new multimedia communication systems will likely create such a huge volume of subscribers that the price will plummet and make access by all possible. But if billions of dollars of losses to thieves are compounded by billions more required to repair damages created by system terrorists, the cost might become prohibitive to all but the wealthy.

CYBERCRIMES AGAINST THE GOVERNMENT

In 1995, the U.S. Internal Revenue Service instituted stringent new regulations on electronic tax filing and returns. This move was to stop a rash of fraud that cost taxpayers millions in 1994: Returns that were processed quickly via this method turned out to be for tens of thousands of fictitious corporations and individuals. Similarly, in an attempt to stop food-stamp fraud, the government issued electronic debit cards to a trial population and plans to go nationwide with the system later in the decade. However, early reports show that many recipients are selling their benefits for cash—50¢ to 60¢ on the dollar—to merchants who then receive full payment.

Cyberpunks regularly break into government computer systems, usually out of curiosity and for the thrill of the challenge. They often intercept classified data and sometimes even interrupt and change systems. One U.S. Justice Department official reported that military computers are the most vulnerable, "even less secure than university computers." This official noted that, during Operation Desert Storm, hackers were able to track both actual and planned troop movements.

James V. Christy II, director of an Air Force unit of computer-crime investigators, set up a team of hackers to test the security of military computer systems. He reported that the hackers broke into Pentagon systems "within 15 seconds" and went on to break into over 200 Air Force systems with no one reporting or even recognizing the break-ins.

Ironically, computer hackers often beat the system using the very technology intended to stop them. For example, federal law-enforcement agencies use an Escrowed Encryption Standard to protect classified information and a chip-specific key to decrypt the system. Experienced hackers can easily discover the key and use it to obtain passwords, gaining full access to encrypted systems.

Newer, more secure encryption systems for protecting government and international business transactions require storing the "keys" in "escrow" with a specific government agency—usually the U.S. Treasury Department. Hackers and civil libertarians find this security solution unacceptable because it impedes the free flow of information and puts almost all sensitive and important data in the hands of government officials. This is seen by many as being dangerous to individual freedoms and a major step in the direction of creating a class structure based on the "information rich" and "information poor."

As more government data is stored in computers, protection will become both more vital and more difficult. When the livelihood of an individual depends on data in government computers, the temptation to "adjust" that record to increase benefits and reduce charges will be great. Many will try to do the adjusting themselves; others will be willing customers for a burgeoning black market of professional crackers. For those who have little need for government benefits but would like to eliminate their tax liability, a highly destructive method would be to plant a computer virus in government computers to destroy large members of records. In this way, suspicion would not fall on an individual.

TARGETING BUSINESS

Today, most banking is done by electronic impulse, surpassing checks and cash by a wide margin. In the near future, nearly all business transactions will be electronic. Thus, access to business computers equals access to money.

Recently, computer hacker John Lee, a founder of the infamous "Masters of Deception" hacker group, discussed his 10-year career, which began when he was 12 years old and included a one-year prison term in his late teens. Without admitting to any wrongdoing, Lee said that he could "commit a crime with five keystrokes" on the computer. He could: (1) change credit records and bank balances; (2) get free limousines, airplane flights, hotel rooms, and meals "without anyone being billed"; (3) change utility and rent rates; (4) distribute computer software programs free to all on the Internet; and (5) easily obtain insider trading information. Though prison was "no fun," Lee admitted that he would certainly be tempted to do it all again.

In a groundbreaking study published in *Criminal Justice Review* in the spring of 1994, Jerome E. Jackson of the California State University at Fresno reported the results of a study of a new group of criminals he called "fraud masters." These professional thieves obtain credit cards via fake applications, or by electronic theft, and pass them around among their peers internationally for profit. These young men and women want the "good life" after growing up in poverty. They are proud of their skills of deception and arrogant enough to feel they won't be caught. Indeed, none of those in the five-year case study were caught.

As seen in the $50-million-plus losses in the MCI case, a far greater threat to businesses than hackers are disgruntled and financially struggling employees. As internal theft from retail stores has always been many times greater in volume than theft from shoplifters, robbers, and burglars, theft by employees armed with inside information and computer access is and will continue to be a much larger problem than intrusion by hackers, crackers, and terrorists combined. By the turn of the century, 80% of Americans will process information as a major part of their employment, according to a United Way study.

In addition, the future portends new and brighter "for-profit" invasion of business computers. As one Justice Department official warns, "This technology in the hands of children today is technology that adults don't understand." The first generation of computer-literate citizens will reach adulthood shortly after the turn of the century and will surely open a new age in the annals of crime and crime-fighting.

CYBERSTALKING

One frightening type of cybercriminal emerging rapidly is the cyberstalker. Possibly the most disturbing of these criminals is the pedophile who surfs computer bulletin boards, filled with bright young boys and girls, in search of victims. He develops a cyberspace relationship and then seeks to meet the child in person to pursue his sexual intentions. Already recognized as a serious problem, cyberstalking has spawned the cybercop—a police officer assigned to computer bulletin boards in search of these pedophiles. Once a suspect is spotted, the cybercop plays the role of a naive youngster and makes himself or herself available for a meeting with the suspect in hopes of gaining evidence for an arrest.

Also surfing the network, in search of pedophiles, are computer pornography sellers who offer magazine-quality color photographs of young boys and girls in a variety of sexually suggestive or actual sexual acts. Such a ring was broken up in 1994 and was found to have clients in several countries, with the pictures themselves transmitted from Denmark.

Another type of stalker expected to be seen more in the future is the emotionally disturbed loner, seeking attention and companionship through cyberspace, and who often becomes obsessed with a bulletin board "friend." If this person obtains personal information about the cyberspace acquaintance, he or she sometimes seeks a close, often smothering relationship. If spurned, the stalker launches a campaign of cyberspace harassment, moving into real-space harassment if adequate information is obtained. Cyberspace vengeance can take many forms, from ruining credit records and charging multiple purchases to the victim to creating criminal records and sending letters to employers informing them of the "shady background" of the victim.

What effect do computers have on the developing morals of children?
Courtesy of Simon & Schuster/Merrill Education

In the twenty-first century, with access to the information superhighway available to all and information from data banks networked into dossiers reserved for "official use only" (but easily accessible to hackers and crackers), stalking will not only increase but be facilitated by a new generation of portable computers. Organic nanocomputers may one day be implanted in the human brain, making possible a new crime: mindstalking. Unauthorized intrusion and seduction will reach directly into the victim's brain, making the stalker harder to evade and even more difficult to escape.

REMOTE TERRORISM

In London a couple of years ago, terrorists placed deadly missiles in the back of a truck and remotely sent them flying toward the home of the British prime minister. The missiles exploded on the lawn without harm to the prime minister or the house, but they could have killed him and created an international crisis—clearly the intent of the bombers.

Today, terrorists have the capacity to detonate explosives in another country by means of computers and radio signals bounced off satellites. Because the emerging information superhighway is without borders, computer viruses and other information-destroying instruments can be hurled at business or government officials and facilities from anywhere on the globe.

In the future, information will be so crucial to success in business and personal life that being cut off from it will be like being held hostage or kidnapped. Terrorists who can cut communications off to an individual, group, community, or wider society will have the power and ability to spread fear and panic.

As with stalkers, terrorists will find new opportunities when computer implants in human brains become widely available. Borrowing a twentieth-century technique from psychology—subliminal conditioning—terrorists might recruit unsuspecting accomplices via low-intensity audiovisual messages aimed directly at individuals with brain-implanted computers. Unsuspecting implantees might unconsciously begin to modify their attitudes in the direction sought by the terrorists, or worse, even begin to join in terrorist activities. Political terrorists, whose agenda often is to change the world to suit their beliefs, are the most likely candidates to embrace this new approach and other emerging technologies to gain direct access to the minds of the populace.

VIRTUAL CRIMES

Stock and bond fraud is already appearing in cyberspace—stocks and bonds that appear on the markets, are actively traded for a short time, and then disappear. The stocks and bonds are nonexistent; only the electronic impulses are real.

In a recent case, a trader was paid $9 million in commissions for what appeared to be some $100 million in sales of bonds. But investigators now feel that these bonds may never have changed hands at all, except in cyberspace. In the future, a virtual-reality expert could create a hologram in the form of a respected stockbroker or real estate broker, then advise clients in cyberspace to buy certain stocks, bonds, or real estate. Unsuspecting victims acting on the advice might later find that they had enlarged the coffers of the virtual-reality expert, while buying worthless or nonexistent properties.

This is just the tip of the iceberg in what might be tagged as "virtual crime"—offenses based on a reality that only exists in cyberspace. As virtual reality becomes increasingly sophisticated, it is the young adults in the first decade of the twenty-first century who—having grown up with virtual reality—will create the software and determine the legal and criminal uses of this technology. And with virtual reality potentially reaching directly into the brains of recipients via "organic" computers, the ability to separate cyberspace reality from truth outside cyberspace will be one of the greatest challenges of the twenty-first century.

TWENTY-FIRST CENTURY EXPECTATIONS

The outlook for curtailing cyberspace crime by technology or conventional law-enforcement methods is bleak. Most agencies do not have the personnel or the skills to cope with such offenses, and to date all high-tech approaches have been met by almost immediate turnabouts by hackers or crackers.

As individuals see and talk to each other over computers in the next few years, and as nanotechnology makes computers even more portable, new technology will emerge to protect data. But simplifying systems to make them more universally acceptable and accessible will also make them more vulnerable to intruders.

Control of access by optical patterns, DNA identification, voice spectrographs, encryption, and other methods may slow down hackers, but no method is foolproof or presents much of a challenge to today's most-talented cyberpunks. The trouble is that in the future many more users will have skills far beyond those of today's crackers—a process one expert termed "the democratization of computer crime."

Still, there is much to be gained by easy access to the information superhighway. The "cyberpunk imperatives," a code subscribed to many hackers, include: (1) information should be free so that the most capable can make the most of it; (2) the world will be better off if entrepreneurs can obtain any data necessary to provide needed or desired new products and services; and (3) decentralization of information protects us all from "Big Brother."

Cybercrime probably cannot be controlled by conventional methods. Technology is on the side of the cyberspace offender and motivation is high—it's fun, exciting, challenging, and profitable. The only real help is one that has not proven very successful in recent decades: conscience and personal values, the belief that theft, deception, and invasion of privacy are simply unacceptable.

Behavioral psychologists argue that all values are learned by a system of rewards and, to a lesser extent, punishment. Thus, if these values are necessary for survival, children should consciously be conditioned to live by them. If all citizens—all computer users—were taught these values and sought to live by them, cyberspace could become the wondrous and friendly place its creators have envisioned.

Ironically, the greatest possible allies to be found in this search for values in cyberspace are the adolescent hackers of the 1980s, many of whom are the software programmers of the 1990s. In his book, *Secrets of a Super-Hacker,* a hacker named "Knightmare" says that "true hackers" love to break into systems and leave proof of their skills, but do not hurt individuals by stealing tangible goods or money, or destroying files or systems.

"Hacker ethics," Knightmare writes, include informing computer managers about problems with their security and offering to teach and share knowledge about computer security when asked. Increasingly, government and business computer managers are asking. Many of the Fortune 500 companies and numerous government agencies have hired hackers to test their systems and even design new security protocols for them.

Thus, hackers are helping to protect the information superhighway from crackers and terrorists. As one hacker says, "Hackers love computers and they want the Net safe."

Questions

1. Do you believe that there will be a cashless society?
2. What would be the ethical issues involved in implanting monitors and chemical drips to keep sexually and physically violent offenders "under control"?
3. Define the term "cyberspace offender." How old are cyberspace offenders? What do they do? Do you believe that the number of cyberspace crimes will increase or decrease in the new century? Why?
4. How do you think cybercrimes will change in the next 10 years? What part will regulations and laws play in those changes?
5. List and describe three cybercrimes. How can they be prevented?
6. How can the Internet be used safely by children?

QUOTES AND FACTS ABOUT CYBERCRIME

"Technology is changing every 60 days, so we're playing catch-up. We're trying to legislate very difficult areas. Criminals can be somewhat anonymous, and the ways of concealing their identities make it easier [for them] to commit a fraud. When we read something on the Internet, we tend to take it as gospel, but it doesn't have to be right. You have to take it with a grain of salt."

Master Sgt. James Murray, Illinois State Police

"A 1994 FBI report estimated that economic loss from Internet crime ranged from $164 million to $5 billion per year. It is difficult to get accurate calculations, because many people who are taken advantage of on the Internet don't report it; also, it is difficult to enforce because many people are known by a one-word screen name and leave few options for verification."

Erica Harrington, "Authorities Playing Catch-Up Against Cybercrime,"
Chicago Tribune, December 15, 1996

" 'We face a unique, disturbing and urgent circumstance, because it's children who are the computer experts in most families,' said Indiana Republican Senator Dan Coats, who is interested in cleaning up the Internet. The result of Senator Coat's interest and concern was the creation of the Communications Decency Act. This act extends regulations written to govern the dial-a-porn industry into computer networks. The Communications Decency Act was designed to impose fines up to $100,000 and prison terms of two years on anyone who knowingly makes 'indecent' materials available to children under 18."

Phillip Elmer DeWitt, "Cyberporn," *Time,* July 3, 1997

"Another form of cybercrime is extortion. A computer hacker can obtain bits of information from the Internet and then transmit an extortion through e-mail demanding money. If they are not paid, they might threaten with a 'mail-bomb,' which is the transmission of constant e-mail until the system overloads and becomes dysfunctional."

Jones International, LTD, "Crime on the Internet," April 1996,
http://www.digital century.com/encycl/update/crime/html

"The Internet can also be used to fight crime. The FBI Web site receives 100,000 visits a day from people with information about the most wanted fugitives or missing persons posted there. The FBI also uses the Web page to request information about various crimes, like the Oklahoma City bombing. There are also private groups specializing in finding missing persons. The most effective tool in finding a child is a photograph. The National Center for Missing and Exploited Children receives between 25,000 and 30,000 visits a week about missing children. It is less expensive to put a picture of a missing child on the 'Net than it would be to do a mass mailing. Because of the Internet, pictures of missing children reach many quickly."

Erica Harrington, "Authorities Playing Catch-Up Against Cybercrime,"
Chicago Tribune, December 15, 1996

"President Clinton signed a crime bill which contains a two-page revision to the federal computer crime statute. The bill makes it illegal to transmit viruses and worms over the electronic network. An important change in the law is the creation of two levels of computer crime: Actions taken 'with reckless disregard' for the damage they could cause are classified as misdemeanors and intentionally harmful acts are classified as felonies."

M.B. Betts, "Statute Outlaws Viruses," *Computerworld,* October 1994, p. 65

"Search and seizure laws still need clarification. Currently the law requires that a warrant be specific in what can be seized and the seizure must be the original document. This is difficult when dealing with computers, because obtaining a specific original file could mean that the entire hard drive would be confiscated. It is hard to get a warrant that allows the police to find the information without jeopardizing the privacy of the rest of the information in the hard drive."

L. Reynolds, "Constitutional Law in the Electronic Age,"
Management Review, 1995, pp. 24–25

Conclusion

Technologies allow us to transport people more quickly, communicate in a variety of formats (e.g., by telephone, videophone, e-mail, chat boxes, etc.), warm up our food rapidly in the microwave, and access and store data efficiently. Technologies envelop our very existence.

The intent of this part of the book has been to highlight the social implications of technology through the article on ethics and then to reemphasize them with the presentation of a classical and newer case study. The goal of this part of the book is not simply to present cases for which the social responsibility of those involved should have been stronger, but also to ask you to think about how often technology must be used in a socially responsible way.

The next part of the book, health and technology, discusses ethical concerns in the medical field. It presents information and arguments concerning the ethics of antiboitic use, the genome project, organ transplants and xenografts, and it lays out a history of medical research done over the past few decades.

Internet Exercise

1. Use any of the Internet search engines (e.g., Alta Vista, Yahoo, Infoseek, etc.) to research the following topics:

    a. The definitions of whistle-blowing, cybercrime, and cyberporn.

    b. Additional factors about the tragedies of the Challenger, the Nuclear Warriors, the molasses spill, and Bhopal. Try to find new areas of interest that are not presented within the articles. What was the financial impact of each of these tragedies?

    c. The amount of money spent in lawsuits nationally or within specific states on legal fees resulting from whistle-blowing.

    d. What is the current status of the Communications Decency Act?

    e. Find five ways that technology provides positive experiences for each of us daily.

Beyond the Bridge: Future Options . . .

Use any of the Internet search engines (e.g., Alta Vista, Yahoo, Infoseek, etc.) to research the following topics:

1. Roger Boisjoly and the Nuclear Warriors are only two examples of whistle-blowers. Find two more examples using the Internet. Create a summary of each whistle-blowing experience and cite the Internet address(es) at which you found your information.

2. Search for information or opinions on psychological, social, or moral reasons for blowing the whistle.

3. Update the story of the Nuclear Warriors. What did the NRC do about this situation?

Useful Web Sites

URL	Site Description
http://www.chem.vt.edu/ethics.htm	Ethics in science
http://www.sjsu.edu/dept/social-resp.html	Social responsibility
http://www-rohansedu.edu/faculty/corlett/se.html	Society for Ethics
ftp://alternatives.com/library/enforst/wj150050.txt	Forest Service Whistle-blower
http://www.digitalcentury.com/encycl/update/crime/html	Crime on the Internet
http://www.hb.edu/sis/whistle/pathfinder.nun	National Whistleblower Center
http://www.fas.org/spp/stspike.htm	Challenger efficiency vs. safety
http://www.va.gov/OIG/hotline/whistle.nun	VAOIG Hotline: Whistle-blowing
http://www.ethics.ubc.ca/papers/science.html	Science and technology ethics resources
http://www,math.ou.edu/~pgoodey/classes/eng1/tacoma.html	Tacoma bridge disaster
http://www.gloucester-online.co.uk/articles/nationalnews/article124.html	German rail disaster

500 BC Chinese use moldy soybean curd as an antibiotic to cure boils	**1590** The microscope is invented by Janssen	**1663** Cells are first described by Hooke	**1675** Leeuwenhoek discovers bacteria	**1797** Jenner vaccinates a child to protect him from smallpox
1805 Morphine used as a pain reliever	**1863** Mendel discovers genes when studying peas	**1869** Miescher discovers DNA in trout sperm	**1883** First rabies vaccine developed	**1899** Aspirin developed by F. Serturner
1928 Flemming discovers penicillin	**1935** Sulfonamides discovered	**1938** First heart surgery performed	**1951** Oral contraceptive developed	**1955** Succesful kidney transplant
1965 Implanted mechanical devices help diseased hearts	**1967** Christiaan Barnard performs a whole-heart transplant from one person to another	**1972** DNA composition of humans is discovered to be 99% similar to that of chimps and gorillas	**1980** U.S. patent of gene cloning is awarded to Cohen & Boyer	**1982** Permanent artificial heart implanted
1983 First artificial chromosome synthesized	**1984** First genetically engineered vaccine developed	**1986** First genetically engineered human vaccine to prevent Hepatitis B developed	**1988** Congress funds the Human Genome Project	**1994** First breast cancer gene is discovered
1993 EPA concludes that secondhand smoke is a lung carcinogen	**1996** Scottish scientists clone identical lambs from an embryonic sheep	**1997** Scottish scientists clone a sheep from adult sheep cells		

Health and Technology

PART

VII

Time line adapted from the following sources:
"Historical Timeline of Biotechnology." Available: http://www.ncbiotech.org/timeline.htm.
"Milestones in Cardiology." Available: http://sin.fi.edu/biosci/history/first.html.
Clayman, C. (1989). *The American Medical Association: Encyclopedia of Medicine.*
New York, Random House.

You have probably heard the saying, "If you have your health, you have everything." Most would agree that our health is vital to the quality of our lives; this part of the book explores the ethical considerations that the doctor and the patient need to examine when trying to create a life of health. In this part, the interplay between health, medicines, and medical interventions is explored within the foundation of bioethics.

When you get sick, do you go to the doctor and receive an antibiotic? Do you finish all of your medicine? Do you sometimes use a friend's, child's, or spouse's antibiotic rather than going to get your own? Both of these latter practices could relate to antibiotic ineffectiveness or resistance. Dr. Stuart Levy explores this thought further in the chapter entitled "Reliance on Medicines and Self-Medication: The Seeds of Antibiotic Misuse."

"End of the Rainbow" is an extremely controversial article about the Human Genome project. Some people believe that this project is an effort to map and sequence *the* set of human genes. Others argue that this statement does not reflect the actual goal of the project. As you read the chapter, try to pinpoint the areas that bring out mixed feelings in you. Decide whether or not you feel that this research is critical to understanding past and future cultures.

When a patient's heart, kidneys, lungs or other organs fail, what options does the patient have? For some, the only option is death; without their essential, functioning organ, the patients will die. In recent years, however, organ transplants have offered hope for survival to very sick patients. The chapter entitled "Organ Concert" discusses the surgical techniques that enabled Dr. Thomas Starzl to perform the first successful liver transplant, techniques that "have added years—decades in some cases—to the lives of hundreds of thousands of men, women and children." However, if you needed an organ transplant but were not able to receive an organ from another human, would you consider receiving a cow, pig, or baboon organ? Xenotransplants—organs that are transplanted from animals to humans—could be the wave of the future. Animal organs are both easy to find and inexpensive, and eventually, researchers may be able to work through the current problems people are experiencing with rejection of animal organs. "Organ Concert" discusses this up-and-coming issue as well.

Another issue that is highly relevant to the topics of health and technology is the controversial question of euthanasia. Should individuals who are critically ill and who have no chance for recovery be allowed to die, or should medical heroics keep them alive? When should the medical technology keeping such people alive be deimplemented to allow those people to die? Should the infamous Dr. Kervorkian be allowed to help people who are in chronic pain or who are technology dependent (e.g., dependent on ventilators, feeding tubes, etc.) die with the aid of his "death machine"? These are questions that are explored in the last chapter, "Physician-Assisted Suicide."

Modern medical technology has increased the average life span of people and, in many cases, the quality of life. Yet, it is important to analyze and study all sides of bioethical questions relating to medical care. This chapter just touches the surface of these issues, but it should provide enough information for you to look differently at medical care from this day forward.

Reliance on Medicines and Self-Medication: The Seeds of Antibiotic Misuse

STUART LEVY, MD

Antibiotics are a medical treasure, perhaps the most important therapeutic discovery in the history of medicine. But they are being misused. In some cases, they are taken when they are not needed at all; in others, they are prescribed and used inappropriately. For example, they are given in too small or too large amounts or for too long or too short periods of time. The old adage applies here. "Too much of a good thing can be bad." In the case of antibiotics, we must add, "so can too little." Not only quantity, but length of usage, either too long or too short, can affect the therapeutic and environmental consequences of these agents.

Misuse has led to the decreased effectiveness of antibiotics because of the emergence of bacteria that are resistant to them. Antibiotics, like other pharmaceuticals, "suffer" from the present day reliance on medication to cure every ailment, the "pill for every ill" belief. In the quest for a rapid relief of symptoms, medicines that are freely available to people are being misused. So it is with antibiotics. They have been overused and used inappropriately, creating in their wake an environment where antibiotic-resistant bacteria survive.

Overreliance on medicine to treat an array of illnesses is not unique to antibiotics. It reflects humanity's understandable desire for relief from illness, the rush to use medicines in order to return to a normal daily life. This attitude, however, was not always so prominent. In early times, when medicinal substances were not plentiful, the

power of the word and communication with the spirits played an important role. The inclusion of a nonmedicinal approach to therapy was retained for a long time during and after the discovery of effective medications. Eventually, however, the chant and the communication were replaced almost completely by medicines.

HISTORICAL OVERVIEW

A brief account of the history leading to modern-day medicine is worth noting, since it sets the background in which antibiotics were discovered and may help to explain society's current expectations and attitudes toward these drugs.

Early ancestors believed that each and every distinct "thing"—whether a tree, a stone, or a drinking vessel—was imbued with a spirit. When someone suddenly fell ill, it was assumed that an object was taking vengeance for a slight or grievance that had been committed against it—an unacceptable offering, a felled tree, an overturned stone. Suffering from headache, fever, stomach cramps, or aching muscles, the patient would seek out a healer to calm the spirits and dispel the symptoms. This healer, whether self-proclaimed or appointed, would proceed, as he and his forebears had done many times before, to address the "souls in conflict" and, thereby, cure the illness. The healer returned the patient and the object to a proper balance or relationship.

The healer believed he communicated with and appeased the spirits through his invocations. Some healers made cuts in the body to let blood or pus run out—to encourage the evil spirit to leave. Sacrifices or offerings were often made to the gods to abate their anger. In very early times, it was the voice of the healer and his accepted, even magical, powers that were valued even above those of the natural substances that accompanied the ritual.

That nonmedicinal approaches worked attests to the power of suggestion that can mobilize processes in our own body and help relieve symptoms. Today, we call this the "placebo effect"—the relief of disease or symptoms caused by the mere suggestion that the medication will work and that the person will get better. The "placebo effect" is that force or reaction that influences disease via changes in the body in response to positive feelings about treatment. In testing the efficacy of a drug, contemporary clinical researchers always give a placebo, usually a sugar or chalk pill, to half the patients in the test while the other half receives the real medication. Even the doctors giving out the drug do not know which pill they are dispensing. If the drug shows a statistically higher benefit over the placebo, then it is considered truly therapeutic. It has demonstrated its potency. While yet to be fully understood, the placebo effect may be linked to products that the cells of our bodies make in response to certain stimuli, such as positive suggestion.

In time, new discoveries led to changes in therapeutic approach. As they were found effective, they were passed on to future generations as part of oral tradition and later written. In the 3500-year-old Egyptian papyri and the 3000-year-old Babylonian cuneiform tablets, we find evidence that a multitude of different natural products were mixed into pumice or potion to treat illnesses. In general, the role ascribed to these medicinals was to drive out the "demons" that had invaded the bodies. In the tradition of their predecessors, healers believed, by and large, that it was still the "soul" of an herb that appeased the "soul" of an offended spirit. In one ancient account, a physician-priest directed his colleagues to combine a medicinal herb, which assuaged the soul, with some bitter substance, generally a form of animal dung, to drive evil spirits away. Such inventive potions served to reinforce the overriding faith in verbal appeals directed to spirits. Even today, while modern medicine no longer attributes disease to evil spirits, people still accept bitterness in certain preparations, believing in its enhanced ability to cure. Perhaps the sense of sacrifice or pain must accompany the treatment in order for the medicine to work.

The earliest written documents, from the 16th to 17th centuries B.C., present details of pathology and diseases, as well as of treatments. In one Egyptian papyrus, discovered by George Ebers in 1872–73, we find complete descriptions of medications used in 1552 B.C., a time when Moses was only 21 years old. They probably represent medicinal preparations that had been passed down to sub-

sequent generations for a thousand or more years. These prescriptions were apparently prepared by an ancestral precursor to our modern pharmacist. The preparations, while hardly like any we use today, represented remedies that had been found to abate disease symptoms. They included whole parts of plants and animals, living and dead. Generally, a special chant accompanied the medication. Verbal appeal was an important component of the therapy.

For diarrhea, the ancient Egyptians suggested a mixture of figs, grapes, sycamore fruit, gum, and yellow ochre—along with a special chant. For headache, "skull of silicrus fish is boiled with oil and the head is rubbed therewith for four days."

The cuneiform tablet writings of ancient Assyria, dating from over 2500 years ago, also document the mixture of healing substances:

- For a headache, the following direction was given. "Thou shalt beat up fennel in cow's milk or cow's urine, wash his head (therewith), reduce *barhus*, bray (it) press it on his head, annoint with oil . . ."

- For an eye problem this advice was given. "Thou shalt disembowel a yellow frog, mix its gall in curd, apply to the eyes."

- For toothache, people were advised, "Thou shalt slit a leek, rub on the root of the tooth and he shall recover."

These writings highlight the extent of medicinals known and used and the importance placed on their proper preparations and applications.

The prescription of medicinals to the afflicted was not uniformly accepted. As Greek mythology relates, Aesculapius angered the gods by taking the ability to cure disease away from them and giving it to mankind. Aesculapius, regarded by most as an ancient physician and by some as a deity, reportedly made house calls to visit his patients in bed. From writings of this time, we can deduce that he probably used emetics and purgatives, incisions, and ointments. When his medicines failed, he relied on his faith in music and incantations to heal. His disciples, advocates of medicines, were seen as enemies of the traditional priesthood, which believed its members had exclusive power over disease. According to them, offerings should be made not to the patient, but to the holy shrines. The Aesculapians, however, who were priests as well as physicians, developed their own religious followings and temples. Their delivery of medicinals directly to the ill person clearly defined the movement away from purely spiritual appeal to tangible cures, residing in organic materials found in natural sources.

During a large part of our later recorded history, sickness was attributed to having too much or too little of necessary bodily substances. Ancient Greeks defined illness as the imbalance of four body humors—blood, phlegm, yellow bile, and black bile—that embodied a mixture of four universal qualities: moist, dry, cold, and warm. Hippocrates, and later Aristotle in the 4th century B.C., articulated this fundamental concept in their teachings. In disease, something either had to be replaced or had to be removed in order to restore health. Influenced by this interpretation, medical practitioners often removed humors; hence, the practice of using leeches attached to the body to suck blood. Under the guidance of this theory, physicians tested and found other effective, natural substances. We know today that these substances, such as plant leaves and roots, contained active chemical ingredients, including antibiotics, that were the agents responsible for the relief of symptoms and cure of the disease. The treatments became classified according to their abilities to correct disturbances in the body, such as fever, rapid heart beat, and muscle weakness.

These ideas formed the rationale for a more organized approach to disease introduced in the second century by a Greek physician named Galen (130–200 A.D.), who is perhaps history's most influential doctor. His more than 22 volumes of teachings greatly influenced medicine and attracted followers for more than 14 centuries. It was Galen who first showed that blood, not air, flowed through arteries. He also proved that urine came from the kidneys. But his fame came from his approach to healing, which led to the discovery and use of other substances as medicinals. Galen based his medical theories and ideas on how natural products found in their native surroundings fit the particular needs of the body as defined by the "humors." Believing "contraria contrarius curantum," or "that which is opposite cures," he was led to try interesting, new substances. Galen chose an item because it appeared to represent one of the four universal qualities making up the human temperament and gave it to patients based on its ability to restore what he considered absent or off balance. For instance, vinegar was recommended for the burning heart. He borrowed from the old Greek writings, widely from Hippocrates and added much more of his own scholarship. Some estimate that he more than doubled the medical literature of the time.

The "galenicals" he gathered were simple organic or mineral ingredients. No substance was outside the realm of potential use—the bark of trees, the juices of berries or algae found in still waters. Galen's preparations were, by their very essence, hard to standardize but were more understandable and more directed to particular disease symptoms than those prominent in the years preceding him. Some were prepared by Galen and his followers and given to the patient; others were made by the patients themselves on advice of the Galenist physicians. No details on amounts were provided. Galen let each patient or physician decide. By consequence, during this extended period of Galen's influence, drug-making by pharmaceutical professionals, who were beginning to surface, progressed very slowly.

Although viewed as separate entities, medicine (the science of diagnosis and treatment) and pharmacy (the science of drug production and drug activity) evolved alongside each other. Certain early physicians devoted their energies to both. Aristotle carried his own medicines with him and had them available to give directly to his patients. To a large extent, so did Galen and his followers. But the pharmacist emerged where his expertise was needed, particularly with the demand for defined medicinal substances. In the 13th and 14th centuries in England and Germany, apothecary shops appeared and a real separation of physician and pharmacist took place. With the establishment of the pharmacist and the apothecary, attention was increasingly focused on the disease and its symptoms.

Consumer confidence and quality control of the product became important early on. In the 13th century, Frederick II, emperor of Spain and Italy, issued an edict that required every medical man to give information against any pharmacist who sold "bad" medicine:

> Every physician given a license to practice must take an oath that he shall faithfully fulfill all the requirements of the law, and in addition, whenever it comes to his knowledge that any apothecary has for sale drugs that are of less than normal strength, he shall report him to the court . . . .

He went on to disallow any physician from owning an apothecary himself, a desirable mandate not practiced in parts of the world today. The Emperor saw clearly how a conflict of interest could emerge.

Today we obtain our medications from pharmacies, generally through the prescription of a physician. The pharmacy represents, therefore, the physical provider of medication and also assures its quality. The two professionals, doctor and pharmacist, are thus intertwined in the delivery of medicine to the patient. In certain countries and for certain drugs, however, medicines can be obtained without a doctor's prescription, that is, as an over-the-counter item. This practice, which we shall discuss further, has broken the tie between these two professions, permitting and encouraging self-medication.

Galen's influence extended into the 16th century. Then Paracelsus, the son of a country physician from Basel, introduced methods for extracting the active components. Not readily accepted by his peers because of his flamboyant style and ideas, he argued for understanding the essence of medical treatment. He simplified and gave uniformity to Galen's prescriptions. But he took a vastly different approach from the established Galenical method. He treated the diseased organ, not the symptom. He discarded the concept of the "humors." In fact, he publicly burned the works of Galen.

In contrast to Galen, who chose medicinals that represented the opposite of the disease symptoms, Paracelsus believed in the doctrine of "signatures" or "similars." Thus, the flower or the leaf of a plant that most closely resembled the diseased organ was often selected to heal the organ. Historians tell us that the discovery of digitalis, the single most important drug used to treat heart disease today, came from the ancient, traditional use of the extract of the heart-shaped foxglove leaf to treat symptoms then that we now know were related to the heart.

Instead of Galen's ill-defined proportions, Paracelsus and followers described exact amounts of particular ingredients to be used. More than ever before, the pharmacy began to find its role in society. This novel approach, however, was not accepted universally, and, throughout the 17th century, followers of Paracelsus remained in conflict with the Galenists.

The therapeutics of the Middle Ages and Renaissance continued to be a mixture of superstition from ancient times and experimental daring of the great physicians of the day. Potions, strange mixtures concocted for good and evil intent and used throughout recorded ancient civilization, continued in use into the Middle Ages. As Shakespeare reminded us in the witches' song in his play *Macbeth* (Act IV, Scene 1):

Fillet of a fenny snake
In the caldron boil and bake
Eye of newt and toe of frog
Wool of bat and tongue of dog
Adders' fork and blindworm's sting
Lizard's leg and howlet's wing
For a charm of powerful trouble
Like a Hell broth boil and bubble.

Belief that disease is caused by evil spirits held sway. Into the 18th century, people wore purple amulets around their necks to ward off the plague and other diseases. They contained bits of frog, other animals, and the ever-potent animal dung. Often extracts of human skulls taken from dead bodies were part of these preparations. Exorcisms, used to drive out altered disease states in the human body, continued into the late 1800s.

But the times were being primed for the appearance of "modern" medicines, that is, those bottled and sold as preparations to relieve health problems. Throughout the 17th and 18th centuries, various medicines became commonly available for a variety of ailments. Some from England were imported to the United States. Advertisements for these medications filled almanacs in the United States and England. As early as 1685, Samuel Atkins carried this advertisement in his first almanac:

Some experienced medicines, sold by William Bradford at Philadelphia. Charles Marshall's Spiritus Mundus, being an excellent medicine against all sorts of Fevers and Agues, Surfeits, Gripes, Pleurisies, etc. A present remedy for the Gravel and Stone, which seldom fails to give ease in half an hour.

The practice continued into the 18th century. Nathaniel Whittimore from Boston offered in 1721, "Sundry very excellent medicines found out to cure both hot and cold gouts, dropsies, consumptions, perilous coughs, fevers, ague and most other diseases incident to Mankind . . . To be had at a reasonable price, of N. Whittemore."

These advertisements for over-the-counter medications epitomize the already prevalent trend toward self-treatment. This was further realized in whole books devoted to self-medication. To some extent these books fulfilled a real need; they also played on people's search for easy cures. One book by John Theobald first appeared in 1764 and was already in a third edition by the end of the same year. In it, Theobald put together a compendium of remedies that he had collected from different sources. He explained that "these receipts are published chiefly for the use of persons residing in the country whose convenience or abilities will not allow of the attendance of a physician or apothecary."

The ingredients of these remedies were in part galenicals but had the details of a modern pharmaceutical preparation. For instance, one such home remedy for pleurisy states, "Bleed frequently till the pain abates, apply a blister to the side, and take half a pint of the following infusion twice a day: take fresh horse-dung six ounces and pour on it a pint of boiling Pennyroyal water, strain it when cold and add a quarter of an ounce of Venice treacle, mix for use." Theobold credited this remedy to the London physician John Quincy, who published a list of dispensaries during the early part of the 18th century.

It can be argued that these books and almanacs may have offered benefits to some, in terms of easy harmless "home remedies," but they opened up opportunities for quackery, playing on people's wishes to find a ready cure for their ailments. Most pertinent to present-day antibiotic misuse, however, was the encouragement for self-medication. This practice, prominent today, has potentially harmful effects not only on the individual, but in the case of antibiotics, on the sustained efficacy of these drugs. While present-day societies have reaped the rewards of past discovery, they have also inherited a potentially harmful relaxed attitude toward medications, particularly evident in regard to antibiotics.

A significant development in understanding disease appeared in the 19th century and led to yet another change in the direction of drug discovery. Although the concept of a diseased state of man, rather than a causal agent, was still in vogue, as we noted earlier, Louis Pasteur, working and writing in Paris at the time, produced convincing observations that "êtres vivants," "living creatures" or microorganisms, were causing human disease. Linking these microscopic beings to disease was a major step into the modern era of medicine. With the "germ" as a causative agent, the scene was set for tremendous advancement in the field of medical science.

This framework encouraged scientists to look for drugs as defined therapeutic entities directed to fight bacteria.

The ability of these agents to kill bacteria and cure previously fatal diseases was nothing less than a miracle. Their discovery satisfied the never-ending appeal of miraculous curing agents able to restore well-being to the patient and to society.

The mindset of the individuals looking for new drugs and the attitude of the public toward medicines have shaped historical developments of medicine and in turn antibiotics. Self-medication and the ready availability of medical products has played into the present-day attitude that antibiotics are cure-alls. A naive confidence that antibiotic use is only beneficial has led to misuse and overuse and the consequent selection of mutant forms of bacteria resistant to their killing effects.

Questions

1. What complications arise when antibiotics are misused?
2. What is the "pill for every ill" belief? How does it correlate to the misuse of antibiotics?
3. Describe two "cures" that were used by the ancient Egyptians for their ills.
4. How does the Greeks' definition of illness differ from the descriptions of illnesses today?
5. What influence did Galen have on the distribution of medicines?
6. What does Dr. Levy mean when he says that "overuse and the consequent selection of mutant forms of bacteria are resistant to their [antibiotic] killing effects"?

45 End of the Rainbow

JOANN C. GUTIN

When Henry Greely is perplexed or troubled, his body English tells you as clearly as his words: the Stanford law professor and bioethicist leans back in his chair, stares into the middle distance, and slowly, absently tousles his own hair.

In his modest office this morning he's discussing the challenges of his two-year stint as one of the bioethicists on the organizing committee of the North American arm of the Human Genome Diversity Project. ("Has it only been since '92?" he wonders aloud. "It feels longer.") After two and a half hours spent grappling with variations on a single theme—"Why are some people so mad about the Human Genome Diversity Project?"—Greely's hair is decidedly the worse for wear.

That it should upset people seems curious. On paper, which is really the only place it exists so far, the project appears to be a singularly uncontroversial idea. It is merely a call for a coordinated effort by scientists on every continent to record the dwindling regional genetic diversity of *Homo sapiens* by taking DNA samples from several hundred distinct human populations and storing the samples in gene banks. Researchers could then examine the DNA for clues to the evolutionary histories of the populations and to their resistance or susceptibility to particular diseases.

Yet today the architects of the three-year-old program— a group of geneticists and anthropologists with irreproachable academic and political credentials—stand accused of being neocolonialists, gene pirates, and pawns in a conspiracy to develop race-specific biological weapons. The at-

mosphere surrounding the work is thick with suspicion: Greely recently heard one rumor about a medical researcher whose ongoing study in the Caribbean was abruptly shut down by charges that he would use his subjects' blood samples to clone a race of slaves. "Obviously *Jurassic Park* didn't help us," Greely says, managing a wan smile.

Clearly, though, reaction to the diversity project far exceeds mere blockbuster-induced paranoia about the perils of genetic engineering. University professors and indigenous peoples alike are voicing objections, and while the academic critique tends to be less vivid than what appears in the popular press, racism is the shared subtext. Is the Human Genome Diversity Project scientific colonialism, using the genes of Third World people to answer obscure academic questions or—worse—provide expensive medical cures for the privileged citizens of the developed world? Might it backfire and inadvertently supply more fodder for ethnic battles, as if any more fodder were needed? Or are its organizers merely victims of bad timing? Are the 1990s an impossible moment in human history to launch a project touching two of the rawest nerves in the culture: genes and race?

The Human Genome Diversity Project began innocently enough in 1991 with an impassioned open letter to the readers of the journal *Genomics* by a number of prominent researchers, among them the geneticists Luigi Luca Cavalli-Sforza of Stanford and Mary-Claire King and Allan Wilson of the University of California at Berkeley. The genus *Homo,* argued the letter's authors, has reached a critical juncture: indigenous peoples are being absorbed into the larger gene pool at an escalating rate, and if the information contained in their DNA is not collected quickly, it may be lost to humankind forever. "The genetic diversity of people now living harbors the clues to the evolution of our species," they wrote, "but the gate to preserve these clues is closing rapidly." They urged members of the Human Genome Organization—an international consortium of scientists who are interested in human genetics—to "grasp a vanishing opportunity to preserve a record of our genetic heritage."

Their plea was heard not only by the nonprofit Human Genome Organization but by funding agencies that included the National Institutes of Health, the Department of Energy, and the National Science Foundation; all gave the letter's authors seed money, charging them with devising a way to collect a wider range of DNA.

Backers of the project saw it as a necessary adjunct to the much larger and better-funded Human Genome Project. The Human Genome Project often gets billed as the effort to map and sequence *the* set of human genes, but as Diversity Project organizers gently point out, that isn't quite accurate. Molecular anthropologist Ken Weiss, head of the North American Diversity Project committee, notes that the literal human genome is "the whole ball of wax," the sum of 5 billion people's DNA. What Human Genome Project researchers are actually analyzing is a sort of composite genome: 23 chromosome pairs donated by a mere handful of U.S. and European scientists. (As one wag observed, when they're finally mapped, those chromosomes will tell researchers everything there is to know "about one French farmer and a lady from Philadelphia"). And even *that* will take about 15 years and cost some $3 billion.

That's where the Human Genome Diversity Project would come in—it would supplement, particularize, and colorize the chromosome maps drawn by the Human Genome Project. As Weiss observes, "If we don't go ahead with this, then in ten years when the Human Genome Project is done, a Navajo, say, will look at those results and ask, 'Why did they bother? How well does that represent *me?*'"

From the outset, all the scientists involved called for sensitivity toward the sampled populations. These groups would include "historically vulnerable" people, warned the original *Genomics* letter, and using them merely as research subjects would inevitably lead to a "sense of exploitation and abandonment."

Yet the critiques began almost immediately. "The Human Genome Diversity ('Vampire') Project," reads a communiqué from the Central Australian Aboriginal Congress, "is legalized theft." "Your process," says a letter to the Na-

tional Science Foundation from Chief Leon Shenandoah of the Onondaga Council of Chiefs, "is unethical, invasive, and may even be criminal. It violates the group rights and human rights of . . . indigenous peoples around the world."

The project's friends are perplexed by the commotion, believing that aside from its giant scale, the work doesn't constitute anything fundamentally new. Researchers have been collecting biological materials from indigenous groups for years; the Diversity Project is merely a way to organize that collection. Far from being a high-tech threat, say its backers, the project will do a better job of safeguarding subjects' rights and will generate better science than the scattershot data collection that preceded it.

As the guidelines stand today, anthropologists and geneticists around the world will be asked to gather blood samples from the groups they routinely study; the groups will participate in the Human Genome Diversity Project only if they want to. In addition, all the researchers will adhere to strict and uniform standards of informed consent; the property rights of donor populations to their DNA will be protected; and the material will be stored in a gene library accessible to all qualified researchers rather than disappearing into a refrigerator in one scientist's lab. The establishment of cell lines that will survive for 20 to 25 years—an expensive process—will guarantee that scientists into the next century will be able to ask questions of the genes that no one has yet thought of.

Why is the project necessary? After all, all humans, no matter what their ancestry, share most of their DNA. As Mary-Claire King is fond of saying, "We are all different, yet we are all the same." Every human carries about 6 billion base pairs—the chemical rungs of the DNA ladder—in the nuclei of his or her cells. Our personal DNA code differs from that of a random stranger by two rungs for every thousand, or .2 percent of the whole. The differences are smaller between family members and larger between people whose ancestors are unlikely to have intermingled in recent history. Still, a random sample of people in any small group from any location in the world—from rural Sweden to the Ituri Forest to Tierra del Fuego—will turn up 85 percent of all the genetic variation our species contains.

Nevertheless, the remaining 15 percent of human genetic variation isn't distributed randomly. It has a geographic pattern, which stems from past population movements and matings. Interestingly, the larger part of that 15 percent difference is not racial: almost 9 percent is reflected in differences among ethnic and linguistic groups within any given race. Only 6 percent represents genetic differences between races.

These kinds of patterns interest anthropologists and geneticists. The interest isn't merely historical: some of the variation finds expression in physical differences that intrigue medical researchers. The Navajo, for example, have very high rates of high blood pressure, some of which may be genetic in origin. Genetic research without Navajo samples won't illuminate that problem. African Americans, as another example, experience high failure rates in organ transplants, partly because donors and recipients, even if both are of African origin, may have geographically different ancestries. If geneticists understood DNA variation on the African continent, tissue matching could be done more efficiently.

But—and this is the message that Diversity Project proponents repeat like a mantra—the patterns of variation that appear at the genetic level cut across visible racial divisions. Moving from the physical traits that scientists call phenotype—things like skin color and hair type—to the genetic level is like moving closer and closer to a pointillist painting. Twenty feet from Seurat's *La Grande Jatte,* for instance, you see Parisians and their dogs, but at two feet the image dissolves into dabs of pigment that might belong to a Parisian, a dog, or a tree. It's the same way with the human phenotype and the human genotype. "The closer in you go from what you see on the surface," notes Diversity Project planner Marc Feldman of Stanford, "the more unity there is."

This genetic unity means, for instance, that white Americans, though ostensibly far removed from black Americans in phenotype, can sometimes be better tissue matches for them than are *other* black Americans. "After the Diversity Project," predicts planning-committee member Georgia Dunston of Howard University, "we won't have the luxury of drawing distinctions between one another based on skin pigmentation anymore."

That day, however, may be a long time coming, judging from the initial criticism of the project. Perhaps what's most ironic about such criticism is that the scientists most involved in the project have established track records in human rights. As Feldman observes, "All of us have worked throughout our lives in an antiracist framework. Our political credentials are in order."

Charter member and 1960s activist Mary-Claire King, for instance, was putting her genetic expertise on the political line long before the Diversity Project was proposed: in Argentina she used DNA analysis to help reunite the kidnapped children of "disappeared" political prisoners with their grandmothers. In El Salvador she's been helping UN workers identify the remains of the 794 villagers of El Mozote, who were massacred by the American-trained military in 1981.

Throughout the 1970s, three-year project veteran Feldman publicly took on Nobel Prize-winning physicist William Shockley, who argued that whites are intellectually superior to blacks, debating him at the podium and in the press; Feldman currently heads the Morrison Institute for Population and Resource Studies at Stanford, which trains scientists and government officials from the developing world in ecology, population biology, and demographics.

And then there's Luca Cavalli-Sforza. It's Cavalli-Sforza, professor emeritus of genetics at the Stanford medical school, who remains both the project's biggest booster and the biggest target for the flak it takes. "Any sensible person can see this is important research," he says with characteristic aplomb. "But I must tell you, I was completely unprepared for the negative reactions we have encountered."

Straight-backed, silver-haired, and courtly—he registers somewhere between Marcello Mastroianni and David Niven on the charm meter—Cavalli-Sforza comes by his confidence honestly. A member of the Royal Society and the National Academy of Sciences, a recipient of the Huxley Medal for Biology and the Order of Merit of the Italian Republic, the 72-year-old Cavalli-Sforza is widely regarded as one of the world's leading geneticists. Though he has worked in the United States for most of his adult life, he remains an Italian in everything from his citizenship to his accent to his style of dress, which by American scientific standards is extraordinarily debonair.

Cavalli-Sforza has spent his entire career decoding the genetic clues to our hidden past, and he recently summed up his life's work in a 1,032-page magnum opus called *The History and Geography of Human Genes.* In the preface, he and coauthors Paolo Menozzi and Alberto Piazza note that written history, linguistics, and archeology are flawed tools for reconstructing the history of human evolution: "Only genes . . . have the degree of permanence necessary," they say, for discussing *Homo sapiens'* 100,000 years of "fissions, fusions, and migrations of populations."

Yet if Cavalli-Sforza is a man entranced by genes and the evolutionary patterns they reveal, he is acutely aware of how genetic information can be willfully misused, particularly when mixed with notions of race. "I get hate mail from neo-Nazi groups all the time," he says, gesturing at the pile in his office that awaited him on his return from a six-month sabbatical in Italy.

Cavalli-Sforza considers visible racial traits mere physiological frosting, functional adaptations of an organism to its environment, but his correspondents don't agree. "To say that race doesn't exist is a lie. And only an idiot would believe it," reads one laboriously handwritten example, which attributes Cavalli-Sforza's intellectual stance to a degenerative mental disease. Others are nastier, even frightening; all are anonymous. He shrugs dismissively, immune after years of attacks. "People like this never sign their names."

The criticism that's harder to shrug off, however, comes from more respectable quarters, including some members of the scientific community, for "crimes" ranging from colonialism to outright racism. Some anthropologists suggest that Cavalli-Sforza got off on the wrong foot in 1991 by referring to African "tribes" but European "ethnic groups" before a large audience of anthropologists whose support for the project he was trying to enlist. "That's when he lost us," says one critic, who implies that the choice of words revealed a disturbing glimpse of a colonial mentality at the highest level of the project.

Ken Weiss heatedly rejects this interpretation. As for raising awareness of indigenous peoples, "I would say categorically that Luca has done more than anyone in the history of the species." He has his own explanation for the negative reaction to the project among some of his colleagues. "Many anthropologists," he contends, "are lamentably ignorant about genetics." And that ignorance breeds unwarranted suspicion, he thinks. "Laypeople sometimes have this idea that there's a black gene or a white gene, or a gene for criminal behavior. And there are a lot of anthropologists who don't know much more than that. If some anthropologists are worried that the project might be used for racist purposes, then maybe that's because deep down they really believe that there is a gene for race, and they are afraid to find it. But I'm not afraid of that, because I know a race gene doesn't exist. And that's what the project will show."

It seems clear that the high-profile Diversity Project has brought a long-simmering anthropological unease with genetics to a rolling boil. In particular, cultural anthropologists fear that the Human Genome Diversity Project gives intellectual legitimacy and—at a hoped-for $5 million a year for five years—a financial leg up to an approach they think shortchanges human complexity. Not surprisingly, they argue that it's more important to study and preserve the world's cultures than its genes. Greely, who has a long-standing amateur interest in anthropology, first became aware of this strain at a project-related meeting in Mount Kisco, New York, in 1993. "It was sort of like going out with somebody and being invited to Christmas dinner at her parents' house, with all of the family there," he recalls. "And suddenly they're reliving old arguments—what Uncle Joe said to so-and-so 20 years ago—and you don't have the foggiest idea what's going on. Fascinating, but I had the sense of being an outsider at a family fight."

Cavalli-Sforza attributes this family fight to a fundamental misunderstanding of how science itself works. "Some people say we should take a more *holistic* approach," he says, using quasi-audible italics to convey just how naïve an idea this is. "What they don't see is that any science involves initial reductionism. You must simplify first, so you can get a handle on the problem." In an aside not calculated to win converts, he adds, "I don't think cultural anthropologists are scientists at all—more philosophers or social critics."

But cultural anthropologists are not the only ones taking serious issue with the Diversity Project. Biological anthropologist Jonathan Marks of Yale thinks its potential for answering evolutionary questions is being oversold. "You don't need molecular genetics to tell you that Danes are more closely related to Swedes than they are to Iroquois—just look at a map!" he says. "And it's not going to be able to tell you whether they're more closely related to Austrians than to Swiss, because at that level we're *all* mutts. This is 1990s genetics applied to questions anthropologists stopped asking in the 1940s."

Yet even the harshest scientific critics stop short of accusing project members of anything worse than naïveté ("a grand naïveté," Marks amends). "I think what you have here," says anthropologist Jason Clay, "is a bunch of honor roll scientists who are in way over their heads."

Clay, who founded and edited a journal focusing on the problems of indigenous peoples, supports the Diversity Project in theory. "You can't be afraid of information," he says. Yet as the head of Rights and Resources, an organization that brings together Third World agriculturists and "green" businesses like Ben & Jerry's and the Body Shop, he wonders about the details. Judging from his own experience with indigenous peoples, Clay says, well-intentioned explanations of why researchers want individuals' DNA will be useless. "Some of these groups don't know about germs, much less about genes or property rights," he explains. "What could 'informed consent' possibly mean to them?"

He also worries about the uses to which the samples might be put. In the past, botanicals taken from Third World countries have been used to develop new pharmaceuticals that are then sold back to their countries of origin at a profit. What if the Diversity Project were to uncover a gene that confers resistance to, say, an environmental toxin? "Indigenous peoples have been mined for their resources by big companies, and mined for their ideas by anthropologists," he says. "Now are they being mined for their molecules?"

Jon Marks concurs. "Just imagine how it seems to indigenes," he says. "'We've taken your land, we've eradicated your life-ways, we've killed your people, but—guess what?—we're going to save your cells.'"

In response to these criticisms, Feldman simply sighs. "Look, if the Malaysian government is going to allow the Negrito population to be eliminated by selling their land to the Japanese timber companies," he replies wearily, "there's not much the Genome Diversity Project can do about that. We're scientists, not politicians."

Still, however acrimonious it got, the debate about the Diversity Project was confined mostly to the laboratory, the seminar room, and the faculty lounge until 1993. That's when the Rural Advancement Foundation International got into the act. RAFI, an advocacy group concerned with issues of biodiversity and intellectual property, has for a decade been sounding the alarm over what it considers to be biopiracy: the theft of intellectual property rights of indigenous peoples. And it doesn't see the Diversity Project as an exception. "I think they're very naïve with regard to the commercialization of cell lines," says Hope Shand, the research director of RAFI-USA. "If the cells are in repositories that are open to everyone, what's to prevent somebody from patenting them?"

According to RAFI's point of view, First World agribusiness has made a fortune from plant strains developed by Third World agriculturists, without funneling any of the profits back to the original openers. The fledgling Diversity Project, RAFI believes, could easily become a vehicle for similar abuses—not so much by project scientists as by outside researchers who might well be less scrupulous in their use of the sampled DNA. "There is nothing in international law," notes RAFI member Jean Christie, "that assures us those abuses won't take place."

RAFI workers have told indigenous leaders of their suspicions, buttonholed delegates at conventions, and E-mailed activist groups worldwide. Partly as a result of this lobbying, the European Green party, joined by the World Council of Indigenous Peoples and the Guaymi General Congress, has called for suspension of the Human Genome Diversity Project.

All this troubles Hank Greely very deeply; he sees the intellectual property issues as a misplaced concern. "There's no reason the project and RAFI should be ene-

mies," he says. "There's no commercial money in the project, no pharmaceutical-industry backing. This is pure science." He concedes that the patent question is a knotty one but insists "we're happy to do what's right. It's just not clear, yet, exactly what's the best way to do that."

While the patent question may eventually yield to time, legislation, and good intentions, it may take more heroic measures to counter the darkest charge leveled against the project: genocide. "Unscrupulous parties," warns a RAFI newsletter, could "devise cheap and targeted biological weapons," effective against specific races, by using data collected by the researchers. The Diversity Project, in RAFI's view, makes the specter of genocide a biotechnological reality.

This claim is the one that sends project scientists around the bend. "If people understood human genetics," snaps Feldman, "they'd know it can't be done."

"It's ludicrous," says University of Florida anthropologist and project committee member John Moore, "to suggest that we could be indifferent to the destruction of what most interests us."

"This is the most incredible rubbish, this DNA-poison idea," says Cavalli-Sforza. "It is part of a hate campaign waged against us."

But RAFI won't back down from its claims. "We're not scientists," says Christie, "but we've done research on biological warfare. People say our protests are naïve, radical, or ill-conceived, but they're not."

Predictably, Hank Greely has a more measured response to even this dire accusation. "Governments *have* engaged in biological warfare," he says, recalling that in the nineteenth century the United States gave blankets impregnated with smallpox virus to Native Americans. "Indigenous people are right to be skeptical when people from the developed world come to them saying they want to help. It's a kind of survival trait—groups that didn't have it are probably gone now."

Greely doesn't for a moment think these fears are warranted vis-à-vis the Diversity Project, but in his view that's not the point. "If people are worried," he says, in what amounts to the ethicist's credo, "you have to deal with their fears, whether or not they have any basis."

It appears that his credo will guide the future progress of the Diversity Project. Feldman admits that they've made some mistakes—"You could call it arrogance," he says; "we sort of took it for granted that everyone would see this was a great project"—but he's certain they're on the right track at last. The MacArthur Foundation has awarded the North American committee a grant to develop an ethics program, and project leaders will be holding informational meetings for groups whose cooperation is being sought—meetings to explain the project as well as to answer questions about it. Feldman describes the first few such meetings, held in the spring of 1994, as "frank and good." Jon Marks applauds the trend. "Look, I think the project is a great idea; you can never have enough scientific data. The collection just has to be done right. It has to be done respectfully."

And Cavalli-Sforza, father of the Diversity Project, is heartened by the progress he's been seeing. The Chinese have established a Diversity Project committee, he reports, and collection has started in the British Isles, where the people of Cornwall have begun giving DNA samples. "We are still working on the ethics here," he says, "but that's very important. There cannot be any misunderstanding. We need to be—is the word *fireproof?* No—*bulletproof.* We need to be bulletproof."

Questions

1. What is the purpose of the Human Genome Diversity project? Why is it controversial? Why do the researchers running the project collect blood samples from various groups of people?
2. Why are the geneticists and anthropologists working on the project considered by some to be "neocolonialists, gene pirates and pawns in a conspiracy to develop race-specific biological weapons"?
3. What was the Human Genome Organization? What was its original purpose?
4. Do you believe that the Human Genome Diversity project is necessary? Provide research and specific examples to substantiate your opinion.

46

Organ Concert

B.D. COLEN

Of all the wonders of modern medicine, none has captured the public imagination as fully as organ transplantation. Since 1967, when South African surgeon Christiaan Barnard kept 55-year-old Louis Washkansky alive for 18 additional days by giving him a heart taken from a 24-year-old woman killed in an auto accident, these spectacular feats of surgical legerdemain—often involving teams of physicians toiling meticulously for as long as 48 hours—have won headline coverage and created instant heroes of patients and doctors alike.

One of those heroes is Dr. Thomas Starzl, the doctor who, in the same year Barnard replaced Washkansky's heart, performed the first successful liver transplant in Denver. It was Starzl's team at the University of Pittsburgh's Transplantation Institute that made liver transplants routine and fine-tuned the intricate balance of immunosuppression drugs to fight the rejection of transplanted organs by the body's immune system. Now, as he approaches retirement after three decades of spectacular achievement, Starzl has reached the conclusion that he and his colleagues had, for all those years, been going about organ transplantation the wrong way.

"We've made some discoveries that would suggest there was an epistemologic collapse 30 years ago in the understanding of why transplants work," says Starzl. "This was a classic example of how you can get caught up in the snowstorm of details—learning more and more about less and less and let the great truth escape."

The great truth Starzl now sees is this: the mystery was not about [the body's] rejection. It is about the intermingling of cells, the achievement of a peaceful truce between the patient and the donated organ. Rather than beating the patient's immune system into submission with drugs until it accepts the donor organ, Starzl realized, the trick is to convince both the body's defense mechanism and the new organ that the intruder is really "self," a recognized member of the host body.

Starzl's epiphany—which he calls a "paradigm shift" in transplant thinking—in no way diminishes the work already accomplished. The surgical techniques used by him and his colleagues have added years—decades in some cases—to the lives of hundreds of thousands of men, women and children. From the 1950s through today, physicians like Starzl, Barnard, Toronto's Joel Cooper and Stanford's Norman Shumway have moved mountains' worth of kidneys, pancreases, livers, hearts and lungs from one human body to another.

Moreover, the doctors did all this in direct defiance of the human immune system, a formidable foe whose chief goal is to reject any and all foreign objects. It accomplishes this by deploying highly specialized cells trained to recognize interlopers, then hunt them down and kill them—even if doing so destroys the very life the donated organ was meant to save. The doctors believed the best weapons they had at their disposal were drugs designed to disable the immune system, if only partially. A mixture of azathioprine, prednisone and antilymphocyte globulin was the choice in the 1960s. In the '80s, cyclosporine proved even more effective. It was assumed that these drugs worked simply by disarming the body's built-in commandos—the human leukocyte antigens (HLAS) and T cells—long enough for the invading organs to gain a foothold.

By and large it worked. More and more patients were surviving beyond a year, an established milestone of transplant success. But in 1992 Starzl and his colleagues discovered that there was something different about those recipients who had lived much longer—10, 20, as many as 30 years. By testing these patients, they discovered that white blood cells from the recipient's immune system had migrated into the donated organs—and vice versa. What is more, with the encouragement of the antirejection drugs, body and organ had learned to coexist in peace. If scientists could somehow find a way to facilitate that long-term assimilation, Starzl recognized, they could establish the tolerance of transplants more readily and perhaps minimize the use of drugs.

Starzl acknowledges that this insight had also occurred to other researchers. Scientists, going back as far as 1960 Nobel prizewinner Peter Medawar, had come to recognize that tolerance was possible. If bone marrow, for instance, would only accept an interloping cell, the larger system would follow suit. The trouble was the only way to achieve that was to kill off the body's entire current bone-marrow supply and replace it with another—a technique oncologists use as a last-ditch weapon to try to cleanse patients of such systemic cancers as leukemia and breast cancer. (See Figure 46.1.)

But bone-marrow work and solid-organ transplant work have traditionally been two separate fields of medicine. "The big misconception," says Starzl, "was not realizing that the acceptance and tolerance of solid-organ grafts are due to the same mechanism described by Medawar. There is a seamless wonder of transplantation immunology. It's so damn simple, it's crushing."

Simple in theory, perhaps. But there is a long way to go before mutual cell assimilation, known as chimerism, between a donor organ and its recipient can be achieved with such relative ease. And much of the work being done is with mice, dogs and monkeys, which have been used successfully in assimilation studies by James Gozzo, dean of the Bouve College of Pharmacy and Health Sciences at Boston's Northeastern University, as well as by other researchers, including Judith Thomas, director of the Transplant Center at the University of Alabama. They have found that by first transplanting some donor bone marrow into the recipient animal, it is possible to trick the animal's immune system into accepting a solid-organ transplant almost as if it were native to its own body—just as Starzl

suggests will be the case in humans. That in turn allows them to use lower doses of immunosuppressive drugs—and then phase out the use of those drugs entirely. "For a short time, drugs are used to keep the body's leukocytes from attacking the bone marrow, until it can induce tolerance of the organ," says Thomas. If she and Gozzo are successful, experiments in humans might not be far off.

A melancholy irony, however, hangs over such progress. The greater the success level in human-to-human organ transplantation, the more demand there is likely to be for such procedures—and the longer the waiting list for organs will become. Already, thousands of frustrated and often desperately ill candidates are waiting fretfully for donor organs. According to the United Network for Organ Sharing (UNOS), the organization that coordinates the registration for transplants in America, 3,448 men, women and children died in 1995 while awaiting transplants. As of the first week in August, there were some 47,000 Americans on transplant waiting lists—but for all of last year there were only enough organs available to permit 19,136 transplants.

Some of this bad news is a direct result of good news: physicians are keeping sicker and sicker patients awaiting transplants alive longer, and surgeons are successfully transplanting into patients who are sicker, and older, than they have in the past. All this means that the pool of those awaiting transplants will continue to increase. To fill this gap, medicine is exploring a variety of alternative, if sometimes only temporary, solutions. Among them:

XENOGRAFTS

Virtually everyone in the field says greater use of animal-organ transplants, or xenografts, enhanced through genetic engineering, will help meet the demand for healthy organs. Though much attention was paid to early experiments with primate (mostly baboon) organs, the most productive research is being done with pigs. "We're really looking at pigs because pigs are readily available," says Dr. Jon Kobashigawa, medical director of UCLA's heart-transplant program. "We already use pig valves [to replace damaged human heart valves], and I think most people have less trouble with the concept of using pigs than with using primates."

To pre-empt the recipient's defense against the invasion of a pig liver or heart, scientists are prepping their donor pigs genetically by introducing human genes that will render their organs less foreign. "We want to prevent the pig antigens from being expressed [produced] and prevent the

Cornea and Sclera

More than 44,000 cornea and 6,200 sclera (coating around the eyeball) operations for repair and replacement take place every year

Cartilage

Latest technique uses cells cultivated from humans, then grafted onto joints

Lung

Between 1988 and 1993, patients' one-year survival rate improved 30%

Liver

Of the more than 23,000 transplanted since 1988, 211 have been partial or whole lobes donated by other living patients.

Pancreas

The world's longest living recipient survived 18 years

Kidney-Pancreas

As of July 31, 1,385 people were waiting for this combination transplant

Kidney

One of the veteran organs, with transplant survival rates of more than 90% in the first year.

Blood

Around 14 million pints are donated every year by 8 million volunteers

Artery and Vein Allografts

The same polymer in sutures–now used to build a framework or "scaffold" that guides the growth of new cells–works for everything from skin grafts to heart valves

Knees

Approximately 150,000 rebuilt annually

Pericardium

In 1992 and 1993, there were a total of 696 replacements of this membrane sac, which encloses the heart and the vessels leading into and out of it

Heart-Lung

657 performed through 1995

Heart Valves

Doctors perform approximately 60,000 replacements annually

Heart

361 hearts were replaced in 1995. Others remained in place with the help of LVADs (left-ventricular assist devices), mechanical boosters that are often "bridges" to eventual full transplantation

Hip Replacements

On average, new hips last 10 to 15 years after surgery

Bone Marrow

Despite an average of 89 transplants each month, the National Marrow Donor Program still cannot find matches for nearly a third of its applicants

Skin

6,668 sq. ft. grafted in 1993 alone

Muscles and Tendons

Total muscle transfers move whole muscles–tendons, vessels and all– to other parts of the body, where they are reconnected under a microscope

Figure 46.1

A host of transplant possibilities, if the parts are in stock.

Sources: United Network for Organ Sharing. Eye Bank Association of America. American Association of Tissue Banks. Baylor College of Medicine. National Marrow Donor Program. Columbia-Presbyterian Medical Center human recipient from identifying the pig heart as foreign," says Kobashigawa. In anywhere from 2 to 10 years, there could be genetically engineered pigs with hearts that produce no foreign antigens, only human ones. The Institute of Medicine in Washington recently recommended the development of dedicated colonies of swine to reduce the chance of virulent animal-borne diseases being transported to humans—a widespread concern.

ARTIFICIAL HEARTS

When Dr. Robert Jarvik's artificial heart sustained the life of dentist Barney Clark for 112 days in the winter of 1982–83, it looked for a brief period as if some form of artificial pump—as crude a device as that first contraption was—might be the answer to the shortage of hearts. But after Clark's death, and a number of less than successful similar attempts in the years following, interest waned. The mechanical pumps required the use of cumbersome external power supplies. More worrisome, they tended to throw off blood clots that led to devastating strokes.

Meanwhile, though, other medical engineers were developing partial artificial hearts, called left-ventricular assist devices (LVADS), which are installed to assist a weakened heart at its steady work. Since the first LVAD was implanted a decade ago, more than 700 patients have used them for periods as long as 17 months while awaiting full heart transplants.

Unlike the earlier, totally artificial hearts, the newest LVADS encourage the body to form a smooth layer of cells, like those that line the interior of arteries, on the pump's inner surface. These naturally slick surfaces help prevent coagulation and thus the formation of dangerous clots.

LVADS are not meant to be permanent organ supplements but rather "bridges" that keep patients alive until donor hearts are found, and they can actually improve the recipients' overall condition. "If you put these devices in at an optimal time, you can turn a very high-risk transplant patient into a very low-risk transplant patient," says Dr. Robert Kormos, clinical director of the University of Pittsburgh's artificial-heart program.

CELL TRANSPLANTS

Though not in the same class as solid organs, cells may be the ultimate unit of transplantation. Bone-marrow transplants represent the wholesale transfer of stem cells that can correct a range of problems. Cells taken from fetuses have been used with varied success to reverse autoimmune disorders, Parkinson's disease and certain types of diabetes. These young cells, unjaded by exposure to the world's defense-inducing impurities, have not yet developed the ability to trigger counterattacks and are therefore ideal for implantation with minimal risk of rejection.

But the future of fetal-cell use is darkly clouded by moral and ethical considerations. The great majority of donations come from abortion clinics, since they constitute the healthiest and most predictable supply of fetuses. Right-to-Life proponents passionately oppose their use and succeeded in getting a nationwide moratorium on federally funded research related to fetal-tissue transplants in human subjects that lasted for nearly five years. A less controversial source of innocent young cells is umbilical-cord blood. Rich in the same kinds of stem cells found in bone marrow, cord blood could provide an alternative to fetal transplants.

Ethical questions loom over almost every aspect of organ transplantation. Donor shortages force doctors to rank candidates according to standard criteria established by the medical community. Although many people suspect that economic or celebrity privilege plays a role, UNOS maintains that the allocation policy is designed to give equal access to all. To get on its waiting lists, doctors must agree that a transplant is necessary for long-term survival. Once patients are on a list, allocation is based on specific criteria, including severity of illness, organ match and even logistics.

The use of animal organs and artificial parts only adds another layer of concern. Some animal-rights advocates recoil at the prospect of breeding beasts solely for organ harvest. Religious fundamentalists argue that all of this messing with Mother Nature amounts to a perversion of the natural order.

By adhering more closely to nature's order, the research spurred by Starzl's "paradigm shift" may yet lead to a more elegant solution. But any form of transplantation, says Dr. Peter Libby of Harvard Medical School and Boston's Brigham and Women's Hospital, must be recognized as a "halfway technology." Transplantation, he says, "is an admission of our failure to deal with the underlying diseases. I would like to see the day when we don't need transplantation."

While science may not soon achieve that ideal, the advances in the transplantation of bone-marrow and stem cells, and the progress made toward assimilation of donor organs through the exchange of immune cells, augur well for a peaceful solution. Much the way cancer specialists hope that they may one day look back at chemotherapy and radiation as primitive, brutish weapons used in desperation against tumors, so experts in the organ-transplant field may eventually view the work done in the latter half of the 20th century as a crude precursor to a model of subtle cellular persuasion.

Questions

1. Write a summary of this chapter, and list three new concepts that you learned from it.

2. What does Starzl's epiphany—a "paradigm shift"—refer to? What have doctors done to prevent the rejection of new organs by the human body?

3. What is chimerism? How does it relate to organ transplants?

4. What is your opinion of xenografts, the transplantation of animal organs to humans? What ethical issues should be considered with regard to xenografts?

5. What are cell transplants? When are they used? What are the ethical issues in using fetal cells to reverse autoimmune or other disorders?

Physician-Assisted Suicide

47

What I do is relieve suffering . . . . Unfortunately, death is the result.

DR. JACK KERVORKIAN

Dr. Jack Kervorkian is a delicensed pathologist often referred to as "Dr. Death" because he participates in doctor-assisted suicide for terminally ill patients. Dr. Kervorkian has assisted in at least 50 suicides. He has been involved in three trials and three acquittals and shoulders the responsibility of being the "standard-bearer" for ethical doctor-assisted suicide. (Worthington, August 1993)

In Illinois, hospitals have been turning off ventilators or pulling out the feeding tubes of terminally ill patients at relatives' requests since September 1991, when the Health Care Surrogate Act went into effect. In addition, there are 43 other states that allow medical proxy laws that give a person permission to dictate before the onset of a catastrophic illness that in the event of a hopeless medical situation, his or her life would not be prolonged (Hilkevitch, 1993).

"Pulling the tubes," "euthanasia," and "physician-assisted suicide" are terms that are used interchangeably when discussing the ultimate death of an individual who is terminally ill and wants to die. (This wish is either verbally stated by the patient to his or her doctor or family or via a living will.) Historically, euthanasia was defined as a peaceful death with minimal suffering, regardless of whether the death is natural or deliberate. Recently, however, the meaning has been changed to refer to the deliberate killing of people with chronic illnesses or disabilities (Sosby, 1994). Dr. Kervorkian is quick to point out that euthanasia and physician-assisted suicide are the same thing. He states that euthanasia is a Greek word and means "easy death" (Laurence, 1997). Whatever words are used, however, are only symbols of the emotional process of making

the decision to die or the decision to allow a loved one to die. It is an ethical dilemma that individuals and families face when they encounter a terminal illness.

One ethical question often asked is that of what point a terminally ill patient should end his or her life? When does life become hopeless enough to ask for Dr. Kervorkian to bring his "Mercitron" suicide machine so that the patient can kill him or herself? This particular machine lets the patient release a clamp that injects a lethal combination of anesthesia and poison into him or herself. When does life

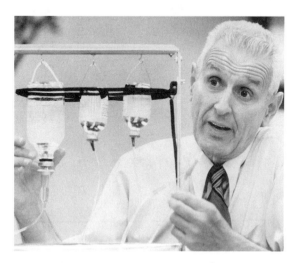

Dr. Jack Kervorkian and his death machine.
Photo courtesy of Gamma-Liaison, Inc.

365

become hopeless enough that parents make the decision to pull life-support systems from a six-year-old child who has already been comatose for four weeks? When does life become hopeless enough that the children of a 77-year-old, paralyzed stroke patient adhere to her request that a feeding tube not be provided, an act that will ultimately kill her (Worthington, October 1993)?

As if these questions are not tough enough, there are others to consider when contemplating physician-assisted suicide. If a patient is in his or her "right mind," is terminally ill, and wants to die with Dr. Kervorkian's aid, is his or her death to be counted as murder? How would you even know if the patient was in his or her right mind or if he or she was exercising good judgment in the midst of such great physical and emotional suffering? What part should the law play in this decision, or should the decision be a private doctor–patient decision? Should religion be integrated in the final decision of doctor-assisted suicide? Should pain management be used instead of death? Should doctor-assisted suicide happen only when there is intolerable, unrelenting pain and suffering with no chance for recovery? If so, how would you know definitively that there *really* is no chance for recovery? How would courts of law measure "suffering" or "unrelenting pain" or the determi-

nation of "no chance for recovery" if the cases went to court (Laurence, 1997)?

Dr. Kervorkian has brought to light a dilemma that many families, medical professionals, and counselors have struggled with in private. It is a difficult issue that should be contemplated, struggled with, and understood by each human prior to finding him or herself in that type of situation.

References

Hilkevitch, J. (1993, February 15). Euthanasia Debate is Heating Up. *Chicago Tribune.*

Laurence, C. (1997, April 27). Some Difficult Questions for "Dr. Death." *Chicago Sun-Times.*

Sosby, D. (1994, September 30). *An Issue of Autonomy: Questioning Physician-Assisted Suicide and Euthanasia.* The Special Senate Committee on Euthanasia and Assisted Suicide, Winnipeg, University of Alberta Developmental and Disabilities Center.

Worthington, R. (1993, August 18). Suicide Doctor Finally to Have Day in Court. *Chicago Tribune.*

Worthington, R. (1993, October 23). Kervorkian Fires up Ethics Debate: 19th Suicide Disturbs Even Some of His Sympathizers. *Chicago Tribune.*

Conclusion

Between 1980 and 1995, life expectancy has increased globally by 4.6 years: by 4.4 years for males and by 4.9 years for females. Leprosy has been reduced by 82% worldwide in the last 11 years. There are currently 380 million people aged 65 and above (Subramamian 1997). As of December 18, 1998 there were 63,833 people waiting for transplants. The number waiting breaks down as follows: 41,982 kidney transplants, 11,814 liver transplants, 4,161 heart transplants, and 3,142 lung transplants (Gift of Life Foundation, 1999). These facts speak strongly to the positive effects of medical technology. By reading this part of the book and examining the history of technological advancements in medicine, you now have an enhanced awareness of where medical technology has been (e.g., the invention of antibiotics, the irradication of smallpox, etc.) and where it is headed (e.g., tissue and genetic engineering, antibiotic resistance, and organ transplants).

What about the future? You have been asked in this part to access Web sites to find out additional information about medical technology in the future. What did you find? Did you find that xenotransplants may be a part of medical technologies in the future? There have been approximately 30 experimental xenotransplants since the turn of the century. According to Rebecca Williams, in an article entitled "Organ Transplants from Animals: Examining the Possibilities,"

> [I]n April 1995, with FDA permission, doctors at Lahey Hitchcock Medical Center in Burlington, Mass., injected fetal pig brain cells into the brains of patients with advanced Parkinson's disease. The hope was that the fetal tissue would produce dopamine, which the patient's brains lack. The experiments were done primarily to test the safety of the procedures. Other xenotransplant experiments have involved implanting animal hearts, livers and kidneys into humans.

The major concern in conducting xenotransplants is that the body may reject the transplants from other animals. One way to counteract this problem is to prescribe very strong drugs that suppress the immune system—and thus, its negative response to the transplanted organ. Even if the body did not reject the new organ, the drugs may cause the organ recipient to be vulnerable to infections. The hope is that genetic engineering will pave the way for the human body to accept xenotransplants more readily in the future.

Throughout this part of the book, many ethical and social issues were outlined that should cause you to stop, ponder, wonder, and reevaluate the social implications of medical technologies. It is impossible to read this part and not wonder about the amazingly positive effects of medical technology. Yet, this part may also force you to ponder quality-of-life issues, ethical considerations in medical treatment, the choices you have as a patient, and what you will do if you ever have to decide about euthanasia.

The next part of the book will discuss the effects of technology on Third-World countries. It will provide a clearer understanding of the part that technology plays in the development of these countries.

References

Subramamian, Director of the Office of the World Health Reporting. "Facts from the World Health Report 1997." Available: http://www.who.ch/whr/1997/facts.htm. Access Date: 2/18/99

Gift of Life Foundation. (1999) "Gift of Life-Statistics." Available: http://www.giftoflife-sc.org/statistics.asp. Last updated: 1/26/99

Williams, R. (1996) "Organ Transplants from Animals: Examining the Possibilities." Available: http://www.fda.gov/fdac/features/596_xeno.html.

Internet Exercise

Using any of the Internet search engines (e.g., Alta Vista, Yahoo, Infoseek, etc.) answer the following questions:

1. Internet questions

   a. What constraints and rules must researchers follow today when working with animals and humans? What is "informed consent"?

   b. What are the legal ramifications of doctors using clients for research without obtaining informed consent?

   c. Find information on current research on the misuse of antibiotics. What are the current medical concerns about patients who fail to finish antibiotic prescriptions or who use others' antibiotics without a doctor's prescription?

   d. What is the current status of the Human Genome Project?

   e. What is the current trend in the field of organ transplants? In what geographical locations are organ transplants done the most? The least? What age groups usually receive the most organ transplants?

   f. Define the following terms:
      colonization
      tissue engineering
      bioengineered tissue
      cell transplant
      euthanasia
      biotechnology

2. Xenotransplants questions

   a. What is a xenotransplant?

   b. Describe the first animal-to-human transplant. When was it? Who did the surgery? What kind of animals were used? Did the recipient live? Did the animals live?

   c. Why is it difficult to keep patients who have had xenotransplants alive? Does the body usually reject the transplanted organ? What effect do immunosuppressive drugs have on the human body?

   d. Why do doctors not want to use baboons for xenotransplants? Why, medically, might baboons be the best animal to use for xenotransplants?

   e. Ethically, why might pigs be better to use for xenotransplants than baboons?

3. Tissue engineering questions

   a. What parts of the body can be re-created through tissue engineering? Can a heart valve, liver, uterus, bone, skin, eye, or brain be recreated? It is doubtful that eyes could be grown in cultures, but some researchers hope to create artificial vision systems instead. What research can you find on each topic?

   b. Some biotech companies are waiting to gain approval from the Food and Drug Administration for skin substitutes that would help patients suffering from burns and serious wounds. Until recently, doctors used cadaver tissue to replace dead tissue, but the cadaver tissue is sometimes rejected by the patients' immune system. By growing skin in the lab, the need for cadaver skin is eliminated. What research can you find on this technological phenomenon?

   c. Tissue engineering today may start with neonatal foreskin; cow tendons may be used as replacement connective tissues. Try to find more details on this type of tissue engineering.

Useful Web Sites

URL	*Site Description*
http://www.ornl.gov/TechREsources/Human_Genome/home.html	Human Genome Project
http://www.ccf.org/transplant/allvol.html	Organ transplants
http://www/pslgroup.com/dg/3f226.htm	Tissue engineering
http://www.who.ch/whr/1997/factse.htm	Medical facts
http://www.who.ch/whr/1997/fig2e.gif	Global causes of death
http://sln.fi.edu/biosci/history/firsts.html	Historical medical timeline
http://www.giftoflife-sc.org/statistics.asp	Gift of Life statistics

Technology
and the Third World

The first world...the third world
...the rich....the poor
...where are the
boundaries...?

One Planet...One People

Photo courtesy of NASA Headquarters

371

One billion people in the developing world still lack access to clean water . . . nearly 2 billion lack adequate sanitation . . . electric power has yet to reach 2 billion people.

WORLD DEVELOPMENT REPORT, WORLD BANK, 1994

As we approach the end of the 20th century, the advances in information technologies have transformed the world into a global village. People of this global village find themselves so close as they witness world events unfolding on the television screens and computer monitors, and yet they still remain oceans apart in terms of their economic conditions and living standards. The gap between the world's poor and its rich is wide and has been getting even wider. The following facts illustrate the dilemma:

- According to the United Nations Development Program (UNDP), in 1991 the richest 20% of the world's people earned 61 times more income than the poorest 20%.

- Thirty years ago, the richest 20% of the world's people received 30 times more than the poorest 20% did—half as wide a gap as today. Since then, the poorest fifth saw its share of global income drop from 2.3 to 1.4%, while that of the richest group rose from 70 to 85%.

- Of the $23 trillion gross world product (GWP) in 1993, $18 trillion was generated in the industrial world, and only $5 trillion circulated in the developing world.

- The gap in per-capita income between the industrial and developing worlds tripled over the past three decades—from $5,700 in 1960 to $15,400 in 1993.

- Economic conditions and growth have been failing during the last 15 years in about 100 countries, home to a quarter of the world's population. The income of 1.5 billion people living in these countries was lower in the 1990s than in earlier decades.

- One fifth of the world's population—those people living in developed nations—now accounts for 70% of the world's energy use.

- More than 80% of the world's population resides in developing countries.

- According to the president of the World Bank, James Wolfensohm, the number of people living in acute poverty could grow from 3 billion to 5 billion in the next 30 years if world leaders do not act now to prevent the trend.

Many developing nations gained independence from the colonial powers after the second World War. But their dreams and aspirations of economic growth and prosperity have yet to materialize. People in developing countries wonder if the colonial era has really ended or if it has merely been replaced by an economic system in which international financial institutions and multinational corporations rule over developing nations.

This part of the book presents an array of issues and challenges that the Third World faces today. The chapters in this part will enable readers to gain insights to the problems of the developing world and their potential solutions. As the developed world prepares itself to enter the 21st century and a new millennium, people in many developing countries, due to their lagging technological level, are still struggling to enter the 18th, 19th, and 20th centuries.

One Planet: Many Worlds

AHMED S. KHAN

The Earth is one but the world is not. We all depend on one biosphere for sustaining our lives. Yet each community, each country, strives for survival and prosperity with little regard for its impact on others.

WORLD COMMISSION ON ENVIRONMENT AND DEVELOPMENT (WCED), *OUR COMMON FUTURE*

As we approach the new millennium, the great technological accomplishments of the 20th century in the areas of telecommunications, computers, energy, agriculture, materials, medicine, genetic engineering, and defense have transformed the world and brought people closer, yet millions of people worldwide still go to bed hungry at night. These technological advances have enabled us to design advanced early warning systems to warn against missile attacks, but we have failed to develop an advanced early warning system to warn against and prevent global famine or the spread of disease. Thanks to state-of-the-art technologies, we are able to design spaceships to explore life on other planets, yet we have failed to preserve life on planet Earth. Millions of children worldwide continue to die due to malnutrition, disease, and poverty.

In this information age, thanks to the Internet, the world has been transformed into a global village. But in this global village, the economic gulf between the developed and the developing countries, commonly known as the Third World, is wide and growing. This economic disparity is one of the most challenging issues in world affairs.

In 1952, when the French demographer Alfred Sauvey coined the phrase "Third World," he observed that the aspirations of the nations gaining independence from the colonial powers were similar to those of the Third Estate in France at the time of the French Revolution. Like the French commoners, who in the later part of the 18th century struggled against the clergy and the elite, these nations wanted to become the masters of their own destinies (Grimm, 1990). The usage of the phrase "Third World" led to the coinage of the phrases "First World" and "Second World." The "First

World" represents mainly economically developed western countries. The "Second World" was meant to represent the communist countries of eastern Europe during the Cold War era, but the term never really caught on. Today, in the post–Cold War era, these countries are referred to as former Soviet-bloc countries. Some of these countries are economically worse off than Third-World countries, but they are never called Third-World countries. Today, the phrase "Third World" is exclusively used to describe a group of nations that are struggling to feed, house, clothe, and educate their people while restrained by poverty, climate, oppression, war, the aftereffects of colonialism, and the economic bondage of the IMF and the World Bank. The phrase "Third World" is also used in a discriminatory manner. According to William J. Grimm, associate editor of Maryknoll Magazine, the Third World is "any nonwhite country whose economy is as bad as or worse than Poland's. No matter how desperate the economic situation may be in eastern Europe or on parts of the Iberian Peninsula, those places are never spoken of as being the Third World, which is a world of brown-, black-, or yellow-skinned people. No white nation is described with the term, though the country may be economically worse off than, for example, Thailand. When whites ruled Rhodesia, it was not the Third World. Now that it is black-ruled Zimbabwe, it is" (Grimm, 1990).

Many African and Asian nations gained independence from the colonial powers after the second World War. But their dreams and aspirations of economic growth and prosperity have yet to materialize. People in developing countries wonder if the colonial era has really ended or if it has merely been replaced by an economic system in which international financial institutions and multinational corporations rule over developing nations. As the developed world prepares itself to enter the 21st century and a new millennium, people in many developing countries, due to their lagging technological level, are still struggling to enter the 18th, 19th, and 20th centuries.

Development in the Third World is inhibited due to a number of extrinsic and intrinsic factors. The extrinsic factors include political interference by the superpowers during the Cold War era, political and economic instability caused by international financial institutions, and economic exploitation of resources by multinational companies. The intrinsic factors are illiteracy; poverty; social injustice; corruption; lack of resources; population pressures; and power-hungry political, feudal, and military elite.

The developed nations have portrayed themselves to the Third World as role models of development and modernization while simultaneously producing a disproportionate share of pollutants emitted into the atmosphere through the burning of fossil fuels relative to the size of their population as compare to the population of the Third World. The Third-World nations confront numerous environmental problems of their own, with water, soil, and air pollution being among the most common. Other problems include desertification, deforestation, the extinction of animal and plant species, international trade in wildlife, the export of toxic waste by developed countries to the Third World, and the disposal of garbage and human waste (Myers, 1990; Mennerick and Mehrangiz, 1991).

Efforts to industrialize by Third-World countries are often hindered by the developed countries in the name of

Table 48.1

Development Indicators for the Five Most Populous Low-Income Countries

	China	India	Pakistan	Bangladesh	Nigeria
Population (1995) in millions	1,200	929	130	120	111
Percent of population with access to safe water	83	63	60	83	43
Infant mortality rate per 1,000 births	34	68	90	79	80
Fertility rate (1995)	1.9	3.2	5.2	3.5	5.5
Energy use in (oil eq.) kg	664	248	254	64	162
Carbon dioxide emission per capita	2.3	0.9	0.6	0.2	0.9
Adult illiteracy					
% Female	27	62	76	74	53
% Male	10	35	50	51	33
1990–1995 annual growth rate (GDP) %	12.8	4.6	4.6	4.1	1.6
Exports (million $)	148,797	30,674	7,992	3,173	11,670
Imports (million $)	129,113	34,522	11,461	6,496	7,900
External debt (million $) (1993)	118,090	93,766	30,152	16,370	35,005
External debt as % of GNP (1995)	17.2	28.2	49.5	56.3	140.5
Debt service as % of exports of goods and services (1995)	77.3	201.2	257.9	298.2	274.5

Source: Worldbank, World Development Indicators (http://www.worldbank.org/html/iecdd/products.htm)

reducing pollution. How would the developed countries respond if the power relationship were reversed? How would they respond if Third-World nations had the economic and technological power to exert pressure on these countries to reduce, for example, the use of fossil fuels and curb industrial processes in order to reduce pollution?

Despite the fact that the average incomes for both the developed and the developing countries have increased, the gap between them has widened during the most recent years. Since 1960, the developed countries have become richer by an average of $5,400 in gross national product (GNP) per capita, while the developing countries have advanced by only $800. Latin American citizens are, on average, poorer than they were in 1970. Countries like Burundi, Somalia, Burkina Faso, Chad, Bangladesh, and Sri Lanka have the lowest per-capita GNP (less than $610), whereas in most developed countries it is more than $14,000 (Mansbach, 1994; Gardner, 1995).

The debt of developing countries is estimated to have grown to over $1.8 trillion in 1994, up from $1.77 trillion in 1993. The worst debt is that of sub-Saharan Africa, excluding South Africa. Collectively, the region's debt amounts to $180 billion, three times the 1980 total, and is 10% higher than the region's entire output of goods and services. Many developing nations have committed a third to a half of their foreign currency earnings to pay the interest and principal, and it is not enough. In Latin America, all of the major debtors, especially Brazil, Argentina, Mexico, Venezuela, Peru, and Chile, are in default and have had to reschedule their repayments (Gardener, 1995).

The developing countries also lag behind in areas like health and education. In the developing countries, the infant mortality rate declined from 109 per 1,000 live births in 1970 to 71 per 1,000 in 1991. Yet, these rates are still much higher than in the developed countries. In 1970, the infant mortality rate in developed countries was 20 per 1,000 live births and declined to about 8 per 1,000 by 1991. Life expectancy rose from an average of about 50 years in 1965 to slightly more than 62 in 1991 in developing countries, but remained far behind the figure for most developed countries (Mansbach, 1994). The story is the same for adult literacy rates, which improved in poor countries but remained far behind those of developed countries. (See Tables 48.1 through 48.4 and Figures 48.1 through 48.3.)

Today the developed countries have set the membership standards for the First and the Third Worlds. Basically,

Table 48.2

Development Indicators for Low-, Middle- and High-Income Countries

	Low-Income Countries	Middle-Income Countries	High-Income Countries	World
Population in millions (1995)	3,180	1,591	902	5,673
Energy use (oil eq.) kg (1994)	369	1,475	5,066	1,433
Carbon dioxide emission per capita (metric tons) (1992)	1.3	4.8	11.9	4.0
Infant mortality rate per 1,000 live births (1995)	69	39	07	55
Fertility rate (1995)	3.2	3.0	1.7	2.9
Adult illiteracy				
% Female	24	19	—	—
% Male	45	23		
1990–1995 Annual growth rate (GDP)	6.8	0.1	—	2.0
Exports (million $) (1995)	245,456	893,331	3,997,288	5,144,770
Imports (million $) (1995)	251,806	987,309	4,037,671	5,246,326
External debt (1995)	534,794	1,530,883	—	—
External debt as % of GNP	38.7	39.9	—	—

Source: Worldbank, World Development Indicators (http://www.worldbank.org/html/iecdd/products.htm)

Table 48.3

Literacy, Per-Capita GNP, and Electricity Use for Selected Developed and Developing Countries

Country	Literacy % of the Population	GNP Per Capita $ US	Electricity Use Per Capita (kWh)
Afghanistan	29	NA	39
Algeria	57	3,480	587
Australia	100	20,720	8,021
Austria	99	17,000	6,300
Bangladesh	35	1,000	75
Belgium	99	17,700	6,790
Bolivia	78	2,100	250
Brazil	81	5,000	1,531
Burma	81	950	65
Canada	97	22,200	17,900
Chad	30	500	15
Chile	93	7,000	1,630
China	78	2,200	630
Comoros	48	700	50
Colombia	87	5,500	1,050
Denmark	99	18,500	6,610
Djibouti	48	1,200	580
Egypt	48	2,400	830
El Salvador	73	2,500	390
Finland	100	16,100	11,050
France	99	18,200	7,430
Gabon	61	4,800	920
Germany	99	16,500	7,160
Ghana	60	1,500	290
Haiti	53	800	75
India	52	1,300	340
Indonesia	77	2,900	200
Israel	92	13,350	4,600
Japan	99	20,400	6,700
Kenya	69	1,200	100
Laos	64	900	220
Malaysia	78	7,500	1,610
Mexico	87	8,200	1,300
Nepal	26	1,000	50
Netherlands	99	17,200	4,200
New Zealand	99	15,700	9,250
Niger	28	650	30
Norway	99	20,800	25,850
Oman	NA	10,000	3,200
Pakistan	35	1,900	350
Peru	85	3,000	760
Saudi Arabia	62	11,000	3,690
Singapore	88	15,000	6,420
Spain	95	12,700	4,000

Table 48.3

Literacy, Per-Capita GNP, and Electricity Use for Selected Developed and Developing Countries (continued)

Country	Literacy % of the Population	GNP Per Capita $ US	Electricity Use Per Capita (kWh)
Sudan	27	750	40
Turkey	81	5,100	750
Uganda	48	1,200	30
United Kingdom	99	16,900	5,480
United States	97	24,700	12,690
Vietnam	88	1,000	130
Yemen	38	800	120
Zimbabwe	67	1,400	740

Source: CIA World Factbook 1995–96.

these standards are economic (Grimm, 1990). Many people in the Third World believe that they are not allowed to attain these standards because of "economic and technological imperialism" imposed by western nations. According to this belief, the First World does not allow economic growth and transfer of technology to reach the developing countries because it may lead to the elimination of jobs and affect the standard of living in the developed countries.

The Third-World countries have found the global economic order imposed on them by the First World intolerable and have called for a new economic order. Policy makers in the developed countries fear that unrest over unmet economic problems may lead the poor to "desperate politics" versus the rich. The people in the Third World counter that the developed countries are still practicing invisible colonialism via international economic institutions.

In 1961, in order to create a more equitable international economic system, the developing countries formed the "nonaligned movement" (NAM). The efforts by NAM led to the passage of resolutions 3201 and 3202 on May 1, 1974, at the special session of the United Nations General Assembly. These resolutions defined principles and a program to improve international economic relations between the developing and the developed countries. These resolutions were also outlined in the "Charter of Economic Rights and Duties of States," passed by the General Assembly in December 1974. These documents specified six major areas of international economic reform that were needed to resolve conflict between the First World and the Third World. The demands were as follows (Mansbach, 1994):

1. Transnational corporations are to be regulated.
2. Technology should be transferred from rich to poor.
3. The trading order should be reformed to assist the development of poor countries.
4. Poor countries' debt should be canceled or renegotiated.
5. Economic aid from rich to poor countries should be increased.
6. Voting procedures in international economic institutions should be revised to provide poor countries with greater influence.

The First World's response to these demands was mostly negative. The Third-World countries seek economic and technological help from the First-World countries in order to become economically self-sufficient. On the other hand, First-World countries can learn a lot from the Third-World countries. The people in developing countries take pride in family, history, cultural, and religious values, and they consider these values to be more important than economic fulfillment and greed for materialism. For the near future, the developing world will continue to struggle for economic assistance. With the end of the Cold War, and with the former Soviet-bloc countries competing for economic assistance from the West, the future for the developing world remains bleak.

Table 48.4
State of the Environment and Technology in Selected Third-World Countries

Country	Population/ Education (Literacy, Total % of Population) July 1994 Estimate	National Product (GDP– Purchasing Power Equivalent) /External Debt ($ Billion)	State of Technology, Electricity Production, Telecommunications (Number of Telephones)	Environment (Current Issues)
World	5,643,289,771	29 trillion, 1 trillion for less developed countries	11.45 trillion kWh	
Afghanistan	16,903,400 29%	NA	1 billion kWh, limited number of telephones	Soil degradation, overgrazing, deforestation, and desertification.
Algeria	27,895,068 57%	89, 26	16.384 billion kWh, 820,000 telephones	Soil erosion from overgrazing; desertification; dumping of untreated sewage, petroleum refining wastes, and other industrial effluents is leading to pollution of rivers and coastal waters; the Mediterranean Sea, in particular, is becoming polluted from oil wastes, soil erosion, and fertilizer runoff; limited supply of potable water.
Angola	9,803,576 42%	5.7, 8	800 million kWh, 40,300 telephones (4.1 telephones per 1,000 persons)	Population pressures contributing to overuse of pastures and subsequent soil erosion; desertification; deforestation of tropical rain forest attributable to the international demand for tropical timber and domestic use as a fuel; deforestation, contributing to loss of biodiversity; soil erosion, contributing to water pollution and siltation of rivers and dams; scarcity of potable water.
Argentina	33,912,994 95%	185, 73	51.305 billion kWh, 2,650,000 telephones (78 per 1000 persons)	Erosion from inadequate flood control and improper land use practices; irrigated soil degradation; desertification; air pollution in Buenos Aires and other major cities; water pollution in urban areas; rivers becoming polluted due to increased pesticide and fertilizer use.

Table 48.4
State of the Environment and Technology in Selected Third-World Countries *(Continued)*

Country	Population/ Education (Literacy, Total % of Population) July 1994 Estimate	National Product (GDP– Purchasing Power Equivalent) /External Debt ($ Billion)	State of Technology, Electricity Production, Telecommu- nications (Number of Telephones)	Environment (Current Issues)
Bangladesh	125,149,469 35%	122, 13.5	9 billion kWh, 241,000 telephones (1 per 522 persons)	Many people are landless and forced to live on and cultivate flood-prone land; limited access to potable water; waterborne diseases prevalent; water pollution, espe- cially of fishing areas, results from the use of commercial pesticides; intermittent water shortages because of failing water tables in the northern and central parts of the country; soil degradation; deforestation; severe overpopulation.
Bolivia	7,719,445 78%	15.8, 3.8	1.834 billion kWh, 144,300 telephones (18.7 telephones per 1,000 persons)	Deforestation, contributing to loss of biodiversity; overgrazing; soil erosion; desertification; industrial pollution of water supplies used for drinking and irrigation.
Brazil	158,739,257 81%	785, 119	242.184 billion kWh, 9.86 million telephones	Deforestation in Amazon Basin; air and water pollution in Rio de Janeiro, Sao Paulo, and several other large cities; land degradation and water pollution caused by improper mining activities.
Burkina	10,134,661 18%	7, 0.865	320,000 million kWh, NA	Recent droughts and desertification, severely affecting agricultural activities, population distribution, and the economy; overgrazing; soil degradation.
Burma	44,277,014 81%	41, 4	2.8 billion kWh, 53,000 telephones	Deforestation.
Cambodia	10,264,628 35%	6, 1.08	70 million kWh, NA	Deforestation, resulting in habitat loss and declining biodiversity. (In particular, the destruction of mangrove swamps threatens natural fisheries.)

continued

Table 48.4

State of the Environment and Technology in Selected Third-World Countries *(Continued)*

Country	Population/ Education (Literacy, Total % of Population) July 1994 Estimate	National Product (GDP– Purchasing Power Equivalent) /External Debt ($ Billion)	State of Technology, Electricity Production, Telecommu- nications (Number of Telephones)	Environment (Current Issues)
Cameroon	13,132,191 55%	19.1, 6	2.19 billion kWh, NA	Waterborne diseases are prevalent; deforestation; overgrazing; desertification; poaching.
Chad	5,466,771 30%	2.7, 0.492	40,000 kWh, NA	Desertification.
Chile	13,950,557 93%	96, 19.7	22.01 billion kWh, 768,000 telephones	Air pollution from industrial and vehicle emissions; water pollution from untreated sewage; deforestation, contributing to loss of biodiversity; soil erosion; desertification.
China	1,190,431,106 78%	2.61 trillion, 80	740 billion kWh, 11 million telephones	Air pollution from the overwhelming use of coal as fuel, producing acid rain, which is damaging forests; water pollution from industrial effuents; many people do not have access to safe drinking water; less than 10% of sewage receives treatment; deforestation; estimated loss of one third of agricultural land since 1957 to soil erosion and economic development; desertification.
Colombia	35,577,556 87%	192, 17	36 billion kWh, 1.89 million telephones	Deforestation; soil damage from overuse of pesticides.
Congo	2,446,902 57%	7, 4.1	315 million kWh, 18,100 telephones	Air pollution from vehicle emissions; water pollution from the dumping of raw sewage; deforestation.
Costa Rica	3,342,154 93%	19.3, 3.2	3.612 billion kWh, 292,000 telephones	Deforestation, largely the result of land clearing for cattle ranching; soil erosion.
Cuba	11,064,344 94%	13.7, 6.8	16.248 billion kWh, 229,000 telephones	Overhunting threatens wildlife populations; deforestation.

Table 48.4
State of the Environment and Technology in Selected Third-World Countries *(Continued)*

Country	Population/ Education (Literacy, Total % of Population) July 1994 Estimate	National Product (GDP– Purchasing Power Equivalent) /External Debt ($ Billion)	State of Technology, Electricity Production, Telecommu- nications (Number of Telephones)	Environment (Current Issues)
Djibouti	412,599 48%	0.5, 0.355	200 million kWh, NA	Desertification.
Dominican Republic	7,826,075 83%	23, 4.7	5 billion kWh, 190,000 telephones	Water shortages; soil eroding into the sea damages coral reefs; deforestation.
Ecuador	10,677,067 88%	41.8, 12.7	7.676 billion kWh NA	Deforestation; soil erosion; desertification; water pollution.
Egypt	60,765,028 48%	139, 32	47 billion kWh, 600,000 telephones (11 telephones per 1,000 persons)	Agricultural land being lost to urbanization and windblown sands; increasing soil salinization below Aswan High Dam; desertification; oil pollution threatening coral reefs, beaches, and marine habitats; other water pollution from agricultural pesticides, untreated sewage, and industrial effluents; water scarcity away from Nile, which is the only perennial water source; rapid growth in population, overstraining natural resources.
El Salvador	5,752,511 73%	14.2, 2.6	2.19 billion kWh, 116,000 telephones (21 telephones per 1,000 persons)	Deforestation, soil erosion; water pollution; contamination of soil from disposal of toxic waste.
Eritrea	3,782,543 NA	1.7, NA	NA, NA	Famine; deforestation; soil erosion; overgrazing; loss of infrastructure from civil warfare.
Ethiopia	54,927,108 24%	22.7, 3.48	650 million kWh, NA	Deforestation; overgrazing; soil erosion; desertification; famine.

continued

Table 48.4

State of the Environment and Technology in Selected Third-World Countries *(Continued)*

Country	Population/ Education (Literacy, Total % of Population) July 1994 Estimate	National Product (GDP– Purchasing Power Equivalent) /External Debt ($ Billion)	State of Technology, Electricity Production, Telecommu- nications (Number of Telephones)	Environment (Current Issues)
Gabon	1,113,906 61%	5.4, 4.4	995 million kWh, 15,000 telephones	Deforestation; poaching.
Gambia	959,300 27%	0.740, 0.336	65 million kWh, 3,500 telephones	Deforestation; desertification.
Ghana	17,225,185 60%	25, 4.6	4.49 billion kWh, 42,300 telephones	Deforestation; overgrazing; soil erosion; poaching and habitat destruction threatens wildlife populations; water pollution; limited supply of safe drinking water.
Guatemala	10,721,387 55%	31.3, 2.2	2.5 billion kWh, 97,670 telephones	Deforestation; soil erosion; water pollution.
Guinea- Bissau	1,098,231 36%	0.860, 0.462	30 million kWh, 3,000 telephones	Deforestation; soil erosion; overgrazing.
Guinea	6,391,536 24%	3.1, 2.5	300 million kWh, 15,000 telephones	Deforestation; inadequate supplies of safe drinking water; desertification; soil contamination and erosion.
Guyana	729,425 95%	1.4, 1.9	276 million kWh, 27,000 telephones	Water pollution from sewage, agricultural, and industrial chemicals; deforestation.
Haiti	6,491,450 53%	5.2, 0.838	480 million kWh, 36,000 telephones	Deforestation; soil erosion.

Table 48.4
State of the Environment and Technology in Selected Third-World Countries *(Continued)*

Country	Population/ Education (Literacy, Total % of Population) July 1994 Estimate	National Product (GDP– Purchasing Power Equivalent) /External Debt ($ Billion)	State of Technology, Electricity Production, Telecommu- nications (Number of Telephones)	Environment (Current Issues)
Honduras	5,314,794 73%	10, 2.8	2 billion kWh, 7 telephones per 1,000 persons	Urban population expanding; deforestation results from logging and the clearing of land for agricultural purposes; further land degradation and soil erosion hastened by uncontrolled development and improper land use practices, such as farming of marginal lands; mining activities polluting Lago de Yojoa (the country's largest source of freshwater) with heavy metals as well as several rivers and steams.
India	919,903,056 52.11%	1017, 90.1	310 billion kWh, about 1 phone per 200 persons	Deforestation; soil erosion; overgrazing; desertification; air pollution from industrial and vehicle emissions; water pollution from raw sewage and runoff of agricultural pesticides; huge and rapidly growing population is overstraining natural resources.
Indonesia	200,409,741 77%	571, 100	38 billion kWh, 763,000 telephones	Deforestation; water pollution from industrial wastes and sewage; air pollution in urban areas.
Iran	65,615,474 54%	303, 30	43.6 billion kWh, 2,143,000 telephones (35 telephones per 1,000 persons)	Air pollution, especially in urban areas, from vehicle emissions, refinery operations, and industry; deforestation; overgrazing; oil pollution in Persian Gulf; shortage of drinking water.

continued

Table 48.4
State of the Environment and Technology in Selected Third-World Countries *(Continued)*

Country	Population/ Education (Literacy, Total % of Population) July 1994 Estimate	National Product (GDP– Purchasing Power Equivalent) /External Debt ($ Billion)	State of Technology, Electricity Production, Telecommu- nications (Number of Telephones)	Environment (Current Issues)
Iraq	19,889,666 60%	38, 45	12.9 billion kWh, 632,000 telephones	Government water control projects drain inhabited march areas, drying up or diverting the streams and rivers that support a sizable population of Shia Muslims, who have inhabited these areas for thousands of years; the destruction of natural habitat also poses serious threats to wildlife populations; damage to water treatment and sewage facilities during the Gulf War; inadequate supplies of potable water; development of Tigris–Euphrates Rivers system contingent upon agreements with upstream riparians (Syria, Turkey); air and water pollution; soil degradation (salinization) and erosion; desertification.
Jamaica	2,555,064 98%	8, 4.5	2.736 trillion kWh, 127,000 telephones	Deforestation; water pollution.
Jordan	3,961,194 80%	11.5, 6.8	3.814 billion kWh, 81,500 telephones	Lack of adequate natural water resources; deforestation; overgrazing; soil erosion; desertification.
Kenya	28,240,658 69%	33.3, 7	2.54 billion kWh, 260,000 telephones	Water pollution from urban and industrial wastes; degradation of water quality from increased use of pesticides and fertilizers; deforestation; soil erosion; desertification; poaching.
Korea, North	23,066,573 99%	22, 8	26 billion kWh, NA	Localized air pollution attributable to inadequate industrial controls.
Laos	4,701,654 64%	4.1, 1.1	990 million kWh, 7,390 telephones	Deforestation; soil erosion.

Table 48.4
State of the Environment and Technology in Selected Third-World Countries *(Continued)*

Country	Population/ Education (Literacy, Total % of Population) July 1994 Estimate	National Product (GDP– Purchasing Power Equivalent) /External Debt ($ Billion)	State of Technology, Electricity Production, Telecommu- nications (Number of Telephones)	Environment (Current Issues)
Lebanon	3,620,395 80%	6.1, 0.7	3.413 billion kWh, 325,000 telephones (95 telephones per 1000 persons)	Deforestation; soil erosion.
Liberia	2,972,766 40%	2.3, 2.1	750 million kWh, NA	West Africa's largest tribal tropical rain forest, subject to deforestation; soil erosion; loss of biodiversity.
Madagascar	13,427,758 80%	10.4, 4.4	450,000 million kWh, NA	Soil erosion results from deforestation and overgrazing; desertification; surface water contaminated with untreated sewage and other organic wastes; several species of flora and fauna unique to the island are endangered.
Malawi	9,732,409 22%	6, 1.8	620 million kWh, 42,250 telephones.	Deforestation; land degradation; water pollution from agricultural runoff, sewage, and industrial wastes; siltation of spawning grounds endangers fish population.
Maldives	252,077 92%	0.140, 0.148	11 million kWh, 2,804 telephones	Depletion of freshwater aquifers threatens water supplies.
Mali	9,112,950 17%	5.8, 2.6	750 million kWh, 11,000 telephones	Deforestation; soil erosion; desertification; inadequate supplies of safe drinking water; poaching.
Mauritania	2,192,777 34%	2.2, 1.9	135 million kWh, NA	Overgrazing, deforestation, and soil erosion aggravated by drought are contributing to desertification; water scarcity away from the Senegal River, which is the only perennial river.

continued

Table 48.4
State of the Environment and Technology in Selected Third-World Countries *(Continued)*

Country	Population/ Education (Literacy, Total % of Population) July 1994 Estimate	National Product (GDP– Purchasing Power Equivalent) /External Debt ($ Billion)	State of Technology, Electricity Production, Telecommu- nications (Number of Telephones)	Environment (Current Issues)
Mauritius	1,116,923 80%	8.6, 0.991	630 million kWh, 48,000 telephones	Water pollution.
Mexico	92,202,199 87%	740, 125	120.725 kWh, 6,410,000 telephones	Natural water resources scarce and polluted in north, inaccessible and poor quality in center and extreme southeast; untreated sewage and industrial effluents polluting rivers in urban areas; deforestation; widespread erosion; desertification; serious air pollution in the national capital and urban centers along U.S.–Mexico border.
Mongolia	2,429,762 NA	2.8, 16.8	3,740 kWh, 63,000 telephones	Limited water resources; policies of the former communist regime promoting rapid urbanization and industrial growth have raised concerns about their negative impact on the environment; the burning of soft coal and the concentration of factories in Ulaanbaatar have severely polluted the air; deforestation, overgrazing, and the conversion of virgin land to agricultural production have increased soil erosion from wind and rain; desertification.
Morocco	28,558,635 50%	70.3, 21.3	8.864 billion kWh, 280,000 telephones (10.5 telephones per 1,000 persons)	Land degradation/desertification (soil erosion resulting from farming of marginal areas, overgrazing, and destruction of vegetation); water supplies contaminated by untreated sewage; siltation of reservoirs; oil pollution of coastal waters.
Mozambique	17,346,280 33%	9.8, 5	1.745 billion kWh, NA	Civil strife in the hinterlands has resulted in increased migration to urban and coastal areas, with adverse environmental consequences; desertification; pollution of surface and coastal waters.

Table 48.4
State of the Environment and Technology in Selected Third-World Countries *(Continued)*

Country	Population/ Education (Literacy, Total % of Population) July 1994 Estimate	National Product (GDP– Purchasing Power Equivalent) /External Debt ($ Billion)	State of Technology, Electricity Production, Telecommu- nications (Number of Telephones)	Environment (Current Issues)
Namibia	1,595,567 38%	3.85, 0.220	1.29 billion kWh, 62,800 telephones	Very limited natural water resources; desertification.
Nepal	21,041,527 26%	20.5, 2	1 billion kWh, 50,000 telephones	The almost total dependence on wood for fuel and cutting down trees to expand agricultural land without replanting has resulted in widespread deforestation; soil erosion; water pollution (the use of contaminated water presents human health risks).
Nicaragua	4,096,689 57%	6.4, 10.5	1.118 billion kWh, 60,000 telephones	Deforestation; soil erosion; water pollution.
Niger	8,971,605 28%	5.4, 1.2	230 million kWh, 14,260 telephones	Overgrazing; soil erosion; deforestation; desertification; wildlife populations (such as elephant, hippopotamus, and lion) threatened because of poaching and habitat destruction.
Nigeria	98,091,097 51%	95.1, 29.5	8.3 billion kWh, NA	Soil degradation; rapid deforestation; desertification; recent droughts in north severely affecting marginal agricultural activities.
Pakistan	128,855,965 35%	239, 24	43 billion kWh, 7 telephones per 1,000 persons	Water pollution from untreated sewage, industrial wastes, and agricultural runoff; water scarcity; a majority of the population does not have access to safe drinking water; deforestation; soil erosion; desertification.
Panama	2,630,000 88%	11.6, 6.1	4.36 trillion kWh, 220,000 telephones	Water pollution from agricultural runoff threatens fishery resources; deforestation of tropical rain forest; land degradation.
Paraguay	5,213,772 90%	15.2, 1.2	16.2 billion kWh, 78,300 telephones	Deforestation; water pollution; inadequate means for waste disposal present health hazards for many urban residents.

continued

Table 48.4
State of the Environment and Technology in Selected Third-World Countries *(Continued)*

Country	Population/ Education (Literacy, Total % of Population) July 1994 Estimate	National Product (GDP– Purchasing Power Equivalent) /External Debt ($ Billion)	State of Technology, Electricity Production, Telecommu- nications (Number of Telephones)	Environment (Current Issues)
Peru	23,650,671 85%	70, 22	17.434 billion kWh, 544,000 telephones	Deforestation; overgrazing; soil erosion; desertification; air pollution in Lima.
Philippines	69,808,930 90%	171, 34.1	28 billion kWh, 872,900 telephones	Deforestation; soil erosion; water pollution; air pollution in Manila.
Rwanda	8,373,963 50%	6.8, 0.845	130 million kWh, NA	Deforestation; overgrazing; soil exhaustion; soil erosion.
Senegal	8,730,508 38%	11.8, 2.9	760 million kWh, NA	Wildlife populations threatened by poaching; deforestation; overgrazing; soil erosion; desertification.
Sierra Leone	4,630,037 21%	4.5, 0.633	185 million kWh, 23,650 telephones	Rapid population growth pressuring the environment; overharvesting of timber, expansion of cattle grazing, and slash-and-burn agriculture have resulted in deforestation and soil exhaustion; civil war depleting natural resources.
Somalia	6,666,873 24%	3.4, 1.9	NA, NA	Use of contaminated water contributes to health problems; deforestation; overgrazing; soil erosion; desertification.
Sri Lanka	18,129,850 88%	53.5, 5.2	3.6 billion KWh, 114,000 telephones	Deforestation; soil erosion; wildlife population threatened by poaching; coastal degradation from mining activities and increased pollution; freshwater resources being polluted by industrial wastes and sewage runoff.
Sudan	29,419,798 27%	21.5, 17	905 million kWh, NA	Contaminated water supplies present human health risks; wildlife populations threatened by excessive hunting; soil erosion; desertification.
Suriname	422,840 95%	1.17, 0.18	2.018 billion kWh, 27,500 telephones	NA

Table 48.4
State of the Environment and Technology in Selected Third-World Countries *(Continued)*

Country	Population/ Education (Literacy, Total % of Population) July 1994 Estimate	National Product (GDP– Purchasing Power Equivalent) /External Debt ($ Billion)	State of Technology, Electricity Production, Telecommu- nications (Number of Telephones)	Environment (Current Issues)
Syria	14,886,672 64%	81.7, 19.4	11.9 billion kWh, 512,600 telephones (37 telephones per 1,000 persons)	Deforestation; overgrazing; soil erosion; desertification; water pollution from dumping of untreated sewage and wastes from petroleum refining; lack of safe drinking water.
Tanzania	27,985,660 46%	16.7, 6.44	600 million kWh, 103,800 telephones	Soil degradation; deforestation; desertification; destruction of coral reefs threatens marine habitats; recent droughts affected marginal agriculture.
Thailand	59,510,471 93%	323, 33.4	43.75 billion kWh, 739,500 telephones (1987)	Air pollution increasing from vehicle emission; water pollution from organic and factory wastes; desertification; wildlife populations threatened by illegal hunting.
Tunisia	8,726,562 65%	34.4, 7.7	5,096 kWh, 233,000 telephones (28 telephones per 1,000 persons)	Toxic and hazardous waste disposal is ineffective and presents human health risks; water pollution from untreated sewage; water scarcity; deforestation; over-grazing; soil erosion; desertification.
Turkey	62,153,898 81%	312.4, 59.4	44 billion kWh, 3,400,000 telephones	Water pollution from dumping of chemicals and detergents; air pollution; deforestation.
Uganda	19,121,934 48%	24.1, 1.9	610 million kWh, NA	Draining of wetlands for agricultural use; deforestation; overgrazing; soil erosion.
Uruguay	3,198,910 96%	19, 4.2	5.96 billion kWh, 337,000 telephones	NA

continued

Table 48.4

State of the Environment and Technology in Selected Third-World Countries *(Continued)*

Country	Population/ Education (Literacy, Total % of Population) July 1994 Estimate	National Product (GDP– Purchasing Power Equivalent) /External Debt ($ Billion)	State of Technology, Electricity Production, Telecommu- nications (Number of Telephones)	Environment (Current Issues)
Venezuela	20,562,405 88%	161, 28.5	58.541 billion kWh, 1,440,000 telephones.	Sewage pollution of Lao de Valencia; oil and urban pollution of Lago de Maracaibo; deforestation; soil degradation; urban and industrial pollution, especially along the Caribbean coast.
Vietnam	73,103,898 88%	72, 3.4	9 billion kWh, 25 telephones per 10,000 persons.	Deforestation; soil degradation; water pollution and overfishing threatening marine life populations.
Yemen	11,105,202 38%	9, 7	1.244 billion kWh, 65,000 telephones (est.)	Scarcity of natural freshwater resources (shortages of potable water); overgrazing; soil erosion; desertification.
Zaire	42,684,091 72%	21, 9.2	6 billion kWh, NA	Poaching threatens wildlife populations; water pollution; deforestation.
Zambia	9,188,190 73%	7.3, 7.6	12 billion kWh, NA	Poaching seriously threatens rhinoceros and elephant populations; deforestation; soil erosion; desertification.
Zimbabwe	10,975,078 67%	15.9, 3.5	8.18 billion kWh, 247,000 telephones	Deforestation; soil erosion; land degradation; air and water pollution.

Source: CIA World Factbook 1995–96.

Positive change in the Third World will occur only when both the intrinsic and extrinsic factors inhibiting the development of Third-World nations are addressed. The effects of extrinsic factors (i.e., political and economic instability caused by international financial institutions and the economic exploitation of resources by multinational companies) can be rectified only when a great change takes place in the modes of thought of the policy makers of the developed world; those leaders must begin to believe that all people are created equal; no one is superior to another; and treating people with equality and justice is the key to solving man-made economic, political, and environmental dilemmas.

To address the intrinsic factors (i.e., illiteracy, poverty, social injustice, corruption, lack of resources, population pressures, and power-hungry political and military elite), the key is education and appropriate use of technology. Education is a great equalizer for changing socioeconomic

Worldwide Railways Inc.

Figure 48.1

Comparison of the First World, the Second World, and the third world: Worldwide Railways Inc.

Source: Tasneem Khan.

Country by literacy (% total population)

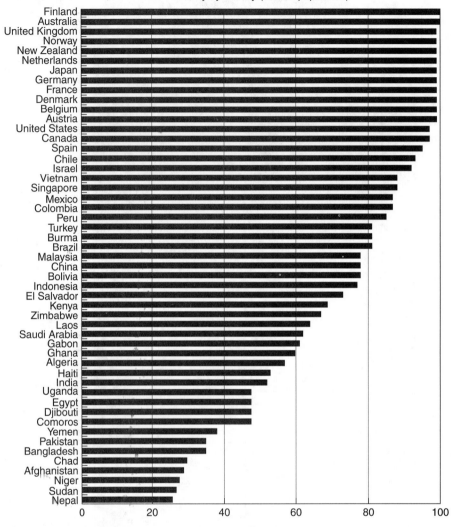

Figure 48.2
Literacy as a percentage of population for selected developed and developing countries.
Source: CIA World Factbook 1995–1996.

conditions. It could provide solutions to many of the problems of developing countries and set them free from economic bondage, autocratic rule, poverty, and disease. The developing nations should give a higher priority to educating their people. The innovative use of telecommunications technologies can provide endless opportunities in educa-

tion (e.g., distance learning), medicine (e.g., telemedicine), and business (e.g., electronic trade) in developing countries. These applications could enable developing countries to increase teledensity and literacy, improve per-capita income, and narrow the technoeconomic gap with developed countries. And in the process of developing economic

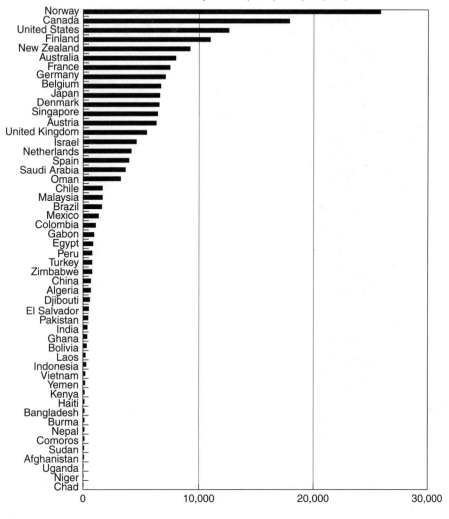

Figure 48.3
Electricity consumption per capita (kWh) for selected developed and developing countries.
Source: CIA World Factbook 1995–1996.

infrastructures, the Third-World countries, through proper planning and appropriate policies, could also minimize the huge cost of industrialization that the developed world has paid in terms of damage to the environment. If the developing countries fail to enter the 21st century with educated populations and technoelites, it will be only a matter of time before they fall victim to a new era of technoslavery.

The terms "First World," "Third World," "less developed countries" (LDC), and "least developed countries" (LLDC) may have significant meanings in an economic context. However, if one looks at earth from space, it is, at this point, the only living planet in the universe, without any boundaries or barriers between the First and the Third Worlds. The people on earth are members of one big

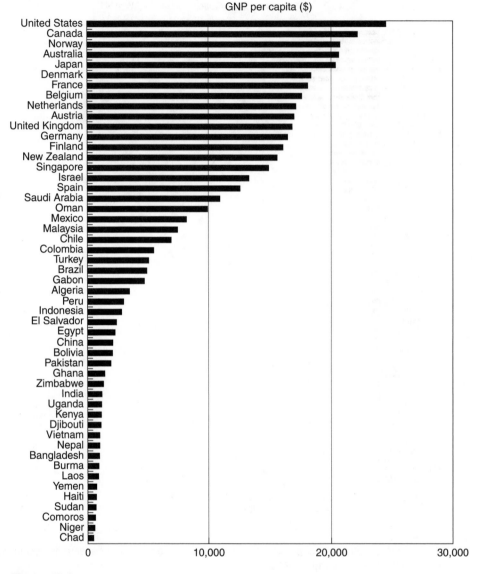

GNP per capita ($)

Figure 48.4
Per-capita GNP ($) for selected developed and developing countries.
Source: CIA World Factbook 1995–1996.

family with a common past and a common destiny. Problems like ozone depletion, global warming, soil erosion, deforestation, poverty, homelessness, illiteracy, and obstruction of world peace are universal problems and cannot be solved as long as the artificial distinction between the First World and the Third World exists. All people are created equal. No one is superior to others on the basis of color, race, or wealth. Treating people with equality and justice is key to solving man-made global economic, political, and environmental crises.

References

CIA World Factbook. (1995). Washington, DC, Brassey's.

Gardner, G. (1995, January/February). Third World Debt is Still Growing. *Worldwatch.* pp. 37–38.

Grimm, W. (1990, May 5). The Third World. *America: National Catholic Weekly.* pp. 449–451.

Mansback, R. (1994). *The Global Puzzle: Issues and Actors in World Politics.* Boston, Houghton Mifflin Company.

Mennerick, L., and Mehrangiz, N. (1991, Spring). Third World Environmental Health, Social, Technological and Economic Policy Issues. *Journal of Environmental Health.* pp. 24–29.

Myers, N. (1990) *The GAIA Atlas of Future Worlds.* New York, Doubleday.

Worldbank IED. (1997, September). *World Development Indicators.* Available: http://www.worldbank.org/html/iecdd/products.htm.

Try being poor for a day or two and find in poverty double riches.

RUMI

"The advanced Western countries completed their escape from poverty to relative wealth during the nineteenth and twentieth centuries. There was no sudden change in their economic output; but only a continuation of year-to-year growth at a rate that somewhat exceeded the rate of population growth."

Nathan Rosenberg and L.E. Birdzell, Jr.

"The gap in the world between the haves and the have-nots is becoming a gulf. Will the so-called Southerners tolerate the absurd imbalances when, to some extent (through inequitable trade terms, for example), they are poor simply because the Northerners are rich when many impoverished people among the have-not nations receive less protein per week than a domestic cat in the North?"

"Intolerable Imbalances," The GAIA Atlas of Future Worlds, Norman Myers

"Sub-Saharan Africa's debt is now higher than its entire output of goods and services. Collectively, the region's debt amounts to $180 billion, three times the 1980 total, and is 10% higher than its entire output of goods and services. Debt service payment comes to $10 billion annually, about four times what the region spends on health and education combined. The burden is choking off economic development over much of the continent."

World Watch Institute's Annual Report, Vital Sign, 1995

"The ending of colonialism does not automatically inaugurate an era of peace and prosperity for liberated peoples. It could equally be the prelude to fraternal wars and new inhumanities. . . . It is my considered opinion that the third world war has already begun—in the Third World. The new war is likely to be a cumulation of little wars rather than one big war. Though the form is new, it is basically a war between the great powers and one fought for the realization of their ambitions and the promotion of their national interests. However, this is not obvious because in this new world war, the great powers are invisible."

Sinathamby Rajaratnam, Singapore's senior minister and veteran delegate to the Nonaligned Movement (NAM)

Questions

1. Define the following terms:
   a. First World
   b. Second World
   c. Third World
   d. LDC
   e. LLDC

2. Many people in the Third World believe that they are the victims of technological imperialism imposed by the First World. The developed countries do not allow economic growth and transfer of technology to developing countries because it may lead to the elimination of jobs and affect the standard of living in the developed countries. Do you agree with this opinion? Explain your answer.

Figure 48.5
Asia.

3. Identify the countries shown on the map of Asia on previous page and define the state of technology in each country.

Country	Name	State of Technology (Developed/Developing)
A		
B		
C		
D		
E		
F		
G		
H		
I		
J		

4. Identify the countries shown on the map below and define the state of technology in each country.

Country	Name	State of Technology (Developed/Developing)
A		
B		
C		
D		
E		
F		
G		
H		
I		
J		

Figure 48.6
Africa

5. Identify the countries shown on the map below and define the state of technology in each country.

Country	Name	State of Technology (Developed/Developing)
A		
B		
C		
D		
E		
F		
G		
H		
I		
J		

Figure 48.7
South America.

Richer and Poorer

Number of billionaires (people with the net worth of a thousand millionaires) in the world in 1989	157
Number of billionaires just five years later, in 1994	358
Number of the world's richest people whose collective wealth adds up to $762 billion	358
Number of the world's poorest people whose combined income adds up to $762 billion	2,400,000,000
Portion of global income going to the richest fifth of the population	83 percent
Portion of global income going to the poorest fifth	1 percent
Number of billionaires in Mexico in 1988	2
Number now	24
Combined income of the poorest 17 million Mexicans last year	$6,600,000,000
Wealth of the richest *single* Mexican	$6,600,000,000
Ratio of income of the richest fifth to the poorest fifth of the U.S. population in 1970	4 to 1
The same ratio in 1993	13 to 1
Combined total R&D expenditures of General Motors, Ford, Hitachi, Siemens, Matsushita, IBM, and Daimler-Benz Corporations in 1993	$31.8 billion
Military R&D expenditures of the United States in the same year	$43.5 billion
GDP of Israel in 1992	$69.8 billion
Sales of Exxon in 1992	$103.5 billion
GDP of Egypt in 1992	$33.6 billion
Sales of Philip Morris in 1992	$50.2 billion

Source: United Nations Research Institute for Social Development, *States of Disarray: The Social Effects of Globalization* (London: UNRISD, 1995). Reprinted with permission from Worldwatch Institute (World Watch July/August 1996)

Who Dominates the World?

Number of people employed by the United Nations	53,589
Number of people employed at Disney World and Disneyland	50,000
Total budget of the United Nations in 1995–96 (two-year budget)	$18.2 billion
Revenue of a single U.S. arms manufacturer (Lockhead Martin) in 1995	$19.4 billion
U.N. peacekeeping expenditures in 1995	$3.6 billion
World military spending in 1995	$767.0 billion
Number of U.N. peacekeepers for every 150,000 people in the world	1
Number of soldiers in national armies for every 150,000 people in the world	650
U.S. contribution to the U.N. budget, per capita	$7
Norwegian contribution to the U.N. budget, per capita	$65
Number of U.S. troops serving in U.N. peacekeeping operations in 1994	965
Number of U.S. troops serving in international missions under U.S. command in 1994	86,451
Cost of the 1992 Earth Summit	$10 million
Cost of the 1994 Paris Air Show and Weapons Exhibition (U.S. portion)	$12 million

Sources: U.S. Arms Control and Disarmament Agency, *World Military Expenditures and Arms Transfers 1995;* Michael Renner, "Peacekeeping Expenditures Level Off," in Lester R. Brown et al., *Vital Signs 1996;* Michael Renner, *Remaking U.N. Peacekeeping: U.S. Policy and Real Reform,* Briefing Paper 17 (Washington, D.C.: National Commission for Economic Conversion and Disarmament, 1995); U.N. Department of Public Information. Compiled by Michael Renner. Reprinted with permission from the Worldwatch Institute, Washington, D.C. (World Watch November/December 1996)

A Bridge to Your 21st Century Understanding

Complete the following flowchart.

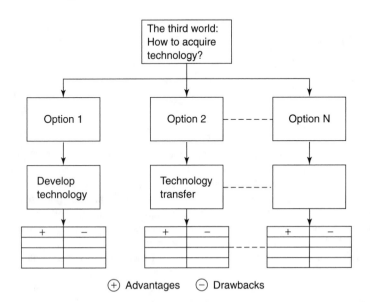

49 Income Gap Widens

HAL KANE

The gap in income among the people of the world has been widening. In 1960, according to United Nations statisticians, the richest 20 percent of the world's people received 30 times more income than the poorest 20 percent. By 1991, they were getting *61* times more. While the poorest one-fifth in 1960 received a meager 2.3 percent of world income, by 1991 that revenue share had fallen to 1.4 percent. The income share of the richest fifth, meanwhile, rose from 70 percent to 85 percent.

These disparities prevail both among countries and within them, and the large gap between individuals world-wide reflects the combination of both of those splits. Almost four-fifths of all people live in the developing world, where incomes are only a fraction of those in industrial countries. In turn, within countries in both categories, gaps in income between citizens can be even wider.

The widest income gap reported within a country is in Botswana, where during the 1980s the richest 20 percent of society received over 47 times more income than the poorest 20 percent (see Table 49.1). Brazil was second, with a ratio of 32 to 1. In Guatemala and Panama, the ratio stood at 30 to 1.

The rapidly growing economies of East Asia have had income patterns similar to those of Western Europe and North America, with the richest one-fifth often earning 5 to 10 times more than the poorest fifth. In South Asia, India, Bangladesh, and Pakistan have had relatively even distributions of income, with the richest 20 percent getting only four to five times more than the poorest quintile. Some countries that have had military conflicts apparently based in part on inequities among citizens, nevertheless have relatively even income distributions.

The split between countries and people can be seen in the marketplace. The value of luxury goods sales world-wide—high-fashion clothing and top-of-the-line autos, for example—exceeds the gross national products of two-thirds of the world's countries. The world's average income, roughly $4,000 a year, is well below the U.S. poverty line.

The poorest fifth of the world accounted for 0.9 percent of world trade, 1.1 percent of global domestic investment, 0.9 percent of global domestic savings, and just 0.2 percent of global commercial credit at the beginning of the 1990s. Each of those shares declined between 1960 and 1990.

These disparities are reflected in the consumption of many resources. At the start of this decade, industrial countries, home to roughly a fifth of the world's population, accounted for about 86 percent of the consumption of aluminum and chemicals, 81 percent of the paper, 80 percent of the iron and steel, and three-quarters of the timber and energy. Since then, economic growth in developing countries has probably reduced these percentages. China's economy, for example, is more than 50 percent larger now than it was in 1990, and developing countries have passed industrial ones in fertilizer consumption.

Reprinted with permission from Worldwatch Institute (*Worldwatch* March/April 1996)

Table 49.1

Income Distribution, Selected Countries, Late 1980s

Country	Ratio of Richest One-Fifth to Poorest
INDUSTRIAL COUNTRIES	
United States	9
Switzerland	9
Israel	7
Italy	6
Germany	6
Sweden	5
Japan	4
Poland	4
Hungary	3
DEVELOPING COUNTRIES	
Botswana	47
Brazil	32
Guatemala	30
Panama	30
Kenya	23
Chile	17
Mexico	14
Malaysia	12
Peru	10
Thailand	8
Philippines	7
China	6
Ghana	6
Ethiopia	5
Indonesia	5
Pakistan	5
India	5
Bangladesh	4
Rwanda	4

Source: UN Development Programs, Human Development Report 1994 (New York: Oxford University Press, 1994).

Uneven income distribution is shaping some of the most important trends in the world today. It raises crime rates, for example. And it drives migration. People have long responded to economic disparities by following a path from poor regions to richer ones, as tens of millions of workers chase higher wages and better opportunities. Some 1.6 million Asians and Middle Easterners were working in Kuwait and Saudi Arabia before they fled war in 1991, and at least 2.5 million Mexicans live in the United States.

The same is true within countries: rising disparities of income are adding to the growth of cities through rural-to-urban migration. Latin America, with some of the highest disparities of income among its citizens, is also the most urbanized region of the developing world—not entirely by coincidence. Since 1950, city dwellers there have risen from 42 percent of the population to 73 percent.

For many years, China had one of the most equal distributions of income in the world. But now that is changing, as incomes in its southern provinces and special economic zones soar while those in rural areas rise much more slowly. Also not coincidentally, the Chinese National Academy of Social Sciences forecasts that by 2010, half the population will live in cities, compared with 28 percent today and only 10 percent in the early 1980s.

In the early 1990s, developing world economies, especially in East Asia, have grown faster than the economies of the industrial countries. This has the potential to shrink disparities of income, if poorer countries continue to catch up. Yet even if the gaps among countries narrow, the gaps between *people* may not, because economic growth is distributed so unevenly within nations. Despite the recent restoration of economic growth in Latin America, for example, U.N. economists say that no progress is expected in reducing poverty, which is even likely to increase slightly.

Meanwhile, in some regions almost no one has been getting richer. The per capita income of most sub-Saharan African nations actually fell during the 1980s. After the latest negotiations of the General Agreement on Tariffs and Trade (GATT) were completed, *The Wall Street Journal* reported that "even GATT's most energetic backers say that in one part of the world, the trade accord may do more harm than good: sub-Saharan Africa," the poorest geographic region. There, an estimated one-third of all college graduates have left the continent. That loss of talented people, due in large part to poverty and a lack of opportunities in Africa, will make it even more difficult for the continent to advance.

The economic growth that has the potential to close income gaps among peoples in the developing world is instead becoming a splitting off, with some parts of societies joining the industrial world while others remain behind. Singapore, Hong Kong, and Taiwan have begun to look like wealthy industrial countries, for example. Now parts of China are following, as are the wealthier segments of Latin American society and of Southeast Asian countries. This is good news for members of the middle-income countries and for the world. But it may do little to help the poorest fifth of humanity.

Questions

1. Define the following terms.
   a. GNP
   b. GDP
   c. GATT

2. Describe the factors that are responsible for the wide gap between the per-capita GNP of the developed and of the developing countries. How could this gap be reduced?

AFGHANISTAN: A LEGACY OF THE COLD WAR

During the Cold War, in various civil conflicts around the globe, the refugee population exploded from about 4.6 million people in the early 1970s to nearly 15 million in 1989 and more than 18.9 million in 1993. In Afghanistan, more than 6 million people (one-third of its total population) alone were displaced by the Soviet invasion in 1979.

Afghanistan, a poor nation with a per-capita gross domestic product of $130 per person, life expectancy of 41 years (about half of that in the United States), and literacy rate of 10%, has suffered the following effects of the ravages of war: 50% reduction in agricultural production, a 50% reduction in livestock, damage to 70% of the paved road, 60% of rural health centers destroyed, 35% of villages destroyed, 40% of the population displaced, and 6% of the population (1 million people) killed (MacFarquhar, 1989). Over the past decade, one third of the population of Afghanistan fled the country, with Pakistan sheltering more than 3 million refugees and Iran about 3 million. About 1.4 million Afghan refugees remain in Pakistan and about 2 million in Iran. Another 1 million probably moved into and around urban areas within Afghanistan. (Brassey's, 1996)

In 1979, when the Soviet Union invaded Afghanistan, millions fled by truck, cart, donkey, and foot to Pakistan and Iran. During the early days of the occupation, Soviet helicopters and planes spread the provinces bordering Pakistan with tens of thousands of plastic "butterfly mines," colored green for vegetated areas and beige for deserts. Even more diabolically, they dropped boobytrapped toys, cigarette packs, pens, and other objects. Designed to maim rather than to kill, these antipersonnel explosives were scattered over mountain passes, caravan routes, and fields as a means of terrorizing the local population. The Hind helicopter gunship (MIL Mi24) carried out thousands of attacks on small villages, killing tens of thousands of innocent civilians (Girardet, 1985).

President Richard Nixon expressed his view about the situation in Afghanistan in the following manner: "Those who have called Afghanistan the Soviet Union's Vietnam tragically misstate the case. South Vietnam was doomed when Congress cut our aid by 80% from 1973 to 1975 and revoked the president's powers to enforce the Paris Peace Accords of 1973, while Moscow poured in massive assistance to North Vietnam. One key lesson of Vietnam is that the United States must do as much for its friends as Kremlin leaders do for theirs. We are not doing that in Afghanistan today" (Nixon, 1990).

Brigadier M. Yousuf, who played a prominent role in the war against the Soviet Union, comments on the Afghan tragedy: "I feel the only winners in the war in Afghanistan are the Americans. They have their revenge of Vietnam, they have seen Soviets beaten on the battlefield by a guerilla force that they helped to finance, and they have prevented an Islamic government replacing a Communist one in Kabul. For the Soviet Union, even their military retreat has been turned into a huge political success, with Gorbachev becoming a hero in the West . . . . The losers are most certainly the people of Afghanistan. It is their homes that are heaps of rubble, their land and fields that have been burnt and sown with millions of mines; it is their husbands, fathers, and sons who have died in a war that was almost, and should have been, won" (Yousuf and Adkin, 1992). As the rest of the world prepares to enter the 21st century, the Afghan people—the victims of technology—are struggling to cope with the socioeconomic wounds inflicted by the technological might of the superpowers.

REFERENCES

CIA World Factbook (1996). Brassey's. Washington, D.C.

Girardet, E. (1985). *Afghanistan—The Soviet War.* New York, St. Martin's Press.

MacFarquhar, E. (1989, February 13). World Report. *U.S. News & World Report.* pp. 33–36.

Nixon, R. (1990, February 6). Afghanistan: Our Job Isn't Done. *Chicago Tribune.*

Yousuf, M. and Adkin, M. (1992). *The Bear Trap— Afghanistan's Untold Story.* London, Leo Copper.

(Source: World Resources. (1988–89). *An Assessment of the Resources Base that Supports the Global Economy: A Report By the World Resources Institute for Environment and Development.* New York, Basic Books.)

BANGLADESH: NATURAL AND MAN-MADE DISASTERS

Global Warming: Impact of Sea-Level Rise

A rise in sea level is probably the most widely recognized consequence of global warming, because in a warmer climate, the oceans will expand when heated, and polar ice caps in Greenland and Antarctica may melt. Scientists calculate that expansion effects alone could raise sea levels 20–40 centimeters if the average temperature rises 1.5–4.5 degrees Celsius. A temperature rise in the middle of this range might increase the sea level by 80 centimeters. Such a rise could inundate low-lying areas, destroy marshes and swamps, erode shoreline, worsen coastal flooding, and increase the salinity of rivers, bays, and aquifers. Nearly one third of the human population lives within 60 kilometers of a coast, and thus many reside on land that would be lost. In Bangladesh, the situation would be particularly severe. Bangladesh would lose 12–28% of its area, which currently houses 9–27% of its population. Floods could penetrate further inland, leaving the nation vulnerable to the type of storm that killed 300,000 people in the early 1970s.

Farakka Barrage: A Threat to the Economy and the Environment

The Farakka barrage was constructed across the Ganges river at Farakka, 11 miles upstream from the border of Bangladesh. The 70-foot-high and 7365.5-foot-long barrage, with 109 bays, was built to divert 40,000 cubic feet per second (cusec) of water from the Ganges into the Bhagirathi–Hooghly River during the low-flow period. The Indian government's objective for building the Farakka barrage was the preservation and maintenance of the port of Calcutta. The Farakka barrage has triggered a series of adverse impacts in Bangladesh:

Low water flows in the Ganges and its tributaries

Profound effects on hydrology and river morphology

Loss in agricultural production

Increase in surface and groundwater salinity

Adverse impact on navigation and fisheries

Desertification

Cyclones

Cyclones coming from the Bay of Bengal claim thousands of lives and cause major economic damage every year. In November of 1970, cyclones and tidal waves killed 200,000 people, and 100,000 were reported as missing (http://wwwinfoplease.com/ipa/). The cyclone of May 1996, the strongest cyclone in a century, killed 139,000 people and damaged or destroyed more than a million homes (http://193.67.176.1/~climate/database/records/).

continued

Figure 49.1
May 3, 1991—Cyclone aftermath—Bangladeshis mill around a devastated settlement on
the south Bangladeshi island of Sandwip Friday after a cyclone hit the area, destroying
large parts of southern Bangladesh. Courtesy of AP/Wide World Photos.

(Source: *Bangladesh's Economy, Environment and the Farakka Barrage,* by Dr. Sufian A. Khondker. Development issues of Bangladesh edited by
Ashraf Ali, et al. University Press Limited, Dhaka, Bangladesh).

China's Challenge to the United States and to the Earth

LESTER R. BROWN AND CHRISTOPHER FLAVIN

During the 1990s, China has emerged as an economic superpower, boasting the world's second largest economy. It is now challenging not only U.S. economic leadership, but the earth's environmental limits.

Using purchasing power parity to measure output, China's 1995 GNP of just over $3 trillion exceeded Japan's $2.6 trillion and trailed only the U.S. output of $6.7 trillion. If the Chinese economy continues to double every eight years, the pace it has maintained since 1980, it will overtake the United States by 2010, becoming the world's largest economy.

Over the last four years the Chinese economy has grown by 10 to 14 percent per year. As its population of 1.2 billion people moves into modern houses, buys cars, refrigerators and televisions, and shifts to a meat-based diet, the entire world will feel the effects. Already, China's rapidly rising CO_2 emissions account for one-tenth of the global total.

In recent decades, many observers noted that the United States, with less than 5 percent of the world's population, was consuming a third or more of its resources. But this is no longer true. In several areas, China has overtaken the United States. For example, China now consumes more grain and red meat, uses more fertilizer, and produces more steel than the United States.

Since China has 4.6 times as many people as the United States, its per capita demands on the earth's resources are still far less. To cite an extreme example, the average American consumes 25 times as much oil as the average Chinese citizen does.

Even with its still modest per capita consumption, China is already paying a high environmental price for its booming economy. Its heavy reliance on coal, for example, has led to air pollution nearly as bad as that once found in eastern Europe. As a result, respiratory disease has become epidemic in China, and crop yields are suffering.

As China, with its much larger population, attempts to replicate the consumer economy pioneered in the United States, it becomes clear that the U.S. model is not environmentally sustainable. Ironically, it may be China that finally forces the United States to come to terms with the environmental unsustainability of its own economic system. If China were to consume as much grain and oil per person as the United States does, prices of both commodities would go off the top of the charts. Carbon dioxide emissions would soar, leading to unprecedented climate instability. Together, these trends would undermine the future of the entire world.

The bottom line is that China, with its vast population, simply will not be able to follow for long any of the development paths blazed to date. It will be forced to chart a new course. The country that invented paper and gunpowder now has the opportunity to leapfrog the West and show how to build an environmentally sustainable economy. If it does, China could become a shining example for the rest of the world to admire and emulate. If it fails, we still all pay the price.

GRAIN HARVEST: CHINA

The United States, long the world's leading grain producer, was overtaken by China in 1983. Over subsequent years,

Reprinted with permission from Worldwatch Institute, Washington, D. C. (World Watch September/October 1996)

Figure 50.1
Grain Production, United States
and China, 1950–95

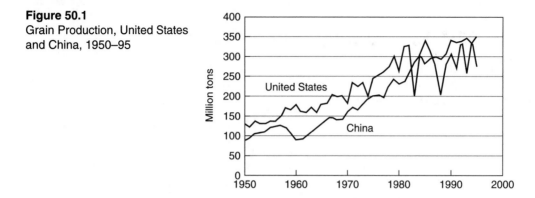

the lead changed hands several times, but since 1986, China's grain harvest has usually exceeded that of the United States. It is also much more stable, because China has 2.5 times as much irrigated land as the United States. U.S. production of corn, which dominates U.S. agriculture, is largely rainfed and, affected by both heat and drought, it fluctuates widely from year to year. In consumption, the gap is far wider. China now consumes 365 million tons per year, and has become the world's second largest grain importer, whereas the United States consumes 200 million tons and remains the world's leading exporter.

FERTILIZER USE: CHINA

U.S. fertilizer use climbed rapidly from mid century onward. By 1980, it exceeded 20 million tons. Then it leveled off, averaging less in the mid-1990s than in the early 1980s. Meanwhile, in China, the 1978 economic reforms in agriculture led to a meteoric climb in fertilizer use. In 1986, China overtook the United States to become the world leader. In 1995, Chinese farmers used 28 million tons of fer-

tilizer, while U.S. farmers used just under 20 million tons. In the United States, and now increasingly in China, fertilizer use is constrained by the physiological capacity of crop varieties to effectively absorb more nutrients.

CONSUMPTION OF RED MEAT: CHINA

The consumption of red meat, particularly beef in the form of steak and hamburgers, has become a defining component of the U.S. lifestyle, but China's total consumption of red meat has eclipsed that of the United States. For all red meat combined—beef, pork, and mutton—China now consumes 42 million tons per year, compared with only 20 million tons in the United States. China's pork consumption of 30 kilograms per person matches the U.S. intake of 31 kilograms, but its beef consumption lags far behind—4 kilograms to 45 kilograms. If China were to close the beef gap, its people would eat an additional 49 million tons each year. Produced in feedlots, this would take some 343 million tons of grain—roughly as much as the entire U.S. grain harvest.

Figure 50.2
Fertilizer use in the United
States and China, 1950–95

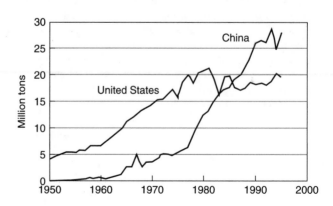

Figure 50.3
Red Meat Consumption, United
States and China, 1960–96

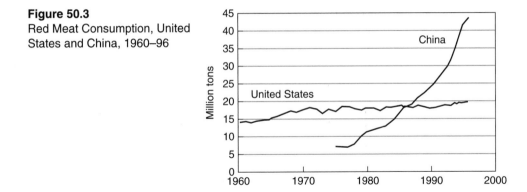

AUTOMOBILE PRODUCTION: UNITED STATES

In the production of automobiles, the United States dwarfed China by some 6.6 million to 239,000 in 1995. U.S. output is not likely to increase much in the future, since most of the automobiles made now are used for replacement rather than for expanding the fleet. China, by contrast, plans to boost production to 3 million per year by the end of the decade, building a fleet of 22 million automobiles by the year 2010. If China's ownership of automobiles were to reach 1 for every 2 people, as in the United States, its fleet of 600 million cars would exceed the 1995 *world* fleet of 480 million cars.

BICYCLE PRODUCTION: CHINA

If a crowded world is compelled to move toward a less polluting, less land consuming mode of personal transport, then the bicycle may well be the transport vehicle of the future. For this shift, China is well positioned. Its bicycle production has averaged over 40 million a year in recent years, compared with less than 8 million a year in the United States. This is perhaps the only major indicator for which the ratio of production between the countries reflects the ratio of population size. In global terms, China accounts for nearly two-fifths of world production of 110 million bicycles annually in recent years.

STEEL OUTPUT: CHINA

In the industrial world of an earlier era, steel production was perhaps the best single indicator of industrial progress. China has recently caught up with the United States in this industry, with both countries turning out 93 million tons in 1995. The big difference is that most of China's steel production is from iron ore. The United States, a more mature industrial society, now gets *roughly half* of its total steel from the reprocessing of scrap metal, a more energy-efficient, less polluting means of production. If China proceeds

Figure 50.4
Automobile Production, United
States and China, 1950–95

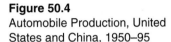

Figure 50.5
Bicycle Production, United
States and China, 1970–94

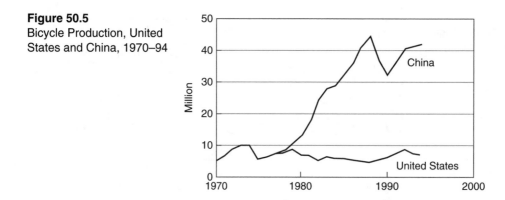

to develop an automobile-centered transportation system as currently planned, its steel needs will soar far beyond those of the United States.

OIL USE: UNITED STATES

Despite its becoming economy, China still consumes only 3.3 million barrels of oil each day, one-fifth the 17 million consumed daily in the United States. U.S. oil use per person is a striking 25 times that in China. With its limited oil reserves, China relies on coal for 75 percent of its energy, whereas the United States relies on coal for just 22 percent. But as China becomes more dependent on automobiles and trucks, its oil use is climbing. Already, it has gone from exporting 500,000 barrels of oil per day in 1990 to *importing* 300,000 barrels per day in 1995. If China were one day to use as much oil per person as the United States does, it would need 80 million barrels daily—more than the whole world now produces or is ever projected to produce.

CARBON EMISSIONS: UNITED STATES

Carbon emissions from fossil-fuel burning totaled 1.394 million tons in the United States in 1995, 73 percent higher than the 807 million tons emitted by China. Fossil fuel burning releases carbon dioxide into the atmosphere—the main gas leading to greenhouse warming. Since 1990, U.S. carbon emissions have grown at roughly 1 percent per year while China's grew at 5 percent annually as use of coal and oil surged. Even so, the United States still emits eight times as much carbon per person as China. If China develops the sort of energy-intensive industries and lifestyles found in the United States, it would further destabilize the world's atmosphere.

COMPUTER POWER: UNITED STATES

If steel production is a key indicator of progress in an industrial society, computer use is a key indicator in the information economy of the late twentieth century. In this

Figure 50.6
Steel Production, United States
and China, 1977–95

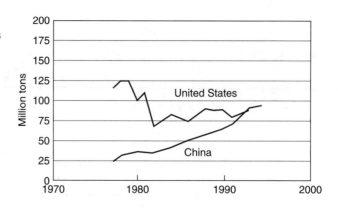

Figure 50.7
Oil consumption, United States
and China, 1950–94

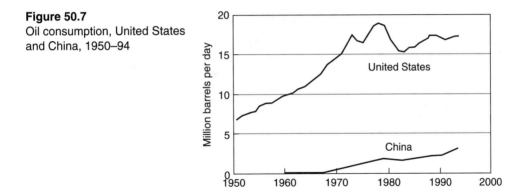

Figure 50.8
Carbon Emission from Fossil
Fuel Burning, United States and
China, 1950–95

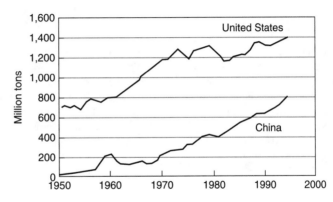

Figure 50.9
Number of Computers, United
States and China, 1993

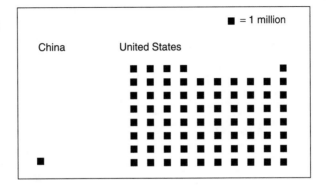

area, there is no contest: the United States has one computer for every three people; China has one for every 1,000 people. With 74 million computers out of a worldwide total of 173 million, the United States leads the world by a wide margin in the computerization of its economy. China, which has just 1.2 million computers, lags far behind not only the United States but much of the rest of the world as well.

Questions

1. Compare China with the United States in terms of the following aspects: population, amounts of carbon emissions, automobile production, and oil consumption.
2. Do you think that China, despite its large population, will emerge as an industrialized nation? Why or why not? Explain your answer.

INDIA: TAJ MAHAL THREATENED BY AIR POLLUTION

Taj Mahal, one of the seven wonders of the world, located in Agra, Delhi, was built by the Mughal emperor Shahjahan in memory of his beloved wife Mumtaz Mahal.

Uncontrolled emissions from factories and plants around Taj Mahal are said to be damaging its marble facade. Agra's air has become so badly polluted that the Taj Mahal—a 350-year-old monument—often disappears behind the murk and smog. Environmentalists claim that clouds of pollution contain sulphur dioxide and nitrogen dioxide that are eating away the monument, turning the brilliant white marble into an ugly shade of gray.

The environmentalists are demanding the area around the monument to be designated a total pollution-free zone. This would mean relocating all of the area's 2,000 potentially polluting industries, such as cast iron foundries, glassworks, and a state-owned oil refinery, to areas located farther from Taj Mahal.

Taj Mahal is the biggest tourist attraction in the country and the source of much-needed foreign exchange. The Indian government has recently announced plans to clean up the environmental pollution that is slowly destroying the monument. Plans call for industries that burn coal or oil to switch to natural gas or liquefied petroleum gas. People living in the city will be required to cut down on their use of kerosene and firewood. Traffic pollution will be curbed with incentives for truck drivers to use diesel with low sulphur content.

Recently, the Indian Supreme Court ordered the closing of 14 industries near the Taj Mahal that had failed to install antipollution devices. It also ordered 190 industries along the Ganges River to take steps to control their effluents.

Source: Impact International, April 1995.

A Bridge to Your 21st Century Understanding

Complete the following flowchart.

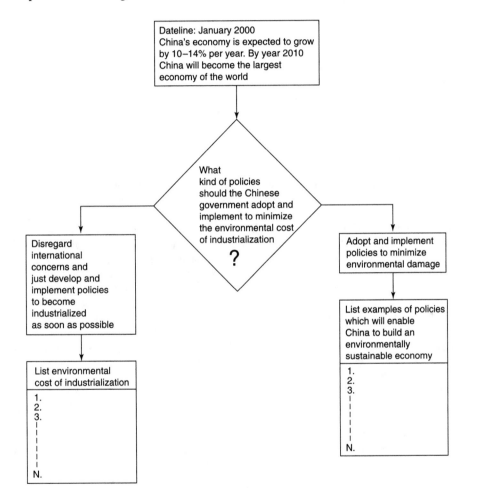

Dateline: January 2000
China's economy is expected to grow by 10–14% per year. By year 2010 China will become the largest economy of the world

What kind of policies should the Chinese government adopt and implement to minimize the environmental cost of industrialization

?

Disregard international concerns and just develop and implement policies to become industrialized as soon as possible

Adopt and implement policies to minimize environmental damage

List environmental cost of industrialization

1.
2.
3.

N.

List examples of policies which will enable China to build an environmentally sustainable economy

1.
2.
3.

N.

51

Pakistan: Karachi's Informal "Recycling Network"

Karachi, with an estimated population of 10 million in 1995, is Pakistan's largest city. The city has been growing at more than 5 percent per annum in recent years and is expected to reach 12 to 15 million inhabitants by the year 2000. Karachi was the world's twenty-fifth largest city in 1985; it is projected to be the fifteenth largest by the end of the century.

Karachi's high rate of population growth, coupled with scarce resources and inadequate planning, have created a number of environmental problems such as water pollution, air pollution, waste disposal, etc.

According to Karachi Municipal Corporation (KMC), the city generates 7,000 tons of domestic waste daily. The city has a nonmechanized system of waste disposal which is able to remove only about one third of the solid waste that is generated daily (Shah, 1993). The waste is removed manually by the city's 9,000 municipal sweepers and then transported by a fleet of 150 refuse vans to a single dumping site located 30 kilometers from Karachi, where it is disposed of by burning. The remaining garbage lies uncollected in city alleys and is processed by the informal "recycling network." This informal network consists of scavengers, middle men commonly known as "Kabaria," and the dealer. The scavengers hunt for recyclable garbage, in community dumpsters and city streets, and sell it to a middle man, (Karabia), who sells the material to the big dealer, and finally the dealer sells recyclable waste to recycling industries.

Unlike the West, where the process of recycling has been initiated in response to environmental concerns. Pakistan's recycling industry is motivated purely by economic motives. The informal recycling network of scavengers, middlemen, dealers and recycling units constitutes an amazing and not widely known phenomenon which performs an essential service under very adverse conditions. This informal recycling effort not only helps KMC in waste removal but also provides a source of inexpensive raw material to local small industry, and sustenance to thousands of inhabitants (Ahmad, 1993).

According to a report by National Training and Consultancy Services (NTSC) for the United Nations Center for Human Settlements (HABITAT), about 40 percent of Karachi's solid waste is recycled in the informal sector, and about 2 percent of the city's population is engaged full-time in the recycling industry. Considering the other participants, like reprocessing workers, housewives, servants, entrepreneurs, and craftsmen, it seems that almost half of Karachi's population is participating in recycling (Shah, 1993).

It is estimated that there are about 25,000 scavengers operating in Karachi. Almost 95 percent of the scavengers are Afghan refugees, (who fled to Pakistan after the Soviet invasion of Afghanistan in 1979), the remainder being Burmese or Bengali. Although no accurate statistics are available, it is estimated that these scavengers reduce the work of government agencies by as much as two-thirds, saving the Karachi Municipal Corporation (KMC) up to 200 million rupees annually in garbage collection and disposal costs. Karachi's informal recycling network has created one of the largest recycling industries in Asia. Paper, glass, metal, plastics, even bones, are all recycled (Table 51.1) and hence provide an inexpensive source of raw

Table 51.1
Karachi's Informal "Recycling Network"

Waste Category	Efforts of "Recycling Network"
Bones	About a dozen bone processing industries have been set up in Karachi, each with a processing capacity of 5 to 10 tons per day. About 80 percent or 30,000 tons of bones find their way to the far eastern markets, particularly Japan. Bones are a vital raw material in the manufacture of photographic film, and Japan's $20 billion photographic film industry makes it the largest market for this Pakistani export.
Iron	Iron, especially scrap recycling, has been known to build fortunes. The leading tycoons of Indo-Pakistan, from Mians of Lahore to the Tatas of Bombay, are basically scrap dealers and scrap recyclers. According to conservative estimates, about 3,000 tons of iron scrap is generated in Karachi daily.
Glass	About 80 percent of the country's demand for glass is also met through recycling locally generated glass waste, saving Pakistan millions of rupees in imports. It is estimated that about 80,000 tons of glass scrap is produced each year in Karachi alone, from both industrial and domestic sources.
Plastic	Research conducted by the NED University's Environment Department, and the Pakistan Council for Scientific and Industrial Research (PCSIR) reveals that more than 1,000 tons of plastic waste is generated daily in Karachi. The material includes discarded polythene bags and the waste from hundreds of plastic factories manufacturing PVC pipes and household items. The scale of plastic recycling can be gauged from the fact that there are about 8,000 polythene bag manufacturing units in Karachi alone.
Paper	Several tons of paper is recycled into paper and cardboard daily. The recycling process involves the low tech process of dumping large quantities of paper scrap in a pool of water and later sifting it through a sieve.

materials for domestic and overseas industrial needs (Ahmad, 1993).

Karachi's informal recycling network has emerged as an indigenous industry of miraculous proportions. About 60 to 70 percent of Karachi's reusable waste is recycled, generating employment for over 2 percent of the city's population and simultaneously saving energy and cutting down on pollution. But the industry has its pit falls, too. More than anything else, unregulated recycling practices pose health hazards especially for those engaged in the separation of waste and reprocessing. Laborers melt batteries to extract lead, electroplated utensils to extract aluminum, photographic films to extract silver, without using any masks. Laborers in the bone industry breathe in bone powder and hence suffer from respiratory disease. In plastic recycling units, laborers breathe toxic emissions (Shah, 1993).

The existence of the vast informal recycling network suggests that, contrary to popular notions about developing countries, Pakistan is a highly waste conscious country where a staggeringly large proportion of garbage is recycled (Ahmad, 1993).

Table 51.2
Daily Garbage Generation per Person for Selected Cities

City	Daily lbs. of Garbage/Person
New York	4
Paris	2.4
Hamburg	1.9
Rome	1.5
Cairo	1.1
Karachi	1.4
Calcutta	1.1
Hong Kong	1.9
Jakarta	1.3
Singapore	1.9
Tokyo	3

416   Part VIII: Technology and the Third World

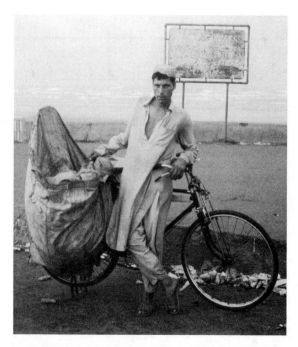

Shah, an Afghan refugee, collects 50–60 kilograms of paper waste daily at Karachi's Clifton beach and earns about Rs. 90 ($2) by selling it to Kabaria. Photo courtesy of Ahmed S. Khan.

References

Ahmed, F. (1993, July). The Waste Merchants. *The Herald (Karachi)*. pp. 107–112.

Carson, W. (1990). *The Global Ecology Handbook: What You Can Do about the Environmental Crisis.* Boston, Tomorrow Coalition, Boston Press.

Population Growth and Policies in Mega-Cities: Karachi, Population policy paper No. 13. (1988). New York, United Nations.

Shah, N. (1993, June). Our Wonderful World of Waste. *Newsline (Karachi)*. pp. 71–77.

Questions

1. Discuss the pros and cons of Karachi's informal "Recycling Network."

Karachi's Informal "Recycling Network"	
(+) Pros	*(−) Cons*

2. What steps need to be taken by the government agencies of Pakistan to make the processes of waste disposal and recycling safer and more efficient?

Karachi's Informal "Recycling Network"

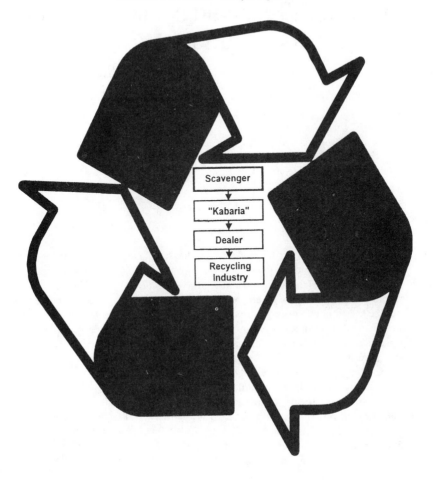

Scavenger
↓
"Kabaria"
↓
Dealer
↓
Recycling
Industry

52

Sri Lanka: Technology and Agriculture, Tractor versus Buffalo

The replacement of traditional animal power by modern tractors could pose serious ecological and environmental problems in Third-World countries. The use of modern technology in agriculture offers the benefits of efficient farming, but also poses the danger of eliminating jobs and a threat to the environment. A good example of the ramifying environmental consequences of technology is the case presented by Senanayake. He studied the effects of replacing buffalo power by tractor power for agriculture (Figure 52.1). At first sight, the substitution of tractor for buffalo power in the villages of Sri Lanka seems to appear a straightforward efficient trade-off between timely planting and labor saving at the expense of milk and manure. But it is not only milk and manure at stake. The substitution of buffalo with tractors could lead to a chain of events that could have an adverse impact on the environment. The buffalo and buffalo's wallows offer a number of benefits that the tractors could not offer. Figure 52.1 illustrates the these benefits.

In the dry season, the wallows are refuge for fish, who then move back to the rice fields in the rainy season. Some fish are caught and eaten by the farmers; others eat the larvae of mosquitoes that carry malaria. The thickets harbor snakes that eat rats that eat rice, and lizards that eat the crabs that make destructive holes in the ricebunds. The

wallows are also used by the villagers to prepare coconut fronds for thatching. If the wallows go, so do these benefits.

If pesticides are used to kill rats, crabs, or mosquito larvae, then pollution or pesticide resistance can become a potential problem. Similarly, if tiles are substituted for the thatch, forest destruction may be hastened, since firewood is required to fire the tiles.

References

Senanayake, R. (1984). The Ecological, Energetic and Agronomic Systems of Ancient and Modern Sri Lanka in Douglas, G.K. Ed. *Agricultural Sustainability in a Changing World Order,* Boulder, Colorado, Westview Press.

Gordon, C. (1990). Agriculture and the Environment: Concepts and Issues in Huq, S., et al. Eds. *Environmental Aspects of Agricultural Development in Bangladesh,* Dhaka, University Press Limited.

Questions

1. What strategy would you suggest for employing tractors for farming in Sri Lankan villages?

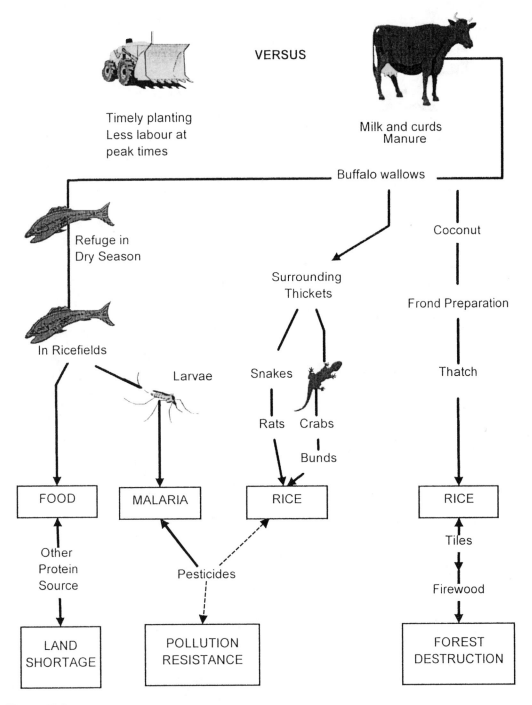

Figure 52.1

Technology and Agriculture: Tractor vs. Buffalo.

Source: Agriculture and the environment: Concepts and Issues," *Environmental Aspects of Agricultural Development in Bangladesh,* University Press Limited, Dhaka, Bangladesh.

A Bridge to Your 21st Century Understanding

Complete and discuss the following flowchart.

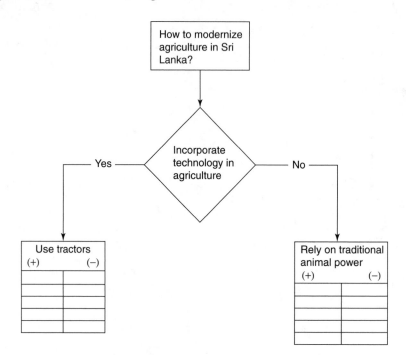

Appropriate Technologies

GADI KAPLAN

The ending of the Cold War has released more energy for tackling the concerns of underprivileged populations. "One billion people in the developing world still lack access to clean water . . . nearly 2 billion lack adequate sanitation . . . Electric power has yet to reach 2 billion people," the World Bank noted in its June *World development report 1994: infrastructure for development.*

A country's infrastructure includes services based on electrotechnology, such as electric power, telecommunications, and road, sea, and air transport. Developing countries in round figures pour US $200,000 million every year into new infrastructure, amounting to 4 percent of their national output and a fifth of their total investment, according to the World Bank report.

In purely human terms, the situation of these people is unacceptable. Technologically, it dares electrical and electronics engineers to devise remedies by applying proven technology at an affordable cost.

One challenge may well be to upgrade the infrastructure in developing countries. At present, for example, about 40 percent of their power-generating capacity is on average unavailable when needed, as a result of malfunction or scheduled maintenance; elsewhere, in the best performing power sectors in the world, the percentage is half that figure, according to the 1994 World Bank report.

To cut back on waste and improve efficiency, the bank is embarking on a thorough reform. Among its goals are to see the infrastructure managed as a business, and not as a bureaucracy; to see competition introduced; and to give those who use the services a stronger voice in and responsibility for their operation than has been the custom.

But what exactly is a developing country? The World Bank often refers to "developing economies" as those with low or middle per-capita income, derived by dividing the gross national product (GNP) by the population count.

Low-income countries, with US $675 or less per capita, include Burundi and Benin in sub-Saharan Africa, Egypt in North Africa, Cambodia in East Asia, Tadjikistan in Central Asia, and Haiti in the Americas. Senegal, though, and Thailand, Turkey, Iran, Algeria, and Chile are representative of middle-income economies, with $675–$8356 per capita income (in 1992). (All dollar figures are for U.S. currency.)

Indeed, a developing country quite often seeks to leapfrog straight into the 21st century, particularly if the leap makes sound economic sense. Indonesia is doing just that. Looking to a rapid expansion of its urban telephone network, it is installing a radio-based, cellular telephone system in Jakarta and West Java for a total of 280,000 subscribers.

The first topic covered in the appropriate technology series is photovoltaics, which has the potential of bringing electric energy to millions of remote rural households, greatly enhancing their quality of life.

So rosy, in fact, is its promise that the 12th European Photovoltaics Solar Energy Conference and Exhibition devoted a parallel symposium to photovoltaics in developing countries. Inspired in part by that symposium, which was held in April in Amsterdam, the Netherlands, the following report includes an overview of the technology's applications and two regional studies, one on a large project in West Africa, and the other about India.

Photovoltaics is attractive because it can help countries avoid the huge expense of expanding electric grids into rural areas, at an estimated cost of $20,000–$30,000 per kilometer, reports Erik H. Lysen, the head of a department at Novem, the Netherlands agency for energy and the environment located in Utrecht. But if affordable power is to be supplied by this means to millions of rural households, the worldwide manufacturing capacity for photovoltaic modules and systems will have to be substantially enlarged, he noted. Furthermore, funding for photovoltaics applications by national and international organizations would have to be increased by orders of magnitude, he said.

International cooperation counts heavily toward the success of photovoltaics applications. Evidence of that comes from projects in Vietnam and the republic of Kiribati in the mid-Pacific.

In West Africa, high grades are scored by a program for installing photovoltaic systems with 1200 peak kilowatt capacity for water pumping, refrigeration, and lighting. And in India, about 62,000 rural photovoltaic systems have already been installed under a government-assisted program, and the installation of 60,000 units that power VHF remote radio links is under way.

From these and other reports it is clear that designing "appropriate" technology may sound easier than it is. In the West Africa project, for instance, inverters for water pumps had to be flexible enough to accommodate various pump capacities, pipe sizes, and water heads, but this flexibility could not be bought by sacrificing efficiency. Protection of the photovoltaic system against lightning and the safety of maintenance personnel also came into the picture in a big way.

Even so, the obstacles that photovoltaics must overcome are more institutional in nature than technological, as became very clear at the Amsterdam meeting. More than 30 years in the making, photovoltaics is mature enough in itself, but will require innovative breakthroughs in financing as well as changes in energy policy, the experts believe.

PHOTOVOLTS FOR VILLAGES: ERIK H. LYSEN

Two billion people are without an electrical connection, but the cost of hooking up their homes to a conventional grid system will be too high for most developing countries.

Photovoltaic solar systems are a cheaper alternative and can reach virtually any site on earth. Granted, new and bold initiatives are necessary to realize the required 20,000-MW peak power of photovoltaic capacity. But the breakthroughs needed are less technical and more in the areas of financing and energy policy.

Energy is not the most pressing problem of the developing countries, partly because oil prices are at present so low. Instead, they have to worry about the poverty of most of the inhabitants, their food supply, the creation of sufficient and meaningful jobs, competition in the international markets for their products, and, sadly enough in some cases, the presence of war. The main energy problem in rural areas still is to find enough wood for cooking meals. In some developing countries, biomass for cooking accounts for over half of the national energy consumption.

For some decades now, photovoltaics (PV) has been on the energy scene in the developing world, particularly in established niche markets such as telecommunications, marine beacons, railway signaling, and cathodic protection of pipelines. The challenge will be to apply PV to the provision of energy to rural homes for lighting, refrigeration, and TV.

The most successful to date is the individually owned solar home system: typically a 50-W solar panel that charges a battery by day and power loads after dark. Owners are proud of having their own power system and are not susceptible to grid failure or inconsiderate neighbors, while the equipment itself can be expanded when required. Of course, the systems must be well designed, properly maintained, and paid for by the owner, because giveaways seldom last long.

On the face of it, it looks strange that people in rural areas and nonindustrialized countries are satisfied with a fraction of a kilowatt-hour a day, whereas residents of industrialized countries "need" 10 kWh or more per day. The explanation is that people are not interested in kilowatt-hours as such, but in light, a working TV set, or a refrigerator. In other words, they want the services of the energy regardless of whether it amounts to 0.1 kWh or 10 kWh per day. And as only a limited number of solar kilowatt-hours are available, people cannot afford to waste them and must use efficient lighting, low-power TV sets (a golden market for future flat-screen TV sets with liquid-crystal displays), and efficient refrigerators.

The only thing that matters to the owner is: how much do I have to pay for these services every week or month? As a first estimate, a reasonable part of the rural population can raise $5 to $8 per month. This is what they are paying now for kerosene lighting and for battery charging at grid-connected centers. (All dollar figures in this article refer to U.S. currency.)

As is well known, nearly all utilities in developing countries are losing money on rural electrification. Investment capital is not the problem, being available at comparatively low rates from large multilateral banks like the World Bank and Asian Development Bank. High costs are the issue, stemming from long transmission lines to remote customers, low consumption, the need to charge only low tariffs, and high technical and nontechnical losses (transmission and distribution losses and illegal connections)— 20–40 percent in some countries. And these high costs are usually cross-subsidized by urban consumers.

Line costs are the heaviest burden, usually accounting for 80–90 percent of the budget of a rural electrification project They typically run $20,000–$30,000 per kilometer. Another factor is the widely variable number of users per kilometer of line, which may be as low as two but in Bangladesh must be at least 75. As a result, the average cost per rural connection also varies wildly: Mohan Munasighe, an energy expert with the World Bank, quotes a range from $200 to $3650 (in 1983 prices). The monthly power consumption of rural consumers is usually low: 20–40 kWh, leading to high per-kilowatt-hour costs of 10–20 cents to $1.

Power to the People

A recent report from the World Bank on its role in the power sector notes that the number of power connections in developing countries in the period 1969–89 grew by 9 percent per year, or 2.5 times the average population growth. In spite of this rapid growth, rather few members of the population are yet connected to an electricity supply. Average real power tariffs declined from 5.2 to 3.8 cents per kilowatt-hour in the period 1979–88 (in 1986 dollars).

Nevertheless, governments and utilities in developing countries have impressive plans for expanding their power sectors. The idea is to increase the total power supply capacity from the 471 GW of 1989 to 855 GW in 1999. It is estimated that no less than $1 trillion will be needed to achieve the desired 384-GW increase. Approximately 40 percent of this sum is in foreign exchange, and it is clear that the $40 billion needed annually cannot be mobilized, even by the large multilateral banks (the present level of World Bank lending for the power sector is around $7 billion per year).

The conclusion seems inescapable. Governments in the developing world will face great difficulties in expanding their power sectors as planned. Obviously, too, priority will be given to industry and the urban sector. This prospect underlines the need to consider other alternatives for rural electrification, such as pre-electrification through PV or other renewable sources.

The Story Till Now

One of the earliest references to photovoltaics in a rural setting is to a system installed in Chile in 1960. In the '60s, PV cell development was dominated by research for space applications (the first satellite was launched in 1957).

Rural energy developments in the '70s were typically the so-called "integrated energy systems" promoted by the United Nations. These projects characteristically exploited various sources of renewable energy (such as the sun and wind, biomass, and organic waste), and they distributed the electricity thus obtained through a regular grid system in the village. In practice these systems never came up to expectation; they demanded too much maintenance, were poorly designed, gave unreliable service and, most importantly, were more or less forced upon the village inhabitants.

Individual solar home systems were introduced more or less independently in the Philippines, the Dominican Republic, and Indonesia in the early 1980s.

The Philippine-German Solar Energy project (1982–88) started with a 13-kW plant for a small village. The plant was found to be not economical for wide dissemination. The second phase emphasized small PV systems for use in rural areas, namely, solar home systems and communal battery-charging stations. The first 100 of these home systems were installed at Burias Island. A would-be owner had to make a down payment of $140 and 36 monthly payments of $13.

An important lesson was learned. Solar home systems have become a status symbol because they are one of the few high-tech systems available outside urban areas and they open the door to radio, TV, and video. At present, about 105 kW of solar systems are installed in the Philippines, of which 70 kW is in residential systems and 35 kW is in systems intended for telecommunications, pumping, and other purposes.

In the Dominican Republic, a true catalyst for the development of photovoltaics was the presence of Richard Hansen, founder of Enersol Associates (USA). In April 1984 the first PV system was installed in Bella Vista. Right from the beginning, owners had to pay for the system (48 monthly installments of $10). Soon a solar credit fund was created (Adesol) with seed money from the U.S. Agency for International Development, and from the installments paid by its clients new systems could soon be bought. Local entrepreneurs were trained for servicing and sales of new systems.

By mid-1987 more than a hundred systems were up and running. That year, the Solar-Based Rural Electrification Concept was introduced, as a model for intervention by a nongovernmental organization, and gradually spread. By 1992 the number of PV systems grew to 4000. More than 10 installation businesses are active in the Dominican Republic.

The development of solar home systems in Indonesia was the fruit of cooperation between individuals and the Dutch PV company R&S (Renewable Energy Systems), the Indonesian Ministry of Research and Technology, and the Indonesian Ministry for Cooperatives. A start was made in 1987 and in 1988 the systems were demonstrated in Sukatani, a village 110 km from Jakarta. The seed money was provided by the three organizations listed above plus the Netherlands Ministry of Foreign Affairs.

Sukatani has a lower than average amount of sunshine. The idea was that if the system worked there (which it did), it would work throughout Indonesia. The local cooperative took responsibility for fee collection and simple maintenance.

The President of Indonesia became so enthusiastic about the Sukatani project that he started the Banpres project, with interest-free credit for 3000 solar home systems, which have since been successfully installed. Additional credit schemes through revolving funds have been started, one example being the $50,000 revolving fund grant from the North Holland utility PEN, for solar home systems in the village of Lebak.

By 1993 more than 10,000 home systems had been installed throughout Indonesia. The average investment has dropped below $400, and with a down payment of 35 percent the solar home system owner pays the equivalent of $8 per month.

Five Types of Problems

As with every new technology, all was not smooth sailing. Problems that arose during the systems' introduction fall into the following five categories: financial, institutional, infrastructural, and technical.

Financing the purchase is still the most forbidding hurdle. The average price of a solar home system is about $500. But in many countries, only 10–20 percent of rural families earn more than $100 per month. Assuming that 10 percent can be spent on a solar home system, this means they can afford a maximum of $10 per month, and preferably less. The problem therefore is how to reduce the monthly installments to, say, $5 per month.

Institutional conflicts are the next concern. Electric utilities are traditionally either hostile or at best indifferent to small autonomous systems such as solar systems for the home. It can happen that a nongovernmental organization pushes hard to install solar home systems in a village, only for the utility to show up with a grid extension a few months later. Confusion is created and part of the investment in home systems suffers. Rural electrification policies seldom include pre-electrification options such as solar home systems, or wind or microhydro supply systems.

Experience has shown that interpersonal relations were often mishandled. People were not properly involved in a timely fashion in the decision to introduce PV systems. They were not informed about the performance of the solar home system and its pluses and minuses compared to a grid connection. Training of the owners was sometimes inadequate, so that batteries were discharged too deeply if poor (or no) controllers were present. Simple but essential repairs took much too long, so that people lost confidence in the system. The key factor here is proper communication with the users.

This situation is closely linked to infrastructural weakness. Often after-sales service was either nonexistent or poorly organized. Publicity was insufficient, wrongly targeted, or even negative. Stories about failures tend to stick in people's minds for a long time, and 10 times as many successes are needed to eradicate them.

Then of course there were the technical problems associated with a new technology. Interestingly, there were hardly any problems with the PV modules. The trouble came from conventional parts of the system—batteries, controllers, and lights and switches. Controllers worked poorly or were omitted to save money, so batteries had a short life. Cheap fluorescent light tubes were used, which blackened quickly; electronic ballasts failed and switches malfunctioned.

In essence, the financing problem can be solved by lowering the investment cost of the PV system and by enabling the customers to pay smaller amounts over longer periods. The first part of the solution is largely for the manufacturers to implement and is influenced by Western development programs. The developing countries' governments can help by lowering or waiving import duties.

Several options for lowering the monthly costs for consumers have been proposed and are being practiced: revolving funds (started with grants); presidential loans (as in Indonesia); local bank loans; the Finesse approach (*fi*-*n*ancing of *e*nergy *s*ervices for *s*mall-*s*cale *e*nergy consumers); and supplier's credit.

Energy experts made a good point during the Finesse workshop held in October 1991 in Kuala Lumpur with the support of the World Bank, the U.S. Department of Energy (DOE), and the Netherlands Ministry of Foreign Affairs. Given that large power companies have access to very cheap capital for new power plants and rural electrification projects, they argued, smaller-scale power options that complement the grid supply should also be allowed to tap just a fraction of those funds, and on the same conditions. Solar home systems were seen as a case in point.

This is in essence the aim of the Asia Technical Alternative Energy unit of the World Bank, which is supported by (among others) the DOE and the Netherlands Ministry of Foreign Affairs. The unit at present is active in Indonesia, India, Sri Lanka, and China.

On the institutional level, clashes with the electricity companies can be avoided if the initiatives in solar home systems are coordinated or even channeled through them. The utilities should permit, spur on, or even contract with the private sector and nongovernment organizations to start offering solar home systems in certain areas. They should make it clear to the customers that this is a pre-electrification option, and that if in the future the utilities have the means to reach the village by the grid, the PV panels can be resold to the private sector (or kept as an emergency option).

Events in the Philippines, Dominican Republic, and Indonesia prove that the early involvement of potential customers is crucial to the success of any PV project. People should be properly taught about system operation and properly informed about comparative performance and costs. A warning system for larger breakdowns should be set up, to ensure quick repairs and maintain confidence in the system. Local cooperatives should be used to collect fees and carry out basic maintenance. Local youths should be trained as PV technicians and paid for their work.

Improvements in product quality have occurred over the last few years, thanks to lessons learned from simple technical problems. Controllers and lamp ballasts have improved, some of them locally produced; battery indicators have now become available so people can "see" how much is left in their battery (as was their custom with bottles of kerosene).

The wattage needed for rural electrification of the 2 billion people as yet without electricity can be estimated. The average bad load of a rural connection is around 350–500 W, so with an average family size of five and 400 million as yet unwired households, an additional capacity of 140–200 GW is needed. At a conservative value of $2500/kW, this capacity would cost $350 billion to $500 billion. In addition, the annual fuel bills of the developing countries will be increased by $5000 to $10,000 million.

Governments in developing countries are already hard pressed to expand their industrial and urban capacity as fast as necessary. They will find it impossible to invest also in rural electrification. If, however, the latter task could be achieved through individual solar home systems, the total investment would be lower, although still considerable. Assume that a 50-Wp solar home system in the future will cost $250 on average, then 400 million solar home systems (20 GWp) will require $100,000 million, or $4000 million annually for 25 years. These systems would have to be financed through long-term loans, not grants.

To put things in perspective, it is perhaps useful to mention the size of the predicted PV market and required capacities. Note that the present market in photovoltaics is about 60 MWp, of which about 5 MWp is for rural off-grid applications. Market analyst Paul D. Maycock, president of Photovoltaic Energy Systems Inc., Casanova, Va., expects the following markets for the off-grid rural segments in the years 1995, 2000, and 2010:

- For a business-as-usual scenario: 8, 20, and 40 MWp.
- For an accelerated growth scenario: 15, 40, and 600 MWp.

Recall the estimate that the electrification of all 400 million households currently without electricity would require 20 GWp of PV capacity, or 800 MWp on average for a period of 25 years. This is even more than is predicted in Maycock's accelerated growth scenario. So probably this target will not be met unless bold new initiatives are taken.

Bold Ideas

One initiative of this nature is the Power for the World proposal put forward by Wolfgang Palz, division head of renewable energies in the European Commission's Directorate General XII, which handles science research and development. To reduce system costs and increase production volume, plants with an annual production capacity of 10 MWp must be built soon; by the year 2000, annual capacity must reach 100 MWp. This can only be done if specific conditions are met, namely, policy changes, better financing options, and system improvements. But the environmental issue must be considered right now.

There are signs of policy changes and a beginning of acceptance by electricity companies, as in Mexico and the Philippines. But there is still a long way to go before solar PV systems are accepted by utilities in developing countries as a reliable means of pre-electrification or even electrification. Sources of capital can be instrumental in changing this attitude by requesting such policy changes (as well as financing renewable options) during the negotiations for conventional power loans.

Several financing initiatives have been offered by both national and international donors; but in terms of total funds required, the efforts have to be increased by orders of magnitude. The easy terms for large power loans should be made available for small off-grid options as well.

Manufacturers, importers, and distributors should ensure the quality of their PV products. National product standards should be established, leaving enough room for product improvement.

With the introduction on a large scale of PV battery-charging systems, the number of batteries in rural areas will soar. Environmental problems could ensue if no measures are taken beforehand. Manufacturers, together with local counterpart companies, should work out optimum and least-cost solutions. National battery recycling is already in effect in Indonesia, for example.

Acknowledgment

This article summarizes the plenary paper presented by the author at the 12th European Photovoltaic Conference, held in Amsterdam in April 1994. The full paper has been published in the conference proceedings.

To Probe Further

Costs of rural electrification are addressed in *Electricity for rural people* by G. Foley (Panos Publications Ltd., London, 1990) and in *Rural Electrification for Development: policy analysis and applications* by M. Munasinghe (Westview Press, Boulder, Colo., 1987).

R.J. Saunders is the author of "The World Bank's role in the electric power sector: policies for effective institutional, regulatory and financial reform," a 1993 World Bank Policy Paper, published in Washington, D.C. The costs of electrification are discussed by R. Turvey and D. Anderson *in Electricity Economics,* a World Bank Research Publication (Johns Hopkins University Press, Baltimore, Md., 1977).

A reference to an early photovoltaic system in Chile is included in *Photovoltaics for Development,* by R. Hill (ed.), United Nations ATAS Bulletin No. 8, 1993.

Integrated Rural Energy Planning was discussed by Y. El Mahgary and A.K. Biswas in a United Nations Energy Planning (UNEP) publication (Butterworth Scientific, England, 1985).

Solar home systems are discussed in *The Philippines' Rural Photovoltaic Electrification Scheme* by G. Santianez-

Yeneza and H. Böhnke in a publication of the National Electrification Administration, Manila, 1992. Photovoltaics applications were addressed by R. Schröer and P. de Bakker in their article, "It All Began on Burias Island," *GATE* magazine, July 1989. *Solar Rural Electrification in the Developing World; Four Country Case Studies: Dominican Republic, Kenya, Sri Lanka, Zimbabwe* was dealt with by M. Hankins, Solar Electric Light Fund, Washington D.C., 1993.

The financing of energy services for small-scale energy consumers (Finesse was discussed during the World Bank workshop, Kuala Lumpur, October 1991. Paul Maycock examines *Photovoltaic technology, performance, cost and market forecast 1975–2010,* in a publication of PV Energy Systems Inc., Casanova, Va., June 1993.

Bold initiatives in rural electrification were proposed by Wolfgang Palz in his paper "Power for the world," which is to be found in the proceedings of the International Solar Energy Society (ISES) Solar World Congress, held in Budapest in 1993.

Energy sources are regularly written about in the papers in *IEEE Transactions on Electron Devices,* while energy conversion by renewable sources is regularly addressed in *IEEE Transactions on Energy Conversion.*

WATER FROM THE AFRICAN SUN: SERGE MAKUKATIN

The most ambitious worldwide program in photovoltaics ever financed by the European Union (until a year ago, the European Community) is nearing realization. Its goal is to better the living conditions of those who live far from population centers. Both short-term and permanent improvements are envisaged.

The first task is to make available drinkable water, the next to irrigate fields under cultivation. A third aim is to supply small communities with electricity for lighting and essential refrigeration. As part of this 1200-kW (peak power) project, Siemens Solar GmbH faced special requirements involving a variety of systems and key components. The project had several important social aspects as well.

The project's beneficiaries are the members of a body set up in 1973 to fight drought in West Africa's Sahel zone, the Comité Inter-Etats de Lutte contre la Sécheresse dans le Sahel (Cilss). Present membership consists of nine countries that suffered greatly from drought in 1968 and 1974: Burkina Faso, Cape Verde, Chad, Gambia, Guinea-Bissau, Mali, Mauritania, Niger, and Senegal.

It was to help these nations that the Programme Régional Solaire (PRS) was established to make use of photovoltaic energy and to that end given 34 million ECU in funding by the then European Community as nonrepayable aid.

The program was divided into three parts, with Siemens Solar GmbH the first to be awarded a contract. The contract called for systems to be installed in five Cilss states—Gambia, Guinea-Bissau, Cape Verde, Mauritania, and Senegal. All in all, Siemens Solar will supply 550 kW, peak, of solar power. Most of this power will be used by 330 pumping systems, the largest number of high-capacity pumping systems of any part of the program.

Also to be provided are a total of 339 so-called community systems—240 for lighting, 63 for refrigeration, and 36 for recharging lead-acid and nickel-cadmium batteries. The DM 30-million contract covers parts supply, installation maintenance, and after-sales support.

Under this contract, Siemens Solar had in addition to establish a service network, train local partners, and support their activities. The execution and coordination of this all-embracing contract required the establishment of a complex project organization. For instance, Siemens was obliged to find a local partner in each of the five countries.

These partners would be responsible for maintaining contact with the local building supervisors, coordinating all essential documents (dealing with orders for installations and technical information resulting from alterations) and dispatching them to Siemens, and stocking spare parts for repairs. The importance of reliable local partners cannot be overemphasized. A lack of spare parts of technical support has wrecked many a past project.

Numerous companies volunteered for the project. The challenge was to identify those that would be most suitable as partners. In the end, there were only a few serious candidates with adequate financial backgrounds.

The partnership benefits both parties. By being involved in the greatest PV project ever carried out, the local partner can earn a good sum of money for the services rendered. Siemens Solar, in turn, can extend its activities in the African market through the aid of the local partner.

For its partner in the Sahel region, Siemens Solar chose a French company that had already been a subcontractor on African projects, successfully performing installation and maintenance services. Wherever it has a local subsidiary in the five regions, Siemens' partner takes care of any tasks there directly. Otherwise, it picks a company in the area to do so.

Future Upkeep

As the main contractor, Siemens has to guarantee all systems and to deliver spare parts for five years free of charge (although consumable materials, such as light bulbs, have a one-year-warranty). After the termination of the five-year guarantee, funds will be needed for maintenance and replacement.

Once a village has inspected and provisionally accepted the PV system, those of its inhabitants who use it pay an annual sum determined by the individual system's maintenance costs. For example, a medium-sized P4 pumping system used in Mauritania will deliver 9000 m^3 of water in a year. Dividing the total US $2000 yearly costs of maintenance ($900) and replacement ($1100) by the annual 9000 m^3 water output, results in 22 cents per cubic meter of water. This is the charge users must be able to afford to keep the system operational; it does not include money for new investments in future PV plants.

Siemens chose its own M50 module, a 50-W, peak, monocrystalline solar panel with an efficiency of 12.4 percent, as the major power component. A requirement of the EC project is that all components be of European origin.

The key components for pumping systems are the pumps themselves and their ac inverters. Standard centrifugal pumps and motors are used for high water output. These pumps are equipped with 3.5-kVA Simovert-P-Solar inverters. This inverter model—a slightly modified version of the more than 10,000 units thus far produced by Siemens—is designed for highly reliable operation even under severe conditions. It has an efficiency of up to 95 percent.

The Simovert-P's microprocessor allows it to be programmed for special site conditions. It drives common three-phase, 220-Vac pumps up to 2.2-kW rated power. There are no known competitive inverters with these features.

Centrifugal pumps with modified motors are employed for the smaller pumping systems. The Grundfos Solartronic SA1500 inverters drive the modified three phase, 65-Vac pumps. (The P1 types are for surface-pumping irrigation systems.)

Both Simovert-P and the Solatronic inverter have dry-running protection and can produce frequencies from 1 to 60 Hz. The actual output frequency at which the inverter operates depends on several factors: the input power from the solar modules, type of pump, piping, and the delivery head (defined as the height of the inlet to the cistern above the well's water level). The efficiency differs with frequency and also with pump type, piping, and the slope from the delivery head. Typical efficiencies of the combined inverter, pump, and motor are in the area of 40 percent at 50 Hz and 10–20 percent at 25 Hz.

Danger Free

The installations need to be safe in two senses. They must be as immune as possible to external events, like lightning strikes, as well as harmless for people to approach and maintain.

There are two types of lightning protection: external and internal. The external variety consists of connecting all parts (not only the modules and inverters, but also the support structures and fences) to earth ground. This is accomplished by burying a ring of copper cable 1 meter deep in the ground around the system and inside its protective fence, and connecting the ring to an earthpole, or plate, in the ground. These measures ensure that, in case of an external overvoltage, no significant difference in electric potential exists between the different components.

The internal protection keeps any overvoltage from damaging the electronic devices—the inverter and solar-cell array. It consists of varistors in the junction box and in the inverter.

Since the operating voltage of the pumping system lies in a hazardous range, measures must be taken to protect the public as well as system maintenance personnel. For this reason, the systems were designed using German industrial safety standards (DIN/VDE-Standards). In addition, each pumping system is fenced off from the public.

The EC office awarding the contract imposed strict quality requirements on components and material for this project. It wanted to ensure that systems would be rugged enough to operate in harsh environments throughout a long service life.

To find accessories and components of suitable quality at acceptable prices, extensive market research was necessary. The materials and components selected had to pass severe tests performed at one or other of the four European research laboratories that are officially accepted by the Cilss organization: Technical Inspection Authority (TUV) Rheinland, Cologne, Germany; LVT/CEA, Cadarache, France; Global Renewable Energy Services (GRES), Swindon, England; or Ciemat, Madrid, Spain. The main purpose of the tests was to ensure that the technical data indicated by the suppliers reflected the specifications required.

For instance, in the case of the inverters, the test criteria used by TUV Rheinland included performance, efficiency, temperature and climate tests, electrical safety, and the examination of packaged devices after a drop from a height of 1 meter. Further, the fabrication processes of the inverters' suppliers were audited. During these tests, some possibilities for optimizing the devices came to light and were later integrated during production.

For instance, the degree of electrical protection was increased from IP54 to IP55, the mechanical mounting of several components was optimized for greater ruggedness, and the steering program within the microcontroller was improved. A 10-g vibration test was also added to production testing.

Although this testing raised the supplier's costs, in the end it was justified by the way the components operated; all devices work perfectly in the field and are highly reliable, which is not typically the case for photovoltaic inverters.

For all PV modules, a certificate (CEC specification 502) from the Ispra Institute of Ispra, Italy, is proof of qualification for the project. No problems arose in complying with the module data for any of the PV systems during the verification of the delivered power.

For the West-African region, the basis for the system design is 6 kWh/m^2 per day (which lasts from 6 AM until 6 PM there) and a daily output of water within a range of 30 percent (-10 to $+20$ percent). All design values (300 W, peak, to 3.8 kWp, rated generator power) were checked and confirmed by the customer.

For a specific site on an average day in a recommended month, a nomograph can be used to determine the characteristics of a photovoltaic pumping system (of the solar generator, the well, and the water output). Note that when water is drawn, its level in the well will drop; this so-called draw down and the rate at which the water returns to its previous level depend on the conditions of the site. No realistic statements on the delivery capacities of the systems can be made without these data. On this basis, characteristic variations for various frequencies were determined for all centrifugal pumps used.

First Results

The first of the project's PV pumping systems were installed in early 1991. As of April of this year, 55 out of the total of 330 deep-well pumping systems had been installed and had provided approximately 270,000 hours of trouble-free operation. The total efficiency (from sun to water) of the completed systems is about 3–4 percent. The efficiency of other systems is about 2–3 percent.

All systems work without any notable problems, so that the local populations can rely on receiving the precalculated quantities of water. The yield of the systems until now amounts to approximately 1,200,000 m^3 of water and is probably unique in its volume. In several villages the water output is so great (50–60 m^3 per day) that the cisterns can be filled up within two or three hours.

Cilss has installed several test PV plants that store all key data: delivery head, water output, insolation, voltage/-current of solar generator, and water output. The goal is to measure performances and water output within a limited time period. So far, the stored data has shown that the systems' output exceeds the Cilss specifications by 10–20 percent (water output per day at a specific insolation).

As of April 1994, 30 of the 339 community systems had been installed, among them 11 cooling systems used for storing vaccine in Mauritanian first-aid hospitals and 6 lighting systems in Cape Verde schools. All the installed systems have satisfied their users and work without trouble.

Essential to this success were the contributions of the local companies. Following a period of well-structured instruction, these local companies assembled, installed, and maintained the pumping systems.

In this way, an excellent base of technical knowledge for system and component has been established within the Cilss organization. The local firms involved with the systems are now familiar with PV systems and their experience should form the basis for further successful applications in this and future projects.

Minor Problems

As with every project, there were some problems, but they were minor in nature. Some Gambian systems are in a region with frequent lightning strikes. To date, four lightning barriers at the input of the 3.5-kVA inverters have been destroyed by indirect lightning strikes. Nevertheless, the devices fulfilled their function because the inverters remained fully operational. The barriers were replaced with locally available spare parts.

The second event, and to date the last, was the failure of four float switches in boreholes, caused by corroding well casings. The problem was remedied by using an additional float switch filter.

Choice of Village

The selection of a village to be equipped with photovoltaic systems is governed by several criteria. There must be a real demand for water supply (population) and the basic infrastructure must be there (water hole, a small hospital). In addition, the villagers must be able to pay some money for replacement and maintenance. The water committees of the local villages take care of the administration of the money. Fees for the water can be individually paid if somebody takes water. Alternatively, it is also possible to pay an annual average per family.

Payment for the water is essential—it ensures the survival of the PV system. In Cape Verde, droughts have often lasted for as long as two years. When this happened,

the villagers had to pay for water brought in tanks from the capital or places with higher rainfall. It was not difficult for these people to understand that water is not free of charge.

The Podor people of Senegal, on the other hand, have traditionally taken drinking water from the river free of charge. Even though this water was often polluted and caused many diseases, it is difficult to explain to the people that they must pay for clean drinking water. So the need to pay for water must often be clarified in lengthy discussions.

PV systems within the region have completely changed the lives of the African village people. Infectious diseases caused by polluted water have greatly diminished. Pure drinking water is available at water taps, and women and children no longer have to walk 3–5 km for water. Freed from this chore, children can go to school while women can tend a kitchen garden watered by the PV system. Because of the electrification of schools and public buildings, it is now possible to educate people after the workday ends at 6 PM.

In each case, the local population must recognize the need for a village organization that is responsible for seeing that the PV installation is kept in good condition. They must also realize that they, too, have an obligation to care for the systems; there cannot always be a solution from an external source for everything.

To solve the problem of collecting money, several sociologists, who are working on the problem of forging an "identification of people with the project," have in the meantime worked out insurance concepts. For example, in Gambia—a relatively well developed country with good business opportunities—a contract being negotiated between the Department of Water Resources and an insurance company covers the possible risks of maintenance and replacement. This had the advantages of lowering costs for maintenance and replacement and of placing financial administration outside the village.

Preliminary Findings

Three years into the project, some interim conclusions can be drawn. Because of its comprehensiveness—including the high requirements set on system quality and the reliance on local firms and local after-sales service, the training of local partners, and the stocking of spare parts within each country—the project is very likely to succeed and to set an example for others like it in the future.

Photovoltaic systems have proved to be a reliable way of offering essential services to rural communities off the electric grid. But for the successful implementation and operation of such systems, well-trained partners located in the developing communities are imperative.

That the components used in the project have shown themselves to be reliable and of high quality indicates that authorized inspection institutions play an important role in the success of large-scale projects. At the same time, projects like Cilss allow manufacturers and suppliers to optimize their systems and components and prove their reliability. This in turn is beneficial for the next customers, increasing confidence in the products.

Last, but by no means least, the Cilss project clearly demonstrates the benefits of appropriate technology to people in remote areas.

To Probe Further

More information about this project can be found in the paper, "PV Energy for a Sustained and Social Development in the Sahel Region," by F. Kabore, in *The Yearbook of Renewable Energies,* a publication of Eurosolar in collaboration with UNESCO sponsored by the Commission of the European Communities, 1994, pp. 146–149.

Acknowledgment

The author thanks Mr. Cunow and Mr. Theissen, engineers from the technical office of Siemens Solar, for their valuable support.

Questions

1. What type of energy technologies are most appropriate for improving the general well-being of Third-World countries?

2. Compare the energy consumption (kW-hour per capita) for the following countries:
   a. USA vs. Bangladesh
   b. UK vs. China
   c. France vs. Nepal
   d. Germany vs. Yemen

3. List the advantages (+) and limitations (−) of various energy technologies available to the developing countries on the table below.

4. A number of developing countries are planning to construct nuclear power plants to meet growing energy needs. Due to scarce resources in the Third World, nuclear energy seems to be the best viable option. The developed countries, however, are trying to prevent the transfer of nuclear technology to the Third World. The developing countries consider this attitude to be one of technological imperialism.
   a. Do you agree that Third-World nations should be denied access to nuclear technology?
   b. What alternative sources would you recommend for Third-World countries to acquire instead of nuclear technology?

5. What is the future of solar power in developing countries? What are the obstacles to its implementation and use?

6. Discuss the status of solar power projects in the following nations:
   a. Indonesia   e. Niger
   b. Chad   f. Senegal
   c. Gambia   g. Guinea-Bissau
   d. Mali   h. Mauritania

Energy Technology	*(+)*	*(−)*
Solar		
Wind		
Hydroelectric		
Nuclear		
Biomass		

Harnessing the Wind

JAY JAYADEV

54

As the new world order takes shape, energy demand in developing countries is growing at an awe-inspiring rate. At present, China and India, with nearly 2 billion people (more than 30 percent of the world's population) consume less than one-tenth the energy of the United States (in which only about 4 percent reside). By the year 2020, economists predict that the energy consumption of a typical Chinese villager will grow by 85 percent and of his Indian counterpart by 145 percent, assuming a high-growth scenario. Even then, the per-capita energy used will be less than one-fifth the amount the average U.S. citizen consumes today.

This need for more energy could lead the developing countries to devour all cheap and available energy resources to feed the furnaces of rapid industrial growth. Such a prospect is alarming. According to projections made by the United Nations' International Energy Agency, based in Paris, these countries would by the year 2010 be producing more than half of the world's emissions of carbon dioxide, a large part of which would come from India and China alone.

Fortunately, developing countries may avoid the paths the developed world took earlier. A renewable energy technology, by now mature enough for wide-scale deployment, can contribute substantial power without spoiling the environment. The world can now feasibly reap energy from the wind.

Only fairly recently has wind power been recognized as the one renewable energy source that will be economically viable in the near future. The Electric Power Research Institute (EPRI), in Palo Alto, Calif., which represents cooperative R&D interests of the U.S. utility industry, stated in a 1992 report: "Alone among the alternative energy technologies, wind power offers utilities with good wind resources, pollution free electricity that is nearly cost-competitive with today's conventional sources."

Since then, several wind power projects from Antarctica and Mexico to India and Indonesia have shown how practical its use can be. Not only is the power supply reliable and easily maintained, but it can also be more competitive in the long run than traditional, more heavily polluting alternatives, as case studies will shortly show.

POSSIBLE PRICES

The market for wind power is alluring. A study entitled "International Wind Power Markets," conducted by Arthur D. Little in November 1994 for the American Wind Energy Association, Washington, D.C., estimated an astounding US $2 billion–$3 billion market by the year 2000. Moreover, wind-energy costs are expected to decline in the near future. A goal of groups such as the U.S. Department of Energy and EPRI is to reach $0.04/kWh by 2000, given 21-km/h winds. (See Figure 54.1.) This achievement would mean a 20 percent reduction in cost compared with today's best technology.

Until 1994, installed capacity of wind turbines in four large developing countries—India, Brazil, China, and Mexico—amounted to only 340 MW, the equivalent of the

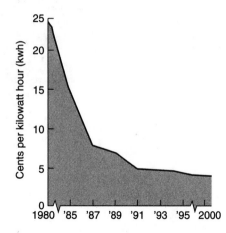

Figure 54.1
The cost of producing electricity from wind power has taken a dive in recent years because of better engineering, materials, manufacturing, and power electronics.
Courtesy of American Wind Energy Association, 1995.

output of a medium-sized conventional power plant. But today the ongoing and projected wind capacity additions for the leading developing countries are quite impressive. (See table 54.1) In addition, vigorous growth is seen for such countries as Brazil, the Philippines, Sri Lanka, and others.

Among the most ambitious plans are those of India, which has created a Ministry of Non-conventional Energy to lead activities there in solar and wind energy. The country wants to become the world's leading producer of wind energy (after the United States) within three years from now. By the end of this year, plants producing more than

Table 54.1
Projected Additions to Wind Energy Capacity, 1994–2000

Country	Capacity, MW
India	700–1200
China	350–1000
Mexico	150–300
Chile	100–200
Argentina	100–150

Source: *Arthur D. Little*, 1994

250 MW of wind power are expected to be installed, and plans for a further 900 MW are in the works. The Indian ministry justifies the expense of the plants on the grounds that the capital costs of new wind energy projects are about the same as for new thermal power plants.

Another country with aggressive plans is China, which in the 1980s began to experiment with wind farms—that is, collections of large or medium-sized wind turbines working together as a power plant. The country announced at an energy conference in Beijing last June that it had set a goal of having available 1 GW of wind power by the year 2000. Meeting this objective would increase China's present wind power capacity of 29 MW by a factor of more than 30. The Government's interest in wind power was sparked by the prediction that pollution would surge if the country's attempt to expand its generating capacity by 10 GW annually overall relied heavily on coal-fired plants.

Additional interest in wind power worldwide has picked up with a steady stream of business announcements of contracts between Western wind energy companies and developing countries. For example, Advanced Wind Turbines, Seattle, Wash., is setting up a wind farm with 220 machines, each rated at 275 kW, in India, while Enercon of Aurich, Germany, is to deploy its wind turbines next year for the first large (130-MW) project in Mexico. For a municipality in Guatemala, New World Power Corp., Waitsfield, Vt., is building a 60-MW wind power plant, and for Inner Mongolia, FloWind Capital Corp., San Rafael, Calif., has signed an agreement with Inner Mongolia Electric Power Co. in China to form an $85 million joint venture for a 110-MW wind-power plant. And a Franco-Danish group has also won a bid to construct a 50-MW wind farm in Morocco.

WIND POWER BASICS

In all wind turbines, the wind rotor is what converts the wind's kinetic energy into rotational energy. The blades of this impeller are turned by the wind, and this rotation is coupled directly or through gears to a generator of some sort.

Wind turbines come in two basic designs: vertical-axis (or "egg-beater" style) and the more common horizontal-axis, used in both small and large wind plants. (Vertical-axis machines are less proven and less efficient at lower wind speeds, but seem to be promising for large-capacity applications.)

In the case of either horizontal- or vertical-axis turbines, good-quality electricity can be generated by two methods. In the well-established approach, induction generators are connected to the grid, resulting in the turbine's being mechanically constrained to a very narrow speed range and therefore producing a constant-frequency output suitable for pumping power to the grid. That means when high velocities or gusts of wind try to speed up the rotation of the shaft, the extra torque must be absorbed by the drivetrain and the tower. This approach causes torsional stresses on the mechanical parts and also wastes wind energy (although often the pitch of the rotor blades can be changed to reduce stress during high winds).

A newer approach, made feasible by advances in power semiconductors, is to allow the turbine speed to vary and then eliminate the fluctuations in amplitude and frequency electronically. (See "Technical Options," p. 438.) By letting the generator speed up during gusts and sustained high winds, this approach both increases the amount of electricity generated and reduces the stresses on the drivetrain.

In general, such technology as high-efficiency blades and generators, along with power electronics for variable-speed drives, has contributed to reducing the cost of wind energy. Wind turbines can produce electricity at $0.05/kWh at a good wind site, with an average wind speed of greater than 5 meters per second.

But in any situation, the fickleness of the wind must be considered. According to the American Wind Energy Association, most modern wind farms operate with a capacity factor of 25–35 percent—that is, the actual power produced over time as compared to the theoretical production of the turbines operating at maximum output 100 percent of the time. (Conventional power plants typically operate at 40–80 percent capacity factors.)

HARVESTING THE BREEZE

An advantage of wind power plants is that they are modular and can be sized to adjust to many situations and accommodate future growth in big or small increments, depending on the needs of a developing country.

The versatility of wind turbines includes both their size and use. Large turbines range from 1 to 5 MW, medium machines fall between 50 kW and 1 MW, while machines of less than 50 kW are considered small. All of these turbines can be used either as utility-connected machines or as independent, stand-alone systems. (See Figure 54.2.) Especially in the latter case, when stand-alone installations are used to provide power for isolated villages, socioeconomic considerations can be as important as technical ones—as will be shown later in illustrating how villagers

in Xcalac, Mexico, updated their energy supply from wind power. Wind farms are in effect centralized power plants situated in windy areas. Because each farm individually assembles a large number of turbines, costs are often reduced.

The farms tie into a grid for their own benefit, too. Because the output of a wind turbine varies with the prevailing winds, the utility serves to absorb power as it becomes available (instead of requiring storage in batteries, for instance). A utility offering favorable buy-back rates is crucial to establishing the economic viability of wind farms.

Many of the wind farms now taking root in developing countries are connected to utilities and vary in power from a few megawatts to a few tens of megawatts. The technology they use is often identical to that of wind farms in California or Europe.

The way a wind farm is run in India, for example, illustrates some technical and economic aspects of the technology's application in developing countries. An arid plain in Gujarat is home to a joint venture supported by state and central governments but run by Vestas-Danish Wind Technology A/S, a large wind-energy company based in Lem, Denmark, and RBB Consultants, a local engineering company. The two concerns have teamed up to run a 10-MW Lamba wind farm, for which Vestas is supplying 50 horizontal-axis wind turbines churning out 220 kW each.

The Lamba project has produced not only energy but also jobs. Just as consequential as providing the turbines, Vestas has trained local engineers to install and maintain them. The project generated more than 200 new engineering and support jobs.

In 1992, two years after the farm's start-up, daily operation and maintenance were taken over by Indian companies and engineers, and the farm produced an impressive 13.4 GWh of electricity.

As in many developing countries where demand grows faster than generating capacity, networks in India are often over-loaded and subject to blackouts and burnouts. This situation adversely affects wind turbines directly connected with the grid because of reduced efficiency and capacity. Engineers are thus challenged by voltage and frequency variations unlike those in industrialized countries. Consequently, the Lamba wind farm's availability in the early years was around 90 percent. In contrast, California wind farms routinely obtain 98 percent availability levels.

Funds spent on Lamba have been modest. The cost of installing the 50 Vestas turbines was $1.7 million per megawatt. The average production cost, based on accumulated data for four years, is 7.4 cents per kilowatt-hour.

Figure 54.2
Two of the many ways in which developing countries use wind turbines are as utility-connected machines and as independent, stand-alone systems.
Courtesy of Jay Jayadev.

This amount is comparable to the life-cycle cost of conventional generators using fuels like diesel oil in India. (And in many developing countries, the wind is more to be depended on than are fuels.)

Another benefit gained from the Lamba project has been the prevention of pollution. In lauding the environmental benefits of wind power over fossil fuel power, Louis Ebler, marketing manager for Vestas, estimates that one 500-kW wind turbine at a good wind site in one year avoids the generation of 1.1 million kilograms of carbon dioxide, 82,000 kg of slag and fly ash, 9000 kg of sulfur dioxide, and 7000 kg of nitrogen oxides.

Similar findings were obtained in the United States. Paul Gipe, a well-known author on wind energy, estimates that if the 2.7 terawatt-hours of power generated annually by wind farms in California were instead generated by modern coal power plants, the atmosphere would be sullied by 2600 million kilograms of carbon dioxide, 13 million kilograms of NO_x and SO_2, 4.1 million kilograms of particulates, and 0.6 million kilogram of solid waste per year. (The estimates are based on data from the Department of Energy on pollution from modern coal power plants.)

END OF THE LINE

Developing countries are using wind turbines in tandem with the utility power supply in another way—by connecting the end of a transmission line to small wind systems to supply power for villages. Individual turbines can be built on windy spots close to the villages and the grid. So the villages' energy resource is increased without adding costly transmission lines.

Such situations are common in countries where the energy demand is growing, but generation and transmission capacity cannot keep up. (This happens in industrialized countries, too. For example, Pacific Gas and Electric Co. of California found that by reducing the loads at the end of heavily used lines, it could avoid having to construct new transmission capacity.)

Like wind farms, such utility-connected wind systems generally use an induction generator, which needs an external source of excitation to operate. The grid absorbs excess power and also serves as an excitation source and frequency reference. Reactive power correction can be made at the individual turbine site with static capacitors. Or a synchronous condenser can be connected at a strategically located distribution center. If the utility lines suffer from frequent blackouts or brownouts, the wind system owner should have a backup generator to ensure availability and meet the loads on demand.

STAND-ALONE TURBINES

To supply villages with electricity, it is often more feasible to give them an independent source of power than to invest in transmission lines to connect them to the utility grid. For the many villages that are farther than 3 km from the nearest transmission line, stand-alone wind systems are usually more economical.

Estimates by the World Bank, Washington, D.C., claim that as much as 40 percent of the world's population—some 2 billion people—live in villages that are not tied to a utility grid. When these villagers move to city areas, as they often do, the urban infrastructure is strained in many ways, not least in its ability to meet the demand for electricity.

The International Energy Agency predicts that if city populations in developing countries double in the next 15 years, energy demand will increase 45 percent, even if national income levels and population remain constant. But social and economic problems are caused by such urbanization, which might be prevented by more rural development.

Thus creating jobs at the rural level in developing countries—somewhat along the lines of village industries envisioned by leaders like Mohandas Gandhi and others—is imperative. These jobs in the modern context may be stuffing printed-circuit boards or producing textile products for export. The prerequisite is energy.

Stand-alone installations are appropriate technology for such applications. Because storage is a necessity in those isolated systems, they are technically more challenging to design and more expensive than are grid-connected generators that simply augment existing power infrastructures.

To boost overall reliability of the electricity supply, engineers can design systems that tie isolated wind machines to other types of generators. These hybrid systems often combine a wind turbine, a battery bank, and a diesel-powered backup generator.

Hybrids may electrify villages, powering lamps and small appliances, small industries, health clinics, schools, and community centers. If the loads are in tens of kilowatts, several small wind turbines, rated at 10–20 kW, and photovoltaic modules of a few kilowatts with a few hundred kilowatt-hours of batteries will suffice.

Photovoltaic panels are also employed in hybrid systems because of the complementary nature of solar and wind energy. But since wind power is lower in cost by a factor of five or so, it gets the lion's share of responsibility in hybrids. In many developing countries where biomass—for example, sugar cane husk or other crop residues—is already used to provide thermal energy, wind-biomass hybrids to furnish electricity should be attractive.

If job creation is an objective a hybrid system of 100 kW or more may be necessary. For sites with an average wind speed of just 4 meters per second, a village power system can be designed using medium-sized wind machines and diesel generators.

Coupling a wind machine to a diesel generator offers several benefits. It not only saves fuel, but is also more dependable because of its reliance on multiple power sources. Further, the hybrid arrangement allows for the expansion of loads (in contrast to the diesel operating alone) and the diesel generator lasts longer because it runs for fewer hours.

Even in a country as technologically advanced as Denmark, farmers often collectively own and operate a medium-sized wind machine of 100–250 kW. An intriguing possibility for a cluster of villages in developing countries is to share a power plant of a few hundred kilowatts.

A MEXICAN VILLAGE'S EXPERIENCE

Having a dependable power supply system can boost the demand for electricity. That experience was shared by Mexican villagers in Xcalac, a fishing village on the Yucatan peninsula that updated its power system with a hybrid wind system. Confident that they could rely on their power system, villagers bought more modern appliances and the village itself became a more attractive place to live in.

Xcalac is located about 50 km from the nearest town of Chetumal, which is where the public grid stops. The estimated cost of a power line from Chetumal to Xcalac was $3 million. But, as developers recognized, Xcalac has average wind speeds of 5.2 meters per second. So in 1991 the State of Quintana Roo decided to electrify the village with a centralized renewable hybrid-energy system, which was retrofitted to the existing diesel system.

Among the institutions participating in the construction, operation, and monitoring of the Xcalac project were Condumex, the Instituto de Investigaciones Eléctricas of

Mexico, and New Mexico State University, as well as Bergey Windpower (a maker of small wind turbines) and Sandia National Laboratories.

Xcalac's prior system had proved to be problematic, to say the least. As is the case in many Latin American villages dependent on diesel electricity, power was limited to lights, television, and radio for only 4–6 hours during the evening. Village refrigerators and ice makers were powered by propane. Fuel was not always available, with the villagers sometimes appropriating the diesel oil for the community fishing vessel, leaving the electric generator high and dry.

Xcalac's hybrid solution consists of six 10-kW Bergey wind turbines, 11.2 kW of a total of 234 Siemens photovoltaic modules, 1738 A·h of 220-V GNB 6-7C23 deep-cycle flooded lead-acid batteries, and a 40-kW inverter built by Advanced Energy Systems, and the existing 125-kW Selmec diesel generator as backup.

The hybrid system produces up to 260 kWh per day, much more than was expected. Since 80 percent of the energy is produced by wind, system availability is dominated by whether the wind blows rather than the amount of sunshine or the diesel fuel supply.

During the project's monitoring period, the total energy provided to the village in October, when there is least wind, averaged 140 kWh per day, close to the predicted performance of 150 kWh per day. In high-wind months, the total energy provided averaged about 240 kWh per day. (See Figure 54.3.)

Wind turbines had a utilization factor that varied from 68 percent in the high winds of May through September to 97 percent during the doldrums of October through December, when the batteries reached full charge less often. (Conversely, in high-wind periods, the utilization factor was lower because the batteries were often fully charged; excess wind power was therefore wasted.)

The total cost for the Xcalac system was about $450,000 (including shipping and installation)—less than one-sixth of the $3.2 million estimated by the public utility for grid extension. Xcalac proved that a total capital cost of $369,000 could result in an average of 77.3 MW-h of wind-generated energy per year, as was shown during the project's monitoring period. At reasonable interest rates, this amount would roughly translate into $0.40/kWh, a cost that is quite competitive with diesel or any other energy source for Xcalac.

By far the most serious problems raised by the Xcalac project were socio-economic concerns. Even though villagers now enjoy over 150 kWh per day of electricity, loads have grown, due in part to the return of villagers and the arrival of newcomers, both groups drawn by the availability of power.

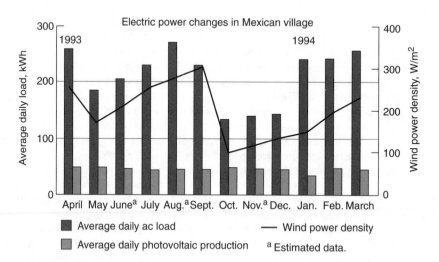

Figure 54.3
Even during the doldrums of October to December, wind power was able to supply enough energy for the entire Mexican village of Xcalac.
Courtesy of Sandia National Laboratories.

Per-capita usage has risen, too. A load survey conducted in August 1993 by the Instituto de Investigaciones Eléctricas revealed two groups of consumers. One group had minimum facilities with low demand, such as a few lights, a radio, and a television set. The other group had acquired appliances such as refrigerators, freezers, and washing machines, using 10 times more energy than the first.

This huge growth has overloaded the Xcalac system. Consequently, a tariff system has been instituted in which the first 36 kWh used per month costs the consumer $0.34/kWh and thereafter the tariff doubles to $0.68/kWh. The money raised will pay three of the local people to operate the system and collect electricity bills. Enough funds are expected to be left over to buy fuel for the diesel engine, replace the battery bank when necessary, and maintain the overall system.

The experience at Xcalac could serve as a guide to village power planners. Still, as Ron Pate, a researcher at Sandia National Laboratories, Albuquerque, N.M., who studied the Xcalac system for a year, warned: a good program does not end after installation. It must have an ongoing institutional structure so that loads are managed, resources are generated for its operation and maintenance, and responsibilities are assigned for continued operation. If these tasks are not performed, as happens in many village projects, the program will fail.

INDEPENDENT OPTIONS

In designing stand-alone systems, engineers can choose from several options. Usually the systems operate in a variable-speed mode. To generate clean constant-amplitude, constant-frequency electricity, they therefore require a rectifier-inverter combination. For dc loads, of course, the rectifier is needed.

Generally, if the average load is greater than 25 kW or so, using a single medium-sized turbine rather than several small ones is better—as long as the logistics are practical. For example, if a village requires 100 kW, and there is good access to the site, a medium-sized machine would be a good choice. Energy from these machines costs a half to a third of that from an array of small machines.

Medium-sized machines have the additional advantages of technical support from stable companies, ease of obtaining spare parts, and so on. A number of villages might even cooperate to use the power from one medium-sized turbine located at the best wind site in the area.

If a medium-sized turbine is not practical, however, a number of small machines will do the trick. Among the 20 companies making smaller turbines are Northern Power Systems, Moretown, Vt., and Bergey Windpower Co., Norman, Okla.

Small wind turbines usually have alternators with permanent magnet excitation. They produce power according to wind speed, reaching maximum power at 12 meters per second. Modern small wind machines have achieved a high level of integration and simplicity, and have proved that they can work well in the field under extreme conditions. Bergey Windpower, for example, integrates the rotor and the hub into one component and the stator and the main frame into another, thus reducing the number of parts and boosting reliability.

WELL, WELL, WELL

A widespread application of wind power is pumping water. For hundreds of years, wind-driven pumps have helped to draw water from wells. Even in the first part of the century, windmills were a common sight in the rural United States.

Recent improvements in wind-powered pumping are a good omen for the developing world. In particular, the use of variable-voltage and -frequency electric turbines without a rectifier-inverter package makes electric pumping especially attractive and affordable.

With the new technology, developed by Bergey Windpower and the U.S. Department of Agriculture, the varying generator output is applied directly to the pump, whose load characteristics match well with such generators. Better yet, electric pumping decouples the location of the pump from its power supply so that the wind turbine may be located at the best and most practical site, such as a nearby hill.

The repercussions of these advances could be enormous. In an average year, the Indian state electricity boards (which oversee state-owned utilities) connect about 500,000 new water pumps to the grid, according to a report, "The Renewables Opportunity in India," by Shering Energy Associates, Princeton, N.J., 1994. During that year, in one state alone, the waiting list for grid extensions to existing wells exceeded half a million.

If the economics can be justified, the market potential for renewables for this application could be huge. A national photovoltaics program is already targeted to occupy 10 percent of the market, and it is a safe bet that wind electricity can supply another 10 percent wherever farms are near sites having an average wind speed of at least 4 meters per second.

TECHNICAL OPTIONS

Wind rotors in small turbines spin 100-300 or so revolutions per minute. Large turbines intended for grid interconnection spin about 30–60 revolutions a minute and sometimes even more slowly.

In small systems, direct drive is preferred to geared drive for its higher reliability. Any standard, off-the-shelf generator can be used with a speed-increasing gear, but reliability is reduced. As a result, manufacturers of small turbine systems develop their own custom generators, and couple them directly to the wind rotor.

For example, in a machine developed by wind turbine manufacturer Bergey Windpower Co., Norman, Okla., a permanent-magnet ring is directly attached to the wind rotor, which envelops and rotates about the stator.

Large wind turbines connected to the grid commonly use induction machines that operate as generators running at higher than their synchronous speeds. The same machines are also used to start the wind turbine by running as induction motors, drawing power for this function from the grid.

Even though wind velocity is fickle, any power output for grid-connected machines needs to be of high quality. A grid-connected wind turbine can operate in a fixed- or variable-speed mode. In either case, however, a controlled-frequency output is required.

For fixed-speed systems that can be hooked up to a grid, maintaining a constant frequency is no problem. Such systems typically employ induction or synchronous machines connected directly to the grid. If induction machines are used, as is generally the case in the wind industry today, they are usually high-efficiency, low-slip machines. In fact, self-excitation of induction machines is possible in isolated systems, but it has not found wide application.

Variable-speed wind turbines have benefited from recent progress in power semiconductors—power MOSFETs and insulated-gate bipolar transistors, for example. These devices enable the turbines to deliver high-quality electricity. As a variable-speed system can absorb the torque transients better, it has the potential for reduced cost and increased reliability.

Currently, two generation schemes are preferred for variable-speed wind systems. One employs the popular induction motor speed control, using power electronics to operate the induction machine in the generating mode by varying voltage and frequency.

The other scheme uses a dc-excited alternator, whose varying output is rectified and then inverted to produce stable ac suitable for grid connection.

In medium-sized and large wind turbines, the controversy over running a turbine at constant speed or at variable speed persists. Nearly constant-speed systems are widely used because of their simplicity and the low cost of induction generators. But proponents of variable-speed systems claim that when the wind rotor speed is allowed to vary with the wind, the turbine can be operated at peak efficiency.

Another benefit of variable speed is that the mechanical stresses caused in structural elements by gusts and varying wind speed are diminished by letting the rotor follow the wind. The necessary power electronics, however, can be expensive—up to four or five times the cost of the generator.

—J.J.

IRRIGATION IN INDONESIA

Most of the farms in eastern Indonesia are so small (approximately 20,000 m^2) that 1.5-kW kerosene-fueled pumps have been used for water pumping. These pumps are inexpensive and readily available, but they are costly to operate and last less than five years.

To overcome this problem, Indonesia's Ministry of Public Works has installed a 1.5-kW wind-electric water pumping system supplied by Bergey Windpower at its demonstration farm in Oesao, 30 km east of Kupang on Timor Island. This proof-of-concept system, installed in October 1992, was supported by the Japanese Overseas Economic Cooperation Fund and the U.S. Agency for International Development.

Oesao irrigation calls for 150 m^3 of water per day pumped from a depth of 4–6 meters. On the basis of that requirement and available wind data, a 1.1-kW multi-stage, surface-mounted centrifugal pump was chosen, along with the 1.5-kW wind-electric system.

Performance predicated on scaled wind data yielded an average daily water delivery of 60–350 m^3, depending on the time of year. This variation was fully acceptable because the strongest winds blow (and the most water flows) during the dry season.

The wind resource in Timor has proven to be better than the initial data indicated, and the system has had nearly 100 percent availability since installation. Average energy production has been some 130–180 m^3 per day. So far, windless periods have not presented a big problem at this site. The soil holds enough water not to require the pumps to operate during calm periods. So no energy storage system is required.

Advantages of the wind-electric water-pumping system include its being nearly automatic, with less maintenance and lower replacement costs than the kerosene pumping systems needed. And, of course, it requires no fuel. While kerosene pumps must be replaced every two to four years, wind-electric systems require only about $25 worth of scheduled maintenance each year and have a design life of 30 years.

The equipment cost for the Desao was $7000. This amount is roughly six times the cost of a kerosene system designed to deliver the same amount of water. But these initial costs are more than offset by the reduced costs for fuel, operations, and maintenance. A value calculation comparing the two systems shows that wind-electric water pumping is about 50 percent less expensive than the kerosene systems over a life of 30 years.

FUTURE MANUFACTURERS?

In their recent book, *Power Surge*, Christopher Flavin and Nicholas Lenssen of the WorldWatch Institute, Washington, D.C., construct a scenario in which renewable energy systems play a major role in an energy revolution involving both the developed and developing countries. In this prediction, developing countries are seen as taking the lead in the utilization of renewables and even emerging as suppliers of renewable energy components.

Whether or not this comes true, at least part of the scenario may be unfolding. Already, a British company is setting up a joint venture with an Indian partner to develop and manufacture turbine blades in India.

On the horizon, wind power costs will further decline, and business is expected to accelerate because of technical advances in wind machines, cost-cutting improvements in manufacturing techniques, and environmental concerns. Moreover, wind power technology is straightforward—unlike solar cells, for example. It does not involve sophisticated processing of high-purity materials. Because of that advantage, developing countries, with their relatively cheap labor, might turn to building their own manufacturing capability in the technology.

Questions

1. List the benefits gained from the Lamba project.
2. Describe the advantages of the wind–electric system used in eastern Indonesia.
3. What benefits does the Xcalac hybrid system offer to the inhabitants of villages in Mexico?
4. Discuss the limitations of the wind-power systems.

55

Application of Telecommunications Technologies in Distance Learning

AHMED S. KHAN

ABSTRACT

Recent advances in telecommunications technologies (computer networks, satellite communications, fiber-optic systems, the Internet, and so forth) have transformed the modes of learning and teaching. The dissemination of knowledge is no longer confined to constraints of physical premises, with an instructor and a textbook, and it is no longer the only educational resource. The use of telecommunication technologies in distance learning overcomes the barriers of distance and time, and allows students in developed as well as in developing countries to learn in a synchronous or asynchronous manner. This paper presents an overview of various telecommunications technologies that are used in distance education. The discussion includes evolution of distance education, synchronous and asynchronous learning, and characteristics of broadcast television, instructional television fixed service (ITFS), microwave systems, satellite systems, direct broadcast satellite (DBS), cable systems, private fiber, and the Internet.

INTRODUCTION

Distance education or learning is a discipline that links people with information through a variety of technologies.[1] Distance learning has been practiced for over 100 years, primarily in the form of correspondence courses. These print-based courses solved the problem of geographic dispersal of students for specialized courses of instruction. In the late 1960s and early 1970s, emerging technologies afforded the development of a new generation of distance learning, aided by open universities, which combined television, radio, and telephone with print.

Today, advances in telecommunications technologies are again changing the face of distance learning. With the explosion of Internet tools over the last few years, distance learning has become more accessible to people whether they live in urban or rural areas. In this time of increasing technological advances, it is no surprise that college enrollment is on the rise. The increasing enrollment, coupled with yearly budget cut requests, opens the door for distance learning.

With the advent of distance-learning technologies, the dissemination of knowledge is no longer confined to the constraints of physical premises. Distance-learning technologies overcome the barrier of distance to allow face-to-face communication between students and teachers from different locations. With rapid technological change in developed countries, educational institutions are challenged with providing increased opportunities without increased budgets. In developing countries, the policy-makers face a dilemma: how to provide educational opportunities to an increased population while considering lack of resources. Distance education offers a solution to the problems of educators in developed as well as developing countries. In developed countries, there are three major motivations for an educational institution to incorporate distance learning in its program offerings:

- to compensate for the lack of specialist courses at its own institutions

- to supplement an existing curriculum to make it more enriched

- to compete with other institutions which offer distance-learning courses via the Internet

For developing countries, distance education offers a unique approach to promote literacy and enhance higher education in a cost-effective way.

MODES OF DISTANCE LEARNING

Distance learning can be employed in a synchronous as well as an asynchronous mode. In a synchronous mode, the student and teacher interact in real time, whereas in an asynchronous mode, the student learns at a convenient time and place.

Advances in computer and communication technologies have greatly contributed to asynchronous access. Asynchronous learning is time- and place-independent; learning takes place at the convenience and pace of the learner. A student can contact a college or teacher via e-mail or engage in discussion with a group through a conferencing system or bulletin board. A learner can participate interactively in a team project with other students that requires problem analysis, discussion, spreadsheet analysis, or report preparation through modern commercial groupware packages. Similarly, lectures can be transmitted through computers, videotape, or CD-ROM. Learning becomes a distributed activity, and participants in these distributed classes access resources and interact asynchronously, more or less at their own convenience.[2]

Asynchronous learning has been categorized into three different levels. They are on-campus, near campus, and far from campus. The on-campus level meets in the traditional classroom, but through computer labs students participate in asynchronous communication through listservs, bulletin boards, and the World Wide Web (WWW). The near campus level (50–60 miles from campus) requires students to meet on campus occasionally for tests, teacher consultation, or labs, but use the Internet or another electronic medium for lectures, class information, and communication. The far from campus level is the "true" asynchronous delivery. This is where the student never sets foot on the campus, and the entire course is delivered through tools such as the Internet, videos, or CD-ROMs. All three levels meet the needs of different learners. One of the benefits of asynchronous learning is that it meets the needs of many "non-traditional" students who would normally not have access to an education due to distance or time constraint.[3]

From Britain to Thailand and Japan to South Africa, distance learning is an important part of national strategies to educate large numbers of people rapidly and efficiently. In the United States, educators are finding distance learning effective not only for outreach to new populations, but also as an important medium for new instructional models. Distance learning, used as a term associated with new technologies offering a full-fledged alternative to classroom education, got its biggest boost internationally with the founding of the British Open University (BOU) in 1969. BOU gained rapid visibility and recognition by broadcasting its video course components weekly throughout the United Kingdom on the BBC network.[4]

Table 55.1 lists the enrollment for distance learners seeking university education in various developed and developing countries. The addition of distance learners, who receive programming in elementary, secondary, training, and noncredit areas would almost quadruple these numbers.[5]

Many agree that distance learning is the fastest growing instructional pattern in the world. Technologies of delivery, particularly those related to telecommunications, have had a "greening" effect on the distance-learning enterprise. The potential to solve access, cost, time, place, and interactivity considerations that have plagued education since the beginning of time has never been greater.[6]

TELECOMMUNICATIONS TECHNOLOGIES

Telecommunications technologies provide opportunities for basic education as well as advanced education for those disadvantaged by time, distance, physical disability, and resources. Table 55.2 lists the evolution of telecommunication technologies. Table 55.3 lists the breakdown of voice, data, and video technologies used in distance education.[7]

Distance learning blends technological infrastructure and learning experiences. The experiences and applications that can be provided depend on the appropriate infrastructure. Current technologies have favored applications where a central source controls information flow. Emerging networked technologies allow for both centralization and decentralization. While centralized and decentralized approaches each have advantages and disadvantages, networked computer technologies and the

Table 55.1
Major Open Universities in Developed and Developing Countries

Institution	Country	Year Established	Enrollment
University of South Africa	South Africa	1951	50,000
Open University	United Kingdom	1969	50,000
Universidad Nacional	Spain	1972	83,000
Fernuniversitat	Germany	1974	37,000
Open University of Israel	Israel	1974	12,000
Allama Iqbal Open University	Pakistan	1974	150,000
Athabasca University	Canada	1975	10,000
Universidad Nacional Abierta	Venezuela	1977	29,000
Universidad Estatal a Distancia	Costa Rica	1977	11,000
Sukhothai Thammathirat OU	Thailand	1978	200,000
Central Radio and TV University	China	1978	1,000,000
Open University of Sri Lanka	Sri Lanka	1981	18,000
Open Universiteit	Netherlands	1981	33,000
Andrha Pradesh Open University	India	1981	41,000
Korean Air and Correspondence University	South Korea	1982	300,000
University of the Air of Japan	Japan	1983	22,000
Universitas Terbuka	Indonesia	1984	70,000
Indira Ghandi Open University	India	1986	30,000
National Open University of Taiwan	Taiwan	1986	48,000
Al-Quds Open University	Jordan	1986	not available
Universidade Aberta	Portugal	1988	3,800
Open University of Bangladesh	Bangladesh	1992	not available
Open University of Poland	Poland	Proposed	
Open University of France	France	Proposed	

distributed-learning applications they enable have not only practical benefits for information management but also attributes that are more congruent with newer educational paradigms based on cognitive approaches to learning.[8]

Broadcast Television

Broadcast TV involves the transmission of video and audio over standard VHF and UHF channels to reach a large number of sites in a limited geographic area (e.g., campus, metropolitan, county, multi-county, and so forth). Most educational programming broadcast over television does not allow real-time interaction with the television instructor but interactively can be designed into live or recorded telecourses using the telephone, computer networks, and Internet tools. This mode of transmission lacks security and confidentiality.

Instructional Television Fixed Service (ITFS)

ITFS refers to a band of microwave frequencies originally set aside by the Federal Communications Commission (FCC) in 1963 exclusively for the transmission of educational and cultural programming. ITFS is similar to broadcast television but is used in a more limited geographic area for simplex point-to-multi-point transmission. ITFS uses omni-directional microwave signals in the 2.5-GHz band to transmit standard 6-MHz video signals to remote locations. An ITFS network can serve as a stand-alone distance education-delivery system, transmitting locally originated programming directly to local schools or cable companies for redistribution through their network. It offers limited or no interaction and a moderate level of security and confidentiality.

Table 55.2
Evolution of Telecommunication Technologies

Year	Technological Development
1832	Telegraph
1875	Telephone
1895	Radio
1945	Audiotape
1953	Broadcast Television
1960	Videotape
1960	Audio Teleconferencing
1965	Cable Television
1975	Computer Assisted Instruction
1980	Audiographic teleconferencing
1980	Satellite Delivery
1980	Facsimile
1980	Videoconferencing
1984	Videodisc
1985	CD-ROM Compact Disc
1988	Compressed Video
1989	Multimedia
1990s	Lightwave systems, LANs, HDTV, Internet

Table 55.3
Telecommunication Technologies
in Distance Learning

	Technology
Voice	Telephone
	Radio
	Short-wave
	AM
	FM
	Audiotapes
Data	LANs
	WANs
	Internet
	Computer-assisted instructions (CAI)
	Computer-mediated education (CME)
	Computer-managed instruction (CMI)
Video	Pre-produced videotapes
	Digital video disc (DVD)
	Videoconferencing
	Broadcast television
	ITFS
	Satellite System
	DBS
	Internet

Microwave Systems

Terrestrial microwave systems require a line-of-sight transmission between the transmitter and the receiver site. Microwave systems allow simplex or half duplex/duplex point-to-point audio, data, and video transmission. There are two types of point-to-point microwave systems: short haul and long haul. Short-haul systems typically have a range of 5 to 15 miles, suitable for local communications between two schools or campuses. Long-haul systems typically have a range of up to 30 miles between repeaters, depending on transmitter power, terrain, dish size, and receiver sensitivity. Microwave systems offer a high level of interaction, security, and confidentiality.

Satellite Communications

Satellite communication involves the transmission of a broadcast signal from an earth station via an uplink signal to a geosynchronous satellite, where the signal is processed by the transponder and sent, via a downlink signal, to a receiving dish antenna. Satellite communication is used to cover a large number of sites over a wide geographic area (e.g., statewide, nationwide, and continent-wide) for simplex point-to-multi-point audio and video transmission. Analog satellite systems offer low levels of security and confidentiality, and digital

systems offer high levels of security and confidentiality. Satellite systems offer limited or no interaction.

Direct Broadcast Satellite (DBS)

These high-powered satellites transmit programming directly to the general public. The received dish antennas used in DBS systems are very small (<1 meter). DBS systems allow programmers to beam educational programming directly to homebound students, providing an alternative to over-the-air broadcast or cable television. DBS technology employs data-compression technologies that enhance the efficiency of video channels.

Televised education offers the following advantages:[9]

• Televised courses can actually enhance instruction by allowing instructors to present material in novel ways and thus to increase interest in it.

• Televised courses provide access to education for those who might not otherwise have it.

• Televised courses can help the instructor become a better teacher.

- Televised courses are often better organized and more highly developed than traditional courses.
- Televised courses offer an opportunity for faculty members to learn from their students as well as teach them.

Satellite communications is one of the most cost-effective modes to promote literacy and enhance higher education in developing countries. Table 55.4 lists the typical cost for leasing a video channel for satellites that provides large footprints in Asia and Africa.

Cable Systems

Cable-television systems use coaxial and fiber-optic cable to distribute video channels to local subscribers. Programming is received from local broadcast channels and national programming services at the cable "head end" and is sent out over the cable in a tree configuration. A cable head end can receive many types of signals, such as satellite or microwave transmission, which can then be retransmitted to schools over the normal cable system.

Cable-television systems are primarily one-way (simplex) broadcast (point-to-multipoint) type transmission systems. Many systems also have a limited number of reverse channels, providing some measure of two-way interaction. There is a high-level inter-system security and confidentiality.

Private Fiber

Optical fiber is used for full-duplex point-to-point audio and video transmission. It allows a high degree of interaction and offers a high level of security and confidentiality. It also has the highest information-carrying capacity. The bandwidth for mono-mode step index fiber is 10–100 Gbps; multimode step index fiber is around 200 Mbps.

Public Telephone Service

Public telephone service is used over a limited to wide geographic area (local, regional, national, and international) for full-duplex point-to-point or point-to-multipoint audio transmission. It is used in conjunction with other technologies (television, satellite, etc.) to provide a feedback channel for students at remote sites to interact with the instructor and other sites. Table 55.5 compares the characteristics of distance-learning technologies.

The Internet

The Internet offers full-duplex point-to-point and point-to-multipoint audio, video, and data transmission over a wide geographic area (regional, national, and international). It allows a high degree of interaction. Generally, it has a low level of security and confidentiality but, with the use of data encryption, it has a high level of security and confidentiality.

With a computer, minimal software, and an Internet connection, people anywhere in the world can access on-line sites and programs. In addition, these programs can be accessed almost instantaneously through a user-friendly "point and click" interface, using almost any type of computer without producing and distributing printed materials, floppy disks, or CD-ROMs and with no training delivery cost. Furthermore, training can be delivered to a potentially unlimited audience, updates can be easily made on-line, and programs can link to a vast collection of other on-line resources.[10]

Although the Internet can be accessed worldwide, current access for many people is still limited. Even when access is available, bandwidth for accessing the Internet is frequently low. Low bandwidth severely limits capabilities such as on-line interactive multimedia training. Other disadvantages are that students need a moderate degree of computer literacy; sensitive/classified training requires

Table 55.4

Typical Cost for Leasing a Video Channel for Satellites Providing Large Footprints in Asia and Africa

Satellite	Footprint Coverage Area	Typical Hourly Cost for Leasing a Video Channel
Panamsat	South Asia	$1850
TDRS-5	South Asia	$1680
Chinasat 1	Southeast Asia	$990
Asiasat 2	Southeast Asia	$990
Measat	Southeast Asia	$990
Palapa-B2	South Asia	$885
Intelsat-k	Western Africa	$2000
GESTAR-4	Western Africa	$2000
Inmarsat-3	Western Africa	$2000
Intelsat	South Africa	$1000
Orion 2	South Africa	$1000
Panamsat PAS3	South Africa	$1000

Table 55.5
Comparison of Distance-Learning Technologies

Technology	Characteristics
Broadcast Television	Simplex mode of transmission One site to multi-site video and audio transmission (point-to-multipoint transmission) Limited or no interaction Public system Lack of security or confidentiality
Instructional Television Fixed Site (ITFS)	Similar to broadcast TV Semi-public system Moderate level of security and confidentiality
Broadband Cable	Similar to broadcast TV Public and private systems High degree of interaction possible High level of inter-system security and confidentiality
Microwave	Point-to-point audio and video transmission over limited area (one site to another) FDX mode of transmission High level of interaction Private system High level of security and confidentiality
Satellite	Simplex mode of transmission Point-to-multipoint audio and video transmission over wide area Limited or no interaction Private or public system Low level of security and confidentiality for older analog systems; higher level of security and confidentiality for digital systems
Private Fiber	Point-to-multipoint transmission over limited area FDX audio/video transmission High degree of interaction possible Private system High level of security and confidentiality
Public Switched Digital Service	Point-to-point and point-to-multipoint audio and video transmission over short and long distances Moderate to high degree of interaction possible Public system High level of security and confidentiality

continued

Table 55.5
Comparison of Distance-Learning Technologies *(Continued)*

Technology	Characteristics
Public Telephone Service	Point-to-point and point-to-multipoint audio transmission over short and long distances. Used in conjunction with satellite and other simplex technologies to provide a way for remote site to interact with instructor and other sites
Public Packet Network Services	Point-to-point SPX transmission Used in conjunction with other technologies to provide a way for students to interact with the instructor

Source: http://www.oit.itd.umich.edu/reports/DistanceLearn/sect3.html

additional security measures; and the high level of current Internet "hype" makes it difficult to determine what is practical for the near future.[11]

In addition to these technologies, a number of high-speed non-switched and switched lines could be incorporated in wide-area networking strategies in distance learning. Table 55.6 lists various switched and non-switched services provided by U.S. carriers.

A recent report entitled "Distance Education in Higher Education Institutions" issued by the National Center for Education Statistics highlights the following facts:[12]

- By fall 1998, 90 percent of all institutions with 10,000 or more students and 85 percent of those with enrollments of 3,000 to 10,000 expect to offer at least some distance education courses. Among the smallest institutions (those with fewer than 3,000 students), only 44 percent plan to offer distance education courses.

- More than 750,000 students were enrolled in distance education courses in 1994–95. That year, some 3,430 students received degrees exclusively through distance education.

- More students enroll in distance education courses through public two-year institutions than through any other type of institutions.

In terms of the type of technology used to deliver courses, 57 percent of the institutions offering distance education courses in 1995 used two-way interactive video, and 52 percent used one-way prerecorded video (institutions frequently used more than one type of distance-learning tech-

nology). Twenty-four percent used two-way audio and one-way video, 14 percent used two-way on-line interactions, 11 percent used two-way audio, 10 percent used one-way audio, and 9 percent used one-way live way.

A key point to note, however, is that because of the many logistical factors involved, distance education

Table 55.6
High-Speed Wide-Area Networks

Non-switched (Leased)	
Analog	4.8–19.2 kbps
Digital Data Service (DDS)	2.4–56 kbps
T-1	1.54 Mbps
T-3	44.736 Mbps
Frame Relay	1.54 Mbps–44.736 Mbps
Synchronous Optical Network (SONET)	51.84 Mbps–2.488 Gbps

Switched	
Dial-up/modem	1.2–28 kbps
X.25 packet switching	2.4–56 kbps
Integrated Services Digital Network (ISDN)	64 kbps–1.544 Mbps
Frame Relay	1.54 Mbps–44.736 Mbps
Switched multimegabit data service (SMDS)	1.54 Mbps, 44.736 Mbps
Asynchronous Transfer Mode (ATM)	25 Mbps–155 Mbps
B-ISDN (broadband ISDN)	155 Mbps, 600 Mbps

courses typically require considerable investments of money and time. Distance education courses can be cost-effective when a large number of students take the courses over the long run. It is important to realize that such courses are costly to produce and deliver. The costs rise even more when the courses are presented with advanced one-way or two-way real-time video.[13]

The incorporation of new telecommunications technologies in distance education has abolished the barriers of location and time. However, the success of distance education in higher education depends on:[14]

- the availability of high-quality, full-motion video via the Internet

- the electronic accessibility at a reasonable cost of content currently available only in print format

- development and documentation of effective teaching/learning processes that rely on advanced technology

- the ability of distance learning to comply with an accreditation process for engineering education that is outcome-based

Conclusion

Distance education has come far since its humble beginnings as correspondence courses conducted by mail. To excel in the 21st century, higher education must undergo a paradigm shift. It must be transformed from an environment and culture that defines learning as a classroom process shaped by brick-and-mortar facilities and faculty-centered activities to an environment defined by "learner-centered" processes and shaped by telecommunications networks with universal access to subject content material, learner support services, and technology-literate resource personnel.[15] The use of telecommunication technologies in distance learning will promote literacy and enhance higher education. Thus, distance learning will narrow the techno-economic gap between the developed and developing world of the 21st century.

Notes

1 *www.fsu.edu/~lis/distance/brochure·html#program*
2 Mayadas, F. and P. Alfred (1996) *Alfred P. Sloan Foundation Home Page.* (Online). Available at *www.sloan.org/Education/ALN.new.htm.*

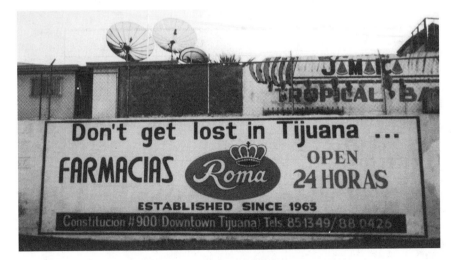

Satellite dish antennas are popping up on rooftops everywhere in developing countries. However, satellite broadcasts are used purely for entertainment purposes. The educational use of satellite technology is very limited. The use of satellite communications coupled with computer networks is not only a very cost-effective delivery mode to educate millions, but also has the potential to revolutionize the educational structure in developing countries in order to narrow the technoeconomic gap that exists between the First and the Third Worlds. The appropriate use of telecommunications technology is the key to solving problems of illiteracy, poverty, and disease in the developing world. Photo coutesy of Ahmed S. Khan

3 *Linking for Learning: A New Course for Education,* Office of Technology Assessment (OTA), U.S. Congress, Washington, D.C, 1989.

4 Granger, D., "Open Universities: Closing the Distance to Learning, Change," *The Magazine of Higher Learning,* 22 (4), pp. 42–50.

5 Brown, B., and Y. Brown, "Distance Education Around the World," *Distance Education Strategies and Tools,* edited by Barry Willis, Educational Technology Publications, NJ, 1994.

6 IBID.

7 Willis, B., *Distance Education Strategies and Tools,* Educational Technology Publications, Englewood Cliffs, NJ, 1994.

8 Locatis, C. and M. Weisberg, "Distributed Learning and the Internet," *Contemporary Education,* vol. 68, no. 2, Winter 1997.

9 Richard, Larry G., "Lights, Camera, Teach," *ASEE Prism,* February 1997, p. 26.

10 Collis, B., *Tele-Learning in a Digital World: The Future of the Distance Learning,* International Thompson, London, 1996.

11 IBID.

12 *ASEE Prism,* February 1998.

13 Martin, B., P. Moskal, N. Foshee, and L. Morse, "So You Want to Develop a Distance Education Course?" *ASEE Prism,* February 1997, p. 18.

14 *ASEE Prism,* February 1997, p. 4.

15 Dubols, Jacques R., "Going the Distance, A National Distance Learning Initiative," *Adult Learning,* September/October 1996.

Questions

1. Define the following terms:
   a. Distance learning
   b. Asynchronous learning
   c. Open university
   d. DBS
   e. Synchronous learning

2. What telecommunications technologies could be used to educate millions of illiterate children and adults in the developing countries?

3. Compare the pros (+) and cons (−) of distance education.

Pros (+)	Cons (−)

MATTERS OF SCALE

The Plight of the Displaced

Number of people in the past decade displaced by infrastructure projects, such as road and dam construction	80 to 90 million
Number of people in the past decade left homeless by natural disasters including floods, earthquakes, hurricanes and landslides (based on an annual average over 25 years)	50 million
Number of people in 1981 who were landless or near-landless	938 million
Number of people expected to be landless or near-landless in 2000	1.24 billion
Number of people per square mile in the five boroughs of New York City	23,700
Number of people per square mile in Jakarta, Indonesia	130,000
Number of people per square mile in Lagos, Nigeria	143,000
Number of international refugees in the early 1960s	1 million
in the mid-1970s	3 million
in 1995	27 million
Number of refugees displaced within the borders of their own countries, in 1985	9.5 million
in 1995	20 million
Number of people currently living in coastal areas vulnerable to flooding from storm surges	46 million
Number of people living in vulnerable areas if global warming produces a 50-centimeter rise in sea level	92 million
Number of people living in vulnerable areas if global warming produces a 1-meter rise in sea level	118 million

Reprinted with permission from Worldwatch Institute, Washington, D.C. (World Watch Jan/Feb '96)

MATTERS OF SCALE

Human Health and the Future

Number of people now living within the reach of malaria-transmitting mosquitoes (potential transmission zone), worldwide	2.5 billion
Number of people who will live in the transmission zone by the latter half of the 21st century, after projected expansion of the transmission zone by global warming	4.8 billion
Average number of heat-related deaths in Atlanta each summer	78
Average number projected by 2050, assuming no change in the city's population size or age profile, but with projected global warming	293
Predicted decline in production of cereal grains (rice, corn, wheat, etc.) as a result of climate change (climate effects only) by 2060, in the developed countries in the developing countries	23.9 percent 16.3 percent
Additional decline in grain production from physiological effects of CO_2, in developed countries in the developing countries	3.6 percent 10.9 percent
Number of people at risk of hunger in 2060, without global warming	640 million
Number at risk with projected warming	680 to 940 million
Life expectancy in the most developed countries in 2000	79
Life expectancy in the least developed countries in 2000	42
Share of worldwide AIDS/HIV cases that are in developing countries	90 percent
Share of AIDS stories with non-U.S. settings in the U.S. media	4 percent

Reprinted with permission from the Worldwatch Institute, Washington, D.C. (World Watch September/October 1996)

WHO OWNS INDIGENOUS PEOPLES' DNA?

Aboriginal leaders have long struggled to control native lands. Now some have begun to worry that they may have to fight for control of native genes.

In August 1993, Pat Mooney, the President of Rural Advancement Foundation International (RAFI), a non-profit concerned with third-world agriculture, discovered that the U.S. government was trying to patent a cell line derived from a 26-year-old Guaymi woman. The Guaymi people are native to western Panama. The cell line, a type of culture that can be maintained indefinitely, came from a blood sample obtained by a researcher from the U.S. National Institutes of Health in 1990. The application claimed that the cell line might prove useful for the treatment of the Human T-lymphotropic virus, or HTLV, which is associated with a form of leukemia and a degenerative nerve disease.

RAFI notified Isidro Acosta, President of the Guaymi General Congress, who demanded that the United States withdraw its claim and repatriate the cell line. Acosta also appealed to the General Agreement on Tariffs and Trade, and to an intergovernmental meeting on the Rio Biodiversity Convention. But GATT does not forbid the patenting of human material, and Acosta's case before the Biodiversity Convention fared no better. The convention does provide for sovereign rights over genetic resources, but the meeting did not rule on whether the Guaymi cell line came within its jurisdiction. As a growing number of nongovernmental organizations voiced their disapproval, however, the United States dropped its patent claim last November.

The story might have ended there had not a European researcher uncovered two similar claims in January of this year. Miges Baumann, an official at Swissaid, a Swiss NGO that supports rural initiatives in developing countries, discovered that the U.S. government had filed applications on a cell line derived from the Hagahai people of Papua New Guinea, and another from the Solomon Islanders. These lines might also prove useful for treating HTLV. Baumann's discovery came as a shock to the governments concerned but despite their protests, the U.S. has refused to withdraw the applications. In a letter dated March 3, 1994, Ron Brown, the U.S. Secretary of Commerce, explained the U.S. position to a Solomon Island official. "Under our laws, as well as those of many other countries," Brown wrote, "subject matter relating to human cells is patentable and there is no provision for considerations relating to the source of the cells that may be the subject of a patent application."

Patenting indigenous peoples' genes invites an obvious comparison with the patenting of the developing world's other biological resources, and native leaders have tended to take a dim view of the entire trend. "I never imagined people would patent plants and animals. It's fundamentally immoral, contrary to the Guaymi view of nature," said Acosta, who considers the patenting of human material a violation of "our deepest sense of morality."

But the rapid growth of biotechnology is driving a boom in human patents that may prove difficult to resist. The patenters are looking for genes that could be used to produce substances with commercial potential, usually for treating a disease. To patent a "product of nature," patent laws generally require some degree of human alteration. But in the United States, the simple act of isolating a DNA sequence removes it from nature, as far as the law is concerned.

The accessibility of the patent has fueled a growing commercial interest in the field. Companies that prospect in the human genome use a highly automated process called sequencing to decode bits of DNA from large numbers of samples. One company, Human Genome Sciences, of Rockville, Maryland, is reported to have sequenced over 200,000 chunks of DNA thus far. Patent claims may follow if the sequences obtained look novel—and in some cases, even if they don't. In one of the more spectacular instances of "driftnet patenting," as critics call the practice, Incyte Pharmaceuticals, of Palo Alto, California, filed claims on 40,000 sequences.

Observers say it's a good bet that other applications on indigenous DNA have already been filed. "I'm not aware of any others," says Hope Shand, RAFI's Research Director, "but it would surprise me if there weren't any more of them."

Reprinted with permission from Worldwatch Institute, Washington, D.C. (World Watch·November/December 1994)

Conclusion

No great improvement in the lot of mankind are possible until a great change takes place in fundamental constitution of their modes of thought.

JOHN STUART MILL, PHILOSOPHER

The world may have become a global village as a result of technological advancements, but billions of people in the developing countries will continue to live with poverty, disease, and illiteracy. Changes in the Third World will occur only when both the intrinsic and extrinsic factors inhibiting its development are addressed. The effects of extrinsic factors (e.g. political and economic instability caused by international financial institutions, and economic exploitation of resources by the multinational companies) can be rectified only when a great change takes place in the modes of thought of the policy makers of the developed world. These leaders must begin to believe that all people are created equal, no one is superior to another and treating people with equality and justice is the key to solving man-made economic, political and environmental dilemmas that the world faces today.

And to address the intrinsic factors (e.g. illiteracy, poverty, social injustice, corruption, lack of resources, population pressures, and power-hungry political and military elite) the key is education. Education is a great equalizer for changing the socio-economic conditions. It could provide solutions to many of the problems of developing countries and set them free from economic bondage, autocratic rule, poverty and disease. The developing nations should give a higher priority to educating their people. By incorporating innovative telecommunications technologies, the developing countries could increase their literacy rates and therefore produce a humanistic techno-elite that could then promote social justice, economic growth, and a sustainable environment, and thus narrow the technoeconomic gap with the developed countries.

Throughout this book, a spectrum of issues related to a wide array of topics (e.g. energy, ecology, population, war and technology, social responsibility, health and technology, and the technology and the Third World) has been presented. The next and final part discusses the state of technologies of the future.

Internet Exercise

1. Visit NASA's Multimedia Gallery at http://www.nasa.gov. (The site contains a large collection of photos of earth, taken from space by various space shuttle missions, depicting the impact of various human interactions, such as deforestation, desertification, pollution, oil well fires, soil erosion, mining, urbanization, irrigation, and oil drilling.) Complete the following table by listing the impact of human interaction in the developed and developing countries listed in the left-hand column.

Country	Impact of Human Interaction
Argentina	
Australia	
Bangladesh	
Brazil	
Bolivia	
Cameroon	
Canada	
China	
Ethiopia	
Egypt	
India	
Indonesia	
Japan	
Kuwait	
Libya	
Madagascar	
Malaysia	
Mexico	
Nepal	
Panama	
Philippines	
Sudan	
Tajikistan	
Tanzania	
Turkey	
USA	
Venezuela	
Vietnam	

2. The Chinese government is building an enormous dam—The Three Gorges Dam—on the Yanatze River to control flooding and to transform its hydropower into electric power. The project is expected to be completed in 2009 to have a power-generating capacity of 18,200 megawatts. This enormous capacity will enable China to move into the 21st century with a hydropower bang.

    Use any of the Internet search engines (e.g., Alta Vista, Yahoo, Infoseek, etc.) to research the following questions:

    a. How many people will be displaced due to The Three Gorges Dam project?

    b. How many towns and villages will be resettled?

    c. What are the environmental costs of this project?

    d. What are the benefits and the drawbacks of this project?

3. Use any of the Internet search engines (e.g., Alta Vista, Yahoo, Infoseek, etc.) to research the following topics:

    a. Define the following terms:

        i. GNP

        ii. GDP

    b. Compare the per-capita GNP for the following groups of developed and developing countries:

Developed Country	Per-Capita GNP	Developing Country	Per-Capita GNP
United States		Afghanistan	
France		Bangladesh	
United Kingdom		China	
Japan		Ethiopia	
Australia		Ghana	
Norway		India	
Sweden		Indonesia	
Canada		Kenya	
Switzerland		Malaysia	
Italy		Pakistan	
Singapore		Venezuela	

c. Describe the factors that are responsible for the wide gap between the per-capita GNP of developed and developing nations.

d. List five benefits of recycling.

e. Compare the following groups of developed and developing countries in terms of their recycling efforts:

Developed Country	Garbage Produced Per Year	% of Garbage Recycled	Developing Country	Garbage Produced Per Year	% of Garbage Recycled
United States			Bangladesh		
France			China		
United Kingdom			Chile		
Japan			Ethiopia		
Australia			Ghana		
Norway			India		
Sweden			Indonesia		
Canada			Malaysia		
Switzerland			Pakistan		
Italy			Philippines		
Singapore			Thailand		

f. What strategies are being used at personal, national, and international levels to promote recycling of this garbage?

Personal Level	National Level	International Level

g. Define the following terms:

   i. Photovoltaic

   ii. Inverters

h. Determine the solar (photovoltaic) power–generating capacity for the following developed and developing countries:

Developed Country	Solar Power–Generating Capacity (megawatts)	Developing Countries	Solar Power–Generating Capacity (megawatts)
United States		Bangladesh	
France		China	
Japan		Ethiopia	
Australia		Ghana	
Norway		India	
Sweden		Indonesia	
Switzerland		Kenya	
Italy		Malaysia	
Singapore		Pakistan	
United Kingdom		Venezuela	
Germany		Zimbabwe	

i. Define the following terms:

   i. kWh

   ii. MOSFET transistor

   iii. Bipolar transistor

   iv. Kinetic energy

j. Determine the wind power–generating capacity for the following developed and developing countries:

Developed Country	Wind Power–Generating Capacity (Megawatts)	Developing Countries	Wind Power–Generating Capacity (Megawatts)
United States		Bangladesh	
France		China	
Japan		Ethiopia	
Australia		Ghana	
Norway		India	
Sweden		Indonesia	
Switzerland		Kenya	
Italy		Malaysia	
Singapore		Pakistan	
United Kingdom		Venezuela	
Germany		Zimbabwe	

A Bridge to Your 21st Century Understanding

1. The history of the 20th century reveals that the First World has always imposed its will via its technological might on the Third World in dealing with the economic and political problems. (a) Do you believe that the level of confrontation between the First and Third World has increased during the last decade of the 20th century? Explain your answer. (b) How could the conflicts between the Third World and the First World be resolved in order to achieve a win–win situation in the 21st century?

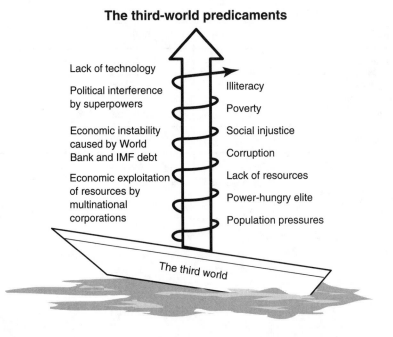

The third-world predicaments

Lack of technology

Political interference by superpowers

Economic instability caused by World Bank and IMF debt

Economic exploitation of resources by multinational corporations

Illiteracy

Poverty

Social injustice

Corruption

Lack of resources

Power-hungry elite

Population pressures

The third world

2. What actions must be taken by the developed countries as well as the developing countries to improve the human suffering in the Third World?
3. What kind of relationship (cooperation vs. confrontation) do you envision will emerge between the First and the Third World in the 21st century? Explain your answer.

Useful Web Sites

URL	Site Description
http://www.worldbank.org	World Bank
http://www.un.org	United Nations
http://www.worldwatch.org	World Watch Institute
http://www.envirolink.org	Environment-related links
http://www.igc.apc.org/worldviews	
http://www.sipri.se	Military expenditure statistics
http://www.citinet.com	Country information database
http://www.sunsite.unc.edu/lunarbin/worldpop	World population estimates
http://www.undp.org	United Nations Development Program
http://www.nrel.gov/business/international	Alternative energy sources
http://www.lib.umich.edu/libhome/Documents·center stats·html	Statistical resources on the Web
http://www.worldvillage.org	What if the world were a village?

Technology
of the Future

PART

IX

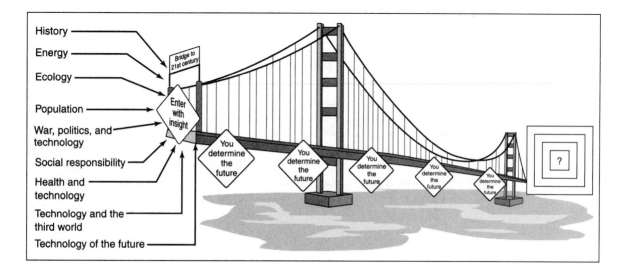

History
Energy
Ecology
Population
War, politics, and technology
Social responsibility
Health and technology
Technology and the third world
Technology of the future

Bridge to 21st century

Enter with insight

You determine the future

You determine the future

You determine the future

You determine the future

You determine the future

?

461

As man proceeds into the future with unprecedented technological powers, it is time to pause and ponder the technological and ethical issues that bridge the past to the present, and the present to the future. The decisions made today will determine the directions of decision making into the new century. These decisions will carry implications of historical, scientific, ecological, and sociological significance as man moves rapidly through space and time. Part IX presents a time and space approach to our examination of technology, enabling the reader to reflect on the issues of the previous eight parts and project their future development and applications to the future. The purpose of this approach is to refocus and converge the thoughts across the "bridge of now" so that they guide us to the "bridge of the 21st century."

This part begins by crossing over the bridge into the 21st century and envisioning and creating a preferred future. Specific case studies examine new technological applications that will affect the medical, military, and ecological aspects of our lives. Chapters also focus on predictions of future developments. In "Creating the Future," Norman Meyers dicusses ways to evaluate technology and its "multifarious impacts" in the new century. In his article "Head Start," Samuel Greengard outlines the work being done at the University of Southern California linking the computer and the brain in a parallel-processing network that could restore physcial and mental functions to patients who have battled an array of physical and psychological maladies.

Part IX continues the exploration of future medical issues in "Telemedicine: The Health System of Tomorrow" by Thomas Blanton and David Balch. This article explores the use of telemedicine in prisons, rural settings, and other areas where medical treatments have been sporadic because doctors cannot see patients on a regular basis. Even though telemedicine has been around since the late 1950s and has been a theme of science fiction films, it has only recently emerged as a viable way to reach out to medically underserved areas.

"Keys to the Kingdom," by Leon Jaroff, presents the issues associated with gene therapy. Readers will find themselves anticipating the results of researchers who hope to introduce genes into existing cells that could prevent or cure a wide range of diseases, including cancer. It is possible that within thirty years, scientists will have identified approximately one hundred genes that predispose people to common diseases. Medical researchers are creating tests to determine the presence of genes that could predict a patient's potential for developing specific diseases. Based on these findings, the research being done today in medical labs could have long-standing positive ramifications for the prevention of diseases in the future.

"Future Genetic Testing" presents the ethical issues of genetic tests. Would you want to know as a ten-year-old that you might develop cancer when you are thirty? Would you want your insurance company to have this information? After reading this short atricle, you may have an entirely different perspective on the ethical issues involved in genetic testing.

Ellison C. Urban explains in "The Information Warrior" how the world of the military will be transformed in the next century. Laser rangefinders, live videos of battle scenes, body-hugging computers, computer-generated maps, and humionics will drastically change the battlefield. Predictions for the new century and the new millennium tie together many issues that have been presented in this text. These predictions relate to the part that will be played by hyperlinks, microprocessor miniaturization, optical networks, gene alteration, artifical intelligence, and nanotechnology in the 21st century.

Part IX concludes with commentaries from each of the authors, describing our own view of how to interpret our steps into the future as we walk across our very significant bridge, the bridge of the 21st century.

56 Creating the Future

Norman Myers

The future can still be *our* future. We can possess the future, provided we do not let it possess us. All we have to do is to choose. Or rather, to choose to choose.

To do that we shall need to keep an eye better fixed on the long-term future. This is hard, since we have grown adapted to thinking about the short-term future. When the marketplace decrees an interest rate of 10 percent, investors must recoup their investment within seven years, which is akin to saying there is no future to bother about thereafter. Our political systems proclaim the future extends only till the next election. To enable us to cater for the future beyond this foreshortened perspective, we shall have to engage in much restructuring of society. Otherwise we run the risk of an unguided future descending on us, a future with upheaval abounding. Make no mistake: for the first time in human history, the next generation could find itself worse off than the previous one to an extent without parallel. A worst-case outcome—a prospect far from impossible—would entail the end of civilization as we know it. The only way to avoid that is to reconstruct our civilization from top to bottom.

Many of our options are already foreclosed through our penchant for muddling through. As a result, we face an immediate bottleneck of restricted choices. Much of Part Three presents ways for us to squeeze through this bottleneck. We look at measures to contain the greenhouse effect, to move to new energy paths, to reverse biomass shifts, to halt deforestation, to defuse the population bomb, to refashion our economies, to promote "soft" technologies, to build an organic agriculture, to establish green governance, to devise planetary medicine, to foster dynamic peace, and to undertake the many other prerequisites of a sustainable world.

Most of all, these changes in our outer world depend on still more revolutionary changes in our inner world. So the concluding pages look at the greatest transitions of all: from knowledge to wisdom, and from constant chatter to a readiness to listen—to listen to each other, to ourselves, and to Gaia.

We shall gain the future we deserve. Part Three points the way, a way with portents, pitfalls, and hopes. Whatever tough times lie immediately ahead, this book, like the expansive promise of the longer-term future, is for optimists.

TOWARD 2000

As we head toward the new millennium, a number of organizations have been making ambitious plans. Well might they be ambitious: only by thinking a great deal bigger than we have in the past will we be ready to tackle the challenges ahead.

Health for All

This World Health Organization plan aims to: counter the malnutrition suffered by at least 1 billion people; supply primary health care to everyone; ensure life expectancy reaches 60 years; cut infant mortality to 50 per 1000 live

From THE GAIA ATLAS OF FUTURE WORLDS by Norman Myers. Copyright © 1990 by Gaia Books Ltd, London. Used by permission of Doubleday, a division of Bantam-Doubleday Dell Publishing Group, Inc.

births; ensure all infants and children enjoy proper weight (half of developing-world children are poorly nourished); and supply safe water within 15 minutes' walk. All this is to be accomplished by the year 2000. Just to provide primary health care for all would cost $50 billion a year, and safe water plus sanitation would cost $30 billion a year. The plan also proposes much greater attention to the greying communities in the developed world.

Education for All

This UNESCO plan aims to supply basic education for every person on Earth by the year 2000. Today, 105 million developing-world children enjoy no schooling at all, and more than 900 million adults, or one out of every four, are illiterate. Cost: around $5 billion a year.

Population 2000

According to the International Forum on Population in the 21st Century, convened in late 1989 by the UN Fund for Population Activities, the aim is to "hold the line" on the medium population projection of 6.25 billion people by the year 2000. To achieve this, we need to: reduce developing-world fertility to 3.2 children per family; increase developing-world use of contraceptives to 56%; upgrade the status of women, especially their literacy; and achieve universal enrollment of girls in primary schools. In order to accomplish just the first two items, we shall need to increase the budget for family-planning services in developing countries to $9 billion annually, or twice as much as today.

Anit-Desertification Action Plan

The United Nations' plan seeks to halt the spread of human-made deserts, now threatening one-third of the Earth's land surface. There has been next to no progress on this issue since it was first formulated in 1978, due to government indifference. Yet it would be an unusually sound investment at $6 billion a year for 20 years, against the continuing costs of inaction worth $32 billion a year in agricultural losses alone. In 1986 the world spent more than $100 billion in drought-relief operations that saved lives but did nothing to halt further desertification.

Tropical Forestry Action Plan

The plan, already in action, seeks to slow deforestation by supplying: tree farms for commercial timber; village woodlots and agroforestry plots for fuelwood; more pro-

tected areas for threatened species; more research and training, plus public education; and better management all round. Cost: $1.6 billion per year. But the plan does next to nothing to address the main source of deforestation, the slash-and-burn cultivator, who reflects an array of non-forestry problems such as population growth, pervasive poverty, maldistribution of existing farmlands, lack of agrarian reform, and hopelessly inadequate development for rural communities generally.

Climate Change Programme

Focused on global warming, and undertaken by the Intergovernmental Panel on Climate Change leading up to a proposed global-warming treaty, the Programme proposes to stabilize the concentration of greenhouse gases in the atmosphere by cutting emissions of carbon dioxide by 80%, of methane by 15-20%, of nitrous oxide by 70-80%, and of CFCs and related HCFCs by 70-85%. In the case of carbon dioxide, which accounts for roughly half the greenhouse effect, developed nations would have to reduce their fossil-fuel burning by 20% by 2005, by 50% by 2015, and by 75% by 2030. Developing nations would have to stabilize their emissions by 2010, allowing them to rise to no more than double today's levels as they continue to industrialize (developing nations would also have to halt deforestation by 2010 and engage in grand-scale tree planting). All this would mean that global emissions of greenhouse gases would fall to one-quarter of their present levels by 2050, limiting the rate of warming to 0.1° C per decade, and eventually holding it at 2° C above today's average temperatures—still a highly disruptive outcome.

Global Change Programme

Formerly known as the International Geosphere-Biosphere Programme, this research effort aims to provide the information we need to assess the future of the planet for the next 100 years, with emphasis on such areas as biogeochemical cycles, the upper layer of the oceans, Earth's soil stocks, and the sun's radiation. With an operational phase beginning in the early 1990s, the plan will last for ten years.

Beyond 2000?

As worthy as all these organizations' plans are, they all suffer from a serious shortcoming. They are targetted at the year 2000: what about longer-term goals, which must be established *now* if we are to avoid much costlier efforts later on, with much less prospect of success? Regrettably the plans reflect the timid and short-term attitudes of the governments that approve the strategies. It is not in the nature of governments to see beyond the end of their noses, let alone beyond the end of the decade.

GREENHOUSE TACTICS: OPTIONS FOR RESPONSE

The greatest environmental upheaval of all, the greenhouse effect, offers much scope for positive response. While it is not possible to tame the problem entirely—there is already too much change in the pipeline—there is still time to slow it, perhaps even to stabilize it, and buy ourselves precious decades in which to devise longer-term answers. But this will require immediate and vigorous action on a broad front, plus international collaboration and individual initiatives on an unprecedented scale.

First and foremost we need to consume less energy, through energy conservation and more efficient use of energy. In fact these two strategies represent our best energy source: from 1973 to 1978 some 95 percent of all new energy supplies in Europe came from more efficient use of available supplies—an amount 20 times more than from all other new sources of energy combined.

Since the oil crises of 1973 and 1979, most of the fuel-guzzling industrialized countries have expanded their economies by a full 30 per cent while actually cutting back on total energy consumption. In 1985 came a third oil shock, this one of plunging oil prices, whereupon we quickly reverted to our energy-wasting ways.

But the energy-saving technologies are still there, waiting to be mobilized (see below). And at the same time as we cut back on fossil-fuel burning, so we reduce acid rain, among many other forms of environmental pollution.

Burning fossil fuel for energy, however, is only about one-third of the greenhouse problem. Another source is agriculture: nitrous oxide from nitrogen-based fertilizers; methane from rice paddies and ruminant livestock. With more mouths to feed around the world, we cannot allow food production to plateau—though we could do it differently and more productively with genetically engineered breeds. A halt to tropical deforestation would prevent at least 2.4 billion tons of carbon from entering the atmosphere each year, while reforestation would soak up carbon as well as restore vital watershed functions among many other purposes.

Through multiple linkages, then, the greenhouse problem reflects the myriad ways we all live. It will only be through myriad shifts in economic sectors and lifestyles alike that we shall get on top of the problem.

Public Perception

Look out of a window and you view a world in the thrall of climatic upheaval. Although nothing can be seen, the world is undergoing an environmental shift of a type and scale to rival a geological cataclysm—and one of the most rapid ever to overtake the Earth. To confront it we need a parallel change in our inner world, our world of perception and understanding.

Changing Energy Policies

To mitigate the effects of the greenhouse we must reduce fossil-fuel burning. In the short term the greatest savings will come from buildings and products that use energy more efficiently. Many U.S. electricity utilities offer their customers energy surveys, rebates on energy-efficient appliances, and loans to finance energy-saving improvements. In the long term we need to replace fossil fuels with environmentally benign renewables, such as wind, wave, and solar. As for nuclear power, and leaving aside the unacceptable risks in its use, plus its uncompetitive price in the marketplace, to replace the world's coal-burning stations would entail building one nuclear plant every three days for the next 36 years at a cost of $150 billion annually.

A Climate Convention

A worldwide convention will need to decide how much greenhouse effect we are prepared to live with and the degree of remedial action to be taken, and by whom, in order to reduce the problem. This will mean a cap on greenhouse-gas emissions by all nations. But how hefty a cap for such disparate cases as Britain and Bangladesh, the U.S. and Brazil, Germany and China, the Soviet Union, and India? Should the industrialized nations indemnify the industrializing nations in order to safeguard the climate of all nations? Should there be special dispensations on the part of the entire community of nations to help those worst affected? The questions multiply and ramify, and we have no precedents to guide us.

Rethinking Agricultural Practices

Population growth and the intensification of food production are likely to set limits to reductions in certain greenhouse gases. Actively reducing the extent of intensive cattle-rearing operations would curtail some methane production; reducing fertilizer use, or implementing more efficient means of fertilizer application would do the same for nitrous oxide. An even more important answer lies with new varieties of crops that require less fertilizer.

DYNAMIC PEACE

Just as health is more than the absence of disease, so peace is much more than the absence of war. It is a state of dynamic stability that has to be actively maintained. It is an end to violence among human beings and, by extension, to the planet. When this relationship is understood and accepted and when basic needs are met, there exists the opportunity for positive peace. While many people talk about peace building, they rarely specify what it means. Not that they have had much chance to practice it, since peacebuilding activities have not received even 1 percent of 1 percent of what has been spent on war activities.

First and foremost, peace on Earth means peace with the Earth. We are engaged in World War III, a war against the planet, a war that is no contest. We must negotiate terms of surrender to the new environmental dictates, recognizing that victory over the Earth would be a no-win outcome. In turn, this postulates a new form of security, environmental security. As past president Gorbachev was one of the first to point out, the threat from the sky is no longer missiles but climate change. Stealth bombers cannot be launched against this uniquely threatening adversary—just as tanks cannot be mobilized to counter rising sea levels, nor troops dispatched to block the advance of the encroaching desert.

So peace with the Earth implies peace with each other, a peace comprising three essential components: relations of harmony among people in society; co-operation for the common good; and justice based on the concept of equity. Much environmental ruin derives from inequity. Economic and political imbalance drives the marginal Third Worlder into marginal environments—ones that are too dry, too wet, too steep for sustainable livelihoods, and where vast environmental damage is caused through desertification, deforestation and soil erosion.

To achieve dynamic peace at global level, there must be a submerging of the narrow interests of individual nations in an effort to conduct international affairs in a manner that befits a global community. But unless it is based on general consensus and it is environmentally and economically sound, there is scant hope of success.

Green Security

With the thawing of the Cold War, some of the erstwhile military outlays could be directed toward building a more secure world. According to Robert McNamara and other experts, NATO countries could soon release $175 billion a year from military budgets. Soviet leaders indicate they could release perhaps $100 billion a year, funds needed to rebuild the Soviet economy. According to Lester Brown, President of the Worldwatch Institute, to restore environmental security would cost: protecting topsoil around $9 billion in 1991; restoring forests $3 billion; halting the spread of deserts $4 billion; supplying clean water $30 billion; raising energy efficiency $10 billion; developing renewable energy $5 billion; slowing population growth $18 billion; and retiring developing world debt $30 billion. This total of $109 billion would need to rise to $170 billion a year by 2000—still no more than eight weeks' military spending at late 1980s levels.

The Role of Nonviolence

Nuclear power has forced us to contemplate both extinction and new forms of conflict resolution. The latter could soon become much more common. Nonviolence however goes far beyond ensuring peace by reducing military budgets or halting environmental destruction. As well as the weapons, we must also eliminate the "mind" that brought them into being and contemplated their use.

"Vulnerable" to Peace

The arms race has tied the economies of many nations to the military. Now there is a fear that an outbreak of peace will take jobs, shareholders' dividends too. To counter this, communities are developing "economic conversion projects." The objective is to retrain workers and adapt factories to civilian production. To this end, citizens, workers, and managers plan their future with local politicians, technocrats, and economists. In the US, 70 cities have passed "Jobs with Peace" initiatives and are beginning the conversion process.

PLANETARY CITIZENSHIP

We started out on our human enterprise with loyalty to a hunting band of a few dozen people. From there we successively expanded our allegiance to the village, town, city, region, and eventually the nation. At each stage our sense of community grew, until today we feel a part of societies of millions. Yet the greatest loyalty leap awaits us. Can we now raise our vision to embrace the whole of humanity? So great is this challenge that it will rank as the second true step away from the cave's threshold.

First, we need to identify with a global community of individuals whose names we do not know, whose faces we shall never see, whose traditions we may not share, and whose hopes we shall not know, but who are all, whether they are aware of it or not, *de facto* members of a single society. Second, we must foster a super-allegiance to Gaia, and frame our actions accordingly. Can we learn in time to identify with these two ultimate communities?

This need not present any conflict of interest. When we salute our countries' flags, we are not thereby denying bonds with families or neighborhoods. We are simply acknowledging a greater context of kindred spirits, a loftier level of allegiance. So our new planetary loyalty will not diminish established links; rather it will enhance them by adding perspective to local attachments.

There could, however, be some exceptions. What when a country asks us to do something against the global good? To hold back for the sake of the national economy on anti-global-warming measures, for example, or to consume for the sake of the balance of payments, when that means supporting unduly polluting activities? As we head farther into an interdependent future, there may well arise numerous occasions when we shall feel torn by planetary obligations that should outweigh "state dues." On such occasions it will not be easy to rise above past practices or to keep our attention fixed firmly on the universal need. We cannot live in isolation, whether from one another or from the planetary home. Either we shall become involved through joint effort as global citizens, or we shall become involved through jointly suffering global catastrophe.

Transcending Politics

Traditional politics concerns itself with the managing of social systems. This view will need to be considerably broadened to take into account the concept of planetary citizenship. The best politics will enable people and communities to create their own solutions to their own problems within a larger context. But a prerequisite will be the moulding of a new environmental/political consensus from the present anti-environmental world. Among initiatives that could soon become commonplace is an Earth Corps, an organization providing a framework for people, young and old, to make a personal contribution to the planet. The potential is vast, not only in terms of work to be done but the reservoir of people and energy waiting to be mobilized on behalf of the Earth.

Rising Above the Nation-State

We are suspended at a hinge of history, between two ages—that of competitive nationalism and that of cooperative internationalism. Nationhood is becoming a pernicious anachronism, a primitive phenomenon like feudalism or slavery. Future generations will surely consider that nationhood was a transient phase in society's development, a holding measure until the emergence of planetary citizenship.

Our Evolutionary Conditioning

When we attempt to identify with the global community, we may find that our evolutionary conditioning stands in the way. Our individual nurturing has derived primarily from the 99% of human history spent as hunter-gatherers, dependent for survival on sinking individual interests with those of a few dozen others. So we have inherited a set of sensibilities that, however capable they were for our formative years, may have left us deficient for our future worlds. Can we develop the extra faculties we need to cooperate as a band of more than 5 billion people?

A LAW UNTO OURSELVES

In a new-age world we shall learn to be our own legal experts, in that we shall have to devise rules for living in a crowded global community without treading on anybody else's prerogatives. We shall need to recognize that planetary citizenship entails responsibilities as well as rights; and we shall have to learn that it is in our own best interests to be our own private law enforcer. Not that this concept is anything new in itself. The rule of law has always depended on a strong supporting consensus of the citizenry, without which the best-intentioned laws fail. Consider, for example, the debacle of the Prohibition years in America. But this time around there will be such an abundance and complexity of laws, regulations, and rules, whether formal or unwritten, that there cannot be enough police to keep everyone on the straight and narrow. We must devise our own path ahead, and follow it because it is in our own best interests.

This mode of behavior will be in stark contrast to the free-wheeling years of a simpler and less vulnerable world, one where there was no threat of terminal breakdown in society through outright environmental collapse. With multiplying numbers of people, multiplying demands, and multiplying linkages through our increasing interdependency, both environmental and economic, there will be multiplying scope for disruption and dislocation. The answer will lie with the dictum of "Mutual coercion, mutually agreed upon". But this need not be a fraction as "Big Brotherish" as it may sound. It will replace the unlicensed liberty of yesterday with new forms of freedom for tomorrow—an expansive and disciplined freedom.

Above all, the new "world of laws" will be all the more acceptable in that it will not be a top-down affair, by contrast with the situation in the past. It will be a grass-roots process, a home-grown homage to largely local imperatives. Communal laws will be more like social codes, finely tuned to local needs—a world away from the rigidity of conventional laws.

Local Control in Sweden

Flexible, local systems of sharing and control are becoming a feature of codes of conduct of certain smaller nations. In Sweden, for example, most of the unionized workforce is solidly behind its government's new program of economic decentralization. In each one of Sweden's two dozen counties, a proportion of the workforce's earnings is automatically paid into a public fund administered by an elected board. The accumulated funds are used to purchase shares in local industries, which are then publicly controlled. Local economic control is thus back in the hands of the community, where decisions can be made in light of local needs.

Roundabouts or Traffic Lights?

Law-abiding societies of the future must operate by consensus, rather than by the threat of punishment. Communally agreed codes will be the order of the day, not dictates passed down from some distant national assembly. When we all agree to drive on the same side of the road we make no sacrifice of personal freedom—rather our freedom is enhanced by communal consensus. As we progress into the future we shall find that we will be driving ever-more sophisticated models (of the figurative type) at higher speeds, and sharing the road with ever-more drivers. This will necessitate more "traffic control" to facilitate everybody's journey. These controls can take the form of roundabouts (communal codes with which people have licenses to assess, evaluate, and make decisions) or traffic lights (specific laws that require simple acquiescence).

THE GENIE OUT OF THE BOTTLE

Our technological capacities are such that it is now possible to reshape our world from top to bottom—not only our planetary living space, but our social relations, our individual inner worlds, all that we are and do. The record to date does not presage a future as constructive and bountiful as we might wish. Unbridled technology already threatens our very life-support systems. Yet technology could be one of the greatest boons for the human condition, pro-

vided we ensure that it serves our overall interests. We need to take a long look at the role of technology in our future world and to ask how we can take systematic control of its multifarious impacts. We have released the genie from its bottle, and even if we perversely wished, we cannot return it. The present challenge is to control the genie before it controls us in unwitting ways that we cannot remotely discern.

What then is to be the future role of technology, as of its scientific underpinnings? The new physics shows us that what scientists observe in nature is intimately conditioned by their minds. Hence scientific and technological applications are also conditioned by the mind and thus by human values. Scientists are not only intellectually responsible for their research, they are also morally responsible. In turn, should not scientists and technologists now be required to take methodical cognizance of the impacts of their endeavours, whether environmental, social, or even political?

True, this would mark a profound change in our attitudes to science, as to its role in society. Many scientists would be aghast at the notion that their research should somehow be trammelled. But this is not to assert that all science should be subject to detailed constraints. There must always be abundant place for the pursuit of knowledge and understanding, whatever it reveals. Yet the overall context of science should surely be examined to see whether we can determine some limits to its unfortunate technological by-products. It is this new dimension, placing a check on undesirable fall-out, that is the key to controlling the genie.

Human Hubris

Our overweening attitude toward the natural world is a recurring theme in cultures right from the Ancient World. For stealing fire from the gods, Prometheus was chained and tortured. It seems always to have been accepted that there are some areas of enquiry that are simply off limits in view of the potential costs they entrain. The question now is to determine which precisely these areas are. While we understand so little of the world about us, especially the expanding world of the future, we must move from hubris to humility and practice a cautious rather than a Promethean approach.

Self-Imposed Audits

Already some ecology professors are proposing that students' dissertations should include a chapter on the social implications of their findings. In some cases, these implications will be virtually nil, in many others they will be of marginal consequence, in certain others they will be significant. Whatever the outcome, the exercise will induce an explicit awareness that science and technology can no longer be practiced in a vacuum.

Genetic Engineering

To date, genetic engineering has caused no regrettable spillovers on to the environment. The potential, however, is certainly there as new organisms are introduced into natural communities at an increasing rate. After all, an earlier effort at improved breeding of livestock in the form of a goat variety adapted to harsh environments—hailed as an undoubted success at the time—led to semi-arid lands becoming arid lands. The new breeders, for example, gene splicers using recombinant DNA technology, need to exercise far more scrupulous care as they release multitudes of entirely new organisms. While it is unlikely that the newcomers could ever become dominant on a broad scale, they could well cause local ecological disasters that could not readily be controlled. Unfortunately there is a tendency for expectations and benefits to be overestimated, while costs and problems receive short shrift—as is often the case during the early stages of the development of any new technology. The prospect of hosts of newly minted organisms warrants exceptional caution rather than a "rush-in" approach. Yet we have scarcely started to assess the legal, let alone ethical, issues at stake.

RESPONSIBLE TECHNOLOGY

Modern society is hooked on technology, one that gives us life-saving hospital units and liberating communications, also nuclear weapons and soulless production lines. We are led to believe that there is a technofix for every social ill and global problem—and if technology goes wrong, then technology will put it right again. Yet we continue to feed off ecodestructive agriculture, to use products from energy-wasteful industries, and to live lives in technology-ravaged environments.

Our notions of wealth and welfare, competition and efficiency, are grounded in technology. The progress of technology is supposed to be unstoppable: it represents the crowning achievement of human enterprise, and other notions of progress come second. But our resource-intensive, overcentralized technology is making itself obsolete. Petrochemical agribusiness, nuclear power, fuel-guzzling cars are environmental disasters. Yet we still have to devise guidelines for our present technology, let alone the

fast-expanding technology of the future. What technology is "right"?

The answer lies with technology that supports humankind in our need to live in accord *with* the planet rather than in dominion *over* it: technology with a planetary face. Many technologies for sustainability already exist in the form of so-called "soft technologies," for instance those that utilize renewable resources and recycled materials. A good number of these technologies are already familiar to us: energy-saving devices; ultra-efficient motors; solar energy conversion; wind, wave, and tidal power utilization; organic farming; semiconductors; and superchips. The challenge is to create a flexible, benign, and humane technology—a process that will allow us to exercise our full creativity. Indeed a crucial factor in this new technology will be its readiness to draw much more on a resource we already possess in abundance—human ingenuity.

In this regard, the soft technologies are often ideal, since they tend to be small scale and decentralized. And, being generally labor intensive, they help to establish a local economy, one that is flexible and sensitive to local conditions.

A New Orientation

To solve the multiple crises we face, we don't need more energy-intensive technologies. We need to shift our emphasis from nonrenewable to renewable resources, from hard to soft technologies. But this alone will not be sufficient without a thorough-going cultural change—a move away from the mechanistic "we can fix it" mentality to a more careful and caring approach. This in turn will require the most basic retooling of all: wholescale shifts in our attitudes, lifestyles, and values.

The Solar Future

The planet's principal energy source is the sun, with its potential for limitless, nonpolluting energy. Life has evolved to make optimum use of this form of energy. Plants photosynthesize food with the aid of the sun's radiation, and in turn provide the conditions, directly or indirectly, for practically all other forms of life. Solar energy can either be "passive", as when the fabric of a building heats up and then releases its energy, or "active", as in the example of solar collectors. As well, the sun's energy raises air masses that drive wind turbines, and it also energizes the water cycle, which we harness as hydropower. Bear in mind that solar energy is not only available everywhere, it is a source of diverse energy types, hence adapted to decentralized technologies in local communities.

People's Technology

Grass-roots technology is not always accorded the recognition it deserves. In the 1960s, traditional fishermen of the Arabian Sea protested that the introduction of mechanized trawling would destroy local fishing stocks. Their detailed ecological insights were dismissed by fisheries experts. Today, and through their own technological expertise, the fishing communities are pioneering the use of artificial reefs and species-specific baits, exploiting them in a manner that is both sustainable and finely tuned to local circumstances. More, their efforts are starting to be supported by the government, strengthening their organization.

FROM KNOWLEDGE TO WISDOM

As T. S. Eliot once asked: "Where is the knowledge we have lost in information? Where is the wisdom we have lost in knowledge?" Obviously knowledge is an essential component of wisdom, but there is more to it than that. While we possess knowledge in abundance, the world about us proclaims that we are falling woefully short of the step from knowledge to wisdom.

Our long tradition of reductionist analysis has brought us to a state where we often find that we are learning more and more about less and less. Result: our attention is diverted from the whole that is more than the sum of its parts. Confronted with the disjunct pieces of a watch, would we guess that when reassembled they would make up a mechanism for telling the time? Yet we meddle with the intricate components of our planetary ecosystem, no less, and suppose we can do so with impunity, even concluding that certain pieces are forever dispensable. We are unwittingly engaged in global-scale experiments, not only environmental but technological and social experiments, without a thought for their global consequences. Yet these grandiose experiments demand the most scrupulous care, and would tax the faculties of the wisest.

Moreover there is much that we, whether scientist or not, can discern in terms of values without understanding the details. We do not need to understand the physical or chemical make-up of a weapon to realize it is designed to destroy. We do not need endless reports on the influence of the media to see their power to misinform.

Thus far we have tended to head blithely toward a "universal horizon" and have limited ourselves to doing a better job in getting from here to there—"there" being something that reflects the common understanding of most people. We make sure that we travel along smoothly in a car that is in good order and with enough fuel. Beyond our present crossroads, however, that will not suffice. Often enough we shall need to consider the proper road to follow. The landscape ahead is no longer preordained by "where we have always been going before." Increasingly we shall find that we need to choose a different route, change the car, even ask whether we want to travel at all. All the fast-growing knowledge in the world will not help us if we do not have the wisdom to look out all over the world, and to decide where we feel most at home.

Dinosaur of the Mind

"But we learn no lesson, give no moral to our children. We go on not having understood what is meant by our technological act of knowing. Some day, in the far, far future, the evolutionary processes will perhaps have gotten rid of this failing attempt at gaining knowledge; either we will be the ancestral progenitors (of a wiser species), or else we will be discarded, an unsuccessful offshoot, a dinosaur of the mind, one of nature's failures." Professor Phillip Siekevitz, Rockefeller University

Analysis and Vision

The knowledge business—not only science but telecommunications, media, advertising—means we can generate more information than ever before, and mobilize it more efficiently. This is far from enough, even though it is the credo of government, business, and the general ethos of "advancement". For we see only what we are disposed to see. When we analyse information to produce new ideas, we do no more than find new slots for old ones. To generate truly new ideas—to strive toward "wise" insights—we must bring into play our creativity, our powers of inspiration, above all our sense of vision. All these are a world beyond the nose-to-the-microscope approach of conventional understanding.

Knowledge as Private Property

The trend toward privatized knowledge is regrettable. While the patenting of ideas is a valid safeguard, the wholesale locking away of knowledge as private property, walled by legal defenses, can only redound to our collective detriment. Instance the North-South gap: whether wittingly or not, the technological underpinnings of the knowledge explosion in the developed nations are acting to exclude developing nations from one of the most productive phenomena of our age. How ironic if the knowledge resources in the North serve to impoverish further the South. Surely we will recognize that knowledge should be generally available in the public domain, serving the needs of everyone. Only as the walls around knowledge crumble away will the shared experience of all contribute to dawnings of wisdom.

THE FUTURE OF THE FUTURE

For however much is uncertain about the future, one thing is definite: new worlds will constantly unfold, with their new problems *and* their new possibilities. In some senses, in fact, there will be as many possible futures as there are people. We are all deeply involved, whether we appreciate it or not; we shall all play our individual parts. Indeed there has never been a time like the present when the individual can *count*. So a prime aim has been to show the reader how to envision the future, and to decide how to contribute—if only at the local level, which will often be the best level.

The shadows over our future remind us that the optimist proclaims this is the best of all possible worlds, while the pessimist responds that is regrettably true. We must stay hopeful, otherwise we might as well go to the beach until the sky falls in. But let us not be seduced by an airy hope that somehow all will work out in the wash: the laundry water likely contains too many pollutants. There are prophets who assert we should not worry about the prospect of feeding 10 billion people when it is theoretically possible to feed four times as many. As Paul and Anne Ehrlich point out, it is theoretically possible too for your favorite football team to win every game for the next ten years. In any case, the Ehrlichs continue, what is the sense in converting the Earth into a gigantic human feedlot? How about more quality of life for fewer people? Moreover a future of "the same as usual, only more so" would be a future that for many people would simply not arrive.

If further persuasion is necessary, recall that of the 31 major civilizations in history, only one remains a dominant force, so-called Western civilization. As the historian Arnold Toynbee demonstrates, the rest disappeared because they tried to become dominant on every side—over their neighbors, their environments, whatever else they cast their eyes on. Western civilization, materialist to beat any other, shows plenty of signs of dominating the entire world into an ultimate crunch.

No doubt about it, we stand at a hiatus in the human enterprise. The present is so different from the past, and the present so different from the future, that it is as if we are at a hiatus in the course of human affairs. It is a unique time: a time of breakdown or breakthrough.

To break through into a future of undreamed potential, we must enable a new sort of society to be born. Indeed the stresses of the present are like the stresses of being born, a time of utmost threat yet with new life ahead. Or, to shift the analogy, our society is like a human being growing up. From the start it shows boundless appetite for resources of every type. This appetite continues throughout the first two decades of physical growth, expanding all the while. Then it suddenly levels off. This does not mean the person's growth is at an end. On the contrary, the richest stage of growth begins—mental, intellectual, emotional, and spiritual growth, growth that extends many times longer than the early phase.

Our global society is still adolescent—lusty, vigorous, and assertive. Can we move on to maturity—assured, stable and sensitive, displaying all the attributes of adulthood? Are we ready to grow up? To shift from egosystem to ecosystem, to social compact and whatever else is needed for us to become citizens of the globe?

Are we ready, in fact, to engage in the most salient experience of adulthood, the mutuality of love? Nothing less will do. Finally we can recognize that there is no longer any "we' and "they." For the first time, and for all time, there is only "us"—all of us humans, together with all our fellow species.

This will be the greatest of our global experiments. As we measure up to the challenge, we shall need to become giants of the human condition. As we approach our climacteric—never attempted before, surely never to be repeated with such instantaneous speed—let us count ourselves fortunate to be living at this hour. No generation of the past has been presented with such a chance to rise above the tide of human history. No generation of the future will have our chance, because if we do not do the job they will have little left but to pick up the pieces. What a privileged generation we are.

WHAT'S POSSIBLE; WHAT'S PROBABLE

What lies ahead? This section looks at an array of possibilities that may prompt us to speculate on what else is in store. The following list is highly selective and no more than illustrative. The items derive from analyses of experts who use techniques such as scenario planning to think methodically about the future. Futurists based at universities have set up entire departments for futures studies. There are commissions on the future, established by individual governments, United Nations agencies, the City of Tokyo, and the like. The World Future Society, based in Washington DC, organizes regular conferences on all aspects of the future. But the most remarkable feature of this futurist community is not that there are so many people thinking about what the future holds, but that there are so few. Among some prospective developments are the following.

Global Environment

As the greenhouse effect takes hold, we could witness persistent droughts over much of North America, sub-Saharan Africa, and China. Together with repeated failures of the Indian monsoon and other climatic quirks, plus the most expansive phase of the population explosion, there could ensue a greater outbreak of starvation in a single year early next century than throughout the 1980s, even culminating in the deaths of one billion people in just one decade. This worse-case scenario, by no means implausible, would amount to a human catastrophe of unique proportions.

In the longer-term future, a one-metre rise in sea level by the middle of next century could, when combined with storm surges reaching far inland, plus saltwater intrusions up rivers, threaten a total area of 5 million sq km—or one-third of today's croplands and home to one billion people already. Also on the cards is the prospect of mass migrations in the wake of the greenhouse effect. On the Chinese side of the Sino-Soviet border there are already acute pressures from 1300 persons per square kilometre, by contrast with only one person to every 2.5 square kilometres on the Siberian side. What when China starts to suffer the full rigors of global warming?

Geopolitics

Consider the following scenario. In the year 2000 the world has 350 billionaires, at least 4 million millionaires, and 250 million homeless. The average income of the top 1 billion people has reached 50 times more than that of the bottom 1 billion. More than 50 nations no longer qualify as developing nations; they are disintegrating nations. Americans spend $10 billion per year on slimming diets, while 1 billion people are so undernourished that they are semi-starving. Water from a single spring in France is still shipped to the affluent around the world, while a full 2.5 billion people lack access to clean water for basic needs. It has become plain that poverty is a luxury we can no longer afford.

Furthermore, there has been a series of crises on top of widespread starvation. Chernobyl-type accidents have occurred in four nations. the North Sea has been declared beyond foreseeable recovery. The most bountiful marine ecosystem on Earth, the Southern Ocean, has collapsed after UV-B radiation knocks out the phytoplankton. A nu-

clear terrorist has destroyed Cairo. Drug barons have declared jurisdiction over much of South America. The Pope has been added to Willy Brandt, Stevie Wonder, and Steffi Graf as hostages held by extremists. The latest Live World concert has been watched by two and a half billion people, and has led to mass protests throughout the world.

This all pushes governments into finally acknowledging that there is only one track ahead: global collaboration with a vengeance, and for the first time ever. As European President Joan Ruddock puts it at the World Conference for the World: "The biggest problem is no longer others, it is ourselves. We are suspended at a hinge of history, between two ages—that of competitive nationalism and that of cooperative internationalism. At long glorious last, we recognize that traditional nationhood is an anachronism, a pernicious phenomenon like feudalism or slavery."

What emerges is a system of government based on concentric circles: local councils, regional assemblies, national governments, groupings such as the European Community, and global bodies such as the United Nations (supplied with teeth). This vertical structure is paralleled by a horizontal structure of NGOs with real power, made up of professions, trade unions, Friends of the Earth, major charities, academics, service clubs, Oxfam, and the like. These NGOs receive collective representation through the long proposed Second Assembly of the Untied Nations. Under these twin structures of government, citizens can cheer equally for Edinburgh, Scotland, Britain, Europe, the Commonwealth, the world, tropical forests, Antarctica, and Action Aid.

Science and Technology

As a result of scientific advances, techno-jumps could include a breakthrough with photovoltaics that transforms the energy prospect from top to bottom, especially for tropical countries; backpack nuclear weapons, with all that means for terrorism; sex selection on the cheap, leading to a massive majority of male babies; and genetically engineered trees that sprout like mushrooms ("plant the seedling and jump aside"), allowing reforestation to do a better job of soaking up excess carbon dioxide from the atmosphere. But note that genetic engineering could lead to some unfortunate consequences of economic and social sort. It will soon be possible to "grow" cocoa in the laboratory, which could devastate those developing-world countries that now earn $2.6 billion a year from the field-grown crop.

A related technology is nanotechnology, enabling us to redesign cellular structures. This will lead to, for example, exceptionally strong and lightweight alloys, leading in turn to organically manufactured aircraft that fly much more speedily and cheaply than today's dinosaur-style devices. Among more "way out" applications of nanotechnology could be steaks from hay, without the help of cows. These, like many other techno-jumps, will derive in part from the fast-growing capacity of supercomputers. Already the latest Cray model, standing no taller than its human operator, can solve problems at a sustained rate better than one "gigaflop," or one billion calculations every second (the term gigaflop comes from "giga" meaning one billion, and FLOP for "floating point operation," a common form of computerized arithmetic). Soon to become available is a computer capable of 22 gigaflops per second, while we should soon see a machine speeding along at 128 gigaflops per second.

As for the car of the future, that is already with us. A Volvo prototype, with lightweight synthetic materials, weighs only half as much as a conventional model. Its lean-and-clean engine, backed up by a continuously variable transmission and a flywheel energy-storage unit, achieves almost 150 km per gallon in average traffic conditions. A further prospect for the petrol-driven car is that there will simply be far fewer of them in urban areas, their place having been taken by vehicles powered by electricity or hydrogen fuel. In any case, there will be far less need for them in the face of competition from efficient and cheap mass-transit systems (in Tokyo today, only 15% of commuters drive cars to the office). Moreover there will be an increasing trend for offices to be connected by electronic lines rather than crowded highways. Note too that if China were to devote as much land to asphalt as the United States does per head, it would lose over 40% of its croplands.

Health

What price an end to drug addiction? There is prospect of a final solution in the form of "opiate antagonists" that block the effects of, for example, cocaine for a month or so, whereafter the euphoric impact dissipates and the addict loses interest.

More broadly, we can anticipate a growing disaffection with established ideas about health. As more people recognize that health is intrinsically a holistic affair, so they will be inclined to accept personal responsibility for cures of "disease." There will thus be an increase in wholesome diets, exercise, and sports, stress-reducing activities, self-rehabilitation, and recreation in the sense of recreation. Sooner than we might suppose, self-help health will become mainstream.

In developing countries the technique of oral rehydration therapy (ORT) could soon become as familiar as cola—otherwise we shall witness 25 million children die of dehydration during the 1990s. Ironically, as we bring about an end to the human hemorrhage represented by child mortality in developing countries—one of the great success stories in human history—we may well witness another scourge overtaking hundreds of millions, the ravages of tobacco, as cigarette corporations of the developed world, losing their clientele at home, peddle their wares to the last corners of the developing world.

Lifestyles

Already many households feature a personal computer. A child has hardly learned to read and write before he or she starts to work with a device that, a couple of decades earlier, would have had to be as big as a house to contain the computing power of the tabletop model. It is this new skill, backed by global-scope telecommunications networks, that is opening up worlds for youngsters way beyond the dreams of their parents.

Within just a few years a majority of women will be engaged in paid work, whether in a formal workplace or in homes linked to offices by computer networks. At the same time, many men will accept a greater role in the family and home. In response to the cocktail party question, "What do you do?" the answer will increasingly be, "I'm a househusband."

Questions

1. What are the problems and challenges with our current thinking for the future?
2. What are some of the immediate needs that we must address for the future?
3. In order for population growth to be held at 6.25 billion people by the year 2000, what must be the average number of children per family worldwide? What is the current average?
4. What is the problem with current plans for the year 2000? These plans were written in 1990; do you feel that they are realistic? Explain from our current historic view.
5. Compare the Climate Change Program with the outlined plans of the Kyoto Climate Treaty of December 1997. What are the differences between the two?
6. When discussing the greenhouse effect or global warming, what is the main issue that has to be addressed? Name three approaches suggested to deal with the global warming issue.
7. Identify three approaches for developing world peace strategies.

8. Explain two views of global politics that expand planetary political unity.
9. What are some of the considerations and concepts behind planetwide laws?
10. What is being suggested of engineers, scientists, and technologists when they design new systems and technologies?
11. What is meant by the term "responsible technology"? Give two examples of it.
12. How can we attain wisdom for the future?
13. What is the biggest challenge to sustaining our world and ourselves in the future?
14. Comment on your impressions of the predictions of the future with regard to the global environment, geopolitics, science and technology, health, and lifestyles. Do you agree with these future predictions? Give some of your own predictions as a contrast.

A Bridge to Your 21st Century Understanding

Complete and discuss the following flowchart.

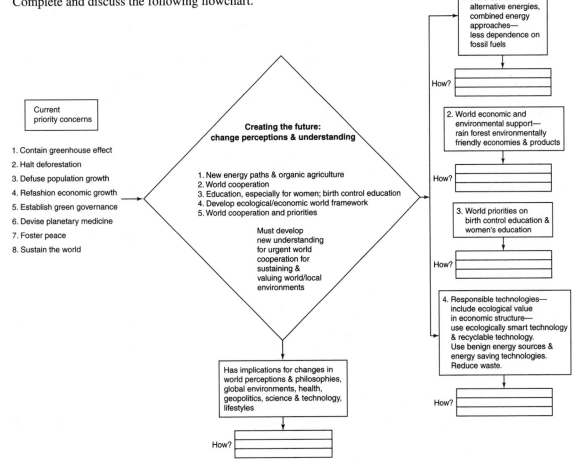

Current priority concerns

1. Contain greenhouse effect
2. Halt deforestation
3. Defuse population growth
4. Refashion economic growth
5. Establish green governance
6. Devise planetary medicine
7. Foster peace
8. Sustain the world

Creating the future: change perceptions & understanding

1. New energy paths & organic agriculture
2. World cooperation
3. Education, especially for women; birth control education
4. Develop ecological/economic world framework
5. World cooperation and priorities

Must develop new understanding for urgent world cooperation for sustaining & valuing world/local environments

1. More use of alternative energies, combined energy approaches— less dependence on fossil fuels

How?

2. World economic and environmental support— rain forest environmentally friendly economies & products

How?

3. World priorities on birth control education & women's education

How?

4. Responsible technologies— include ecological value in economic structure— use ecologically smart technology & recyclable technology. Use benign energy sources & energy saving technologies. Reduce waste.

How?

Has implications for changes in world perceptions & philosophies, global environments, health, geopolitics, science & technology, lifestyles

How?

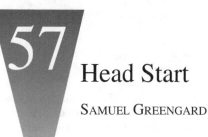

57 Head Start

SAMUEL GREENGARD

Clad in slacks and a dress shirt, Theodore Berger sits in his cluttered office, surrounded by the flotsam and jetsam of his work: modems, Zip drives, electrostatic bags, manuals, floppy disks, white cotton gloves, books. The intense neurobiologist is talking neurons and silicon chips, dendrite tissue and advanced photonics.

Beneath the wall-mounted photographs of brain tissue and schematic diagrams of VLSI chips sit a pair of Gateway 2000 Pentium PCs. Their hard plastic outer cases have been removed, the inside electronics ready for quick exploration. It's an unmistakable metaphor for a guy who finds the bony cranium an incidental obstacle to studying gray matter.

During the past four years, Berger and a seven-member team of scientists—experts in everything from semiconductors to the neurophysiology of tissue cultures—have worked ceaselessly at the University of Southern California in Los Angeles to unlock the brain's complex mathematical model so they can bridge the gap between silicon and cerebrum. "If we can speak to the brain in its own language then we begin to understand the biological basis of thought and learning," says the 46-year-old scientist. "It's a matter of understanding the way neurons act and react in every conceivable situation, then building a device that can duplicate their basic functions and transmit the appropriate electrical impulses."

If Berger can link the two—computer and brain—he may create a parallel-processing network that could func-

tion as a brain implant. Such a device would restore physical and mental functions lost to stroke, head trauma, Alzheimer's, epilepsy, and an array of other maladies. His plan to create a bionic brain is bold, brash, and just a bit, well, mind-blowing. Berger—scientist, tinkerer, dreamer—wants to be the man who implants microchips between your ears. And the amazing thing is that he just might succeed.

SIMPLE PROBLEM, COMPLEX SOLUTION

Understanding the human brain is a formidable task. Parked inside the average cranium are between 1 and 10 billion neurons. Extensions called dendrites relay electrical impulses to other neurons, the brain cells that serve as the basic building blocks of thought and activity. The electrical impulses are carried on fibers called axons. The result is a neural network of remarkable complexity.

The power of neurons is that they can work together in different ways to produce speech, vision, hearing, and thought. Only when something goes terribly wrong are we aware of how serious it is to lose these connections. Only then are we able to recognize how difficult it is to regain what's lost and how much therapy may be required.

That's the part intriguing Berger, who earned his doctorate in physiological psychology in 1976 from Harvard University and has been hooked on the brain ever since. Even in his early researching days at the University of Pittsburgh, when he first began to explore the idea of building a bionic brain, Berger found himself puzzling over some fascinating questions: If brain tissue dies, can it be replaced with a small computer that sends the same signals? Can we build an electronic bridge to restore the brain's full function? Says Berger: "The problem is simple; the solution is incredibly complex."

Neuroscience, a field that didn't exist until the mid-1960s, has struggled to map the human brain and comprehend how all the pieces fit together. It's analogous to a space alien dissecting computers, robots, and other devices stuffed with semiconductors. Without a road map, it would be virtually impossible to know what each chip does and how it interacts with other microprocessors.

A decade ago, when Berger began studying "wet" brain tissue taken from animals, he saw how little was known about the way neurons process information, or how populations of neurons can work together.

Although scientists know a great deal about the functioning of the individual nerve cells that compose the hippocampus—the part of the brain that oversees memory—there's still no clear idea of how their interaction produces the cognitive function known as learning. "A great deal of classical neurophysiology is devoted to trying to understand how the neurons process the signal and what the output represents," he explains.

That's not a nagging concern for Berger. Instead, he spends 12 to 14 hours a day identifying and cataloging predictable and repeatable neural electrical patterns, continuing a pattern of neural/technical intervention that has been explored for decades. In the 1950s, for instance, a stir was caused by a famous experiment on rats by J. Olds and P. Milner. Electrodes were implanted in each rat's lateral hypothalamus and connected to a stimulator that could be activated by pressing a small button. Since the electrical stimulation caused feelings of pleasure, the rats soon learned to stimulate themselves, choosing that button rather than another that would provide them with food, even when they were hungry.

A decade later, American neurophysiologist J. M. R. Delgado used stereotactic instruments to implant microelectrodes in precisely targeted areas within the brain. Their signals were transmitted wirelessly, making it possible to send high-voltage current. That led to drastic changes in emotional, sexual, and social behavior.

In one dramatic demonstration, Delgado implanted an electronic receiver in the medial region of the hypothalamus of a bull and then challenged the animal to do battle in a bullfighting ring. Delgado stopped the charging bull at the last minute by activating electrodes with a radio transmitter.

More recent experiments by researchers like Caltech's Carver Mead have shown that the elementary operations found in the nervous system can be realized by analog circuits created with standard silicon fabrication technology. Many neural areas are organized as thin sheets and carry two-dimensional representations of their computational space. These structures map well onto the two-dimensional silicon surface. Coincidentally, in both neural and silicon technologies, the active devices (synapses and transistors) occupy no more than a small percentage of the space—"wire" fills the remaining area.

Berger and fellow team member Vasilis Marmarelis, a professor of biomedical engineering, have built on those insights through an elaborate game of copycat, developing a complicated mathematical model that precisely replicates the input and output signals that a natural neural system uses. Just as a basketball player doesn't require a degree in advanced trigonometry to toss a jump shot through a hoop, Berger doesn't need to unlock the vast secrets of the brain to make an implant work.

Wander into Berger's lab and you begin to see where he's going with all this. Alongside a workbench covered with beakers and tubes, a researcher (in the finest tradition of a Carnegie Deli chef) slices human brain tissue into ultrathin sections. These samples are then inserted into test tubes filled with oxygen and artificial cerebral-spinal fluid, which keeps the fresh tissue alive for several hours. The sample is transported to another part of the lab, where a series of electrodes and probes are inserted. This leads to a smorgasbord of electronic amplifiers and oscilloscopes.

For the next few hours, the tissue is subjected to a series of electronic impulses designed to simulate every possible combination that the brain can throw at it. A Pentium computer charts the data, creates a unique profile for each piece of tissue, and then slots the information into an enormous database.

Berger & Co. repeat this process thousands of times. It's not enough to know how a piece of brain tissue reacts to different circumstances. They must understand the *range* of responses to the same stimulus at different times.

HARDWIRING THE HEAD

Constructing a brain implant is more than a meat-and-test-tube operation, however. Even with a growing understanding of the mathematics involved in driving such a system, today's digital microprocessors are not fast enough to execute the complex instructions in real time. Minutes, hours, even days could elapse before a software-driven brain implant could process even the most basic task, such as moving a finger that has been paralyzed by stroke or restoring a fragment of memory lost to Alzheimer's. Imagine trying to surf the Web on a 300-bps modem or commute to work in a go-cart. Possible? Yes. Practical? Definitely not.

That's where silicon and hybrid analog/digital microchips enter the picture. By hardwiring the algorithms that represent, say, 100 neurons onto a microchip, it is possible to rapidly accelerate the data processing. A calculation that might have taken 10 seconds or more in the past is now completed in only about 100 nanoseconds. What's more, these neural microchips can operate as parallel-processing devices.

But there's still a long way to go. Putting the function of perhaps 100 or 200 neurons on a single chip and then hardwiring tens of thousands of chips together would replicate only a fracton of the 4 or 5 million neurons in the hippocampus. You'd need an implant device the size of a pickup to get anywhere near the processing power of the brain.

Armand R. Tanguay Jr., director of the Center for Neural Engineering at USC and a key member of the team, hopes to solve the scaling and bandwidth problems through a combination of holography and laser optics. By using light signals to replace physical wiring, it's possible to tightly stack 1-by-1-centimeter chips, which can then communicate with each other. This tiny parallel-processing network potentially allows for real-time response, and might eventually fit into a space the size of a peanut or, more important, the human skull.

Such an implant could be tailored to replace a lost ability in humans. "Because the brain is such an adaptive organ," Berger says, "the device wouldn't have to precisely mimic the lost functions. If the brain is provided with a basic set of instructions, it would fill in the blanks and regain the lost functions. Over days and weeks, the person might make a full recovery."

It's tough, time-consuming work, but engineering an implant from the silicon up is a bit easier when you've got your own photonic fabrication facility on the premises. Just a few hundred feet from Berger's lab is a US$10 million setup that has the ability to make the photonic elements that "wire" the silicon chips together, as well as the multielectrode probes that act as an interface between living and man-made neural circuits.

Surrounded by an array of equipment that would seem more fitting in Silicon Valley than downtown LA—including a bonding machine and clean room that can filter down to 10 particles per cubic foot—assistant professor Chris Kyriakakis shows off a hybrid optical electronic device that contains a set of stacked chips. "It has the built-in electronics to power the entire device," he explains. "The first chip drives another optical chip that can modulate light. Ultimately, that's what runs the tiny computer network."

The final and most difficult step is placing such a device inside the skull and connecting it to a living brain. Crosswiring such wildly divergent universes—one brains, the other bytes—isn't for the faint of heart or the intellectually timid. It's certainly not difficult to let your imagination run amok and conjure up an image of some crazed zombie straight out of a Boris Karloff flick. But Berger is no Boris. Although Berger eschews much of the conventional wisdom that permeates the rarefied field of neuroscience—particularly traditional reductionist thinking that says every piece of the puzzle must be fully understood in order to build a scientific model—he also knows that it's crucial to retain credibility within the discipline by adhering to accepted standards and practices.

You might call his attitude skeptically reverent. "History is littered with the debris of firmly established explanations that have suddenly been overturned by new information," he says. "There are countless cases where humanity believed that an explanation was absolutely right, and then someone else came along with a radically different explanation that washed the old theory down the drain. So, it is very difficult to accept the truth of the day. It's crucial to look at various perspectives and explanations, to always keep the big picture in mind."

Berger seems to do that pretty well, though his approach perturbs some in the scientific community. Having grown up in a household that placed a high premium on introspection and accomplishment ("Not necessarily the accomplishment that comes with dollars, but the accomplishment of having an impact on the people around you," he explains), and with a father who helped pioneer transistor research at IBM, he realized early on that he wanted to make a real difference in the world.

Berger studied mathematics and psychology at college but shied away from a career in psychology, opting instead for the hands-on world of neuroscience. "I realized that psychology doesn't have the tools to fully understand the cause and effect of behavior," he says. "It is a very incomplete part of the puzzle."

Fast-forward a couple of decades, and Berger's life puzzle is mostly assembled. He lives in a pleasant split-level home overlooking the bluffs and beaches of Palos Verdes, commuting the 40 minutes to work in a 1992 Honda Accord. He spends spare moments gardening or tinkering with computers; both allow him to further explore elaborate relationships as well as evolution. Then there's his wife and his 7-year-old daughter, the latter serving as his most prized experiment. "Watching her brain develop is fascinating," he observes. "You realize that there are some things you can influence and some things you can't. You can try to teach something to someone, but if the brain isn't ready or willing to accept it, it ain't goin' in."

Which is precisely the challenge of Berger's odyssey into the mind. Dropping a functioning brain implant into a person's head and expecting it to work requires a voyage beyond the flat earth of today's neuroscience. For starters, the shape of the hippocampus doesn't remotely resemble a computer board, so inserting a conventional microchip into the brain and trying to send electrical waves back and forth would be like speaking into a telephone that's not connected to anything. Berger has circumvented this problem with a digital interface chip that will serve as the gateway between the brain's cells and the stacked set of chips that creates a group of artificial neurons.

Since transistors and neurons both send and receive electrical signals, it all boils down to arranging the chip's conductors in a pattern that matches the layout of neurons in a particular part of the brain. The brain then believes it's receiving its own signals, when in fact they're originating from the computer network.

"A transistor can send electricity and so can a neuron," Berger says. "So, instead of using a computer chip that has transistors on it, you build a chip with a piece of exposed metal. You place the metal right next to the neuron, so that it can sense the electrical signals sent out by the neuron and send signals to the neuron." By slightly overbuilding the device—designing a layer of electrodes that are perhaps 30 microns thick compared with the cell's layer of 20 microns—Berger increases the odds of a successful contact.

"THE EVER PRESENT SCALING ISSUE"

In almost all cases, electrical signals trigger the release of chemical reactions in the brain, which in turn stimulate other cells to produce electrical reactions. These result in additional chemical activity. In fact, Berger points out that cells cannot talk to each other without the release of chemicals that effectively bridge the gap between neurons. So, the brain implant would need only to stimulate electrical activity to work. Many chemical imbalances would still be treated by medication, which allows the brain to restore the proper electrical activity.

With all the parts in place, Berger will have essentially created a circuit between the device and the gray matter that operates much like a dedicated phone line.

Brain cells could actually grow on top of the silicon or metal surfaces, further blurring their distinction. A pair of the team's scientists—Michel Baudry, a professor of biological sciences, and Roberta Brinton, an associate professor of molecular pharmacology—have begun developing such cultures with animal tissue. When their research is finalized, says Berger, "We will have created a physical connection, or synapses, between the brain cells and computer chips. We have the basic ingredients for a brain replacement."

The most remarkable aspect of all, says fellow team member Tanguay, is that such a device represents the sheer oddity of today's science. Increasingly, researchers are able to find solutions without fully understanding the underlying process. "We may never really know how the brain works, but we might be able to understand enough about how neurons correlate and work together to run the mathematical model," he explains. "By connecting a silicon neural circuit to a probe chip and allowing it to 'learn' and then feed data back, it's possible to diagnose and fix the problem without having a clue how the system achieved the results. The brain would use its natural adaptive abilities to reestablish all the correct connections."

In other words, the device could learn the brain's native language and speak it, but not interpret it to the outside world.

The research is also yielding data that can be plugged into an array of other, seemingly divergent, scientific disciplines. Says Joel Davis, program manager at the Office of Naval Research: "Once you understand the algorithms that drive the brain, you can apply them to all sorts of real-world problems that require computing. You can use reverse engineering to solve problems in communications, sonar, and neural networks."

One spin-off has been a new type of parallel-processing network that could dramatically improve the quality of wireless and cellular communication. By embedding an existing algorithm in a microchip that mimics a biological model, it is possible to drastically reduce the effects of noise and distortion. Yet another prototype design, which used the same biological processing model, promises to improve speech recognition.

Of course, connecting all the dots on the brain implant remains the team's central focus—and their enormous challenge. For one thing, there's a dizzying array of experimental technologies that must intertwine and complement one another perfectly. It's one thing to create computer simulations onscreen in a highly controlled environment, but it's quite another to make them work in the real world of chemistry, biology, and neurophysiology. Stimulating a neuron or two in the brain is a pretty good achievement but mere child's play compared with stimulating thousands of neurons and running electrical channels through each.

Then there's the profound question of how many artificial neurons scientists can fit on a microchip, and how many chips they can pack into a cranium. "The ever present scaling issue," as Tanguay puts it. Even the simplest prototype versions of the device will require far more exotic and sophisticated chips and interconnections than the group has so far managed to design and build.

Alas, there's also the humbling reality that if any member of the highly skilled research team drops out or dies, the project could quickly crumble. So far, the team has steered remarkably clear of ego and turf battles, but the irony remains inescapable—the development of what could be the most advanced parallel-processing network on earth hinges on the most basic and tenuous: fellow humans.

Berger believes the team is about five years away from designing a brain implant for animals and about 10 to 15 years away from the first device for humans. With custom microchip designs taking weeks or months and other technical hurdles at every turn, it's certainly not a project for anyone with less than the patience of Buddha and the persistence of someone who sells insurance.

That suits Berger just fine. Nobody ever said that building an electronic brain would be easy, and it's clear that he's just as infatuated with the process as with the thought of changing people's minds.

"You build it neuron by neuron and chip by chip," he says. "You enjoy each experiment and piece of the puzzle while keeping a focus on the bigger picture." Berger won't rest until he has built a bionic brain. He definitely wants to get inside your head.

Questions

1. What are Theodore Berger and his team trying to accomplish in understanding as well as in technological development?
2. What is the major technological problem in creating a bionic person?
3. What is "neuroscience," and how old is it?
4. What are the scientists' strategies in trying to understand how nerve cells produce learning?
5. How has Theodore Berger dealt with the problem of there being no physical connection between a microchip that would be inserted into the brain and the brain's existing neurons?
6. How and why is photonics used in the brain microchips?
7. Could brain cells actually grow on top of the metal or silicon surfaces? Explain.
8. Is it possible for electronic devices to simulate brain processes without our full understanding of how the brain works? Explain.
9. What are some possible spin-offs from such a "brain microchip"? Name three.
10. What are the most formidable problems of such spin-offs?
11. How far are Berger and his team from successfully designing a brain implant chip?

A Bridge to Your 21st Century Understanding

Complete and discuss the following flowchart.

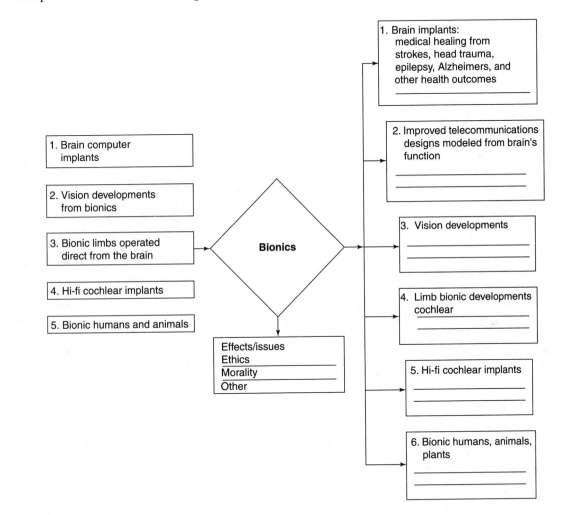

58

Telemedicine: The Health System of Tomorrow

Thomas Blanton and David C. Balch

• •

The place: North Carolina's Central Prison in Raleigh.

The problem: Inmate No. 35271 (not his real number) has an unusual skin rash that the prison doctor can't diagnose. The prison administration does not want to be sued for inadequate medical care for its prisoners, but at the same time, it does not want to run the security risk of transporting a dangerous felon to an outside specialist. Bringing the specialist to the prison would also present problems.

The solution: A telemedicine link with East Carolina University School of Medicine. In a special telemedicine booth a hundred miles away, a dermatologist sits in front of a video console and interviews the patient while directing the prison nurse where to point the tiny dermatology camera. He diagnoses the condition and prescribes a course of treatment.

The result: The prisoner's condition is treated, the prison doesn't get sued, and the state saves potentially thousands of dollars.

A far-flung view of the future? Not at all. Telemedicine is already in practice in settings such as this and may become nearly universal in the not-too-distant future.

CREATING PORTABLE HEALTH CARE

The phrase "health care reform" has been used in recent political years to describe changes in the way health care is

Originally appeared in September–October 1995 issue of THE *FUTURIST.* Used with permission from the World Future Society, 7910 Woodmont Avenue, Suite 450, Bethesda, Maryland 20814. 301/686-8274. ⟨http://www.wfs.org⟩

financed. Even though health-care-financing reforms failed to make it through the last Congress, health care is changing in the United States. The real reform is developing in the way health care is delivered.

As technology has developed over the years, medical diagnoses have become more accurate and treatments more effective. But the x-ray, magnetic resonance imaging machines, and other tools are not portable. Treatment and therapeutic facilities have been centralized in hospitals and rehabilitation centers, so that patients have to travel distances and wait in doctors' offices to be seen. As a result, doctors don't get to see patients on a regular basis and end up treating symptoms and diseases rather than people.

Proposed solutions have been varied, from holistic health to formerly fringe ideas such as herbal medicine and massage therapy, which are gaining in popularity. But technology may soon allow the house call to return to mainstream medicine, with data being transported rather than people.

The idea of telemedicine has been around for almost as long as there has been science fiction and has been in actual practice since the late 1950s. But the recent upsurge in medical costs, combined with advances in technology, are now making telemedicine a widespread reality.

TELEMEDICINE IN PRACTICE

There are now 25 telemedicine projects in the United States, according to the American Telemedicine Association. At present, these programs tend to serve rural areas where population is sparse and income low. Areas such as western Texas, eastern North Carolina, rural Georgia, and

West Virginia are the most active in using telemedicine. A recent study by the consulting firm of Arthur D. Little, Inc., showed that healthcare costs could be reduced by as much as $36 billion a year if health information technologies such as telemedicine were widely used.

In 1989, the U.S. Public Health Service gave partial funding to Texas Tech's MedNet program, which linked health-care practitioners in hospitals and clinics from 37 rural communities in western Texas. In its first year, this project reported a net savings of 14% to 22% in the cost of health-care delivery. The agencies involved reported a decrease in salaries and ambulance costs along with an increase in earned revenue.

One important issue in developing telemedicine has been states' costs in providing health care in prisons. California alone spends $380 million per year on prison health care. With the popularity of laws such as "Three Strikes and You're Out," prison populations will increase. So will the cost of prison health care.

In 1990, a prison inmate sued the state of Florida over inadequate health care and won a $1-million settlement. That prompted Florida to begin prison telemedicine on a pilot basis.

The next year, North Carolina's largest prison—Central Prison in Raleigh—contracted with the East Carolina University School of Medicine to provide telemedicine services. Since that time, physicians from the medical school have provided more than 350 consultations with the prison. In 1994, the school built the first "telemedicine suite" in the nation—four consultation booths specially designed for telemedicine.

In addition to the prison, two hospitals in rural eastern North Carolina have consultation links with the East Carolina medical school, and two more are scheduled to come on-line in 1995. The Medical College of Georgia, too, is building a network of 60 sites around the state for telemedicine consultations.

Just as cable television began as a way of serving rural areas outside of broadcasters' range, telemedicine is beginning as a way of reaching out to medically underserved areas. As the possibilities of cable television offerings became better known, metropolitan areas became its heaviest users. Similarly, as physicians and patients see the possibilities in telemedicine, it should spread more widely and into urbanized areas.

Patients recovering from heart attacks can already put on a headset, connect the electrocardiogram (ECG) wires to their chests, and ride their stationary bikes. The patients stay at home and communicate by telephone with the hospital. The same phone wires that carry their conversation also carry the ECG information to the medical technician on the other end. Up to five patients at a time can be served this way, and they are in contact with each other as well as the hospital.

A pilot program for this type of cardiac rehabilitation took place at St. Vincent Charity Hospitals in Cleveland, Ohio, during the late 1970s and worked so well that it became a model for other areas, including Nashville, Tennessee, and Greenville, North Carolina. Doctors at East Carolina University are setting aside a cable channel so that the cardiac rehab patients can have visual contact with the hospital staff. As technology advances, there may eventually be two-way video interaction between the patient and the hospital.

HEALTH CARE AT HOME AND WORK

As the technology advances, telemedicine will spread out over the information superhighway to link rural hospitals with smaller medical centers; then local doctors' offices will come on-line; and, finally, telemedicine will reach into private homes.

Questions

1. Why is telemedicine gaining popularity and becoming more of a reality?
2. How much in annual health-care costs could be saved if technologies such as telemedicine are used?
3. Why is telemedicine an especially attractive option for use in prisons?
4. Have telemedicine sites proved to be successful? Explain.
5. What are other possible applications of telemedicine?
6. If you lived in a rural area hundreds of miles from a hospital or doctor, would you favor the use of telemedicine? Explain your position.
7. Explain the pros, cons, and implications of using telemedicine as a future approach to medicine.

A Bridge to Your 21st Century Understanding

Complete and discuss the following flowchart.

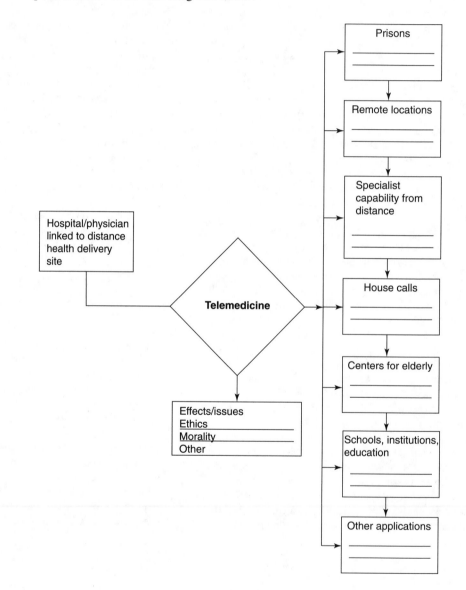

Keys to the Kingdom

Leon Jaroff

- -

As he chats with the young mother, the doctor flicks a cotton swab into the mouth of her infant son, collecting a small sample of mucus from inside his cheek. In the back room of his office, he inserts the sample into a machine, which extracts DNA from the mucus cells and compares it with the genetic material on a dime-size chip. Minutes later, a computer printer begins to spit out a list of the infant's genes. Fortunately, all but a few of the genes are labeled "normal." It is those few that the doctor discusses as he explains the results to the mother. "Your son's genetic inheritance is generally good," he says, "but he is somewhat predisposed to skin lesions. So starting right away, he should be protected against excessive exposure to the sun." And, the doctor warns, "he may well be susceptible to cardiovascular disease later in life. To lessen his risk, after about age two he should begin a lifelong low-fat, high-fiber diet."

Fanciful as it seems, this scenario may soon be commonplace. It is based on the heady progress that medical researchers are making these days as they discover new genes and their role in disease. More than that, it reflects the fact that virtually all disease, to some degree, has a genetic component. As a result of these discoveries, tests for the presence of genes that either cause disease or make people more susceptible to it are becoming increasingly available. "We are entering an era when disease will be predicted before it occurs," says William Haseltine, chairman of Human Genome Sciences, a Maryland biotech firm. "Medicine is

basically going to change from a treatment-based to a prevention-based discipline."

Seizing on the new findings about disease genes and how they function, pharmaceutical companies are rushing to develop drugs that will either neutralize the effects of dangerous genes or take the place of vital proteins that, because of aberrant genes, are missing from an individual's system. Equally promising, researchers are honing their skills in a technique that may cause one of the most significant changes in the history of medicine. It is known as gene therapy: the introduction of genes into existing cells to prevent or cure a wide range of diseases, including cancer.

"Thirty years down the line, we'll have identified a hundred or so genes that predispose to many common diseases," predicts Dr. Leroy Hood, chairman of the molecular-biology department at the University of Washington. "So we'll be able to do a genetic fingerprint showing your potential future health history, and we'll have preventive measures that can circumvent whatever limitations your genes impose on you." Looking even further ahead, Haseltine anticipates the use of genes "to re-generate, replace and repair what's broken."

That kind of optimism is endemic among the legions of medical researchers now engaged in the most momentous technological effort since the Manhattan atom-bomb project: decoding the messages contained in human DNA. Aided largely by grants from the federally funded Human Genome Project, they are striving toward the major goal of mapping the genome and identifying all its estimated 50,000 to 100,000 genes by the year 2005.

Reprinted with permission from *Time* magazine. Jaroff L. "Keys to the Kingdom" *Time*, Fall 1996.

485

The human genome is the famed double helix, the long stretch of DNA containing some 3 billion chemical code letters on which the gene—actually discrete segments on the strand—are located, much like cities and towns along a major highway. Coiled in the nucleus of the human cell, the genome is in effect a blueprint of the human body. When it is fully mapped, says Eric Lander, director of the Whitehead/M.I.T. Center for Genome Research, it will provide for medicine the kind of dramatic insights that the periodic table—which categorized the elements so that scientists could predict how they would react—contributed to chemistry.

Genome researchers are making steady progress toward their goal, discovering new genes almost daily. As of mid-1996, they had identified more than 6,000 human genes. And, of particular interest to doctors, a number of these are disease genes, those with defects or mutations that can cause or predispose to illness. Last year alone, at least 11 new disease genes were discovered, including a second gene for breast cancer.

Once a gene is located and its sequence of chemical code letters discerned, scientists can devise a test for the presence of that gene in any patient. Among the many diagnostic tests available are those for such genetic disorders as cystic fibrosis, Huntington's disease, breast cancer, Duchenne muscular dystrophy, neurofibromatosis and retinoblastoma.

The cystic fibrosis (CF) test, in particular, is already playing a significant role in many families afflicted with this life-threatening disease, which occurs in individuals who have inherited two CF genes, one from each parent. One of every 25 Americans is a CF carrier, free of the disorder but endowed with a single, recessive CF gene. By the laws of Mendelian genetics, any offspring of two carriers has a 25% chance of inheriting two CF genes and being stricken with the disorder, a 1-in-2 chance of being a carrier and a 25% chance of inheriting no CF gene.

Before the cystic-fibrosis test was developed, those statistics posed a dilemma for couples with CF in their families. They could only hope that they did not carry the gene or that, if they did, their offspring would not be afflicted. But now the test affords them the chance to know whether they are carriers and, if so, precisely what the risks are in having children.

Even more hopeful is an experimental procedure in which doctors mix the sperm and eggs from a CF-carrier couple in a laboratory dish, allow the fertilized eggs to grow into four-to-eight-celled embryos, then flick off a few cells and test their DNA. Upon finding an embryo that is free of the CF gene, they implant it in the woman's uterus, ensuring that the resulting baby will neither carry the gene nor be afflicted by the disease.

Carriers of the Huntington's disease gene have fewer options. The Huntington's gene is causal, which means that people with even a single copy of it are invariably doomed to a lingering, unpleasant death from an illness that is yet incurable. This also means that the test results will sound either a death sentence or a reprieve—a fact that must be made clear during pretest counseling, says Nancy Wexler, the Columbia University clinical psychologist whose research led to the discovery of the Huntington's gene. Because of their decision to take the test, she says, some 50,000 Americans are living without symptoms but with the dismaying knowledge that they have the Huntington's gene and will someday succumb to the disease (see Figure 59.1).

The widely heralded test for the breast-cancer gene BRCA1, on the other hand, provides information that gives women many options. Unlike the Huntington's gene, BRCA1 is a "predisposing" gene; it increases vulnerability to cancer but does not make it inevitable. While the gene apparently confers an 85% risk of developing breast cancer and a 40%-to-60% risk of ovarian cancer, women who test positive may reduce that risk considerably, says Mark Skolnick, who led the team at Salt Lake City's Myriad Genetics that isolated the gene. He suggests they adopt a program that includes, among other things, exercise and a low-fat diet, and that they avoid doses of estrogen after menopause. Some go further, opting to have their ovaries removed or even choosing prophylactic mastectomies.

Developing successful drug treatments for these disorders depends not only on the discovery of the appropriate disease gene but also on the identification of the protein that it controls. Each human gene consists of a coded chemical "message" that directs the cell to produce a particular protein necessary either for body structure or for a metabolic process. After researchers have zeroed in on a gene and learned its code sequence, they are able to identify its protein and eventually discover the larger role this protein plays in the body.

Researchers are making good use of the new technology and gene discoveries to develop an array of novel drugs. "Now that we have an increasing ability to identify and sequence genes, there is no doubt that there will be an improvement in the way we go about drug development," says Dr. C. Thomas Caskey, senior vice president of basic research at Merck, in Whitehouse Station, New Jersey.

For example, explains Caskey, researchers know that there are at least three or four forms of Alzheimer's disease,

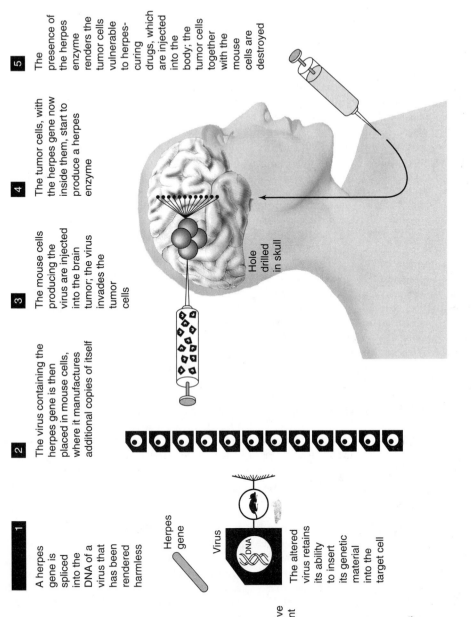

1
A brain tumor is formed by rapidly dividing cancer cells

The reason for this rapid division is that genes within the cells are defective

Defective segment

Genes are segments of DNA, the tightly coiled strands that are found in chromosomes; there are 23 pairs of chromosomes in each human cell

A herpes gene is spliced into the DNA of a virus that has been rendered harmless

Herpes gene

Virus

The altered virus retains its ability to insert its genetic material into the target cell

2
The virus containing the herpes gene is then placed in mouse cells, where it manufactures additional copies of itself

3
The mouse cells producing the virus are injected into the brain tumor; the virus invades the tumor cells

Hole drilled in skull

4
The tumor cells, with the herpes gene now inside them, start to produce a herpes enzyme

5
The presence of the herpes enzyme renders the tumor cells vulnerable to herpes-curing drugs, which are injected into the body; the tumor cells together with the mouse cells are destroyed

Figure 59.1
How It Works

each of which may be caused by a different defective gene. "If I develop a drug for gene A," he says, "it may not have any influence on a patient who has a defect on gene C. So it's easy to understand how genomics research would be critical to the development of very precise and effective drugs."

The strategies pharmaceutical firms are using in drug development for genetic disorders vary widely. If the gene defect results in a protein that does not function, says Myriad's Skolnick, "you would try to replace that function by introducing a correct version of the protein into the body. Or you would try to mimic the function of the missing protein with a synthetic compound."

Pharmaceutical companies synthesize large sets of these compounds, Skolnick explains, and then test them, one at a time, seeking one that will perform the same function as a missing protein. "You try to find one that's effective and doesn't have side effects," he says. "That's the normal process of drug delivery."

Yet for all the emphasis on the development of new drugs, many medical researchers believe the ultimate solution to gene-based disease lies in gene therapy. None is more outspoken on that subject than Dr. W. French Anderson, director of the gene-therapy program at the University of Southern California/Norris Comprehensive Cancer Center in Los Angeles and the undisputed champion of the still adolescent art. "Twenty years from now, gene therapy will have revolutionized the practice of medicine," he predicts. "Virtually every disease will have gene therapy as one of its treatments."

In 1990, with two colleagues, Anderson, then at the National Institutes of Health, performed the first federally approved gene therapy. Their patient was Ashanthi DeSilva, 4, a girl with a severe immune-deficiency disease caused by a faulty gene that failed to order the production of a vital enzyme. The NIH team extracted some of her white blood cells and exposed them to genetically engineered viruses that carried normal versions of the faulty gene. The viruses invaded the white blood cells, which were then transfused back into the child's bloodstream. There, the cells, newly endowed with the normal gene, began producing the proper enzyme. While Ashanthi still needs follow-up treatments—the altered cells eventually die off—she leads a relatively normal childhood.

The widely heralded success of that treatment unduly raised public expectations that permanent cures achieved by gene therapy would soon become commonplace. But as researchers wrestled with a host of technological problems in subsequent human trials, some disenchantment set in. It culminated last spring when an NIH committee on gene therapy suggested that such NIH-funded research be con-

fined to lab animals until more details of the technology are ironed out.

"It's easy to become superenthusiastic and say everything is going to change," says Dr. Arno Motulsky, a University of Washington geneticist who was co-chairman of the NIH committee. Motulsky believes it is going to change—but not overnight. "Gene therapy makes good sense in terms of the theory—putting in a good gene for a bad one," he says, "but the problem is to make it realistic." Dr. David Rimoin, chairman of pediatrics at Cedars-Sinai Medical Center in Los Angeles and president of the American College of Medical Genetics, agrees. "You need a smart bomb to get the DNA to the right place, and a smart detonator to set it off at the right time," he says, "and for the most part, those mechanisms are not yet available."

In gene therapy, most of the current "smart bombs," as in the case of Ashanthi DeSilva, are viruses, which by their nature invade cells and deposit their genetic material into the cell nucleus. Researchers have learned how to strip the viruses of their reproductive genes, insert into the viral DNA the beneficial gene they want to deliver, and then let the virus infect a patient's cells. The virus inserts its own now harmless genes, as well as the beneficial one, into the cellular DNA. If all goes well and the gene "expresses" itself, the cell begins producing the needed protein.

The problem is that the altered viruses do not always seek out the target cells and sometimes insert themselves in the wrong place in the cellular DNA. Then too, once in place, the new genes sometimes fail to express themselves. "There are still a few walls to get over," Anderson concedes. He points out that in the initial trial, viruses used for cystic fibrosis, for example, produced an inflammatory response: "So the trials were halted, and another generation of viral vectors was developed. Now we're going to restart the clinical trials with these new-generation vectors," which he thinks will do the job.

Another problem is getting viral vectors into bone-marrow stem cells, from which all of the blood's white cells are descended. Even when the rare stem cells are found, inserting genes into them is difficult because they divide infrequently, and the vectors used in gene therapy insert genes only into cells that are dividing. Had Anderson's group been able to use stem cells in the landmark therapy with little Ashanthi DeSilva, for example, follow-up treatments would not have been necessary. Endowed with the normal gene, the marrow stem cells would have produced a continuing supply of new white blood cells carrying that gene, and Ashanthi's cure would have been permanent.

Despite these technological obstacles, medical researchers are sanguine about the future of gene therapy. To date, they have injected about 1,500 patients with some form of altered genes as part of the more than 200 gene-therapy trials taking place worldwide. Among the 30-odd illnesses targeted in these trials are cystic fibrosis, vascular disease and 15 forms of cancer.

The fledgling field took another step forward in July, when doctors at the University of Pittsburgh Medical Center performed the first gene therapy on a woman with rheumatoid arthritis, a chronic disease caused by the immune system's running amuck and attacking the body's connective tissue. Their strategy was to expose cells in the swollen tissue lining their patient's finger joints to genetically engineered viruses. These viruses carried a gene responsible for a protein that blocks the action of interleukin-1, a substance that stimulates immune-system activity. Without that stimulation, the doctors hope, the immune system will halt its assault on the joint linings.

Such trials on human patients are vital, Anderson believes, "because you can't just work everything out in test tubes and animal models." He pleads for public understanding and patience as researchers refine their gene-therapy techniques. "People don't understand that the development of an ordinary drug, from time of concept to product, is 10 years," he says. "What we're talking about is a revolutionary new approach to therapy, and we're only five years into it."

Many researchers are looking well beyond today's possibilities and are not averse to a little crystal-ball gazing. The University of Washington's Hood, who heads a large-scale family study to track down the genes that predispose to prostate cancer, predicts that it will not be the "medical" genes but the behavioral genes that will eventually stir the greatest public interest. "We now know that there are genes that predispose to risk taking, and almost certainly there are genes that predispose to violence," Hood says. Such genes, and the neurotransmitters they most likely are

responsible for, he suggests, can lead eventually to drugs "that will do away with mental disease."

The potential of genetic medicine seems virtually limitless, underscoring the words of Nobel laureate James Watson as he spoke before a congressional committee considering the start-up of the Human Genome Project. "We used to think that our fate was in our stars," said Watson. "Now we know that, in large measure, our fate is in our genes."

Questions

1. Explain what is meant by the following quote: "Medicine is basically going to change from a treatment-based to a prevention-based discipline."
2. Discuss some of the pros and cons of gene therapy. What is the future goal of gene therapy?
3. What is the Human Genome Project, and what are the implications of its findings?
4. Explain the findings of the cystic fibrosis test.
5. Name some of the diseases that have been detected from gene findings.
6. How does gene discovery influence drug development?
7. What are some of the practical problems of gene therapy?
8. How many illnesses to date have been treated in gene-therapy trials worldwide?
9. How long is the typical development of a drug from concept to product?
10. Explain the rationale that "drugs will do away with mental disease."
11. What is your opinion of gene therapy? What kind of medicine and medical prevention do you expect to see in 10 years? 20 years? 30 years? 100 years?

Scenario I

Gene Therapy
Consider the following hypothetical news broadcast:

January 20XX New York, NY
Excerpted from the NBC six o'clock news:

> Researchers reported today that they can replace genes that cause disease by using artificial human chromosomes. This treatment will "fix" genes that are not working right and will replace missing genes; the concern is, however, that there could be serious medical risks. There is still hope that artificial chromosomes will be sold soon.

Discussion:
   How can artificial human chromosomes replace genes? What are the medical risks of such replacement? What ethical issues relate to the sale of artificial human chromosomes? Can artificial chromosomes be used to treat disorders caused by a single gene?

Scenario II

Xenotransplants
Consider the following scene:

October 10, 20XX Chicago, IL

   John's kidney has become diseased. He has been on a donor list for months, waiting impatiently for a new kidney. The outlook for the transplant or for returning to a healthy lifestyle seems grim. However, John does not want to give up hope. As he is waiting in the examining room for the doctor, he reviews two detailed reports about xenotransplants and quickly scribbles a list of questions.
   John is sitting on the examining table as the doctor walks in. Before the doctor can say a word, John says, "Dr. Michaels, I have been reading reports on xenotransplants, and I want one."
   "John, let's discuss this idea of yours a little further," Dr. Michaels replies.

Discussion:
   Select a year for this scenario to occur (20??). Based on the time period that you choose, answer the following questions: What kind of animal should be used for John's kidney transplant? What complications might occur? How would researchers prevent animal viruses from being transferred to John? Could animals be kept in pathogen-free environments in order to prevent virus transfer? Should there be concern for the possibility that animals carry as-yet-unknown viruses that are fatal to man? If you were John, what five questions would you want Dr. Michaels to answer for you (not including the previously listed questions)?

Future Genetic Testing

60

DO YOU REALLY WANT THE RESULTS OF YOUR GENETIC TEST?

Genetic testing brings about many ethical, legal, moral, and personal issues that need to be resolved. For example, what would happen if an insurance company knew that you were predisposed to certain diseases because of the results of your genetic tests? Would the company cancel your insurance or not offer you insurance in the first place? Would companies refuse to hire you on the basis of your genetic tests for fear that you would cost them money in sick days, insurance costs, or lack of productivity? What if you had to have a genetic test prior to being hired by a new company. Would you refuse? Could a company demand that you either take a genetic test or be fired?

Other important issues revolve around the availability versus privacy of genetic test results. Would the results of a person's genetic tests be available to anyone who asked for them? Does genetic testing correlate to an invasion of privacy, and would it stigmatize anyone who is found to have cellular deficiencies?

The role of genetic testing in relation to reproduction and children must also be considered. Could prenatal ge-netic testing lead to an increase in abortions? Should children be tested so that parents know what diseases they will have? Would the genetic testing of children help parents prevent their children from getting diseases, or would it cause psychological trauma to the children instead? What would be the psychological and legal effects of incorrect genetic test results?

Many health professionals believe that counseling provided by health professionals before and after genetic tests are taken will soon be medicine's fastest growing specialty. The prediction is that doctors will be required to take courses in how to explain the effects of genetic predictions to patients. Explaining a genetic prognosis is a complicated process; yet, health professionals must learn how to do it so that the great advances in genetics will not be surpassed by unnecessary anguish, dispute, or lawsuits.

Reference

Jaroff, L. (1996, Fall). Keys to the Kingdom. *Time,* pp. 24–29.

A Bridge to Your 21st Century Understanding

Complete and discuss the following flowchart.

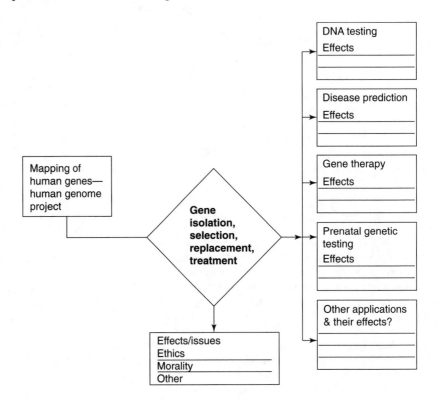

The Information Warrior

Ellison C. Urban

61

In war, in the end, it all comes down to the soldier. Electronics already equips him to fight day or night, whatever the weather, move with extraordinary speed and agility and shoot with unprecedented precision and deadliness. At the same time, it arms staff officers with the means to gather and evaluate a host of strategic and tactical information. Regrettably, the two tasks have yet to be well integrated. The soldier making life-and-death decisions in the thick of battle is seldom aware of the bigger picture. Often neither his fellows nor his commanders have good ways of dispersing what is aptly known as the fog of war.

In future wars, control of lethal weaponry and "information weaponry" will as never before be shared at all ranks of combat personnel. Combat and intelligence gathering will take place simultaneously and synergistically with the advent of the tactical information assistant—TIA, as it is called by the Advanced Research Projects Agency (ARPA) of the U.S. Department of Defense. This gentle name is applied to devices that use not bullets for ammunition, but bits.

Several types are currently in field trial. To pick out a few, there are laser rangefinders that instantly send coordinates and detailed descriptions of targets, as well as live video of the battle scene, to fellow soldiers and to remote intelligence officers and commanders; body-hugging computers and head-mounted displays with which a soldier can walk up to equipment and diagnose its status; computer-generated maps that change scale and overlay

differing types of information in response to voice requests. In design stages is a vest and display that will integrate *all* electronic systems, from voice-controlled computers to radios.

HUMIONICS ON THE MARCH

In the early days of aviation, electronic equipment was simply jammed into any available space on an aircraft without much consideration for aerodynamics, weight distribution, power requirements, interoperability, or user interface. The problems caused by this haphazard approach led to the development of a discipline called avionics. "Integrating" electronics with humans requires the creation of a similar discipline, what I have termed humionics.

The related field of ergonomics, and traditional human-factors studies in general, is primarily concerned with a person's functioning in relation to manifestly physical objects and situations. Ergonomics clearly is important for the already weight-burdened soldier, who before each mission often makes tradeoffs among food, water, bullets, and equipment. Humionics, in contrast, considers the human as a system and addresses how that system operates in its electronic environment.

Humionics is especially important for the increasing number of soldiers who carry computers, radios, Global Positioning System (GPS) displays, cameras, microphones, and sensors, along with all of their other mission-essential equipment. Soldiers commonly use straps or Velcro to affix each piece of equipment on their bodies and connect them with wires. A humionics approach eliminates

Repeated with permission from Urban E. "The Information Warrior." *IEEE Spectrum,* November 1995. ©1995 IEEE.

duplicate components among all these devices, such as keypads, displays, batteries and associated electronics, and uses only the unique front-end circuitry of, say, radios and GPS units.

The resulting system, managed by a vest-pocket computer, would use one battery, one display, one input device, and so on, with a concomitant reduction in overall size, weight, and power consumption. Equipment would be designed with uniform interfaces (either serial or wireless) to the body-worn local-area network (bodyLAN) within the vest which would eliminate the current babel of incompatible specifications. And, as discussed in more detail below, humionics covers safety issues such as placement of equipment on the body, heat dissipation, radio frequency energy, and prevention of electrical shock.

FIRST STEPS

The TIA program of the Advanced Research Projects Agency (ARPA), Arlington, Va., was started just this year. In keeping with the agency's overall mission, much of the technology has never been explored before, and is being developed with extensive cooperation between corporate and university research laboratories.

But TIAs are not blue-sky projects. Despite the short time that has been devoted to their development, all but one (the bodyLAN vest) are now undergoing field tests in the U.S. armed forces. They are critical components in warfare in the information age, part of what is being called the "horizontal battlefield." In this arena new strategy and tactics are required as decision-making becomes more and more decentralized and information flows in all directions among battle echelons.

The Technology Advanced Mini Eyesafe Rangefinder (Tamer) exemplifies a special-purpose TIA. Its prime contractor is Motorola Inc.'s Government and Space Technology Group, based in Scottsdale, Ariz. Tamer adds information technology to Melios, a widely used U.S. Army laser rangefinder. Melios, which in some versions has an internal compass and meter for vertical tilt, is hand-held or mounted on a tripod. To use the rangefinder, the operator puts its 7×50 optics on a target. That target is either a true military target or any landmark that, if it is marked on the soldier's paper map, will help him find out where he is.

Once he has identified his own location, the soldier presses a button to fire an eye-safe laser. The range to the target, which can be up to 10 kilometers away, is displayed on a light-emitting diode in the optics module. The operator then performs what is known in the U.S. Army as a Salute report, the word being a mnemonic for the size of the target or targets (how many of them), activity, location, unit (what type they are, say, armor), time, and equipment (say, T-72 tank). The soldier reads the Salute report information over a radio voice channel to a command post, which relays the information to a gun emplacement.

The entire operation, from self-location to ascertaining the Salute information, typically takes 5 to 10 minutes. The target's location is derived from the soldier's own position and its range bearing, and elevation in relation to the target. Further time is then spent by the recipient of the message, who calculates the coordinates of the target.

Moreover, the accuracy of the target coordinates depends on the skill of the soldier using the rangefinder and the hospitality of the terrain. Examples were demonstrated time after time in the Gulf War: it is extremely difficult to determine a location in the desert because there are few mapped terrain features to lock on to.

TAMER IN ACTION

Tamer was tested with the U.S. Army 2nd Armored Division in Fort Hood, Texas, and with the U.S. Army's Program Manager for Night Vision at Fort Belvoir, Va. (the developer of Melios). Fort Hood gave ARPA only three months to move Tamer from the drawing board to hardware. The tight deadline, fortunately enough, made for some effectively pragmatic decisions, if only for this version. The original Melios was simply sliced more or less down its middle, between its optics module and battery compartment, and the new components added.

The additional components include a 3.8-by-3.8-cm multi-chip module to communicate with the Global Positioning System, as well as a microcontroller, display driver, and input-output circuitry (the GPS circuitry was developed by the Advanced System Technology Office at ARPA). All circuitry is mounted on PCM-CIA cards (now known as PC cards) and connected via a standard bus. A 3.8-by-3.8-cm GPS antenna and display were added on the outside of Melios, as were two control buttons on the bottom.

The Global Positioning System was developed by the U.S. Department of Defense to allow simple, but accurate, navigation anywhere in the world at any time. The system depends on a constellation of 24 satellites that orbit the earth at a very high altitude. The GPS satellites transmit periodic coded messages that can be picked up by GPS receivers located on earth. A receiver can determine its own location only if it picks up at least three satellite signals.

Soldiers and officers in a future battle will use tactical information assistants (TIAs), now in trials or development. This soldier's position is monitored by a global positioning system (GPS) satellite; his position and tactical data are automatically updated on his map, which he queries orally. He aims a laser rangefinder at a target, while filling out an intelligence report on it. The reflected laser beam and GPS data provide target coordinates, which, along with the images he sees through the rangefinder, are sent to the rear, where command and control officers transmit the coordinates to an attack aircraft. The soldier's position and video data are shared with others down the line.

A Future Battle Scenario Using TIAs

The satellite signals are transmitted in two distinct forms: one for civilian use and the other for military use. The military code provides higher positional accuracies and protection against jamming. Civilian accuracies can be increased by a method called differential GPS, in which two receivers are used. One receiver is placed at a known base location while the other is free to roam. A location derived from the signals received by the satellites at the base station is compared with the known location. The difference is then transmitted to the roaming receiver so that it can modify the location that it derives from the satellites. Currently Tamer uses only civilian code accuracies, but both differential GPS and military code devices are being investigated.

When an operator positions the crosshairs on a target and fires the laser, the coordinates of his location are acquired from the satellite by the GPS unit. The Tamer computer takes the latitude and longitude of the rangefinder and its compass bearing and tilt angle and from them calculates the latitude and longitude of the target. These coordinates, along with associated time measurements supplied by the GPS satellite, are automatically loaded into a Salute report form displayed on a liquid-crystal display. Other items in the report are added by the operator, using the two thumb buttons, through menus and submenus for each item.

When the Salute report is completed, it is sent by means of an RS-232 connector to an Army radio, and then transmitted to its destination. The soldier may also fill in reports requesting an attack on the target (call for fire) or on the battlefield's Nuclear, Biological, or Chemical (NBC-1) status.

Current development work on Tamer will eliminate the external display and insert a miniature, high-resolution display in the optical path—the view through the eyepiece—so that no light will be visible at night. The form is laid over, but does not obscure, the view through the eyepiece. It will also add a solid-state compass developed by Honeywell Inc., plus a pedometer and auxiliary computational circuits. Battery life will be increased by using the GPS only to acquire a quick fix. The computerized compass and pedometer will then perform dead-reckoning calculations until another GPS fix is obtained.

Even more significant improvements to the system are planned with installation of an electrically erasable programmable ROM or miniature hard drive (currently a gigabyte can be stored on a 2.5-in. drive). Either will permit maps to be displayed along with a dot indicating current position. Adding a charge-coupled video device in the optical path will allow pictures to be recorded and then annotated with Salute data. A wireless transmitter at standard radio frequencies will be added, as will a receiver that will allow messages and updated tactical information—from soldiers on the field or from back-base intelligence officers—to be shown on the miniature display.

Other ideas, such as obtaining accurate bearing information from GPS data, improved lasers, and night vision, are under investigation by Motorola. It is not envisioned that each Tamer contain all the functions mentioned. Rather, because of the Tamer's modular architecture, an operator will be able to specify a particular configuration that meets his needs with minimum weight and cost.

A MAP THAT LISTENS

Pathfinder is a TIA program at BBN Systems and Technologies Corp., Cambridge, Mass., that should enable a small team to navigate and coordinate its movements with electronic maps. The Pathfinder is based on a Grid computer with a touch-sensitive liquid-crystal display. A hand-held GPS unit and small radio are connected to the computer. Typically, 1 : 50 000-scale maps are displayed on the screen. Using the touch-sensitive screen, the mission commander enters the way points selected; lines linking the points complete the planned travel route. Symbols and lines can be overlaid on the map to show the current tactical battle plan.

From the GPS data, a dot appears on the map showing the user's position. As the user (and map) move, tracks are drawn on the map to indicate travel history and make visible any deviation from the plan. Information on location is transmitted over the radio to other team members to help them coordinate their movements and improve everyone's knowledge of the military situation. A limited amount of message traffic can also be transmitted and received.

Pathfinder has been demonstrated in a variety of field exercises, primarily with the Marines in the Adriatic Sea. Its most important application for the time being is in helicopter navigation. Using Pathfinder, pilots have learned to navigate over long distances without looking outside, a feat that typically cuts 20 minutes off a one-hour trip over unknown terrain. In addition, pilots sometimes become disoriented or miss visual way points when flying low and close to the earth. Pathfinder allows them to follow the way points on the map and correlate the map better with the terrain.

The light from the Pathfinder display, however, interfered with the night vision goggles of pilots. One remedy was to coat the display with a blue gel. But this only created another problem: it is hard to use a touch-sensitive screen, even with pens, when it is smeared with gel. This problem is one of the principal reasons ARPA is working towards voice input for the system.

Pathfinder also has proven useful in training, because it logs and retains all information about its position. The positions of teams in exercises are transmitted to a central site where the entire mission is observed in real time on a single screen. The information may also be replayed for debriefings after the exercise, and may be utilized for future classroom training sessions.

TALKING YOUR WAY OUT

The VoiceMap TIA takes Pathfinder to a higher level. It relies on a smaller, lighter computer from Texas Microsystems Inc., Houston, called the Grunt, which can be strapped to a pilot's leg. The pilot's hands are not tied down, because the computer accepts voice commands and queries and does so regardless of the user. (This so-called speaker-independent voice recognition is computationally tougher than training the computer to recognize just one speaker.)

One intractable problem is that large maps cannot easily be displayed on small computer screens. Instead, the user quickly scans large areas by telling VoiceMap to zoom in and out of the map display, go left or right, and so on. Another problem is the loss of detail due to the poorer resolution and inferior color range of small computer screens. However, details—of any type—can be embedded in databases carried with the unit and selectively applied as graphical overlays, which in fact is a significant improvement over single maps with a welter of information.

The soldier asks VoiceMap for what he or she wants depending on the situation. Questions such as "Where is the water tower?" or "Which way to the river?" are answered instantly by a graphical updating of the map. Other queries might involve information not contained in the user's database, but which is supplied by radio from other databases, such as "Where is Company B?"; in a related scenario, the user would send commands to update remote databases, for instance, "Send my location to the 1st Squadron."

SMART MAPS AND HYBRIDS

Under development is the addition of artificial intelligence to Voice Map. With these techniques in place, the user will be able to ask more general questions, such as, "What is the best route to way-point Delta?" Developing the artificial intelligence techniques is a formidable task. Depending on fuel level, enemy fire, mission goals, or a host of other considerations, imagine what in this example the concept "best" could signify.

Another project in the works is connecting VoiceMap to Tamer, the GPS-aided rangefinder/report-generation system. In a typical scenario where this hybrid technology would be used, Tamer grabs the coordinates of a distant object and loads them into VoiceMap. The user then annotates the data by voice, saying, for example, "enemy tank," and the object's icon appears in the correct position on the map. The information is transmitted to the command headquarters of other soldiers.

This simple scenario shows how intelligence officers can multiply their assets in the field using TIAs. Even while executing his or her combat roles, each soldier is also an intelligence agent. Moreover, the military expects that soldiers will generate entirely novel and unplanned uses for TIAs.

All military equipment must be kept in repair—a job that can also be aided enormously by TIAs. The VuMan TIA is a wearable form-fitting computer and head-up display at present used in equipment maintenance. (A head-up display can be seen through but also superimposes on the field of view computer-generated data and graphics.) The user interacts with the computer (which is hardened against shock, temperature, water, and dirt) by way of a rotary dial and a single selection ring. Menu options are presented on the head-mounted display, and the user scrolls through them by turning the dial, and choosing options with three buttons that surround the center dial. The dial and buttons are purposely made large so that they can be handled through layers of clothing.

The menu selections are simple but extensive. Different software and datasets for different pieces or classes of equipment are uploaded to the VuMan by means of a serial cable. For example, one software package now in trials contains some 600 menu and sub-menu choices. The software is based upon the VuMan Hypertext Language (VHTL), developed at Carnegie Mellon University, Pittsburgh. The VHTL simplifies the task of creating document systems that integrate forms, references, images, and complex nested menus.

When not clambering over, around and under equipment, the maintainer needs to inform logistics officers of the status of the equipment, order parts, and perform other file-keeping operations. For these tasks a plug-in serial port connects VuMan and another computer, usually a personal computer (which itself could be networked to remote databases). VuMan then simply disgorges itself of the data entered by the user as he went about the inspection and repair.

Experience using VuMan in the maintenance of heavy vehicles—predominantly tanks and tracked vehicles—has been encouraging. First off, maintenance no longer needs the usual minimum of two people, one to actually perform the repairs or inspection, and the other to guide him through it by reading aloud from the manuals. Other results have been a 40 percent reduction in the time taken to perform inspections, and a reduction of about one third in the time it takes to fill out the mandatory forms about the procedures undergone and the status of the equipment.

And, of course, the system features one of the saving graces of computer storage: the VuMan is, on average, less than one thousandth of the weight of bound documentation and manuals needed to hold the equivalent amount of data. As for VuMan's "sponsors," the prime contractor is Carnegie Mellon University, while subcontractors are Stanford University, Lockheed Martin, Telxon Corp., Apple Computer, and IBM.

THE BODYLAN VEST

Architecture and component requirements (the CPUs, memory, bus, and so forth) are now being defined for what in some ways is the most ambitious TIA program: an electronic vest that will be a TIA routing station, so to speak. The fundamental design includes the vest, a head-mounted display, and a microphone. Initially the components will include a computer, data storage devices, GPS device, wireless modem, and a plug-in diagnostic interface module.

The first application being developed is the maintenance and repair support system (Marss). The Marss vest will contain components in communication with each other by wireless radio within the vest as well as with the outside world, which ordinarily add up to the equipment being maintained plus logistics databases. Communication with the computers will be by voice, and information—manuals, status reports, reports from other sites, for example—will appear on the head-up display.

Marss is being developed by McDonnell Douglas Aerospace, headquartered in Huntington Beach, Calif. All decisions regarding the content of the software for maintenance are coordinated by the U.S. Army's Program Manager for Test, Maintenance and Diagnostic Equipment. Human-factors studies of the vest are being coordinated by the U.S. Army Soldier System Command (formerly the

Natick Research, Development and Engineering Center), in Natick, Mass.

BATTERIES AND BULLETS

The design of the vest is a prototypical case of the need for good humionics. First, old-fashioned human-factors issues—traditional ergonomics—must be addressed. The vest must be lightweight, so it can be worn underneath a soldier's bulletproof Kevlar vest. If it is made waterproof, the electronics will be better protected; but it also must be porous enough to allow heat to escape and sweat to evaporate.

When the ergonomic and human factors and health issues come up against electronic design, humionics comes into play. Some issues have been studied in a general way for years—for example, the effects of close proximity with radio frequencies. New in the TIA program is the soldier's intimate proximity, one might say, with all sorts of electromagnetic radiation. Health issues related to electromagnetic radiation are under the purview of the Human Research and Engineering Directorate Command of the U.S. Army Research Laboratory, Aberdeen Proving Ground, Md.

Other humionics questions concern the vest itself. For instance, one design under review has flex cables running up either side of the chest over the breasts, with plug-in connections from components to power modules. An alternative has batteries next to the components they power.

Whichever design is adopted, a fundamental factor of war must be addressed: soldiers get shot. Being shot is bad enough under any circumstances, but consider the added dangers of just one of the vest's components, the batteries. Under review for the TIAs are lithium-ion batteries of 2.2 ampere-hours, at around 3.6 volts. Now, someone touching a 1.5-V household battery with a finger would feel nothing; touching it with the tongue would mean a relatively benign buzz. But under certain conditions, batteries put into direct contact with the conductive bloodstream, as could happen in battle, could have more serious effects.

In addition, the designers of the vest's power system naturally want the greatest energy density. But the higher the energy density, the greater the batteries' explosiveness. Finally, surprising as it may seem considering the human cost of war, the environmental impact of equipping entire armies with batteries is quite a concern. Scorched-earth tactics aside, the battlefield should not be further damaged after the end of hostilities. In addition, in field training, huge numbers of batteries could litter the arena.

Optic fibers changing the dimensions of information transmission
Courtesy of AT&T Bell Laboratories.

These applications herald a revolutionary change in the soldier's armament. And new armaments, in turn, bring new ways of waging war. Obviously, the ranks of the military will be interconnected as never before. Surely, too, the soldier's personal weapons will be slaved to computer-assist systems. Nothing better signifies the new battlefield realities than the two vests to be worn by combat troops: the mechanical, Kevlar, variety, to protect them from incoming firepower, over an electronic one, with its own kind of firepower.

Questions

1. What will be the differences in the level of and types of information used in future wars?
2. Explain what a TIA is, and give four examples of it.
3. What is "humionics," and why is it important for the soldier?
4. What can the Tamer (Technology Advanced Mini Eyesafe Rangefinder) do for the soldier and other supportive operations?
5. What is "Pathfinder"? What are its various applications?
6. What is the "VoiceMap" TIA?
7. What can artificial intelligence add to VoiceMap applications?
8. What is the purpose of "VuMan" TIA?
9. Why is the bodyLAN vest the most ambitious TIA program?
10. What are the effects and implications of the use of TIAs by soldiers in warfare?

SCENARIO: TECHNO WARS

Dateline: 19:19:01 GMT December 21, 20XX

The Northern Economic Trading Block (NETB) Authority has accused the Southern Economic Trading Block (SETB) of illegal trading practices in winning major trading export contracts worth more than $35 billion from the Eastern Trading Zone (ETZ).

A global videoconference between the leaders of the Northern and Southern trading blocks has resulted in a stalemate and increasing frustration. The leaders of the Northern economic block have accused the Southern block of technoimperialism.

The Southern block leaders think that the Northern block is trying to pressure them to revoke the contracts they signed with the African Economic Block for the development of carefree oil fields, which are estimated to contain 30% of the oil reserves. The carefree oil fields were recently developed by the Southern economic zone after it won the development bid in the international market. The Northern block accused the Southern block of offering billions of dollars to the royal families of the African Trading Zone in exchange for the bid. During the past 10 years, the Northern economic block has lost manufacturing and high-tech jobs to the Southern block. A number of multiblock global corporations have moved operations from north to south. The gross domestic products of the Southern economic block are expected to be equal to those of the Northern economic block. The experts in the North have predicted that if the Southern development is not curbed, it will seriously impact the Northern economy, which stands to lose $100 billion exports globally. The leaders of the North have issued an ultimatum to the South to vacate the carefree oil fields by January 1; otherwise, the North will declare a technowar. The South has refused to bend to what it calls technoimperialism.

The Untied Nations has failed to find any solution to this crisis. The last meeting on the GLOBALNET between the five trading blocks resulted in futile attempts to solve the crisis, and all efforts have been in vain. The North has superior high-tech electromagnetic weapons as compared to the South, where for the last 50 years there has been little development of technoweaponry; the South has instead emphasized the development of business technology to gain an edge on global consumer businesses.

QUESTIONS

1. Is the Northern Economic Trading Block justified in issuing an ultimatum to the Southern Economic Trading Block? Discuss future economic and political scenarios for this situation.

2. What kind of high-tech electromagnetic weapons might the NETB use against the SETB? Discuss real and prospective weaponry of this type.

3. Do you think that in the future, business conflicts will be resolved by technowar?

4. What type of actions and resolutions would you recommend to prevent future technowars?

A Bridge to Your 21st Century Understanding

Complete and discuss the following flowchart.

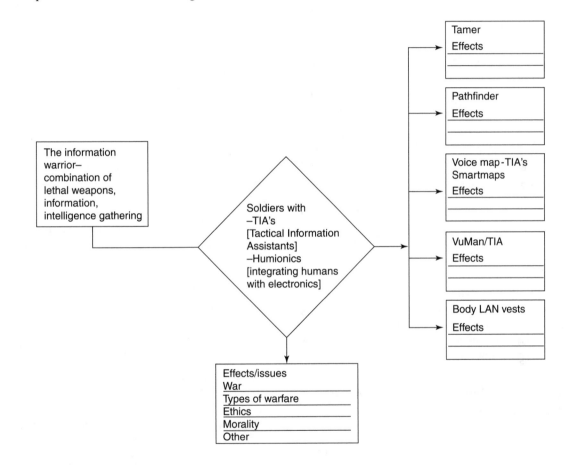

62 Predictions: Technology of the New Century and the New Millennium

Progress will proceed even more exponentially in everything technological. . . .

THE DIGITAL REVOLUTION

Digital World

By 2010, voice recognition will be available in computers and all sorts of digital devices. We should be able to carry on direct conversations with computers, Internet browsers, automobiles, thermostats, TVs, VCRs, microwaves, and other pieces of equipment.

Personalized World through Computers and Hyperlinks

In the future, bandwidth, the capacity of fiberoptics and other "pipelines" to carry digital communications, will become freer, which means that all types of content—including data, all forms of shows, books, and home videos—will be on-line and available to anyone in the world. The practical applications of this ability would allow marketing and subscriptions to be tailored to the specific needs and tastes of individuals. This ability to customize information then would allow the products to be specialized for each user and will change the world from a mass-market world to a more personalized one (Isaacson, 1998).

Further Miniaturization of Microprocessor Design

The following items represent future advances in the design of microprocessors:

- The use of quantum dots and other single-electron devices, for which electrons can be used as binary registers to represent the 0 or 1 of a data bit.

- The development of data storage systems using biological molecules, resulting in molecular computing. Optical computers for which streams of photons could replace electrons would be possible if a biological light-sensitive molecule were used. With biological molecules, self-synthesis would be possible through the life systems of the microorganisms. For some estimates, some photonically activated biomolecules could be linked to a three-dimensional memory system that would have a capacity 300 times greater than that of today's CD-ROMs.

- Nanomechanical logic gates where beams one atom wide would be physically moved to carry out logical operations (Patterson, 1995).

All-Optical Networks

Already, fiberoptic networks transmit data 10 to 100 times faster than standard electronic wiring, but in the future, light waves will be used for most of the transmission of voice, video, and other data along the networks's pathways. The speed and capacity of fiberoptics in the future will be used such that—in theory—a single fiber has the capacity to transmit 25 terabits (trillions of bits) each second, which is comparable to transmitting all U.S. Mother's Day telephone calls simultaneously in a second. The only time the signal would become electronic would be when it moves into the circuits of a computer or into a lower speed electronic network (Chan, 1995). At present, the state of technology allows data rates of the order of tens of billions of bits per second. Once the potential capacity is developed, the transmission rates will allow hundreds of trillions of bits per second. The future potential of optical networks will allow the transmission of 25 billion telephone calls simultaneously. In other words, consider that with the population of the earth at 6 billion people, every person on earth could talk at the same time using one fiber whose dimensions are ten times smaller than a human hair.

THE BIOTECHNOLOGICAL REVOLUTION

In the future, we will have the technological capacity to engineer and change human DNA and build on the emerging capabilities that we have already demonstrated with plants and animals. The challenges will not only be scientific, but also moral.

The Human Genome Project

With the mapping of all of our genetic material, which should be completed by the year 2005, scientists will begin a new age for biology in which we will understand biological processes and the causes of disease and behavior from the level of genes. Central control genes for the formation of organs, behavior characteristics, and other genetic human traits can be studied and understood. Genetic flaws connected to cancers, leukemia, dyslexia, Alzheimer's disease, and even alcoholism and obesity will be traceable, and their discovery contribute to the development of more effective treatments for these disorders. The moral issues of knowing genetic codes and their outcome, predicting susceptibility to disease, the relation of genetic testing to employment and insurance issues, manipulating genes, and knowing the genetic makeup of potential mates are just some of the complex ethical topics that accompany genetic knowledge and its effects (Olesen, 1995).

Plant and Animal Gene Alteration

Some scientists feel that the alteration of genes to modify and create new plants and animals has the potential to alter

the 21st century even more dramatically than computers altered the 20th century. The alteration of plant and animal life-forms has the potential to feed the hungry, alleviate human suffering, provide new medicines and transplant organs, and open possible new sources of energy. But the moral decisions and consequences of such genetic procedures are complex and include the issues of genetic determination, discrimination, and unforeseen long-range problems due to the release of new genetically engineered life forms. As an example of such a public-policy and moral issue, cell biologist Stuart A. Newman and Jeremy Rifkin, president of the Washington-based Foundation on Economic Trends, have applied for a patent on genetically engineered life-forms that fuse human and animal embryonic cells. The purpose behind their patent application is to prevent or delay the use of such technology to better control and regulate such use and to give the public time to develop its moral policy on these issues (Travis, 1998).

TELECOMMUNICATIONS

In the next decade, cellular services and wireless networks will increasingly provide personalized service all over the globe, regardless of the remoteness of the location or the previous lack of telephone services. Cellular networks and other personal communications services will use digital air-interface standards and will shrink the size of the cell station, providing more compactness, quality, and efficiency. Every year and a half, the digital chips required for wireless operations shrink by 50% so that applications can also continue to shrink. Smaller and smaller cellular devices, such as high-quality wireless wristphones, tiny telephone devices in computers, and radio modems are part of this outcome. In just a few years, wireless faxes and video mail will be commonplace globally. Telephone service will be available where it has never been before; today, half of the people in the world have never made a telephone call, but in the future, anyone in any location will be able to do so. Some developing countries will soon be jumpstarting their telephone technology by eliminating the traditional network foundation and beginning with a wireless infrastructure (Zysman, 1995).

THE INFORMATION REVOLUTION

Artificial Intelligence

In the future, computers will be able to make thinking decisions and create new thoughts from stored information. Software will also become intelligent and will act independently in order to ease burdens on computers. Within just a few years, computers will build information and conclusions and automatically coordinate applications and output such as spreadsheets, databases, document preparation systems, and on-line search engines. Content will be automatically checked by word processors to determine completeness, accuracy, and the existence of adequate explanations. Searches for specific content will be possible not just from key-word searches, but also from actual content searches (Lenat, 1995).

The Internet

Information will continue to be increasingly available on the Internet and increasingly used by a predicted 30 million households by the year 2000. Cyberspace will continue to transform with new "non-PC devices" such as Internet TVs and Internet telephones. Commerce, all types of information, games, and personal buying-pattern databases, will all continue to become even more available and part of our everyday lives as cyberspace continues to develop into its global potential (The Web: Infotopia or Marketplace?, 1997).

Additional Leaps

As time goes by, software will become increasingly autonomous with the use of software "agents" that help complete users' goals. These agents will be like many digital proxies, simultaneously guiding users through technical complexities, teaching them, searching for information, performing transactions, or even representing people in their absence. They could even perform as personal secretaries—helping to remind, coordinate, and extend capabilities. Rather than manipulating a keyboard or a mouse, the user would use his or her voice or gestures to communicate with the software, and the agents would appear on the screen as people with simplified facial expressions to communicate their current state (Maes, 1995).

Virtual reality (VR) will also be used to a greater extent in a variety of applications, since it permits people to respond in a re-created environment. Presently, VR provides perceptions of sight, hearing, touch, and response to movement. This range will be extended to perceptions of force, resistance, texture, and smell as well. Applications of VR will include the performance of complex and delicate tasks in hazardous or alien environments, extensive and detailed training operations, the design of prototypes and models of all sorts of systems, and the creation of new artistic and social humanistic expressions and dimensions (Laurel, 1995).

THE WORLD OF WORK

In the future, the equivalent of today's upper crust of white-collar workers will need a graduate degree, and they will be classified as some type of "symbolic analyst," possessing some of the most intensive knowledge in the future economy. At the bottom of the ladder will be low-skill and low-paid personal service workers whose jobs will not have been too affected by the computer or information explosion. Most of the changes will occur in the middle class, made up of "technicians"—the mechanics of the computer age; their positions will require education beyond the high school diploma. This middle class will require more education and training than today's middle class. The highly educated, high-earning professionals to be known as "knowledge workers" will be exposed to downsizing with the arrival of more consultant-type, "paid by the job" employment arrangements. These knowledge workers will telecommute to their various offices and contract sites. Many people feel that workers might move to a 25-hour workweek, with higher pay and benefits allowing more time for cultural activities and nonprofit work (McGinn and Raymond, 1997–98).

NANOTECHNOLOGY

Many futurists feel that nanotechnology will provide man with the ability to participate in the creation of materials on the atomic level and that some of this capability will be realized in the next 10 to 20 years. Nanotechnology is technology that occurs on the microscopic scale of nanometers. (One billion nanometers are in a meter.) Atoms at this microscopic size level join together to form molecules that, in turn, form materials. In the nanotechnological universe, atoms can be positioned in various configurations to design different specified materials according to the material's specific atomic formula. The technology of MEMS—microelectromechanical systems—already exists. These systems are tiny micromachines that react to stimuli like light, sound, and motion. When connected to microchips, MEMS can be programmed to take actions such as those of sensing devices for human health needs and can perform the unlimited applications of control devices. "Microprocessors defined the 1980s, and cheap lasers allowed the telecommunications revolution of the 90s. MEMS and sensors generally will shape the first decade of the next century," states Paul Saffo, an analyst with the Institute for the Future in Menlo Park, California. The process of MEMS becoming less expensive and smaller will result in such applications as smart materials that react to stimuli, houses programmed for energy needs, unlimited technological sensing devices, and tiny robots that detect disease in the bloodstream—and, of course, this is only the beginning (Rogers and Kaplan, 1997–98).

THE MEDICAL FUTURE

New Surgical Techniques

In the 21st century, surgeons will develop more precise and less invasive techniques. Radio waves and lasers will replace scalpels, while light-activated drugs will pinpoint cancer treatments to be more specific and less harmful. Surgery involving small incisions and keyhole surgery are becoming developed procedures, using thin probes, cameras, miniaturized lights, and tiny and remotely controlled surgical tools. Even organ extraction and transplants can be accomplished with less invasive surgery requiring smaller incisions. Doctors are also discovering that directing radio waves by the use of electrodes and radio-wave generators can diminish injuries without the pain and difficulties of surgery. The possibilities of the use of this medicine include the tightening of ligaments, the destruction of tumors and other unwanted tissues, the cessation of abnormal uterine bleeding, the treatment of benign prostate enlargement, and the treatment of heart arrhythmias. Prescription medicines for the 21st century will also be more narrowly targeted and will have few side effects (Cowley and Underwood, 1997–98).

Gene Therapy

Gene therapy will also be part of the new technological medicine bag of the 21st century, and it will cause another medical revolution, since the use of selected corrective genes in a patient's cells can potentially cure or ease many of today's diseases. This new approach can be very effective, as so many diseases derive from the malfunctioning of one or more genes. For example, more than 4,000 conditions, such as severe combined immunodeficiency and cystic fibrosis, are caused from the developmental damage of a single gene. With gene therapy, new genes can be delivered through modified viruses to provide for new genetic coding to prevent or treat diseases. Other methods of delivery involve directly introducing the corrective gene into the tissue where it is needed. While not possible now, in the future it is hoped that physicians will simply be able to inject the new gene carriers into the bloodstream, where the new genetic carriers will locate their targets cells and simply transfer the new genetic information. Within 20 years, it is predicted that gene therapy will be part of the regular approaches to treat and cure diseases. Today, many diseases are already being treated in clinical trials of gene therapy (Anderson, 1995).

OTHER NEW SCIENTIFIC TECHNOLOGIES

Microchip Sensor

A microchip sensor is an optical version of a microchip with tiny lenses and filters that use laser light. The chip is an inexpensive sensor that can be made to detect or sense just about anything. Food processing plants are interested in using this sensor to detect potentially deadly bacteria. It also could be used to detect chemicals in medical patients, replacing their need to undergo frequent blood tests. Other applications of microchip sensors would be to detect pollutants in smokestacks, streams, and automobile exhaust systems and to detect pesticides and fertilizers in farming areas (*Scientists Say Tiny Sensor Has Giant Potential,* 1996).

Molecular Design of Materials

Material design and manufacturing in the future will involve manipulating molecules to change their characteristics. A material could be made stronger or lighter or could be altered to make a new material by changing its molecular structure. The strengths of this approach to design and construction are its access to unlimited resources and its versatility, since the number of molecules in the world is virtually unlimited (Olesen, 1995).

The Futurist's Top Ten Technologies for the Next 10 Years

1. Understanding the genetic basis for human disease and characteristics on the gene level and being able to treat them on that gene level
2. Supermaterials designed on the molecular level
3. High-density energy sources that are very small and portable
4. High-definition digital television
5. A laptop computer that is interactive, wireless, and about the size of a pocket calculator, and smart cards that perform many daily activities such as those of keys, records, money, etc.
6. Smart manufacturing processes that will create individual products for individual consumers

7. Antiaging cosmetics and products
8. Diagnostic health sensors to detect diseases and physiological anomalies
9. Automobile hybrid fuel using reformulated gasoline along with some other type of fuel to be more efficient, economic, and to produce fewer emissions
10. Computer software and other products that combine education and entertainment (Oleson, 1995)

Questions

1. What do you think are the most important technological discoveries mentioned in this chapter for the 21st century? Rank the five most important ones, explain why they are important, and give the reasons for your particular ranking.
2. Of the subheadings in this article, only three include the word "revolution": the digital, the biotechnical, and information revolutions. Why do think those classifications were made in this way? Do you agree with these classifications and subheadings? Explain why or why not. What would you change about them?
3. Can you name some important developments and technologies for the 21st century that were not mentioned in this chapter?
4. Examine the technologies mentioned in this chapter, and describe in a brief narrative what would be the cumulative effect of all these technologies. Give a brief description of what you think life will be like in the future due to the effects of these technologies. What are the pros and cons of this future projection?
5. Think about and describe the specific type of education that will be needed in this future life.
6. Which new technology interests you the most? What applications do you see for it? Describe possible innovative designs or applications for that technology.
7. Research additional specific applications for the new technologies mentioned in this chapter in various periodicals and articles.
8. Find and list new projected technologies for the 21st century that are not mentioned in this chapter.

References

Anderson, W.F. (1995, September). Gene Therapy. *Scientific American: Key Technologies for the 21st Century.* pp. 124–128.

Chan, V.W.S. (1995, September). All-Optical Networks. *Scientific American: Key Technologies for the 21st Century.* pp. 72–76.

Cowley, G., and Underwood, A. (1997–98, Winter). Surgeon, Drop That Scalpel. *Newsweek Extra 2000: The Power of Invention.* pp. 77–78.

Isaacson, W. (1998, April 13). Our Century and the Next One. *Time.* pp. 70–75.

Laurel, B. (1995, September). Virtual Reality. *Scientific American: Key Technologies for the 21st Century.* p. 90.

Lenat, D.B. (1995, September). Artificial Intelligence. *Scientific American: Key Technologies for the 21st Century.* pp. 80–82.

Maes, P. (1995, September). Intelligent Software. *Scientific American: Key Technologies for the 21st Century.* pp. 84–86.

McGinn, D., and Raymond, J. (1997–98, Winter). Workers of the World, Get Online. *Newsweek Extra 2000: The Power of Invention.* pp. 32–33.

Olesen, D.E. (1995, September–October). The Top Technologies for the Next Ten Years. *The Futurist.* pp. 9–13.

Patterson, D.A. (1995, September). Microprocessors in 2020. *Scientific American: Key Technologies for the 21st Century.* pp. 62–67.

Rogers, A., and Kaplan, D. (1997–98, Winter). Get Ready for Nanotechnology. *Newsweek Extra 2000: The Power of Invention.* pp. 52–53.

Scientists Say Tiny Sensor Has Giant Potential. (1996, November 20). *CNN Interactive.* Available: http://www.CNN.com

The Web: Infotopia or Marketplace? (1997, January 27). *Newsweek: Beyond 2000.* pp. 84–88.

Travis, J. (1998, May 9). Patenting the Minotaur? *Science News.* p. 299.

Zysman, G.I. (1995, September). Wireless Networks. *Scientific American: Key Technologies for the 21st Century.* pp. 68–71.

New Horizons of Information Technology

63

AHMED S. KHAN

● ●

The exponential growth in fiberoptics technology during the past two decades has significantly changed global telecommunications. Today, fiber is the medium of choice for short- and long-haul broadband applictions. Numerous new applications of fiber are proving to be the impetus for the technological developments in the field. With rapid advances in optoelectronic devices, low-loss zero-dispersion fibers, and optical amplifiers—coupled with innovations in optical computing and switching—fiberoptics systems are transforming the 20th-century electronic era of telecommunications towards an optical era of the 21st century.[1]

Oceanic fiberoptics systems have revolutionized global telecommunications. Oceanic lightwave systems have been in service since 1988 across the Atlantic Ocean and since 1989 across the Pacific Ocean. These high-capacity digital communications systems have brought about a revolution in available system capacity and service quality compared to prior analog coaxial systems. On the drawing board are the systems with capacities of 5000+ Megabits per second (Mbps). The oceanic fiberoptics systems are transforming the world into a global village.

Approximately 60 million kilometers of fiber have been installed worldwide. The double-digit growth rate continues unabated, as nations strengthen and extend their infrastructure, and as societies enter the information age.[2] The key developments that have revolutionized light-wave communications are the advances in rare-earth optical amplifiers that are used for data transmission. Optical amplifiers have matured into one of the most significant advances in fiberoptic technology since the fiber itself. With the advent of erbium-doped fiber amplifiers (EDFA),

transmission capacities have increased from hundreds to ten thousands of gigabit-kilometers per second.[3] Optical solitons that exploit both the nonlinearity and dispersion of the fiber medium to maintain a constant pulse shape offer a potential for high-capacity ultralong distance systems. Researchers at AT&T have reported achieving error-free soliton data transmission at 10 Gbps over a distance of 1,000,000+ km using recirculating EDFA loop.[4] There exists a wide technoeconomic gap between the developed and the developing countries, especially in the area of telecommunication networks. In developed countries, telecommunications have played a key role in technoeconomic growth. In most developed countries, the teledensity is close to 50%, and the literacy rate is over 80%. In contrast, a vast majority of the developing countries have very low teledensities and low literacy rates (less than 40%). More than three billion people living in African, Asian, and South American developing countries have little access to telecommunications services.

With the globalization of business, it has become a universally acknowledged truth that telecommunications will play a critical role in the global economy. Developed nations want a sophisticated telecom infrastructure to provide a competitive edge for their business interests. Developing nations need a basic telecommunications infrastructure to provide a foundation for economic growth. According to International Telecommunications Union, an investment of $318 billion is required to add 212 million lines in developing countries. The development of a number of global, regional, and national fiberoptics systems will play an important role in meeting the demands for developed as well as developing countries and will help in narrowing the technoeconomic gap between the two.

The development of global, regional, and national lightwave systems will not only satisfy the growing telecommunication needs of developing countries, but will also provide the required infrastructure for creating endless opportunities in education (e.g., distance learning), medicine (e.g., telemedicine), and business (e.g., e-commerce). The lightwave systems will provide an impetus for economic and technological development and enable developing countries to increase their teledensity and literacy rate, improve public health, and increase per-capita income, thus narrowing the technoeconomic gap with the developed countries and allowing them to enter the 21st century with state-of-the-art optical networks.

NEURONS AND PHOTONS: THE LIMITS OF HUMAN KNOWLEDGE AND THE VASTNESS OF THE UNIVERSE

When the potential of fiberoptics communication technology is discussed, new perceptions of accumulated human knowledge can be made that can be visualized with our new understanding of the laws of physics. Fiberoptics technology has a potential transmission capacity of hundreds of trillions of bits of information per second. We can use the holdings of the Washington, D.C., Library of Congress as an example to provide an understanding of the enormous potential information-carrying capacity of the optical fiber.

In 1997, the Library of Congress held 17,402,100 books. If we assume that each book has 300 pages, with 450 words per page, this totals about 126,000 words per book, or 15.3 trillion words. If we further assume that each word averages about 7 letters, the information can be digitized using ASCII code, where each letter represents 7 bits. Therefore, all of the holdings of the Library of Congress would amount to 107.44 trillion bits of information. Using fiberoptics, an optical fiber that has the capability of transmitting 100 trillion bits per second, the entire Library of Congress book collection could be transmitted anywhere in the world in 1.07 seconds.

If we further assume that the total accumulation of human knowledge over the past 5,000 years was represented by 1,000 Libraries of Congress, all of the accumulation of the recorded knowledge of man could be transmitted through an optical fiber in 17.9 minutes. Therefore, in less than 20 minutes, all known human knowledge could be transmitted anywhere in the world. This analogy helps to build our awareness and appreciation of the finite nature of man's knowledge in contrast to the vast dimensions of the universe and the infinite possibilities of the time–space continuum. It also builds our awareness of how limited our knowledge really is, how finite we are on the infinite time–space axis of the ever-expanding cosmos, and how great our future dimensions of knowledge are.

SCENARIO: OPTICAL ERA OF INFORMATION SOCIETY

Date line: 10:01 AM, March 10, 20XX

The MTT Labs has announced that their scientists have successfully developed a micro-optical logic gate. A logic gate is the basic building block of a computer. The state of the current electronics technology allows CPUs to operate at speeds of 500+ MHz. The development of the optical gate will lead to the development of optical computers that will operate at 100+ THz speed ("T" = Tera = 1000,000,000,000 Hz). During the last decade of the 20th century, high-speed optical fibers have already been developed that allow data transmission rates of Tbps (tera bits per second). The present technology of optical storage permits the storage of 100 Terabytes of information per optical compact disc (OCD). The development of a micro-optical logic gate at MTT Labs will enable the development of an end-to-end optical communications system. An end-to-end optical system will use optical computing, optical data storage, and optical data transfer. The development of the miniature optical gate has transformed the electronic era of telecommunications into an optical era of information.

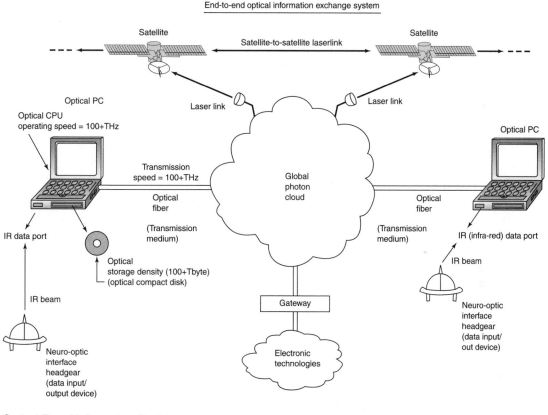

Optical Era of Information Society
Source: Tasneen Khan

Answer the following questions:
a. Discuss the pros and cons of the optical computer.
b. The speed of optical computers and optical data transfer will be much faster than human response times and will thereby force users to process information in their brain much faster and to interact more quickly, thus increasing the stress level of the average computer user. Do you think that optical end-to-end information networks will help or harm the health of a computer user in terms of stress levels?
c. Discuss the implications of the development of end-to-end optical information exchange systems on society.

References

1. Khan, A. (1994). Fiber Optics Communications: An Introduction to Technology and Applications. *Annual Review of Communications Vol. 47.* p 503.
2. Li, T. (1995, January). Optical Amplifiers Transform Lightwave Communications. *Photonics Spectra.* p. 115.
3. Desurvire, E. (1992, January). Lightwave Communications: The Fifth Generation. *Scientific American.* pp. 114–121.
4. Desurvire, E. (1994, January). The Golden Age of Optical Fiber Amplifiers. *Physics Today.* pp. 20–27.

Questions

1. Why will telecommunications and fiberoptics be the information technology of the future?
2. How soon do you think we will have end-to-end optical communications systems? Do you agree with its progressive advances? How do you think it will impact society?
3. What are some of the problems of the advancement of telecommunications and fiberoptics technologies?

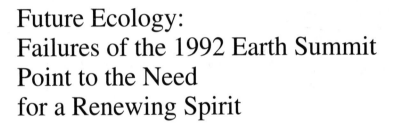

Future Ecology:
Failures of the 1992 Earth Summit
Point to the Need
for a Renewing Spirit

The 1992 Earth Summit of the United Nations Conference on Environment and Development (UNCED), in Rio de Janeiro, Brazil with over 100 heads of state in attendance, making it one of the largest gatherings of world leaders in history, raised high hopes for the commitment of the world's communities to saving the earth. The summit was the first global effort devoted to making world progress on issues of environment and poverty. In the years that have passed since 1992, however, not too much has happened in the way of progress. A five-day review session, held in June, 1997, called "Earth Summit II," visited by about 70 heads of state, reviewed the progress over the years since the 1992 summit, but not too much was actually accomplished. Progress is urgently needed, but not much has been made.

The global environment has continued to decline with

- increasing levels of toxic pollution
- increasing levels of greenhouse gas emissions
- increasing amounts of solid waste
- increasing levels of rainforest destruction
- decreasing levels of biodiversity
- an increasing need for financing for developing nations so that they may adopt strategies and technologies that produce less pollution.

Progress from the 1992 summit included the creation of a climate change convention (held in Kyoto, Japan, in December 1997), a biodiversity convention, a collection of forest principles and other declarations, and Agenda 21, an overarching agreement for a sustainable, environmentally sound development pattern for the 21st century. One important step taken by the summit was the creation of a recommendation, signed by 166 nations, that called for the reduction of emissions of greenhouse gases to their 1990 levels by the year 2000, but the recommendations did not contain tight guidelines and strong-enough measures to actually curb emissions. Furthermore, President Clinton disappointed environmentalists at Earth Summit II by not committing to specific reductions and firm standards for U.S. greenhouse gas emissions.

DISCUSSION

The 1992 Earth Summit was an event for which many people had high expectations. What are some ideas you have to keep Earth Summit priorities urgent, the agendas working, the issues focused, the countries cooperating, and progress advancing on these issues? Do you think that summits of this kind are the best approach to use for such world problems? What influence do you think the United States has on the rest of the world? What level of leadership do you think the United States should assume regarding the amelioration of such environmental problems if these problems are going to be addressed by all nations? What influence can citizens have on U.S. government positions? Should these kinds of summits be sponsored by the United Nations or by a different entity or entities? How can such summits be made more effective? What other ways can you think of to address the world's pollution problems?

References

No Decision on Global Warming. (1997, Fall). *The Amicus Journal,* p. 3.

Swanson, S. (1997, June 22). Was Anyone Listening? Failures of '92 Earth Summit Spur a New One. *Chicago Tribune,* p. 6.

Future Ecology: Kyoto Climate Agreement Is Historic First Step

65

As an outcome of the 1992 Earth Summit, a convention on world climate change was held in December 1997 in Kyoto, Japan, with representatives from about 160 nations in attendance. These nations adopted an historic agreement that placed legally binding limits on their emissions of heat-trapping greenhouse gases in order to protect the environment. The resulting tough agreements mark this conference as one of the most important meetings in the history of the environmental movement and a critical and remarkable first step to stabilizing the earth's climate.

At the Kyoto conference, progress was slow and stalemated until the 8th hour of the 10th day of the conference, when Vice President Gore addressed the delegates and implied U.S. willingness to commit to greater emissions reduction if other nations also strengthened their positions on key issues. At this juncture, the opponents of an agreement, including some oil-producing countries and some countries known for their tendencies to pollute heavily, increased their efforts to thwart negotiations. Several environmental organizations, such as the Environmental Defense Fund, the World Wildlife Fund, Greenpeace International, the Natural Resources Defense Council, and other nongovernmental organizations (NGOs), then joined forces and issued a statement of priorities necessitating a strong stance against harming the environment, a reduction of emissions to below 1990 levels, the elimination of loopholes, and the adoption of strong compliance measures. Through the efforts of these NGOs, the intense level of negotiation was held, communications remained focused, oppositions were effectively deferred, and a binding agreement was successfully attained. The resulting treaty "was prompted by NGOs urging action

. . . [and] underscores the strengthened role of NGOs in world affairs. . . . Virtually unified international NGO support for [emissions] trading and ambitious targets was key to saving the treaty. We were able to bring along a number of developing countries," stated Fred Krupp, Director of the Environmental Defense Fund (Krupp, 1998).

The final agreement that emerged from the Kyoto conference included nine critical points that the NGOs fought for, seven of which included the following measures:

1. The placement of binding limits on emissions.
2. The reduction of emissions to at least 5% below their 1990 levels.
3. The occurrence of reductions by a specified time period, between 2008 and 2012.
4. The placement of limits on all six significant greenhouse gases—not just carbon dioxide, methane, and nitrous oxide, but also hydrofluorocarbons, perfluorocarbons, and sulfur hexafluoride.
5. The awarding of credits on emissions levels for enhancing carbon "sinks," such as forests that remove carbon dioxide from the atmosphere.
6. The implementation of incentive-based mechanisms, such as emissions trading, to encourage early, cost-effective emissions reductions.
7. The institution of a provision, called the "Clean Development Mechanism," to promote greenhouse gas reductions in developing countries. Reduction projects could be financed by industrial nations as a cost-effective way of meeting some of the emission-reduction obligations.

513

The other two points included a compliance agreement that places penalties on industrial nations that fail to meet emissions limits and various explicit commitments for developing nations. Intensive work is still needed on these two points as well as on making the Kyoto agreement become a political and a global reality. (Kyoto Climate Agreement is a Critical First Step, 1998.)

The Kyoto Protocol stipulates that, collectively, the industrial nations must drop emissions levels of the six previously mentioned pollutants to 5.2% below their 1990 levels by the years 2008–2012. Individually, the nations agreed to differential limits: the European Union at 8% below 1990 levels; the United States at 7%; Japan at 6%; Australia at 8%; Iceland at 10%; and the Russian Federation, Ukraine, and New Zealand at 1990 levels. The treaty also divides the industrial countries into two composite "bubbles" that provide trading and selling pollution rights (not to exceed excess) to other countries. The protocol also allows industrial nations to obtain credit (in terms of allowance for emissions) for newly forested land since 1990, but these nations also must balance their reductions to account for deforested land. The treaty imposes binding emission limits on 39 countries, but it does not affect 121 less developed countries, many of which are already emitting large amounts of greenhouse gases (Raloff, 1997).

In order to meet U.S. commitments, predictions are that the United States may be cutting U.S. energy use by a third in the next 10 years. This reduction in energy use will involve not only commitments from industry, but also from the consumer. The United States already failed to comply with the stipulations made at the 1992 Earth Summit in Rio de Janeiro, Brazil, where it promised to cut emissions to 1990 levels by the year 2000. Instead, the United States has created even more emissions and used greater amounts of fuel. (The United States alone emits one fourth of the world's total CO_2 emissions and is the world's greatest polluter of global warming gases.) U.S. fuel use increased by 3.5% in 1997, the largest annual increase on record. By the year 2000, the United States will be burning 15% more fossil fuels—and will therefore be creating 15% more emissions—than it did in 1990, thereby making it necessary to reduce emissions by 22% over 10 years rather than its original goal of 7% (McKibben, 1998).

FACTS

- Since the 1992 convention in Rio de Janeiro, the worldwide level of greenhouse gas emissions has risen by 2% percent each year.

- According to the World Watch Institute, emissions of greenhouse gases in the United States have grown by as much as 13% over the last decade. In 1997 alone, U.S. emissions rose 3.4% to a level that is 7.4% above 1990 levels.

- The United States is the world's largest producer of greenhouse gases by almost double. In 1992, the top 10 CO_2 emitters were the United States, which emitted about 5 million metric tons of CO_2; China, with under 3 million; Russia, with about 2 million; Japan, with about 1 million; and Germany, India, Ukraine, the United Kingdom, Canada, and Italy, with under 1 million.

- Between 1990 and 1994, carbon dioxide emissions from the developing world have risen rapidly, with Brazil increasing emissions by 16%, India by 24%, South Korea by 44%, and China by 13%.

- The problem is that the universal appetite for energy and coal is growing with energy demand and has been forecasted to increase by almost 40% by the year 2015 (Lynch, 1998).

HOW GLOBAL WARMING WORKS

Global warming is part of the natural protection and function of the atmosphere, but when it gets too hot, that warming becomes dangerous, causing severe weather, weather pattern changes, and climatic change. When the sun's rays reach the earth's atmosphere (a 12-mile-thick protective layer of natural greenhouse gases made up mostly of water vapor, but also of carbon dioxide, methane, nitrous oxide, and chlorofluorocarbons, that keeps the earth's average temperature at about 60 degrees), about one third of the sun's solar radiation bounces back into space. The other two thirds of the sun's energy is absorbed into the oceans, forests, and soil, where heat energy is generated and released back into space in the form of heat, not solar radiation. Some of this heat energy is then captured by greenhouse gases. Scientists are concluding that the buildup of greenhouse gases by industrialization and slash-and-burn farming practices is responsible for the heating of the earth's natural heating system. (There has been approximately a 25% increase of CO_2 in the earth's atmosphere in the last century.) It has been concluded that the earth's average temperature has increased by 1 degree in the past century, and it is predicted that it will increase by another 3.6 degrees within the next hundred years. This kind of increase would cause serious problems for the global warming system, where such an increase represents the most rapid warming in 10,000 years. This temperature change would not only change climatic weather patterns, but would also produce a rise in sea level between 1.5 to 3 feet due to melting glaciers, flooding coasts and islands around the world (Lynch, 1998).

Questions

1. How did the Kyoto conference differ from the 1992 Earth Summit in terms of its approach and results?
2. Discuss the roles and effectiveness of NGOs with regard to global policy on the environment. Do you think that coordination and involvement of grassroots organizations are necessary for humanitarian and ecological causes?
3. What does this Kyoto protocol illustrate as far as government negotiations and priorities?
4. The Kyoto Protocol is regarded as a critical and remarkable first step toward overall improvement of the environment. Why is this agreement so remarkable? Do you feel that this agreement represents hope for the 21st century in dealing with critical global issues?
5. Why do you think the United States did not take a leading role in reducing emissions, as it is the world's number-one polluter?
6. If the Kyoto protocol is just the first step, what are the other steps that are necessary to make it an effective and binding agreement?
7. What do you think of the concept of selling and trading pollution rights and allowing emissions credits?
8. Discuss the issues of global warming with regard to the following aspects: increasing amounts of gases in the atmosphere; sources of emissions; and various future strategies to abate the emissions of these gases, with the possible consequences of a global temperature rise and other effects. In your opinion, is the Kyoto protocol on the right track to begin to limit emissions? Are the limits placed on emissions by the protocol enough? What are the steps necessary for the protocol's goals to be met?

References

Krupp, F. (1998, April). A New Force at Kyoto. *Environmental Defense Fund Letter.* Vol. XXIX, No. 2, p. 3.

Kyoto Climate Agreement is a Critical First Step. (1998, April). *Environmental Defense Fund Letter.* Vol. XXIX, No. 2, pp. 1, 5.

Lynch, C. (1998, Winter). Stormy Weather. *The Amicus Journal.* pp. 15–19.

Making History in Kyoto. (1998, Spring). *The Amicus Journal.* pp. 3–4.

McKibben, B. (1998, March–April). Warming Up to Kyoto. *Audubon.* pp. 54–58.

Raloff, J. (1997, December 20/27). Nations Draft Kyoto Climate Treaty. *Science News.* p. 388.

66 Future: Population Growth Estimates

United Nations general projections of population growth for 150 years from now, in the year 2150, range as high as 28 billion people and as low as 4 billion people, with the medium being somewhere around 11.5 billion people. New estimates from the United Nations, however, are stating that the global population will peak at about 11 billion in the year 2200. This new estimate is 6% lower, or 600 million people lower, than 1992's projection of 11.6 billion. The reduction in numbers is caused chiefly from more sharply declining fertility rates than those estimated in 1992. It is turning out that fertility rates are falling steadily and, in some cases, dramatically. For example, in Bangladesh, the fertility rate has declined from 6.2 to 3.4 children per woman in 10 years. This decline is not a temporary decline due to war or depression, but instead seems to be a sustained decline, perhaps caused by increasing modernization. Some of the reasons demographers cite for the correlation between modernization and declining fertility rates are that urban populations do not need extra farm workers as rural populations do, women's status and education is improving as many countries modernize, and family planning programs and methods are more available in modernizing countries (Swanson, 1998).

Population growth is still a problem, however, since even with a decline in fertility rates, the world's population is still increasing by about 80–90 million people a year. This number represents about a 3% growth per year, which, when compounded over decades, is an explosive population growth that can strain and devastate local life support systems (Brown, *Full House,* 1994). Additionally, the number of people will continue to increase quickly, since most of the world's people are young, meaning that there will be more women entering childbearing years in the near future. Predictions are that the world's population will increase to 9.4 billion people in 2050, an increase in about half of a century of 65% of the current population (Swanson, 1998).

About 50 countries, most of them industrialized nations, have fertility rates below the 2.1 children-per-woman "replacement level." The challenge is then for the unindustrialized countries, with the remaining 86% of the world's population, to reach levels below the replacement level (Brown, 1996).

Questions

1. Declining fertility rates seem to be a positive note in the overall picture of a population explosion that has been predicted. Discuss the positive implications of this decline.
2. Considering the readings in Part 4, what do you think are some of the reasons for the declining fertility rates? Explain what you think are some of the most significant reasons for such declines and for future declines in the next 200 years.
3. Do you think that these declining fertility rates provide hope for an abatement of the population growth problem? Explain.

4. Research some of the implications of the high population-growth patterns of unindustrialized nations with regard to food supply, economic hardship, environmental degradation, and availability of seafood. Suggest some ways to help abate these countries' high population-growth patterns.

References

Brown, L., and Kane, H. (1994). *Full house*. New York, W.W. Norton.

Brown, L. (1996). The Acceleration of History. *State of the World, 1996*, W.W. Norton. p. 12.

Swanson, S. (1998, February 17). UN Analysts Trim Global Population Forecasts. *Chicago Tribune*. pp. 1, 9.

Internet Exercise

1. Use any of the Internet search engines (e.g., Alta Vista, Yahoo, Infoseek, etc.) to research the following topics:

    a. Nanotechnology

    b. Responsible technology

    c. Biotechnology

    d. Neuroscience

    e. Telemedicine

    f. Genetic medicine

    g. Human chromosomes and DNA

    h. Xenotransplants

    i. Virus transfer

    j. Humionics

    k. Bionics

    l. Ergonomics

    m. Tactical Information Assistants (TIAs)

    n. Any words you have listed from your research and reading of future issues

2. Use any of the Internet search engines (e.g., Alta Vista, Yahoo, Infoseek, etc.) to research the following issues:

    a. The concepts of responsible technology—what does this responsibility entail?

    b. What are the fields of neural engineering and neuroscience?

    c. Research the progress and developments of the Human Genome Project. What are some of the implications of this project?

    d. What is the capacity and capability of the latest most highly developed computer?

    e. What are the latest developments in human bionics? Are there any animal bionic developments? What are some of the ethical issues involved in bionics?

    f. Research world educational levels. Then identify world educational levels for women. Draw any possible conclusions as to correlations with population levels.

    g. Discover the criteria needed for sustainable world development. What are some of the necessary philosophies involved?

    h. What are some alternative energy systems? How effective can they be?

    i. What is meant by the concepts of population stabilization? When can that happen on a global level?

j. Explain what is meant by the biotechnological revolution. What are some of the technologies involved, and why are they so revolutionary?

k. Explain possible ways that ecology and ecological resources can be included in global economic planning.

l. Research more about military Tactical Information Assistants (TIAs).

m. Discover the latest pros and cons and progress in the field of xenotransplants.

n. What is the U.S. space exploration plan for the next 15 years?

o. Explain some of the newest developments in telecommunications.

p. Research the available material on the military power of two or more unindustrialized nations and two or more industrialized nations. Discuss the implications of the differences you find.

q. Research the ecological priorities for the United States and the world. Explain the differences.

3. What is meant by the year 2000 computer bug/millennium bug/Y2K problem?

4. Discuss the impact of the Y2K bug on the following systems.

   a. Mainframe computers

   b. Personal computers

   c. Telecommunication networks

   d. Embedded devices

   e. Military hardware

5. List and describe various strategies employed to solve the Y2K problem at the:

   a. Personal level

   b. Corporate level

   c. Community level

   d. National level

   e. International level

6. List any potential problems similar to the Y2K computer bug that might cause impairment of computers and telecommunication networks in the 21st century. Explain in detail.

Useful Web Sites

URL	Site Description
http://www.tmn.com/wfs/futurist.html	The Futurist: Official publication of the World Future Society
http://www.discover.com	Discover Magazine
http://www.extrophy.com/eo/index.html	Extropy Magazine on-line
http://www.press.umich.edu/jep	Journal of Electronic Publishing
http://www.nanothinc.com/news/current.html	Nano (nanotechnology) News
http://www.nasa.gov/today/index.html	Today @ NASA
http://www.america.nature.com	Nature
http://www.ci.cambridge.ma.us	Science
http://www.sciencenow.org	Science Now Newsletter
http://www.science.org	Science Newsletter
http://www.ieee.org/society/ssit	IEEE Technology and Society
http://www.cnn.com/TECH/index.html	CNN News: Science and Technology
http://jefferson.village.virginia.edu/pmc	Postmodern culture
http://www.wired.com/news	Wired Magazine
http://www.worldwatch.org	World Watch
http://www.amsci.org/amsci/	American Scientist

Authors' Commentaries

TECHNOLOGY AND THE FUTURE: THE MILITARY PICTURE

When dawn first broke on the typical battlefield several hundred years ago, it must have revealed a surreal picture. Rays of sunlight, cutting through the early morning mist, found their way to the polished steel of the sabres and spears of the armies facing each other. Bright, almost gaudy uniforms stood in stark contrast to the surrounding terrain. At a given signal, usually drums, bugles, or bagpipes, the two forces converged on a designated point, slugging it out until one side disengaged, defeated, but not destroyed. There were always other dawns and other battlefields.

Move to that next battlefield a few generations later. The sun that illuminated that same field of battle might catch not only the glare of sabres and spears, but also the spurs of cavalry and the sight of artillery. The uniforms might still have been garish, given the surrounding terrain. This time, the hostilities began not with the burst from a bagpipe, but most likely with an artillery barrage, as one side tried to use technology to soften up the opposition prior to the assault. And when that assault finally came, it was not led by the screams of men rushing headlong into the breach, but by pounding hooves, as the cavalry, attacking from the flanks, sought to collapse the enemy's perimeter, dash to the rear, and panic the troops headlong into the advancing infantry. There would be no disengagement this time—only total victory, as one side destroyed the other.

The sun that broke over the early battlefields of World War I helped to illuminate not just the familiar past, but also the wave of the future. Men on horseback, sabres and spurs glinting in the sun, prepared to race across an open field to wreak havoc on the enemy's position. However, this time the men on the other side did not quail; instead, they retaliated with machine guns, hand grenades, and poison gas. The technical advantage had shifted, if only temporarily, while the horsemen dismounted and climbed into tanks for a second attack.

And so it has been over the years. In war, technology has proven to be a decisive edge. It has helped to make offensive efforts irresistible, defensive stands impregnable, and for those who found themselves facing superior numbers, it made them equal. However, the edge did not remain so for long. In time, the other side would have the secret, or perhaps go it one better. And so, the search for technological superiority in war has become an escalating factor. Where will it all lead? Here are a few possibilities:

1. *Fewer high-tech wars:* Given the escalating cost and complexity of the new military technologies, only those nations with deep pockets and high-tech capability will be able to use these weapons effectively. Cruise missiles, like the kind used during the Gulf War, can cost $1,000,000 each—not the kind of thing to shoot off willy-nilly. Planes like the F-22 also pack budget-busting price tags. The bottom line is, or should be, that because of the cost of these weapons, nations may want to think twice about the reasons they go to war. Are these reasons sound enough to mortgage their financial present and future?

No one should be naive enough to think that swearing off high-tech weapons will put a stop to warfare. There are plenty of older, more conventional weapons to go around. Millions of antipersonnel devices, also known as land mines, are still buried on battlefields around the world. They are cheap and have a terrific shelf life. ABC News reported in September 1997 that an Egyptian girl was killed when she stepped on a land mine buried by the German Army during World War II. Nations that want weapons don't have to go high tech; low tech will do just fine. The complexity of high-tech weapons might also be a deterrent to war. Nations wanting sophisticated weapons systems might someday realize that these systems are of no use unless they have the trained personnel to use them or an infrastructure that can support them. And even then, there's no guarantee that the weapons will get the job done. After the glow of praise for the Patriot missile's achievements during Operation Desert Storm had faded, a reevaluation of the system revealed that the missiles were not as effective as everyone had thought they were. Now, if the United States cannot get the expected results out of a weapons system, especially one it built, can we honestly expect anyone else to?

2. *Fewer casualties, less political fallout:* High-tech wars, if they are fought, can produce unexpected benefits. For starters, those personnel committed to the battlefield will be better armed and better prepared than previous fighting forces. Equipment could make 1 soldier's firepower equal to that of 10. Therefore, fewer troops will have to be put in harm's way. Because of that fact, wars may become more politically sustainable. Taxpayers may be less likely to question their government's intentions if only a few hundred troops are being jeopardized. And, given the high-tech equipment available, those troops will have a better chance of survival and success than ever before. Medical technologies will make it possible for seriously injured troops to receive immediate attention right there on the battlefield, where it really counts. Communications technology will help locate the wounded and get them to a rear area for more care. "Soft Kill" weapons systems will be used not to kill, but to blind, disorient, or otherwise incapacitate the opposition. Having to deal with thousands of sick or wounded soldiers is actually more difficult than tending to the dead ones.

3. *Simulated war as conflict resolution:* Iraqi forces are on alert. All reservists have been called up, and the Republican Guard has been mobilized. Scud missiles are being repositioned, and the Iraqi Air Force has been given new targets. The front page of the *New York Times?* No, the latest data from satellites tracking Iraq's military operations. Those satellites have been watching for some time now, cataloging troop strength and weapons capability. The data produced has been sifted through by analysts who conclude what Iraq is up to, how it intends to achieve its goals, and the proposed order of battle. Furthermore, those analysts have produced a number of scenarios that the United States might execute to blunt anything Saddam Hussein tries. Iraqi intentions and U.S. responses have been loaded on a floppy disk. The U.S. ambassador at the United Nations delivers the disc to his Iraqi counterpart. "We know what you're doing," he says, "and we think we know where and when. Here's what will happen. We have developed a simulation of the impending conflict, and you will lose. Don't believe me? Load this on your computer and make your own decision." Several days later, satellites record that the Iraqi military machine has stood down from its alert. Saddam's advisors have realized that even before the war has begun, it has already been lost. Just as high-tech weapons can be the edge in conflict, they can also be an effective deterrent. Just knowing what the other guy has and what he might be contemplating is half the battle. Of course, the reverse of this scenario might be that Iraq vows to upgrade its weapons systems until they are on par with those of the United States before trying anything. But there should always be room for optimism.

John C Morello

John Morello, Ph.D.

THOUGHTS ON MEDICAL TECHNOLOGY

I still recall vivid memories from my childhood of Civil War stories as told by my grandfather. His grandfather was a medical doctor in the Civil War. Not only did Gramps talk about the scarcity of medicines and pain killers, gangrene and unbearable pain, his detailed accounts of a time period long gone also revolved around treatments. In his accounts, he described a small black box (approximately $4'' \times 2''$) with a handle on top and razor blades on the bottom. When a patient had an infection, Dr. Stevens, my great-great-grandfather, would pull out the box, place it on one of the patient's arteries, and push hard on the handle, forcing the blades into the skin and causing blood to gush; the goal was to extinguish the patient's ills. The theory behind the technologically simple black box was that infection and impurities would be extracted from the body through the relentless blood flow caused by the "bleeder's" gashes on the skin's surface. The treatment for gangrene, often correlated with bullet wounds, was to remove the tainted limb, aided only by primitive forms of anesthesia.

In recalling these stories, I still remain amazed at the dramatic historical changes in medical technology. When thinking of "bleeders" or primitive amputations, I feel revulsion and confusion. Because today's medicine is more humane, complex, and progressive, it remains difficult to imagine the limitations of doctors in past times. If my grandfather had told his grandfather that in the 1990s, antibiotics (penicillin was discovered in 1928), computed tomography (CAT scans were discovered in 1972), test-tube babies (the first one was born in England in 1978), eradication of smallpox (a very serious disease in his time, and one that was wiped out in 1977), organ transplants (including the successful transplant of genetically altered pig hearts into baboons in 1995), and DNA analysis for disease prevention (1999) would be available or had occurred, I am sure that he would have told his grandson that he was either "nuts" or grandiose (Nuland, 1996, pp. 12–13).

As new medical technologies are created, families are grateful because life spans are extended, low-weight babies are saved and sight can be restored, as can life after death. However, I remain convinced that my great-great-grandfather would still shake his head in dismay at some of the current ethical issues that doctors face today. His stories were gruesome, bold, and primitive, but the stories for the new millennium are amazing, technological, and sometimes ethically disconcerting. If Grandpa Doc were alive today, what would he say about baboon-heart and pig-stomach transplants, tissue engineering, or Dr. Kervorkian's "death machine"? I am not sure, but I do know that he would express a concern that all medical technology be used with caution, remembering that its purpose is to increase the quality of life, not necessarily to make life technology-dependent.

Linda Stevens Hjorth

Linda Stevens Hjorth

REFERENCE

Nuland, S.B. (1996, Fall). An Epidemic of Discovery. *Time*. pp. 12–13.

TECHNOLOGY AND THE FUTURE OF THE FUTURE

The future belongs to those who are willing to learn from the experiences of the present and the past. Indeed, no one can predict the future. But with the lessons learned during the gigantic explosion of technology in the 20th century, we can chart pathways to a future that will enable us to control the fission-like chain reaction of technology's growth for its appropriate, humane, and responsible utilization.

As we approach the new millenium, the great technological accomplishments of the 20th century in the areas of telecommunications, computers, energy, agriculture, materials, medicine, genetic engineering, and defense have transformed the world and brought people closer, yet millions of people worldwide still go to bed hungry at night. These technological advances have enabled us to design advanced early warning systems against missile attacks, but we have failed to develop an advanced early warning system to warn against and prevent global famine or the spread of disease. Thanks to state-of-the-art technologies, we are able to design spaceships to explore life on other planets, yet we have failed to preserve life on planet Earth. Millions of children worldwide continue to die due to malnutrition, disease, and poverty.

We have made tremendous strides in science and technology, but at the cost of numerous environmental, social, and moral dilemmas. Technological advances and economic expansion could become meaningless if moral and social implications are not considered in charting the course of the future.

In developed countries, technology has provided an impetus for economic growth at the cost of many social and environmental problems. In developing countries, the lack of advanced technology has resulted in low economic growth. Many developing nations aspire to become technologically advanced, but lack the required infrastructures and skilled manpower and are reluctant to consider the social and environmental costs that the industrialized nations have paid in the course of their industrialization. The key question for developing nations is how to increase the pace of industrialization without paying the same cost that the developed nations have paid for becoming industrialized. The answer to this question lies in the appropriate use of technology. For example, telecommunications technologies can provide endless opportunities in education (e.g., distance learning), medicine (e.g., telemedicine), and business (e.g., e-commerce) in developing countries. These applications could enable developing countries to increase teledensity and literacy, improve per-capita income, and narrow the technoeconomic gap with developed countries.

As we march into a new millennium with our technological might, we ought to be aware not only of the short-term gains and advantages of technology, but also of its long-term impact and associated problems. In the preceding text, we have attempted to present a spectrum of issues related to a wide array of topics (i.e., energy, ecology, population, war and technology, social responsibility, health and technology, technology and the Third World, and technology of the future) that deal with the impact of technology in the developed and the developing world. I hope that our endeavor will serve as a guide to help the reader understand, anticipate, and address the impact of technology on the various facets of society in order to make future decisions for the humane, just, and responsible utilization of technology.

Ahmed S Khan

Ahmed S. Khan

IT IS NOW THE TIME FOR WISDOM

The *future* is that concept that we who have embraced Western civilization and the concepts of progress, change, improvement, and technology can hardly wait for! The future is ours. We only have to design it, and through technology, it will service us and give us greater pleasures than ever before. The future adventures, the daring, the excitement, and the new luxuries appeal unlimitedly to those of us in the industrialized societies and are dazzling and changing the unindustrialized societies. Anticipating the future gives us a telescopic sight of the accomplishment of our greater hopes, dreams, and visions . . . new reaches for our graceful hand of knowledge.

But this future represents many changes from the futures that were imagined by past generations. This future represents social and economic differences from previously imagined futures, which were more predictable, less multidimensional, less exponential, and less critical. Yes, most futures represent change, growth, and variation from the "comfortable known," but this one is really different. This future is not only a telescopic graceful vision; it is also a multimedia-accelerated production based on technology everywhere, with increasingly faster machines and tools to aid, support, and satisfy mankind. Along with the mach speed of technologies are accompanying critical concerns that have to be addressed before we blindly ride the technological acute paths. We have to ask ourselves some basic questions, for we are at a critical juncture. Critical ecological issues emerge because of our new technological development. Questions and concerns about population emerge because of our progress in the fields of health and medicine and due to our expanded life spans. War can be globally devastating both easily and quickly. Moral and ethical concerns of actions increasingly parallel all of the thoughtful use of technology. The unindustrialized world hopefully tries to adopt some of the technologies to help its economic development, but has a problem with the expense, consequences, and appropriateness of Western technology.

This part's objective has been to converge the thoughts of the other eight parts to their implications for the 21st century so that issues from those parts can find a responsible bridge to the future, a future that is sustainable and fulfills its potential exciting promise. The path, however, is not automatic. Because of the steeper acceleration of technology and accompanying critical humanitarian and ecological issues, all actions have to include more than economic appetites and a gratification of needs and wants; they must also contain larger understandings of technological responsibility and global sustainability. The concern for the quality of life in the future—for a natural sustainable life—depends on our understanding and accompanying actions. This is the challenge and ultimate flow chart for the 21st century: wise decisions and wise and caring actions.

Barbara A. Eichler

Barbara A. Eichler

Beyond the Bridge. . . Explore Future Options

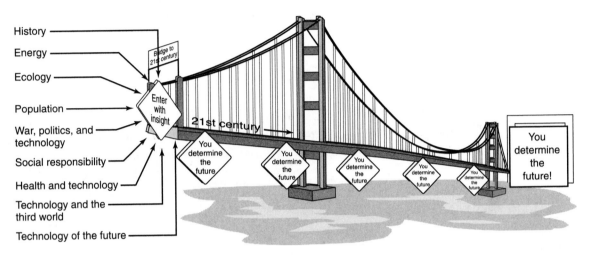

It is a great advantage that man should know his station and not erroneously imagine that the whole universe exists only for him.

—MAIMONIDES
(Dalalat al-ha'irin, Part iii, Chapter xii, c. 1190)

Index

Goldwater, Barry, 176
Gore, Al, 513
Gozzo, James, 361
Grain production, China and the U.S.,
    407–408
Grasman, Keith, 144
Great Leap Forward, 30, 37–39
Greely, Henry, 354, 358
Greenhouse effect, 53–54, 128–129, 466–467,
    473
Green Revolution, 16
Grimm, William J., 373
Guatemala, 402
Guaymi, 451
Guillette, Louis, 143
Guinea-Bissau, 426, 427

H

Habitat destruction, 124–125, 126, 214–215
Hadley, Ernest, 328
Hair trigger military defense systems, 305
Haiti, 421
Hancock, Judith, 177–178
Hansen, Richard, 423
Harris, Ann, 329
Harrison, Paul, 214
Haseltine, William, 485
Hayes, Denis, 176
Hazardous waste, 147–149
Health Care Surrogate Act, 365–366
Health for All, 464–465
Health issues
    antibiotic misuse, 349–353
    future, 464–465, 474
    gene therapy, 505
    high treatment costs, 304
    Human Genome Diversity Project, 354–359
    Human Genome Project, 485–503
    miracle drugs, 182–189
    organ transplants, 360–364
    physician-assisted suicide, 365–366
    science and, 14–15
    surgical techniques, 505
    technology and, 14–15
    technology of the future, 522–523
Heating and cooling, 64
Heron, Ella, 179
Heron, Percy, 179

Hobbes, Thomas, 25
Holdren, John, 261
Holmes, Oliver Wendell, 311
Homer-Dixon, Thomas, 262
Homo erectus, 31–32
Homo habilis, 22–23, 31
Homo sapiens, 31–32
Hong Kong, 403
Hood, Leroy, 485
Hook 112, 285
Horiuchi, Shiro, 237
Human Genome Diversity Project, 348,
    354–359
Human Genome Project, 485, 503
Human rights, 307
Humionics, 493–500
Humvee, 287
Hunger. *See* Food supply
Hydroelectricity, 60

I

IAEA (International Atomic Energy Agency), 78
Income gap, 372, 402–406, 403, 507
India
    photovoltaics in, 422
    pollution in, 412
    population growth in, 246–250, 402
    wind power in, 431–432, 435–437
Indonesia
    as a developing country, 421
    irrigation in, 438–439
    photovoltaics in, 424
Industrial Revolution, 44–45
Industry, energy demand in, 64–65
Infant mortality, in developing countries, 375
Infra-Cams, 284
Instructional Television Fixed Service (ITFS),
    442
Intergovernmental Panel on Climatic Change,
    44–45
International Conference on Population and
    Development (Cairo, 1994), 225–226,
    263
International Geosphere-Biosphere
    Programme, 465
Internet
    BosniaLink, 284
    as a communal technology, 27

M

MacCready, Paul, 102–103
Magic Twist, 37–39
Main Battle Tanks (MBTs), 274
Maine Yankee Plant, 329
Maintenance and repair support system
    (Marss), 498
Makukatin, Serge, 426
Mali, 426
Malthus, Thomas, 196–197, 198
Manhattan Project, 19
Marks, Jonathan, 357, 358, 359
Marmarelis, Vasilis, 477
Marss vest, 498
Martel, L., 221
Materialism. *See* Consumption
Materials design, 506
Mauritania, 426, 427, 429
Maycock, Paul D., 425
Mead, Carver, 477
Mead, Margaret, 176
Medawar, Peter, 361
Medical issues. *See* Health issues
Mendelsohn, Robert, 183
Menozzi, Paolo, 356
Mercury, 143
Methyl isocyanate (MIC), 335
Mexico
    bioprospecting in rain forests of, 182
    debt of, 375
    pollution in Mexico City, 167
    population growth in, 255–256
    wind power and, 431–432, 433, 435–437
MFCMA (Magnuson Fishery Conservation
    and Management Act), 155–156
Michellamine B, 182
Microchip sensor, 505
Microelectromechanical systems (MEMS),
    504–505
Microprocessors, 502
Microwave systems, 443
Military issues
    F–22, 277–279
    friendly fire, 289–290
    humionics, 493–500
    information warfare, 284–288
    science, 14–15
    sponsors, 271–273

Tacit Blue, 280–281
tanks and mechanized warfare, 274–276
technology, 14–15, 293–294
technology and the future, 282–283, 521–522
USS Thresher, 291–292
Miller, Donald, 325, 330
Miller, Margaret, 179
Miller, Timothy, 29
Millstone Unit I nuclear plant, 323–332
Milner, P., 477
Mind control experiments, 310
Misrepresentation, in research, 313
Mocarelli, Polo, 142
Molasses Flood, 333–334
Monopolistic makers, 271–273
Mooney, Pat, 451
Moon landing, 15
Moore, G.E., 301
Morton Thiokol, Inc. (MTI), 310, 318
Motulsky, Arno, 488
M-16 rifles, 272–273
Muellner, George, 280
Munasighe, Mohan, 423
Munson, Ronald, 304
Munzer, Alfred, 167
Murdock, George Peter, 27
Myers, David, 29

N

Nader, Ralph, 272
Nanotechnology, 341–342, 473–474, 504–505
National Environmental Policy Act of 1969,
    19, 177
Natural gas, 54
Natural Resources Defense Council, 168
Neanderthals, 30–35
Needleman, Herbert, 142
Nelson, Gaylord, 176
Nesse, Randolph, 27
Neutron bomb, 17
Newman, Stuart A., 503
Newmark, William, 215
Niger, 426
NIMBY (Not in My Back Yard), 83, 326
Nine Mile Point, 329
1992 Earth Summit of the United Nations
    Conference on Environment and
    Development (UNCED), 511–512